Computers

INTRODUCTORY
TENTH EDITION

are your Future

DIANE M. COYLE

PEARSON

Upper Saddle River, New Jersey 07458

Library of Congress Cataloging-in-Publication Data

Coyle, Diane, 1958-
    Computers are your future. Introductory / Diane M. Coyle. —
Introductory, 10th ed.
        p. cm.
    ISBN-13: 978-0-13-714693-2
    ISBN-10: 0-13-714693-0
    1.   Microcomputers. I. Title.
    QA76.5.C669 2008b
    004.16—dc22

                                        2008046069

VP/Editorial Director: Natalie E. Anderson
Editor in Chief: Michael Payne
AVP/Executive Acquisitions Editor, Print: Stephanie Wall
Director, Product Development: Pamela Hersperger
Product Development Manager: Eileen Bien Calabro
Editorial Project Manager: Virginia Guariglia
Development Editor: Linda Harrison
AVP/Director of Online Programs: Richard Keaveny
AVP/Director of Product Development: Lisa Strite
Editorial Media Project Manager: Alana Coles
Production Media Project Manager: Lorena Cerisano
Marketing Manager: Tori Olson Alves
Marketing Assistant: Angela Frey
Senior Managing Editor: Cynthia Zonneveld
Associate Managing Editor: Camille Trentacoste
Production Project Manager: Mike Lackey
Manager of Rights & Permissions: Charles Morris
Senior Operations Specialist: Nick Sklitsis
Operations Specialist: Natacha Moore
Senior Art Director: Jonathan Boylan
Art Director: Anthony Gemmellaro
AV Project Manager: Rhonda Aversa
Cover Design: Anthony Gemmellaro
Cover Illustration/Photo: © Beathan/Corbis
Director, Image Resource Center: Melinda Patelli
Manager, Rights and Permissions: Zina Arabia
Manager: Visual Research: Beth Brenzel
Manager, Cover Visual Research & Permissions:
    Karen Sanatar
Image Permission Coordinator: Cynthia Vincenti
Photo Researcher: Stephen Forsling
Composition: GGS Higher Education Resources, A Division
    of Premedia Global, Inc.
Full-Service Project Management: GGS Higher Education
    Resources, A Division of Premedia Global, Inc.
Printer/Binder: Quebecor World Color/Versailles
Cover Printer: Lehigh-Phoenix Color/Hagerstown
Typeface: New Century Schoolbook 9.5/12

Credits and acknowledgments borrowed from other sources and
reproduced, with permission, in this textbook appear on
appropriate page within text (or on pages 431-433).

Microsoft, Windows, Word, PowerPoint, Outlook, FrontPage, Visual
Basic, MSN, The Microsoft Network, and/or other Microsoft
products referenced herein are either trademarks or registered
trademarks of the Microsoft Corporation in the U.S.A. and other
countries. Screen shots and icons reprinted with permission from
the Microsoft Corporation. This book is not sponsored or endorsed
by or affiliated with the Microsoft Corporation.

Prentice Hall
is an imprint of

www.pearsonhighered.com

10 9 8 7 6 5 4 3 2 1
ISBN-13: 978-0-13-714693-2
ISBN-10: 0-13-714693-0

With love and thanks to my parents, Don and Cass, who've given me a lifetime of love; to my children, Amy and Steven, who keep life fun and interesting; and to Alan, Norma, and Stephanie for unexpected, but greatly appreciated, opportunities.

ACKNOWLEDGMENTS

This book would not have been possible without the help and support of many individuals. Special thanks go to Stephanie Wall, Associate Vice President and Executive Editor Extraordinaire. An opportunity like this one doesn't come along every day—thank you for opening the window on a cold January day! My project manager, Virginia Guariglia, juggled more schedules than any one person should have to juggle and did it all with a smile—thanks for keeping me on track! I'm especially thankful for Linda Harrison's editing skills, experience, and cheerfulness. As my developmental editor, Linda was just what I needed and this book is better because of her. I'm also grateful to my technical editors, Alan Evans and Julie Boyles, whose keen eyes brought an extra level of care and expertise to this project. I also appreciate the tireless efforts of Mike Lackey, production project manager, and Stephen Forsling, photo researcher, both of whom worked hard to make this book look so good and made it seem easy. Many thanks also to the supplements authors and all the fine Pearson folks who worked on this book. I may not know all your names, but I know you helped! Finally, thanks to my family, friends, and students for your encouragement and support. I couldn't have done it without you!

Contents At a Glance

Preface   x
Visual Walkthrough   xii

CHAPTER 1   Computers & You 2

SPOTLIGHT 1   Ethics 34

CHAPTER 2   The Internet & the World Wide Web 46

SPOTLIGHT 2   E-Commerce 86

CHAPTER 3   Wired & Wireless Communication 100

SPOTLIGHT 3   Home Networks 134

CHAPTER 4   System Software 142

SPOTLIGHT 4   File Management 176

CHAPTER 5   Application Software: Tools for Productivity. 188

SPOTLIGHT 5   Microsoft Office 218

CHAPTER 6   Inside the System Unit 236

SPOTLIGHT 6   Buying and Upgrading Your Computer System 266

CHAPTER 7   Input/Output and Storage 280

SPOTLIGHT 7   Multimedia Devices 312

CHAPTER 8   Networks: Communicating and Sharing Resources 324

SPOTLIGHT 8   Emerging. 352

CHAPTER 9   Privacy, Crime, and Security 366

Acronym Finder   405
Glossary   406
Illustration Credits   431
Index   435

Table of Contents

Preface xi
Visual Walkthrough xiv

| **Chapter 1** | Computers & You . . . . **2** |

Computer Fundamentals . . . . **.7**
- Understanding the Computer: Basic Definitions .7
- Input: Getting Data into the Computer .9
- Processing: Transforming Data into Information 10
- Output: Displaying Information 10
- Storage: Holding Programs and Data for Future Use 10
- Communications: Moving Data between Computers 11
- The Information-Processing Cycle in Action 11

Types of Computers **12**
- Computers for Individuals 13
- Computers for Organizations 15

Computers, Society, & You **17**
- Advantages and Disadvantages of Using Computers 18
- Don't Be Intimidated by Hardware 19
- Recognize the Risks of Using Flawed Software 20
- Take Ethics Seriously 21
- Societal Impacts of Computer Use 22
- The Effect of Computers on Employment 23
- Being a Responsible Computer User 24
- Staying Informed about Changing Technology 25

| **Spotlight 1** | Ethics . . . . **34** |

| **Chapter 2** | The Internet & the World Wide Web . . . . **46** |

How the Internet Works **48**
- Interoperability 48

Accessing the Internet: Going Online **51**
- Internet Service Providers and Online Services 51

The Internet and the Web: What's the Difference? **53**
- The Hypertext Concept 54
- Web Browsers and Web Servers 55
- Web Addresses (URLs) 57
- Browsing the Web 60

Finding Information on the Web **63**
- Using Search Engines 63
- Using Search Techniques 64
- Evaluating Information 67
- Using the Web for Schoolwork 68

Exploring Internet Services **70**
- E-mail: Staying in Touch 70
- Instant Messaging: E-mail Made Faster .73
- Internet Relay Chat: Text Chatting in Real Time 74
- Social Networking: Helping People Connect 74
- File Transfer Protocol: Transferring Files 75
- Usenet: Joining Online Discussions 75
- Electronic Mailing Lists 77

Spotlight 2 E-Commerce **86**

Chapter 3 Wired & Wireless Communication......................... **100**

Moving Data: Bandwidth & Modems **102**
Bandwidth: How Much Do You Need? 102
Modems: From Digital to Analog and Back 103

Wired and Wireless Transmission Media **104**
Twisted Pair 104
Coaxial Cable 104
Fiber-Optic Cable 105
Infrared 105
Radio 106
Microwaves 107
Satellites 107

Wired Communication via the Public Switched Telephone Network **108**
Last-Mile Technologies 109

Convergence: Is It a Phone or a Computer? **113**
Cellular Telephones 114
Web-Enabled Devices 117

Wired and Wireless Applications **117**
Internet Telephony: Real-Time Voice and Video 117
Faxing: Document Exchange 120
Satellite Radio, GPS, and More 120
Text, Picture, and Video Messaging and More 122

Spotlight 3 Home Networks **134**

Chapter 4 System Software **142**

The Operating System **144**
Starting the Computer 145
Managing Applications 147
Managing Memory 148
Handling Input and Output 150
Providing the User Interface 151

Exploring Popular Operating Systems **153**
Microsoft Windows 153
Mac OS 155
UNIX 155
Linux 155
MS-DOS 156
PC versus Mac versus Linux 157

System Utilities: Housekeeping Tools **159**
Backup Software 159
Antivirus Software 161
Searching for and Managing Files 162
Scanning and Defragmenting Disks 163
File Compression Utilities 164
System Update 165
Troubleshooting 165

Spotlight 4 File Management **176**

Chapter 5 Application Software: Tools for Productivity **188**

General-Purpose Applications **190**
Personal Productivity Programs 190
Multimedia and Graphics Software 192
Internet Programs 197
Home and Educational Programs 197
Tailor-Made Applications **198**
Custom Versus Packaged Software 199
**Standalone Programs, Integrated Programs, and
Software Suites** **199**
Web-hosted Technology: A New Way to Share Files 201
System Requirements and Software Versions **202**
Software Upgrades 202
Distribution and Documentation 204
Software Licenses and Registration **204**
Commercial Software, Shareware, Freeware, and Public
Domain Software 205
Installing and Managing Application Software **206**
Installing Applications 206
Launching Applications 208
Choosing Options 208
Exiting Applications 209

Spotlight 5 Microsoft Office. **218**

Chapter 6 Inside the System Unit. **236**

How Computers Represent Data **238**
Representing Data as Numbers 238
Representing Characters: Character Code 240
Introducing the System Unit **240**
Inside the System Unit **240**
What's on the Motherboard? **244**
The CPU: The Microprocessor 245
The Chipset and the Input/Output Bus .251
Memory 251
What's on the Outside of the Box? **253**
The Front Panel 253
Connectors and Ports 254

Spotlight 6 Buying and Upgrading Your Computer System. **266**

Chapter 7 Input/Output and Storage **280**

Input Devices: Giving Commands **282**
Keyboards 282
The Mouse and Other Pointing Devices 285
Additional Input Devices 287
Output Devices: Engaging Our Senses **288**
Monitors 288
Printers 291
Additional Output Devices 292

Storage: Holding Data for Future Use **293**
    Memory versus Storage 293
    Hard Disk Drives 295
    Flash Drives and Storage 298
    CD and DVD Technologies 300
    Solid-State Storage Devices 302
    Storage Horizons 303

| **Spotlight 7** | Multimedia Devices . . . . **312** |

| **Chapter 8** | Networks: Communicating and Sharing Resources . . . . **324** |

Network Fundamentals **326**
Advantages and Disadvantages of Networking **329**
Local Area Networks (LANs) **330**
    Peer-to-Peer Networks 331
    Client/Server Networks 331
    LAN Topologies 333
    LAN Protocols 334
Wide Area Networks (WANs) **339**
    Point of Presence (POP) 339
    Backbones 340
    WAN Protocols 340
    WAN Applications 341

| **Spotlight 8** | Emerging . . . . **352** |

| **Chapter 9** | Privacy, Crime, and Security . . . . **366** |

Privacy in Cyberspace **368**
    The Problem: Collection of Information Without Consent 368
    Technology and Anonymity 369
    Protecting Your Privacy 372
Computer Crime & Cybercrime **377**
    Types of Computer Crime 377
    Meet the Attackers 384
Security **387**
    Security Risks 387
    Protecting Your Computer System 389
The Encryption Debate **392**
    Encryption Basics 393
    Public Key Encryption 393
    Encryption and Public Security Issues 394

Acronym Finder   405 / Glossary   406 / Illustration Credits   431 / Index   435

Preface

A Reference Tool for Today's Students

You asked for a book that addresses the everyday needs of the students you teach. Today, students aren't wowed by technology—it is part of their daily lives. This book has been revised so that it matches what we believe they already know with what you've told us they should know.

This new edition can serve as a reference tool without being overwhelming or intimidating. Today's students want a practical "what it is" and "how it works" approach to computers, with less explanation of "why." We've applied this approach to each Chapter and Spotlight in this edition. For example, Spotlight 3 clearly identifies the different types of home networks that are available and explains how to set one up. Today's students also want practical tips that help them understand chapter concepts. We've included our

Concept Tips, at the end of each chapter. It serves as a one-page mini-reference tool on topics such as how to capture a screenshot and how to backup data.

You also asked for a text-specific, interactive Web site that enhances your students' learning with valuable additional resources and practice exercises-and for your students to be led intuitively to key information that is concise, intelligent, and clearly laid out. Wait until you experience what we've created! In this edition you will find new and updated coverage; new **Spotlights, Currents,** and **Impacts** features; and an updated accompanying Web site. This text is ready for the challenge of teaching even your most diverse class-without sacrificing quality, integrity, or choice.

ABOUT THIS BOOK

Spotlight sections cover the practical, as well as the innovative, in various subject areas. For example, ethics, home networks, file management, and buying and upgrading a computer system focus on the practical, whereas Microsoft Office, multimedia devices, and emerging technologies cover innovation in software, hardware, and technology for the future. We've added reinforcing exercises at the end of each Spotlight.

Impacts and **Currents** features focus on cutting-edge computer technology as well as controversial topics that relate to students' lives. Students are introduced to thought-provoking bites of information that will stimulate class discussion or team debates on all aspects of technology's impact on life today. These features examine technical issues in computing as well as the societal implications of computing resulting from emerging technologies, security, crime, and ethics.

Teamwork exercises are included as an end-of-chapter activity to reinforce chapter concepts by requiring students to work in teams to conduct research and interviews and to create group papers and presentations.

Green Tech Tips provide eco-friendly solutions to living and working with technology. These range from actions students can apply on their own to those that are initiated by companies in an effort to preserve the environment.

Ethics boxes offer an ethical perspective on decisions and situations that involve computers and technology. They raise "what if" type of questions in a "what would you do format" to prompt thoughtful discussion and debate on complicated issues.

The **Concept Tips** at the end of each chapter present guidelines on how to complete different computer-related tasks. Each Concept Tip serves as a one-page mini-reference tool. The following list shows the Concept Tip presented at the end of each chapter:

CHAPTER 1   Storing and Transporting Your Data
CHAPTER 2   Creating an E-mail Filter to Fight Spam
CHAPTER 3   Surfing Safely at Public Wireless Hot Spots
CHAPTER 4   Viruses: How to Tell if Your System Is Infected
CHAPTER 5   Capturing a Screenshot and Sending It as an E-mail Attachment
CHAPTER 6   CPUs—What's the Difference?
CHAPTER 7   Backing Up Your Data
CHAPTER 8   Choosing an ISP
CHAPTER 9   Safer Surfing

INSTRUCTOR'S RESOURCE CENTER CD-ROM

The Prentice Hall Instructor's Resource Center on CD-ROM includes the tools you expect from a Prentice Hall Computer Concepts text, such as:

- Instructor's Manual
- Solutions to all questions and exercises from the book and Web site
- Customizable PowerPoint slide presentations for each chapter
- An image library of all of the figures from the text

TESTGEN SOFTWARE

TestGen is a test generator that lets you view and easily edit test bank questions, transfer them to tests, and print the tests in a variety of formats best suited to your teaching situation. Powerful search and sort functions enable you to easily locate questions and arrange them in the order you prefer.

TOOLS FOR ONLINE LEARNING

COMPANION WEB SITE

This text is accompanied by a companion Web site at www.pearsonhighered.com/cayf. This new site offers an interactive study guide, downloadable supplements, additional Internet exercises, Web resource links such as Careers in IT and crossword puzzles.

ONEKEY

OneKey, available at www.pearsonhighered.com/onekey, offers you the best teaching and learning resources all in one place. OneKey for *Computers Are Your Future* is all your students need for anywhere, anytime access to your course materials conveniently organized by textbook chapter to reinforce and apply what they've learned in class. OneKey is all you need to plan and administer your course through Blackboard, WebCT, or CourseCompass. With OneKey, all of your instructor resources are in one place, maximizing your effectiveness and minimizing your time and effort. OneKey for convenience, simplicity, and success . . . for you and your students.

COURSECOMPASS

CourseCompass, available at www.coursecompass.com, is a dynamic, interactive online course-management tool powered exclusively for Pearson Education by Blackboard. This exciting product allows you to teach market-leading Pearson Education content in an easy-to-use, customizable format.

BLACKBOARD

Prentice Hall's abundant online content, combined with Blackboard's popular tools and interface, results in robust Web-based courses that are easy to implement, manage, and use-taking your courses to new heights in student interaction and learning.

WEBCT

Course-management tools within WebCT, available at www.pearsonhighered.com/webct, include page tracking, progress tracking, class and student management, a grade book, communication tools, a calendar, reporting tools, and more.

Visual Walkthrough

SPOTLIGHT sections highlight important ideas about computer-related topics and provide in-depth, useful information to take your learning to the next level.

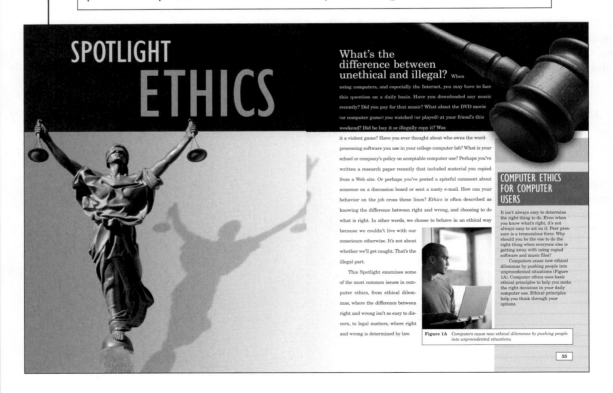

SYSTEM SOFTWARE **161**

IMPACTS

Safety and Security
The Making of Malware

Malware, or malicious software, is installed on a computer without the owner's knowledge or consent. Computer viruses, worms, Trojan horses, rootkits, spyware, and adware are all forms of malware. They can damage your computer and data, spread to other computers, distribute spam, or threaten your privacy and compromise your computer's security. Malware is the Internet's latest security nightmare, causing billions of dollars of damage by destroying or corrupting data, stealing personal information, and clogging networks. Some malware can spread so quickly it causes a chain reaction affecting thousands or even millions of computers within a day or two.

In the past, malware writers tried to erase data on hard drives or disable PCs in other ways. Today's malware writers typically use hard drives as springboards for multiplying and spreading software to as many PCs as possible, rather than erasing files. The profitability of black market schemes and identity theft has made malware big business for organized crime as well. Despite intense attention from cybersecurity experts and law enforcement officials, the pace of malware attacks is increasing, as are their severity and sophistication.

Meanwhile, malware's enemies are fighting back. Sites like the National Cyber Security Alliance (**www.staysafeonline.org**) and the SANS Institute (**www.sans.org**) offer security advice, workshops, and training to individuals and businesses to help prevent cyber attacks; identify potential threats;

and protect computer systems and the information they contain.

How can you guard against malware? Just logging on to the Internet can expose you to malware—even if you've installed antivirus and antispyware software. For security, set your software for automatic updating, because even daily updates may not provide enough protection against the constant onslaught of malware. Don't download files or open attachments with suspicious names or unknown origins. Many antispyware programs, such as Spybot Search and Destroy (**www.safer-networking.org**) and Ad-Aware (**www.lavasoftusa.com**), are free and will catch things your antivirus program won't (Figure 4.21). Finally, strengthen your defenses by downloading the latest security patches for your operating system and other software.

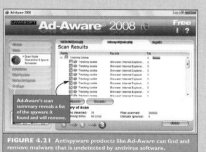

FIGURE 4.21 Antispyware products like Ad-Aware can find and remove malware that is undetected by antivirus software.

Backup option solves that problem with the File Backup Scheduling Wizard. Choose the time and backup location you prefer and Vista will do the rest! You can also obtain stand-alone backup or imaging software from local or online retailers, or check for user reviews and find free utility programs on sites like Download.com (**www. download.com**).

ANTIVIRUS SOFTWARE

Antivirus software protects a com[puter] from computer viruses (Figure 4.22). [...] software uses a pattern-matching tec[hnique] that examines all of the files on a dis[k look]ing for telltale virus code "signatures[." A] limitation of such programs is that th[ey can] detect only those viruses whose signa[ture...]

IMPACTS boxes in each chapter illustrate thought-provoking cultural, ethical, and societal implications of computing.

WIRED & WIRELESS COMMUNICATION **123**

CURRENTS

Computers & Society
Electronic Voting: What's Your Vote?

Electronic voting is in your future, if it isn't already in your neighborhood polling place. What could be simpler? Touch a computer screen or click a mouse and you've had your say about the candidates and the issues on the ballot.

Voting wasn't always this easy for citizens or for the officials who tally election results. In the 19th century, paper ballots were state-of-the-art voting technology. They kept personal choices secret, but counting all those pieces of paper took time—and opened the door to mistakes or outright fraud. By the 20th century, depending on the preferences of the local government, voters were pressing levers on machines, poking holes in punch-card ballots, or inking ovals on optically scannable ballots.

FIGURE 3.26 Electronic voting machines have many advantages and disadvantages—and they are the wave of our voting future.

Fast-forward to the 21st century. In the search for a quick, easy, private, yet secure voting method, more than half the states have installed touch-screen electronic voting machines. In fact, Georgia and Maryland won't let you mark your ballot in any other way. Meanwhile, Michigan and other states are testing systems in which you vote from your home or office PC using an ordinary Internet connection. Your vote is

encoded for secure transmission, just as retailers encode credit card numbers for security (Figure 3.26).

But is electronic voting a boon to society? Proponents argue that the technology is more reliable and more convenient, eliminating many of the problems that plagued elections in the past. Sometimes mechanical voting equipment broke down; sometimes punch-card ballots had to be checked by hand if the holes indicating choices didn't go all the way through. What's more, advocates believe that more people would participate if they could vote from home or by a couple of taps on a computer at the polling place. And with electronic voting, officials could tally the results immediately, instead of counting for hours, or even days.

Critics of electronic voting have four main concerns. First, they worry about security. Can such systems withstand hacker attacks? Can the software or hardware be manipulated to add, change, hide, or prevent votes? Second, critics raise concerns about malfunctions. What if the software doesn't work correctly or the screen blanks out for a time on election day? What if the Internet or wireless connection goes down?

Third, critics worry about verifying votes. How can voters and officials confirm that votes are recorded properly? How can votes be recounted without a paper trail or other proof? Finally, critics are concerned that electronic voting could widen the digital divide. Will people avoid voting if they are wary of computers, can't afford a PC, or don't have Internet access? Will the outcome of an election be affected if people can vote from their homes or offices instead of going to a central polling place?

Experts are already working on solutions. Some rely on paper—for example, you might get a printout after casting your vote electronically at a polling place. If the printout is correct, you would give it to officials for safekeeping so it would be available for a recount. Other solutions rely on technology. You might receive a special card or device to prove your eligibility and to record your choices, either at your own PC or at the local polling place. Once you submit your card, election officials would verify it and hold it in case a recount is needed. Is electronic voting on its way to a polling place near you?

CURRENTS boxes in each chapter examine cutting-edge issues in computing and computer technology.

Finding Information on the Web

Although browsing by means of hyperlinks is easy and fun, it falls short as a means of information research. Web users soon find themselves clicking link after link, searching for information that they never find. If you can't find the information you're looking for after a bit of browsing, try *searching* the Web. You've no doubt heard of Google, Yahoo!, Live Search, and Ask. Although these and other Web search tools are far from perfect, knowing how to use them effectively (and knowing their limitations) can greatly increase your chances of finding the information you want.

Some search sites offer a **subject guide** to the Web, grouping Web pages under headings such as business, news, or travel (Figure 2.17). These guides don't try to include every Web page on the World Wide Web. Instead, they offer a selection of high-quality pages that the search site believes represent some of the more useful Web pages in a given category. If you're just beginning your search for information, a subject guide is an excellent place to start.

USING SEARCH ENGINES

If you can't find what you're looking for in a Web subject guide, you can try searching databases that claim to index the full Web, but with more than 110 million Web sites, and billions of Web pages, in existence, that's a pretty daunting task. These **search engines** maintain databases of the Web pages they've indexed, but it is estimated that more than 75 percent of the Internet is yet to be mined.

More than 10 billion searches were conducted just in January 2008! Of the five core search engines used that month, Google was used more often than all of the other search engines combined. Yahoo! was a distant second, followed by Microsoft, AOL, and Ask (Figure 2.18).

Although an enormous pool of information is available on the Web, chances are that by using these search engines you'll find information relevant to the subject you're researching.

Techtalk

clickstream
As you click from site to site on the Web, you leave a clickstream in your wake. A clickstream is the trail of Web links that you have followed to get to a particular site. Internet merchants are quite interested in analyzing clickstream activity so they can do a better job of targeting advertisements and tailoring Web pages to potential customers.

FIGURE 2.17 Subject guides can help you

Select a category or subcategory to start your search.

Many subject guides include a search tool for searching their site.

The System Stability Index indicates your computer's performance level.

Select a specific date to view alerts.

The report area provides incident details.

FIGURE 4.28 The Windows Reliability Monitor can help you identify problems with your system's performance.

problems, you can undo your last action or installation and see if the problem goes away.

Help and Support
Sometimes the best place to look for troubleshooting guidance is right on your own computer. Microsoft Windows includes a Help and Support utility. You can explore its contents by clicking the Start button and then clicking Help and Support. The Windows Help and Support Center includes a variety of ways to manage and maintain your computer. For example, you could choose Security and Maintenance from the Find an answer section. A security checklist appears with links to various topics, such as Windows Security Center, User Account Control, Back up and Restore, and Windows Firewall. Clicking on a topic will provide more information, including how to access and use specific tools, as well as links to more detailed topics. The Troubleshooting option provides assistance with various problems. The Help and Support Search box at the top of the window can also be used to locate information. Take the time to explore some of these topics; you may be surprised

at the confidence you will gain by interacting with your operating system.

Shutting Down Your System
When you've finished using the computer, be sure to shut it down properly. Don't just switch off the power without going through the full shutdown procedure. In Microsoft Windows Vista, click Start and then click the arrow next to the Lock button and click Shut Down. In Mac OS, click Special in the Finder menu and then select Shut Down. If you switch the power off without shutting down, the operating system may fail to write certain system files to the hard disk. File fragments that result from improper shutdown could result in permanent damage to the operating system or to personal files.

An alternative to completely shutting down your system is to put it in **sleep** mode, a low-power state that enables you to restore your system to full power quickly without going through the lengthy boot process. Sleep mode is available in both Windows and Mac OS. In fact, this is the default shutdown method for Windows, and it occurs when you click Start and then click the Power button.

Destinations

You can find all sorts of troubleshooting sites for both PCs and Macs on the Web. Some offer free advice and user forums, whereas others, such as Ask Dr. Tech, offer support packages for a price. Type "troubleshooting" into your favorite search engine or visit sites such as **www.macfixit. com** or **www. askdrtech.com** to find out more.

TECHTALK margin notes define commonly used computer jargon.

DESTINATIONS margin notes direct you to related Web sites where you can explore chapter topics in more depth.

COMPUTERS & YOU   **15**

Subnotebooks, or **ultraportables**, are notebook computers that omit some components (such as a CD or DVD drive) in order to cut down on weight and size. A significant advantage of subnotebooks is that some of them weigh less than three pounds. For example, the newest Apple MacBook Air weighs only 3 pounds and is less than 1 inch thick. One disadvantage of subnotebooks is that users must often carry along external disk drives and their attendant wiring. A subnotebook might be used by a UPS driver or by salespeople whose specific computing needs do not require all of the peripherals and accessories that are available with desktops and notebooks. Subnotebook manufacturers include many familiar names like Apple, Dell, and Sony but also some newer entries like Asus and Everex.

A **tablet PC**, sometimes called a convertible notebook, can be used in two different configurations. Tablet PCs typically have a keyboard or a mouse for input and can be used like a notebook. However, the LCD screen also swivels to lie flat over the keyboard. In this position, the user can write on it with a special-purpose pen, or stylus. Handwriting-recognition software can then convert the user's handwriting to digital text, if desired. HP's Pavilion brand is an industry leader; however, the Toshiba Portégé, Lenovo Thinkpad, and Dell Latitude are other popular brands from the top manufacturers.

Personal digital assistants (PDAs), sometimes called **handheld computers**, pack much of a notebook's power into a much lighter package. PDAs generally include software for managing contacts, scheduling appointments, and sending and receiving e-mail. Data may be input using a stylus or a keyboard. **Smartphones** are handheld devices that have many of a PDA's characteristics, while integrating mobile phone capability and Web access. The line between PDAs and smartphones is blurring as these devices continue to adopt many of each other's features. In fact, this convergence has been blamed for the decline of many PDA manufacturers. Some well-known examples of these devices include the Apple iPhone, the BlackBerry Curve, the Palm Treo and

All-in-one computers, such as the Apple iMac, are essentially a monitor with everything else built in. The only external devices are a keyboard and a mouse. The microprocessor, memory, storage, and speakers are all contained within the monitor case. This design may be the wave of the future. The Gateway One, the Sony Vaio LT, and the Dell XPS One are all major players in the all-in-one market. All-in-one computers combine the space-saving features of a notebook with the performance of a desktop.

Network computers (NCs) and **Internet appliances** are devices with limited memory, storage, and processing power, used primarily to connect to a network or the Internet. However, interest in these devices has decreased considerably as retail PC costs have declined.

Professional workstations are high-end computers designed for technical applications requiring exceptionally powerful processing and output capabilities. Used by engineers, architects, circuit designers, financial analysts, and other professionals, they are often more expensive than desktop PCs. Manufacturers include HP, Dell, Lenovo, and Sun Microsystems.

COMPUTERS FOR ORGANIZATIONS

Servers are computers that make programs and data available to people who are connected to a computer network. They are not designed for individual use and are typically centralized or operated from one location. Users connect to the network on **clients**, which can be desktops, notebooks, workstations, or any other computer for individuals, to contact the server and obtain the needed information. This use of client computers and centralized servers is called a **client/server network**. These play an important role in today's businesses (Figure 1.14). Servers can be as small as a personal computer or as [large as a] mainframe and are typica[lly housed in a] secure, temperature-regul[ated environ]ment to protect them from [damage or] accidental damage. The to[...]

Destinations

To learn more about the different types of computers, go to **http://computer .howstuffworks.com/ question543.htm.**

Ethics

Smartphones are becoming very popular and can be powerful tools. You can send text messages, take pictures, access your e-mail, and surf the Web. And, it's often possible to do these things without anyone even noticing. Is texting in public more acceptable than holding a conversation over the phone? Some places, such as concerts or museums, prohibit cameras. But what about your smartphone? Does that count? Would you admit that you had one and surrender it, if necessary, or leave it behind before entering such a venue? As technology continues to evolve, these questions will need to be resolved.

ETHICS BOXES highlight ethical issues for students to think about.

Green Tech Tips share ways to be aware of the effects of technology on our earth.

---

114   COMPUTERS ARE YOUR FUTURE: CHAPTER 3

Green Tech Tip

Cell phones made of recycled materials are still in the concept stage, and it may be a while before they reach production. In the meantime, what can you do to dispose of your used phone responsibly? Nokia's We: Recycle program will recycle your phone at no cost to you. Verizon's HopeLine project refurbishes or recycles old phones and uses the proceeds to help prevent domestic violence. Since its inception, more than 60,000 phones and over $5 million have been donated. Sites like Collective-Good (**www. collectivegood. com**) can help you recycle your phone and help the charity of your choice at the same time.

phones (battery life, spotty connectivity, dropped calls), approximately 10 percent of U.S. households have opted to disconnect their conventional landline telephones and rely on cellular service only. Industry professionals expect this migration away from land-based telephones to continue. At the end of 2007, there were approximately 3.3 billion cell phones in use—enough for more than half the world's population!

Why should you care about convergence? Because understanding convergence will help you make more informed decisions about current and future technology purchases. This section explores some of the dimensions of computer-telephony convergence, a process of technological morphing in which previously distinct devices lose their sharply defined boundaries and blend together. As you'll see, it's creating some interesting hybrids.

CELLULAR TELEPHONES

Cellular telephones are computing devices. Although cell phones started out as analog devices, the current generation of cell phones (**3G**, for third generation) are all digital (Figure 3.15). Cell phone

systems use radio signals to transmit voice, text, images, and video data.

In 1971 AT&T built a network of transmitters that automatically repeat signals. This network of transmitters, which are called **cell sites**, broadcasts signals throughout specific, but limited, geographic areas called **cells**. When callers move from cell to cell, each new cell site automatically takes over the signal to maintain signal strength. But who or what monitors your cell phone's signal strength so that you have the best reception? That's the job of the **mobile switching center (MSC)**, and each cellular network contains several MSCs that handle communications within a group of cells (Figure 3.16). Each cell tower reports signal strength to the MSC, which then switches your signal to whatever cell tower will provide the clearest connection for your conversation.

MSCs route calls to the gateway mobile switching center (GMSC), which in turn sends calls to their final destination. If the call is headed for a land-based phone, the GMSC sends the call to the PSTN. Otherwise it forwards the call directly to another cellular network.

Terrain, interference, weather, antenna position, and battery strength can

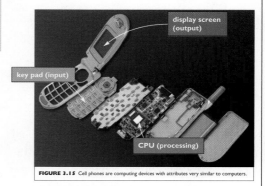

FIGURE 3.15 Cell phones are computing devices with attributes very similar to computers.

What You've Learned

THE INTERNET & THE WORLD WIDE WEB

- The Internet is *the* network of networks. The Internet allows every connected computer to directly exchange data with any other computer on the network. It enables any connected computer to operate a remote computer by sending commands through the network. The Internet is able to work this way because of interoperability, the ability to work with a computer even if it is a different brand and model.
- Users access the Internet by way of a public or private Internet service provider (ISP). Public providers include libraries and schools; private providers are those who provide access for a fee. You can connect to your ISP by way of a telephone modem, a digital service line (DSL), a cable modem, a satellite, or a fiber-optic cable.
- Whereas the Internet is a global computer network that connects millions of smaller networks, the World Wide Web is a global system that contains billions of hypertext documents and uses the Internet as its transport mechanism. Millions of users turn to the Web to research current events, general information, product information, scientific developments, and much more.
- With hypertext, related information is referenced by means of links instead of being fully explained or defined in the same location. On the Web, authors can link to information created by others.
- A Web browser is a program that displays a Web document and enables you to access linked documents. A Web server is a computer that retrieves documents requested by browsers.
- A URL consists of a protocol (such as http://), a domain (such as www.domain.com), a path (such as /windows/), and a resource name (such as default.aspx). To access a Web page, you can click a hyperlink, type a URL into a browser's Address bar, or click a tab in a browser window.
- Web subject guides index a limited number of high-quality pages, whereas search engines enable you to search huge databases of Web documents.
- Most Web searches retrieve too many irrelevant documents. You can improve search results by using inclusion and exclusion operators, phrase searches, and Boolean operators. Search operators such as the + and – signs or the Boolean AND and NOT operators can help limit the results of your search to the particular subject you are interested in.
- To evaluate information you find on the Web, you should look critically at the Web page author's credentials and purpose for publishing the page. Other criteria are whether reputable sources are cited, who provides or pays for the server that hosts the page, and whether the content seems biased, inaccurate, or out of date.
- Popular Internet services include e-mail and instant messaging (IM) for sending messages, Internet relay chat (IRC) for text chatting, social networking sites for online communities, File Transfer Protocol (FTP) for file exchange, Usenet for joining discussion groups, and electronic mailing list managers for broadcasting content to subscribers.

Go to **www.pearsonhighered.com/cayf** to review this chapter, answer the questions, and complete the exercises.

Key Terms and Concepts

anonymous FTP	75
Boolean searches	67
channels	74
cyberspace	48
dead links (broken links)	55
distributed hypermedia system	54
domain name	58
domain name registration	59
Domain Name System (DNS)	59
downloading	61
electronic mailing lists	77
e-mail (electronic mail)	70
e-mail address	70
e-mail attachment	70
exclusion operator	66
fiber-optic service (FiOS)	52
File Transfer Protocol (FTP)	75
flames	77
history list	60
home page (index page)	53
host name	59
hyperlinks (links)	54
hypertext	54
Hypertext Markup Language (HTML)	54
Hypertext Transfer Protocol (HTTP)	58
inclusion operator	66
instant messaging (IM) systems	73
Internet	48
Internet Protocol (IP) address	57
Internet Relay Chat (IRC)	74
Internet service	70
Internet service providers (ISPs)	51
interoperability	48
nesting	67
netiquette	77
newsgroups	75
online service	51
phrase searching	67
plug-ins	56
portal	64
search engines	63
search operators	64
social networking	74
spam	72
specialized search engines	64
subject guide	63
tabbed browsing	60
thread	75
top-level domain (TLD) name	59
truncation	67
uploading	61
URL (Uniform Resource Locator)	57
Usenet	75
Web 2.0	55
Web beacons	73
Web browser	55
Web page	53
Web server	57
Web site	53
wildcards	67
World Wide Web (Web or WWW)	53

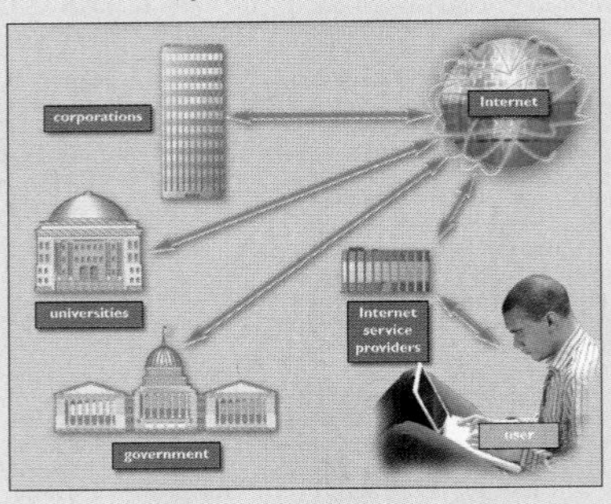

Go to **www.pearsonhighered.com/cayf** to review this chapter, answer the questions, and complete the exercises.

END-OF-CHAPTER MATERIAL includes updated multiple-choice, matching, fill-in, and short-answer questions, as well as Web research projects so you can prepare for tests.

Fill-In

In the blanks provided, write the correct answer for each of the following.

1. A(n) ____________ ____________ site permits users to upload or download files without a user name and password.
2. Web browsers maintain a(n) ____________ ____________ of all the sites that have been visited.
3. A top-level ____________ ____________ indicates the type of organization in which a computer is located.
4. A for-profit firm that uses a proprietary network and limits access to subscribers is known as a(n) ____________ ____________
5. Also known as the Internet, ____________ is the nonphysical place that is accessible only by computer.
6. A(n) ____________ ____________ uses special keywords to provide more precise control of search results.
7. ____________ ____________ often result when a Web page is moved or a site closes down.
8. Someone who violates netiquette rules on a newsgroup may receive a(n) ____________.
9. Every computer, server, or device connected to the Internet has a numeric address known as a(n) ____________ ____________ ____________, which uniquely identifies it to the network.
10. If an e-mail containing a(n) ____________ ____________ is opened, it could alert a spammer.
11. A network-based content development system that uses resources such as sound, video, and text as a means of navigation is known as a(n) ____________ ____________ ____________.
12. A URL consists of a protocol, ____________ ____________, path, and resource name.
13. Surrounding a series of search terms with quotation marks is known as ____________ ____________.
14. A(n) ____________ ____________ ____________ provides individuals and businesses with access to the Internet via phone, DSL, cable, satellite, or fiber-optic lines for a fee.
15. A(n) ____________ ____________ displays Web pages and enables users to access linked documents.

Short Answer

1. Describe your experiences with the Internet. Specifically, identify the browser and e-mail software applications that you have used. Have you used other Internet-related software? If you have, describe these applications.
2. Explain the difference between downloading and uploading files. Have you ever used FTP to transfer files? What types of files did you transfer? What type of software did you use?
3. Are you a member of a social networking site? How often do you use it? Do you take any special precautions to maintain your safety online?
4. What are some rules of thumb for evaluating content on the Web?
5. Now that you have completed this chapter, you should be able to conduct more effective searches. List three search engines that you frequently use and explain why you prefer these search engines over others. Explore the advanced search options these sites offer and explain what you find.

Go to **www.pearsonhighered.com/cayf** to review this chapter, answer the questions, and complete the exercises.

On the Web

1. Internet Statistics
The speed at which the Internet is growing is phenomenal, and the total number of users can only be estimated. To compare the growth of the Internet with that of other media, visit the Computer Almanac site at **www.cs.cmu.edu/~bam/numbers.html**. This site is an online treasury of statistical information about computers. How many years did it take radio to have 50 million listeners? How many years did it take television to achieve 50 million viewers? How many years did it take the Web to reach 50 million U.S. users? (This is a lengthy Web site, so use your browser's Find feature to search for "50 million.")

2. Internet2 Near You
Internet2, or I2, is a collaborative effort among educational institutions, government agencies, and computer and telecommunications companies to increase Internet bandwidth. Visit the I2 site at **www.internet2.edu**. How many university members does it have? Does your school belong to I2? If not, locate and identify the nearest institution that does. What are the annual membership fees and estimated annual institutional costs to participate in I2? What are the annual membership fees and estimated annual corporate partnership costs to participate in I2? Name two corporate partners and two corporate sponsors. In addition to I2, the U.S. government also sponsors its own advanced Internet initiative. Identify this initiative and list two governmental agencies that participate in it and in I2.

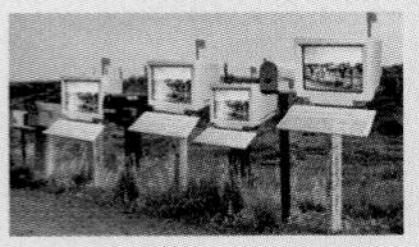

3. Register a Domain Name
Have you ever thought about getting your own domain name? What would you like it to be? Visit **www.register.com** and try different top-level domain names (.com, .net, .org, and so on) to see if they're available. If they are, what is the annual registration cost? If the domain names are already taken, who owns them, when did they acquire them, and when do they expire? What is the minimum bid amount that can be offered to purchase domain names?

4. Online Gaming
Locate a few sites that offer online gaming. You might start out by typing "computer games" or "online games" into your favorite search engine, or you could go to the games link at Yahoo! or visit **www.pogo.com**. Write a short paper that answers the following questions about the sites you have visited: Can you play games without registering? Did the registration process require you to enter your e-mail address? If so, what do you think they will do with it? Roughly how many people were on the site with you at the same time? (Hundreds, thousands, more?) Did you play games? Which ones? What reasons can you think of to explain why people become addicted to playing online games?

5. Term Papers for Sale
Use the search techniques discussed in this chapter to locate two sites that sell research or term papers. Identify the URLs of these sites, describe how to find a paper on a specific topic, and find out how much it costs to purchase a paper. Do these sites post any disclaimers about students using their papers? Do they provide sample papers? If so, what is the quality of the paper? Do you know anyone who has purchased an online paper? Discuss the ethics of using one of these sites to purchase a research or term paper.

Go to **www.pearsonhighered.com/cayf** to review this chapter, answer the questions, and complete the exercises.

Computers Are Your Future

What You'll Learn . . .

- **Define the word *computer* and name the four basic operations that a computer performs.**

- **Describe the two main components of a computer system: hardware and software.**

- **Provide examples of hardware devices that handle input, processing, output, and storage tasks.**

- **Give an example of the information-processing cycle in action.**

- **Discuss the two major categories and the various types of computers.**

- **Explain the advantages and disadvantages of computer usage.**

- **Understand the risks involved in using hardware and software.**

- **Recognize the ethical and societal impacts of computer usage.**

- **Discuss how computers affect employment.**

- **List ways to be a responsible computer user.**

Computers & You

CHAPTER OUTLINE

Computer Fundamentals 7
    Understanding the Computer: Basic Definitions 7
    Input: Getting Data into the Computer 9
    Processing: Transforming Data into Information 10
    Output: Displaying Information 10
    Storage: Holding Programs and Data for Future Use 10
    Communications: Moving Data between Computers 11
    The Information-Processing Cycle in Action 11

Types of Computers 12
    Computers for Individuals 13
    Computers for Organizations 15

Computers, Society, & You 17
    Advantages and Disadvantages of Using Computers 18
    Don't Be Intimidated by Hardware 19
    Recognize the Risks of Using Flawed Software 20
    Take Ethics Seriously 21
    Societal Impacts of Computer Use 22
    The Effect of Computers on Employment 23
    Being a Responsible Computer User 24
    Staying Informed about Changing Technology 25

You're here. Your computer's here. Out there's the Web. What do you need to know to get from here to there? You may be thinking, "Not much," or, "Quite a bit." Computers have become so integral to our day-to-day lives, it's difficult to think of a time without them. They're used at home, at work, in school. You've explored the Web and have used the Internet. You text friends and family or post updates to your MySpace page, take classes online, download music and video files, and burn CDs and DVDs every day. You've been there and done that. What more could you possibly need to know? What more is there to know?

You might be able to perform all of these tasks, but your future isn't just about performing tasks. That's part of it, but hardly all of it. Your future is about having choices and making decisions.

The reason to learn more about any subject is to equip yourself with the knowledge and skills you will need to make informed decisions. Some decisions

FIGURE 1.1 Computers were once considered to be tools for an information age. Today, they are simply a part of our everyday environment.

FIGURE 1.2
Workers with computer and Internet skills tend to make more money and have more satisfying careers than workers without such skills.

you make will be major life decisions; others will have minor consequences. But there will always be facts to gather, opinions to hear, and choices to weigh.

Learning about and understanding computers and technology will help you make informed choices. How can you judge the direction and speed at which technology is moving? What knowledge do you need to capitalize on technological advancements? What current knowledge about your life can you use for perspective?

Think about the changes that have occurred as a result of technological innovation during the most recent 40 years. When your parents were born, there were no telephone answering machines, no cell phones, no handheld calculators, and no personal computers. People wrote letters by hand or with a typewriter, kept track of numbers and data in ledgers, and communicated in person or through the use of the telephone. In fact, telephones were physically connected—cordless handsets didn't come onto the market until the late 1970s, and cell phones followed in the 1980s.

In the 1980s only the U.S. government and colleges and universities were able to access the Internet (including e-mail), cell phones were just coming into use, and fax machines were the fastest way for most people to share documents across great distances. The World Wide Web would not become viable until 1993. Today millions of people use the Internet every day, not only in their professional lives but also in their personal lives. Cell phones are a seemingly necessary part of everyday life, fax machines are becoming obsolete, and retail e-commerce—which didn't begin until 1995—is projected to grow to $335 billion by 2012.

Today it's becoming harder and harder to find an activity that doesn't involve computers and technology (Figure 1.1). Clearly, you'd be wise to learn all you can about computers, the Internet, and the World Wide Web. You should know how to use a computer, the Internet, and popular software such as word-processing and spreadsheet programs. Computer and Internet skills are needed to succeed in almost every occupational area. Studies consistently show that workers with computer and Internet skills tend to make more money and have more satisfying careers than workers without such skills (Figure 1.2).

But skills alone aren't enough. To be a fully functioning member of today's computerized world, you need to know the concepts that underlie computer and Internet technologies, such as the distinction between hardware and software and how to manage the plethora of files that

are created each day. As computers and the Internet play an increasingly direct and noticeable role in our personal lives, understanding the difference between their proper and improper use also becomes increasingly difficult. Should you shop on the Internet on company or school time? Is your credit card information, Social Security number, or personal communication safe from intrusion or misuse? In the past, the only way to shop during work or school was to leave the premises, and the only time you needed to worry about your personal information was if your wallet or mail were stolen!

You also will need to know enough to make decisions about what types of technology to use, whether in your personal or your professional life (Figure 1.3). How much power and speed do you need to perform everyday tasks? How soon do you need it? What will a more powerful and faster computer enable you to do better? What types of technology tools do you need? Do you need advanced training or just enough for a beginner? This text provides answers to these questions as well as the knowledge and skills required to make informed decisions about technology in all areas of your life. When you understand these concepts, you'll be able to:

- Decide whether to purchase new equipment or upgrade specific components

- Judge the likely impact of computer innovations on your personal and business life

- Sort through the difficult ethical, moral, and societal challenges that computer use brings

The more you work with computers, the deeper and richer your understanding of computers and technology will become. Instead of being intimidated by new technologies, you will become quietly confident in your abilities. As your confidence and knowledge grow, you will become more and more adept in your use of computers. Let's start out by describing the machine that's at the center of what you need to know.

FIGURE 1.3 Expanding your knowledge of computers and the latest technology tools will help you become more confident in your abilities.

Computer Fundamentals

Learning computer and Internet concepts is partly about learning new terms. So let's start with the most basic term of all—*computer*.

UNDERSTANDING THE COMPUTER: BASIC DEFINITIONS

A **computer** is a machine that performs four basic operations: input, processing, output, and storage (Figure 1.4). Together, these four operations are called the **information-processing cycle**. Input, processing, output, storage—that's what computers do. The processing function relies on input, output depends on the results of processing, and storage is where output may be kept for later use. Because these operations depend on one another, the information-processing cycle is always performed in sequence.

You'll often hear the term *computer system*, which is normally shortened to *system*. This term is more inclusive than *computer*. A **computer system** is a collection of related components that have been designed to work together. These components can be broken down into two major categories: hardware and software. A computer system's **hardware** includes the physical components of the computer, including the system unit itself, as well as keyboards, monitors, speakers, and so on (Figure 1.5).

Destinations

To learn about the development of computers over time, see the "Timeline of Computer History" at **www.computer. org/portal/cms_ docs_computer/ computer/timeline/ timeline.pdf.**

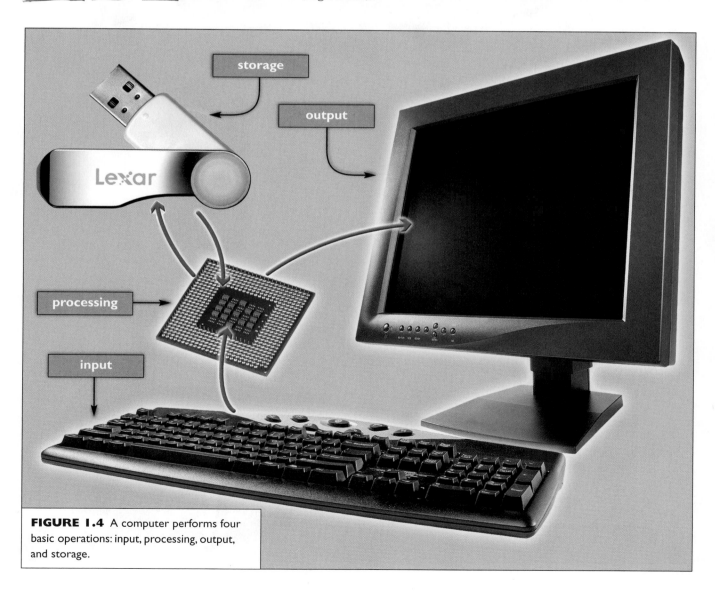

FIGURE 1.4 A computer performs four basic operations: input, processing, output, and storage.

FIGURE 1.5
A typical computer system includes these hardware components.

- **a** Keyboard
- **b** Monitor
- **c** Mouse
- **d** System unit
- **e** CD or DVD drive
- **f** Media card reader
- **g** Headset with Microphone
- **h** Speakers
- **i** Printer
- **j** Cable or DSL modem
- **k** Network interface card

For a computer system's hardware to function, a computer needs a program. A **program** is a list of instructions that tell the computer how to perform the four operations in the information-processing cycle to accomplish a task. **Software** includes all of the programs that give the computer its instructions. You can divide software into two categories: system software and application software. **System software** includes all of the programs that help the computer function properly. The most important type of system software is the computer's operating system (OS), such as Microsoft Windows. Other parts of the system software include system utilities such as backup and disk cleanup tools. **Application software** consists of all of the programs you can use to perform a task, including word-processing, spreadsheet, database, presentation, e-mail, and Web browser software.

To better understand how computer system components are interrelated, you might compare a computer system to an aquarium. The computer hardware is like the fish tank, the operating system is like the water, and the software applications are like the fish (Figure 1.6). You wouldn't put fish in an empty aquarium. Fish can't survive without water, just as software applications can't function without an operating system. And without the water and fish, an aquarium is an empty box, just as computer hardware isn't much use without an operating system and applications.

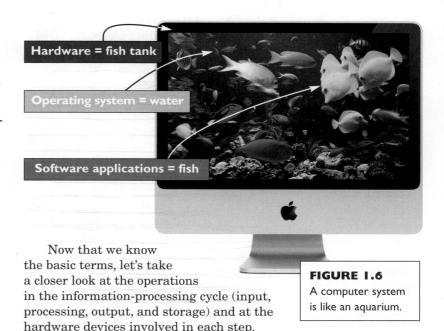

Hardware = fish tank

Operating system = water

Software applications = fish

FIGURE 1.6
A computer system is like an aquarium.

Now that we know the basic terms, let's take a closer look at the operations in the information-processing cycle (input, processing, output, and storage) and at the hardware devices involved in each step.

INPUT: GETTING DATA INTO THE COMPUTER

In the first operation, called **input**, the computer accepts data. The term **data** refers to unorganized raw facts, which can be made up of words, numbers, images, sounds, or a combination of these.

Input devices enable you to enter data into the computer for processing. The most common input devices are the keyboard and mouse (Figure 1.7). Microphones, scanners, and devices such as digital cameras and camcorders offer other ways of getting data into the computer.

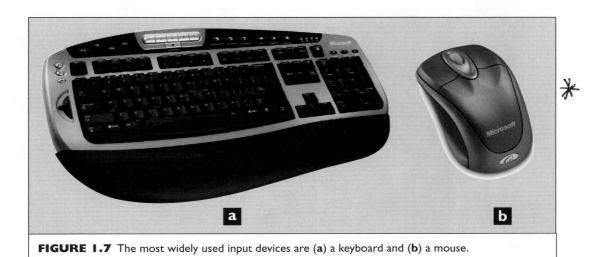

a

b

FIGURE 1.7 The most widely used input devices are (**a**) a keyboard and (**b**) a mouse.

PROCESSING: TRANSFORMING DATA INTO INFORMATION

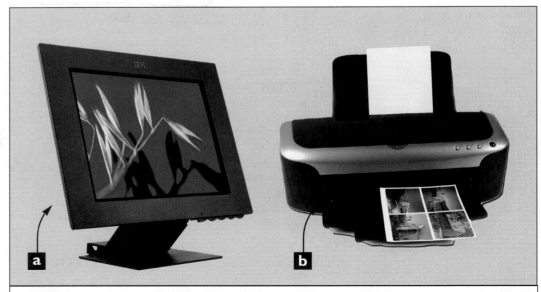

FIGURE 1.8
The CPU (micro-processor, or processor) performs operations on input data.

In the second operation, called **processing**, comput-ers transform data into infor-mation. **Information** is data that has been simplified and organized in a way that people can use. During processing, the computer's processing circuitry (Figure 1.8), called the **central processing unit (CPU)** or **microprocessor** (or just **processor** for short), performs opera-tions on the input data. The processor is located within the computer system's case, also called the **system unit**.

Even though the CPU is often referred to as the "brain" of the computer, comput-ers don't really "think" at all. They are capable only of simple, repetitive process-ing actions organized into an **algorithm**—a series of steps that result in the solution to a problem.

Because the CPU needs to juggle multiple input/output requests at the same time, it uses memory chips to store program instructions and data. Memory is essential to the smooth operation of the CPU. A typical computer includes several different types of memory, but the most important of these is **random access memory (RAM)**, which temporarily stores the programs and data with which the CPU interacts.

OUTPUT: DISPLAYING INFORMATION

In the third operation, called **output**, the computer provides the results of the processing operation in a way that people can understand. **Output devices** show the results of processing operations. The most common output devices are monitors and printers (Figure 1.9), or if the com-puter is processing sounds, you may hear the results on the computer's speakers.

STORAGE: HOLDING PROGRAMS AND DATA FOR FUTURE USE

In the fourth operation, called **storage**, the computer saves the results of processing to be used again later. **Storage devices** hold all of the programs and data that the com-puter system uses. Most new computers include a hard disk drive, a CD or DVD drive (or both), and often a media card reader too (Figure 1.10). These devices are usually not removable and are mounted inside the system unit.

Some older systems may have a floppy disk drive or Zip drive, but such

a

b

FIGURE 1.9 The most common output devices are (**a**) monitors and (**b**) printers.

FIGURE 1.10 The most common storage devices are (**a**) hard disk drives, (**b**) CD and DVD drives, and (**c**) media card readers, which can be used with USB drives and flash memory cards.

devices are quickly becoming obsolete and are often referred to as **legacy technology**.

COMMUNICATIONS: MOVING DATA BETWEEN COMPUTERS

Communications, which some consider to be the fifth operation in the information-processing cycle, involves moving data within a computer or between computers. To move data between computers, communications devices are necessary. **Communications devices** enable computers to connect to a computer network. A **network** is a group of two or more connected computer systems, usually for the purpose of sharing input/output devices and other resources.

Most computers are equipped with a **modem**, a communications device that enables the computer to access the Internet via telephone lines, cable, satellite, and even wireless connections. Many computers have an internal modem that can be used for dial-up Internet access over a standard telephone line. External modems are used for high-speed access to the Internet via cable, DSL, or satellite.

Another important component is a **network interface card**, often referred to as a **NIC**, used to connect a computer to a network. Many computers already have a NIC installed, but external NICs are available and can be plugged into a USB port or inserted into a specially designed slot. NICs can be used with wired or wireless networks.

Now that you understand how hardware and software work in the information-processing cycle and where they are located in a typical computer system, let's look at an example of how the computer uses the basic functions of input, processing, output, and storage.

THE INFORMATION-PROCESSING CYCLE IN ACTION

Even if you haven't wondered what goes on "behind the scenes" when using a computer, the following example illustrates your role and the computer's role in each step of the information-processing cycle (Figure 1.11).

- **Input.** You've just finished writing a research paper for one of your classes. You think it's probably riddled with misspellings and grammatical errors, so you run your word-processing program's spell checker. In this example, your entire word-processed document is the input.

- **Processing.** A spell checker makes use of the computer's ability to perform very simple processing operations at very high speeds. To check your document's spelling, the program begins by constructing a list of all of the words in your document. Then it compares these words, one by one, with a huge list of correctly spelled words. If you've used a word that isn't in the dictionary, the program puts the word into a list of apparent misspellings.

Techtalk

peripheral
A computer device that is not an essential part of the computer; that is, any device that is not the memory or microprocessor. Peripheral devices are usually separate components used for input, output, storage, or communication purposes. A peripheral can be an external device, such as a mouse, keyboard, printer, monitor, scanner, modem, or external hard drive. An internal peripheral device, also known as an integrated peripheral, can be a CD drive, DVD drive, or internal modem.

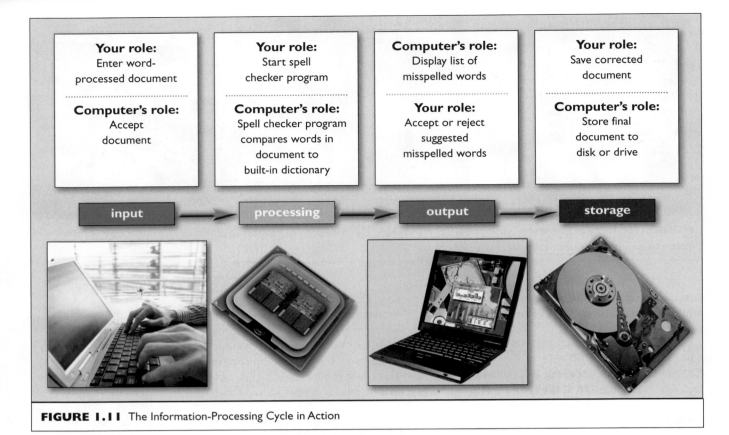

Your role:	Your role:	Computer's role:	Your role:
Enter word-processed document	Start spell checker program	Display list of misspelled words	Save corrected document
Computer's role:	**Computer's role:**	**Your role:**	**Computer's role:**
Accept document	Spell checker program compares words in document to built-in dictionary	Accept or reject suggested misspelled words	Store final document to disk or drive

input → processing → output → storage

FIGURE 1.11 The Information-Processing Cycle in Action

Destinations

To learn more about the information-processing cycle, go to www.pcguide.com/intro/works/exampl-c.html.

Note that the computer isn't really "checking spelling" when it performs this operation. The computer can't check your spelling because it doesn't possess the intelligence to do so. All it can do is tell you which of the words you've used do not appear in the dictionary list. Ultimately, only you can decide whether a given word is misspelled.

- **Output.** The result of the processing operation is a list of apparent misspellings. The word *apparent* is important here because the program doesn't actually know whether the word is misspelled. It is able to tell only that these words aren't in its massive, built-in dictionary. But many correctly spelled words, such as proper nouns and technical terms, aren't likely to be found in the computer's dictionary. For this reason, the program won't make any changes without asking you to confirm them.

- **Storage.** After you've corrected the spelling in your document, you save or store the revised document to disk.

In sum, computers transform data (here, a document full of misspellings) into information (a document that is free of misspellings).

Up to this point, we've been talking about computers in general. We now need to examine the specific types of computers used in a wide variety of tasks and job situations.

Types of Computers

Computers come in all sizes, from large to small. It's convenient to divide them into two categories: computers for individuals and computers for organizations. Computers for individuals are mainly designed for one user at a time. They process and store smaller amounts of data and programs, such as a research paper or a personal Web page (Figure 1.12). In contrast, computers for organizations are designed to meet the needs of many people concurrently. They process and store large amounts of data and more complex programs, such as all the research papers for every class on campus or the school's entire Web site. Computers are also categorized by power (their processing speed) and purpose (the tasks they perform).

COMPUTERS FOR INDIVIDUALS

A **personal computer (PC)**, also called a microcomputer, is designed to meet the computing needs of an individual. The two most commonly used types of personal computers are Apple's Macintosh (Mac) systems and the more numerous IBM-compatible systems, which are made by manufacturers such as Dell, Gateway, Sony, Hewlett-Packard (HP), and many others. These PCs are called "IBM-compatible" because the first such computer was made by IBM. The price range of personal computers has dropped steadily over the years, even as they have become more powerful and useful.

Designed for use at a desk or in an office environment, a **desktop computer** is a personal computer that runs programs to help individuals accomplish their work more productively or to gain access to the Internet. Dell is one of the leading producers of desktop computers.

A **notebook computer** is small enough to fit into a briefcase or backpack, making it ideal for mobile computing and popular with both students and business people who travel frequently. The original term for this type of computer, *laptop*, is being phased out in favor of the more accurate name, *notebook*. Few people actually use a notebook on their lap, because the heat it emits can be uncomfortable. Many notebook computers are as powerful as desktop computers and include nearly all of a desktop computer's components, such as speakers, a DVD drive, and a modem. Notebooks range in size from large, desktop-replacement models with displays measuring up to 17 inches to smaller, lighter-weight models with 13-inch screens. Some of the most popular notebook computers are Dell's Inspiron and XPS series, Toshiba's Satellite and Tecra series, Lenovo's Thinkpad, HP's Pavilion, and for Mac lovers, the MacBook and MacBook Pro.

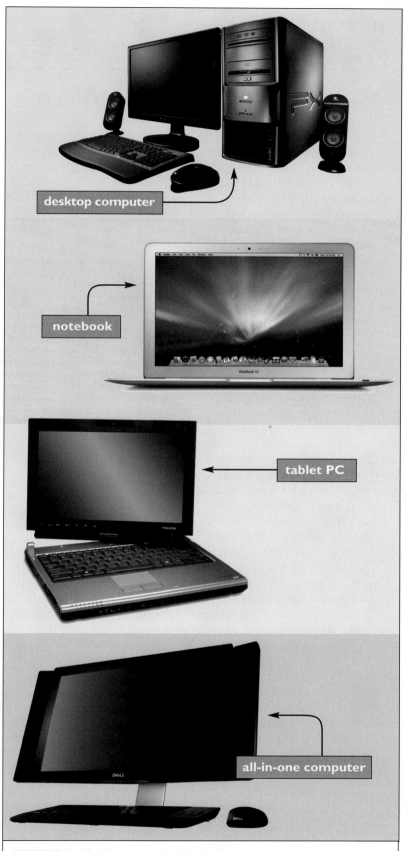

FIGURE 1.12 Computers for Individuals

IMPACTS

Ethical Debates

Digital Piracy: What's the Big Deal?

Most of us wouldn't consider walking into a store and stealing a notebook computer. But when it comes to software (or music or videos) for that notebook, well, that's a different story. How many people do you know who have "borrowed" software, downloaded movies from the Web, shared music files with friends, or illegally burned copies of music CDs? If you ask around, you'll find that you're surrounded by people who don't think it's wrong to steal digital data, even though global losses to digital piracy amount to more than $40 billion annually.

What's the big deal? It may be that when you buy a computer or a CD, you buy a physical, tangible item that you then own. But when you buy software, you're only purchasing the right (or a license) to use the software, not the copyright. So if you install software on your computer and then install it on a friend's computer, you're stealing. And if you download music or videos off the Web without paying, you're stealing just as if you grabbed a DVD off the shelf in a store without paying. You may not see it that way, but the companies creating and distributing the software and other digital data do, as does the law (Figure 1.13).

It's tempting to steal software or music. Consider a school system with 1,000 computers, all of which need to have Microsoft Word. Licensing all those could amount to quite a hefty bill. Do you think it's okay for a school system to have unlicensed proprietary software on its computers? After all, the software is benefiting students. If you think the law bends for schools, think again. Institutions that don't honor software licensing agreements may be subject to

inspection by antipiracy agencies, such as the Business Software Alliance, that work with software companies to determine whether pirated software has been installed. If piracy is discovered, an institution can face steep fines.

What if the school system buys just 500 copies of the software instead of the full 1,000? They're still paying for a lot of software, why should they pay for it all? Do a quick calculation and you'll find that this kind of rationalization is expensive. If the value of each copy is $50, the school is actually stealing $25,000 worth of software. Multiply that by the number of other schools in the district, state, country, and world and suddenly billions of dollars of programs are being stolen.

You may think it's no big deal to download a new song off the Web or to burn a copy of your friend's CD or DVD. But what about the artists who wrote or performed the song, the record company that produced the song, the programmers who worked on the software, and all the other people down the line who rely on honest consumers to purchase their products? They lose money every time somebody illegally copies their software, music, or movies—and that translates into higher prices for everyone who buys these items legitimately.

The Business Software Alliance reports that reducing U.S. piracy rates by just 10 percent over the next four years could create more than 32,000 new jobs, generate $6.7 billion in tax revenues, and result in $40 billion in economic growth, and that's good for all of us!

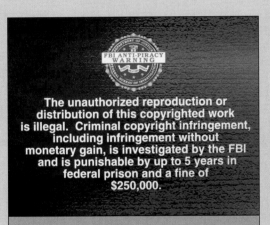

The unauthorized reproduction or distribution of this copyrighted work is illegal. Criminal copyright infringement, including infringement without monetary gain, is investigated by the FBI and is punishable by up to 5 years in federal prison and a fine of $250,000.

FIGURE 1.13 Music and movie companies use an FBI warning logo to warn users against illegally copying digital data. Offenders face $250,000 in fines and up to five years in prison if convicted.

Subnotebooks, or **ultraportables**, are notebook computers that omit some components (such as a CD or DVD drive) in order to cut down on weight and size. A significant advantage of subnotebooks is that some of them weigh less than three pounds. For example, the newest Apple MacBook Air weighs only 3 pounds and is less than 1 inch thick. One disadvantage of subnotebooks is that users must often carry along external disk drives and their attendant wiring. A subnotebook might be used by a UPS driver or by salespeople whose specific computing needs do not require all of the peripherals and accessories that are available with desktops and notebooks. Subnotebook manufacturers include many familiar names like Apple, Dell, and Sony but also some newer entries like Asus and Everex.

A **tablet PC**, sometimes called a convertible notebook, can be used in two different configurations. Tablet PCs typically have a keyboard or a mouse for input and can be used like a notebook. However, the LCD screen also swivels to lie flat over the keyboard. In this position, the user can write on it with a special-purpose pen, or stylus. Handwriting-recognition software can then convert the user's handwriting to digital text, if desired. HP's Pavilion brand is an industry leader; however, the Toshiba Portégé, Lenovo Thinkpad, and Dell Latitude are other popular brands from the top manufacturers.

Personal digital assistants (PDAs), sometimes called **handheld computers**, pack much of a notebook's power into a much lighter package. PDAs generally include software for managing contacts, scheduling appointments, and sending and receiving e-mail. Data may be input using a stylus or a keyboard. **Smartphones** are handheld devices that have many of a PDA's characteristics, while integrating mobile phone capability and Web access. The line between PDAs and smartphones is blurring as these devices continue to adopt many of each other's features. In fact, this convergence has been blamed for the decline of many PDA manufacturers. Some well-known examples of these devices include the Apple iPhone, the BlackBerry Curve, the Palm Treo and Centro, and the HP iPAQ.

All-in-one computers, such as the Apple iMac, are essentially a monitor with everything else built in. The only external devices are a keyboard and a mouse. The microprocessor, memory, storage, and speakers are all contained within the monitor case. This design may be the wave of the future. The Gateway One, the Sony Vaio LT, and the Dell XPS One are all major players in the all-in-one market. All-in-one computers combine the space-saving features of a notebook with the performance of a desktop.

Network computers (**NCs**) and **Internet appliances** are devices with limited memory, storage, and processing power, used primarily to connect to a network or the Internet. However, interest in these devices has decreased considerably as retail PC costs have declined.

Professional workstations are high-end computers designed for technical applications requiring exceptionally powerful processing and output capabilities. Used by engineers, architects, circuit designers, financial analysts, and other professionals, they are often more expensive than desktop PCs. Manufacturers include HP, Dell, Lenovo, and Sun Microsystems.

COMPUTERS FOR ORGANIZATIONS

Servers are computers that make programs and data available to people who are connected to a computer network. They are not designed for individual use and are typically centralized or operated from one location. Users connect to the network on **clients**, which can be desktops, notebooks, workstations, or any other computer for individuals, to contact the server and obtain the needed information. This use of client computers and centralized servers is called a **client/server network**. These play an important role in today's businesses (Figure 1.14). Servers can be as small as a personal computer or as large as a mainframe and are typically housed in a secure, temperature-regulated environment to protect them from deliberate or accidental damage. The top three server manufacturers are HP, Dell, and IBM.

Destinations

To learn more about the different types of computers, go to **http://computer .howstuffworks.com/ question543.htm.**

Ethics

Smartphones are becoming very popular and can be powerful tools. You can send text messages, take pictures, access your e-mail, and surf the Web. And, it's often possible to do these things without anyone even noticing. Is texting in public more acceptable than holding a conversation over the phone? Some places, such as concerts or museums, prohibit cameras. But what about your smartphone? Does that count? Would you admit that you had one and surrender it, if necessary, or leave it behind before entering such a venue? As technology continues to evolve, these questions will need to be resolved.

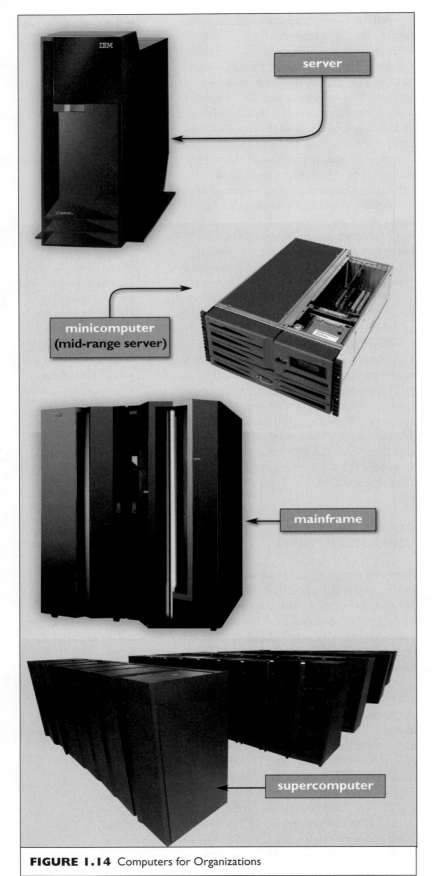

FIGURE 1.14 Computers for Organizations

[image labels: server; minicomputer (mid-range server); mainframe; supercomputer]

Minicomputers, also known as **mid-range servers**, are mid-size computers that handle the computing needs of a smaller corporation or organization, usually as part of a network. They can handle complex tasks and enable users to connect to them simultaneously through PCs or terminals. **Terminals** are computers that lack processing capabilities. They receive input via a remote keyboard and display output on a monitor. In size and capability, minicomputers fall between workstations and mainframes, but as these markets have evolved, demand for minicomputers has decreased.

Mainframes are designed to handle huge processing jobs in large corporations or government agencies. For example, an airline may use a mainframe to handle airline reservations. Some mainframes are designed to be used by hundreds of thousands of people at the same time. People connect to mainframes using terminals or PCs. Mainframes are usually stored in special, secure rooms that have a controlled climate. They are manufactured by firms such as IBM, Sun Microsystems, and HP; cost hundreds of thousands to millions of dollars; and are very powerful.

Supercomputers are ultrafast computers that process large amounts of scientific data and then display the underlying patterns that are discovered. The TOP500 list (**www.top500.org**) tracks the most powerful systems worldwide. As of June 2008, the IBM "Roadrunner," located at the Department of Energy's Los Alamos National Laboratory, topped the list. Using almost 7,000 dual-core processors, the Roadrunner set a new performance record, reaching a processing speed of over one petaflop—over one million billion calculations per second. This equals the combined computing power of over 100,000 of the fastest notebook computers and is twice as fast as the next supercomputer on the list. IBM stated it would take the entire world population (over 6 billion people) performing one calculation per second with a handheld calculator over 46 years to do what the Roadrunner can do in one day!

Now that you know about the variety of computers available, let's look at how their use has an impact on you as an individual and on society in general.

Computers, Society, & You

A computer can work with all types of data. That is one of the major reasons for its remarkable penetration into almost every occupational area and more than 70 percent of U.S. households. Although it is true that computers are becoming commonplace, computers and the Internet aren't readily accessible in some segments of society. Computer and Internet use cuts across all educational, racial, and economic boundaries, but there are still inequities.

The higher your education level, the more likely you are to own a computer and have Internet access. Studies show that approximately one-third of people in the United States have a bachelor's degree and 91 percent of college-educated individuals use the Internet, but only 59 percent of people with a high school education do.

Age, race, and income are also factors in the United States. A survey released by the Pew Internet and American Life Project in February 2008 indicated that only 37 percent of adults older than 65 use the Internet, compared with more than 85 percent of people between 18 and 49. The same report shows that more than 75 percent of whites and English-speaking Hispanics are online, but less than 60 percent of African Americans are. Similarly, only 60 percent of U.S. households with income levels less than $30,000 have access to the Internet. Internet usage increases as income levels rise, with more than 90 percent of households earning $50,000 or more reporting Internet usage. This disparity in computer ownership and Internet access isn't limited to the United States. Known as the **digital divide**, this is a global problem.

Some studies have shown that the digital divide is shrinking because of government programs to bring computing access to all citizens. However, other studies show that the digital divide is continuing to grow.

Computers enable us to collect, organize, evaluate, and communicate information. Although computers are merely a tool, we can use them for a variety of common activities to make our daily lives easier (Figure 1.15). Rather than going to the mall to buy the latest movie on DVD, you can now purchase it, or even view it, online. To organize your movie collection before computers, you would have had to physically sort through the DVDs and arrange them on your shelf. A computer makes it possible to organize your entire collection and sort it in a variety of ways, including by title, artist, release date, or genre, making it simple to reorganize and update your collection whenever you wish. And there's no need to wait for reviews to come

FIGURE 1.15 Computers enable us to collect, organize, evaluate, and communicate information.

out in the newspaper—simply go online to find the latest reviews from critics and other moviegoers. To spread the word to family and friends, simply post this information to your Facebook account and organize your next night out even quicker than by phone or e-mail.

Computers also help us be more productive and creative, reducing the amount of time spent on tedious tasks. A good example of this is using a word-processing program to create a term paper. The computer provides the student with spelling and grammar help and formatting suggestions and also makes it easy to include graphics. Without a computer, the student would need volumes of dictionaries and encyclopedias, not to mention style guides and other special resources, along with extra time to gather and go through all of these sources.

Computers help us not only perform individual activities more efficiently and effectively, but also work, teach, and learn better together. Computers facilitate collaboration with others to solve problems. For instance, computers are increasingly part of law enforcement activities. Computers facilitate quick and efficient communication between jurisdictions and enable patrol officers to obtain critical information about potential suspects. Criminal databases like the Automated Fingerprint Identification System (AFIS) allow pertinent data to be shared nationally and globally. Additionally, as cybercrime becomes a bigger concern, police are using the Internet and computer forensics to find and apprehend these criminals. Using collaboration software, computers permit people to share ideas, create documents, and conduct meetings, regardless of

location or time zone. Whether you're an employee of a multinational firm developing a new product with a group of colleagues located halfway around the globe or a student enrolled in a distance-learning course, computers make these tasks possible.

Computers also facilitate learning and bolster critical thinking through the use of computer-based study guides, problem sets, and educational games. For instance, a CD or DVD that offers tutorial training might have been provided with one or more of your textbooks. Or you might visit this book's companion Web site, **www.pearsonhighered.com/cayf**, to browse the learning aids provided.

Students working on a group project may conduct research using the Internet and use an online application like Google Docs to develop a presentation that is accessible by the entire group. To share ideas and facilitate conversation, they may create a wiki or a Google Groups site. After the project is finalized, the computer is used to produce, print, and present it.

Even though computers offer us many advantages in today's hectic world, the responsible computer user should also be aware that computer use has its advantages *and* disadvantages.

ADVANTAGES AND DISADVANTAGES OF USING COMPUTERS

A computer system conveys certain advantages, such as speed, memory, storage, hardware reliability, and accuracy, to its users. However, with these advantages of computer use come some disadvantages (Figure 1.16), including information overload, the expense of computer equipment, data inaccuracy, and an increasing dependence on unreliable software. Computer technology is growing at such an incredible rate that we are spending more and more time just trying to keep up.

A computer processes data at very high speeds. The most brilliant human mathematicians can perform only a few operations per second, whereas an inexpensive computer performs hundreds of millions—even billions—of them in a second.

FIGURE 1.16 Advantages and Disadvantages of Computer Use

Advantages	Disadvantages
Speed	Information overload
Memory	Cost
Storage	Data inaccuracy
Hardware reliability	Software unreliability

A 2003 study by University of California Berkeley's School of Information Management and Systems found that the amount of new information generated is increasing by more than 30 percent each year. In fact, people are generating so much information today that they often succumb to **information overload**, feelings of anxiety and incapacity experienced when people are presented with more information than they can handle.

Computers store and recall enormous amounts of data in a variety of formats, including text, graphic images, audio, and video. Even an inexpensive desktop PC can store and provide quick access to a complete encyclopedia, a world atlas, an unabridged dictionary, an extensive CD collection, home videos and photos, and much more. This computing power enables users to increase productivity, gain ideas and insight through collaboration with others, and solve real-world problems.

How do computers help us perform these tasks so quickly? The answer is RAM. RAM provides very fast access to resources, but it's more expensive than other forms of storage. As a result, most computers are equipped with just enough RAM to hold programs and data while the computer works with them. Additionally, data held in RAM can be lost if the power is turned off. The alternative is storage devices, which are typically much slower than RAM, but offer increased storage capacity at a more affordable price.

Not only do they hold and generate huge amounts of information but computers are exceptionally reliable and accurate, too. Even the least expensive PCs perform several million operations per second, and they can do so for years without making an error caused by the computer's physical components. For example, you can equip a computer to transcribe your speech with an accuracy of 95 percent or more—which is better than most people's typing accuracy. In fact, almost all "computer errors" are actually caused by flaws in software or errors in the data people supply to computers. Computers store these mistakes for long periods and then replicate the errors with amazing speed.

Along with computers' strengths and weaknesses, there are additional points to consider in your quest to become a responsible user.

DON'T BE INTIMIDATED BY HARDWARE

Many people feel threatened by computers because they fear that computers are too complicated. But without humans, computers have no intelligence at all. The processing operations they perform are almost ridiculously simple. The average insect is a genius compared with a computer.

There is nothing scary about computer hardware. Without a person and a program to tell it what to do, the computer is no more frightening—or useful—than an empty fish tank.

Computer hardware components should be treated with the same care as any other electronic device. Be mindful that electronic devices are sensitive to dust, moisture, static electricity, and magnetic interference. To maintain a safe working environment for you and your hardware, you should heed the following advice (Figure 1.17):

- Use a surge protector and avoid overloads by not plugging too many devices into the same electrical outlet.

- Place hardware equipment in a secure position, so it won't fall or cause accidents.

- Leave plenty of space around hardware for sufficient air circulation to prevent overheating.

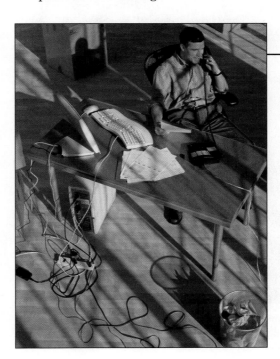

FIGURE 1.17
A messy computer environment is an unsafe one.

Destinations

Ergonomics is an important issue for many computer users. To learn more about ergonomics, go to **http://ergo. human.cornell.edu**

- Make sure computer cables, cords, and wires are fastened securely and not strung haphazardly or left lying where you could trip over them or where they could cause a fire.

Although you shouldn't be intimidated by hardware, you should be aware that using it for long periods can result in injuries or health conditions such as eye, back, and wrist strain.

To prevent injuries, become familiar with the available ergonomic computer products as well as healthy computing practices. If something is **ergonomic**, it means that the product matches the best posture and functionality of the human body (Figure 1.18). For example, prolonged keyboard use can cause **carpal tunnel syndrome** (also known as cumulative trauma disorder or repetitive strain injury). This type of injury is caused by repeated motions that damage sensitive nerve tissue in the hands, wrists, and arms. Sometimes these injuries are so serious that they require surgery. To help prevent these problems, ergonomic keyboards, such as the Microsoft Natural Keyboard, keep your wrists flat, reducing (but not eliminating) your chance of an injury. Many hotel chains try to attract business travelers by promoting their ergonomic desk chairs along with high-speed Internet access.

In addition to using ergonomically designed equipment, you can promote a safe and comfortable computer environment by arranging your chair, lighting, and computer equipment properly and using antiglare computer screens. You should also take periodic breaks from working at your computer to rest your eyes and stretch your legs.

Treat the physical components of your computer with respect and you will get the most return for your money and health.

Computer hardware can be amazingly reliable, but software is another matter.

RECOGNIZE THE RISKS OF USING FLAWED SOFTWARE

All programs contain errors, and this is why: Computers can perform only a limited series of simple actions. Many programs contain millions of lines of programming code (Figure 1.19). In general, each line of program code tells the computer to perform an action, such as adding two numbers or comparing them. Consider this: The program that allows you to withdraw cash from an ATM contains only 90,000 lines of code. But when you file your taxes, the Internal Revenue Service (IRS) program that calculates your refund contains 1,000 times that—100 million lines of code!

With so many lines of code, errors inevitably occur—and they are impossible to eradicate completely. On average, commercial programs contain between 14 and 17 errors for every 1,000 lines of code. This means that an ATM is likely to have 1,350 errors in its code, and the IRS program code might have as many as 1.5 million or more errors! Thankfully, most errors simply cause programs to run slowly or to perform unnecessary tasks, but some errors do cause miscalculations or other inconveniences.

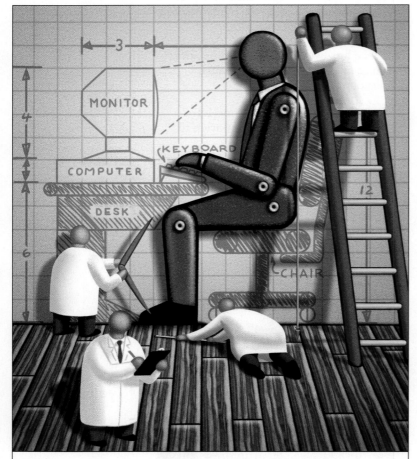

FIGURE 1.18 Ergonomics involves matching the best posture and functionality of the human body to the physical characteristics of various devices.

Another phenomenon worth mentioning is that the more lines of code you add, the more complex the program becomes—and the harder it becomes to eradicate the errors. Because every computer program contains errors, all computer use entails a certain level of risk. A bug might occur when you least expect it and cause your computer to freeze up. You may be forced to restart your computer, losing your unsaved work.

The situations described above provide ample reasons why it's not a good idea to put off writing a paper until the night before your assignment is due. Bugs in a word-processing program aren't usually life threatening, but computers are increasingly being used in mission-critical and safety-critical systems. Mission-critical systems are those essential to an organization's viability, such as a company's computerized cash register system. If the system goes down, the organization can't function—and the result is often a very expensive fiasco. A safety-critical system is one on which human lives depend, such as an air traffic control system or a computerized signaling system used by high-speed commuter trains (Figure 1.20). When these systems fail, human lives are at stake. Safety-critical systems are designed to much higher-quality standards and have backup systems that kick in if the main computer goes down.

FIGURE 1.19 Programs often contain millions of lines of code

Program	Lines of Programming Code
Bank ATM	90,000
Air traffic control	900,000
Microsoft Windows 2000	35 million
Microsoft Windows XP	40 million
Microsoft Windows Vista	50 million (estimated)
IRS	100 million (all programs)

The disturbing thing about computers isn't the computers themselves but what people might do with them—which leads us to consider the issue of computers and ethics.

TAKE ETHICS SERIOUSLY

Ethics is the behavior associated with your moral beliefs. You have learned what is right and wrong from your parents, teachers, and spiritual leaders. By this stage of your life you know what is right and wrong.

Techtalk

bug
An error or defect in software or hardware that causes a program to malfunction. The term is often attributed to Rear Admiral Grace Murray Hopper, whose team of programmers located a moth that had flown into the Mark II computer's relay, causing a fault. However, the term *bug* had been used to describe technical glitches for some time before this discovery.

FIGURE 1.20 Air traffic control systems use safety-critical software whose code must be written to the highest possible standards.

However, people's use of computers and the Internet has created ethical situations that we might not have otherwise encountered. **Computer ethics**, a branch of philosophy that continues to evolve, deals with computer-related moral dilemmas and defines ethical principles for computer usage.

Responsible computing requires that you understand the advantages and disadvantages of using a computer as well as the potential harm from computer misuse. Every day there are stories in the news of people misusing computerized data. Names and e-mail addresses are distributed freely without permission or regard for privacy. Viruses are launched against unsuspecting victims. Credit card information is stolen and fraudulently used. Children and women are stalked. Pornography abounds. Illegitimate copies of software are installed every day. Professional musicians, actors, and others in the entertainment industry lose

tens and hundreds of thousands of dollars a year in unpaid royalties because of illegal downloading and digital copying. Research papers are bought and sold over the Internet. Homework assignments are copied and then modified to appear as though they are original work. The Internet is a hotbed of illicit and sometimes illegal content. The list of ethical considerations goes on and on.

Computers are very powerful tools. They can be used to magnify many aspects of our lives, including unethical behavior. The Spotlight following this chapter provides an in-depth discussion of computer ethics. But computers and the Internet can also be used to improve our lives and society.

SOCIETAL IMPACTS OF COMPUTER USE

Almost everyone has been affected by computers and the Internet. Although most people are able bodied, consider the effect of technologies that support or provide opportunities to the disabled and disadvantaged (Figure 1.21). To meet the requirements of the Americans with Disabilities Act of 1990, your school must provide computer access to people with disabilities. A college's computing services department must provide special software, such as speech-recognition software, to help people with vision impairments use computers. Input and output devices specifically designed for the physically disabled can be installed or existing devices can be modified to accommodate users with hearing or motor impairments. Home and school computers equipped with speech-recognition software can help children and those with learning disabilities learn to read.

Computers also help stroke victims lead more independent lives. From robotic treadmills to muscle stimulators to therapy that involves playing video games, computers give many patients hope of almost full recovery of their former abilities.

In schools, students can use computers to take advantage of inexpensive training and learning opportunities. **E-learning** is the use of computers and computer programs to replace teachers and the time-place specificity of learning. People also can access computers and the Internet from libraries, Web cafés, and public Internet centers to look for work or find online training and résumé-creation tools.

FIGURE 1.21 Continued innovations in computers, software, and other related technologies provide mobility, hearing, speech, and vision assistance to individuals with myriad disabilities. Shown above, the Alternative Computer Control System (ACCS) manufactured by Gravitonus is designed to provide computer access for severely motor-impaired people.

CURRENTS

Computers & Society

Hello, ASIMO: Meet a Computer-Guided Robot

From fire fighting to fetching eyeglasses, Honda's ASIMO (Advanced Step in Innovative Mobility) robot could one day take on dangerous tasks as well as everyday functions such as lifting items or opening doors. ASIMO is a 4-foot-tall humanoid robot controlled wirelessly by a notebook computer and powered by the batteries in its backpack (Figure 1.22).

Sound like science fiction? ASIMO is very real, the result of more than two decades of research and experimentation by Honda engineers. Unlike earlier clunky robots, this humanlike robot has highly flexible arms, legs, and neck so it can move around under its own power much like we do. And because it's programmed to maintain proper posture and balance as it moves, ASIMO can easily and effortlessly walk up and down stairs, step in any direction, and check around corners.

Think of the possibilities. Computer-guided robots like ASIMO could become helpful assistants to people with physical disabilities—turning lights on and off, finding and moving household objects, opening and closing doors, and taking care of dozens of other daily tasks. Walking independently—with or without packages in hand—they could also guide people through buildings and streets.

Of course, ASIMO is still a work in progress. Behind the scenes, Honda's engineers are continuing to refine the robot's computers, software, and physical structure. Meanwhile, ASIMO has demonstrated its capabilities at industry meetings and even served brief stints as an attention-getting greeter for other companies. Visitors to the Disneyland park in Anaheim, California, can see ASIMO in action at the Honda ASIMO Theater inside the Innoventions attraction.

Looking ahead, as Honda perfects the technology, such robots may become commonplace as stand-ins for scientists, fire fighters, and police officers facing risky situations. ASIMO robots might shift dangerous chemicals from one storage place to another or climb several flights of stairs to position fire-fighting equipment inside a burning building. Or they might act as the eyes and ears of emergency personnel, exploring the scene of a natural disaster, gathering data about the extent of the damage, and helping to carry out rescue missions. You may never meet ASIMO, but sometime in the near future, your life might change because of such computer-guided robots.

FIGURE 1.22 Honda's ASIMO robot

THE EFFECT OF COMPUTERS ON EMPLOYMENT

Although computers are creating new job opportunities, they're also shifting labor demand toward skilled workers, particularly those with computer skills. As a result, skilled workers earn more; wages paid to unskilled workers have stagnated over the past 20 years. As a consequence, the gap between the rich and the poor has widened as educated, skilled workers have taken

FIGURE 1.23 Computer-guided robots are taking over many manufacturing jobs that people once held.

advantage of new technology-based opportunities. Computer skills have never been more important to a person's future.

Advanced technology can free people from hazardous working conditions and from repetitive tasks, thereby making workflow safer and more efficient and increasing productivity. However, the result is that fewer workers may be required to perform a task. **Automation** (the replacement of human workers by machines) and computer-guided robots are taking over many manufacturing jobs that people once held (Figure 1.23).

More than 1 million robots are in use worldwide, mostly in Japan, though the United States ranks second. In 2007, robotic orders for North American manufacturers totalled over $1 billion in sales, a 24 percent increase from the previous year. Contrary to popular opinion, less than 50 percent of robots used in the United States are found in automotive plants. The remainder are used in industries such as health care and in locations such as warehouses, laboratories, and energy plants.

Technology has also contributed to globalization, which has led to outsourcing. Outsourcing is blamed for eliminating many jobs, but studies show that increased productivity is the real cause. Increasing productivity by as little as

1 percent can eliminate up to 1.3 million jobs a year. In comparison, it is estimated that 250,000 U.S. jobs are lost to outsourcing annually—less than 2 percent of the unemployment total.

Structural unemployment results when advancing technology makes an entire job category obsolete. Structural unemployment differs from the normal up-and-down cycles of layoffs and rehires. People who lose jobs because of structural unemployment are not going to get them back. Their only option is to retrain themselves to work in other careers.

Consider this: Half of all the jobs that will be available in 10 years don't even exist today. So who will survive—and flourish—in a computer-driven economy? The answer is simple. The survivors will be people who are highly educated, who know that education is a lifelong process, and who adapt quickly to change. Being a responsible computer user is just as important.

BEING A RESPONSIBLE COMPUTER USER

How can you become a responsible user of computers and the Internet? Knowing how your computer and Internet usage affects others in your school, family, community, and the environment is a start. Don't hog public computer resources. If you are using a computer and Internet connection at a library or in a wireless hotspot, don't download or upload large files. Be considerate of others who might be sharing the same connection. Responsible users help the environment by recycling paper and printer cartridges.

A larger concern is how to dispose of obsolete computer equipment, also called **e-waste**. More than 100 million computers, monitors, and TVs become obsolete each year, and these numbers keep growing. By 2009, the number of cell phones sold worldwide is expected to reach 2 billion, adding another element to the mix. Because monitors, batteries, and other components contain hazardous materials, they can't just be thrown in the trash. Unfortunately, only 12.5 percent of this e-waste is properly recycled. At least 24 states either have passed or are considering passing laws regarding e-waste disposal. Responsible users will look for computer and electronics equipment disposal and recycling companies in their areas or check state and federal Web sites, such as the Environmental Protection Agency site (**www.epa.gov**) for tips on computer disposal. Some schools also offer guidelines for discarding old computers (Figure 1.24).

Another way to solve the disposal problem and to give back to your community is by donating old computer equipment to local charities that could refurbish it to help new users learn the basics. Who knows, you might even donate a little of your time to help!

Being a responsible user also means being aware of how computers and Internet use can affect your own well-being and personal relationships. Researchers at Carnegie Mellon University were surprised to find that people who spent even a few hours a week on the Internet experienced higher levels of depression and loneliness than those who did not. These people interacted with other Internet users online, but this interaction seems to have been much shallower than the time formerly spent with friends and family. The result? According to these researchers, Internet use leads to unhealthy social isolation and a deadened, mechanized experience that is lacking in human emotion. Interestingly, other studies show just the opposite. These studies demonstrate that there is no

difference in socialization between those who use the Internet and those who do not. So who is right? It will take years of studies to know. But for now, keep in mind that computer and Internet overuse may promote unhealthy behaviors.

STAYING INFORMED ABOUT CHANGING TECHNOLOGY

It is important to stay informed about advances in technology. One benefit of staying informed is getting the latest product upgrades. Upgrading the software on your computer helps you enjoy the most current features the software manufacturer has to offer. Staying informed also helps you thwart the latest computer viruses from invading and harming your computer. Viruses wreak havoc on computers every day. By knowing all you can about the latest viruses and how they're spread, you can prevent your computer from getting infected.

One constant in today's changing technology is the steady advance of computing power. Faster processors and cheaper storage mean that next month's computer will be more powerful than this month's computer.

You can stay informed about the latest technology by reading periodicals, visiting Web sites such as CNET (**www.cnet.com**), subscribing to print and online newsletters and publications, and reading technology columns in your local newspaper. Learning about computers and technology will help you be a more responsible computer user.

Green Tech Tip

Is your old computer a good candidate for donation? Answer these questions to find out:

1. Is it less than five years old?
2. Does it still work?
3. Do you have the original software and documentation (operating system and other applications)?
4. Have you used disk-cleaning software to remove your personal data?
5. Have you checked to be sure the organization to which you're donating your equipment can actually use it?

If you were able to answer "Yes" to all these questions, it's very likely your computer can be put to good use by someone else.

FIGURE 1.24 Responsible computer use includes recycling old computers, monitors, printers, and other types of e-waste.

What You've Learned

COMPUTERS & YOU

- A computer is a machine that performs four operations: input, processing, output, and storage. These four operations are called the information-processing cycle.

- A computer system is a collection of related components that have been designed to work together. It includes both the computer's hardware (its physical components such as the computer, keyboard, monitor, and speakers) and software (the programs that run on it).

- In a typical computer system, a keyboard and a mouse provide input capabilities. Processing is done by the microprocessor (CPU) and RAM (random access memory). You see the results (output) on a monitor or printer. A hard disk is typically used for long-term storage.

- Spell checking a word-processed document is a good example of the information-processing cycle. The input consists of the original document, which contains spelling mistakes. When the computer processes the document, it detects and flags possible spelling errors by checking every word in the document against a massive spelling dictionary. Output consists of a list of words that the spell checker is unable to find in its dictionary. User interaction is required to confirm whether the apparent misspelled words need to be corrected. The user saves the corrected document to storage for future use.

- There are two major categories of computers: computers for individuals and computers for organizations. Types of computers for individuals include personal computers (PCs), desktop computers, notebooks, subnotebooks, handheld computers (for example, PDAs, smartphones, and tablet PCs), all-in-one computers, network computers (NCs), and Internet appliances. Types of computers for organizations include servers, minicomputers, mainframes, and supercomputers.

- Responsible computing requires that you understand the advantages and disadvantages of using the computer. Advantages include speed, memory, storage, hardware reliability, and accuracy. Disadvantages include information overload, the expense of computer equipment, data inaccuracy, and dependence on unreliable software.

- Using hardware and software involves some risk. It is important to pay attention to the proper care and use of hardware to avoid damage to the equipment and potential computer-related injuries to the user. Recognize that all programs contain errors that typically cause programs to run slowly or produce other inconveniences.

- Computers can be misused or used to benefit individuals and society. Examples of misuse include distributing personal information without permission; exposing users to unwanted solicitations or viruses; and illegally copying or sharing software, music, or videos. Benefits include using computers to assist those with disabilities or no access to otherwise available goods and services.

- Although computers are creating new job opportunities, they're also shifting labor demand toward skilled workers, particularly those with computer skills. As a result, skilled workers earn more, whereas unskilled workers' wages have stagnated over the past 20 years. Computers and technology also affect employment through automation, outsourcing, and the elimination of less technical occupations.

- Being a responsible computer user means knowing how your computer and Internet usage affects others in your school, family, community, and the environment. Using recycled paper, fairly sharing access to public resources, properly disposing of computers and peripherals, being aware of computer and Internet overuse, and staying informed about changing technology demonstrate responsible computer use.

Key Terms and Concepts

algorithm.................. 10
all-in-one computer.......... 15
application software.......... 9
automation................ 24
carpal tunnel syndrome...... 20
central processing unit (CPU),
    also microprocessor or
      processor................ 10
clients.................... 15
client/server network........ 15
communications............ 11
communications devices...... 11
computer.................. 7
computer ethics............. 22
computer system............ 7
data...................... 9
desktop computer........... 13
digital divide............... 17
e-learning................. 22
ergonomic................. 20
e-waste................... 25

handheld computers......... 15
hardware.................. 7
information................ 10
information overload........ 19
information-processing cycle... 7
input..................... 9
input devices............... 9
Internet appliance.......... 15
legacy technology........... 11
mainframes................ 16
microprocessor, also
    processor................ 10
minicomputers (mid-range
    servers)................. 16
modem.................... 11
network................... 11
network computers (NC)..... 15
network interface card (NIC).. 11
notebook computer.......... 13
output.................... 10
output devices.............. 10

personal computer (PC)...... 13
personal digital assistants
    (PDAs)................. 15
processing................. 10
professional workstations.... 15
program................... 9
random access memory
    (RAM)................. 10
servers................... 15
smartphones............... 15
software.................. 9
storage................... 10
storage devices............. 10
structural unemployment.... 24
subnotebooks.............. 15
supercomputers............ 16
system software............ 9
system unit................ 10
tablet PC................. 15
terminals................. 16
ultraportables............. 15

Matching

Match each key term in the left column with the most accurate definition in the right column.

_____ 1. application software

_____ 2. ultraportable

_____ 3. smartphone

_____ 4. modem

_____ 5. random access memory

_____ 6. input

_____ 7. professional workstation

_____ 8. tablet PC

_____ 9. computer ethics

_____ 10. output device

_____ 11. program

_____ 12. storage

_____ 13. mainframe

_____ 14. system unit

_____ 15. information-processing cycle

a. a high-end computer designed for technical applications

b. shows the results of the processing operation

c. the four basic operations of a computer

d. program used to perform a task, such as word-processing

e. processed results are saved for later use

f. a convertible notebook that can be used in two different configurations and accepts handwritten input

g. handheld device integrating communications with features of a PDA

h. case for the computer system

i. the computer accepts data in this first step of the information-processing cycle

j. designed to handle huge processing jobs in large corporations or government agencies

k. a subnotebook computer that omits certain components to reduce weight

l. list of instructions telling the computer how to perform the four operations in the information-processing cycle

m. needed to temporarily store data and programs with which the CPU interacts

n. a new branch of philosophy dealing with computer-related moral dilemmas

o. a communications device that enables a computer to access other computers and the Internet

Multiple Choice

Circle the correct choice for each of the following.

1. Which of the following is a common output device?
   a. mouse
   b. printer
   c. disk drive
   d. processor

2. Which of the following is an example of a storage device?
   a. modem
   b. DVD drive
   c. microphone
   d. program

3. Which type of memory temporarily stores the programs and data with which the CPU interacts?
   a. read-alone memory
   b. refreshable auxiliary memory
   c. random access memory
   d. read-only memory

4. Which of the following is an ultrafast computer that processes large amounts of scientific data?
   a. minicomputer
   b. ultraportable computer
   c. mainframe computer
   d. supercomputer

5. What does the acronym PDA stand for?
   a. personal data aid
   b. professional digital attachment
   c. personal digital assistant
   d. programmable data acquisition

6. Which of the following is *not* an input device?
   a. speakers
   b. mouse
   c. scanner
   d. digital camera

7. What are the four basic operations of the information-processing cycle?
   a. input, output, storage, communication
   b. processing, communication, storage, data creation
   c. input, printing, storage, retrieval
   d. input, processing, output, storage

8. Which of the following computers is *not* designed for individual use while travelling?
   a. workstation
   b. notebook
   c. tablet PC
   d. ultraportable

9. Which of the following is *not* an example of a client?
   a. tablet PC
   b. server
   c. subnotebook
   d. desktop computer

10. Which device enables the computer to access a wired or wireless network?
    a. keyboard
    b. server
    c. network interface card
    d. smartphone

Fill-In

In the blanks provided, write the correct answer for each of the following.

1. The most common _____ _____ are the monitor, printer, and speakers.

2. The physical components of the computer, including the computer itself and the keyboard, monitor, and speakers, are known as _____.

3. Hard drives and DVD drives are examples of _____ _____.

4. _____ _____ includes all of the programs that enable a computer to function, the most important being the operating system (OS).

5. _____ is a term used to describe unwanted or obsolete computer equipment.

6. Smartphones and PDAs are examples of _____ _____.

7. A(n) _____ lacks processing capabilities, receives input via a remote keyboard, and displays output on a monitor.

8. _____ _____ _____ provides temporary storage for the programs and data used by the CPU.

9. A(n) _____ is a group of two or more connected computer systems that share devices and resources.

10. A(n) _____ computer is essentially a monitor with everything else built in.

11. A(n) _____ computer is used to connect to a network and contact the server to obtain needed information.

12. The replacement of human workers by machines is known as _____.

13. When advancing technology makes an entire job category obsolete this is known as _____ _____.

14. The _____ _____ describes the disparity between groups who own computers and have Internet access and those who do not.

15. A collection of related components designed to work together is known as a(n) _____ _____.

Short Answer

1. What is system software? Discuss the two types of software in this category.

2. Provide a brief description of a microcomputer, a minicomputer, and a mainframe. Be sure to include information on the power and size of each.

3. What is the difference between hardware and software?

4. Define the terms *data* and *information* and explain how they are different from one another.

5. Define *server*. Briefly describe how a server is used.

6. Discuss the advantages and disadvantages of computer use.

7. List three to five characteristics of a responsible computer user.

Teamwork

1. Outsourcing Jobs

Your team is to investigate how computers affect global shifts in employment. For this exercise you will divide into two teams to research the pros and cons of outsourcing jobs. Use your favorite search engine to explore this topic and locate appropriate research materials. Read and cite at least three articles. Each side will prepare a presentation to make to the rest of the class.

2. Whose Music Is It?

Locate articles that cover the areas of legal and illegal music downloading. You will find hundreds of articles by typing "legal versus illegal music downloading" into your favorite search engine, such as Yahoo! or Google. You should read at least two articles and then report your findings to the larger group. When all team members have completed their research, work together to develop a group report and present your findings to the class. How big of a problem is illegal music downloading? Be sure to include statistics to support your answer.

3. Desktop or Notebook—You Decide

As a team, determine whether you would purchase a desktop or a notebook computer. Use the Internet or contact a local vendor and compare the prices for similarly equipped desktop and notebook computers. Based on your needs and finances, prepare a report to explain which computer you would buy and give reasons that support your decision.

4. Mac or PC?

Divide your team into two groups: Mac and PC. Each group should research its assigned system and provide a report that summarizes what they've learned. Be sure to cover all of the components of the basic computer system (input devices, processors, output devices, and the type and amount of storage).

5. Exploring the Information-Processing Cycle

As a team, examine advertisements for computers and peripherals from local or regional newspapers. Compare a desktop computer with a notebook or PDA. Which input, processing, output, and storage devices look the same? Which are different? Prepare a group presentation that describes the products in the ads, identifying them as input, processing, output, or storage devices.

On the Web

1. Owning the Music

Go to **www.apple.com/itunes**, **www.napster.com**, and **www.rhapsody.com** to learn more about legal music downloading. You may visit other sites as well. For each site, answer the following questions: What is the price per song? How is the site funded? What process ensures that the music you are downloading is legal? Is illegal downloading possible? Write a one-page report that addresses these questions.

2. Servers: Network Workhorses

Use Google (**www.google.com**) or **www.howstuffworks.com** to locate information on servers and the work they perform. Write a one-page report that summarizes what you've learned.

3. Hunting for Easter Eggs

Easter eggs are special, fun screens or information that software developers put into commercial versions of software. Many different programs include Easter eggs. You can find out about Easter eggs at the Easter Egg Archive (**www.eeggs.com**). Using the information from the Web site, can you locate any Easter eggs in the programs on your computer? How difficult is it to display Easter eggs in some programs? Which Easter eggs surprised you the most? Prepare a presentation on the information you found.

4. Supercomputers—Super Fast!

Compared with other types of computers, there are few supercomputers. Some major universities (such as the University of Tokyo), specialized governmental agencies (such as NASA), and businesses (such as Verizon) use these extremely fast and expensive computers. Visit the list of the world's most powerful computing sites at **www.top500.org** for other types of organizations, agencies, and companies that have supercomputers. Write a brief report that summarizes the following:

- What is the minimum processing speed needed to be included in this list?
- What type and speed of supercomputers are used by the following?
  - Audi AG for designing automotive frames?
  - NASA/Ames Research Center/NAS for critical NASA missions?
  - Harvard University for research on the human heart and circulatory system?
  - Merck & Co. to develop new drugs?

5. International News—The Big Picture

People use media such as radio, television, newspapers, and of course, the Internet to obtain information about current events. The Internet Public Library maintains a worldwide list of newspapers at **www.ipl.org**. International students attending schools in the United States can use this site to read (in their native languages) about events that are happening in their home countries. U.S. students can use this site to read (in English) about global political, financial, or cultural events from the perspective of other nations. Prepare a report that includes reasons why someone would read foreign newspapers as well as the headline or lead story in the following newspapers:

- the *Cape Argus*, published in Cape Town, South Africa
- the *Viet Nam News*, published in Hanoi, Vietnam
- the *Buenos Aires Herald*, published in Buenos Aires, Argentina
- the *Moscow Times*, published in Moscow, Russia
- the *Kuwait Times*, published in Kuwait City, Kuwait

Storing and Transporting Your Data

The computer ate my homework! That's something no one should ever say again with all the storage and backup options now available. Gone are the days when your only option for transporting files was a floppy disk. In fact, most new computers aren't even equipped with a floppy disk drive. You've invested a lot of time and energy in your education, and it's worth a few extra dollars to adopt some of today's improved storage solutions so you can properly store and transport your files. Here's a brief overview of some of the newest products, as well as some advice for minimizing your risk of data loss no matter what type of storage you choose.

One of the most popular new products is the USB flash drive. This drive is small enough to carry in your pocket, but can hold as much as 8 GB (gigabytes) of data. USB flash drives use solid-state flash technology and plug into a computer's USB port. They can be found in most retail and computer stores in an array of styles and capacities. You can even buy one that looks like a rubber ducky or your favorite Star Wars character!

If you have an older PC, it probably has a rewritable CD drive (CD-RW), which can save, or "burn," up to 700 MB (megabytes) of data on inexpensive CD-RWs. Many newer computers often include a rewritable DVD drive. DVDs are available in several different formats, including traditional, double layer, and Blu-Ray. Storage capacity ranges from 4.7 GB to 50 GB, depending on the selected format.

You can also transfer a file via e-mail, if it isn't too large. If you have a Web-based e-mail account such as Yahoo! or Gmail, simply send yourself an e-mail and include the appropriate file as an attachment. However, this is not a good long-term storage solution.

USB drives, CDs, and DVDs are fine for transporting files or making a backup copy of essential data, but for long-term storage consider investing in an external hard drive (Figure 1.25) and starting a regular backup routine. Some external hard drives can store as much as 2 TB (terabytes) of data—that's more than 2,000 GB! Probably more than enough space to store the contents of your entire computer with room to spare.

FIGURE 1.25 Back up your files to an external hard drive.

Backing files up can be as simple as copying your critical files from your hard drive to another storage device, but experts recommend regularly backing up your entire computer. Having a complete backup is critical if you ever experience data loss due to a virus or hard drive failure, and it can also be handy if you need to retrieve a file you deleted accidentally.

The important thing to remember about backups is that your computer is a machine and machines can and do fail. Preparing for such a disaster doesn't have to be difficult. Microsoft Windows includes a backup program and a scheduling tool; however, many different software products are available. When choosing among the many options, consider how often you want to back up—daily, weekly, monthly? Do you want to back up manually or automatically? Automate your backups for one less thing to worry about! And last but not least, where do you want to keep your backup files? Ideally, critical files should be kept off-site in case of flood or fire. Remote backup storage solutions are available, though they usually charge a monthly fee and require high-speed Internet access.

So whether you need to bring your presentation to school for today's speech or want to protect the contents of your computer, you've got great storage options available.

ETHICS

JUSTICE
DELAYED
JUSTICE

What's the difference between unethical and illegal?

When using computers, and especially the Internet, you may have to face this question on a daily basis. Have you downloaded any music recently? Did you pay for that music? What about the DVD movie (or computer game) you watched (or played) at your friend's this weekend? Did he buy it or illegally copy it? Was it a violent game? Have you ever thought about who owns the word-processing software you use in your college computer lab? What is your school or company's policy on acceptable computer use? Perhaps you've written a research paper recently that included material you copied from a Web site. Or perhaps you've posted a spiteful comment about someone on a discussion board or sent a nasty e-mail. How can your behavior on the job cross these lines? *Ethics* is often described as knowing the difference between right and wrong, and choosing to do what is right. In other words, we choose to behave in an ethical way because we couldn't live with our conscience otherwise. It's not about whether we'll get caught. That's the illegal part.

This Spotlight examines some of the most common issues in computer ethics, from ethical dilemmas, where the difference between right and wrong isn't so easy to discern, to legal matters, where right and wrong is determined by law.

COMPUTER ETHICS FOR COMPUTER USERS

It isn't always easy to determine the right thing to do. Even when you know what's right, it's not always easy to act on it. Peer pressure is a tremendous force. Why should you be the one to do the right thing when everyone else is getting away with using copied software and music files?

Computers cause new ethical dilemmas by pushing people into unprecedented situations (Figure 1A). Computer ethics uses basic ethical principles to help you make the right decisions in your daily computer use. Ethical principles help you think through your options.

Figure 1A *Computers cause new ethical dilemmas by pushing people into unprecedented situations.*

ETHICAL PRINCIPLES

An **ethical principle** defines the justification for considering an act or a rule to be morally right or wrong. Over the centuries, philosophers have come up with many ethical principles. For many people, it's disconcerting to find that these principles sometimes conflict. An ethical principle is only a tool that you can use to think through a difficult situation. In the end, you must make your choice and live with the consequences.

Three of the most useful ethical principles are:

- *An act is ethical if, were everyone to act the same way, society as a whole would benefit.*

- *An act is ethical if it treats people as an end in themselves, rather than as a means to an end.*

- *An act is ethical if impartial observers would judge that it is fair to all parties concerned.*

If you still find yourself in an ethical dilemma related to computer use even after careful consideration of these ethical principles, talk to people you trust. Make sure you have all the facts. Think through alternative courses of action based on the different principles. Would you be proud if your parents knew what you had done? What if your action was mentioned in an article on the front page of your local newspaper? Always strive to find a solution you can be proud of.

FOLLOWING YOUR SCHOOL'S CODE OF CONDUCT

When you use a computer, one of the things you will need to determine is who owns the data, programs, and Internet access you enjoy. If you own your computer system and its software, the work you create is clearly yours, and you are solely responsible for it. However, when you use a computer at school or at work, it is possible that the work you create there might be considered the property of the school or business. In short, you have greater responsibility and less control over content ownership when you use someone else's system than when you use your own.

Sometimes this question isn't just an ethical one but a legal one as well. How companies and schools enforce computer usage rules tends to vary. So where can you, the college computer user, find guidance when dealing with ethical and legal dilemmas? Your college or place of employment probably has its own code of conduct or **acceptable use policy** for computer users. You can usually find this policy on your organization's Web site (Figure 1B), in a college or employee handbook, or included in an employment contract. You might call the help desk at your computing center and ask for the Web site address of the policy or request a physical copy of it. Read the policy carefully and follow the rules.

- **Respect yourself.** If you obtain an account and password to use the campus computer system, don't give your password to others. They could do something that gets you in trouble. In addition, don't say or do anything on the Internet that could reflect poorly on you, even if you think no one will ever find out.

- **Respect others.** Obviously, you shouldn't use a computer to threaten or harass anyone. You should also avoid using more than your share of computing resources, such as disk space. If you publish a Web page on your college's computers, remember that your page's content affects the college's public image.

- **Respect academic integrity.** Always give credit for text you've copied from the Internet. Obtain permission before you copy pictures. Don't copy or distribute software unless the license specifically says you can.

Figure 1B *Many organizations publish their computer use (or acceptable use) policy on their Web site.*

TEN COMMANDMENTS FOR COMPUTER ETHICS

The Computer Ethics Institute of the Brookings Institution, located in Washington, D.C., has developed the following "Ten Commandments for Computer Ethics" for computer users, programmers, and system designers:

1. *Don't use a computer to harm other people.*

2. *Don't interfere with other people's computer work.*

3. *Don't snoop around in other people's files.*

4. *Don't use a computer to steal.*

5. *Don't use a computer to bear false witness.*

6. *Don't copy or use proprietary software you have not paid for.*

7. *Don't use other people's computer resources without authorization or proper compensation.*

8. *Don't appropriate other people's intellectual output.*

9. *Do think about the social consequences of the program you write or the system you design.*

10. *Do use a computer in ways that show consideration and respect for your fellow humans.*

NETIQUETTE

General principles such as the "Ten Commandments for Computer Ethics" are useful for overall guidance, but they don't provide specific help for the special situations you'll run into online—such as how to behave properly in chat rooms or while playing an online game (Figure 1C). As a result, computer and Internet users have developed a lengthy series of specific behavior guidelines called **netiquette** for the various Internet services available (such as e-mail, mailing lists, social networking sites, discussion forums, and online role-playing games) that provide specific pointers on how to show respect for others—and for yourself—while you're online.

Here's a sample, based on Albion.com's Netiquette Home Page (**www.albion.com/netiquette**) and other Internet sources:

- **Discussion forums.** Before posting to a discussion forum, review the forum and various topics to see what kinds of questions are welcomed and how to participate meaningfully. If the forum has an FAQ (frequently asked questions) document posted on the Web, be sure to read it before posting to the forum; your question may already have been answered in the FAQ. Post your message under the appropriate topic or start a new topic if necessary. Your post should be helpful or ask a legitimate question. Bear in mind that some people using the discussion forum may not speak English as their native tongue, so don't belittle people for spelling errors. Don't post inflammatory messages; never post in anger. If you agree with something, don't post a message that says "Me too"—you're just wasting everyone's time. Posting ads for your own business or soliciting answers to obvious homework questions is usually frowned upon.

- **E-mail.** Check your e-mail daily and respond promptly to the messages you've been sent. Download or delete messages after you've read them so that you don't exceed your disk-usage quota. Remember that e-mail isn't private; you should never send a message that contains anything you wouldn't want others to read. Always speak of others professionally and

Figure 1C *Netiquette offers guidelines for how to behave properly in chat rooms or while playing an online game.*

courteously; e-mail is easily forwarded, and the person you're describing may eventually see the message. Check your computer frequently for viruses that can propagate via e-mail messages. Keep your messages short and to the point; focus on one subject per message. Don't type in all capital letters; this comes across as SHOUTING. Spell check your e-mail as you would any other written correspondence, especially in professional settings. Watch out for sarcasm and humor in e-mail; it often fails to come across as a joke. Be mindful when you request a return receipt that some people consider this to be an invasion of privacy.

Figure 1D   *Some computer games are both engrossing and violent.*

- **Instant messages (IM) and text messages.** IM and text messages are ideal for brief conversations but complex or lengthy discussions may be better handled in person or by e-mail or phone. IMs can be easily misinterpreted because tone is difficult to convey. Never share bad news or a major announcement in a text message or send an IM while you are angry or upset. Don't assume that everyone knows what IM acronyms such as BRB and LOL mean. Be mindful that some smartphone plans still charge for text messages. Also, remember to set away messages and use other status messages wisely.

Besides respectful use of Internet services, playing computer games is another area where you might face ethical dilemmas.

COMPUTER GAMES: TOO MUCH VIOLENCE?

Computer gaming isn't universally admired. More than one-third of all games fall into the action category; among these, the most popular are so-called "splatter" games, which emphasize all-out violence of an especially bloody sort. Parents and politicians are concerned that children who play these games may be learning aggressive behaviors that will prove dysfunctional in real life—and they may be right.

In one study, 210 college students were observed before and after playing an especially violent computer game. Researchers found that the students were more hostile and reacted more aggressively after playing the game. Another study found that young men who played violent computer games during their teenage years were more likely to commit crimes.

Fears concerning the impact of violent computer games were heightened by the Columbine High School tragedy in 1999, in which two Littleton, Colorado, teenagers opened fire on teachers and fellow students before committing suicide. Subsequently, investigators learned that the boys had been great fans of splatter games, such as Doom and Quake, and may have patterned their massacre after their gaming experiences.

Still, psychologists disagree on the effect of violent computer games. Some point out that they're little more than an extension of the World War II "combat" games that children used to play on street corners before the television—and the computer—came along. Others claim that violent video games provide an outlet for aggression that might otherwise materialize in homes and schools.

One thing's for certain: Computer games are becoming more violent. In the past few years, the video game industry has released a slew of new titles that offer a smoother gaming experience, particularly when a player is connected to the Internet in multiplayer mode—and of course, much more realistic portrayals of violent acts (Figure 1D).

So who's responsible? Is it the software manufacturers who create the programs? Is it the consumers who purchase and use the programs? Parents certainly have a responsibility over what their children do, but what about you—do you make "good" decisions when it comes to exposure to violence? More importantly, is there anything you can do about it? Refer back to the "Ten Commandments for Computer Ethics," especially numbers 9 and 10.

Now that you know about the ethical issues individuals face, let's take a look at how organizations deal with computer ethics.

COMPUTER ETHICS FOR ORGANIZATIONS

Every day, newspapers carry stories about people getting into trouble by using their computers to conduct personal business while they're at work. In many cases, the offenders use company computers to browse the Web and send personal e-mail on company time or to commit crimes such as cyberstalking or distributing pornography. Although most companies have an acceptable-use policy for computers, you should be aware that using a computer for non-business-related tasks is generally banned within an organization. You should check with your system administrator, supervisor, or human resources department to obtain a copy of the company's acceptable use policy.

But that's just individuals' behavior while at work. What ethical responsibilities do the companies themselves have? To serve its customers and the public effectively, a business or organization must protect its data from loss and damage and from error and misuse.

Protecting data from loss is often simply a matter of following proper backup procedures. **Backup procedures** involve making copies of data files to protect against data loss or damage from natural or other disasters. Without backup procedures, an organization may place its customers' information at risk (Figure 1E). What would happen to a bank, for example, if it lost all of its data and didn't have any backups?

Data errors can and do occur. It is the ethical responsibility of any organization that deals with data to ensure that its data is as correct as possible. Data that hasn't been properly maintained can have serious effects on the individual or organization it relates to.

Data misuse occurs when an employee or company fails to keep data confidential. A breach of confidentiality occurs when an employee looks up data about a person in a database and uses that information for something other than what was intended. For example, U.S. government workers accessed the passport files for 2008 presidential candidates John McCain, Barack Obama, and Hillary Clinton, in addition to more than 100 celebrities. Such actions are grounds for termination.

Companies may punish employees for looking up customer data, but many of them think nothing of selling it to third parties. A mail-order company, for example, can gain needed revenue by selling customer lists to firms marketing related products. Privacy advocates believe that it's unethical to divulge customer data without first asking the customer's permission. These advocates are working to pass tougher privacy laws, so the matter would become a legal concern, not an ethical one.

As an employee, what can you do to stop companies from misusing data or to protect your customers' privacy? Often, there's no clear-cut solution. If you believe that the way a company is conducting business poses a danger to the public or appears to be illegal, you can report the company to regulatory agencies or the press, an action called **whistle-blowing**. The Business Software Alliance (BSA) helps to combat software piracy by educating the public and businesses about the legal and safety issues regarding commercial software use. You can even fill out a confidential piracy-reporting form on their Web site at **https://reporting.bsa.org/usa**. But what if your whistle-blowing causes your company to shut down, putting not only you but all of your coworkers out of work? As this example illustrates, codes of ethics don't solve every ethical problem; however, they at least provide solid guidance for most situations.

Figure 1E *A backup system can help protect a business's information assets. It would be unethical not to keep regular backups, because the loss of the company's data could negatively impact the stakeholders in the business.*

COMPUTER ETHICS FOR COMPUTER PROFESSIONALS

No profession can stay in business for long without a rigorous (and enforced) code of professional ethics. That's why many different types of professionals subscribe to ethical **codes of conduct**. These codes are developed by professional associations, such as the Association for Computing Machinery (ACM). Figure 1F is an excerpt from the Code of Ethics of the Institute for Certification of Computing Professionals.

THE ACM CODE OF CONDUCT

Of all the computing associations' codes of conduct, the one developed by the ACM (**www.acm.org**) is considered the most innovative and far-reaching. According to the ACM code, a computing professional

1. *Contributes to society and human well-being*

2. *Avoids harm to others*

3. *Is honest and trustworthy*

4. *Is fair and takes action not to discriminate on the basis of race, sex, religion, age, disability, or national origin*

5. *Honors property rights, including copyrights and patents*

6. *Gives proper credit when using the intellectual property of others*

7. *Respects the right of other individuals to privacy*

8. *Honors confidentiality*

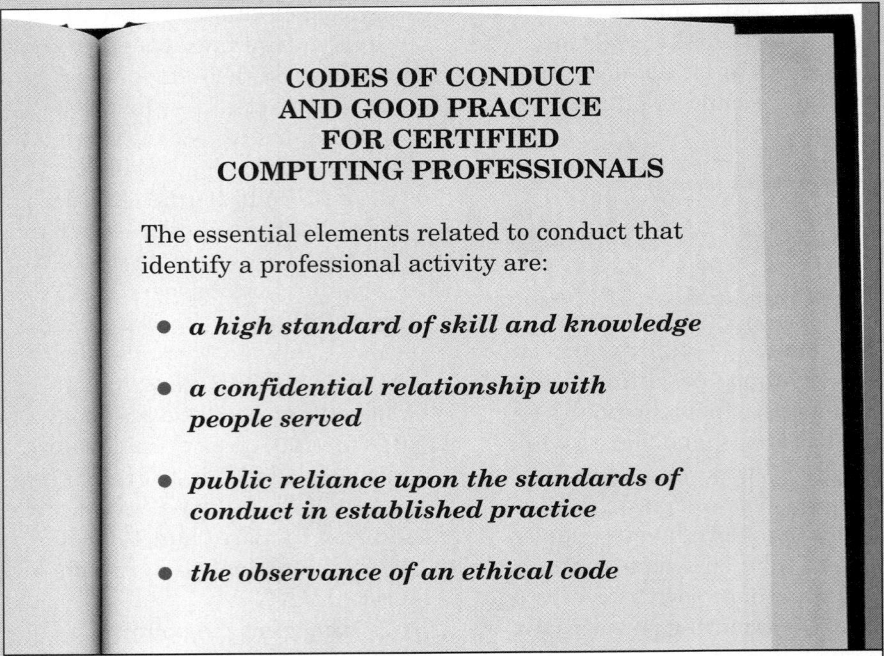

CODES OF CONDUCT AND GOOD PRACTICE FOR CERTIFIED COMPUTING PROFESSIONALS

The essential elements related to conduct that identify a professional activity are:

- *a high standard of skill and knowledge*

- *a confidential relationship with people served*

- *public reliance upon the standards of conduct in established practice*

- *the observance of an ethical code*

Figure 1F *Excerpt from the Code of Ethics of the Institute for Certification of Computing Professionals*

Like other codes of conduct, the ACM code places public safety and well-being at the top of the list.

SAFETY FIRST

Computer professionals create products that affect many people and may even expose them to risk of personal injury or death. Increasingly, computers and computer programs figure prominently in safety-critical systems, including transportation monitoring (such as with air traffic control) and patient monitoring in hospitals (Figure 1G).

Consider the following situation. An airplane pilot flying in poor visibility uses a computerized autopilot to guide the plane. The air traffic control system also relies on computers. The plane crashes. The investigation discloses minor bugs in both computer programs. If the plane's computer had been dealing with a person in the tower rather than a computer, or if the air traffic control program had been interacting with a human pilot, the crash would not have occurred. Where

does the liability lie for the loss of life and property?

Experienced programmers know that programs of any size have bugs. Most complex programs have so many possible combinations of conditions that it isn't feasible to test for every combination. In some cases, the tests would take years; in other cases, no one could think of all the possible conditions. Because bugs are inevitable and programmers can't predict all the different ways programs interact with their environment, most computer experts believe that it's wrong to single out programmers for blame.

Software companies are at fault if they fail to test and document their products. And the organization that buys the software may share part of the blame if it fails to train personnel to use the system properly.

At the core of every computer code of ethics, therefore, is a professional's highest and most important aim: to preserve and protect human life and to avoid harm or injury. If the public is to trust computer

Figure 1G *Computer professionals create products that affect safety-critical systems, including transportation monitoring (such as air traffic control) and patient monitoring in hospitals.*

professionals, they must have the ethics needed to protect our safety and welfare—even if doing so means the professional person or the company they work for suffers financially.

Unlike the ethical dilemmas we've discussed up to now, right and wrong are more easily defined when it comes to matters of the law.

IT'S NOT JUST UNETHICAL, IT'S ILLEGAL, TOO

What else can cause problems for computer users? Let's start with something that gets many college students into serious trouble: plagiarism.

PLAGIARISM

Imagine the following scenario. It's 4 a.m., and you have a paper due for your 9 a.m. class. While searching for sources on the Internet, you find a Web site with an essay on your topic. What's wrong with downloading the text, reworking it a bit, and handing it in? Plenty.

The use of someone else's intellectual property (their ideas or written work) is called **plagiarism**. Plagiarism predates computers; in fact, it has been practiced for thousands of years. But computers—and especially the Internet—make the temptation and ease of plagiarizing even greater. It's not only very easy to copy and paste from the Internet but some sites are actually set up specifically to sell college-level papers to the lazy or desperate. The sites selling the papers aren't

guilty of plagiarism, but you are if you turn in the work as your own.

Plagiarism is a serious offense. How serious? At some colleges, the first offense can get you thrown out of school (Figure 1H). You might think it's rare for plagiarizers to be caught, but the truth is that college instructors are often able to detect plagiarism in students' papers without much effort. The tip-off can be a change in the sophistication of phraseology, writing that is a little too polished, or errors in spelling and grammar that are identical in two or more papers. Software programs are available that can scan text and then compare it against a library of known phrases. If a paper has one or more recognizable phrases, it is marked for closer inspection. Furthermore, even if your actions are not discovered now, someone could find out later, and the evidence could void your degree and even damage your career.

The more well-known you are, the more you're at risk of your plagiarism being uncovered. Take noted historian and Pulitzer Prize–winning author Doris Kearns Goodwin, for example. In 2002, she was accused of plagiarizing part of her best-selling 1987 book *The Fitzgeralds and the Kennedys*. Although she claimed her plagiarizing was inadvertent and due to inadequate research methods, she suffered a significant decline in credibility and even felt obligated to leave her position at the PBS news program *NewsHour with Jim Lehrer*. It took 15 years for Goodwin's plagiarism to come to light.

Plagiarism is a unique offense because it's both unethical and illegal. The unethical part is the dishonesty of passing someone else's work off as your own. The illegal part is taking the material without permission. Plagiarizing copyrighted material is called **copyright infringement**, and if you're caught, you can be sued and may have to pay damages in addition to compensating your victim for any financial losses due to your theft of the material. Trademarks, products, and patented processes are also protected. If you're tempted to copy anything from the Web, bear in mind that the United States is a signatory to international copyright regulations, which specify that an author does not need to include an explicit copyright notice to be protected under the law.

Does this mean you can't use the Internet source you found? Of course not. But you must follow certain citation guidelines. In college writing you can make use of someone else's effort if you use your own words and give credit where credit is due. If you use a phrase or a few sentences from the source, use quotation marks. Attach a bibliography and list the source. For Internet sources, you should list the Web site's address or Uniform Resource Locator (URL), the date the article was published (if available), the date

Figure 1H *At some colleges, plagiarism can get you thrown out of school on the first offense.*

and time you accessed the site, the name of the article, and the author's name. You can usually find a link at the bottom of a Web site's home page that outlines the owner's copyright policy. If not, there is usually a "contact us" link that you can use to contact the owner. You cannot assume that it is legal to copy content from a Web site just because you cannot find a disclaimer.

You'll often hear people use the term **fair use** to justify illegal copying. The fair use doctrine justifies *limited* uses of copyrighted material without payment to or permission from the copyright holder. This means that a *brief* selection from a copyrighted work may be excerpted for the purposes of commentary, parody, news reporting, research, and education. Such excerpts are short—generally, no more than 5 percent of the original work—and they shouldn't compromise the commercial value of the work. In general, the reproduction of an entire work is rarely justifiable by means of the fair use doctrine.

As a responsible computer user, you should worry about not only wrongly using someone else's

words, but also the content you create yourself. The written word carries a lot of power. If those words are untrue, you could be crossing into dangerous, and illegal, territory.

LIBEL

The power of computers and the Internet as a means of communication makes them ripe for involvement in libel. In the United States, **libel** is the publication of a false statement that injures someone's business or personal reputation. A plaintiff who sues for libel must prove that a false statement caused injury and demonstrate some type of resulting damage. This could include being shunned by friends and associates or the inability to obtain work because potential employers believed the false accusations. Some states allow for a jury to assess damages based generally on harm to the person's reputation. It is in your best interest to ensure that any electronic publication statement you make about an individual or a corporation is truthful.

SOFTWARE PIRACY

Here's another common situation. You need to have Microsoft Office 2007 for your computer class. A friend has a copy that she got from her mom's office. You've just installed a copy on your computer. Have you done something wrong? Yes, of course you have! In fact, so has your friend. It is illegal for her to have a copy of the software from her mom's office in the first place.

Just like written works, most computer software (including computer games) is copyrighted, which means that you can't make copies for other people without infringing on the software's copyright. Such infringements are called **software piracy** and are a federal offense in the United States (Figure 1I).

How serious is software piracy? The information technology industry loses billions of dollars a year because of piracy. If you're caught pirating software, you may be charged with a felony. If you're convicted of a felony, you could spend time in jail, lose the right to vote, and ruin your chances for a successful career.

When you purchase commercial software you're really purchasing a **software license**, which generally grants you the right to make backups of the program disks and install the software on multiple machines as long as you're using only one copy of the software at a time. Providing the program to others or modifying the program's function is not allowed.

Free programs that users can copy or modify without restriction are called **public domain software**. However, don't assume that a program is public domain unless you see a note (often in the form of a Read Me text file) that explicitly identifies the file as being copyright free.

Unlike public domain software, you can't copy or modify **shareware** programs without permission from the owner. You can almost always find the owner and licensing information by accessing the Help

Figure 1I   *The Software & Information Industry Association (SIIA) is trying to raise consciousness about software piracy.*

menu or by locating and reading a Read Me file that is usually placed in the same directory as the program. You may, however, freely copy trial or evaluation versions of shareware programs. When the evaluation period expires, you must pay a **registration fee** or delete the software from your computer.

Other programs qualify under the provisions of the Free Software Foundation's **General Public License** (**GPL**), which specifies that anyone may freely copy, use, and modify the software, but no one can sell it for profit.

Organizations with many computers (including colleges) also have to be concerned about software piracy. A **site license** is a contract with the software publisher that allows an organization to use multiple copies of the software at a reduced price per unit. Taking copies outside the organization usually violates the contract.

Software manufacturers are working very hard to develop **copyright protection schemes** to thwart the illegal use of their programs. Increasingly, software is becoming **machine dependent**.

This means that the program captures a machine ID during the installation process and writes that ID back to the software company's server during a mandatory online registration process. If you attempt to install the program on another machine, the code will be checked and the installation will terminate.

How can you tell whether you're guilty of software piracy? All of the following actions are illegal:

- *Incorporating all or part of a GPL program in a commercial program that you offer for sale.*

- *Continuing to use a shareware program past the evaluation version's expiration date without paying the registration fee.*

- *Violating the terms of a software license, even if you've paid for the program. For example, if you have copies of the same program on your desktop and notebook computers but the license forbids this, you are in violation of the license.*

- *Making copies of site-licensed programs that you use at work or school and installing them on your home computer.*

- *Giving or selling copies of commercial software to others.*

Do you have pirated programs on your computer? The police aren't likely to storm into your home or dorm room and take you away, kicking and screaming. Most software piracy prosecutions target individuals who are trying to distribute or sell infringing copies or companies that have illegally made multiple copies for their employees.

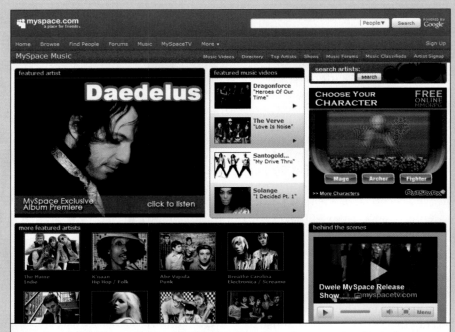

Figure 1J *Sites such as MySpace offer fans the opportunity to learn about their favorite bands.*

If you have any pirated software, you should remove these programs from your computer right away. And in the future, consider whether your actions constitute software piracy before the software is installed on your computer. If you still don't see the need to delete pirated software from your computer, consider this: It's very, very wise to become accustomed to a zero-tolerance approach to pirated software. If you're caught with an infringing program at work, you could lose your job. A company can't risk retaining employees who expose the firm to prosecution.

FILE SHARING: MUSIC, MOVIES, AND MORE

You may have heard that it's okay to download a copyrighted MP3 file as long as you keep it for no longer than 24 hours, but that's false. If you upload music copied from a CD you've paid for, you are violating the law. You can't justify spreading a band's copyrighted music around by saying it's "free advertising"; if the group wants advertising, they'll arrange it themselves (Figure 1J). And don't fall into the trap of thinking that sharing MP3s is legal as long as you don't charge any money for them. Anytime you're taking royalties away from copyright holders, it's illegal.

A 2008 survey found that the average digital music player contains 842 illegally copied songs. Although many people seem to believe that illegal file sharing is okay because so many others are doing it, the entertainment industry is fighting back. Ohio State University recently led the nation in music piracy—its students received more than 2,300 warning letters about pirated music in just one school year. Students can face fines or even jail time for copyright infringement, but schools may also be penalized. Some colleges are taking steps to reduce their liability, such as limiting bandwidth and providing students with free, legal download services.

SPOTLIGHT EXERCISES

1. Have you ever made a copy of software that you've bought for yourself? Did you ever give a copy of it away? What are your feelings about software piracy? Do you own or have access to a CD or DVD burner? What are your thoughts about burning copies of software installations or other CDs or DVDs? Ask four or more other students these same questions and write a report summarizing your findings.

2. A music fan sets up a Web site about his favorite band. On his site, he posts photos he's downloaded from other sites, as well as the lyrics of all the band's songs. He doesn't obtain permission for the photos or lyrics but figures this is fine because his site serves only to promote the band he loves. Write a brief essay on whether he acted ethically and provide support for your position.

3. Online file-sharing sites continue to be popular Internet attractions. Detractors claim that such sites make it easy for users to violate copyright laws. The sites themselves claim that they don't support copyright violations; they simply allow users to share files. Are the users who exchange files on such sites acting ethically? What about those who want to prevent such sites from existing at all? Go to the Web sites for Napster.com, Kazaa.com, or Ruckus.com to learn about their different schemes for allowing the copying of music and video files while still protecting copyright. Write a short paper that describes the scheme of the site you chose.

4. An employee at a small nonprofit organization often uses her home computer to do work for her organization. To complete her work from home, she copies the software program she uses at work to her home computer. The only time she ever uses the software is when she is performing work for the organization. Is what she has done unethical or illegal? Defend your position in a brief essay.

5. A computer tech person working at a campus repair center finds child pornography on a computer he is repairing. He knows that possession of child pornography is illegal and that he should contact the authorities. However, he also knows that he shouldn't have been looking at the contents of the customer's hard drive so closely and that he may lose his job if his employer finds out he did. He doesn't report his discovery to the police. Instead, he permanently erases all the files containing child pornography from the customer's hard drive. What do you think is wrong with this situation?

6. Working with one or more of your classmates, do the following and write a short report: Obtain a copy of your institution's acceptable use policy for computers. What restrictions does the institution place on your computer use that you might not apply when using your own computer or a commercial Internet connection? What are the advantages of connecting to the Internet through an institution instead of through a commercial connection? Are there time restrictions? Are there volume restrictions? Are there any content restrictions? Are there ethical concerns when using the school's system that you wouldn't have if you were using your own system?

What You'll Learn . . .

- Explain how the Internet works.

- Describe methods for accessing the Internet.

- Define and differentiate the Internet and the World Wide Web.

- Explain the concept of hypertext.

- Contrast Web browsers and Web servers.

- Explain the parts of a URL and how to access Web pages.

- Contrast Web subject guides and search engines.

- Explain how search operators can improve Web search results.

- Evaluate the reliability of information on a Web page.

- List the most popular Internet services and explain what they do.

The Internet &
the World Wide Web

CHAPTER OUTLINE

How the Internet Works **48**
    Interoperability 48

Accessing the Internet: Going Online **51**
    Internet Service Providers and Online Services 51

The Internet and the Web: What's the Difference? **53**
    The Hypertext Concept 54
    Web Browsers and Web Servers 55
    Web Addresses (URLs) 57
    Browsing the Web 60

Finding Information on the Web **63**
    Using Search Engines 63
    Using Search Techniques 64
    Evaluating Information 67
    Using the Web for Schoolwork 68

Exploring Internet Services **70**
    E-mail: Staying in Touch 70
    Instant Messaging: E-mail Made Faster 73
    Internet Relay Chat: Text Chatting in Real Time 74
    Social Networking: Helping People Connect 74
    File Transfer Protocol: Transferring Files 75
    Usenet: Joining Online Discussions 75
    Electronic Mailing Lists 77

Destinations

If you'd like to learn about Internet history, the best place to start is the Internet Society's "Histories of the Internet" page at **www.isoc.org/internet/history**. The Internet Society is an organization for professionals who are interested in supporting the Internet's technical development.

Techtalk

Internet2 (I2)
The Internet2 (I2) project is a nonprofit consortium of universities, government agencies, and leading computer and telecommunications companies in more than 50 countries. Members of the I2, including more than 200 U.S. universities, are developing and deploying advanced networking applications and technologies to provide high-speed bandwidth access to enhance partnerships among academia, industry, and government.

As you may already know, the **Internet** is a global computer network made up of thousands of privately and publicly owned computers and networks, and it's growing rapidly. Today, hundreds of thousands of networks and more than 1 billion computers of all types and sizes are directly connected to the Internet. According to one estimate, the total amount of information available on this worldwide network doubles each year. But defining the Internet as a fast-growing global network understates its significance.

The Internet was originally planned to be nothing more than a communication and file-exchange network for academics and government agencies. However, it has become a medium for discovering and exploring information that even novices can enjoy (Figure 2.1). Today, we're witnessing the birth of the first major mass medium since television; more than 70 percent of U.S. residents are Internet users. What's more, the Internet isn't simply a new mass medium; it's the *first* mass medium that involves computers and uses digitized data. And it's more interactive than TV, radio, and newspapers, which limit user interaction to content consumption. With the Internet, people can create information as well as consume it. With the growing popularity of Web 2.0 applications such as wikis and blogs, it's the first truly democratic mass medium, allowing anyone to add content to the growing mass of information available online.

Most college students have used the Internet—it's hard to imagine students these days not having heard of a Web page, a URL, or a Web link. But no matter how familiar you think you are with this part of the Internet, this chapter will help you fully understand the concepts behind the Web and Web browsers. In addition, this chapter will show you how to use the Web effectively for research and how to evaluate the quality of the information you retrieve.

Now that you know what the Internet is, let's explore how it works and how it is used.

How the Internet Works

The Internet is best thought of as *the* overarching network of networks. In this network of networks, theoretically every connected computer can exchange data with any other computer on the network. The Internet is also referred to as **cyberspace**—territory that isn't an actual, physical place and that is accessible only with computers. The networks that make up the Internet are maintained by large organizations, such as corporations and universities, as well as by service providers that sell Internet subscriptions to the public (Figure 2.2).

INTEROPERABILITY

The Internet does more than merely allow any one of millions of computers to exchange data with any other. One key to the Internet's success is called **interoperability**, the ability to work with a computer even if it is a different brand and model. This remarkable characteristic of the Internet comes into play every time you use the network. When you access the Internet using a Mac, for example, you contact a variety of machines that may include other Macs, Windows PCs, UNIX machines, and even mainframe computers. You don't know what type of computer you're accessing, however, and it doesn't make any difference (Figure 2.3).

The Internet's interoperability helps explain the network's popularity. No network could match the Internet's success if it forced people to use just one or two types of computers. Many home computer users have IBM-compatible PCs, but others

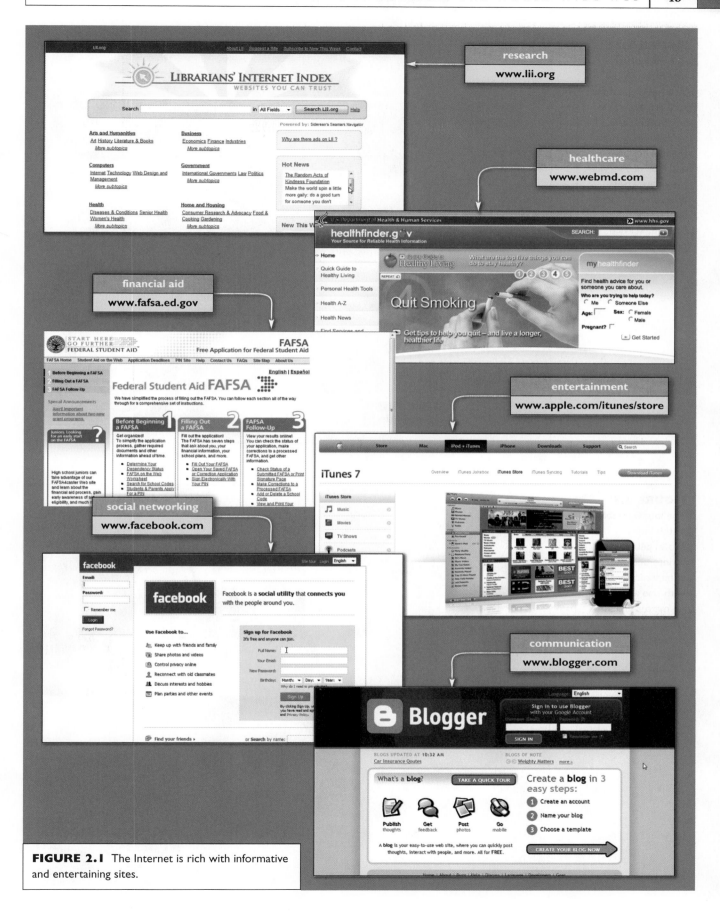

research
www.lii.org

healthcare
www.webmd.com

financial aid
www.fafsa.ed.gov

entertainment
www.apple.com/itunes/store

social networking
www.facebook.com

communication
www.blogger.com

FIGURE 2.1 The Internet is rich with informative and entertaining sites.

FIGURE 2.2
The networks that make up the Internet's infrastructure are maintained by corporations, universities, government agencies, and Internet service providers. Users interact with them all through their Internet service provider.

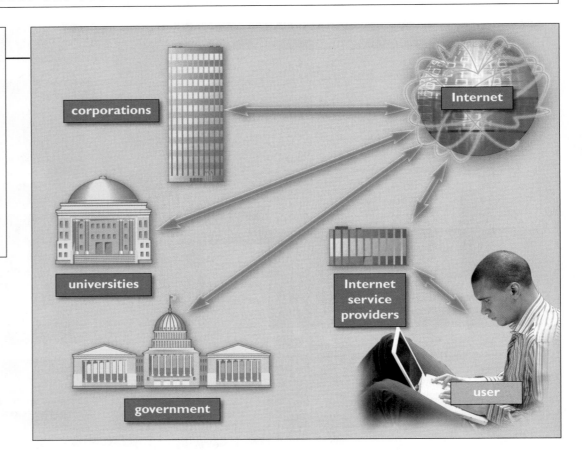

FIGURE 2.3
The interoperability of the Internet allows people to interact and communicate with one another, no matter which type of computer or operating system they use.

have Macs or other types of computers or communications and browsing devices. The Internet enables these computers to exchange data and even to control each other's operations, regardless of the system being used, allowing greater flexibility for communication and collaboration.

Now that you've learned about how the Internet works, the next section explores how you go about getting online.

Accessing the Internet: Going Online

When you access the Internet, it is referred to as *going online*. You need two things to go online: an Internet account and a method of connecting or gaining access. How do you get both of these? By contacting an Internet service provider.

INTERNET SERVICE PROVIDERS AND ONLINE SERVICES

Internet service providers (ISPs) are companies that provide access to the Internet, primarily to individual and business users. Users receive an Internet account, which often includes several password-protected user names. Access may be provided via telephone lines, cable, satellite, or fiber-optic technologies. SBC, Verizon, AOL, and Comcast are all examples of ISPs (Figure 2.4). An **online service** is a for-profit firm that provides a

proprietary network offering special services that are available only to subscribers. Members may participate in chat rooms and discussions and take advantage of fee-based content, such as magazines and newspapers.

So what's the difference between an ISP and an online service, such as MSN or AOL? Not much anymore. As the Internet grew in popularity during the late 1990s, online services began to offer Internet access in an attempt to keep existing customers and attract new ones. While retaining their proprietary network and custom content, they have become ISPs.

To enable users to access the Internet, ISPs distribute software that runs on users' computers, makes the connection, and guides them through the available content and activities. These various providers usually charge a monthly fee for Internet access, but you can sometimes obtain free trial accounts for a certain number of days or hours.

ISPs have several roles and responsibilities. They are responsible for providing and maintaining a connection to the Internet. It might help to think of an ISP as an on-ramp to a highway. When you want to travel that highway, you must first get on the highway via one of its on-ramps. ISPs must also support the hardware and software needed to service that connection. They need to protect their site and network from external threats such as viruses, hacker attacks, and other illegal activities. And finally, they should provide 24-hour customer service and technical support.

In addition to obtaining an Internet account, you need to decide how you will

ISPs require users to sign in to access their e-mail and account information.

Many ISPs provide links to current events, weather, sports, and entertainment information.

ISPs may also offer the ability to customize the information displayed.

FIGURE 2.4 Internet service providers, such as Comcast, provide Internet access to individuals and businesses.

Destinations

Looking for an ISP? A good place to start is The List (www.thelist.com), which is a buyer's guide to ISPs. You can search for an ISP by area code or country.

access the Internet (Figure 2.5). Your choices typically include the following options:

- **Dial-up access.** Some home users still connect to the Internet using a dial-up connection, which requires a modem and a telephone line. With this method, your computer is directly connected to the Internet, but it's usually only temporarily connected. That is why you sometimes get bumped off or disconnected when online. Dial-up access is typically the most affordable option for many people. Because most homes have at least one phone line and many PCs include an internal modem, equipment cost is minimal. But dial-up is also the slowest type of Internet access.

- **Digital subscriber line (DSL).** DSL connections offer high-speed access and a permanent online connection. Like dial-up, DSL uses phone lines but also requires a special external modem. One drawback of DSL is that service doesn't extend more than a few miles from a telephone switching station or central office (CO). Although this distance is being extended, DSL service may be unavailable in some rural areas.

- **Cable access.** Many cable TV companies provide permanent online connections and offer high-speed Internet access, comparable to—and sometimes surpassing—DSL speeds. No phone line is needed, but a cable modem is required.

- **Satellite access.** Capable of fast downloads, satellite access requires a phone line and a modem for uploading data, as well as a satellite dish. Satellite access provides a temporary connection and works better in rural or less congested areas where signal interference is not an issue.

- **Fiber-optic service (FiOS).** Fiber-optic lines running directly to the home provide users with incredibly fast Internet access, easily surpassing other methods. With more than 1.5 million customers in at least 13 states, FiOS is rapidly becoming a challenger to DSL and cable providers, especially in the suburbs. However, this service is still unavailable in many cities and rural areas and is only provided by Verizon. No modem is needed, but fiber-optic cable may need to be run to and within your home.

FIGURE 2.5 Types of Internet Access

Type	Price Range per Month	Speed of Access (receiving data)	Advantages	Disadvantages
Dial-up	$5 to $25	Slow: 56 Kbps	Availability Low user cost	Slow speed
DSL	$20 to $60	Average : 1.5 Mbps Maximum 6+ Mbps	Speed Reliability	Availability High user cost
Cable	$30 to $60	Average : 3 Mbps Maximum 30+ Mbps	Speed Reliability	Availability High user cost
Satellite	$60 to $100	Average : 700 Kbps Maximum 1.5 Mbps	Availability Speed	High user cost Reliability
FiOS	$40 to $180	Average : 15 Kbps Maximum 50+ Mbps	Speed	Availability High user cost

Many ISPs also provide direct connections on special leased lines for businesses, educational institutions, and large organizations. Internet access is attained through the organization's network and is usually free to the users, because the company or institution pays the bill.

Now that you understand the various ways to access the Internet, let's differentiate the Internet from its most popular entity, the World Wide Web.

The Internet and the Web: What's the Difference?

What's the difference between saying "I'm on the Internet" versus "I'm on the Web"? Although many people talk as if the Internet and the Web were the same thing, they aren't. As we learned earlier, the Internet is a network through which any computer can directly access other computers and exchange data. The **World Wide Web** (or **Web** or **WWW**) is a portion of the Internet that contains billions of documents. The Web *uses* the Internet as its transport mechanism, but it's a separate entity (Figure 2.6). The Internet is the physical connection of millions of networks, whereas the Web is an information resource that enables millions of Internet users to research products, get medical advice, read about current events, and much more.

Who owns or controls the Internet and the Web? No one. The Internet is made up of thousands of publicly and privately owned computers and networks, all of which agree to follow certain standards and guidelines and share resources on the network. A variety of organizations are responsible for different aspects of the network (Figure 2.7). For example, the World Wide Web Consortium (W3C), based in Cambridge, Massachusetts, issues standards related to all aspects of the Web.

A **Web site** is a location that is accessible from the Internet and makes Web pages available. A **Web page** is any document on a Web site that includes text, graphics, sound, animation, or video. Web sites are collections of related Web pages. A Web site typically contains a **home page** (also called an **index page**), which is a default page that's displayed automatically when you enter a site at its top level.

It's amazing to think that the Web's billions of documents are almost instantly accessible by means of the computer sitting on your desk. Tens of thousands of new Web pages appear every day. The Web is also appealing because of its graphical richness, which is made possible by the integration of text and graphics.

In the following section, you'll learn how all of these pieces work together on the Web, starting with the concept of hypertext.

FIGURE 2.6 The Internet provides the infrastructure used to transport the ideas, queries, and information available on the World Wide Web to and from users.

FIGURE 2.7 Internet Management Organizations

Name	Purpose
ISOC—Internet Society **www.isoc.org**	Nonprofit, international organization consisting of over 80 organizations and 28,000 individual members, formed to provide leadership in Internet-related standards, education, and policy and to ensure the open development, evolution, and use of the Internet for the benefit of people throughout the world.
IETF—Internet Engineering Task Force **www.ietf.org**	International community of information technology (IT) professionals, including network designers, operators, vendors, and researchers, responsible for improving the operation of the Internet by developing protocol standards, best current practices, and informational documents.
IAB—Internet Architecture Board **www.iab.org**	Advisory body to the ISOC, this international committee of the IETF comprises 13 volunteers from the IT community who oversee the development of Internet architecture, protocols, procedures, and standards.
IRTF—Internet Research Task Force **www.irtf.org**	A task force comprising individual contributors from the research community working together in small, long-term research groups that report to the IAB and explore important topics relating to the evolution of the Internet.
ICANN—Internet Corporation for Assigned Names and Numbers **www.icann.org**	Nonprofit, international organization responsible for keeping the Internet secure, stable, and interoperable by coordinating the Internet's Domain Name System and assigning IP addresses.
Network Solutions **www.networksolutions.com**	Organization responsible for managing the central domain name database. Network Solutions was the first and only public domain name registrar until 1999, when the registration process was opened to competition.
W3C—World Wide Web Consortium **www.w3.org**	An international consortium of over 440 organizations in more than 40 countries responsible for ensuring long-term growth for the World Wide Web and promoting Web interoperability through the publication of open standards for Web languages and protocols.

THE HYPERTEXT CONCEPT

The Web's billions of documents are created using special coding known as **Hypertext Markup Language (HTML)**. **Hypertext** is a method of preparing and publishing text that is ideally suited to be read with a computer. You can think of hypertext as active text that is linked to text or graphics contained within the document you are reading or in other documents in cyberspace.

Hypertext works by means of hyperlinks. **Hyperlinks** (also called **links**) are words or images you can click to bring another document into view (Figure 2.8).

In addition to being a global hypertext system, the Web is a distributed hypermedia system. A **distributed hypermedia system** is a network-based content development system that uses multimedia resources, such as sound, video, and text, as a means of navigation or illustration. In this system, the responsibility for creating

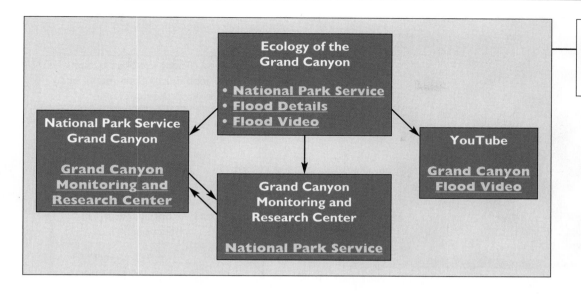

content is distributed among many people. The next generation of the Web, known as **Web 2.0**, provides even more opportunities for individuals to collaborate, interact with one another, and create new content by using applications such as blogs, wikis, and podcasts. The more people who create content, the easier information creation and dissemination becomes. For example, if you are creating a Web site on the ecology of the Grand Canyon you might link to the National Park Service for a general overview, link to the Grand Canyon Monitoring and Research Center for details on the flood the dam operators released in 2008 to improve the canyon's ecosystem, and link to a site such as YouTube for a video of the event.

The Web's distribution of content creation responsibilities does have a drawback: You can link to any page you want, but you can't guarantee that the page's author will keep the page on the Web. The author can delete it or move it at any time without notice. For this reason, **dead links** (also called **broken links**), which are links to documents that have disappeared, are common on the Web.

Now that you understand hypertext, let's move on to what enables us to use it: browsers and servers.

WEB BROWSERS AND WEB SERVERS

The first graphical Web browsers (which make hypertext become "live" on your computer screen) were developed in 1993. A **Web browser** is a program that displays a Web document and enables you to access linked documents. Figure 2.9 illustrates how to connect to the Web via your browser.

The first successful graphical browser, called Mosaic, helped launch the Web on the road to popularity. Developed by the National Center for Supercomputing Applications at the University of Illinois, Mosaic was followed by two commercial products, Netscape Navigator and Microsoft Internet Explorer. Initially, Netscape was extremely successful, but it eventually lost ground to Internet Explorer. The last version of Netscape was released in 2008. However, Mozilla Firefox, a new browser built using the Netscape model, began challenging Internet Explorer in 2004.

Both major browser programs use similar features, such as tabbed browsing, navigation buttons, a search box, an address bar, and a status bar, as shown in Figure 2.10. When you first launch a browser it may default to a preset home page from your ISP or the publisher of the browser software. You can either keep this as your home page, which will be displayed each time you start your browser, or you can change the browser's default home page, also referred to as customizing your browser. You can find the default home page settings in Internet Explorer under the Tools, Internet Options menu (Figure 2.11).

Browsers display and act on documents that are created using hypertext. It is the browser that allows the text and graphics on a hypertext document to be

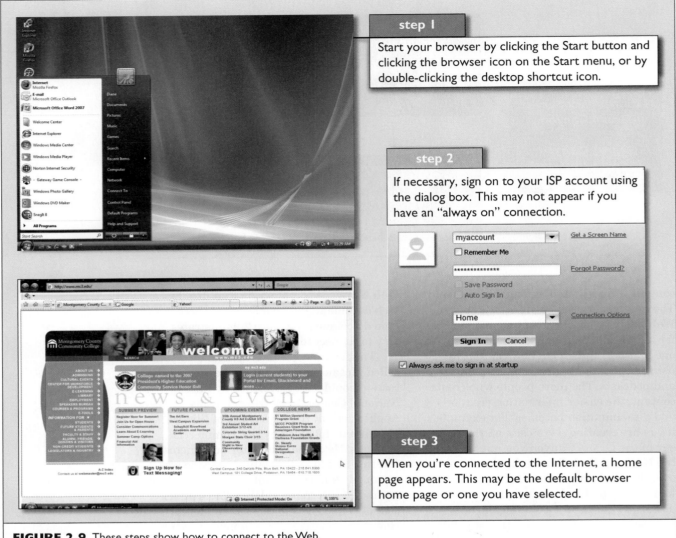

step 1

Start your browser by clicking the Start button and clicking the browser icon on the Start menu, or by double-clicking the desktop shortcut icon.

step 2

If necessary, sign on to your ISP account using the dialog box. This may not appear if you have an "always on" connection.

step 3

When you're connected to the Internet, a home page appears. This may be the default browser home page or one you have selected.

FIGURE 2.9 These steps show how to connect to the Web.

Destinations

The Opera Web browser is known for its advanced cross-platform technology for desktop computers, mobile phones, and other products. Visit **www.opera.com** for more information about the Opera Web browser.

active. In short, browsers are meant to work with Web pages. Sometimes you need to upgrade your browser to the latest version so that you can fully enjoy the features of a Web site. New Web page creation software is being developed all the time, and eventually older browsers won't have the capability of displaying the newest features or animations. Browsers use **plug-ins**, which are software programs that allow you to derive the full benefits of a Web site, such as sound or video. If a Web site requires a plug-in to function properly, a pop-up message will appear in newer browsers, indicating which plug-in is needed, with an option to install the plug-in or cancel the installation.

Another feature that browsers share is the ability to cache, or store, Web page files and graphics on your computer. When you browse a Web page the first time, it is stored on your hard drive in a specially assigned storage space. This allows Web pages to be retrieved faster the next time you want to browse them because they don't have to be transferred across the Internet. The positive aspect of this feature is that you can retrieve Web pages faster; the downside is that a Web page you retrieve from your hard disk may not be the most current version. This does not happen often, but if it does, simply click the Refresh button on your browser's toolbar to obtain the latest content.

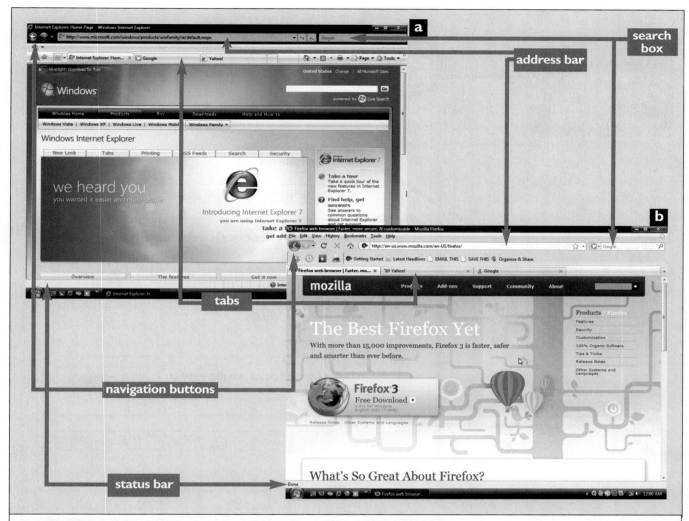

FIGURE 2.10 (a) Microsoft Internet Explorer and (b) Mozilla Firefox are the two most popular graphical Web browsers. They use similar features, such as tabbed browsing, navigation buttons, a search box, an address bar, and a status bar.

Web sites and their affiliated materials are housed on Web servers. Millions of Web servers are located all over the world. When you click a hyperlink, the browser sends a message to a Web server, asking the server to retrieve the requested information and send it back to the browser through the network. A **Web server** is a computer running server software that accepts requests for information, processes those requests, and sends the requested documents. If the file isn't found, the server sends an error message.

WEB ADDRESSES

To locate a resource on the Web, you have to know how to find the Web server on which it resides. Every computer, server, or device connected to the Internet is assigned an **Internet Protocol (IP) address** that uniquely identifies it to the network. The IP address consists of four groups of numbers, separated by periods. The value in each group ranges from 0 to 255. An example would be the IP address *128.30.52.38*, which corresponds to the W3C Web site. Although this numeric system works well for computers, it doesn't work as well for people. You could type the numeric address into your browser, but most of us find that it's much easier to use text names, such as those found in a URL. A **URL (Uniform Resource Locator)** is a string of characters that precisely identifies an Internet resource's type and location. It is much easier to access the W3C Web site by typing **http://www.w3.org** than it

1. Click Tools, then Internet Options (Tools, Options for Firefox users).

2. Add a URL for each site you want to include.

3. Click OK.

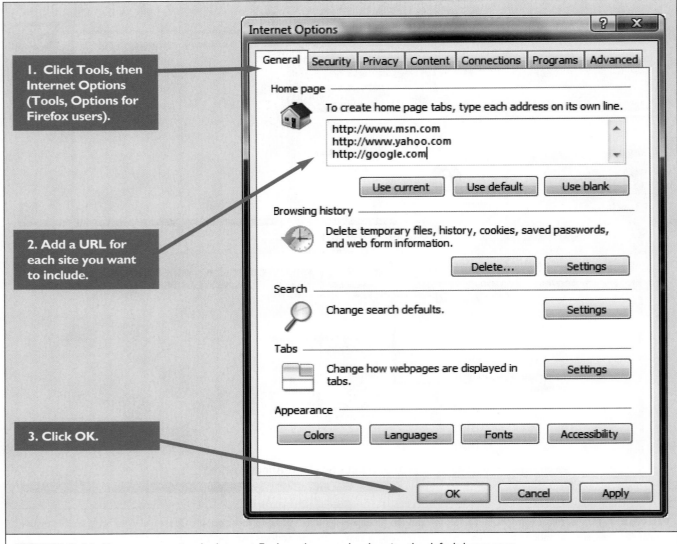

FIGURE 2.11 You can customize the Internet Explorer browser by changing the default home page.

is to remember *128.30.52.38*. The URL is a Web site's address, and the IP address identifies the Web server's location.

A complete URL has four parts: protocol, domain name, path, and resource name (Figure 2.12).

Protocol

The first part of a complete URL specifies the **Hypertext Transfer Protocol (HTTP)**, the Internet standard that supports the exchange of information on the Web. Most browsers can also access information using FTP (File Transfer Protocol) and other protocols. The protocol name is followed by a colon and two forward slash marks (//). You can

generally omit the *http://* protocol designation when you're accessing a Web page, because the browser assumes that you are browsing hypertext Web pages. For example, you can access **http://www. pearsonhighered.com/cayf** by typing **www.pearsonhighered.com/cayf**.

Domain Name

The second part of a complete URL specifies the Web site's **domain name**, which correlates to the Web server's IP address. The domain name has two parts: a host name and a top-level domain name. Some domain names also include a prefix, the most common of which is "www." Early Web servers adopted the name "WWW," but this has become less common. The **host name** is usually the name of the group or institution hosting the site. The **top-level domain (TLD) name** is the extension (such as .com or .edu) following the host name and indicates the type of group or institution to which the site belongs.

The Domain Name System

The Internet uses a system called the **Domain Name System (DNS)** to link domain names with their corresponding IP addresses, functioning like a phone book for the Internet. The Domain Name System enables users to type an address that includes letters as well as numbers. A process called **domain name registration** enables individuals and organizations to register a domain name with a service organization such as InterNIC. You can use your favorite search engine to search for domain name registrars to find other sites that provide this service.

Domain names can tell you a great deal about where a computer is located. For Web sites hosted in the United States, top-level domain names (the *last* part of the domain name) indicate the type of organization in which the computer is located (Figure 2.13). Outside the United States, the top-level domain indicates the name of the country in which the computer hosting the Web site is located, such as .ca (Canada), .uk (United Kingdom), and .jp (Japan).

Path

The third part of a complete URL specifies the location of the document on the server. It contains the document's location on the computer, including the names of subfolders (if any). In the example in Figure 2.12, the path to the default.aspx file on the Web server at **www.microsoft.com** is **/windows/default.aspx**.

Resource Name

The last part of a complete URL gives the filename of the resource you're accessing. A resource is a file, such as an HTML file, a sound file, a video file, or a graphics file. The resource's extension

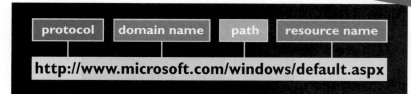

FIGURE 2.12 A complete URL has four parts: protocol, domain name, path, and resource name. This is the URL for the default Microsoft Windows home page.

(the part of the filename after the period) indicates the type of resource it is. For example, HTML documents have the .html or .htm extension.

Many URLs don't include a resource name because they reference the server's default home page. If no resource name

FIGURE 2.13 Common Top-Level Domain Names

Top-Level Domain Name	Used By
.com	Commercial businesses
.biz	Businesses
.edu	Educational institutions
.info	Information
.gov	Government agencies
.pro	Professionals
.mil	Military
.aero	Aviation
.net	Network organizations (such as ISPs)
.coop	Cooperatives
.org	Nonprofit organizations
.museum	Museums
.name	Names

Destinations

Visit the Internet Corporation for Assigned Names and Numbers (ICANN) at **www.icann.org** for more information on domain names.

Techtalk

spiders
The Web contains more than just a vast network of information links. "Spiders" exist there, too. A spider is a small piece of software that crawls around the Web, picking up URLs and information on the pages attached to them.

is specified, the browser looks for a file named *default* or *index*—a default page that's displayed automatically when you enter the site at its top level. If it finds such a file, it loads it automatically. For example, **www.microsoft.com/windows** displays the default Microsoft Windows home page. Other URLs omit both the path name and the resource name. These URLs reference the Web site's home page. For example, **www. microsoft.com** displays Microsoft's home page on the Web.

BROWSING THE WEB

When you have installed browser software and are connected to the Internet, you're ready to browse the Web. To access a Web page, you can do any of the following (Figure 2.14):

- **Type a URL in the address bar.** You don't need to type http://. Watch for spelling errors, and don't insert spaces. A common mistake is typing a comma instead of a period to separate the components of a URL.

- **Click a tab in the browser window.** Both major browsers offer **tabbed browsing**, which enables a user to quickly switch between Web sites. You can customize your home page by adding tabs for sites that you frequently access.

- **Click a hyperlink.** Hyperlinks are usually underlined, but sometimes they're embedded in graphics or highlighted in other ways, such as with shading or colors. To tell whether a given portion of a Web page contains a hyperlink, position your mouse pointer over it and watch for a change in the pointer's shape. Most browsers indicate the presence of a hyperlink by changing the on-screen pointer to a hand shape.

As you browse the Web, your browser keeps a list of the Web pages you've accessed called the **history list**. If you'd like to return to a previously viewed site and can't find it by clicking the Back button, you can consult the history list and choose the page from there. You'll soon find some Web pages you'll want to

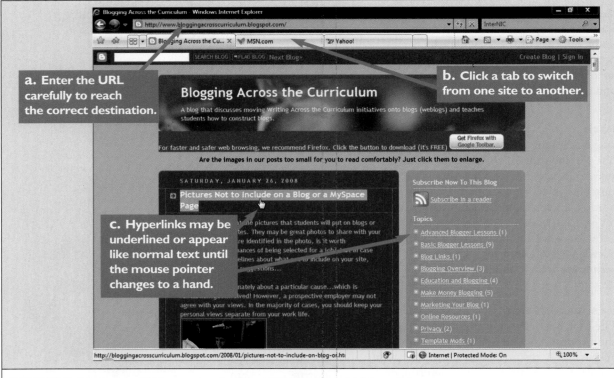

FIGURE 2.14 A typical Web page showing (**a**) a URL, (**b**) tabs, and (**c**) hyperlinks.

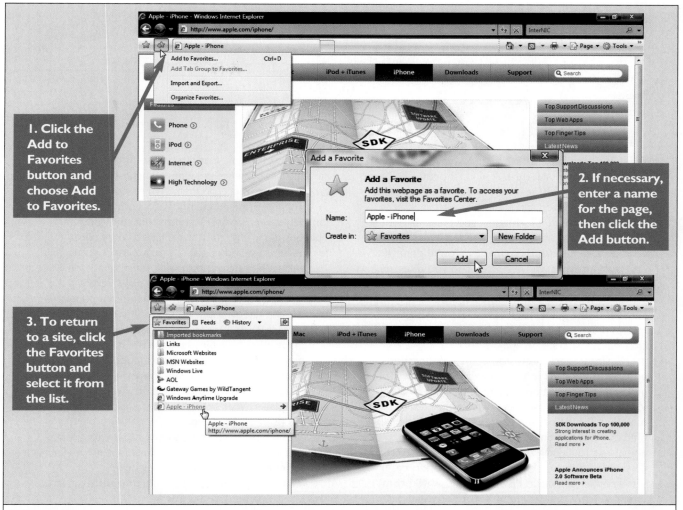

1. Click the Add to Favorites button and choose Add to Favorites.

2. If necessary, enter a name for the page, then click the Add button.

3. To return to a site, click the Favorites button and select it from the list.

FIGURE 2.15 Follow the steps shown to save a Web page to your Favorites in Internet Explorer. Creating Bookmarks in Mozilla Firefox is very similar.

return to frequently. To return easily, you can save these pages as Favorites (Internet Explorer) or Bookmarks (Mozilla Firefox) (Figure 2.15). After you've saved these pages as Favorites or Bookmarks, you'll see the names of these pages in the Favorites or Bookmarks menu.

Uploading and Downloading

After you have browsed the Web and accessed various Web pages, you may want to try downloading or uploading data. With **downloading**, a document or file is transferred from another computer to your computer. With **uploading**, you transfer files from your computer to another computer.

You should exercise caution when downloading files of unknown origin from the Web. If you download software from a site that doesn't inspect files using up-to-date antivirus software, you could infect your computer with a virus. Most Internet users believe that it's safe to download software from Web sites maintained by software companies. However, be aware that some viruses are spread in the data files of popular programs, such as Microsoft Word or Excel. Be sure to check any software or data files that you download with an antivirus program.

Now that you understand the basics of the Internet and Web, let's examine how to conduct research on the Web.

IMPACTS

Emerging Technologies

Wiki, Blog, Podcast: Sharing Information—Fast

Want to share information fast? A wiki, blog, or podcast may be in your future. A wiki (short for *wiki-wiki*, the Hawaiian word for "fast") is a simple Web page on which any visitor can post text or images, read and change posted information, and track earlier changes. No elaborate coding needed—just click to post, click to refresh the page, and you're done. If a visitor changes what you've posted and you disagree, just click to revert to an earlier version. See a wiki in action by visiting **www. wikimusicguide.com**, an open-content music guide. Fans can create new pages about music or artists, share information, and edit entries created by others.

Businesses are interested in the collaboration possibilities of wikis. It is estimated that at least 50 percent of organizations will be using wikis by 2009. Wikis can be public, or they can be restricted to specific members. Businesses using wikis have found that real-time communications improved and time spent on e-mail was reduced. Wikis also provide a way to share corporate knowledge with the entire workforce. Try setting up a free wiki at PBwiki (**http://pbwiki.com**) next time you work on a group project to eliminate the

scheduling problems that often arise. Group members can share documents and ideas and collaborate at any time, from anywhere, on their own schedule.

The Internet equivalent of a journal, blogs (short for Weblogs) allow users to post their thoughts and opinions, along with photos or links to other sites, for the entire world to see. There are more than 15.5 million blogs covering a wide range of personal, political, or professional topics. Blogs by Microsoft employees (see **http://blogs.msdn.com**) are popular because of their insightful observations and tech know-how (Figure 2.16). Visit **www.blogsearchengine.com** to search for blogs by subject and for FAQs about blogging.

If you'd rather get your information in audio or video format, podcasts may be the answer! Despite the name, you can listen to podcasts on your PC or on an MP3 player. Visit sites that host podcasts or sign up for one using an RSS feed. Imagine taking a physics class at MIT or listening to an interview with your favorite musician. Check the Podcast Directory (**www.podcast.net**) to hear what's new!

Whether you use a wiki, blog, or podcast, interactivity is the name of the game.

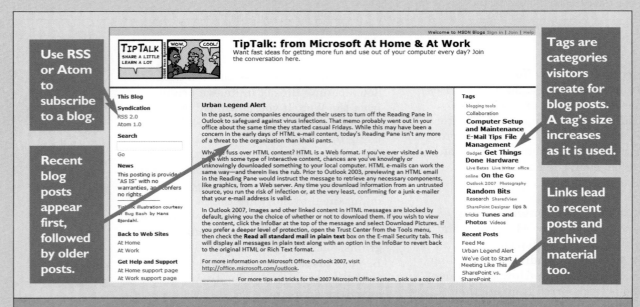

FIGURE 2.16 Blogs can be entertaining or provide information on a wide variety of subjects.

Finding Information on the Web

Although browsing by means of hyperlinks is easy and fun, it falls short as a means of information research. Web users soon find themselves clicking link after link, searching for information that they never find. If you can't find the information you're looking for after a bit of browsing, try *searching* the Web. You've no doubt heard of Google, Yahoo!, Live Search, and Ask. Although these and other Web search tools are far from perfect, knowing how to use them effectively (and knowing their limitations) can greatly increase your chances of finding the information you want.

Some search sites offer a **subject guide** to the Web, grouping Web pages under headings such as business, news, or travel (Figure 2.17). These guides don't try to include every Web page on the World Wide Web. Instead, they offer a selection of high-quality pages that the search site believes represent some of the more useful Web pages in a given category. If you're just beginning your search for information, a subject guide is an excellent place to start.

USING SEARCH ENGINES

If you can't find what you're looking for in a Web subject guide, you can try searching databases that claim to index the full Web, but with more than 110 million Web sites, and billions of Web pages, in existence, that's a pretty daunting task. These **search engines** maintain databases of the Web pages they've indexed, but it is estimated that more than 75 percent of the Internet is yet to be mined.

More than 10 billion searches were conducted just in January 2008! Of the five core search engines used that month, Google was used more often than all of the other search engines combined. Yahoo! was a distant second, followed by Microsoft, AOL, and Ask (Figure 2.18).

Although an enormous pool of information is available on the Web, chances are that by using these search engines you'll find information relevant to the subject you're researching.

Techtalk

clickstream
As you click from site to site on the Web, you leave a clickstream in your wake. A clickstream is the trail of Web links that you have followed to get to a particular site. Internet merchants are quite interested in analyzing clickstream activity so they can do a better job of targeting advertisements and tailoring Web pages to potential customers.

FIGURE 2.17 Subject guides can help you quickly find the information you seek.

FIGURE 2.18 In 2008, the Google search engine was used more than all of the others combined.

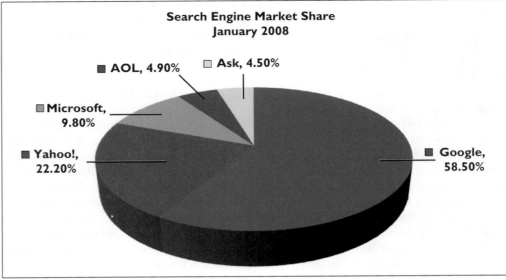

**Search Engine Market Share
January 2008**

- AOL, 4.90%
- Ask, 4.50%
- Microsoft, 9.80%
- Yahoo!, 22.20%
- Google, 58.50%

Green Tech Tip

Environmental concerns generate a lot of interest. Now there's even a "green" search engine—Green Maven (**www. greenmaven.com**). Use it to find environmentally conscious Web sites and news.

To use a search engine, type one or more words that describe the subject you're looking for into the search text box and click Search (or press Enter). Generally, it's a good idea to type several words (four or five) rather than just one or two. If you use only one or two words, the Web search will produce far more results than you can use.

Why do search engines sometimes produce unsatisfactory results? The problem lies in the ambiguity of the English language. Suppose you're searching for information on the Great Wall of China. You'll find some information on the ancient Chinese defensive installation, but you may also get the menu of the Great Wall of China, a Chinese restaurant; information on the Great Wall hotel in Beijing; and the lyrics of "Great Wall of China," a song by Billy Joel.

Specialized Search Engines

Full Web search engines generally don't index specialized information such as names and addresses, job advertisements, quotations, or newspaper articles. To find such information, you need to use **specialized search engines**. Examples of such specialized search engines include Indeed, a database of more than 1 million jobs, and Infoplease, which contains the full text of an encyclopedia and an almanac (Figure 2.19).

You can save the results of your searches—the Web pages you visit by following the results links of a search engine—to your hard drive by using your browser's Page (or File), Save As menu sequence. If you don't want or need the entire Web page, you can right-click the various

elements of the page and choose from a variety of options (Save, Print, Copy). You can also use your mouse and cursor to highlight and then copy text on a Web page for pasting into a word-processing file or other document. Sometimes you might want to view a Web page that you've saved *offline*; that is, without connecting to the Internet. This is easily accomplished by opening your browser and then choosing the File, Open menu sequence. Simply browse through your folders and files to locate the file and then open it.

Search engines are not the only way to find information on the Web. Sites such as MSN, AOL, and Yahoo! offer many services, including search features, on their home pages. These sites are also referred to as portals. A **portal** is a gateway that provides a conveniently organized subject guide to Internet content, fast-breaking news, local weather, stock quotes, sports scores, and e-mail (Figure 2.20). Portal sites usually use indexes and lists of links to provide you with a jumping-off place for your search.

Some Web sites have their own site search engines. You will often find this feature on the site's home page. It is usually a clearly marked box into which you type the keywords of what you are looking for. Some home pages will have a Search icon or button that will take you to the site's search page.

USING SEARCH TECHNIQUES

By learning a few search techniques, you can greatly increase the accuracy of your Web searches. **Search operators**, which are symbols or words used for advanced

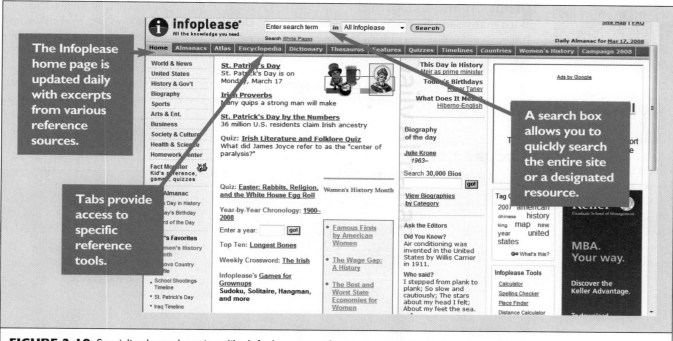

FIGURE 2.19 Specialized search engines, like Infoplease, provide access to selected reference tools and resources.

FIGURE 2.20 The Yahoo! portal to the Web provides a conveniently organized subject guide to Internet content, news, local weather, stock quotes, and much more.

searches, can be helpful. Most search engines include a link for advanced searches or provide search tips to explain which search operators you can use. Although specific methods may vary, some or all of the following techniques will work with most search engines.

Destinations

Feel like you're stuck in a rut? Try using a different search engine. Visit sites like Mahalo (**www.mahalo.com**), KartOO (**www.kartoo.com**), Dogpile (**www.dogpile.com**), FindSounds (**www.findsounds.com**), or SurfWax (**www.surfwax.com**) and see what you find!

Inclusion and Exclusion

With many search engines, you can improve search performance by specifying an **inclusion operator**, which is generally a plus (+) sign (Figure 2.21). This operator states that you don't want a page retrieved unless it contains the specified word. By listing several key terms with this search operator, you can exclude many pages that don't contain one or more of the essential terms.

If the list of retrieved documents contains many items that you don't want, you can use the **exclusion operator**, which is

FIGURE 2.21 Improving Your Search Results

Search Operators

Symbol	Example	Result
Plus sign (+)	CD+Aerosmith	Web pages that contain all search terms listed, in any order. In this case, pages would include BOTH the word **CD** AND the word **AEROSMITH**.
Minus sign (−)	CD+Aerosmith−eBay	Web pages that contain all included search terms, but not the excluded term. In this example, pages would include BOTH the word **CD** AND the word **AEROSMITH** but NOT the word **EBAY**.
Wildcards (*)	CD*	Web pages that include variations of the search term or additional words. For example, pages could include the terms **CD, CDS, CD RIPPING, CD FILES**, etc.
Quotation Marks (" ")	"Aerosmith Just Push Play CD"	Web pages that contain the exact phrase in the order listed.

Boolean Search Terms

Term	Example	Result
AND	CD **AND** Aerosmith	Returns the same results as using the plus sign (+).
OR	CD **OR** Aerosmith	Web pages that include either or both of the search terms listed, usually providing a large number of hits. For this example, results would include EITHER the word **CD** OR the word **AEROSMITH** or BOTH.
NOT	CD **AND** Aerosmith **NOT** eBay	Returns the same results as using the minus sign (−).
Parentheses ( )	(CD **OR** MP3 **OR** Record) **AND** Aerosmith	Search terms in parentheses are located first, using the search operators provided. In this case, results would include pages that included any combination of **CD, MP3,** or **RECORD** AND the word **AEROSMITH**.

generally a minus (−) sign. You can exclude the undesired term by prefacing it with the exclusion operator.

Wildcards

Many search engines enable you to use wildcards. **Wildcards** are symbols such as ? and * that take the place of zero or more characters in the position in which they are used, also known as **truncation**. Wildcards help you improve the accuracy of your searches and are useful if you are unsure of the exact spelling of a word. Wildcards may be handled differently, depending upon the search engine used. So the search term *bank** might return *bank, banks, banking, bankruptcy, bank account*, etc.

Phrase Searches

Another way to improve the accuracy of your searches is through **phrase searching**, which is generally performed by typing a phrase within quotation marks. This tells the search engine to retrieve only those documents that contain the exact phrase (rather than some or all of the words anywhere in the document).

Boolean Searches

Some search engines enable you to perform Boolean searches. **Boolean searches** use logical operators (AND, OR, and NOT) to link the words you're searching for. By using Boolean operators, you can gain more precise control over your searches. Let's look at a few examples.

The AND, OR, and NOT Operators. When used to link two search words, the AND operator tells the search engine to return only those documents that contain both words (just as the plus sign does). You can use the AND operator to narrow your search so that it retrieves fewer documents.

If your search retrieves too few documents, try the OR operator. This may be helpful when a topic has several common synonyms, such as car, auto, automobile, and vehicle. Using the OR operator usually retrieves many documents.

To exclude unwanted documents, use the NOT operator. This operator tells the search engine to omit any documents containing the word preceded by NOT (just as the minus sign does).

Using Parentheses. Many search engines that support Boolean operators allow you to use parentheses, a process called **nesting**. When you nest an expression, the search engine evaluates the expression from left to right and searches for the content within the parentheses first. It then uses the other keywords and operators to search these results and provide the final results. Such expressions enable you to conduct a search with unmatched accuracy.

EVALUATING INFORMATION

After you've found information on the Web, you'll need to evaluate it critically. Anyone can publish information on the Web; many Web pages are not subject to the fact-checking standards of newspapers or magazines, let alone the peer-review process that safeguards the quality of scholarly and scientific publications. Although you can find excellent and reliable information on the Web, you can also find pages that are biased or blatantly incorrect.

Rules for Critically Evaluating Web Pages

As you're evaluating a Web page, ask yourself the following questions:

- Who is the author of this page? Is the author affiliated with a recognized institution, such as a university or a well-known company? Is there any evidence that the author is qualified with respect to this topic? A page that isn't signed may signal an attempt to disguise the author's lack of qualifications.

- Does the author cite his or her sources? If so, do they appear to be from recognized and respected publications?

- Who provides the server for publishing this Web page? Who pays for this page?

- Does the presentation seem balanced and objective, or is it one sided?

- Is the language objective and dispassionate, or is it strident and argumentative?

Destinations

Go to **www.internet tutorials.net/search. html** to learn more about search engines and their specialized capabilities.

Ethics

Copyright violations and infringements often occur with material that is available online. Make sure you understand your rights and responsibilities. Visit the Electronic Frontier Foundation (**www.eff.org**) or the U.S. Copyright Office (**www.copyright.gov**) for more information.

- What is the purpose of this page? Is the author trying to sell something or promote a biased idea? Who would profit if this page's information were accepted as true? Does the site include links to external information, or does it reference only itself?

- Does the information appear to be accurate? Is the page free of sweeping generalizations or other signs of shoddy thinking? Do you see many misspellings or grammatical errors that would indicate a poor educational background?

- Is this page up to date? When was it last updated?

In the next section, you will explore the practical applications of Web research to both the work and school environments.

USING THE WEB FOR SCHOOLWORK

Finding information on the Web can help you as a consumer. But how can it help you as a student? The following sections provide some helpful hints.

Authoritative Online Sources

Many respected magazines and journals have established Web sites where you can search back issues, giving you the best of both worlds—the power and convenience of the Internet, plus material that is more reliable than the average Web page.

Locating Material in Published Works

Remember that the Web is only one of several sources you can and should use for research. Many high-level research tools can be found in your institution's library. Additionally, librarians are trained research professionals who are there to assist you. As institutions have begun to offer distance-learning courses, student access to library materials has become a critical issue. To meet the needs of distance-learning students, many college libraries now provide online access to

their services. Check your library's home page to find out what Internet services are available. In addition to standard card-catalog information—such as author, title, and publication date—you can often access full-text versions of books and periodicals online. Some libraries provide these materials directly, whereas others use a third party to provide these services. You can almost certainly access and search your library's inventory of books and can often order them online. The library's books and articles search engine will allow you to search by author, title, or key term. Your library may also provide access to valuable search tools such as EBSCOhost, LexisNexis, and other professional databases. Sometimes you can access these online materials from off campus as well as on campus. Materials may be accessible only to faculty and students, or they may also be available to the general public.

Also, visit Google Scholar (**scholar. google.com**) to search for scholarly literature from many academic disciplines. You can use advanced search methods and even personalize your searches to have Google Scholar indicate when materials are held by your local library. Google Scholar can help you locate peer-reviewed papers, theses, books, abstracts, and articles from academic publishers and professional sources (Figure 2.22).

Citing Online and Offline References

Including citations in your work is an important way to honor copyright and avoid accusations of plagiarism. Because citing Internet-based sources is not the same as citing traditional references, visit University of California Berkeley's General Guides site at **www.lib.berkeley. edu/Help/guides.html** to learn how to properly cite online and electronic resources. You should know how to cite Web sites, e-mail messages, and online databases. When citing electronic resources, it is important to include the date the site was last accessed. Even more than the written and published word, electronic words are time sensitive.

Now that you're familiar with how to find and evaluate information on the Web, let's look at some of the Internet's most useful services.

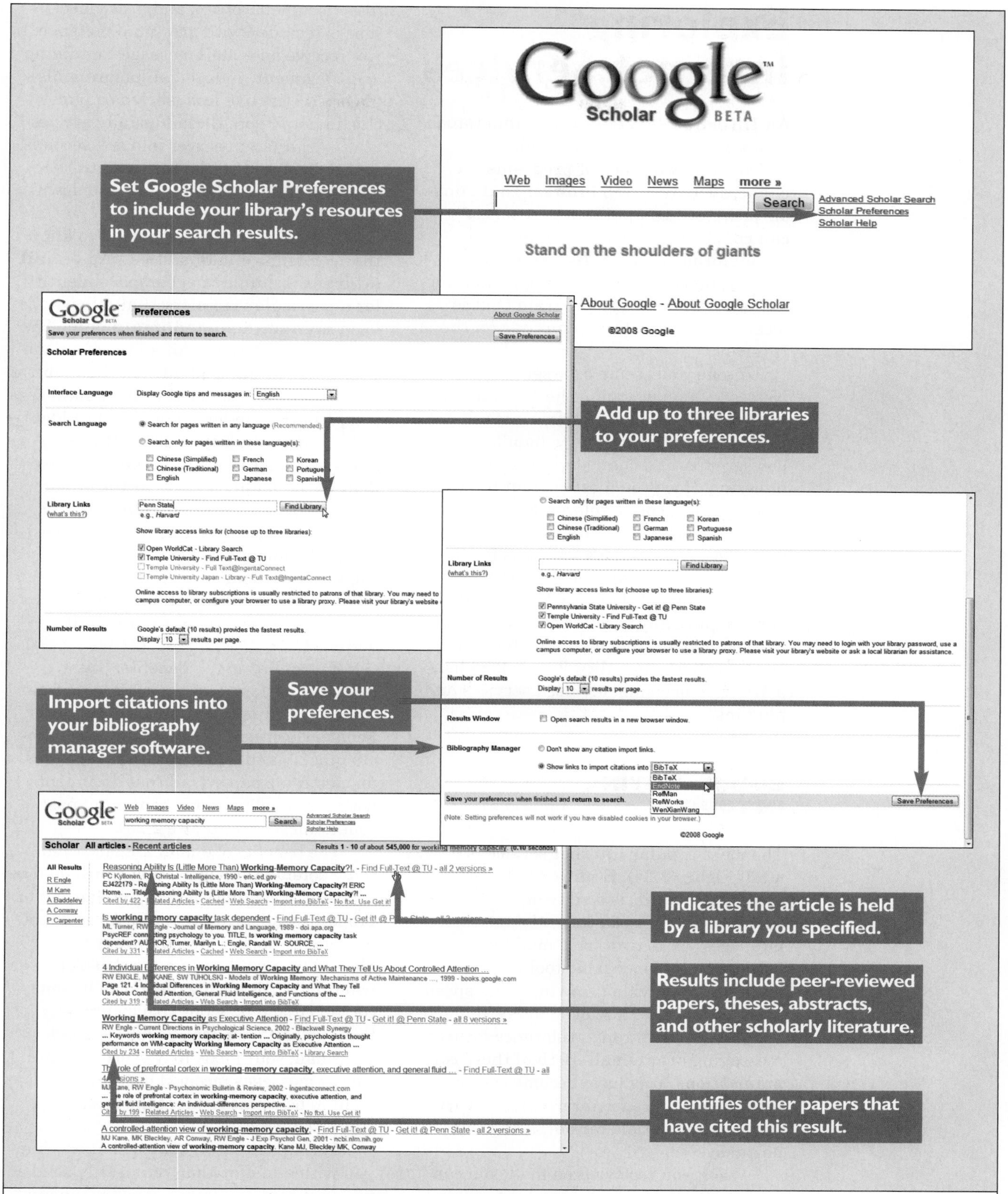

FIGURE 2.22 Google Scholar uses the power of Google to search scholarly literature and provide high-quality results for academic research.

Exploring Internet Services

An **Internet service** is best understood as a set of standards (protocols) that define how two types of programs—a client, such as a Web browser that runs on the user's computer, and a server—can communicate with each other through the Internet. By using the service's protocols, the client requests information from a server program that is located on some other computer on the Internet.

At one time, some browsers, such as Netscape Navigator and the Mozilla Suite, were distributed as software suites that included client programs to handle e-mail, newsgroups, and chat services, as well as browsing. However, most current browsers, including Internet Explorer, Firefox, and Safari (for Macs), operate as stand-alone programs. Although it's still possible to obtain client software for some of these services, many of them are Web-based and don't require any special software to use, but you may need to install a plug-in to ensure full functionality. Figure 2.23 lists a selection of commonly used services and plug-ins.

E-MAIL: STAYING IN TOUCH

The most popular Internet service is e-mail (Figure 2.24). **E-mail** (short for **electronic mail**) is a software application that enables you to send and receive messages via networks. E-mail has become an indispensable tool for businesses and individuals owing to its speed and convenience. However, many younger people report a strong preference for text messaging over e-mail. Both of these communications tools have become the medium of choice for interpersonal written communication, far outpacing the postal system.

When you receive an e-mail, you can reply to the message, forward it to someone else, store it for later action, or delete it. In addition to the text message, you can include an e-mail attachment. An **e-mail attachment** can be any type of computer file—document, photo, audio, or video—that is included with an e-mail message. If you receive an e-mail message containing an attachment, your e-mail program displays a distinctive icon, such as a paper clip, to notify you. E-mail usually arrives at the destination server in a few seconds. It is then stored on the server until the recipient logs on to the server and downloads the message.

To send an e-mail, you need to know the recipient's e-mail address. An **e-mail address** is a unique cyberspace identity for a particular recipient that follows the form **myname@somedomain.com**. The components of an e-mail address are the user name or other identifier, the name of the domain that is hosting the e-mail service, and the top-level domain that identifies the provider's type of institution. For instance, you can send mail to the president of the United States at the e-mail address **president@whitehouse.gov**. In this instance, the user name is "president," the domain is "whitehouse," and the top-level domain is ".gov" (for government). You can often tell quite a bit about someone just by seeing their e-mail address!

E-mail has many benefits. It is inexpensive, fast, and easy to access from almost any Internet-connected computer. People use e-mail to collaborate with others quickly and efficiently. It also creates an electronic paper trail that documents both the timeliness and content of past communications (Figure 2.25).

The benefits of e-mail are tempered by some potential problems that you should be aware of. Sometimes e-mail systems fail to properly send or receive mail. Attachments may not be delivered or they may be blocked by e-mail system administrators as potentially unsafe. Messages can become corrupted and may not display properly. Sometimes, if you don't regularly check your mail, your inbox may overflow, which causes messages received past the overflow point to be bounced out of the box and never delivered.

Perhaps the worst thing that can happen with e-mail is that you hastily send a message that you later wished you hadn't or you use the Reply All or Forward feature to send inappropriate or irrelevant messages that can embarrass you or that inconvenience the recipient.

FIGURE 2.23 Commonly Used Internet Services and Plug-ins

Service	Client	Web-based	Comments
E-mail			
AOL Mail	X	X	Available with AOL Desktop installation or as Web-based service
Google Gmail		X	
Microsoft Outlook	X		Part of the Microsoft Office suite
Microsoft Windows Mail	X		Replaced Outlook Express in Windows Vista
Mozilla Thunderbird	X		Coordinates with Mozilla Firefox
Windows Live Hotmail		X	Replaced MSN Hotmail
Yahoo! Mail		X	
Instant Message			
AOL AIM	X	X	Available with AOL Desktop installation or as Web-based service
Google Talk	X	X	Available for download or as Web-based service
meebo.com		X	Users can access other IM clients on the meebo site
ICQ	X	X	Available for download or as Web-based service
Yahoo! Messenger		X	
Windows Live Messenger		X	Formerly MSN Messenger
Internet Relay Chat (IRC)			
mIRC	X		
Mozilla ChatZilla	X		Runs only in a Mozilla Firefox browser
Trillian	X		Also supports instant message clients
Plug-ins			
Adobe Reader	X		Viewer for Adobe PDF files
Adobe Flash Player	X		Viewer for web animation (Flash) files
Adobe Shockwave Player	X		Used for interactive games, multimedia, graphics, and streaming audio and video
Apple QuickTime Player	X		Used for animation, music, MIDI, audio, and video files
RealPlayer	X		Used for streaming audio, video, animations, and multimedia presentations
Windows Media Player	X		Used for MP3 and WAV files, live audio, movies and live video broadcasts

FIGURE 2.24
More than 147 million people in the United States use e-mail almost every day; almost three-quarters have more than one e-mail account.

Spam: Can It Be Stopped?

Many e-mail users receive unsolicited e-mail advertising called **spam**. In fact, according to recent estimates, as much as 85 percent of all e-mail is spam. This mail is sent by spammers, businesses or individuals that specialize in sending such mail. Spammers believe that they're doing only what direct-marketing mail firms do: sending legitimate advertising. But they don't acknowledge a crucial difference between unsolicited postal advertising and spam. With postal advertising, the advertiser pays for the postage. With spam, the recipient pays the postage in the form of lost time and productivity for individuals and businesses. A 2007 study estimated that managing spam costs U.S. businesses more than $71 billion annually. That's $712 per employee!

Most Internet users detest spam, but feel helpless to prevent it. For businesses, spam is a costly nuisance. It's not unusual for a massive amount of spam messages to overwhelm mail servers, resulting in impaired service for legitimate, paying customers.

In most cases, little or nothing of worth is being peddled: pornographic Web sites, get-rich-quick scams, bogus stock deals, rip-off work-at-home schemes, health and diet scams, and merchandise of questionable quality.

Can you filter out spam? You can try. It's often possible to set up a spam or bulk mail folder in your e-mail account. Check your mail options to enable this service (Figure 2.26). Most spam, however, originates from a new account, which is almost immediately closed down after the service provider receives hundreds of thousands of outraged complaints. The spammer just moves on to a new account. One thing you can do to help prevent spam is to avoid posting your e-mail address in any public place. In fact, you should be very selective when providing your e-mail address to anyone. Companies like Cloudmark and ChoiceMail provide businesses with

FIGURE 2.25 E-mail enables collaboration and keeps a record of past communications.

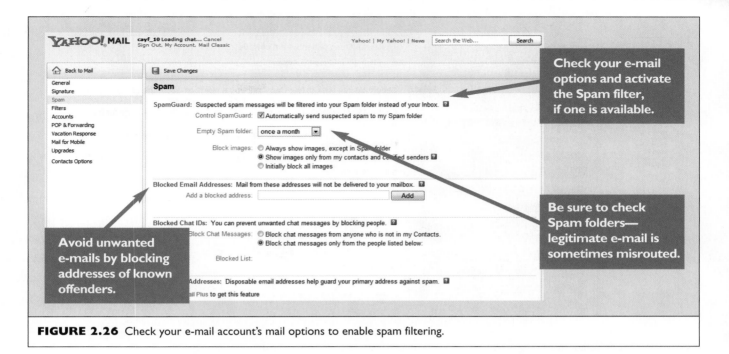

FIGURE 2.26 Check your e-mail account's mail options to enable spam filtering.

enterprise-level protection from spam. Antivirus software manufacturers like Symantec and McAfee incorporate antispam features in their products to help home users recognize and avoid opening spam. Free or low-cost alternatives such as SpamBully and MailWasher attempt to clear spam out of your inbox. Some e-mail providers offer on-site spam-filtering services that try to filter out spam before it is even sent to your mailbox, but so far there is no way to get rid of spam entirely.

Don't reply to spam or request to be removed from a spammer's mailing list. All that does is verify to the spammer that your e-mail address is valid. If possible, you should also modify your e-mail account to disable graphics, since some graphics, known as **Web beacons**, alert the sender that the message has been opened. Your address will be added to a list of validated addresses, so all that will happen is that you'll get even more spam.

Increasingly, state and federal legislatures are attempting to pass laws against spam. Bills have been introduced in Congress, and the Senate's CAN-SPAM act is aimed at deceptive e-mails, unsolicited pornography, and marketing. The Direct Marketing Association (DMA), an advocacy group for both online and offline direct marketers, counters that the appropriate solution is an opt-out system, in which spam recipients request that the sender of spam remove their names from the mailing list—but that's just what e-mail users have been trained not to do because of fear that they'll receive even more spam. In addition, efforts to outlaw spam run afoul of free-speech guarantees under the U.S. Constitution's First Amendment, which applies to businesses as well as individuals. Furthermore, many spammers operate outside the United States, making effective legislation even more difficult. One solution under consideration is a congressional measure that would give ISPs the right to sue spammers for violating their spam policies.

Although it's no fun, most of us have learned to live with spam—just don't open it!

INSTANT MESSAGING: E-MAIL MADE FASTER

What's faster than e-mail and more convenient than picking up the phone? **Instant messaging (IM) systems** alert you when a friend or business associate who also uses the IM system (a buddy or contact) is online (connected to the Internet). You can

Destinations

Check out the Federal Trade Commission's spam site at **www.ftc.gov/spam** for more information and tips on how to avoid spam.

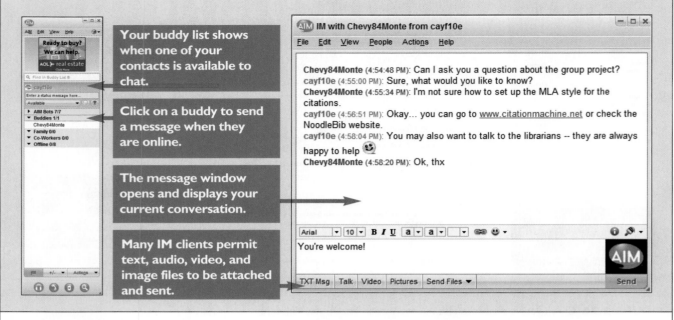

FIGURE 2.27 Instant messaging is a popular way for Internet users to exchange near real-time messages.

then contact this person and exchange messages and attachments, including multimedia (Figure 2.27).

To use IM, you need to install instant messenger software from an instant messenger service, such as AOL's AIM or Microsoft's Windows Live Messenger, on your computer. You can use IM systems on any type of computer, including handhelds. Many IM services also give you access to information such as daily news, stock prices, sports scores, and the weather, and you can keep track of your appointments. There is no standard IM protocol, which means that you can send messages only to people who are using the same IM service that you are.

An increasing number of businesses and institutions are trying out IM services, with mixed results. On the one hand, IM is a novel and convenient way to communicate. On the other hand, voice communication is faster and richer. Additionally, the tone of an instant message can easily be misinterpreted and privacy and security concerns also exist.

Another threat to the use of IM is a phenomenon known as *spimming*. Spimming is to IM as spam is to e-mail. Be very careful about opening files or clicking on a link sent in an instant message by an unknown sender.

INTERNET RELAY CHAT: TEXT CHATTING IN REAL TIME

Internet relay chat (IRC) is an Internet service that enables you to join chat groups, called **channels**, and participate in real-time, text-based conversations. Popular in the early days of the Internet, IRC has been replaced by tools like IM. Today it is mostly the province of specialized communities, such as gamers or programmers.

SOCIAL NETWORKING: HELPING PEOPLE CONNECT

Social networking is a way to build expanding online communities. On a social networking site like MySpace or Facebook, you can create an online profile, invite friends and acquaintances to join your network, and invite their friends to join too (Figure 2.28). Some sites, like LinkedIn, are used by business professionals to expand their network of business contacts.

Many privacy and security concerns surround social networking sites. A 2007 Pew Internet report revealed that more than 55 percent of 12- to 17-year-olds use these sites. Cyberstalking and harassment are legitimate concerns. Once posted,

Destinations

Tired of MySpace or Facebook? Why not start your own social network? Ning (**www.ning.com**) is a free site that encourages people to start their own social networking community. Artists, hobbyists, educators, athletes . . . , the list continues to grow. Find a community to join or start your own!

FIGURE 2.28 Social networking sites like Facebook are creating extensive online communities.

pictures and content are easily shared and distributed to others, sometimes with detrimental effects. Users should give thought to the information they publicly display and consider the possible consequences.

FILE TRANSFER PROTOCOL: TRANSFERRING FILES

File Transfer Protocol (FTP) is one way that files can be transferred over the Internet, and it is especially useful for transferring files that are too large to send by e-mail. Although you can use special FTP client software, such as WS_FTP Home, you can also transfer files to and from an FTP server simply by using your browser or Windows Explorer. FTP can transfer two types of files: ASCII (text files) and binary (program files, graphics, or documents saved in proprietary file formats).

In most cases, you need a user name and a password to access an FTP server. However, with **anonymous FTP**, files are publicly available for downloading (Figure 2.29). FTP sites are structured hierarchically—that is, they use a folder and file structure similar to that used on your own computer. Depending on how you access the site, downloadable files may appear as hyperlinks. Just click the link to download the file. If you access the

site using Windows Explorer, you can use the same file management techniques you use to organize your own files.

FTP is also used to upload Web pages from your computer to the ISP or hosting service's Web server, making your Web site available to other Internet users.

USENET: JOINING ONLINE DISCUSSIONS

Usenet is a worldwide computer-based discussion system accessible through the Internet. It consists of thousands of topically named **newsgroups**, which are discussion groups devoted to a single topic. Each newsgroup contains articles that users have posted for all to see. Users can respond to specific articles by posting follow-up articles. Over time, a discussion thread develops as people reply to the replies. A **thread** is a series of articles that offers a continuing commentary on the same general subject.

Usenet newsgroups are organized into the following main categories:

- **Standard newsgroups.** You're most likely to find rewarding, high-quality discussions in the standard newsgroups (also called world newsgroups). Figure 2.30 lists the standard newsgroup subcategories.

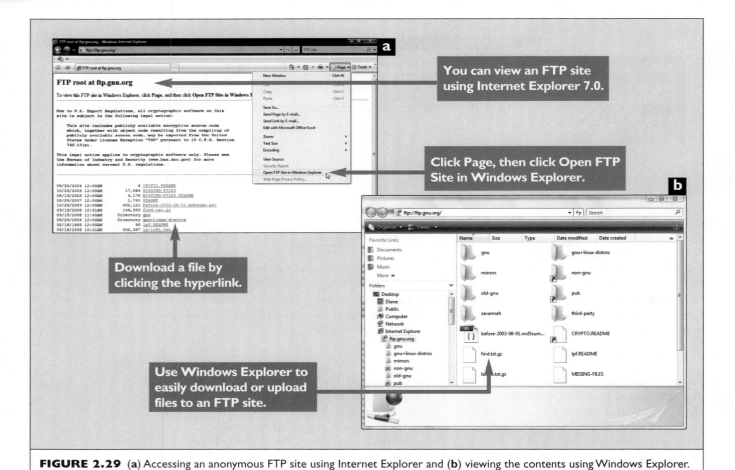

FIGURE 2.29 (a) Accessing an anonymous FTP site using Internet Explorer and (b) viewing the contents using Windows Explorer.

FIGURE 2.30 Standard Newsgroup Subcategories	
Subcategory Name	**Description of Topics Covered**
Comp	Everything related to computers and computer networks, including applications, compression, databases, multimedia, and programming
Misc	Subjects that do not fit in other standard newsgroup hierarchies, including activism, books, business, consumer issues, health, investing, jobs, and law
Sci	The sciences and social sciences, including anthropology, archaeology, chemistry, economics, math, physics, and statistics
Soc	Social issues, including adoption, college-related issues, feminism, human rights, and world cultures
Talk	Debate on controversial subjects, including abortion, atheism, euthanasia, gun control, and religion
News	Usenet itself, including announcements and materials for new users
Rec	All aspects of recreation, including aviation, backcountry sports, bicycles, boats, gardening, and scouting

- **Alt newsgroups.** The alt category is much more freewheeling. Anyone can create an alt newsgroup (which explains why so many of them have silly or offensive names).

- **Biz newsgroups.** These newsgroups are devoted to the commercial uses of the Internet.

The easiest way to access Usenet is through Google Groups (**groups.google.com**). You can read and post messages, but be careful what you post on Usenet. When you post an article, you're publishing in the public domain. Sometimes articles are stored for long periods in Web-accessible archives.

Also be aware that you'll be expected to follow the rules of **netiquette**, guidelines for good manners when you're communicating through Usenet (or any Internet service). To avoid errors, check the group's FAQs to see how they operate. If you violate netiquette rules, you may receive **flames** (angry, critical messages) from other newsgroup subscribers.

ELECTRONIC MAILING LISTS

Electronic mailing lists of e-mail addresses are similar in many ways to newsgroups and forums, but they automatically broadcast messages to all individuals on a mailing list. Because the messages are transmitted as e-mail, only individuals who are subscribers to the mailing list receive and view the messages. Some colleges and universities host electronic mailing lists. Eric Thomas developed the first electronic mailing list program, Listserv, in 1986 for BITNET. The most common freeware version of an electronic mailing list manager program is Majordomo.

CURRENTS

Internet Security
Protecting Children in Cyberspace

Are there angels in cyberspace? A couple in Fanwood, New Jersey, has a ready answer to this question: Yes! After their computer-addicted 13-year-old daughter ran away from home, the parents began to suspect that she had fled to the residence of an adult man who had been romancing the child online. They then contacted CyberAngels (**www.cyberangels.org**), a volunteer organization of thousands of Internet users worldwide. The group's purpose: to protect children in cyberspace.

CyberAngels was founded in 1995 by Curtis Sliwa, who also started the Guardian Angels (the volunteer organization whose members wear red berets as they patrol inner-city streets). Today, CyberAngels volunteers scour the Internet for online predators, cyberstalkers, and child pornographers, and they've been responsible for a number of arrests. Their Web site and newsletter provide many useful articles about practical safety measures to keep you and your loved ones safe. They recently launched their own social networking site—CyberAngels Global Community—and have brought their Children's Internet Safety Program to thousands of schoolchildren across the United States.

The Internet can be a dangerous place for young children, and older ones too! Cyberbullying occurs when one child targets another for some form of torment or abuse through digital tools. Online stalkers and sexual predators haunt social networking sites. Speaking with children about Internet safety practices, being aware of where and when they surf, and knowing who their cyberfriends are should be a top priority. Concerned parents can implement the parental controls that are provided by their ISPs or included in safety and security software. Web site blocking and content-filtering software and monitoring programs like Net Nanny, Bsafe Online, and myspaceWatch can add another level of security.

And what about the New Jersey couple? Their daughter is home and safe thanks to the CyberAngels who successfully used their network to identify the child's online contact.

Destinations

To learn more about how to protect yourself or the children in your household, visit Stop Cyberbullying (**www.stopcyberbullying.org**), SocialSafety.org (**www.socialsafety.org**), and the Family Online Safety Institute (**www.fosi.org/resources/parents**). Also, Ken Leebow's blog, Crossing the Digital Divide (**http://crossingthedigitaldivide.blogspot.com**), tries to keep adults up to date on cyberactivities of their children.

What You've Learned

THE INTERNET & THE WORLD WIDE WEB

- The Internet is *the* network of networks. The Internet allows every connected computer to directly exchange data with any other computer on the network. It enables any connected computer to operate a remote computer by sending commands through the network. The Internet is able to work this way because of interoperability, the ability to work with a computer even if it is a different brand and model.

- Users access the Internet by way of a public or private Internet service provider (ISP). Public providers include libraries and schools; private providers are those who provide access for a fee. You can connect to your ISP by way of a telephone modem, a digital service line (DSL), a cable modem, a satellite, or a fiber-optic cable.

- Whereas the Internet is a global computer network that connects millions of smaller networks, the World Wide Web is a global system that contains billions of hypertext documents and uses the Internet as its transport mechanism. Millions of users turn to the Web to research current events, general information, product information, scientific developments, and much more.

- With hypertext, related information is referenced by means of links instead of being fully explained or defined in the same location. On the Web, authors can link to information created by others.

- A Web browser is a program that displays a Web document and enables you to access linked documents. A Web server is a computer that retrieves documents requested by browsers.

- A URL consists of a protocol (such as http://), a domain (such as www.domain.com), a path (such as /windows/), and a resource name (such as default.aspx). To access a Web page, you can click a hyperlink, type a URL into a browser's Address bar, or click a tab in a browser window.

- Web subject guides index a limited number of high-quality pages, whereas search engines enable you to search huge databases of Web documents.

- Most Web searches retrieve too many irrelevant documents. You can improve search results by using inclusion and exclusion operators, phrase searches, and Boolean operators. Search operators such as the + and − signs or the Boolean AND and NOT operators can help limit the results of your search to the particular subject you are interested in.

- To evaluate information you find on the Web, you should look critically at the Web page author's credentials and purpose for publishing the page. Other criteria are whether reputable sources are cited, who provides or pays for the server that hosts the page, and whether the content seems biased, inaccurate, or out of date.

- Popular Internet services include e-mail and instant messaging (IM) for sending messages, Internet relay chat (IRC) for text chatting, social networking sites for online communities, File Transfer Protocol (FTP) for file exchange, Usenet for joining discussion groups, and electronic mailing list managers for broadcasting content to subscribers.

Go to **www.pearsonhighered.com/cayf** to review this chapter, answer the questions, and complete the exercises.

Key Terms and Concepts

anonymous FTP 75
Boolean searches. 67
channels 74
cyberspace. 48
dead links (broken links) 55
distributed hypermedia
    system. 54
domain name. 58
domain name registration 59
Domain Name System
    (DNS) 59
downloading 61
electronic mailing lists 77
e-mail (electronic mail). 70
e-mail address. 70
e-mail attachment 70
exclusion operator. 66
fiber-optic service (FiOS) 52
File Transfer Protocol
    (FTP). 75
flames 77
history list. 60
home page (index page) 53
host name 59

hyperlinks (links) 54
hypertext 54
Hypertext Markup
    Language (HTML) 54
Hypertext Transfer Protocol
    (HTTP) 58
inclusion operator. 66
instant messaging (IM)
    systems 73
Internet 48
Internet Protocol (IP)
    address 57
Internet Relay Chat (IRC) 74
Internet service. 70
Internet service providers
    (ISPs) 51
interoperability. 48
nesting. 67
netiquette 77
newsgroups 75
online service 51
phrase searching. 67
plug-ins 56
portal. 64

search engines. 63
search operators 64
social networking 74
spam 72
specialized search
    engines 64
subject guide 63
tabbed browsing 60
thread 75
top-level domain (TLD) name . . 59
truncation 67
uploading. 61
URL (Uniform Resource
    Locator). 57
Usenet 75
Web 2.0 55
Web beacons 73
Web browser 55
Web page 53
Web server 57
Web site 53
wildcards. 67
World Wide Web
    (Web or WWW). 53

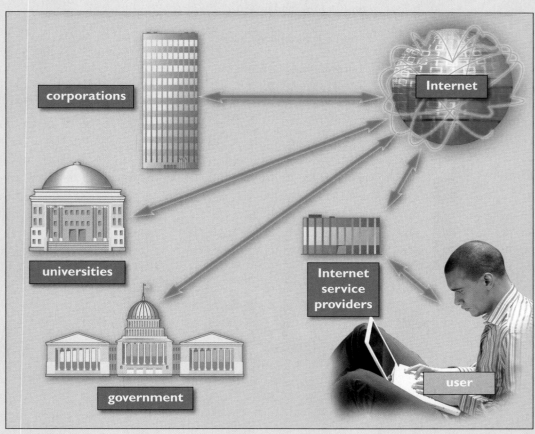

Matching

Match each key term in the left column with the most accurate definition in the right column.

_____ 1. nesting

_____ 2. subject guide

_____ 3. netiquette

_____ 4. dead link

_____ 5. tabbed browsing

_____ 6. interoperability

_____ 7. exclusion operator

_____ 8. channel

_____ 9. Domain Name System

_____ 10. portal

_____ 11. Boolean search

_____ 12. e-mail address

_____ 13. social networking

_____ 14. Web server

_____ 15. spam

a. results from a missing Web page

b. IRC chat group

c. gateway to a conveniently organized subject guide used as a jumping-off point for searches

d. a technique used when search terms and Boolean operators are enclosed in parentheses

e. the process of creating an online community

f. logical operators include AND, OR, and NOT

g. a search tool that groups useful Web pages in categories to provide high-quality results

h. identifies a search term that should not be returned

i. unsolicited e-mail advertising

j. describes the Internet's ability to work with computers of different makes and models

k. unique cyberspace identity

l. feature of newer browsers

m. a computer that runs special software to accept and process information requests and return the requested documents

n. rules or guidelines for good Internet behavior

o. used by the Internet to link a domain name with its corresponding IP address

Multiple Choice

Circle the correct choice for each of the following.

1. Which of the following is an example of a wildcard?
   a. (
   b. +
   c. *
   d. @

2. Which of the following is *not* an example of a top-level domain?
   a. asp
   b. org
   c. biz
   d. gov

3. Which of the following items can be used as a tool by spammers?
   a. flame
   b. channel
   c. TLD
   d. Web beacon

4. Which of the following is the Internet standard that supports the exchange of information on the Web?
   a. Hypertext Markup Language
   b. Top Level Domain
   c. Hypertext Transfer Protocol
   d. Domain Name System

5. Using a wildcard in a search term supports which of the following?
   a. exclusion operators
   b. truncation
   c. Boolean operators
   d. Usenet

6. Which of the following does the World Wide Web use as its transport mechanism?
   a. Uniform Resource Locator
   b. Internet
   c. Internet Relay Chat
   d. Usenet

7. Which of the following is the term for transferring files from your computer to another computer?
   a. downloading
   b. flaming
   c. blogging
   d. uploading

8. Which of the following develops as people respond to a newsgroup discussion?
   a. Listserv
   b. IRC
   c. thread
   d. channel

9. Which of the following describes material that is specially prepared and published to be read by a computer?
   a. hyperlinks
   b. hypertext
   c. index page
   d. protocol

10. Which of the following automatically broadcasts messages to subscribers?
    a. Instant messenger service
    b. wiki
    c. newsgroup
    d. electronic mailing list

Go to **www.pearsonhighered.com/cayf** to review this chapter, answer the questions, and complete the exercises.

Fill-In

In the blanks provided, write the correct answer for each of the following.

1. A(n) _____ _____ site permits users to upload or download files without a user name and password.

2. Web browsers maintain a(n) _____ _____ of all the sites that have been visited.

3. A top-level _____ _____ indicates the type of organization in which a computer is located.

4. A for-profit firm that uses a proprietary network and limits access to subscribers is known as a(n) _____ _____.

5. Also known as the Internet, _____ is the nonphysical place that is accessible only by computer.

6. A(n) _____ _____ uses special keywords to provide more precise control of search results.

7. _____ _____ often result when a Web page is moved or a site closes down.

8. Someone who violates netiquette rules on a newsgroup may receive a(n) _____.

9. Every computer, server, or device connected to the Internet has a numeric address known as a(n) _____ _____ _____, which uniquely identifies it to the network.

10. If an e-mail containing a(n) _____ _____ is opened, it could alert a spammer.

11. A network-based content development system that uses resources such as sound, video, and text as a means of navigation is known as a(n) _____ _____ _____.

12. A URL consists of a protocol, _____ _____, path, and resource name.

13. Surrounding a series of search terms with quotation marks is known as _____ _____.

14. A(n) _____ _____ _____ provides individuals and businesses with access to the Internet via phone, DSL, cable, satellite, or fiber-optic lines for a fee.

15. A(n) _____ _____ displays Web pages and enables users to access linked documents.

Short Answer

1. Describe your experiences with the Internet. Specifically, identify the browser and e-mail software applications that you have used. Have you used other Internet-related software? If you have, describe these applications.

2. Explain the difference between downloading and uploading files. Have you ever used FTP to transfer files? What types of files did you transfer? What type of software did you use?

3. Are you a member of a social networking site? How often do you use it? Do you take any special precautions to maintain your safety online?

4. What are some rules of thumb for evaluating content on the Web?

5. Now that you have completed this chapter, you should be able to conduct more effective searches. List three search engines that you frequently use and explain why you prefer these search engines over others. Explore the advanced search options these sites offer and explain what you find.

Teamwork

1. University Internet Access

Universities usually provide on-campus Internet connections along with free technical support. Some schools even provide students in on-campus housing with special cable channels that broadcast live review sessions or access to legal downloads of streaming music files. But what if you live off campus? Contact your institution's computing services department to find out whether it provides off-campus Internet connections. If it does, do students pay an extra fee for this service, or is it funded by general student fees? If your school does not provide off-campus Internet access, how do you connect to the Internet, and what are the monthly fees? Have each team member explore a different question and write individual answers. When all of the team members have completed their work, combine your answers into a document that you will deliver to your professor.

2. Researching ISPs

Your team's task is to research various ISPs. Each team member should research a different type of provider (such as dial-up, DSL, cable, satellite, or FiOS). Be sure to answer at least the following questions: What is the monthly or annual cost of the service? How many accounts can you create under your name? Why does the company say you should subscribe with them rather than others? Does it offer online storage? If so, how much? How would you feel about your Internet identity being associated with this provider? Write an informative and collaborative paper that answers these questions and that describes your experience.

3. Revisiting Web Sites

Explain the difference between a browser's history list and its Favorites or Bookmarks. Have you used either one? Explain how you have used them. Did you know that you can place frequently visited Web sites in your Links toolbar (Internet Explorer) or in your Bookmarks toolbar folder (Mozilla Firefox)? Select one of these two browsers and explain how you can place links to Web sites in the appropriate toolbar. If you have never done this, use the browser's Help feature to learn how. Research the Web and your browser's Help utility to see what you can learn about manipulating the history and Favorites lists. You may work together on this or assign various tasks to each member. Write a paper that meets your professor's specifications.

4. Using the Internet to Job Hunt

Use the Internet to find two potential jobs in the field of your current or intended major. Give the URLs of the sites that list the positions and describe each job—the organization, location, necessary qualifications, benefits, salary, and so on. Explain why you feel that your major coursework does or does not prepare you to assume either of these two positions. Share your papers with the team. Write a collaborative paper that summarizes your group's work.

5. Is Your E-Mail Really Free?

Most ISPs offer "free" e-mail. But we all know that nothing is truly free. Each team member should research at least one such provider and answer the following questions: Who is the provider? What does it offer? Are you required to allow the provider to advertise in each and every message you send? What type of advertisements will it use? How do you feel about having advertising included in each of your mail messages? Does the site offer a for-pay option to remove the advertising? Besides advertising, what other reasons do you think the ISP has for offering you free e-mail? Write an informative and collaborative paper that answers these questions and that describes your experience.

On the Web

1. Internet Statistics

The speed at which the Internet is growing is phenomenal, and the total number of users can only be estimated. To compare the growth of the Internet with that of other media, visit the Computer Almanac site at **www.cs.cmu.edu/ ~bam/numbers.html**. This site is an online treasury of statistical information about computers. How many years did it take radio to have 50 million listeners? How many years did it take television to achieve 50 million viewers? How many years did it take the Web to reach 50 million U.S. users? (This is a lengthy Web site, so use your browser's Find feature to search for "50 million.")

2. Internet2 Near You

Internet2, or I2, is a collaborative effort among educational institutions, government agencies, and computer and telecommunications companies to increase Internet bandwidth. Visit the I2 site at **www.internet2.edu**. How many university members does it have? Does your school belong to I2? If not, locate and identify the nearest institution that does. What are the annual membership fees and estimated annual institutional costs to participate in I2? What are the annual membership fees and estimated annual corporate partnership costs to participate in I2? Name two corporate partners and two corporate sponsors. In addition to I2, the U.S. government also sponsors its own advanced Internet initiative. Identify this initiative and list two governmental agencies that participate in it and in I2.

3. Register a Domain Name

Have you ever thought about getting your own domain name? What would you like it to be? Visit **www.register.com** and try different top-level domain names (.com, .net, .org, and so on) to see if they're available. If they are, what is the annual registration cost? If the domain names are already taken, who owns them, when did they acquire them, and when do they expire? What is the minimum bid amount that can be offered to purchase domain names?

4. Online Gaming

Locate a few sites that offer online gaming. You might start out by typing "computer games" or "online games" into your favorite search engine, or you could go to the games link at Yahoo! or visit **www.pogo.com**. Write a short paper that answers the following questions about the sites you have visited: Can you play games without registering? Did the registration process require you to enter your e-mail address? If so, what do you think they will do with it? Roughly how many people were on the site with you at the same time? (Hundreds, thousands, more?) Did you play games? Which ones? What reasons can you think of to explain why people become addicted to playing online games?

5. Term Papers for Sale

Use the search techniques discussed in this chapter to locate two sites that sell research or term papers. Identify the URLs of these sites, describe how to find a paper on a specific topic, and find out how much it costs to purchase a paper. Do these sites post any disclaimers about students using their papers? Do they provide sample papers? If so, what is the quality of the paper? Do you know anyone who has purchased an online paper? Discuss the ethics of using one of these sites to purchase a research or term paper.

Creating an E-mail Filter to Fight Spam

Most e-mail clients, including Yahoo! Mail, allow you to designate a series of rules that are applied to each and every e-mail message you receive. If an e-mail message matches any of the rules you have defined, it can be automatically deleted or stored in a folder for you to review at a later date. Building custom e-mail filters can be tedious, but it can also be a great last line of defense against spam. You can also use custom filters to automatically sort and organize your e-mail messages. You can set up a series of rules to automatically put e-mails from friends in one folder, work in another folder, and family in yet another. The following steps will walk you through the process of creating a custom e-mail filter in Yahoo! Mail. You can get a free Yahoo! Mail account by going to the Yahoo! Web site and clicking the Mail icon. Simply follow the registration instructions to sign up and create a username and password.

1. Log on to your Yahoo! Mail account. You may need to use the Mail Classic interface to set up filters.

2. Locate the "Mail Options" page and then, under Management, select Filters. The "Filters" page displays two large text boxes. Add, Edit, and Delete buttons appear above the left-hand text box. You can choose to modify or create a new rule by clicking the appropriate button.

3. To create a new filter, click the Add button. The "Add Message Filter" page displays (Figure 2.31). Give the filter a name that describes the purpose of the filter, because you may decide to build multiple filters for various purposes. Yahoo! permits up to 15 filters for free accounts.

4. Next, you will set a rule to determine how the filter should work. You can apply the rules to one or more of four different areas—the From header, the To/CC header, the Subject, and the Body. From the dropdown list for each rule

option, choose an operator for the rule to follow. In the next text box, add the criteria. You might choose to create a rule that will select all e-mails that contain "junk@nospam.com" in the From header.

5. The next step is to determine what action you want to apply to the filter results. You can select a folder from the "Move the message to" dropdown box. Incoming e-mail can be automatically sorted to a specified folder, including folders that you have created.

6. After you've completed your selections, click the Add Filter button. This returns you to the "Filters" page. You can now see the filter you created. The rule name appears in the left column, and the parameters you've assigned appear on the right. You can edit or delete the rule by selecting it and clicking the appropriate button.

7. When you have configured your filter, return to your inbox by clicking the Mail tab. New e-mails will now be handled according to the filter you have created.

FIGURE 2.31 Many e-mail providers, including Yahoo! Mail, provide functions for creating a custom e-mail filter to help block spam.

SPOTLIGHT
E-COMMERCE

What do you want to buy online today? Many e-tailers (Web-based retailers) hope you're asking yourself this question. Online merchants sell books, CDs, clothes, and just about anything else you might want to buy. If you buy online, you're one of millions engaging in e-commerce.

Sister Blue

Lust, Pain, & Other Temptations
© 2005 Sister Blue (837101031639)

Electric Chicago-styled guitar blues and soul, with a few cuts of acoustic blues, bluegrass, & jazz

notes

Just released in 2005, "Lust, Pain, and Other Temptations", is a seventeen track CD of all original SISTER BLUE material. It has already received airplay on WXPN's Blues Show hosted by Jonny Meister, as well as being heard at their performance next door at Philly's World Live Cafe.

SISTER BLUE'S debut CD entitled "Red, White, & SISTER BLUE", released in 2002, has received international airplay, including her hometown Phila.'s most popular public radio station, WXPN 88.5fm, on Jonny Meister's Blues Show. "Red, White, & SISTER BLUE" is featured in the "top picks" for blues at the most popular online, independent artist CD store www.cdbaby.com. In a review of "Red, White, & SISTER BLUE", Jim Speese of "The Reading Eagle" states, " The original songs are fun and rocking, and played with relish." "Red, White, and SISTER BLUE" is a passionate slab of heartfelt and fun blues…"

add CD to cart
CD price: $11.97

CD IN STOCK. ORDER NOW. Will ship immediately.

SPECIAL: 10% discount if you buy more than one copy of it today!

add MP3 to cart
MP3 price: $11.97

Figure 2A
Hundreds of thousands of independent musicians sell their CDs and distribute their music to online stores through CD Baby.

Commerce is the selling of goods or services with the expectation of making a reasonable profit. **Electronic commerce**, or **e-commerce**, is the use of networks or the Internet to carry out business of any type. E-commerce supports many types of traditional business transactions, including buying, selling, renting, borrowing, and lending.

E-commerce isn't new; companies have used networks to do business with suppliers for years. What is new is that, thanks to the Internet and inexpensive PCs, e-commerce has become accessible to anyone with an Internet connection and a Web browser (Figure 2A).

Internet users are shopping, banking and paying bills, trading stocks, and using other services online more than ever before. The U.S. Census Bureau reported that total retail sales for 2007 grew by 4 percent over 2006 sales. In comparison, e-commerce sales over the same time frame increased by 19 percent, producing $136.4 billion in revenue. E-commerce sales are forecast to grow by 15 percent annually over the next 4 years, to $335 billion in revenue by 2012. Experts predict there will be more than 1 billion online buyers by 2012.

In this Spotlight, you will explore three types of e-commerce: business-to-business (B2B), consumer-to-consumer (C2C), and business-to-consumer (B2C).

BUSINESS-TO-BUSINESS E-COMMERCE

Although most people think of online shopping when they hear the term *e-commerce*, much of the growth of e-commerce involves business-to-business transactions. **Business-to-business (B2B) e-commerce** occurs when a business uses the Internet to provide another business with the materials, services, and/or supplies it needs to conduct its operations.

Even though you might not personally engage in B2B, you'll probably recognize many of the industries and companies that do. Some of the different industries engaged in B2B include agriculture, health care, aerospace and defense, real estate, automotive, and construction, as well as familiar computer and software companies such as Dell, IBM, and Microsoft.

In addition, many traditional and online retailers have special B2B units. For example, the popular office supplies chain Staples has a B2B division that operates the Web site **www.staplescentral. com** for mid-sized and Fortune 1000 companies (Figure 2B). The Staples

Contract division has experienced double-digit growth for the last seven years and launched the office supply industry's first online B2B catalog in 2007. Staples Contract works with business customers to create custom programs to meet individual needs and manage costs.

Unlike B2B, you may have engaged in the next type of e-commerce: consumer-to-consumer.

CONSUMER-TO-CONSUMER E-COMMERCE

Consumer-to-consumer (C2C) e-commerce is the online exchange or trade of goods, services, or information between individual consumers. C2C often involves the use of an intermediary such as eBay—the most popular online auction destination (Figure 2C). eBay has more than 84 million active users in more than 39 global markets. In 2007 eBay reported that more than $59 billion in merchandise was auctioned. At least $2,000 worth of goods changes hands every second. Other C2C sites include craigslist and Amazon Marketplace.

C2C sites continue to grow in popularity. Unfortunately, fraud—especially in auction sites—is also increasing. Responsible sites like eBay strive to protect both buyers and sellers by implementing various protection programs and policies, but consumers still need to exercise common sense.

So what can you do to protect yourself? Perhaps the most important thing you can do is to arm yourself with as much information and understanding of the buying and selling processes as possible. When participating in an online auction, this includes knowing what you are bidding on, the maximum value that you are willing to pay (you can do pricing research on the auction site or through a general search of the Web), and the terms and conditions of the sale. You should also find out as much as you can about the seller, including his or her feedback rating, and pay with a credit card or through PayPal whenever possible.

If you intend to sell something on an auction site, you need to find out what it

Figure 2B
Staples Contract develops tailor-made B2B programs for large regional companies and national organizations.

will cost to register with the site, what it will cost per sales transaction, and the terms or conditions that may exist for using the auction site. You will also need to provide an accurate description of what you are offering for sale and possibly a digital photo of the item (perhaps from different perspectives and including some form of size reference such as a ruler or other object of known size). When you receive e-mail inquiries during the bidding process, you should respond quickly. As soon as the bidding closes, you should contact the highest bidder. Finally, you should take care in packing the item for shipping and ship it as soon as possible after the sale.

Just as you can have fun and enjoy yourself in everyday storefront shopping experiences, online auctions and other C2C shopping venues can be fun as well. Many users of online auctions clearly enjoy the hustle and bustle of bidding and of becoming a part of the online trading community. Most online auction sites have message boards that help collectors and buyers learn from others. These sites include FAQs (Frequently Asked Questions) and often provide an area for threaded discussion groups.

In the next section, you will learn about companies that use the Internet as a part of their business strategy.

BUSINESS-TO-CONSUMER E-COMMERCE

Business-to-consumer (B2C) e-commerce occurs when a business uses the Internet to supply consumers with services, information, or products. B2C is essentially the same as shopping at a physical store—you have a need or want, and the marketplace offers products and solutions. The primary difference is that B2C e-commerce is not place or time specific, which means that you don't have to be in any particular place at any particular time to participate. This freedom of time and place enables you to shop whenever you wish and to choose from more products and services than could ever be assembled in one place.

Figure 2C
eBay is the most well-known C2C trading site.

ONLINE SHOPPING

The trend is for more Web users to purchase merchandise online and many more to use the Web to research purchases from brick-and-mortar stores.

Getting Good Deals Online

Have you ever tried to comparison shop on the Web? After surfing at 10 different sites (or more!), it can be daunting to keep track of where you saw the best price on that new digital camera you want. You might want to turn to shopping portals such as PriceGrabber.com, Shopzilla, NexTag, and others. These sites help you conduct price and product comparisons. They also offer reviews on just about any product you can imagine (Figure 2D). You can search and sort by brand, price range, or product rating. To save even more, you can also check sites that offer coupons and rebates, such as The Bargainist and eCoupons.

What kinds of shopping can you do online? Just about any kind you can imagine—even your groceries.

Online Grocery Shopping

Companies such as Peapod and Netgrocer provide online grocery and sundries shopping. Many local grocery stores are also beginning to offer online shopping options. Initially, that may sound crazy. Why would anyone want to buy groceries over the Internet? Well, if the extra expense isn't a problem, the convenience and time saved by avoiding traditional shopping trips may make online grocery shopping a worthwhile experience. In fact, online grocery shopping accounted for more than $3.3 billion in revenues in 2005.

Once you start looking at the concept more closely, it doesn't sound so crazy. For the price of a good bottle of wine, you can select your groceries from an online grocery store and have them delivered to your home. What's more, the online supermarket "remembers" your last grocery list, so you can see what you bought the last time—and will probably need to buy again. You can even set up recurrent transactions so that you receive needed perishables, such as milk and eggs, on a fixed schedule. Some online supermarkets even offer budgeting, automatically tracking your expenditures so that you can stay within the limits you've set.

Peapod, for example, offers grocery delivery in several U.S. metropolitan areas (Figure 2E). Peapod works with local grocery store retailers to select and pack grocery orders in temperature-controlled bins. The bins are delivered to customers' homes in trucks that Peapod leases. Peapod allows customers to choose the time and date of delivery—an important matter for people with busy schedules. Some consumers have found one very important advantage to online grocery shopping: It cuts down on impulse buying.

Online grocery stores can be broken down into two groups: pure play (there is not a physical store that you can visit) and partnerships (there is a brick-and-mortar store as well as an online presence). Most of the pure-play start-ups have gone out of business due to the large overhead required to warehouse large numbers of items that may or may not sell. Some of the pure-play companies that tried and failed include Webvan, Streamline, Homegrocer, and Shoplink. Peapod was able to transform itself from a pure play to a partnership by buying out a brick-and-mortar grocery chain and then layering its Internet presence over the chain's distribution area.

Conversely, traditional grocery stores are now developing a Web presence. In this case, instead of layering the Internet over a traditional store, the traditional store is layering itself with the Internet. For instance, Albertsons.com and Safeway.com provide online shopping and delivery in

Figure 2D

Shopping portals can help users locate items, compare prices, view consumer feedback, and buy products.

Figure 2E

Peapod (www.peapod.com) offers grocery delivery in several U.S. metropolitan areas.

select areas. Online grocery shopping isn't for everyone, but it may become an integral part of the mix of shopping options. Many other businesses are concluding that they must have an Internet presence or they'll soon be out of business.

THE DOT-COM PHENOMENON

Much e-commerce occurs in the *dot-com world,* the universe of Web sites with the suffix *.com* appended to their names. This unique world has been in existence only since 1995. Before 1995, companies were not able to sell over the Internet. But in 1995, the government eliminated all taxpayer funding of the Internet and opened it up to commercial development. The period between 1995 and 2000 is referred to as the *dot-com boom.*

As the dot-com crash of 2000 made painfully clear, not every online business is able to succeed. The dot-com bubble blew up so quickly because existing businesses and start-ups found that it was fairly easy and relatively inexpensive to establish a Web presence. Many companies grew to hundreds of employees and millions of dollars in revenues as customers decided to give online buying a try. The problem was that many of their business plans failed to materialize because their customer base was not sustainable. For example, Pets.com, with its sock-puppet dog mascot, couldn't seem to find the niche of customers who would buy pet food and supplies online. The company claimed losses of $147 million by September 2000 and couldn't raise additional funds to stay in business. Even though the company had more than 570,000 customers and ran high-profile and expensive TV ads during the Super Bowl, Pets.com was just one of hundreds—if not thousands—of dot-com companies that went out of business during the big bust.

A dot-com company that has held its ground and become profitable is Amazon.com. Amazon quickly discovered that books are a commodity well-suited for online trade but didn't stop there (Figure 2F). Its offerings have grown to include music, videos, groceries, tools, jewelry, and clothing. Amazon entices buyers to access, shop, and complete their

sales online by offering professional and peer product reviews; author, artist, and subject matching; and book excerpts and music samples. Shoppers can choose from a variety of shipping options and track their purchases.

There are some drawbacks to B2C e-commerce. Buyers might miss speaking with a real sales clerk, being able to touch and feel the merchandise, and being able to take it home the same day, but many sellers are adopting creative solutions to these issues by offering online chats with live customer service reps, various ways to view products, and a wide array of shipping options. One of the hallmarks of a successful online business is good customer service. Customers are reassured by sites that clearly post their contact information, offer FAQ pages, and respond quickly to customer inquiries.

Click-and-brick stores—retailers that have both an online and a traditional retail store presence, such as Barnes & Noble, Best Buy, and Wal-Mart—are winning consumer confidence. Why? Shoppers can return products locally if there's something wrong with an online order. In addition, customers like to use the Internet to research products before they make a purchase. A recent study reported that 80 percent of people who bought electronic goods locally conducted online research first, with 53 percent buying from the store at whose site they had spent the most time.

Many Web sites also rely on advertising to generate revenue. Different types of ads may appear—including banner ads;

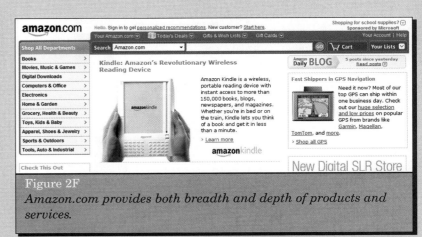

Figure 2F
Amazon.com provides both breadth and depth of products and services.

pop-up ads; text ads such as Google's AdSense (Figure 2G); interstitial ads, which appear before the site loads or as a floating ad on the screen; and rich media ads, which often include sound and

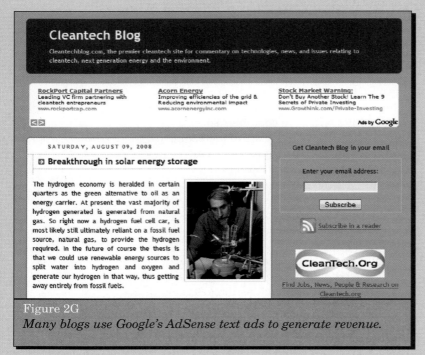

Figure 2G
Many blogs use Google's AdSense text ads to generate revenue.

Figure 2H
Sites such as Bplans.com can help get your small business plan off to a good start.

motion. How do these ads work? When you click on an ad, you're taken to another page or site and the ad host site automatically records how you arrived there. The advertising company then gives the site from which you clicked anywhere from a penny to as much as $50 if a sale occurs as a result of your click.

Another common way for a site to earn money is to become a sponsored site. Sponsors often are large companies that agree to provide financial assistance to small companies or organizations in exchange for advertising space on their sites.

Although online stores are growing in popularity, they won't entirely replace traditional stores. Most people enjoy the instant gratification of obtaining their purchased item at a store. In addition, shipping costs often make Web purchases more expensive than items purchased offline. But despite all of this, e-commerce is taking off because of the convenience it offers.

If one word could sum up what B2C and C2C sites share, it would be **disintermediation**, or the process of removing an intermediary—for example, a bookseller, car salesperson, or auctioneer—and providing a customer with direct access to information and products. B2C and C2C sites put customers in direct contact with incredibly rich sources of information. They enable customers to make their own choices without interacting with a salesperson.

Building Your Own Online Business

One of the tremendous advantages of B2C e-commerce is the low capital investment needed to start an online business. For less than $50, a person can open a Web storefront and start selling products online. In contrast, a brick-and-mortar business requires land, a building, utilities, display shelving, and salespeople. A Web-based storefront requires only an ISP, a Web site, and the ability to ship goods or services to customers.

The first thing you need to do when starting any business is to develop a business plan (Figure 2H). You must decide what products to offer, who your target market is, and how many items you plan to sell and at what price. Who will pay for shipping? Will there be service provided after the sale? Who are your competitors? What profit margin do you expect to achieve?

All businesses need to have a name, and an online business is no different, except that the online business's name is almost always the same as its Web site or domain name. So after you've completed your business plan you will need to shop for a domain name and a Web hosting service. Many Web hosting companies, such as 1&1 (**www.1and1.com**), offer domain name search and registration services as part of their package. You will most likely want a name with a .com extension. Try to pick a name that will be easy for your customers to remember.

In a traditional business, the owner needs to select a building site, develop the company logo and identity, manage the inventory, and provide customer service. These issues are equally important for an online business. Many Web hosting services provide templates and other tools to make it simple to build a professional-looking Web site, even if you don't have any Web design skills (Figure 2I). However, a professional Web designer can be a great help in developing and maintaining a site. When developing a Web site, you will need to consider having the site designed or designing it yourself, budgeting adequate time and money for site development, advertising the site, and ongoing site maintenance. At a minimum, the Web site will need a home page, product pages, and a page for taking orders.

You may also wish to employ an electronic shopping cart. This feature is much like the physical shopping cart you'd use at a grocery store. It remembers your customer's order items and provides the results to the summary order page. Your Web site should project a professional image and be structured to meet your customers' needs to encourage their confidence in your product or service. Go to GoodPractices (**www.goodpractices.com**) for some Web site development guidelines.

Now that you've gotten your name and developed the Web pages for your Web site, you will need to make arrangements for Web hosting, if you haven't already done so. Web hosting services provide server space, make your site available to the public, and offer site management utilities such as preprogrammed shopping cart services. There are thousands of Web hosting companies. Sites such as 1&1, GoDaddy, and Yahoo! offer a variety of pricing plans for personal and commercial sites. Expect to pay a start-up fee as well as a monthly amount that is usually based on a one-year contract.

You can ensure that your site gets listed with search engines by visiting each engine's Web site (**www.google.com**, **www.yahoo.com**, **www.msn.com**, and so on) and searching for "submitting my site." Provide the information requested, and then when someone searches for keywords that match your site, it will be one of the sites that are provided in the search results answer screen.

To operate a business, you need a way to receive payments. Just like in a traditional retail business, perhaps the best option may be to take credit cards. You should be aware that there are many costs involved with setting up and maintaining a credit card acceptance account—but the benefits may well outweigh the costs. Customers are comfortable using their credit cards online, and many feel more secure knowing that the credit card company is there in case of a dispute or fraudulent use.

One of the best and quickest ways to accept credit cards is to use a PayPal

Figure 2I
For your online business, someone will need to create the Web pages for your Web site. Many Web hosting services offer tools and templates to help you develop your Web storefront.

merchant account (Figure 2J). PayPal also acts as a secure intermediary, offering users the ability to make payments from their bank account, credit card, or PayPal account without revealing their personal financial information to the seller. PayPal manages more than 40 million accounts worldwide. Transaction fees range from 2 to 3 percent and there is a per-transaction fee of about 30 cents per transaction. The benefits to such a solution include the relatively easy setup on their site (no local installation is needed), the instant recording of transactions, a resource center with tools and links to help you grow your business, and a fraud protection policy that protects you from those who would attempt to take advantage of the transaction process.

All businesses need monthly and annual reports to know where they stand and where they are headed, so one of the utilities you should look for in a Web host is back-end reporting. Back-end reports will tell you how many hits your site has had, when the site has the most traffic, what your total sales volume is, and a variety of other important information (Figure 2K).

Here's a bonus. Go to Homestead (**www.homestead.com**). This site will help you set up and then host a trial business site for 30 days—for free! You might try setting up a pseudo-business just to see how all the pieces fit together.

ONLINE TRAVEL RESERVATIONS

Another area of e-commerce experiencing rapid growth is online travel reservations. Sites such as Travelocity, Expedia, and CheapTickets enable leisure travelers to book flights, hotels, and car rentals online, as well as find the cheapest fares based on their trip parameters (Figure 2L). Most travel sites provide e-tickets so that you can quickly check in at airport terminals by using small self-service kiosks.

In addition, nearly every hotel and car rental agency is now online, which means you can check room or car availability and book a reservation without making a single call. And if you're looking for backpacking trails at a national park, you're sure to find plenty of free information using any search engine. Travel and travel-related sites not only simplify your trip planning and booking, but also save you money.

Figure 2J
You can accept credit card payments on your site using services such as PayPal.

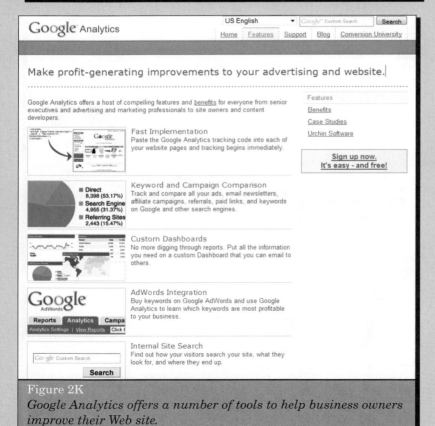

Figure 2K
Google Analytics offers a number of tools to help business owners improve their Web site.

Expedia, for example, provides a very rich booking experience. You can use features that compare fares and then keep a running total price summary as you add hotels, cars, and entertainment packages to your trip. Personalization options allow you to retrieve itineraries and receive notifications when rates change. You can also make use of vacation and cruise wizards that will walk you through the process of developing the best options for your excursion. All of these technologies make a sometimes complex and expensive process work to your advantage.

By 2011, U.S. online travel bookings are expected to account for $128 billion in revenue—representing 38 percent of total U.S. travel revenue. More than $40 billion of this revenue is expected to result from online corporate travel bookings. Expedia's corporate travel division, Egencia, reported more than $1.3 billion in global bookings for 2007. In addition to online travel booking, Egencia also offers corporations 24-hour access to travel agents with whom they can book reservations over the phone, alerts travelers of any changes to their travel plans, and assists with post-trip expense management. Egencia competes well against traditional corporate travel agencies by offering lower fees and better service.

Personal online travel booking does have some drawbacks. Online travel sites get revenues from advertising on their Web pages as well as from fees that are charged to the airlines, car rental agencies, hotel chains, and entertainment venues. Although this is almost always advantageous to the consumer, other businesses have been greatly affected. As more and more consumers use the Web to do their own travel booking, the offline travel agency business continues to decline. It seems that the use of the electronic middleman is making the traditional travel agent obsolete.

Figure 2L
*Sites such as Travelocity (**www.travelocity.com**) are popular because they help travelers find the cheapest fares and reservations available.*

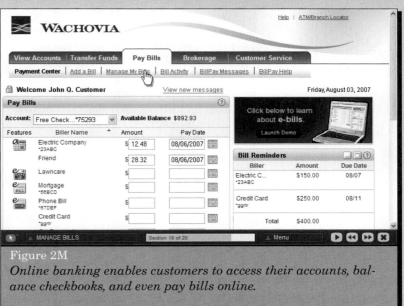

Figure 2M
Online banking enables customers to access their accounts, balance checkbooks, and even pay bills online.

ONLINE BANKING

Online banking enables you to use a Web browser to access your accounts, balance your checkbook, transfer funds, and even pay bills online (Figure 2M). In fact, 40 million Americans used online banking services by the end of 2005. The use of online banking is expected to grow by 55 percent by the end of 2011. By that time, some 76 percent of Americans (72 million households) will be using online banking services. Currently, banks that offer online banking gain a competitive advantage over those that do not, because most customers now consider it a necessary and expected service, like ATMs. What else is in it for banks? Plenty. Online banking helps banks cut down on the expenses of maintaining bank branches and paying tellers and also allows them to provide advanced levels of electronic customer service.

Banks implement online banking in different ways. One method makes use of personal finance programs such as Microsoft Money Plus or Intuit's Quicken, enabling customers to balance their checkbooks automatically. An advantage of this to customers is that Microsoft Money Plus and Quicken offer powerful features for budgeting and analyzing spending habits. The drawback of this method, however, is that you can access your online bank account only from the computer that holds all the Money or Quicken data.

Easier online banking tools are Web-based systems that require only one program: a Web browser. All the data is stored on the bank's computer, not your own, which means that you can access your account from any computer connected to the Internet. Although Web-based online banking doesn't offer the advanced budgeting and analysis features that Money Plus and Quicken do, it's much easier to use because you are directly manipulating your accounts online instead of recording copies of your work in offline programs.

Besides the convenience of doing your banking from home, online banking relieves you from hand-writing checks (and buying stamps!). Online banking is also cheap—many banks offer online banking for free. Some banks even offer customers cash incentives to try online bill paying. However, online banking is not trouble-free. If you switch banks, it can be a time-consuming hassle to switch from one bank's online system to another. You also have to be aware that when you pay a bill online,

the money is deducted from your account much more quickly than with offline bill paying. You can research online banking on sites such as Bankrate.com.

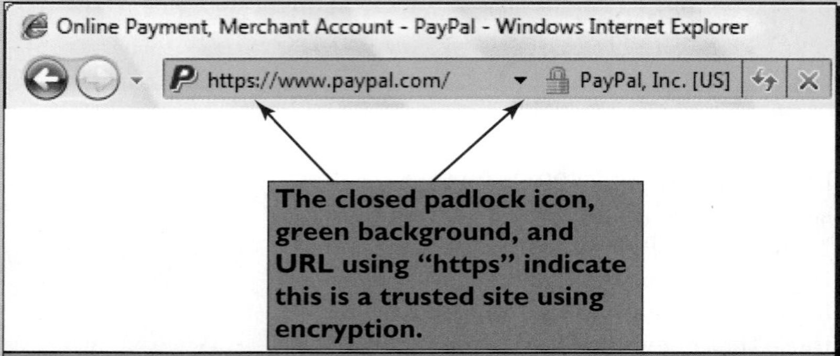

However, the biggest concern for most people is security. Many people who would like to use online banking are concerned about losing their money. As long as you follow certain precautions, you have little need for concern. In fact, you are 10 percent less likely to have your personal information stolen using online versus offline bill paying. When you access a bank account online, be sure you're doing so in your browser's secure mode (Figure 2N). In **secure mode**, the browser scrambles and encodes the data when it communicates with the bank's server. Check your browser's documentation to find out where the secure mode icon appears and what it looks like. Above all else, keep your password safe.

Another concern is the security of the bank's **electronic vault**, the server that stores account holders' information. Because no computer system is totally secure, it's reasonable to be concerned that an intruder could gain access to the vault and steal your money. Still, the threat is minor. Online banks use state-of-the-art security systems, including measures such as **active monitoring**, in which a security team constantly monitors the vault for signs of unauthorized access.

ONLINE STOCK TRADING

Online stock trading (also referred to as e-trading) is the purchase or sale of stock through the Internet. In use only since 1996, online stock trading now accounts for one out of every six stock trades, easily making it the fastest-growing application in B2C e-commerce. Offering secure connections through the customer's Web browser, online stock trading sites enable investors to buy and sell stocks online without the aid of a broker (Figure 2O).

The attraction of online stock trading can be summed up in one word: Cost. Traditional, full-service brokerages charge up to $100 per trade; discount brokerages charge about $50. But the most aggressive e-traders have cut the charges to $10 per trade or less. E-traders, such as E*TRADE and Ameritrade, can offer such low prices because the trading is automatic—no human broker is involved.

Online Payment, Merchant Account - PayPal - Windows Internet Explorer

https://www.paypal.com/   PayPal, Inc. [US]

The closed padlock icon, green background, and URL using "https" indicate this is a trusted site using encryption.

Figure 2N
The Internet Explorer browser has several features used to identify a safe site that uses encryption.

However, many potential online investors are concerned about security and timeliness. The issue of making secure online trades isn't really any different from the general issue of online security. All financial institutions use secure connections. This doesn't mean that transactions can't be intercepted or redirected, but millions of trades are transacted online every day without incident. Online trading of stocks is regulated by the Securities and Exchange Commission (SEC) in the same way other methods of trading are. Most brokerages use trade confirmation methods that help ensure that all trades are transacted properly.

Timeliness is an issue only if a delay in completing a transaction causes you to miss an opportunity. Delays can be caused by power outages, dropped connections, computer overloads, and batch processing. Despite these occasional delays, however, most online transactions take place in a timely manner.

According to investment professionals, online trading does have a disadvantage. Online trading appeals to an amateur investor's worst instincts—namely, buying when the market is at its peak of enthusiasm (and prices are also at their peak) and then selling when prices start to drop. This translates to buying high and selling low. You don't make money that way; you lose money. That's true even when, overall, the market is going up. Most investment counselors believe that amateurs are well advised to avoid frequent trading (sometimes called *day trading*).

NONRETAIL ONLINE SERVICES

Nonretail online services include dating services; credit reports; health and medical advice; news, weather, and sports information; real estate listings (for homes and apartments); and insurance products (Figure 2P). These sites offer various levels of access and services for members and nonmembers. Some services, such as insurance quotes, up-to-the-minute news reports, and severe-weather alerts, are free. You can also post dating profiles or receive diet and other health-related profiles as well as trial passes for sports subscriptions. Many news and

Figure 2O
E-trading sites enable investors to buy and sell stocks online without going through a traditional broker.

newspaper sites give you free access to some online content, but you must pay for additional content, such as archived articles. You can also subscribe to e-mailed newsletters on health, sports, and other related topics.

AVOIDING E-COMMERCE HAZARDS

Although there are many benefits to engaging in e-commerce, it also entails risks. These risks include identity theft, personal information exposure, money loss, and being ripped off by unscrupulous charlatans. To protect yourself you should carefully create user names and passwords, particularly at sites where you must pay for goods or services. You should avoid e-commerce with little-known companies, at least until you've taken the opportunity to check their legitimacy. Checking shopping portals or other review sites to locate feedback from other users or conducting an online search combining the company's name with keywords such as *problem*, *fraud*, or *scam* can help you be better informed. Even though you are most likely protected from monetary losses by your credit card company, you should always be careful when giving out your credit card information, and you should do so only on secure sites. Never share credit card or account numbers or user name and password information with others, even if you receive an e-mail requesting that information from what seems to be a legitimate source. Some of the things you should look for on a secure site (one that is protected from intrusion of your personal business by others) is *https://* in the address of the site instead of the usual *http://*. The added "s" stands for "secure site." Other things you can look for are the VeriSign logo, the locked padlock symbol, or a logo from other site-security entities such as Verified by Visa. Another security alert is a message box that notifies you when you are leaving (or entering) a secure site.

Sometimes you will find that the seller is a person just like you—that the seller doesn't have the ability to take credit cards, and that he or she has set up an account with an online transaction processing system such as PayPal. It is the seller who decides which vendor to use for the payment. For instance, if you see the PayPal logo on an eBay auction item site, it means that you can use PayPal as a payment option. In fact, sometimes this is the only option available. The PayPal Web site even offers a tool to help you manage your buying experience. The PayPal AuctionFinder searches eBay for items you've recently won and prefills your payment form with details taken straight from the item listing. With AuctionFinder, you can eliminate errors and pay for your items instantly. Always use extra care and caution whenever you conduct financial transactions on the Internet. Doing so will help to ensure that your e-commerce experience will be a positive one.

Figure 2P
Many nonretail sites offer various levels of access and services for members and nonmembers.

SPOTLIGHT EXERCISES

1. Use your browser to go to Peapod (**www.peapod. com**). Choose the link to Groceries for your Home in the New Customers area of the screen. Type in your zip code to see if Peapod is available in your area. If it is not, then press the Back button of your browser and type in 20010, which is a Washington D.C. zip code. Browse through the online store and write down the name and price of at least five products. Now use local newspaper ads or a trip to the local grocery store to compare the pricing of the online goods. Factoring in delivery costs, which shopping method is the most economical (include the cost of fuel and time to go to the local store)? Would you shop for groceries online? Why or why not?

2. Have you purchased an item from a merchant over the Internet? Describe the item, the merchant, and the method of payment. Would you use the Internet to make another purchase? Explain why or why not.

3. Type the word *travel* into your favorite search engine's search window. Choose a travel link that will allow you to book a flight. Work through the site's dialog boxes to book a mock trip to a tropical destination. Write down the cost, connections, and total travel time. Now go back to the search engine and choose a competing travel site and repeat the process. How much difference in cost, connections, and travel time do you find? Try booking one of the trips on different days of the week to see whether there is a difference. Finally, list the cheapest itinerary you can find. Would you travel for the cheapest rate or would you choose another option. Why?

4. Are you in the mood to do a little shopping? Visit eBay at **www.ebay.com** and track the sale of an item. Select and describe an item that you wish to purchase. There are two methods for finding your item.

   - You can select a general category and then refine your search by selecting successive subcategories.
   - You can enter a description of the item in the search textbox and then click the Search button.

   Try both methods. Which method do you prefer? How many items met your criteria? If the number is too large, refine your criteria. View the list of items and sellers, and select a specific item. Identify the item, the seller, the first bid, the current bid, the bid increment, the number of bids, and the amount of time left in the auction. Click the bid history link, and identify the bidders and how many bids they have submitted. Click the "See detailed feedback" link to see the seller's rating. What is the seller's overall number of positive, neutral, and negative ratings? Based on buyer activity and the seller's profile, determine the amount of money that you would initially bid for this item. Track the bidding of this item until the auction closes, increasing your imagined bid as necessary. When the auction ends, determine whether you would have been the successful bidder. If not, what was your maximum bid? What was the final bid? Would you consider actually bidding for items in an online auction? Explain why you would or would not use an Internet auction to sell or purchase an item.

5. Online stock trading is one of the fastest-growing applications in consumer-based e-commerce. To see why, visit E*TRADE, one of the most popular online trading sites, at **www.etrade.com**. What were the last levels of the NASDAQ, DOW, S&P 500, and 30-year bonds? Although you will not formally open an account online, look at the steps that are needed to open one. (Enter the requested information, but don't accept the agreement!) What personal information is needed? What information is needed to create your investment profile? How do you feel about this? How much is charged per transaction? What is the annual fee? Would you trust this site? Why or why not?

6. For this exercise, you will create your own business Web site. Use whichever tools you wish (a word processor's Web page design wizard, Yahoo!'s free Web site development section, and so on) to create a home page and at least two other linked pages. Your site does not need to have a registered name, but your home page should clearly identify your business. Post your completed site to the Web and then provide your instructor with the address.

What You'll Learn...

- Define *bandwidth* and discuss the bandwidth needs of typical users.

- Discuss how modems transform digital computer signals into analog signals.

- List transmission media and explain several transmission methods.

- Explain the limitations of the public switched telephone network (PSTN) for sending and receiving computer data.

- Describe multiplexing and digital telephony, including their impact on line usage.

- Provide examples of how digitization and convergence are blurring the boundaries that distinguish popular communications devices, including phones and computers.

- Discuss various wired and wireless applications.

Wired & Wireless Communication

CHAPTER OUTLINE

Moving Data: Bandwidth & Modems 102
    Bandwidth: How Much Do You Need? 103
    Modems: From Digital to Analog and Back. 103

Wired & Wireless Transmission Media 104
    Twisted Pair. 104
    Coaxial Cable 104
    Fiber-Optic Cable 105
    Infrared 105
    Radio 106
    Microwaves 107
    Satellites 107

**Wired Communication via the
Public Switched Telephone Network** 108
    Last-Mile Technologies 109

Convergence: Is It a Phone or a Computer? 113
    Cellular Telephones. 114
    Web-Enabled Devices 117

Wired & Wireless Applications 117
    Internet Telephony: Real-Time Voice and Video 117
    Faxing: Document Exchange 120
    Satellite Radio, GPS, and More 120
    Text, Picture, and Video Messaging and More. 122

Techtalk

throughput

Throughput is often used interchangeably with *bandwidth*, but the two terms are actually different. *Bandwidth* is the theoretical maximum amount of data that can be sent through a specific transmission medium at one time (usually per second). *Throughput* is the actual amount of data that is transmitted. Throughput is almost always lower than bandwidth, especially with wireless communications.

Suppose you're on a trip and need to access your e-mail—but you left your notebook at home. No problem; you just use your Web-enabled cell phone to retrieve your messages. As for sending e-mail messages back, again, no problem; you can do this with most messaging devices. Back at home, you hop on your ultrafast FiOS connection to download and upload files. The whole time, you're experiencing the realities of **connectivity**. Defined broadly, this term refers to the ability to link various media and devices. Connectivity enhances communications and improves access to information. In this chapter, we'll examine the various technologies involved in communications, whether they're **wired** (connected by a physical medium) or **wireless** (connected through the air or space).

Moving Data: Bandwidth & Modems

Communications (data communications or telecommunications) is the process of electronically sending and receiving messages between two points. Communications occurs over communications channels. **Communications channels** (also referred to as links) are the path through which messages are passed from one location to the next. In communications,

a source encodes messages and sends them over the communications channel to a destination that decodes messages (Figure 3.1). When you send a message from your computer, the message is converted into an electrical signal.

In communications, both analog and digital signals move data over communications channels. Old-style phones and phone lines sent and received analog signals. **Analog signals** take data (most often audio of the human voice) and translate it into continuous waveforms that travel over communications channels. An analog signal can carry only so much data, limiting its usefulness.

In contrast, computing devices send and receive digital signals. **Digital signals** convert data into discontinuous pulses in which the presence or absence of electronic pulses represents 1s and 0s (Figure 3.2). Because 0s and 1s are discrete, the data arrives in a much clearer format. As a result, the receiving end knows exactly how to reconstruct the data back into its original form. Digital signals also transfer much more data than analog and at much greater speeds. For instance, digital TV systems can now deliver more than 500 stations across digital cable, which allows not only more stations than analog cable but also more features.

So how are the digital signals from your computer prepared for traveling over analog telephone lines? Let's look at two additional considerations for sending data over communications channels: bandwidth and modems.

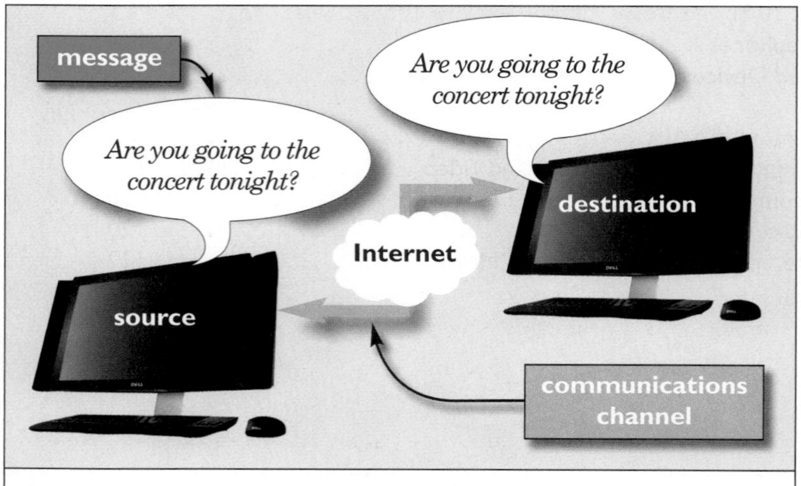

BANDWIDTH: HOW MUCH DO YOU NEED?

Bandwidth refers to the amount of data that can be transmitted through a given communications channel. The physical characteristics of the transmission medium and the method used to represent and transmit data via the transmission medium determine bandwidth. For analog signals, bandwidth is expressed in cycles per second, or hertz (Hz). For digital signals, bandwidth is expressed in bits per second (bps).

Broadband refers to any transmission medium that transports high volumes of data at high speeds, typically greater than

FIGURE 3.1 In communications, a message is encoded into electrical signals at the sending end and then decoded at the receiving end.

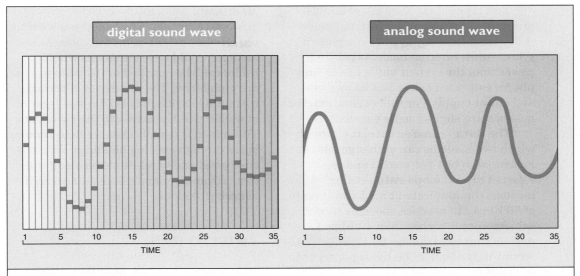

FIGURE 3.2 Digital signals are composed by sampling an analog wave at discrete points in time. The analog wave is then approximated by these discrete measurements.

1 Mbps (megabits per second, or million bits per second). So how much bandwidth do you need? Conventional dial-up connections to the Internet use a relatively low bandwidth of 56 Kbps (kilobits per second, or thousand bits per second) or less. Most users find this painfully slow when searching the Web. But dial-up connections are still cheaper than broadband connections, so some people sacrifice speed for low price.

Broadband digital connections are now widely available in the United States. Approximately 60 million out of 114 million U.S. households had broadband access in 2007, and this is estimated to reach 86 million by 2012.

MODEMS: FROM DIGITAL TO ANALOG AND BACK

Modems are communications devices used to transmit data over telephone lines. On the sending end, a modem uses a process called *modulation* to transform the computer's digital signals into analog tones that can be conveyed through the telephone system. On the receiving end, the process used is *demodulation,* whereby the other modem transforms the signal from analog back to digital. Modems can perform both modulation and demodulation—*modem* is short for modulator/demodulator (Figure 3.3).

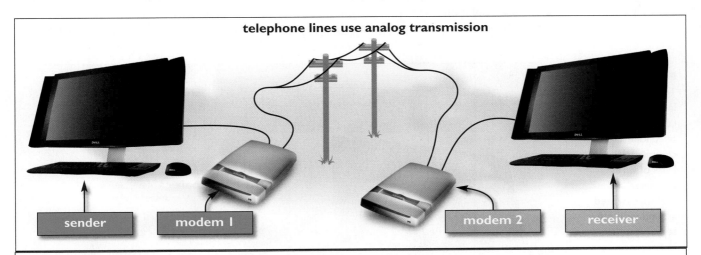

FIGURE 3.3 A modem transforms the computer's digital signals into analog tones that can be conveyed through the telephone system. Once the transmission is received, the modem converts the analog tones back to digital signals.

Two types of modems are available: internal and external. An internal modem is designed to fit inside your computer's system unit. Internal modems get their power from the system unit's power supply. An external modem has its own case and power supply. For this reason, external modems are slightly more expensive.

The **data transfer rate**, the rate at which two modems can exchange data, is measured in bits per second and is referred to as the **bps rate**. Analog modems communicate at a maximum rate of 56 Kbps. (In practice, modems rarely achieve speeds higher than 42 Kbps.) A modem that can transfer 56 Kbps is transferring only about 7,000 bytes per second, or about five pages of text.

Often, a single message travels over several different wired and wireless transmission media, including telephone lines, coaxial cable, fiber-optic cable, radio waves, microwaves, and satellite, before arriving at its destination. We'll look at each of these types of wired and wireless transmission media in more detail.

Wired & Wireless Transmission Media

Unlike communications using wired transmission media such as twisted-pair, coaxial, and fiber-optic cables, wireless media don't use solid substances to transmit data. Rather, wireless media send data through air or space using infrared, radio, or microwave signals. Why would you want to use wireless media instead of cables? One instance would be in situations where cables can't be installed or the costs to do so are prohibitive. The popularity of portable computing devices has led most colleges to now offer wireless access to their students. This option is usually cheaper than running wires through existing buildings. We'll discuss wired and wireless media along with their advantages and disadvantages in the following sections.

TWISTED PAIR

The same type of wire used for telephones, **twisted pair** uses four insulated wires twisted around each other to provide a shield against electromagnetic interference, which is generated by electric motors, power lines, and powerful radio signals (Figure 3.4). Although twisted pair is an inexpensive medium, the bandwidth of traditional twisted-pair telephone lines is too low to simultaneously carry video, voice, and data. Twisted pair carries data at transfer rates of less than 1 Kbps.

COAXIAL CABLE

Familiar to cable TV users, **coaxial cable** consists of a center copper wire surrounded by insulation, which is then surrounded by a layer of braided wire. Data travels through the center wire, and the braided wire provides a shield against electrical interference (Figure 3.5). Coaxial

FIGURE 3.4
Twisted pair refers to inexpensive copper cable that's used for telephone and data communications. Pairs of wires contained in the cable are twisted around each other to reduce interference from electrical fields.

twisted pair cable

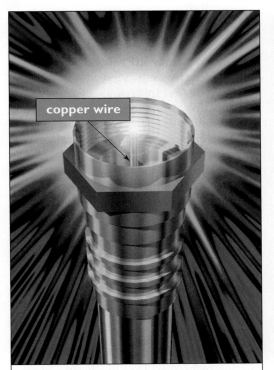

FIGURE 3.5 In coaxial cable, data travels through the center copper wire and is shielded from interference by the braided wire.

copper wire

FIGURE 3.6 Fiber-optic cable consists of filaments of glass or plastic that transmit data by means of pulses of light.

cable carries data at transfer rates of 10 Mbps. In contrast to twisted pair, coaxial cable makes it easy to achieve higher-bandwidth data communications. Your home is probably already wired with coaxial cable if you subscribe to a cable TV service.

FIBER-OPTIC CABLE

Fiber-optic cable consists of thin strands of glass or plastic that carry data by means of pulses of light (Figure 3.6). Broadband uses fiber-optic or coaxial cable to transmit data. Fiber-optic cable can carry more data without loss of signal strength for longer distances than twisted pair or coaxial cable. Fiber-optic cable carries data at transfer rates of 10 Gbps (gigabits per second) or more.

INFRARED

If you use a remote control to change television channels, you're already familiar with infrared signaling. **Infrared** is a wireless transmission medium that carries data via beams of light through the air. No wires are required, but the transmitting and receiving devices must be in line of sight or the signal is lost. When the path between the transmitting and the receiving devices is not obstructed by trees, hills, mountains, buildings, or other structures, infrared signals can work within a maximum of about 100 feet.

To use infrared technology with your computer system, you need an IrDA (Infrared Data Association) port (Figure 3.7). You may encounter an IrDA port on a mobile computing device or peripheral such as a PDA, digital camera, notebook, mouse, printer, or keyboard. The most common use of the IrDA port is to transfer data from your PDA to your desktop or notebook computer or another PDA. To enable data transfer, the IrDA port on the transmitting device must be in line of sight (usually within a few feet) of the port on the

FIGURE 3.7 An IrDA port allows for more flexibility in managing external devices such as a mouse, keyboard, phone, or PDA.

receiving device. IrDA ports offer data transfer rates of 4 Mbps. With all of these restrictions, why would you want to use infrared? If you had a situation where hooking devices together with cables wasn't an option, such as with a wireless keyboard or mouse, infrared would be a good choice. On modern networks, however, IrDA is too slow to be of practical use for transferring large amounts of data.

RADIO

Radio transmissions offer an alternative to infrared transmissions. You probably have experienced one type of radio transmission by listening to your favorite radio station. But you may not realize the impact that radio waves have on your daily life or on society in general. All kinds of gadgets—from cell and cordless phones to baby monitors—communicate via radio waves. Although humans cannot see or otherwise detect them, radio waves are everywhere.

With **radio** transmission, data in a variety of forms (music, voice conversations, and photos) travels through the air as radio frequency (RF) signals or radio waves via a transmitting device and a receiving device. Instead of separate transmitting and receiving devices, radio transmissions can also use a wireless transceiver, a combination transmitting-receiving device equipped with an antenna. Data transfer rates for wireless devices have the potential to reach up to 3 Mbps for cell phones and up to 250 Mbps for wireless networks.

A major disadvantage of radio transmission is noise susceptibility and interference. One of radio's advantages is that radio signals are long range (between cities, regions, and countries) and short range (within a home or office).

Bluetooth

Bluetooth is a short-range radio transmission technology that has become very popular in recent years. Named after the 10th-century Danish Viking and king Harald Blåtand ("Bluetooth" in English) who united Denmark and Norway, Bluetooth was first conceived by Swedish cell phone giant Ericsson (Figure 3.8). Bluetooth technology relies on a network called a **piconet** or a **PAN** (**personal area network**) that enables all kinds of devices—desktop computers, mobile phones, printers, pagers, PDAs, and more—within 30 feet of each other to communicate automatically and wirelessly.

How exactly does Bluetooth work? Bluetooth-enabled devices identify each other using identification numbers that are unique to each device. When these devices are within 30 feet of each other, they automatically "find" and link to one another. You don't have to worry about being connected to Bluetooth devices that you don't want to connect to: The device requires that you confirm a connection before making it final. Up to eight Bluetooth-enabled devices can be connected in a piconet at any one time.

Unlike infrared technologies, Bluetooth doesn't require a direct line of sight to connect devices. Because the frequency used by Bluetooth devices changes often, Bluetooth devices never use the same frequency at the same time and don't interfere with each other. Bluetooth can

Phone with Bluetooth capability

Computer with Bluetooth capability

Bluetooth headset

FIGURE 3.8 Bluetooth-enabled devices make tasks, such as synchronizing your phone calendar with your computer calendar or keeping your hands free while talking on the phone, easier.

accommodate data transfer rates of up to 3 Mbps. At Bluetooth's maximum transfer capacity, you would be able to easily move a document within just a few seconds.

MICROWAVES

Microwaves are high-frequency, electromagnetic radio waves with very short frequencies that are used to transmit data. Using relay stations similar to satellite dishes (including an antenna, transceiver, and so on), microwave signals are sent from one relay station to the next. Because microwaves must travel in a straight line with no obstructions such as buildings, hills, mountains, and so on, relay stations are built at a distance of approximately every 30 miles (the line-of-sight distance to the horizon), or closer if the terrain blocks transmission. Microwave relay stations are also often situated on the tops of buildings or mountains.

Microwave transmission eliminates the need for a wired infrastructure. It is useful in areas where the use of physical wires is impractical or impossible. Microwave technologies are used in the transmission of data across cellular telephone networks. Disadvantages include the 30-mile line-of-sight restriction, sensitivity to electrical or magnetic interference, and the costs of maintaining the multitude of relay stations it takes to transfer messages across long distances.

SATELLITES

Essentially microwave relay stations in space, communications **satellites** are positioned in geosynchronous orbit, which matches the satellite's speed to that of the Earth's rotation, and are, therefore, permanently positioned with respect to the ground below (Figure 3.9). Satellites transmit data by sending and receiving microwave signals to and from Earth-based stations. Devices such as handheld computers and Global Positioning System (GPS) receivers can also function as Earth-based stations.

Direct broadcast satellite (**DBS**) is a consumer satellite technology that uses an 18- or 21-inch reception dish to receive digital TV signals broadcast at a bandwidth

FIGURE 3.9 Communications satellites are often permanently positioned with respect to points on the Earth to provide specific areas of coverage.

of 12 Mbps. Increasingly, DBS operators offer Internet access as well as digital TV service, but at a much lower bandwidth. Currently, DIRECTV offers satellite Internet access at 700 Kbps, but there are a couple of drawbacks. To access the Internet using satellite technology, you need a satellite dish, a satellite receiver, and a relatively clear line of site to the orbiting satellites. Additionally, costs of installation and ongoing fees can be higher than those of cable providers.

Broadband cable is still not available in many rural or other low-population areas, thus many of these areas are prime candidates for DBS. The major weakness of DBS systems is their slow upload speeds. Download speeds are comparable to other Internet connections (1.5 Mbps) but uploading data is often restricted to 256 Kbps. But, if it is the only option available, slow is better than nothing!

To use these various wireless transmission media, a computer system must also use a special communications device called a **network access point**, which sends and receives data between computers that contain wireless adapters. Access points are usually built into wireless routers.

Destinations

A good overview of a DBS can be found at **http://electronics .howstuffworks.com/ satellite-tv.htm**, where you will learn interesting facts about the technical issues surrounding satellite TV and Internet transmission.

So, what is it about wireless connectivity that is so interesting? Well, one answer is that wireless technology removes place-specific restrictions; that is, the need to be in a certain place to receive a service. Some forms of wireless technology allow you to be wherever you choose to be and still have the ability to be connected.

Now that you know more about wired and wireless media, the next section will explore the most common wired communication system: the public switched telephone network.

Wired Communication Via the Public Switched Telephone Network

Although many parts of the phone system have been enhanced to handle digital communications, limitations of the conventional phone system still exist.

The **public switched telephone network** (**PSTN**) is the global telephone system, a massive network used for data as well as voice communications, comprising various transmission media ranging from twisted-pair wire to fiber-optic cable. Some computer users derisively (and somewhat unfairly) refer to the PSTN as plain old telephone service (POTS). The derision comes from most analog telephone lines being based on standards that date back more than a century (Figure 3.10). Although a few parts of the PSTN remain based on analog communications, the majority of the system has been switched over to digital communications.

Many home and business telephones in use today are analog devices. These telephones are linked to subscriber loop carriers by means of twisted-pair wires. A **subscriber loop carrier** (**SLC**) is a small, waist-high curbside installation that connects as many as 96 subscribers; you've probably seen one in your neighborhood. The area served by an SLC is called the **local loop**.

From the SLC on, though, the PSTN is almost a completely digital network. The SLC transforms local analog calls into digital signals, routing them through high-capacity fiber-optic cables to the **local exchange switch**, which is also based on digital technology capable of handling thousands of calls. The local exchange switch is located in the local telephone company's central office (CO). From the local phone company's CO, the call can go anywhere in the world. It continues on the digital portion of the PSTN's fiber-optic cables and can even be converted to radio waves and sent out over cellular networks (Figure 3.11).

Although analog connections are still common, this situation is changing as new digital telephony services become available. **Digital telephony** is the use of all-digital telephone systems: The telephones are digital and the transmission is handled digitally. Compared with analog devices, which are prone to noise and interference, digital phones offer noise-free transmission and high-quality audio. You've probably already used a digital phone: large organizations, such as corporations and universities, typically install their own internal digital telephone systems, called private branch exchanges (PBXs). By using a PBX, an organization avoids the high cost of paying for a line to the local telephone company's exchange

FIGURE 3.10 Digital switches have replaced telephone operators, but some analog technology still exists in many home telephone connections.

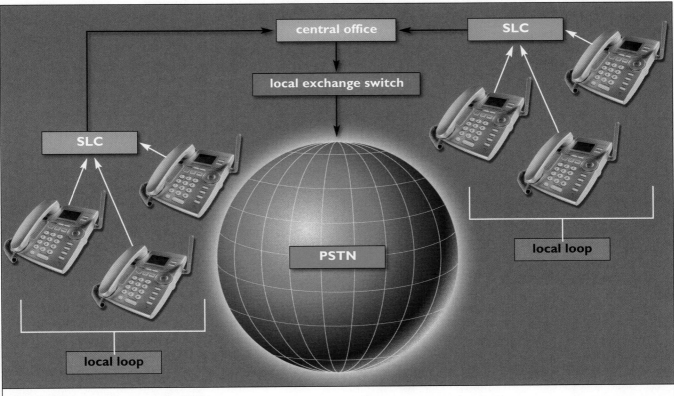

FIGURE 3.11 Pathways on the PSTN

switch for each employee. Calls to the outside must be translated into analog signals to connect to the PSTN.

Because long-distance lines must handle thousands of calls simultaneously (32 calls per second, 24 hours a day, 7 days a week in the United States), a technique called **multiplexing** is used to send more than one call over a single line. The electrical and physical characteristics of copper wire impose a limit of 24 multiplexed calls per line, but fiber-optic cables can carry as many as 48,384 digital voice channels simultaneously. In contrast to the analog local loop, most long-distance carriers use digital signals so that they can pack the greatest number of calls into a single circuit.

The inability of homes or businesses to access the PSTN's high-speed fiber-optic cables, along with the bottleneck of data on the last mile of twisted-pair phone lines connecting homes and businesses, is often referred to as the **last-mile problem**. Here's why. In most areas of the United States, only the local loop is still using analog technology, because nearly all existing buildings were originally constructed with built-in twisted-pair wiring. These analog lines are vulnerable to noise and can't surpass a theoretical limit of 56 Kbps. But things are starting to change. Telephone companies are getting into other businesses (such as providing Internet connectivity) and need to deliver higher bandwidth to homes. Therefore, telephone companies are now replacing analog local loop technology with digital technology (such as FiOS). The last-mile problem might soon be solved in your neighborhood!

LAST-MILE TECHNOLOGIES

Local loops are in the process of being upgraded, but until the upgrade is complete, phone companies and other providers offer a number of interim digital telephony technologies that make use of twisted-pair wiring. Sometimes called **last-mile technologies**, these solutions include digital telephone standards (such as ISDN and DSL) that use twisted-pair wiring as well as always-on high-speed wired services (such as coaxial cable and cable modems).

Destinations

To learn more about today's telephone technologies, check out HelloDirect .com's "Get Informed" tutorials at **http:// telecom.hellodirect. com/docs/Tutorials/ default.asp**.

CURRENTS

Debates

Stealing Bandwidth—Think Before You Surf

Wireless Internet connections are available at more places every day. But with this freedom to surf the Internet no matter where you are comes responsibility.

When you log on to the Internet through a wireless connection at your home, are you sure you're logging on to your own network? With the advances in wireless technology, Internet signals can travel beyond the walls of your home. Many people inadvertently connect to their neighbor's wireless network instead of their own. Using another person's wireless network is known as *piggybacking*. Piggybacking is possible because some users don't take the time to implement security measures on their wireless networks to restrict access.

So why would a neighbor logging on to your network be a big deal? If it only happens occasionally and accidentally, it isn't that significant. But if your neighbor constantly downloads large video files, your network might slow down as your bandwidth is eaten up.

Even worse, what if your neighbor decides to save some money by cancelling her Internet account and using yours without your knowledge? Not only is this stealing, but you could be liable for malicious acts committed by other people using your network—even if they use your network without your consent! Thinking about beating your neighbor to the punch and using her network? Well, think again, because using someone's network without permission is considered a crime in most jurisdictions in the United States.

You can easily avoid such problems by taking a few minutes to set up wireless security on your home network. Check out **www.practicallynetworked.com/support/wireless_secure.htm** for more information.

You could conceivably save money by going to a coffee shop every day and working for a few hours on their free Internet connection. If the coffee shop is advertising free connectivity to customers, you do have their permission to use their network, so this would not be a crime. But what if you aren't buying any coffee? Although not illegal, it certainly is unethical to use the service they are providing for paying customers. You are also being unfair to the paying customers who might be having a less fulfilling experience while you are chewing up bandwidth downloading movies.

So take advantage of Internet connectivity offered by merchants that you patronize, but don't abuse the privilege. To find out about sites with wireless connectivity in your area check out WiFinder at **www.wifinder.com** (Figure 3.12).

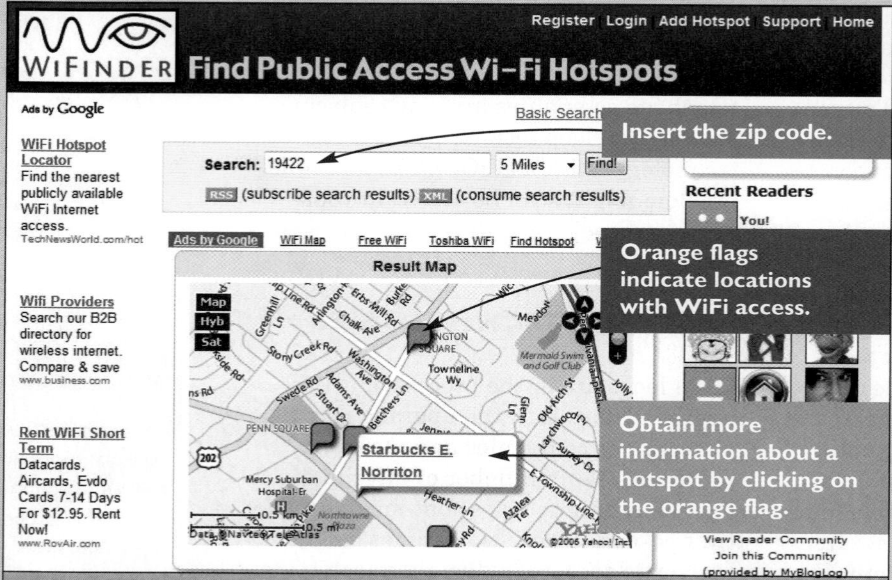

FIGURE 3.12 WiFinder helps you locate businesses with wireless access in your geographic area.

Integrated Services Digital Network

ISDN (integrated services digital network) is a standard that provides digital telephone and data service. ISDN offers connections ranging from 56 to 128 Kbps (basic rate ISDN) or 1.5 Mbps (primary rate ISDN) using ordinary twisted-pair telephone lines. The cost of an ISDN line is often two to three times that of an analog phone line, but there's a payoff. With a 128-Kbps ISDN service, you get two telephone numbers with one ISDN account; you can use one for computer data and the other for voice or fax. When you're using the connection for computer data only, the system automatically uses both data channels to give you the maximum data transfer rate; if a phone call comes in, the connection automatically drops back to 64 Kbps to accommodate the incoming call. What's more, connection is nearly instantaneous. Unlike analog connections with a modem, there's no lengthy dial-in procedure and connection delay.

To connect computers to ISDN lines, you need an **ISDN adapter** (also called a **digital modem**, although it isn't actually a modem; Figure 3.13). Although ISDN has been largely supplanted by faster technologies (such as DSL and fiber optics), ISDN may be the only broadband solution in many rural areas. Keep in mind that ISDN requires that special wiring be installed from the SLC to your home.

Digital Subscriber Line

DSL (digital subscriber line), also called **xDSL**, is a blanket term for a group of related technologies, including ADSL (asymmetric digital subscriber line), that offer high-speed Internet access. DSL technologies can deliver data transfer rates of 2.5 Mbps or higher. DSL is widely available in the United States and is akin to ISDN in that it uses existing twisted-pair wiring. But because DSL achieves much higher throughput than ISDN, it quickly became more popular. SDSL (symmetric digital subscriber line) is superior to ADSL because the download and upload throughput is the same, as opposed to lower upload speeds with ADSL.

To use DSL, you need a DSL phone line and a DSL service subscription. Unlike conventional telephone service, which is available to almost any home, DSL service is limited by the distance from the CO, or telephone switching station, to your home. You also need a **DSL modem**, which is similar to a traditional telephone modem in that it modulates and demodulates analog and digital signals for transmission over communications channels. However, DSL modems use signaling methods based on broadband technology for much higher transfer speeds (Figure 3.13). DSL service

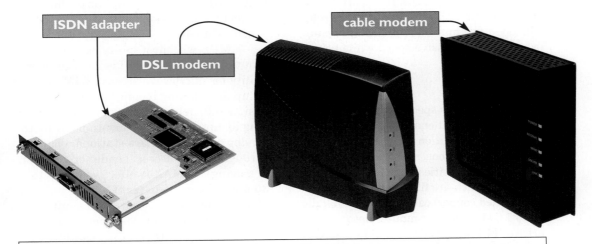

FIGURE 3.13 Various types of modems facilitate the connection between your computer and last-mile technologies.

Destinations

To help you decide which last-mile technology might be right for you, check out the "Cable or DSL" tutorial at **http://telecom. hellodirect.com/ docs/Tutorials/ CableVsDSL.1.030801 .asp.**

is now standardized so that almost any DSL modem should work with the wiring your telephone provider uses. However, it is best to buy a DSL modem that your provider recommends. Check with your provider for a list of approved modems before purchasing one. Although DSL service is more expensive than dial-up, it is usually cheaper than other broadband access options.

Coaxial Cable and Cable Modems

Aside from telephone companies, the leading provider of broadband is your local cable TV company. Approximately 123 million homes in the United States are served—or can easily be served—by cable systems, making Internet access by cable easy to obtain.

When cable and the cabling equipment were originally installed in homes, signals were designed to run in only one direction: to the home. When the Internet became popular, the cable companies invested tremendous amounts of money in equipment and cable to enable two-way communication to capture the Internet market.

For computer users, these services offer data transfer rates that exceed the speed of DSL. **Cable modems**, devices that enable computers to access the Internet by means of a cable TV connection, now deliver data at bandwidths of 1.5 to 6 Mbps or more, depending on how many subscribers are connected to a local cable segment (Figure 3.13). Bandwidth across a cable connection is shared among subscribers who are connected to the cable company in local groups. If you are lucky enough to have subscribers in your group who don't use much bandwidth, you can experience impressive speed while using the Internet.

Leased Lines

A **leased line** is a specially conditioned telephone line that enables continuous, end-to-end communication between two points. Larger organizations, such as ISPs, corporations, and universities, connect using leased **T1 lines**, which are fiber-optic (or specially conditioned copper) cables that can handle up to 1.544 Mbps of computer data. The price of T1 lines has decreased in response to growing demand, making them affordable for small businesses. Leased lines may

use modems, cable modems, or other communications devices to manage the transfer of data into and out of the organization.

Other Last-Mile Technologies

There are also interim technologies that make better use of existing fiber-optic cables. Fiber-optic **T3 lines** can handle 44.7 Mbps of computer data. Although T3 lines can cost between $7,500 and $14,000 per month, Internet service providers, financial institutions, and large corporations that move lots of data find these lines critical to their operations. Another technology that uses fiber-optic cable, **SONET** (**synchronous optical network**) is a standard for high-performance networks. The slowest SONET standard calls for data transfer rates of 52 Mbps; some enable rates of 1 Gbps or faster. SONET is widely used in North America, and a similar standard, synchronous digital hierarchy (SDH), is used in the rest of the world.

In addition to adapting twisted-pair wiring, broadband coaxial cable, and fiber-optic cable, wireless technologies are helping to solve the last-mile problem as well. Here's a look at two wireless solutions.

MMDS (multichannel multipoint distribution service, sometimes called multipoint microwave distribution system) can be thought of as wireless cable. MMDS was originally slated as a wireless alternative to cable television, but now its main application is Internet access. Service providers offer MMDS Internet access within a 35-mile radius of the nearest transmission point at projected speeds of 1 Gbps.

MMDS will most likely be supplanted by WiMAX (worldwide interoperability for microwave access). **WiMAX** is an up-and-coming technology that is designed to deliver high-speed access over long distances, either point-to-point (both sender and receiver are stationary) or through mobile access (sender or receiver is moving). WiMAX is effective for up to 30 miles for point-to-point access and 3 to 10 miles for mobile access. In mountainous areas or other places where there are obstructions, MMDS and WiMAX face challenges because they are susceptible to interference.

In the next section we will explore the phenomenon of the coming together of these communications technologies.

Convergence: Is It a Phone or a Computer?

We've been examining technologies that carry computer data over voice lines as well as through the air. At the core of this process is **digitization**, the transformation of data such as voice, text, graphics, audio, and video into digital form. Digitization enables convergence. **Convergence** refers to the merging of disparate objects or ideas (and even people) into new combinations. Within the IT industry, convergence means two things: (1) the combination of various industries (computers, consumer electronics, and telecommunications) and (2) the coming together of products such as PCs and telephones.

Wireless devices are proliferating at a tremendous pace. Today, it is not unusual for your phone to double as a PDA or talk to your computer or for your computer to be controlled by a wireless mouse or keyboard. Convergence has culminated in the transmission of data. With the advent of Internet telephony (sending telephone calls over the Internet), all forms of information (voice, data, and video) now travel over the same network—the Internet (Figure 3.14).

Digitization also enables media convergence. Media convergence is the unification of all forms of media (including newspapers, TV, and radio). The Internet is already a major source of breaking news, rivaling such traditional sources as newspapers and television. Many telephone calls are now transmitted across the Internet using a technology known as Voice over IP (VoIP). This trend could be signaling the end of the traditional public switched telephone network.

Another threat to the PSTN is the December 2001 legislation on telephone number portability. Under this rule, people can keep their existing phone number when changing providers, whether from traditional land-based or cellular phone service. Despite the ongoing challenges of cell

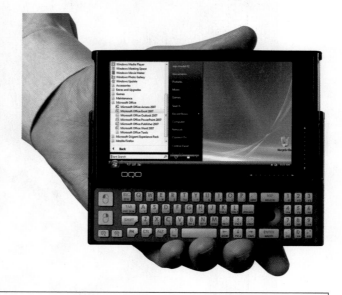

FIGURE 3.14 Convergence means smaller devices do more. The BlackBerry® Curve™ 8320 (left) is a PDA, phone, and Internet access device all rolled into one. The OQO Model 02 is one of the world's smallest computers at 5.6 × 3.3 inches, making it easy to take your computer with you.

phones (battery life, spotty connectivity, dropped calls), approximately 10 percent of U.S. households have opted to disconnect their conventional landline telephones and rely on cellular service only. Industry professionals expect this migration away from land-based telephones to continue. At the end of 2007, there were approximately 3.3 billion cell phones in use—enough for more than half the world's population!

Why should you care about convergence? Because understanding convergence will help you make more informed decisions about current and future technology purchases. This section explores some of the dimensions of computer-telephony convergence, a process of technological morphing in which previously distinct devices lose their sharply defined boundaries and blend together. As you'll see, it's creating some interesting hybrids.

CELLULAR TELEPHONES

Cellular telephones are computing devices. Although cell phones started out as analog devices, the current generation of cell phones (**3G**, for third generation) are all digital (Figure 3.15). Cell phone

systems use radio signals to transmit voice, text, images, and video data.

In 1971 AT&T built a network of transmitters that automatically repeat signals. This network of transmitters, which are called **cell sites**, broadcasts signals throughout specific, but limited, geographic areas called **cells**. When callers move from cell to cell, each new cell site automatically takes over the signal to maintain signal strength. But who or what monitors your cell phone's signal strength so that you have the best reception? That's the job of the **mobile switching center** (**MSC**), and each cellular network contains several MSCs that handle communications within a group of cells (Figure 3.16). Each cell tower reports signal strength to the MSC, which then switches your signal to whatever cell tower will provide the clearest connection for your conversation.

MSCs route calls to the gateway mobile switching center (GMSC), which in turn sends calls to their final destination. If the call is headed for a land-based phone, the GMSC sends the call to the PSTN. Otherwise it forwards the call directly to another cellular network.

Terrain, interference, weather, antenna position, and battery strength can

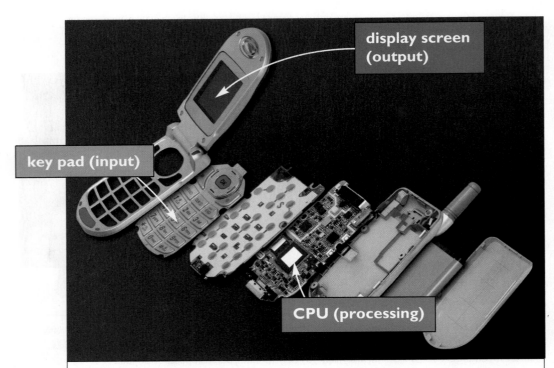

display screen (output)

key pad (input)

CPU (processing)

FIGURE 3.15 Cell phones are computing devices with attributes very similar to computers.

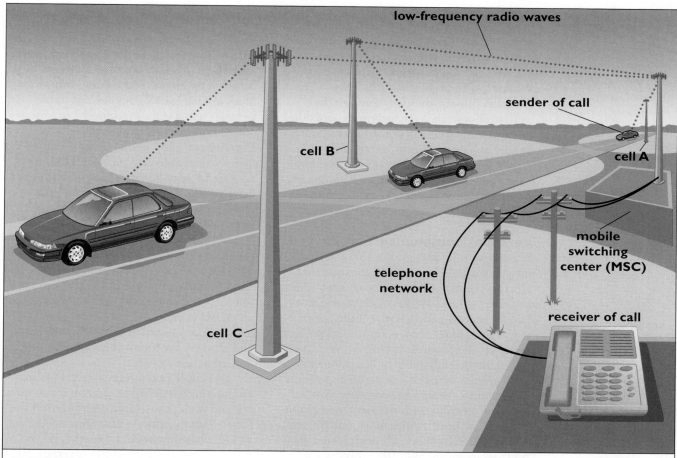

FIGURE 3.16 When callers move from cell to cell, the nearest cell site automatically takes over transmission to maintain the strength of the signal. The mobile switching center (MSC) is the switching office that connects cell towers to the PSTN or other cellular networks.

all affect signal strength. However, there may be times when you've extended your antenna, recharged your battery, have clear weather, and are standing at the top of a hill—and still cannot achieve a good signal. Cell coverage is not perfect, and cellular networks have *holes* (areas in which you can't send or receive calls).

MSCs are also key players in another widely used cellular service, SMS (short messaging service). Better known as text messaging, close to 60 percent of U.S. mobile phone users have used SMS and more than 30 percent are texting daily. The MSC forwards the message to a messaging center for storage and then locates the other cell phone that will receive the message. An appropriate signal is then sent out through the cell in which the receiving phone is located to let it know it will be receiving a message. The receiving phone

sends an acknowledgment to the message center when the message is received.

Cell phone etiquette and safety are other issues to be aware of. Many people may be irritated or concerned by others' careless use of cell phones in public places or while driving motor vehicles. A number of states have banned drivers from using handheld cell phones while operating a motor vehicle. Other agencies have policies on cellular phone use in aircraft, trains, and hospitals. Businesses may limit the use of cell phones in movie theaters and restaurants. In addition, your college or university may restrict the use of cell phones in classrooms.

Besides cell phone etiquette and safety, burgeoning cell phone use has another societal impact. Just as with old computer equipment, you need to think about the proper disposal of your cell phone when you

Destinations

For tips on proper cell phone etiquette (to avoid annoying your friends, family, and strangers), check out **http://cellphones.about.com/cs/miscellaneous/ht/cell_etiquette.htm**.

upgrade or damage it beyond repair. The average life of a cell phone is 18 months; about 125 million phones are disposed of each year in the United States alone. Discarded cell phones are toxic waste. When they end up in landfills, they threaten the environment through the release of arsenic, lead, cadmium, and other heavy metals that can creep into the water supply and cause cancer or birth defects. AT&T, Verizon, and many other providers, as well as indirect retailers, will accept old phones. The bottom line: recycling your old cell phone is good for the environment.

Personal Communication Service

A group of related digital cellular technologies called **PCS** (**personal communication service**) quickly replaced most analog cellular services. PCS is also referred to as **2G**, for second-generation cellular technology, or dual-band service. Digital 2G phones made strides toward solving many of the problems that plagued analog phones. Improvements included decreasing signal interference, increasing reception, providing better protection from eavesdropping, and increasing the difficulty of committing cell phone fraud. In short, 2G design specifications enabled the manufacturers to use convergence to make the **smartphones** we enjoy today, which are combinations of phones and computing devices (Figure 3.17).

For millions of people, 2G made mobile computing a reality. Because 2G technology is digital, it's much more amenable to data communications than analog cellular services. It made it possible to access the Internet by means of a modem connected to an analog cellular phone, but data transfer rates were extremely low because of line noise and poor connections. Throughput of up to 384 Kbps for downloads was enabled by 2G standards.

Technology has marched on with the introduction of 3G technology and the planning of **4G** (fourth generation) cell phones. The main benefit of 3G is that it supports much higher numbers of data and voice customers and provides higher data transfer rates (greater than 384 Kbps while walking and up to 2 Mbps while stationary). Although still under development, 4G is expected to offer improvements in connectivity, data transfer rates, and support for the next generation of multimedia.

So should you dump your 2G phone and opt for a 3G? If your phone is providing you with good, quality service and the feature set is sufficient for your needs, you should probably keep it. However, if you need to regularly access the Internet, you may wish to consider upgrading to a 3G phone to take advantage of the higher data transfer rates.

FIGURE 3.17 The Nokia E90 Communicator is a smartphone that operates as a conventional phone or opens up to function more like a PDA or computer.

WEB-ENABLED DEVICES

A **Web-enabled device** is any device that can display and respond to the codes in markup languages, such as HTML (Hypertext Markup Language) or XML (Extensible Markup Language), typically used to build Web pages. Web-enabled devices include PDAs, smartphones, and notebook PCs.

PDAs are fast disappearing from the market because of convergence. Many smartphones now offer all the functionality that PDAs used to offer, and also act as phones. Windows Mobile and the Palm OS are popular operating systems for smartphones that were originally developed for PDAs. BlackBerry devices (which use their own operating system) continue to be a popular choice for managing business life (which includes checking e-mail, making phone calls, and accessing the Internet). BlackBerry devices actually lead the smartphone revolution as one of the first truly convergent devices.

To work over wireless networks, Web-enabled devices require WAP (Wireless Application Protocol). WAP is a standard that specifies how users can access the Web securely using pagers, smartphones, PDAs, and other wireless handheld devices.

It doesn't matter which operating system your device uses because WAP is supported by all of them. However, WAP-enabled devices do require a microbrowser, a special Web browser that works with small file sizes. Smaller file sizes are necessary because of the low memory capacities of WAP-enabled devices and wireless networks with low bandwidth.

Now that you understand how convergence is blurring the boundaries between phone and computer devices, let's take a look at some wired and wireless applications used with these devices.

Wired & Wireless Applications

The world of wired and wireless applications is receiving more attention every day. You can't open a magazine, surf the Web, or watch TV without seeing ads for the latest wireless solutions. More and more businesses and home users are implementing these various applications to help them communicate, collaborate, and share text, graphics, audio, and video. You can sit in a classroom today and receive instant messages, e-mail, and stock quotes and even browse the Web—all from your cell phone! And it is happening at increasingly faster speeds, higher data transfer rates, and lower costs.

INTERNET TELEPHONY: REAL-TIME VOICE AND VIDEO

Internet telephony, more commonly known as **VoIP (Voice over Internet Protocol)**, uses the Internet for real-time voice communication. Although the Internet isn't ideal for real-time voice, you can place calls via the Internet in a variety of ways. To place free long-distance calls, you'll need a computer equipped with a microphone, speakers or headphones, an Internet connection, and a telephony-enabled program such as Skype (**www.skype.com**). With Skype you can make free calls to other similarly equipped Skype users (Figure 3.18).

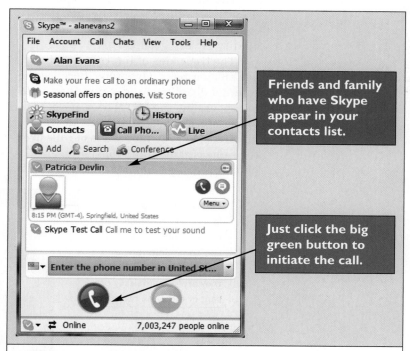

FIGURE 3.18 Skype features a simple interface and offers free calls to other Skype users. All you need is the Skype software, a microphone, and speakers (or headphones).

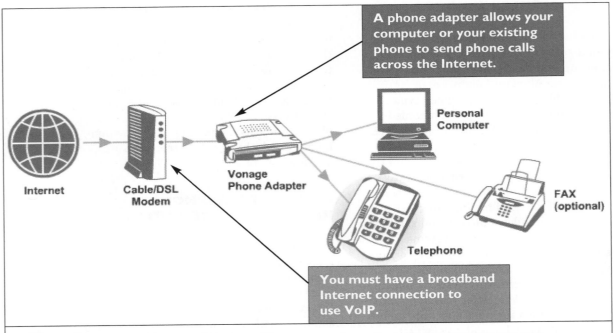

A phone adapter allows your computer or your existing phone to send phone calls across the Internet.

Internet

Cable/DSL Modem

Vonage Phone Adapter

Personal Computer

Telephone

FAX (optional)

You must have a broadband Internet connection to use VoIP.

FIGURE 3.19 VoIP installation is relatively easy. The system can be configured by a novice computer user.

What about placing a call to an ordinary telephone? You can't do it for free. However, VoIP service providers such as Vonage are stepping into the act by offering computer-to-phone and phone-to-phone services that use the Internet for long-distance transmission (Figure 3.19). Rates are cheaper than conventional land-line phones and the quality is very good.

The basic idea of Internet telephony has an enormous advantage: Because the Internet doesn't rely on switches to route messages, like the PSTN does, it's cheaper to operate. Providers can route dozens, hundreds, or even thousands of calls over the same circuit. Many conventional phone companies already send voice calls over the Internet. You may have actually experienced VoIP without even knowing it. You can try Internet telephony by using Skype, which is the cheapest way (free!) to experience VoIP, and see how you like it.

If you and the person you're calling have a digital video camera, you can converse through real-time videoconferencing as well. **Videoconferencing** is the use of digital video technology to transmit sound and video images so that two or more people can have a face-to-face meeting even though they're geographically separated (Figure 3.20). Many notebook computers sold today come with built-in video cameras (Webcams) and Skype software to support video

FIGURE 3.20

In a videoconference, two or more people can see and communicate with each other, even though they are not physically present in the same room.

conferencing. However, you won't always have perfect quality; you'll hear echoes and delays in the audio, and the picture will be small, grainy, jerky, and liable to delays. But there are no long-distance charges (using Skype).

In addition to Internet voice and video calls, Internet telephony products support real-time conferencing with such features as a shared whiteboard, file-exchange capabilities, and text chatting. A **whiteboard**, generally shown as a separate area of the videoconferencing screen, enables participants to create a shared workspace. Participants can write or draw in this space as if they were using a physical whiteboard in a meeting. Combine this with live video and audio and it's like being in a conference room with your group.

A **Webcam** (Figure 3.21) is an inexpensive, low-resolution analog or digital video camera that is integrated into a notebook computer or designed to sit on top of a computer monitor. Sometimes an individual, company, or organization places a Webcam in a public location, such as a street corner, a railway station, or a museum (Figure 3.22). Often, the camera is set up to take a snapshot of the scene every 15 minutes or so. The image is then displayed on a Web page. Some sites offer streaming cams, also called live cams, that provide more frequently updated images.

If you want only to transmit voice over the Internet, and not video, you can use a dial-up modem and connection with transfer speeds of 56 Kbps. But for any high-bandwidth Internet application, such as streaming video, you need a broadband connection with transfer speeds of at least 1.5 Mbps. Network-based delivery of high-quality videoconferencing requires a bandwidth of at least 10 Mbps. Videoconferencing will be a much smoother experience for all participants with broadband's faster upload speeds.

Streaming video wasn't practical for home viewing before broadband and cheap, powerful computers became available for the home market. Now, streaming video sites such as YouTube are some of the most visited sites on the Internet (Figure 3.23).

Powerful, inexpensive computers and increased bandwidth offered by ISPs

FIGURE 3.21 If your computer lacks a Webcam, you can buy one like the Logitech Quickcam Pro 9000, which is designed to be freestanding or placed on top of a monitor (or notebook).

have made Internet telephony and videoconferencing affordable and practical for small businesses. And millions of Internet users employ Webcams and programs such as Skype to stay in touch with friends and family—often for free!

FIGURE 3.22 The EarthCam Web site (**www.earthcam.com**) provides live satellite links to many popular locations, including the world-renowned Eiffel Tower in Paris, France.

Inside of Hard Drive

Ever wondered what happens inside the sealed case of a hard drive? Check out this video and find out!

FIGURE 3.23 Availability of increased bandwidth, powerful home computers, and better compression algorithms have made the display of streaming video across the Internet wildly popular.

Destinations

To learn more about the basics of Webcam use, check out **www.microsoft.com/canada/home/communications-and-mobility/articles/webcam-basics-how-do-they-work.aspx**.

FAXING: DOCUMENT EXCHANGE

Facsimile transmission—or **fax** as it's popularly known—enables you to send an image of a document over a telephone line or the Internet (Figure 3.24). The sending fax machine makes a digital image of the document. Using a built-in modem, the sending fax machine converts the image into an analog representation so that it can be transmitted through the analog telephone system. The receiving fax machine converts the analog signals to digital signals, converts the digital signals to an image of the document, and then prints the image.

Some computer users use fax modems instead of fax machines. A **fax modem** is a computerized version of a stand-alone fax machine. This device and software allow your computer to do everything a fax machine can: send and receive documents, print documents, and store documents. The big difference between using a regular fax machine and using your computer as a fax machine is that the fax modem does everything in a digitized way. So you may need a scanner to put a document into a digital format if you want to fax something that's printed or sketched on paper.

Traditional fax machines are quickly becoming obsolete. Some companies have chosen to use a spare computer as a fax server to handle incoming and outgoing faxes. Desktop software can convert e-mails to faxes and vice versa. This is referred to as *fax-to-mail* or *mail-to-fax* technology and reduces costs significantly, because there is no need for a fax machine or an additional phone line. In addition there is no extra charge for using your Internet connection to send a fax.

Faxes received in this way are usually converted to a PDF file and attached to an e-mail, or they may be sent to a cell phone. Similarly, sent faxes are converted to a PDF file and forwarded to a fax server, which then sends it over the Internet to its destination. If the receiving fax machine is a conventional machine attached to a phone line, the fax is forwarded to the PSTN for delivery.

Because computers can send and receive faxes, it is not a far stretch of the imagination to see that sending and receiving documents will soon be accomplished by network-enabled cell phones or Web-enabled devices, thereby making fax machines as we know them today obsolete.

SATELLITE RADIO, GPS, AND MORE

Many applications use satellite technology, including air navigation, TV and radio broadcasting, paging, and videoconferencing. **Satellite radio** broadcasts radio signals to satellites orbiting more than 22,000 miles above the Earth. The satellites then transmit the signals back to a radio receiver. Unlike ground-based radio signal transmitters, satellite radio is not affected by location, distance, or obstructions. Because of their great height, satellites can transmit signals to a radio receiver wherever it might be located.

Satellite radio is a boon for folks living in areas with limited local radio stations or where regular AM/FM reception is hampered by terrain. Companies that offer

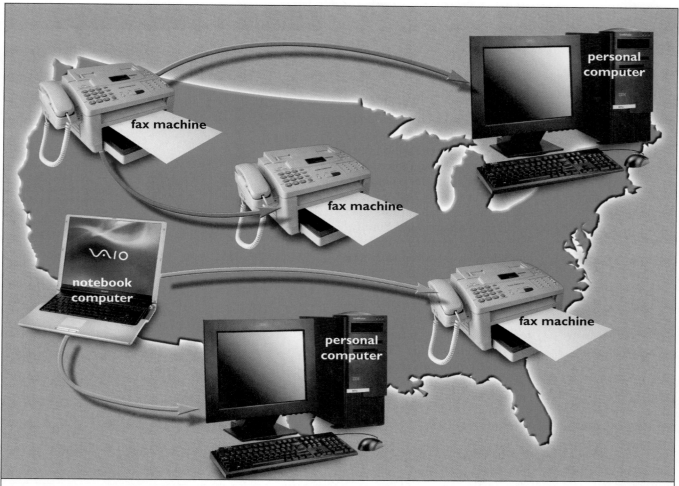

FIGURE 3.24 Facsimile transmission enables you to send an image of a document over a telephone line or through the Internet to anyone who has a fax machine. If your computer has a fax modem, you can send and receive faxes from your computer instead of a fax machine.

monthly satellite radio subscriptions include XM Satellite Radio and SIRIUS Satellite Radio, though these two companies are close to finalizing their merger. Satellite radio can mimic your local radio broadcasting station's style, including commercials. It can provide you with more than 100 channels offering different genres, including continuous music, sports, news, and talk programs. In contrast to music programs that are offered by some cable or satellite in-home providers, satellite radio uses portable receivers that plug into your home or car stereo so it is totally mobile and transportable to wherever you happen to want to listen. SIRIUS now offers Backseat TV, which streams live TV broadcasts to subscribers who have video receivers in their vehicles.

GPS

Another interesting application of satellite technology is GPS. **GPS (Global Positioning System)** is a cluster of 27 Earth-orbiting satellites (24 in operation and three extras in case one fails). Each of these 3,000- to 4,000-pound solar-powered satellites circles the globe at an altitude of 12,000 miles, making two complete rotations every day. The orbits are arranged so that at any time, anywhere on Earth, at least four satellites are "visible" in the sky. A GPS receiver's job is to locate four or more of these satellites, figure out the distance to each, and use this information to deduce its own location.

A GPS receiver can be either handheld or installed in a vehicle. Navigation

Ethics

GPS devices can be extremely useful—ask anyone who has used one to navigate through an unfamiliar neighborhood or the lost hiker whose GPS-equipped cell phone helped searchers find him. But this same technology is viewed as an invasion of privacy by others. New York City cab drivers have protested against a plan to install GPS devices in all cabs, fearing the possibility of constant surveillance. Some schools have begun requiring habitually truant students to carry GPS devices to encourage attendance. Are you aware that many cell phones include GPS technology and can be used to track your location? How do you feel about using GPS technology for monitoring purposes? Do benefits like safety and convenience outweigh the risks of reduced privacy?

systems in rental cars are a typical application of GPS. OnStar is a multifaceted GPS communications system that enables drivers to talk to a service representative to obtain driving directions and information on hotels, food venues, and the like. Drivers can also use OnStar to notify the police, fire department, or ambulance service in case of an emergency. Through in-vehicle sensors, it can even detect when a car has been involved in an accident. Finally, OnStar can unlock car doors should a driver accidentally lock car keys inside (Figure 3.25).

GPS units for cars have become more mobile. Many different models can be easily attached to a dashboard and moved from one vehicle to another. These GPS units even come preloaded with maps and can be updated when connected to the Internet.

Other Satellite Applications

Echelon is a system used by the U.S. National Security Agency to intercept and process international communications passed via satellites. The system uses ground-based listening devices and up to 120 satellites to intercept messages. It combs through the huge volume of intercepted messages, looking for words and phrases such as "bomb" and "terrorist" and other information of interest to intelligence agencies.

Satellites also bring Internet access to areas that don't have a communications infrastructure. The Navajo Nation, which straddles the borders of Arizona, New Mexico, and Utah and covers a 26,000-square-mile area, faces special challenges for connecting its residents to the Internet. Approximately half the households don't even have phone service, and those that do, find the quality of that service sometimes lacking. For data communications, the maximum reliable data speed is often limited to 28.8 Kbps. In addition, Internet access through a private service provider is virtually always a long-distance call.

How OnStar Works

1   A GPS receiver in the vehicle picks up signals from Global Positioning System (GPS) satellites and calculates the location of the vehicle. That location information is stored in the vehicle's OnStar hardware.

2   When the driver pushes the blue OnStar button or red Emergency button, or an air bag deploys, OnStar places an embedded cellular call to the OnStar Center. Vehicle and GPS location data is sent at the beginning of the call.

3   The cellular call is received by a cellular tower and routed to the land line phone system.

4   The OnStar switch sends the call to the first available advisor, who has the location of the vehicle and the customer's information on her computer screen.

FIGURE 3.25 OnStar makes use of a built-in GPS and cell phone system to provide assistance to drivers.

Navajo Nation school administrators purchased a system called HughesNet, which uses a small 18-inch satellite dish to receive information from the Internet and regular telephone or data lines to send information (Figure 3.27). Because Internet use in an educational environment involves massive amounts of downloaded information, the satellite solution was ideal.

TEXT, PICTURE, AND VIDEO MESSAGING AND MORE

A growing niche in cell phone use is within the K–12 student population, with experts predicting that 54 percent of 8- to 12-year-olds will have cell phones within the next three years. Cell phones give teens (and a growing number of preteens) not only a sense of community, but also a sense of freedom. Cell phone ownership is being compared with the freedom and individuality of

Computers & Society

Electronic Voting: What's Your Vote?

Electronic voting is in your future, if it isn't already in your neighborhood polling place. What could be simpler? Touch a computer screen or click a mouse and you've had your say about the candidates and the issues on the ballot.

Voting wasn't always this easy for citizens or for the officials who tally election results. In the 19th century, paper ballots were state-of-the-art voting technology. They kept personal choices secret, but counting all those pieces of paper took time—and opened the door to mistakes or outright fraud. By the 20th century, depending on the preferences of the local government, voters were pressing levers on machines, poking holes in punch-card ballots, or inking ovals on optically scannable ballots.

FIGURE 3.26 Electronic voting machines have many advantages and disadvantages—and they are the wave of our voting future.

Fast-forward to the 21st century. In the search for a quick, easy, private, yet secure voting method, more than half the states have installed touch-screen electronic voting machines. In fact, Georgia and Maryland won't let you mark your ballot in any other way. Meanwhile, Michigan and other states are testing systems in which you vote from your home or office PC using an ordinary Internet connection. Your vote is encoded for secure transmission, just as retailers encode credit card numbers for security (Figure 3.26).

But is electronic voting a boon to society? Proponents argue that the technology is more reliable and more convenient, eliminating many of the problems that plagued elections in the past. Sometimes mechanical voting equipment broke down; sometimes punch-card ballots had to be checked by hand if the holes indicating choices didn't go all the way through. What's more, advocates believe that more people would participate if they could vote from home or by a couple of taps on a computer at the polling place. And with electronic voting, officials could tally the results immediately, instead of counting for hours, or even days.

Critics of electronic voting have four main concerns. First, they worry about security. Can such systems withstand hacker attacks? Can the software or hardware be manipulated to add, change, hide, or prevent votes? Second, critics raise concerns about malfunctions. What if the software doesn't work correctly or the screen blanks out for a time on election day? What if the Internet or wireless connection goes down?

Third, critics worry about verifying votes. How can voters and officials confirm that votes are recorded properly? How can votes be recounted without a paper trail or other proof? Finally, critics are concerned that electronic voting could widen the digital divide. Will people avoid voting if they are wary of computers, can't afford a PC, or don't have Internet access? Will the outcome of an election be affected if people can vote from their homes or offices instead of going to a central polling place?

Experts are already working on solutions. Some rely on paper—for example, you might get a printout after casting your vote electronically at a polling place. If the printout is correct, you would give it to officials for safekeeping so it would be available for a recount. Other solutions rely on technology. You might receive a special card or device to prove your eligibility and to record your choices, either at your own PC or at the local polling place. Once you submit your card, election officials would verify it and hold it in case a recount is needed. Is electronic voting on its way to a polling place near you?

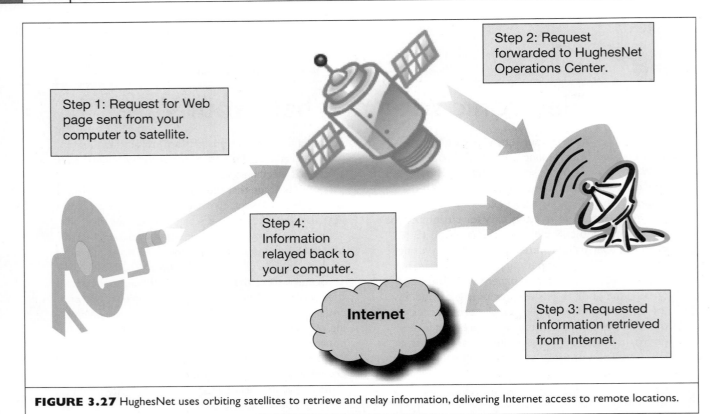

Step 1: Request for Web page sent from your computer to satellite.

Step 2: Request forwarded to HughesNet Operations Center.

Step 3: Requested information retrieved from Internet.

Step 4: Information relayed back to your computer.

Internet

FIGURE 3.27 HughesNet uses orbiting satellites to retrieve and relay information, delivering Internet access to remote locations.

having a driver's license. And the cell phone market for teens is growing rapidly. Approximately 60 percent of teens in the United States now have cell phones. And a recent survey indicates that one-third of them would give up their radio, video games, or a trip to the mall before going without their phone!

More so than adults, teens and young adults use their cell phones to do things besides placing and receiving calls. Text, picture, and video messaging are the hot applications for mobile devices that e-mail and IM

once were for computers. **Text messaging** is similar to using your phone for instant messaging or as a receiver and transmitter for brief e-mail messages (Figure 3.28).

Picture and video messaging are mobile services that will transform the way we electronically interact with each other. People have sent pictures by way of FTP or as e-mail attachments for more than 10 years, but the use of the telephone for such services has exploded in recent years. Today, **picture messaging** allows you to send full-color pictures, backgrounds, and even picture caller IDs on your cell phone. With picture messaging, your phone performs as a camera so that you can send pictures from your vacation or capture spontaneous moments and share them with others (Figure 3.29).

Many people want to use their phones to take pictures instead of carrying a digital camera. In order to have your phone replace your digital camera, you need to consider the resolution of the cell phone camera, which is measured in megapixels. A megapixel is 1 million pixels, or points of light, that make up an image. For pictures that will be printed out in large

FIGURE 3.28
Text messaging enables users to converse without bothering those nearby.

format (8 × 10 inches or larger), you need a camera with a resolution of at least 4 megapixels. Otherwise, the picture will not be sharp.

Images you capture with your phone can be sent by way of e-mail attachments or as a single picture when calling or talking to someone. Note that the user on the other end needs to have a picture-enabled phone as well and that there is a charge for sending pictures or video.

One cell phone application that is more popular with parents than kids is **location** (or **position**) **awareness**. This technology uses GPS-enabled chips to pinpoint the location of a cell phone (and its user). Teens may find location awareness to be a downside of owning a cell phone, because their parents can monitor their location. Teens often complain about such surveillance with statements such as "You're intruding on my privacy," "You're treading on my independence," and "I feel as though I'm always being watched." From the parents' perspective, however, they are simply keeping watch over their children in an effort to help them make better decisions.

Location awareness also has consumer and safety applications. The location-awareness feature enables your cell phone to quickly provide the location of the nearest restaurants and entertainment venues. It also can provide your location to a police station or other emergency service if needed. Law enforcement and government officials with the right credentials can access a Web site and locate a phone to within 35 feet of its actual location.

Cell phones manufactured since the end of 2004 are location aware. The benefit

FIGURE 3.29 Phones like the Nokia N82 include not only high-resolution cameras, but also photo editing features.

for society is that the 911 system can be used to determine the location of a phone, and thus the user, and then provide whatever assistance is necessary.

Today's wired and wireless applications provide us with conveniences that were once unimaginable. If your cell phone or PDA is Bluetooth enabled, you can send files wirelessly from your desktop computer to your printer or to a friend's notebook. You can buy concert tickets online, download the electronic tickets into your Bluetooth-enabled smartphone, and then link to the Bluetooth-enabled scanner at the concert house instead of presenting a ticket. One particularly interesting development is the use of a Bluetooth-enabled earphone that transmits and receives data from your cell phone, even if it is located in your pocket or backpack. Bluetooth radio chips are small and cheap (approximately $5 each) and are growing in popularity. Who knows what tomorrow's wired and wireless applications will enable us to do?

Destinations

Visit **www.u-locate. com** to learn more about location-awareness technology.

What You've Learned

WIRED & WIRELESS COMMUNICATION

- Bandwidth refers to the maximum data transfer capacity of a communications channel and is measured in hertz (Hz) and bits per second (bps). To transmit text, you can get by with low bandwidth (such as a 56-Kbps connection). But for viewing multimedia on the Internet, a broadband connection of at least 1.5 Mbps is preferable.

- To send digital data over dial-up phone lines, it's necessary to modulate the signal (transform it into analog form). On the receiving end, the signal must be demodulated (transformed back into digital form). Modems (modulators/demodulators) perform this service.

- Communications require physical or wireless media, including twisted-pair wire, coaxial cable, fiber-optic cable, infrared, radio, microwaves, and satellite. Last-mile technologies, including DSL, SONET, and cable modems, can increase the capacity of existing physical media. WiMAX and MMDS are wireless technologies used to transmit signals over large geographic areas.

- The public switched telephone network (PSTN) is predominantly digital, except for the local loop, which might still use low-bandwidth twisted-pair wiring. Increased penetration of broadband (cable, DSL, and fiber-optic) in the U.S. means that fewer people are transmitting data across the PSTN.

- Multiplexing is the transmission of more than one telephone call or message on a single line. Digital telephony is the use of all-digital telephone systems: The telephones are digital, and the transmission also is handled digitally. Both technologies enable transmission of more voice data over traditional copper lines as well as fiber-optic cable.

- Digitization is the transformation of data such as voice, text, graphics, audio, and video into digital form. Convergence refers to the coming together of products such as PCs and telephones. Smartphones, PCs, and other Web-enabled devices enable all types of digital information (voice, video, and data) to travel over wireless communication systems.

- Internet telephony and faxing can now be accomplished through the use of the Internet by traditional wired technology. New wireless technologies allow for text and picture messaging, satellite radio, and GPS services.

Key Terms and Concepts

2G 116
3G 114
4G 116
analog signals 102
bandwidth 102
Bluetooth 106
bps rate 104
broadband 102
cable modem 112
cell sites 114
cells 114
cellular telephones 114
coaxial cable 104
communications 102
communications channels . . . 102
connectivity 102
convergence 113
data transfer rate 102
digital signals 102
digital telephony 108
digitization 113
Direct broadcast
  satellite (DBS) 107
DSL (digital subscriber
  line, or xDSL) 111
DSL modem 111
facsimile transmission (fax) . . . 120

fax modem 120
fiber-optic cable 105
GPS (Global Positioning
  System) 121
infrared 105
Internet telephony 117
ISDN (integrated services
  digital network) 111
ISDN adapter
  (digital modem) 111
last-mile problem 109
last-mile technologies 109
leased line 112
local exchange switch 108
local loop 108
location (position)
  awareness 125
microwaves 107
mobile switching center
  (MSC) 114
modems 103
multiplexing 109
network access point 107
PAN (personal area
  network) 106
PCS (personal
  communication service) . . . 116

piconet 106
picture messaging 124
public switched telephone
  network (PSTN) 108
radio 106
satellite radio 120
satellites 107
smartphones 116
SONET (synchronous
  optical network) 112
subscriber loop carrier
  (SLC) 108
T1 lines 112
T3 lines 112
text messaging 124
throughput 102
twisted pair 104
videoconferencing 117
VoIP (Voice over
  Internet Protocol) 117
Webcam 119
Web-enabled device 117
whiteboard 119
WiMAX 112
wired 102
wireless 102

Matching

Match each key term in the left column with the most accurate definition in the right column.

_____ 1. Bluetooth

_____ 2. broadband

_____ 3. Webcam

_____ 4. PSTN

_____ 5. wireless

_____ 6. last-mile problem

_____ 7. convergence

_____ 8. modem

_____ 9. cell

_____ 10. VoIP

_____ 11. T1 line

_____ 12. videoconferencing

_____ 13. twisted pair

_____ 14. 2G

_____ 15. fiber-optic cable

a. refers to the lack of high-connectivity media (such as fiber-optic cable) extending all the way into the home

b. telecommunications line with bandwidth capacity of 1.54 Mbps

c. short-range radio transmission technology often used in personal computing devices

d. the generation in which cellular devices became digital

e. communications technologies with high bandwidth

f. the merging of technologies into a single device

g. transmission media that uses pulses of light

h. technology that facilitates conducting a meeting when participants are in different geographic locations

i. a camera designed for transmitting video over the Internet

j. transmission medium that uses radio signals

k. a device used to translate signal data sent or received by your computer

l. uses the Internet to transmit phone calls

m. cabling that uses intertwined pairs of wires

n. a distinct area of radio coverage in a wireless phone network

o. the global phone network

Multiple Choice

Circle the correct choice for each of the following.

1. Fiber-optic cable uses which of the following to transmit data?
   a. light
   b. sound
   c. electricity
   d. gravity

2. Which medium has the highest bandwidth?
   a. coaxial cable
   b. wireless
   c. fiber-optic cable
   d. twisted-pair wire

3. Which technology is specifically for short-range communication between computing devices?
   a. WiMAX
   b. Bluetooth
   c. DSL
   d. PSTN

4. The Global Positioning System (GPS) tracks locations by using which of the following?
   a. a supercomputer
   b. high-resolution cameras
   c. cellular phone serial numbers
   d. satellites

5. What is the main advantage that 3G cellular devices provide over 2G devices?
   a. 3G devices never drop calls.
   b. 3G devices have higher bandwidth for data reception.
   c. 3G devices are digital, whereas 2G are analog.
   d. 2G devices can't access the Internet.

6. When someone makes a cellular phone call, which of the following eventually handles the call?
   a. public switched telephone network (PSTN)
   b. mobile switching center (MSC)
   c. Global Positioning System (GPS)
   d. synchronous optical network (SONET)

7. Which is an example of convergence?
   a. two friends videoconferencing with Skype
   b. fiber-optic technology being installed in the last mile
   c. smartphones with PDA-like features accessing the Internet
   d. converting a fax into a PDF file before sending

8. Which of the following applies to traditional fax machines that use phone lines?
   a. They are no longer used.
   b. They have been replaced by 3G fax machines.
   c. They are often discarded in favor of Internet faxing technologies.
   d. They are still used because they are cheaper than Internet faxing.

9. A wireless mouse might use which of the following technologies?
   a. IrDA
   b. SONET
   c. 2G
   d. DSL

10. Which of the following is true of VoIP (Internet telephony)?
    a. It is often cheaper than conventional phone service.
    b. It is of such poor quality that businesses refuse to use it.
    c. It is only usable with a dial-up Internet connection.
    d. It is too expensive to install for home use.

Fill-In

In the blanks provided, write the correct answer for each of the following.

1. The _____ _____ _____ _____, or PSTN, is a global communications network used for voice and data transmissions.

2. A mobile computing device may use IrDA to transmit data via _____ signals.

3. Often used for cable TV, _____ _____ consists of a center copper wire surrounded by insulation, which is wrapped in braided wire.

4. Computers using wireless adapters use a special wireless communication device known as a(n) _____ _____ _____ to send and receive data.

5. Measured in bps, _____ refers to the maximum amount of data that can be transmitted through a communications channel.

6. A(n) _____ _____ is the area served by an SLC.

7. Capable of transferring data at speeds up to 1.544 Mbps, _____ _____ are often leased by larger organizations, but are becoming more affordable for small businesses.

8. A(n) _____ _____ translates data into a continuous waveform.

9. Participants in a videoconference can use a(n) _____ to create a shared workspace.

10. The ability of fiber-optic cables to carry more than 48,000 digital voice channels simultaneously is due to a technique known as _____.

11. Devices using _____ technology must be within 30 feet of one another but do not need a direct line of sight to transmit data.

12. To ensure you have the best reception, a(n) _____ _____ _____ monitors your cell phone's signal strength.

13. _____ is a broad term that describes the ability to link various media and devices to enhance communications and improve access to information.

14. Unaffected by location, distance, or obstructions, _____ _____ sends signals 22,000 miles above the Earth and back and is available by monthly subscription.

15. Although mostly surpassed by DSL and fiber-optic technologies, _____ may be the only viable broadband solution in many rural areas.

Short Answer

1. What is the difference between bandwidth and throughput? What Internet applications require high bandwidth?

2. Explain how Internet faxing works and why it is often preferred to using traditional fax machines.

3. In terms of the last-mile problem, explain the limitations of the PSTN for sending and receiving computer data.

4. Define convergence. Provide at least one example of technological convergence.

5. Briefly explain how Bluetooth works. What types of devices use Bluetooth?

6. Explain the difference between the terms modulation and demodulation. Which of these must a modem be able to perform? Explain why.

Go to **www.pearsonhighered.com/cayf** to review this chapter, answer the questions, and complete the exercises.

Teamwork

1. Using Skype

Free telephone calls and videoconferencing are available by using VoIP providers such as Skype. Visit skype.com and download their software. Create a Skype account (free) and have a few of your friends and family do the same. Place voice calls and video calls to some people you know. Note the quality of the calls and the Internet connections used by both parties. What type of Internet connections (dial-up, DSL, cable) provided the best voice call quality? Best video quality?

2. Phone Service Evaluation

Have each team member examine his or her most recent cell phone bill. Answer the following questions and summarize your results:

- How many monthly anytime calling minutes are included in your plan?
- What is the per minute charge if you exceed your allotted minutes?
- Do you have times when you can call for free (nights and weekends)?
- Do you have a data plan (for sending text messages, digital photos, etc.)? How much does it cost per month?
- Are you charged for roaming (that is, making calls when you are out of your local service area)?
- Are long distance calls included in your anytime minutes or is there an additional charge for them?
- How would you rate the quality of your phone, the ability to get a connection when you need it, and your current plan? Does your plan meet your current needs?

3. Replacing Your Cell Phone

Have team members find their ideal phone (not the one they have now) from a cellular phone service provider (Verizon, AT&T, etc.). Each team member should explain why the resulting phone is ideal for them. What is the cost to buy the phone? Can it be used with another network? How much does the cost decrease if you also sign up for the cellular phone plan? How long is the plan commitment? Write a brief paper that summarizes your findings and evaluates each plan.

4. Internet Faxing

Work with your team members to provide the answers to these questions in a one-page summary. Have any team members sent or received a facsimile transmission using a computer? If so, was the fax sent or received from another computer or from an actual fax machine? (Is it even possible to know?) Could you tell the difference? What was the name of the fax software application that was used? Describe the process for sending and receiving the fax. If you sent a fax, describe how you created the document. If you received a fax, did you print it? Why or why not? If not, then find the answers to the preceding questions by either talking with someone who has sent faxes or by doing research on the Web.

5. Cable, Internet, and Phone Convergence

Many cable TV and telephone companies now offer comprehensive communications packages that cover data, phone, and television service. Have each team member contact a different cable TV or phone company in your local geographic area (RCN, Comcast, AT&T, etc.). What hardware is required to participate in the service? Do you buy the hardware or rent it from the company? What are the monthly fees for the various services? Is there an installation charge? Are there cancellation fees if you discontinue your current services? Summarize your results for your instructor.

On the Web

1. 4G Technology

The next generation of mobile communications devices will be known as 4G (fourth generation). Type "4G" into your favorite search engine to learn about this new technology. Which organizations are developing the specifications for 4G? What advantages will 4G provide over 3G devices? What are the expected data transmission rates for 4G? When are 4G devices expected to be widely available? Explain why you would or would not consider upgrading to a 4G phone.

2. Adventure GPS

Go to the Adventure GPS site at **www.gps4fun.com** to learn more about GPS. Then use your favorite search engine to answer the following questions. Who owns the collection of satellites that make up the GPS system? How many GPS satellites are there, and how high do they orbit? How does a GPS receiver determine its position? How accurate is a GPS reading? List a civilian, a military, and a commercial use of the GPS. Do you know anyone who owns a GPS receiver? Have you tried one? Find a GPS device that you would like to own. How would you use it?

3. Using Bluetooth Technology

Go to the official Bluetooth site at **www.bluetooth.com** and research new products

that use Bluetooth. What types of products are profiled on the site? Which products might you be interested in buying? Where can you get the best price on devices that you are interested in purchasing?

4. Camera Sites

Visit EarthCam at **www.earthcam.com**. Follow at least three major category links (for example, computer cams, science cams, traffic cams) until you reach a camera site. Be sure that one of the sites you visit is an international site. Which sites did you successfully visit? How many dead links did you encounter? What was the subject matter? What was the quality of the images from the cameras? Were you satisfied or disappointed with how current the pictures were?

5. Online Images

Go to Google's image search site (**http://images. google.com**) and search for at least three different images that you might use in a project for school. How many results did you get for each image request? For each picture, describe copyright or permission issues that might relate to it. Research the term *fair use* and explain how it applies to using these images without permission (for students and faculty).

CONCEPT
Tip

Surfing Safely at Public Wireless Hot Spots

Finding wireless hotspots is easy because they seem to be everywhere today. McDonald's, Starbucks, and many other merchants often offer Internet connectivity to lure customers. Using sites like JiWire (**www.jiwire.com/ search-hotspot-locations.htm**) and HotSpot Haven (**www.hotspothaven.com**) simplifies the job of locating hotspots. But when you use public hotspots, especially free ones, you need to take some extra precautions to keep yourself and your data safe. Keep these issues in mind:

- **Wireless security is often not implemented on public hotspots.** Because the idea of a free public hotspot is to make connections simple, WEP and WPA encryption (two common wireless security protocols) are usually not implemented. This means that it is relatively easy for hackers, using easily obtainable software, to intercept and read information in data packets being transmitted on the network. Potential information that could be revealed includes the Web sites you are surfing, logon and

password information to nonsecure Web sites (ones that don't use SSL), and e-mail account information—including the content of sent and received messages.

- **Your computing device may be exposed.** Windows Vista is a very sharing-oriented operating system. Access to your shared files and directories may be open to others using the same wireless network.

- **You may be logged on to a malicious network.** Sometimes hackers set up their own hotspots in areas where legitimate hotspots are operating, hoping to fool people into logging on to their network instead. They usually set up a network with a name that sounds plausible. Say Joe's coffee shop has a free network named jcoffee. A hacker might set up a bogus network called Joe's Free WiFi to lure unsuspecting Web surfers. These bogus networks are known as "evil twins" and are used to gather sensitive information such as passwords and credit card data.

Sounds scary, doesn't it? Here are some steps you can take to protect yourself when surfing a public hotspot:

- Use firewall and antivirus software to make it much less likely for anyone to drop a malicious file on your machine.

- Always ask an employee for the name of the legitimate network, to prevent connecting to an evil twin.

- Don't engage in sensitive financial transactions (such as banking or online shopping) when connected to an unsecured hotspot.

- Select the appropriate Windows option (Figure 3.30) to limit sharing of resources and discoverability of your computer while connected to a public hotspot.

So enjoy surfing the Internet, but exercise some basic security practices to minimize the risk of an adverse experience.

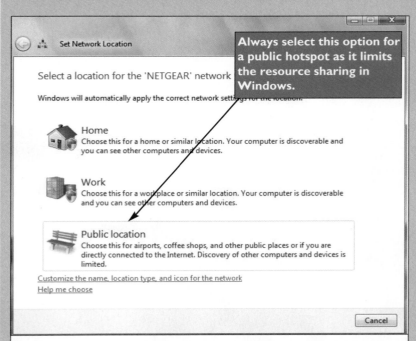

FIGURE 3.30 This screen is displayed when Windows Vista connects to a wireless network. Always choose "Public location" when connecting to an unsecured hotspot.

SPOTLIGHT HOME

When people hear the word *network*, they often think "Oh, that's too technical for me." Although networks require hardware and software technology, you should think of a network as simply a way to share computing power and resources. Setting up a home network may not be as difficult as you think and has many advantages. Today many homes have networks even if the users don't realize it. Because networking capabilities are built into all modern

NETWORKS

operating systems, it is easy to share data among computers and other household media devices. And, of course, you connect to the world's biggest network every time you access the Internet!

Approximately two-thirds of all U.S. households own a computer. And more than 25 percent of those households own two or more computers. Market research indicates that multicomputer households are becoming more common because people who already own PCs are still buying new ones. It is not unusual for each parent and one or more children in a household to have their own computer or mobile device, such as a smartphone (Figure 3A). Why is this important? People in multicomputer households want to share scanners, printers, data, music, movies, and games among multiple users using different computers. In addition, they want the household to share a single Internet connection. The computers in a single household may be of different makes and models (such as a mix of Macs and PCs). How can these computers share information and resources? The answer is a home network.

FIGURE 3A

It is not unusual for each parent and one or more children in a household to have their own computer.

By the end of 2012, it is estimated that there will be more than 160 million home networks in place worldwide, and as many as 70 percent of them will be using wireless technology. A **home network** enables users to quickly and conveniently share files and resources by using network connections between computers and peripheral devices. Home networks, a personal and specific use of network technology, can accommodate both wired and wireless communications. Wired home networks typically use Cat-5 or Cat-6 Ethernet cable, or a home's electrical wiring. Wireless home networks rely on radio signals.

This Spotlight examines the various home network options available to you and explains how to set up a home network.

WIRED HOME NETWORKS

There are two basic types of home network configurations—wired and wireless. Let's first look at wired networks.

HOME ETHERNET NETWORKS

Ethernet is a communications standard that specifies how physically connected computers in a network send data. Ethernet-linked computers send data in small chunks, called *packets*, over wires. You can think of a packet as a letter, addressed for delivery to a different city, that is moving through the mail system. In addition to the actual data, each packet carries your computer's home address and a destination address.

The Ethernet standard also details the types of wires that must be used and how fast data can travel across the network. The most popular type of Ethernet wiring is twisted-pair wire. Home networks use either Cat-5 or Cat-6 wire. These wires are then connected by RJ-45 connectors, which look like large telephone jacks. Cat-5 wire transfers data at speeds of up to 100 Mbps; Cat-6 transfers data at speeds of up to 1,000 Mbps (1 Gbps).

The simplest form of Ethernet network links different computers with a connecting switch or router. A **switch** is an external communications device with multiple connectors (ports) used for transmitting data between devices on a network. A **router** includes the capabilities of a switch, but it also enables communication between two or more networks. Devices connected by a switch can communicate only with other devices on the same network, whereas devices connected by a router can access other networks, including the Internet. See Figure 3B for an example of a simple Ethernet network. In this example, the computer can send a message to the notebook or the printer by way of the router. Routers and switches are available in many configurations. Most have 4 to 12 ports. The majority of home networks use a 100Base-TX router that is capable of a transfer rate of 100 Mbps (100 million bits per second). If you have the money, you can upgrade to a 1000Base-T router with a transfer rate of 1 Gbps. Also known as gigabit Ethernet, 1000Base-T is useful when transferring large amounts of data such as digital multimedia.

With an Ethernet network, each networked computer must have an **Ethernet network adapter**, also called a network interface card (NIC). A NIC is an internal communications device that uses electrical signals traveling across cables to enable computers to communicate with each other. Most newer computers already include a NIC, but a NIC can also be installed as an expansion card on an older system.

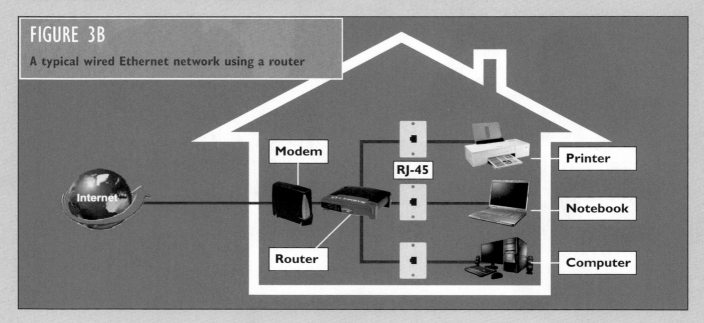

FIGURE 3B

A typical wired Ethernet network using a router

Internet — Modem — Router — RJ-45 — Printer — Notebook — Computer

HOME POWER-LINE NETWORKS

Home power-line networks use a home's existing electrical wiring. Power-line networks use the electrical system to connect computers through power outlets (Figure 3C). They are not as common as Ethernet networks.

One major advantage of home power-line networks is that most homes have at least one electrical outlet in every room. Inexpensive and easy installation is another advantage. In addition, a peripheral that doesn't have to be directly connected to a computer can be located anywhere. For example, whereas a monitor needs to be physically near a computer to be connected and used, a printer could be located in a completely different room or on another floor.

Power-line networks do have some drawbacks. If your home has anything other than 110-volt electrical wiring, you can't install a power-line network. In addition, home power usage and older wiring can affect performance. The devices that power-line networks use to access electrical outlets take up a lot of space inside or outside the walls. Connection speeds are comparable to Ethernet networks, with speeds ranging from 200 to 400 Mbps, but equipment compatibility has been a problem.

WIRELESS HOME NETWORKS

Although several wireless network standards are currently available, Wi-Fi is the wireless standard used for home networking. Wireless network standards have been developed to ensure that companies that build wireless connecting devices do so in compliance with strict definitions and exchange rules. Ultimately, three factors will determine which standard best suits your needs: (1) the cost of the hardware or software, (2) the speed at which data can travel over the network, and (3) the range within which you can reliably transmit between devices.

HOME WI-FI NETWORKS

Home Wi-Fi networks are wireless networks in which each computer on the network broadcasts its information to another using radio signals. Wi-Fi networks use communications devices called **network access points** (also referred to as **wireless access points**) to send and receive data between computers that have wireless adapters. In addition to enabling communication between networked devices and other networks, wireless routers also act as network access points. Network access points enable you to move a notebook with a wireless adapter from room to room or to place computers in different locations throughout a house (Figure 3D).

A peer-to-peer relationship exists among all of the computers in a wireless network (Figure 3E). This means that all the computers are equals, or *peers*, with no particular computer acting as the server. However, some home wireless networks can also be of the client/server type. In a client/server home network, each computer communicates with the server, and the server then communicates with other computers or peripherals. All peripherals in a wireless network must be within the router's range, which is usually 100 to 300 feet, depending on the building's construction and thickness of the walls, floors, and ceilings.

Wi-Fi networks use the 802.11 wireless transmission specifications. Although some older systems may

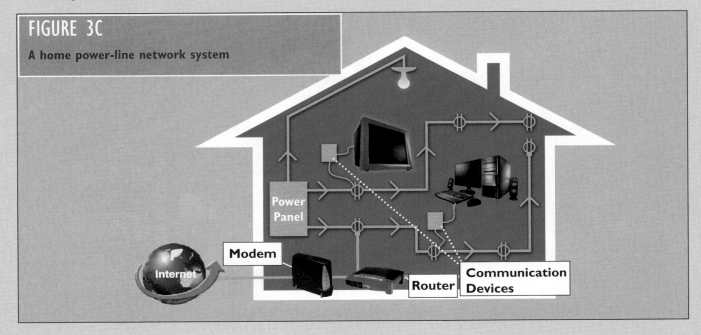

FIGURE 3C

A home power-line network system

Power Panel

Modem

Internet

Router

Communication Devices

FIGURE 3D

Apple's AirPort Extreme is a wireless router that is compatible with Macs and PCs.

still use the 802.11a or 802.11b standards, the most prevalent standards are 802.11g and 802.11n. The 802.11g specification operates in the 2.4 GHz radio band and is capable of data transfer rates of up to 54 Mbps. The newest standard, 802.11n, builds on the 802.11g specification. Although still in draft mode, 802.11n can operate in both the 2.4 GHz and 5 GHz radio band, and the average data transfer rate is about 300 Mbps. The finalized standard is expected to be ratified in 2009 and should be capable of data transfer rates of up to 600 Mbps.

Wireless networks are gaining in popularity because of their ease of setup and convenience. There are no unsightly wires to run through the home, and users are no longer limited to working in just one location. However, there are some disadvantages to wireless networks. Newer notebook computers are usually equipped for wireless access, but older notebooks may require the addition of a wireless adapter card, which plugs into a slot on the notebook. A USB adapter can be connected to the USB port of a notebook or desktop PC. Another alternative is to install a wireless adapter expansion card in a desktop PC (Figure 3F). Wireless

networks may be affected by interference from other devices such as microwave ovens and cordless phones. And some users may find that reception can be a problem if the radio waves are unable to pass through interior walls. Conversely, because radio waves are able to pass through walls, it is important to take appropriate measures to safeguard your privacy from passersby outside your home.

Now that we've examined the various types of home networks, let's look at the steps involved in setting one up.

SETTING UP A HOME NETWORK

Setting up any network, including one for your home, goes much more smoothly if you can follow a series of steps. The steps presented in this section correspond roughly to those followed by computer professionals who develop large-scale networks. Don't let that intimidate you though! You don't have to be a computer professional to set up a home network successfully.

PLANNING

As with any type of project, you must first come up with a plan based on your specific home networking needs. Ask yourself realistic questions: What are you trying to accomplish with your network? Is it for a small business or just for personal use? Is it only for your computer and peripherals or will it support multiple family members? Will the hardware be concentrated in one room (such as an office or den) or be spread throughout many rooms? Based on your answers to these questions and the type of home network you

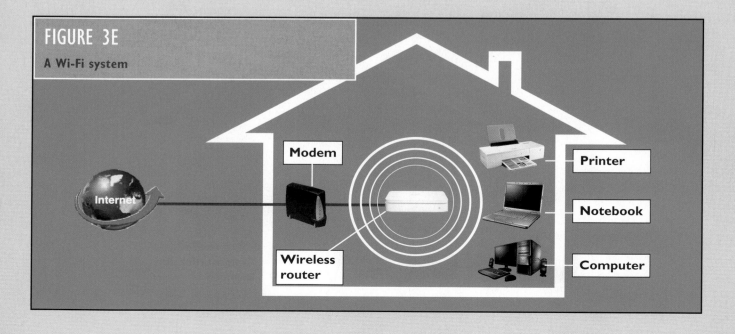

FIGURE 3E

A Wi-Fi system

Internet

Modem

Wireless router

Printer

Notebook

Computer

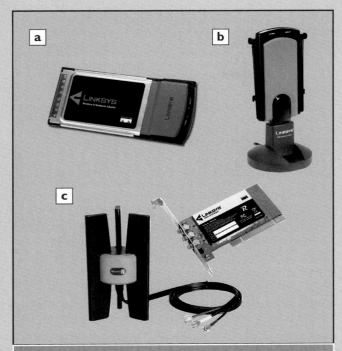

FIGURE 3F

A wireless adapter card (a) can be installed in a notebook's PC card slot. A USB adapter (b) can be used for either notebooks or desktop PCs and a PCI adapter (c) can be used to enable wireless access for a desktop PC.

choose, you should develop a needs, or requirements, checklist. You can determine your specific requirements by visiting your local home electronics store or by reading recommendations you find on the Web.

When planning a home network you will need to do two things. First, you will need to decide which network technology to use. You can choose from the technologies discussed earlier: wired Ethernet, home power line, or wireless 802.11g or 802.11n. Wired networks may perform faster and more reliably, but wireless networks allow for more flexibility, particularly when using one or more notebooks that you might want to move to different locations throughout the house.

Second, you will need to purchase the appropriate hardware. You may want to visit a home electronics store for advice, but many manufacturers such as Linksys and Netgear, as well as retailers such as Best Buy and Circuit City, provide tutorials on their Web sites to help you determine what type of network would best suit your needs and what equipment you will require. You may already have a NIC and a modem but will probably need a router (wired or wireless) and possibly a wireless adapter.

These sites also provide help and advice about setting up a home network:

- Microsoft, **www.microsoft.com/athome/moredone/ wirelesssetup.mspx**

- About.com, **http://compnetworking.about.com/od/ homenetworking/Home_Networking_Setting_Up_a_ Home_Network.htm**

- CNET Reviews, **http://reviews.cnet.com/ wireless-network-buying-guide**

You should also consider purchasing and installing personal firewall software to keep your home network safe from viruses and hackers (Figure 3G).

A wired Ethernet network is best installed during home construction if you want to conceal the wires. When installing this type of network in an existing home, it is possible to route the cables through the walls by use of either attic or basement access, but it will take a lot of work. If you decide to use Ethernet, you will need to determine if you are going to do the job yourself or whether you are going to hire someone to do it. In either case, the installer must carefully plan the routing of the cables through walls and across floors. You can find tutorials on the Web that will help you lay out the appropriate locations to drill into your walls. Search for "home network wiring" in your favorite search engine to find home networking sites.

Once you have purchased the appropriate hardware and software, you must configure the network so that all of the components function together. When your network is properly configured, you will find that a home network improves your home-computing experience.

CONFIGURATION

Depending on which type of network you decide to set up, your configuration options will vary. The main tasks involved with configuration are designating which PCs are to be part of the network; installing the proper hardware and software on those PCs; and designating how files, folders, peripherals (printers and scanners), and an Internet connection will be shared.

Every computer on the network needs a network interface that bundles data into chunks to travel across the network as well as a connection point, or port, for the special wiring that connects all the PCs. The port is either built into the computer or provided as an add-in NIC. The NIC sends data to the network and receives data sent from other computers on the network.

The next step is to configure the router. In a wired network, a wire runs from the back of each computer to the router, which serves as a communications point to connect the signal to the appropriate cable that goes to the intended destination. Printers, scanners, and other peripherals are usually plugged into one of the networked computers and then shared with the others. However, many new peripherals come with network interfaces that allow them to be plugged directly into the router. The router must be placed in a convenient

FIGURE 3G

Personal firewall software is a must for home networks.

location so that you can string individual cables from the router to each port in each room in which you want to use the network.

Windows Vista has a Network Setup Wizard. The Network Setup Wizard can be accessed in several ways. From the Control Panel, go to Network and Internet, then choose the Network and Sharing Center, and select Set up a connection or network (Figure 3H). You can also search for "network" from the Start menu to access the Network and Sharing Center. Setup information may also be available from the store where you purchased your networking supplies or from Web searches on home networks.

MAINTENANCE AND SUPPORT

Computer and network problems can be extremely frustrating. You should set up a regular maintenance schedule for both your computer and your network. The good news is that there isn't much to maintain with today's home networking solutions. You may need to blow off dust and lint that accumulates on your router, wireless adapter, or modem. You may also need to use your operating system's network utilities to refresh your network's settings.

When something goes wrong, you should try to think of what might have caused the problem. Sometimes the solution is as simple as restarting your computer and/or unplugging the power source from your router and other peripherals and then plugging them back in. You may also need to restart each computer that is connected to your system. If these actions do not solve the problem, you have several other options. If the problem produces an error message, write down the subject of the error message and then type it into the search box on your favorite

search engine site. You can also search manufacturers' Web sites. For instance, if you have a Linksys router and Netgear network cards, you could go to **www.linksys.com** and **www.netgear.com** to see if downloads are available to update your network devices.

THE FUTURE OF HOME NETWORKING

Convergence will be the future of home networking systems. You may be skeptical, but someday you may be able to use home networks to control household appliances, prepare food, or maintain a home's appearance. Networked home security systems already help protect us from intrusion or damage from natural events.

In the near future, new houses will have a central control unit that is capable of managing home network events as well as communication, entertainment, temperature regulation, lighting, and household appliances. It is very possible that someday your refrigerator may send you an e-mail informing you of the state of its cooling coils, including a request that you vacuum out the lint that is blocking good air circulation.

In the future, your home networking system will almost certainly be wireless. It will have capabilities that will help it adapt to new technologies as they develop. Wireless technology will be able to provide the flexibility that is required to seamlessly integrate convenience, simplicity, and, hopefully, long-term cost savings.

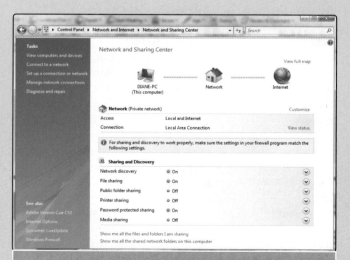

FIGURE 3H

The Network and Sharing Center in Windows Vista helps you set up and manage your network.

SPOTLIGHT EXERCISES

1 The number of households that have more than one computer is increasing. Multicomputer families want to share resources among their respective computers. One of the resources that many want to share is the Internet connection. Although newer versions of Microsoft Windows have software that enables two computers to share an Internet connection, consumers with high-speed connections such as cable or DSL can use a router to share Internet access. Go to a local computer store and investigate cable and DSL routers. How many ports are available? How much do these devices cost? What physical medium is used to connect the computers to the router? Can a router be used to share a printer? What additional hardware is needed to connect computers to the router? If you had a high-speed connection and multiple computers, would you purchase a router? Why or why not?

2 Many homes with cable television service have more than one television set. Connecting multiple televisions to the cable service requires the use of "splitters" to divide the incoming signal and send it to each television set. Some new houses are constructed with coaxial cable running to multiple rooms, but how are multiple television sets connected in older homes? Unfortunately, this usually requires drilling holes in walls, floors, or ceilings or even running cables on the exterior of the residence. Some homeowners and landlords do not want to do this. The same connection problem exists with home computer networks. Fortunately, a wireless access point offers an alternative to running network cables. Go to a local computer store and investigate wireless networking. What are the prices for these wireless access points? How does the wireless connection speed compare with a wired one? What additional hardware is needed to network computers to the wireless access point? If you had a home network, would you consider this networking alternative? Why or why not?

3 Assume that you have both a desktop and a notebook computer and you want them to share a network. To do this, each computer needs a network interface card. Search the Web to find the best price for a NIC for a notebook computer and for a desktop computer. How much does each NIC cost? Which type of card is more expensive? Why do you think one card is more expensive than the other? Some desktop computers now include built-in network connectivity. Locate and name two specific desktop and notebook models that have internal networking capability. If you currently have a desktop or notebook computer, does your computer have internal networking capability? How well does it work for you?

4 Some people need to connect a mobile device such as a smartphone to a desktop or notebook computer. What are the benefits of doing this? Search the Web to determine the most popular methods for networking a smartphone to a PC. Which of these methods require additional PC hardware? Is the use of the word *networking* correct in this instance? Why or why not?

5 Users can protect their personal computers by using firewalls. A firewall can be implemented through software, hardware, or a combination of both. Two of the leading software applications, McAfee Total Protection (**www.mcafee.com**) and Norton Internet Security (**www.symantec.com**), are designed for personal computers running various operating systems. According to these and other security utility sites, why should you purchase firewall software? What are the various pricing structures available for each of these products? After reading descriptions of these products on McAfee's and Norton's Web sites, search the Web to find independent evaluations of each product. Identify the URLs of these additional review sites. Explain which firewall application you would purchase and why.

What You'll Learn . . .

- List the two major components of system software.

- Explain why a computer needs an operating system.

- List the five basic functions of an operating system.

- Explain what happens when you turn on a computer.

- List the three major types of user interfaces.

- Discuss the strengths and weaknesses of the most popular operating systems.

- List the seven system utilities that are considered to be essential.

- Discuss data backup procedures.

- Understand troubleshooting techniques and determine probable solutions to any operating system problems you may encounter.

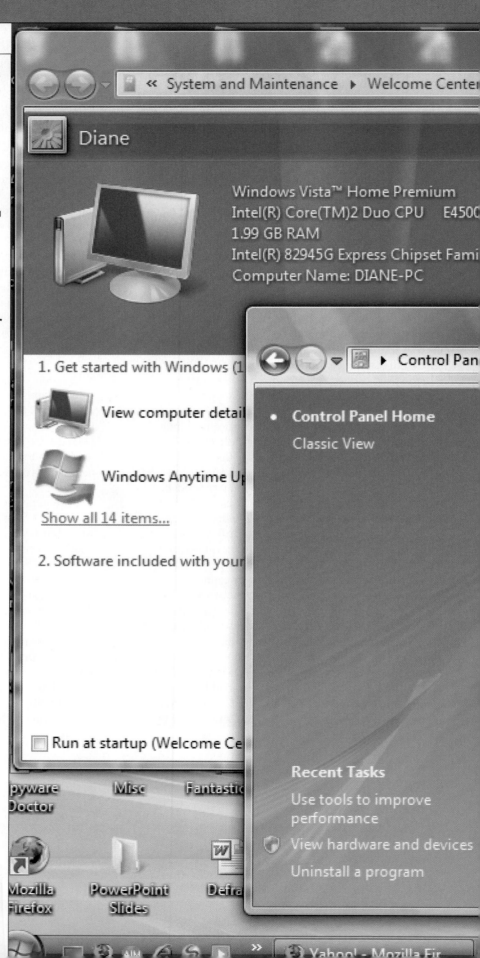

System Software

CHAPTER OUTLINE

The Operating System 144
    Starting the Computer 145
    Managing Applications 147
    Managing Memory 148
    Handling Input and Output 150
    Providing the User Interface 151

Exploring Popular Operating Systems 153
    Microsoft Windows 153
    Mac OS 155
    UNIX 155
    Linux 156
    MS-DOS 157
    PC versus Mac versus Linux 157

System Utilities: Housekeeping Tools 159
    Backup Software 159
    Antivirus Software 161
    Searching for and Managing Files 162
    Scanning and Defragmenting Disks 163
    File Compression Utilities 164
    System Update 165
    Troubleshooting 165

System and Maintenance
Get started with Windows
Back up your computer

Security
Check for updates
Check this computer's security status
Allow a program through Windows Firewall

Network and Internet
View network status and tasks
Set up file sharing

Hardware and Sound
Play CDs or other media automatically
Printer
Mouse

Programs

Without software—the set of instructions that tells the computer what to do—a computer is just an expensive collection of wires and components. You're probably familiar with one type of software: application software. Application software helps you accomplish a task, such as writing a college essay or creating a presentation. The other major type of software is system software. **System software** includes all the programs needed for a computer and its peripheral devices to function smoothly. Although some system software works behind the scenes, some requires your guidance and control.

System software has two major components: (1) the operating system and (2) system utilities that provide various maintenance functions. Learning how to use an operating system and system utilities is the first step you should take toward mastering any computer system. Mastering a computer system is not unlike understanding the fundamentals of any system. The more you know about managing the water, filters, plants, and water temperature in your aquarium, the healthier and happier your fish will be. It's the same with computers; the more you know about and understand the operating system, the better your computer will function. In this chapter, you'll learn what operating systems do, look at the most popular operating systems, and learn which utilities you should use to ensure that your computing experience is safe and enjoyable.

The Operating System

The **operating system** (**OS**) is a set of programs designed to manage the resources of a computer. Its most important role lies in coordinating the various functions of the computer's hardware. The OS also coordinates interaction between application software and the computer hardware. An operating system performs five basic functions: it starts the computer, manages applications, manages memory, handles messages from input and output devices, and provides the user interface—a means of communicating with the user (Figure 4.1).

FIGURE 4.1

An operating system works at the intersection of application software, the user, and the computer's hardware. It starts the computer, manages applications and memory, handles messages from input and output devices, and provides a means of communicating with the user.

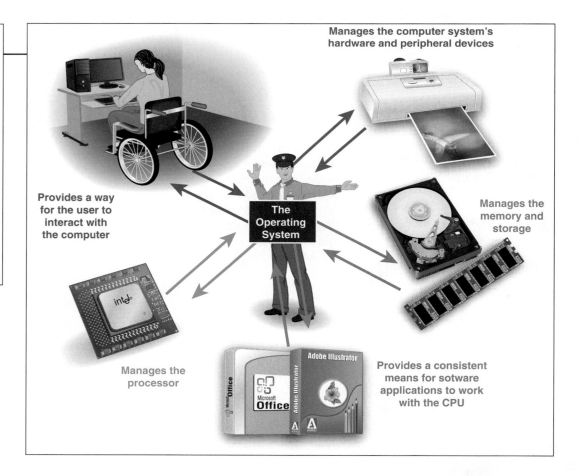

Manages the computer system's hardware and peripheral devices

Provides a way for the user to interact with the computer

The Operating System

Manages the memory and storage

Manages the processor

Provides a consistent means for sotware applications to work with the CPU

The operating system is most often found on a hard disk, although on some small handheld computers it is on a memory chip.

Imagine the traffic at a downtown New York City intersection at rush hour and you'll have a good idea of what it's like inside a computer. Bits of information are whizzing around at incredible speeds, sent this way and that by the operating system, the electronic equivalent of a harried traffic officer. Impatient peripherals and programs are honking electronic "horns," trying to get the officer's attention. As if the scene weren't chaotic enough, the "mayor" (the user) wants to come through right now. Just like a traffic officer, the computer's operating system, standing at the intersection of the computer's hardware, application programs, and user, keeps traffic running smoothly.

Let's examine the five functions of an operating system more closely.

STARTING THE COMPUTER

Starting the computer is the first operating system function. When you start a computer, it loads the operating system into the computer's RAM. (To **load** means to transfer something from a storage device, such as the hard disk, to memory.) RAM is a form of volatile memory. **Volatile** memory is storage that is very fast but that is erased when the power goes off. The process of loading the operating system to memory is called **booting**. This term has been used in computing circles since the very early days. It comes from an old saying that people can pull themselves up by their boot straps, or in other words, get started on their own. With a **cold boot**, you start a computer that is not already on. With a **warm boot**, you restart a computer that is already on. Warm boots are often necessary after installing new software or after an application crashes or stops working. In Windows Vista, you can initiate a warm boot by simultaneously pressing the Ctrl+Alt+Del keys and then choosing the Restart option from the Shut Down menu. (On the Mac, the system will restart when you press the Control, Command, and Eject keys at the same time.)

With both types of booting, the computer copies the kernel along with other essential portions of the operating system from the hard disk into the computer's memory, where it remains while your computer is powered on and functioning. The **kernel** is the central part of the operating system that starts applications, manages devices and memory, and performs other essential functions. The kernel resides in memory at all times, so it must be kept as small as possible. Less frequently used portions of the operating system are stored on the hard disk and retrieved as needed. Such portions are called *nonresident* because they do not reside in memory.

A cold or warm boot is a step-by-step process (Figure 4.2). The following sections discuss the steps followed by the computer during the boot-up process.

Step 1: The BIOS (Basic Input/ Output System) and Setup Program

When you first turn on or reset a PC, electricity flows from the power supply through the CPU, which resets itself and searches for the BIOS. The **BIOS** (**basic input/output system**) is the part of the system software that equips the computer with the instructions needed to accept

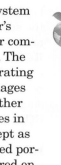

Green Tech Tip

Leaving a computer running when it's not in use is wasteful. By default, a computer running Windows Vista will go into sleep mode after a period of inactivity, saving its owner $70 or more in annual energy costs.

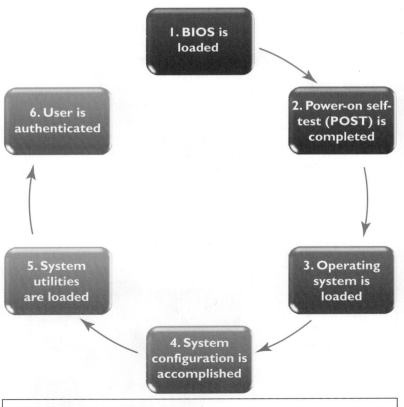

FIGURE 4.2 The six steps involved in starting the computer

keyboard input and display information on the screen. The BIOS is encoded, or permanently written, in the computer's ROM. **ROM**, or **read-only memory**, is **nonvolatile** memory—memory that is permanent and unchanging. Programs, such as the BIOS, that are encoded in ROM are meant to be reliably used over and over again. After the BIOS is located, you may briefly see the BIOS screen, a text-only screen that provides information about the BIOS (Figure 4.3).

While the BIOS information is visible, you can access the computer's setup program by pressing a special key, such as Del or F8. (You'll see an on-screen message indicating which key to press to access the setup program.) The **setup program** includes settings that control the computer's hardware. You should *not* alter or change *any* of these settings unless you are instructed to do so by technical support personnel. We'll look more closely at the setup program in "Step 3: Loading the Operating System."

Step 2: The Power-On Self-Test

After the BIOS instructions are loaded into memory, a series of tests are conducted to make sure that the computer and associated peripherals are operating correctly. Collectively, these tests are known as the **power-on self-test** (**POST**). Among the components tested are the computer's main memory (RAM), the keyboard and mouse, disk drives, and the hard disk. If any of the power-on self-tests fail, you'll hear a beep, see an on-screen error message, and the computer will stop. You often can correct such problems by making sure that components, such as keyboards, are plugged in securely.

However, some failures are so serious that the computer cannot display an error

message; instead, it sounds a certain number of beeps. If this happens, it's time to call for technical support. To help the technician repair the computer, write down any error messages you see and try to remember how many beeps you heard.

Step 3: Loading the Operating System

Once the power-on self-test is successfully completed, the BIOS initiates a search for the operating system. Options (or settings) in the setup program determine where the BIOS looks for the operating system. If multiple possible locations exist (such as an optical drive, a floppy drive, a hard disk), the settings also specify the search order. If no OS is found, the BIOS moves on to the next location. These options are set by default, but can be modified by the user.

On most PCs, the BIOS first looks for the operating system on the computer's hard disk. When the BIOS finds the operating system, it loads the operating system's kernel into memory. At that point, the operating system takes control of the computer and begins loading system configuration information.

Step 4: System Configuration

In Microsoft Windows, configuration information about installed peripherals and software is stored in a database called the **registry**. The registry also contains information about your system configuration choices, such as background graphics and mouse settings.

Once the operating system's kernel has been loaded, it checks the system's configuration to determine which drivers and other utility programs are needed. A **driver** is a utility program that makes a peripheral device function correctly. If a peripheral device that is already installed on the system requires a driver to operate, that peripheral's driver will be installed and loaded automatically. If the driver is missing, you may be prompted to insert a CD or download the needed driver.

Windows operating systems are equipped with **Plug-and-Play** (**PnP**) capabilities, which automatically detect new PnP-compatible peripherals that you might have installed while the power was switched off, load the necessary drivers, and check for conflicts with other devices. Peripheral devices equipped with PnP features identify themselves to the operating system.

FIGURE 4.3
The BIOS screen provides information about your computer's default input and output settings.

Step 5: Loading System Utilities

After the operating system has detected and configured all of the system's hardware, it loads system utilities such as speaker volume control, antivirus software, and power management options. In Microsoft Windows, you can view available custom configuration choices by right-clicking one of the small icons in the System Tray, which is located on the right side of the Windows taskbar. You can access additional system-configuration choices in the Control Panel (Figure 4.4).

Step 6: Authenticating Users

When the operating system finishes loading, you may see a dialog box asking you to type a user name and password. Through this process called **authentication** (or **login**), you verify that you are indeed the person who is authorized to use the computer.

Consumer-oriented operating systems such as Microsoft Windows and Mac OS do not demand that you supply a user name and password to use the computer. However, you can set up profiles on these systems. Associated with a user name and, optionally, a password, a **profile** is a record of a spe-

cific user's preferences for the desktop theme, icons, and menu styles. If you set up a profile for yourself, your preferences will appear on the screen after you log on. You can also enable other users to create and log on to their profiles. They'll be able to see their preferences without disturbing yours.

On multiuser computer systems such as in a university lab or a corporate office environment, you must have an account to access a computer. Your **account** consists of your user name, your password, and your storage space, which is called a *home directory*. The account is usually created by a network system administrator, who is a person responsible for managing the computer network.

Now that the operating system is loaded and running, let's look at another important task that the operating system handles: managing applications.

MANAGING APPLICATIONS

The operating system function that most dramatically affects an operating system's

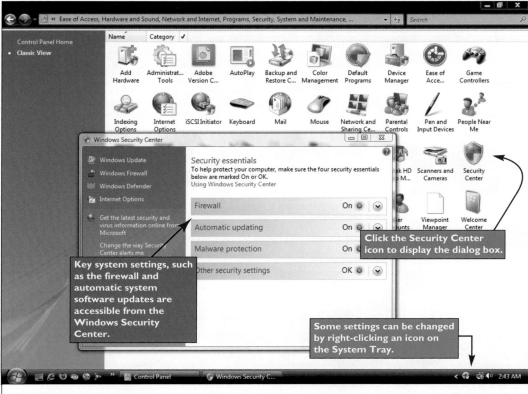

FIGURE 4.4 Many options for managing and customizing your computer system can be found on the Control Panel (accessed from the Start menu) or on the System Tray (on the Windows taskbar).

overall quality is running and **managing applications**. When you start an application, the CPU loads the application from storage into RAM. In the early days of personal computing, **single-tasking operating systems** could run only one application at a time, which was often inconvenient. To switch between applications, you had to quit one application before you could start the second.

Today, multitasking operating systems are the norm. **Multitasking operating systems** enable a user to work with two or more applications at the same time. With multitasking operating systems, the computer doesn't actually run two applications at once; rather, it switches between them as needed. For example, a user might be running two applications, such as Word and Excel, simultaneously. From the user's perspective, one application (the **foreground application**) is active, whereas the other (the **background application**) is inactive, as indicated by how the application appears on the screen (Figure 4.5).

A clear measure of the stability of an operating system is the technique it uses to handle multitasking. If one of the running applications invades another's memory space, one or both of the applications will become unstable or, at the extreme, crash.

Most current operating systems use a more recent, improved type of multitasking called **preemptive multitasking**, which ensures that all applications have fair access to the CPU and prevents one program from monopolizing it at the expense of the others. Even if one program becomes unstable or stops working, the operating system and other applications will continue to run. Although you may lose unsaved work in the application that has crashed, chances are good that everything else will be fine.

Now that you understand how the operating system manages applications, let's take a look at how it manages its primary storage function: memory.

MANAGING MEMORY

If the operating system had to constantly access program instructions from their storage location on your computer's hard

FIGURE 4.5 Multitasking operating systems enable a user to work with two or more applications at once. Here Word is in the foreground and is the active window. Excel is in the background and is inactive. To switch between applications, just click the desired application or its corresponding button on the taskbar.

disk, programs would run very slowly. A buffer is needed to make the processing of instructions more fluid. Computers use a temporary storage medium, called memory, to function as this buffer. The computer's operating systems is responsible for managing memory. The operating system gives each running program its own portion of memory and attempts to keep the programs from interfering with each other's use of memory (Figure 4.6).

Today's operating systems can make the computer's RAM seem larger than it really is. This trick is accomplished by means of **virtual memory**, a method of using the computer's hard disk as an extension of RAM. In virtual memory, program instructions and data are divided into units of fixed size called **pages**. If memory is full, the operating system starts storing copies of pages in a hard disk file called the **swap file**. This file is not an application but a temporary storage space for bits and bytes that the operating system will access as you do your work. When the pages are needed, they are copied back into RAM (Figure 4.7). The transferring of files from the hard disk to RAM and back is called **paging**.

Although virtual memory enables users to work with more memory than the

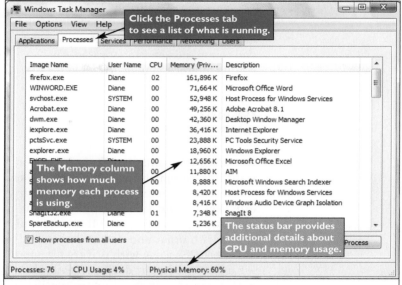

FIGURE 4.6 Use the Windows Task Manager (press Ctrl+Alt+Del and select Start Task Manager) to get information about programs that are currently running.

amount installed on the computer, paging slows the computer. Disks are much slower than RAM. For this reason, adding more RAM to your computer is often the best way to improve its performance. With sufficient RAM, the operating system makes minimal use of virtual memory.

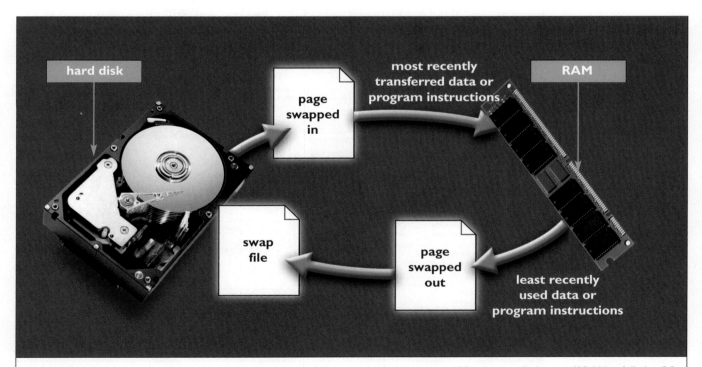

FIGURE 4.7 In virtual memory, program instructions and data are divided into units of fixed size called pages. If RAM is full, the OS starts storing copies of pages in a hard disk file called the swap file. When the pages are needed, they're copied back into RAM.

Once the computer's operating system is running and managing applications and memory, it needs to be able to accept data and commands and to represent the results of processing operations.

HANDLING INPUT AND OUTPUT

How does your computer "know" that you want it to do something? How does it show you the results of its work? Another operating system function is handling input and output, as well as enabling communication with input and output devices.

Most OSs come with drivers for popular input and output devices. Device drivers are programs that contain specific information about a particular brand and model of input or output device. They enable communication between the operating system and the input and output components of a computer system. Printers, scanners, monitors, speakers, and the mouse all have drivers (Figure 4.8). Hardware manufacturers usually update their drivers for new operating systems. You can obtain updated drivers from the manufacturer if they are not already included with the operating system. For many devices, Windows Vista can automatically detect new hardware and install the required driver in less than one minute. Microsoft's Windows Update also handles the retrieval and installation of new drivers as they are needed. But new drivers aren't always needed. If your device is working properly, you may not need to upgrade the driver.

Input and output devices generate **interrupts**, signals that inform the operating system that something has happened (for example, the user has pressed a key, the mouse has moved to a new position, or a document has finished printing). The operating system provides **interrupt handlers**, which are miniprograms that immediately kick in when an interrupt occurs.

Communication between input or output devices and the computer's CPU is handled by **interrupt request** (**IRQ**) lines. Most PCs have 16 IRQs, numbered 0 through 15. If two devices are configured to use the same IRQ but aren't designed to share an IRQ line, the result is a serious system failure called an **IRQ conflict**. In most cases, an IRQ conflict makes the system so unstable that it cannot function. To remedy an IRQ conflict, you may need to shut down the computer and remove peripheral devices, one by one, until you determine which one is causing the conflict. Happily, PnP-compatible OSs and peripherals have made IRQ conflicts much less common. Still, this phenomenon is worth mentioning because it may help you solve a problem with your computer.

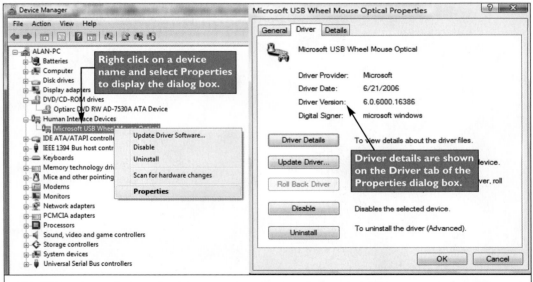

FIGURE 4.8 The Device Manager is accessible from the Control Panel System icon and provides information on the devices connected to your computer and the drivers they are using.

Now we will explore the different interfaces that are used to provide interaction with you, the user.

PROVIDING THE USER INTERFACE

From the user's perspective, the most important function of an operating system is providing the user interface. The part of the operating system that you see and interact with and by which users and programs communicate with each other is called the **user interface**.

User Interface Functions
User interfaces typically enable you to do the following:

- Start (launch) application programs.

- Manage storage devices, such as hard disks, optical drives, and USB drives, and organize files. You can format new disks, copy files from one storage device to another, rename files, and delete files.

- Shut down the computer safely by following an orderly shutdown procedure.

Types of User Interfaces
The three types of user interfaces are graphical, menu driven, and command-line (Figure 4.9).

By far the most popular user interface, a **graphical user interface** (**GUI**; pronounced "goo-ee") takes advantage of the computer's graphics capabilities to make the operating system and programs easier to use. On most of today's computers, GUIs are used to create the **desktop** that appears after the operating system finishes loading into memory. If someone were to ask you about your desktop, you can say that you are running Linux, or Mac OS, or Windows. On the desktop, you can initiate many actions by clicking small images called **icons** that represent computer resources (such as programs, data files, and network connections). Programs run within resizable on-screen windows, making it easy to switch from one program to another (Figure 4.10). Within programs, you can give commands by choosing items from pull-down menus, some of which display dialog boxes. In a **dialog box**, you can supply additional information that the program needs (Figure 4.11).

Menu-driven user interfaces enable you to avoid memorizing keywords (such as *copy* and *paste*) and syntax (a set

FIGURE 4.9 Examples of (**a**) graphical, (**b**) menu-driven, and (**c**) command-line user interfaces

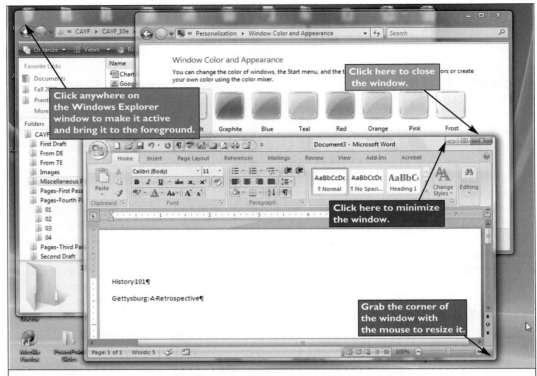

FIGURE 4.10 Programs run within resizable on-screen windows, making it easy to switch from one program to another.

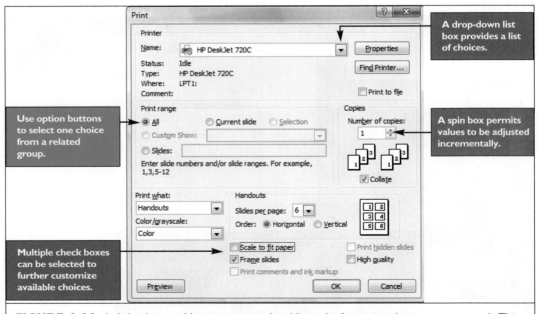

FIGURE 4.11 A dialog box enables you to provide additional information that a program needs. This is the print dialog box.

of rules for entering commands). On-screen, text-based menus show all the options available at a given point. With most systems, you select an option with the arrow keys and then press Enter. Some systems enable you to click the desired option with the mouse or to choose a letter with the keyboard.

Command-line user interfaces require you to type commands using keywords that tell the operating system what to do (such as *format* or *copy*) one line at a time. You must observe complicated rules of syntax that specify exactly what you can type in a given place. For example, the following command copies a file from the hard disk drive C to a removable USB drive in drive F:

```
copy C:\myfile.txt F:\myfile.txt
```

Command-line user interfaces aren't popular with most users because they require memorization, and it's easy to make a typing mistake. Although the commands are usually very simple, such as *copy* and *paste*, others are more cryptic. However, some experienced users actually prefer command-line interfaces because they can operate the computer quickly after memorizing the keywords and syntax.

Now that you've seen how the operating system makes itself available to you, let's explore the most popular operating systems in depth.

Exploring Popular Operating Systems

We will begin with Microsoft Windows and then look at the Mac operating system, UNIX, Linux, and MS-DOS. Although your choice of operating system might be limited by the computer you have, you should know how the various systems have evolved over time and what their strengths and weaknesses are.

MICROSOFT WINDOWS

Microsoft Windows is by far the most popular operating system. Over the years, it has gone through many iterations (Figure 4.12), and it is now considered *the*

FIGURE 4.12 Windows Time Line

Year Released	Version
2007	Windows Vista
2001	Windows XP
2000	Windows 2000/ME
1998	Windows 98
1995	Windows 95
1993	Windows NT
1992	Windows 3.1
1990	Windows 3.0
1987	Windows 2.0
1985	Windows 1.0

operating system of PCs worldwide. When you purchase a computer, it usually comes with an operating system already installed. Microsoft has agreements with the major computer manufacturers to provide Windows on almost all of the personal computers that are made today. Some manufacturers offer a choice of operating systems, but Windows is expected to remain the standard for years to come.

Let's start by looking at the most recent version, Windows Vista, and then we'll look at the other operating systems you might encounter on today's personal and corporate computers.

Microsoft Windows Vista
Released to the general public in January 2007, **Microsoft Windows Vista** (Figure 4.13) replaced the popular Windows XP operating system and is designed for home and professional use. Vista is available in five different versions—Basic, Home Premium, Business, Ultimate, and Enterprise. Vista features a slick new interface called Windows Aero (unavailable in the Basic version) that features translucent windows, three-dimensional animation, and live taskbar thumbnails—just hover the cursor over a button on the taskbar to get a preview

Destinations

Explore the features of Microsoft's latest Windows offerings at the Windows home page at **www. microsoft.com/ windows/default. aspx**.

FIGURE 4.13
Windows Vista focuses on ease of use and multimedia.

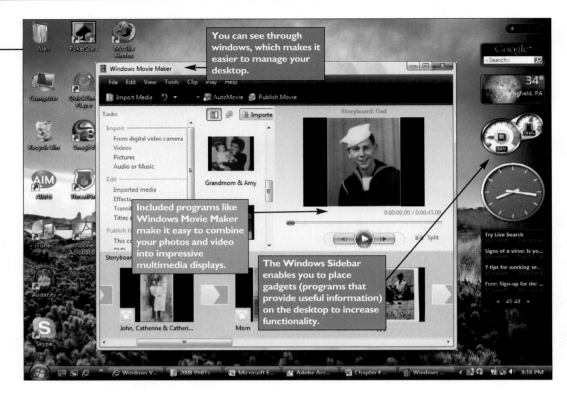

You can see through windows, which makes it easier to manage your desktop.

Included programs like Windows Movie Maker make it easy to combine your photos and video into impressive multimedia displays.

The Windows Sidebar enables you to place gadgets (programs that provide useful information) on the desktop to increase functionality.

of its contents. Vista also addresses the growing popularity of mobile computing. Previously, tablet PCs required the Windows XP Tablet PC Edition operating system, but Vista supports tablet PCs and other mobile devices through the Windows Mobility Center. Responding to concerns about security, the Windows Security Center integrates programs and tools like Windows Defender, Windows Firewall, and Windows Updates for ease of access. It also includes user-installed security programs. Implementing the User Account Control feature can prevent unauthorized users from installing unwanted or malicious programs. However, Windows Vista isn't all work. Windows Media Center, available in the Home Premium and Ultimate versions, allows you to enjoy your audio and video files, including recorded TV shows and DVDs, whenever you want. Watch on your PC, TV, or Xbox, or sync your files to a portable media device. Improved search features and networking tools, integrated speech recognition capabilities, and new multimedia tools help to differentiate this version of the operating system from previous ones.

Microsoft Windows Server 2008

Microsoft Windows Server 2008 is a sophisticated operating system specifically designed to support client/server computing systems in a corporate environment. Servers are special computers used to manage various resources on a network, including printers and other devices, file storage, and Web sites. Windows Server 2008 shares many similarities in architecture and functionality with Windows Vista because the underlying code is closely related. Benefits include the following:

- **Security**. New technologies help prevent unauthorized access to corporate networks, data, and user accounts.

- **Web Server**. Enhanced capabilities are available for developing and hosting Web applications and services.

- **Administration**. All configuration and maintenance is done through the command-line interface or through remote administration.

- **Virtualization**. Multiple servers can be consolidated as separate virtual machines on a single physical server, and multiple operating systems can run in parallel.

Microsoft Windows Mobile

Designed for smartphones and PDAs, **Microsoft Windows Mobile** provides a user interface for simplified versions of

Windows programs, such as Microsoft's own Office applications. Users can create documents on the go and then transfer them to a desktop computer for further processing and printing. Personal information management tools, such as a calendar and address book, along with an e-mail client and a Web browser, are also included (Figure 4.14). Windows Mobile supports handwriting recognition and voice recording. Users can quickly synchronize their mobile devices with corresponding programs on their desktop computers.

MAC OS

The **Mac OS** introduced the GUI to the world. The original Macintosh operating system was released in 1984. By the late 1980s, the Mac's operating system was the most technologically advanced in personal computing. Although Apple eventually lost market share to Microsoft, it has a diehard fan base. Many prefer the Mac OS for its security, stability, and ease of use (Figure 4.15). The current version, Mac OS X, has been gaining ground recently, especially with folks who are dissatisfied with their Windows experience. Macs held an 8 percent market share at the beginning of 2008, reflecting a 28 percent growth in one year.

FIGURE 4.14
Although Windows Mobile can look slightly different depending upon the phone vendor, it still brings Windows functionality to mobile devices.

UNIX

Developed at AT&T's Bell Laboratories, UNIX is a pioneering operating system that continues to define what an operating system should do and how it should work. **UNIX** (pronounced "you-nix") was the first operating system with preemptive

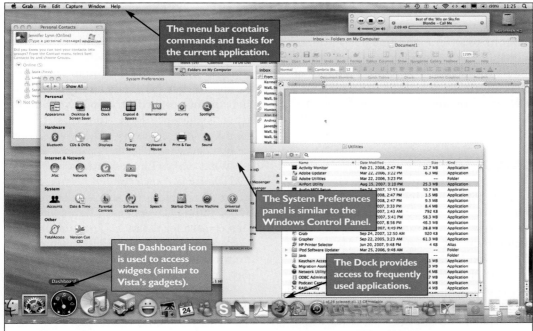

The menu bar contains commands and tasks for the current application.

The System Preferences panel is similar to the Windows Control Panel.

The Dashboard icon is used to access widgets (similar to Vista's gadgets).

The Dock provides access to frequently used applications.

FIGURE 4.15 The Mac OS X interface is similar to the one used by Microsoft Windows.

FIGURE 4.16
A number of GUI interfaces have been developed for UNIX in the past few years, improving the usability of this operating system.

multitasking. It was designed to work efficiently in a secure computer network.

If UNIX is so great, why didn't it take over the computer world? One reason is the lack of compatibility among the many different versions of UNIX. Another reason is that it's difficult to use. UNIX, like DOS, defaults to a command-line user interface, which is challenging for new computer users. In the past few years, a number of GUI interfaces have been developed for UNIX, improving its usability (Figure 4.16). In fact, the Mac OS X is based on UNIX!

LINUX

In 1991 Finnish university student Linus Torvalds introduced **Linux**, his new freeware operating system for personal computers (Figure 4.17). He hoped Linux would offer users a free alternative to UNIX. Linux has since been further developed by thousands of the world's best programmers, who have willingly donated their time to make sure that Linux is a very good version of UNIX. The community approach to Linux has made it a marvel of

the computer world and has made Torvalds a folk legend.

Linux is **open source software**, meaning that its source code (the code of the program itself) is available for all to see and use. Unlike most commercial software, which hides the program's code and prohibits users from analyzing it to see how the program was written, open source software invites users to scrutinize the source code for errors and to share their discoveries with the software's publisher. Experience shows that this approach is often a very effective measure against software defects.

What makes Linux so attractive? Two things: it's powerful and it's free. Linux brings all the maturity and sophistication of UNIX to the PC. Versions of Linux have also been created for the Mac. Linux includes all the respected features of UNIX, including multitasking, virtual memory, Internet support, and a graphical user interface.

Although Linux is powerful and free, many corporate chief information officers shy away from adopting Linux precisely because it isn't a commercial product with a stable company behind it.

Destinations

For the latest in Linux news and developments, visit Linux Today at **www.linuxtoday.com**. Linux beginners can get assistance at **www.justlinux.com** and at **www.linux.org**.

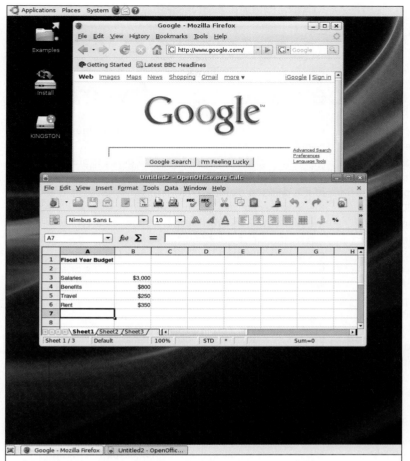

FIGURE 4.17 Ubuntu, a popular version of Linux, features a very Windows-like graphical user interface and includes programs such as OpenOffice and the Firefox Web browser.

When someone needs technical support, they have to find a Web site such as **www. redhat.com** or someone who knows more about Linux than they do—this is not the same as calling technical support when your Mac OS X is on the fritz. Also, Linux can't run the popular Microsoft Office applications, which most corporate users prefer. But Linux is gaining acceptance, especially for use with Web servers.

The beauty of Linux, and its development model, is that it doesn't run on any particular type of computer: It runs on them all. Linux has been translated to run on systems as small as iPods and as large as homegrown supercomputers.

MS-DOS

MS-DOS (or **DOS**, which is short for *disk operating system*) is an operating system for IBM-compatible PCs that uses a command-line user interface. Developed by Bill Gates and Paul Allen's fledgling Microsoft Corporation for the original IBM PC in 1981, MS-DOS was marketed by IBM in a virtually identical version, called PC-DOS. The command-line interface is difficult to learn, and the syntax and commands are not easy for the casual user to remember. It is unlikely that you will ever encounter a command-line interface on a modern personal computer.

PC VERSUS MAC VERSUS LINUX

Traditionally, computer users have had two major platforms to choose from. A **platform** is determined by the combination of microprocessor chip and operating system used by a distinct type of computer, such as a Mac or a PC. Previously, Macs used a Motorola or IBM chip and the Mac OS, while PCs have used an Intel or AMD chip and the Windows OS. Macs have since switched to Intel chips, which has blurred the platform lines a bit, because they can now run the Windows OS too. Depending on which operating system is loaded on a computer, it is simply referred to as a Mac or a PC. As the Linux OS becomes more popular, some people may want to consider this third alternative.

The debate over which platform is best has raged for years, and if market power is anything, PCs are winning by a landslide. But Apple hangs in there with its slew of adherents who choose to "think different." What's the difference between the platforms? Although you'd never know from listening to people who love or hate Macs, there's really not much difference, at least not in terms of power. Still, the debate goes on.

On the one side, Mac lovers say their machines are easier to set up and use. Macs come with everything you need built right in—simply plug them in and you're on your way. Mac lovers also point out that Apple has developed some incredibly advanced technology. (Even PC users will agree to that.)

It's not just the system and the software Mac users love. Most Macophiles love their one-button mice as well as their many shortcut keys. And few will deny

CURRENTS

Emerging Technologies

The Future of Open Source Software

Fee or free? Corporation controlled or user controlled? These two questions are shaping the future of open source software. Originally, Linus Torvalds wrote the Linux operating system because he couldn't afford to run the UNIX operating system on his home computer. At the time, UNIX was priced at $5,000 or more, and it ran only on powerful workstations, which cost $10,000 each. So Torvalds developed Linux and posted it on an Internet newsgroup for free, inviting people to download and improve the software. Thousands of programmers took up the challenge, adding different bells and whistles—not for pay, but for the challenge and the recognition.

The open source model is revolutionizing the software world. Because the basic code is free, you can find pieces of it running iPods, supercomputers, smartphones, and many other computer systems. Need Linux in Hungarian, Thai, or Zulu? Not to worry: Volunteers have translated versions of Linux into dozens of languages, giving computer users of all types—individuals, government organizations, and research groups—a free alternative to buying traditional operating systems. You can even download free open source programs for applications such as word processing and database management.

Although Linux remains free, adapting it to the needs of corporations and other large-scale users has become big business. For example, IBM will customize Linux for corporate customers; Red Hat offers consulting, development, and training services to Linux users. With assistance so readily available and the total price so affordable, it's not surprising that Linux's popularity is growing.

Although Linux held almost 25 percent of the Web server market in 2007, it had less than 2 percent of the desktop market. There are, however, signs that this may be changing. For instance, France's police force, the National Gendarmerie, has switched 70,000 desktop computers from Windows to Linux. And low-cost computers like the OLPC XO, Everex CloudBook, Classmate PC, and the Asus Eee PC are being offered with the Linux operating system (Figure 4.18). Linux is also making inroads in mobile computing, holding approximately 13 percent of the global smartphone market share. Motorola expects to offer Linux on 60 percent of their phones within the next few years. Other devices, such as TiVo and Amazon Kindle, also use Linux-based operating system.

Linux usage is especially strong in the Asia-Pacific market. However, reports indicate that some worldwide purchasers are ordering thousands of new PCs with the Linux operating system installed (because it is free) and are then installing illegal copies of the Microsoft Windows operating system. They do this to lower the cost of the PC package. The effect is that the statistics for PCs shipping with Linux are overstating the adoption of Linux as an operating system and reporting an equal decline in the reported use of Windows, when in fact, illegal copies of Windows are being installed on those very machines. This does not detract from the attractiveness of Linux to its adopters, but it does show that reports of its adoption may be inflated.

FIGURE 4.18 Open source software is being installed on low-cost notebook computers like these and provided to developing nations to help increase computer literacy.

that the Mac design is much more aesthetically pleasing than a PC (Figure 4.19). In addition, certain professions, especially creative fields such as graphic design, rely almost exclusively on Macs.

Linux offers another option. Linux can be installed on a Mac or a PC, and because it is open source software, cost isn't an issue. Security is another benefit. Few types of malware are targeted at Linux machines. But the lack of structured computer support and the level of computer knowledge required to set up a Linux system is often a deterrent to the casual user.

However, PCs still dominate, and the race isn't even close. PCs claim the largest chunk of the marketplace and are the choice of corporate America. And thanks to economies of scale, they also tend to be cheaper in terms of both their hardware and software. Indeed, software is a big plus for PC users, who have far more titles to choose from than their Mac or Linux counterparts. Because so many more people buy the software, it tends to be better, and it is often developed and published more quickly than similar software for Macs.

In recent years, Apple has tried to woo PC users by playing on the idea that Macs are easier to use. However, software products developed for Windows greatly outnumber those written for Macs, one reason PCs have led the marketplace. But now that Mac OS X can run Windows, Mac users are able to run existing Windows software. Unfortunately, as Apple moves into the PC market with its recent innovations, it may make itself more vulnerable to the viruses that have been, until now, mostly a PC headache. In any case, both Macs and Linux have a long way to go to catch PCs—and few experts see that happening any time soon.

All of the operating systems just discussed work in tandem with helper programs called utilities.

System Utilities: Housekeeping Tools

Providing a necessary addition to an operating system, **system utilities** (also called **utility programs**) are used to keep the computer system running smoothly. Sometimes these programs are included in the operating system; sometimes you must purchase them from other software vendors. System utility programs are considered essential to the effective management of a computer system by backing up system and application files, providing antivirus protection, searching for and managing files, scanning and defragmenting disks and files, and compressing files so that they take up less space.

BACKUP SOFTWARE

An essential part of safe, efficient computer usage, **backup software** copies data from the computer's hard disk to backup devices, such as CDs or DVDs, an

FIGURE 4.19 PC manufacturers and Apple have produced all-in-one computers for both Windows and Mac platforms.

external hard drive, or an online storage location. Should the hard disk fail, you can recover your data from the backup disk (Figure 4.20).

Backup software can run a **full backup**, which includes all files and data on the entire hard disk. In an **incremental backup**, the backup software copies only those files that have been created or changed since the last backup occurred. In this way, the backup disk always contains an up-to-date copy of all data. **Drive imaging software** creates a "mirror image" of the entire hard disk—including the operating system and applications, as well as all files and data. In the event of a hard disk or computer system failure, the backup disk can be used to restore the data by copying the data from the backup disk to a new hard disk. Full backups should be made at least once each month. Incremental backups should be made regularly, too—in a business environment, once or more per day.

Even if you don't have backup software, you can still make backup copies of your important files: just copy them to an alternative storage device. Don't ever rely on a hard disk to keep the only copies of your work. Backups should be stored away from the computer system so that, in the event of a fire or flood, they don't suffer the system's fate.

Windows Vista includes a backup utility that is accessed from the Backup and Restore Center on the Control Panel. The Complete PC Backup will create an exact image of your computer—backing up all files and data, plus the operating system and applications, but is only available on the Business, Ultimate, and Enterprise editions. Windows' Automatic Backup option backs up files and data and is available for most versions of Vista, including Home Basic and Home Premium. Although many people know that backing up their files is important, most don't regularly do so. The Automatic

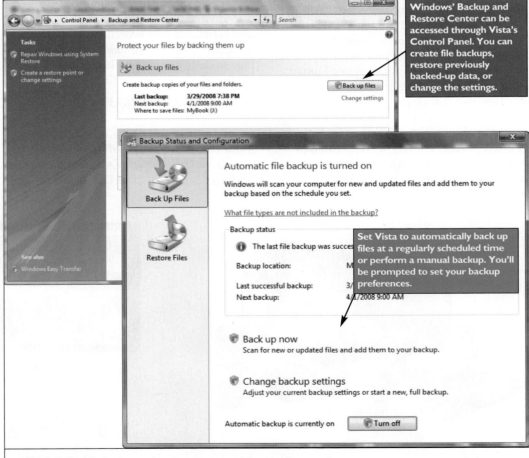

FIGURE 4.20 Backup software is an essential part of computing.

IMPACTS

Safety and Security
The Making of Malware

Malware, or malicious software, is installed on a computer without the owner's knowledge or consent. Computer viruses, worms, Trojan horses, rootkits, spyware, and adware are all forms of malware. They can damage your computer and data, spread to other computers, distribute spam, or threaten your privacy and compromise your computer's security. Malware is the Internet's latest security nightmare, causing billions of dollars of damage by destroying or corrupting data, stealing personal information, and clogging networks. Some malware can spread so quickly it causes a chain reaction affecting thousands or even millions of computers within a day or two.

In the past, malware writers tried to erase data on hard drives or disable PCs in other ways. Today's malware writers typically use hard drives as springboards for multiplying and spreading software to as many PCs as possible, rather than erasing files. The profitability of black market schemes and identity theft has made malware big business for organized crime as well. Despite intense attention from cybersecurity experts and law enforcement officials, the pace of malware attacks is increasing, as are their severity and sophistication.

Meanwhile, malware's enemies are fighting back. Sites like the National Cyber Security Alliance (**www.staysafeonline.org**) and the SANS Institute (**www.sans.org**) offer security advice, workshops, and training to individuals and businesses to help prevent cyber attacks; identify potential threats;

and protect computer systems and the information they contain.

How can you guard against malware? Just logging on to the Internet can expose you to malware—even if you've installed antivirus and antispyware software. For security, set your software for automatic updating, because even daily updates may not provide enough protection against the constant onslaught of malware. Don't download files or open attachments with suspicious names or unknown origins. Many antispyware programs, such as Spybot Search and Destroy (**www.safer-networking.org**) and Ad-Aware (**www.lavasoftusa.com**), are free and will catch things your antivirus program won't (Figure 4.21). Finally, strengthen your defenses by downloading the latest security patches for your operating system and other software.

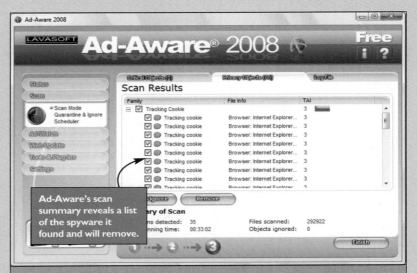

Ad-Aware's scan summary reveals a list of the spyware it found and will remove.

FIGURE 4.21 Antispyware products like Ad-Aware can find and remove malware that is undetected by antivirus software.

Backup option solves that problem with the File Backup Scheduling Wizard. Choose the time and backup location you prefer and Vista will do the rest! You can also obtain stand-alone backup or imaging software from local or online retailers, or check for user reviews and find free utility programs on sites like Download.com (**www. download.com**).

ANTIVIRUS SOFTWARE

Antivirus software protects a computer from computer viruses (Figure 4.22). Such software uses a pattern-matching technique that examines all of the files on a disk, looking for telltale virus code "signatures." One limitation of such programs is that they can detect only those viruses whose signatures

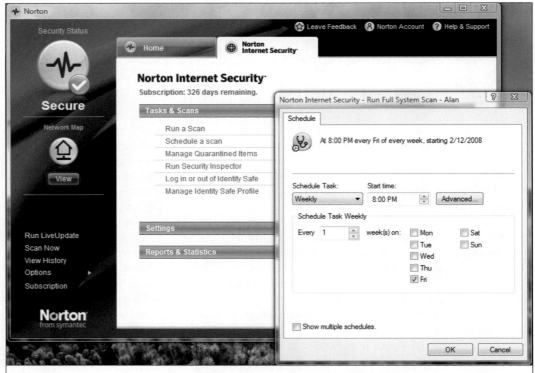

FIGURE 4.22 Norton Internet Security includes an antivirus program that you can schedule to check for viruses regularly.

are in their databases. Most antivirus programs enable you to automatically update the software. However, new viruses appear every day. If your system becomes infected by a virus that's not in the system's database, it may not be detected. Because of this shortcoming, many antivirus programs also include programs that monitor system functions to detect and stop the destructive activities of unknown viruses.

Norton AntiVirus and McAfee VirusScan Plus are the two most popular antivirus applications in use today. Both programs provide users with frequent updates for the term of a license. Licenses are typically issued for a year. Additionally, many ISPs now offer free antivirus protection and other security tools to help keep their customers safe online.

Some viruses do their damage immediately, whereas others hide on your hard disk waiting for a trigger before doing their work. Regardless of when they do their damage, viruses spread quickly and can affect thousands, even millions, of users in a short time. This is why it is important to install and use antivirus

software. It takes only one nasty virus to cause you a lot of grief.

SEARCHING FOR AND MANAGING FILES

Another important system utility is the **file manager**, a program that helps you organize and manage the data stored on your disk. The file manager enables you to perform various operations on the files and folders created on your computer's storage devices. You can use file managers to make copies of your files, to manage how and where they are stored, and to delete unwanted files. Windows Vista uses Explorer, Mac OS X uses Finder, and Linux has various file management utilities. Explorer has been enhanced considerably in Windows Vista and includes many new features (Figure 4.23). These new features help to make Windows Explorer even more versatile.

On a large hard disk with thousands of files, the task of finding a needed file can be time-consuming and frustrating if you try to do it manually. For this reason, most

FIGURE 4.23 A file manager, such as Windows Explorer, enables you to organize your files and folders.

operating systems include a **search utility**, which enables you to search an entire hard disk for a file. In Microsoft Windows, Instant Search is integrated into every Explorer window, and you can search for files in a number of ways, including by name, date, and size (Figure 4.24). The Spotlight utility in the Mac OS performs similar tasks.

SCANNING AND DEFRAGMENTING DISKS

A **disk scanning program**, or error checker, can detect and resolve a number of physical and logical problems that may occur when your computer stores files on a disk. The error-checking and defragmenting

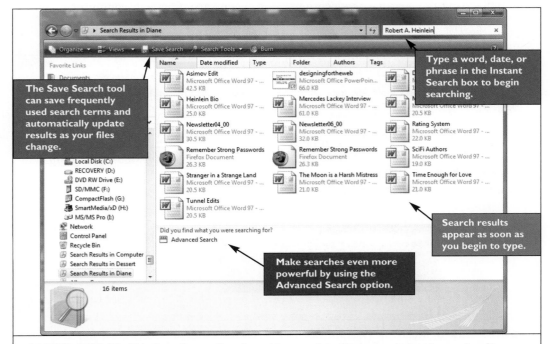

FIGURE 4.24 The Windows Instant Search tool is part of the Explorer window. It searches file names, file properties, and text within files using the search terms you provide.

utilities in Windows are found by clicking Computer in the Start menu, then right-clicking the drive to be checked, and choosing Properties. Select the Tools tab in the Properties dialog box to access the utilities. The Mac OS X scanning utility is called Disk Utility. You can find commercial products that perform this function, but the one that comes with your operating system is usually adequate and best suited for managing your hard disk.

Scanning programs look for a physical problem involving an irregularity on the disk's surface that results in a **bad sector**, which is a portion of the disk that is unable to store data reliably. The scanner can fix the problem by locking out the bad sector so that it's no longer used. Logical problems are usually caused by a power outage that occurs before the computer is able to finish writing data to the disk. **Disk cleanup utilities** can save disk space by removing files that you no longer need.

As you use a computer, it creates and erases files on the hard disk. The result is that the disk soon becomes a patchwork of files, with portions of files scattered here and there. This slows disk access because the system must look in several locations to find all of a file's segments. A disk with data scattered around in this way is referred to as being **fragmented**. A fragmented disk isn't dangerous—the locations

of all the data are known, thanks to the operating system's tracking mechanisms—but periodic maintenance is required to restore the disk's performance. **Disk defragmentation programs** are used to reorganize the data on the disk so that the data is stored in adjoining sectors (Figure 4.25). Scanning and defragmentation utilities should be run anywhere from once every three or four months for the light computer user to as much as once every three to four weeks for the power user.

FILE COMPRESSION UTILITIES

Most downloadable software is compressed. To exchange programs and data efficiently, particularly over the Internet, **file compression utilities** (Figure 4.26) can reduce the size of a file by as much as 80 percent without harming the data. Most file compression utilities work by searching the file for frequently repeated but lengthy data patterns and then substituting short codes for these patterns. Compression enables faster downloads, but you must decompress a file after downloading it. When the file is decompressed, the utility restores the lengthier pattern where each code is encountered. After decompressing the downloaded software, you can save it on your computer.

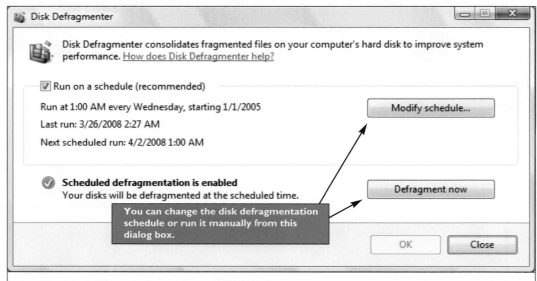

FIGURE 4.25 By default, the Windows Disk Defragmenter is set to run automatically, so you don't have to remember to do it. To change the settings, click Start, All Programs, Accessories, System Tools, Disk Defragmenter.

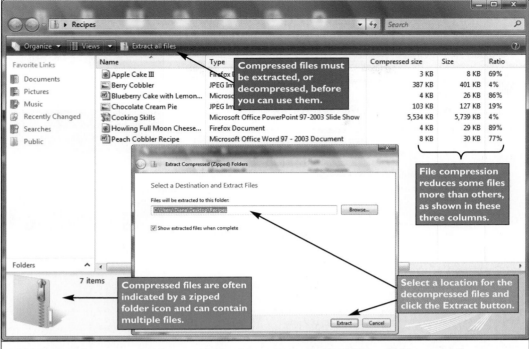

FIGURE 4.26 A file compression utility enables you to create archives and compressed files.

Most compression utilities also can create archives. An **archive** is a single file that contains two or more files stored in a special format. Archives are handy for storage as well as file-exchange purposes because as many as several hundred separate files can be stored in a single, easily handled unit.

To compress, or zip, a file in Windows, right-click it and choose Send To Compressed (zipped) Folder. This creates a new zipped file with the same file name. There are several ways to decompress, or unzip, a zipped file. One way is to double-click the file and use the Extract all files button. Another way is to right-click the zipped file and choose Extract All.

setting Windows Update to automatically download and install updates at a time of your choosing (Figure 4.27). You can also get more information at Microsoft's Security at Home page (**www.microsoft.com/ protect**).

Updates may include service packs, version upgrades, and security updates. They are designed to maintain your computer's security and reliability and to help protect against malicious software and exploits. Software Update provides a similar service for Mac users.

Besides system utilities, there are additional ways to safeguard your data or take care of operating problems.

SYSTEM UPDATE

Because the world of computers is rapidly changing, Microsoft provides an operating system update service called **Windows Update** that is meant to keep your operating system up to date with fixes (service patches) or protections against external environment changes. If you are using Windows Vista, you can ensure that your operating system is current by going to the Security area of your Control Panel and

TROUBLESHOOTING

Almost every user of a computer system experiences trouble from time to time. Whether the trouble stems from starting the computer, running programs, or adding hardware or software, users need troubleshooting tips to get them through a crisis.

If your computer fails to start normally, you may be able to get it running by inserting a **boot disk** (also called an

Destinations

Visit some other compression utility Web sites, such as WinZip (**www. winzip.com**), PKZip (**www.pkware.com**), or StuffIt (**www. stuffit.com**), to learn more about them or to try out an evaluation copy.

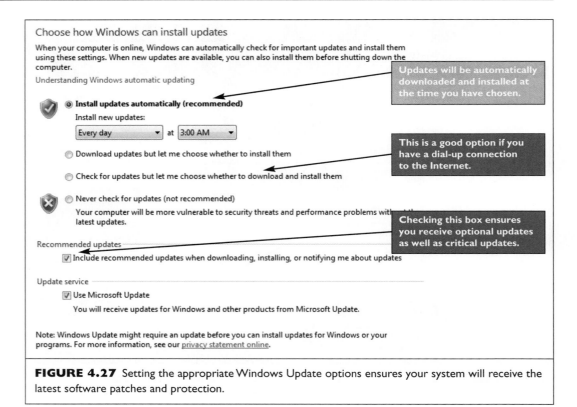

FIGURE 4.27 Setting the appropriate Windows Update options ensures your system will receive the latest software patches and protection.

Destinations

The process used to repair a damaged operating system in Windows Vista is significantly different from previous versions. The recovery information may be found on the original Windows Vista DVD or may have been provided by the computer manufacturer as a Recovery Disk or Recovery Partition on the hard disk drive. Visit the Tech Republic site (**http://blogs .techrepublic.com .com/window-on- windows/?p=622**) to learn more about how to create your own recovery disk.

emergency disk) into the CD or DVD drive. The emergency disk loads a reduced version of the operating system that can be used for troubleshooting purposes. An emergency disk sometimes comes with a new computer, but often you need to create it yourself. Consult the documentation that came with your computer or choose Help and Support from the Windows Start menu to learn about this process.

In Microsoft Windows, configuration problems can occur after adding a new peripheral device such as an external hard drive or new printer to your system. Conflicts can often be resolved by starting the computer in Windows **safe mode**, an operating mode in which Windows loads a minimal set of drivers that are known to function correctly. Within safe mode, you can use the Control Panel to determine which devices are causing the problem. You access safe mode by pressing, for example, the F8 key repeatedly during the initial start-up process. Or you can start the computer in safe mode, which will reset or report any conflicting programs or device drivers, and then simply shut it down and let it boot up normally.

System slowdown can sometimes occur because something has changed gradually over time to cause performance to degrade or there has been a hardware or software change. Windows Vista has a new tool to help diagnose these problems—the Reliability and Performance Monitor. The quickest way to access this tool is to open the Start menu and type "Reliability" in the Start Search text box. The Reliability and Performance Monitor will appear in the top of the list. The Resource Overview page provides real-time usage and performance data for four key resources: CPU, Disk, Network, and Memory. An expandable module for each resource provides additional details. There are also two monitoring tools. The Performance Monitor can be customized to display various performance counters. The Reliability Monitor generates a System Stability Chart that includes a graph and a report showing potential causes of reduced stability, such as botched software installations or hardware failures (Figure 4.28). You can easily check to see when your system's performance began to degrade and get details about individual events that might have caused the problem. The best way to ensure that your system runs optimally is to never change more than one thing at a time. That way, if the system has

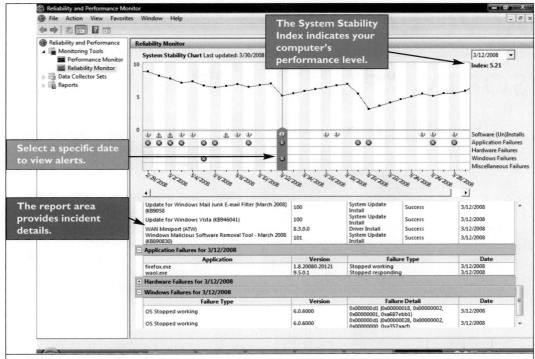

FIGURE 4.28 The Windows Reliability Monitor can help you identify problems with your system's performance.

problems, you can undo your last action or installation and see if the problem goes away.

Help and Support
Sometimes the best place to look for troubleshooting guidance is right on your own computer. Microsoft Windows includes a Help and Support utility. You can explore its contents by clicking the Start button and then clicking Help and Support. The Windows Help and Support Center includes a variety of ways to manage and maintain your computer. For example, you could choose Security and Maintenance from the Find an answer section. A security checklist appears with links to various topics, such as Windows Security Center, User Account Control, Back up and Restore, and Windows Firewall. Clicking on a topic will provide more information, including how to access and use specific tools, as well as links to more detailed topics. The Troubleshooting option provides assistance with various problems. The Help and Support Search box at the top of the window can also be used to locate information. Take the time to explore some of these topics; you may be surprised

at the confidence you will gain by interacting with your operating system.

Shutting Down Your System
When you've finished using the computer, be sure to shut it down properly. Don't just switch off the power without going through the full shutdown procedure. In Microsoft Windows Vista, click Start and then click the arrow next to the Lock button and click Shut Down. In Mac OS, click Special in the Finder menu and then select Shut Down. If you switch the power off without shutting down, the operating system may fail to write certain system files to the hard disk. File fragments that result from improper shutdown could result in permanent damage to the operating system or to personal files.

An alternative to completely shutting down your system is to put it in **sleep** mode, a low-power state that enables you to restore your system to full power quickly without going through the lengthy boot process. Sleep mode is available in both Windows and Mac OS. In fact, this is the default shutdown method for Windows, and it occurs when you click Start and then click the Power button.

Destinations
You can find all sorts of troubleshooting sites for both PCs and Macs on the Web. Some offer free advice and user forums, whereas others, such as Ask Dr. Tech, offer support packages for a price. Type "troubleshooting" into your favorite search engine or visit sites such as **www.macfixit. com** or **www. askdrtech.com** to find out more.

What You've Learned

SYSTEM SOFTWARE

- System software has two major components: (1) the operating system (OS) and (2) system utilities that provide various maintenance functions.

- Without software—the set of instructions that tells the computer what to do—a computer is just an expensive collection of wires and components. The operating system coordinates the various functions of the computer's hardware and provides support for running application software.

- An operating system works at the intersection of application software, the user, and the computer's hardware. Its five basic functions are starting the computer, managing applications, managing memory, handling internal messages from input and output devices, and providing a means of communicating with the user.

- When you start or restart a computer, it reloads the operating system into the computer's memory. A computer goes through six steps at start-up: loading the BIOS, performing the power-on self-test, loading the operating system, configuring the system, loading system utilities, and authenticating users.

- The three major types of user interfaces are graphical user interfaces (GUIs), menu-driven user interfaces, and command-line user interfaces.

- The two major operating systems for the personal computer are Microsoft Windows and Mac OS X.

The major strength of Windows is that it has dominated the market for more than 15 years and is installed and maintained on more than 90 percent of the personal computers in the world. The major strength of OS X is that it has been modified and upgraded for more than 20 years and is the most stable graphical operating system. The biggest weakness of Windows is that Microsoft continues to bring new versions to market before all of the bugs and security holes have been resolved. The main disadvantage of OS X is that it is used on only approximately 8 percent of the computers in the world and thus does not support as many applications as Windows does.

- Essential system utilities include backup software, antivirus software, file managers, search tools, file compression utilities, disk scanning programs, and disk defragmentation programs.

- A sound backup procedure begins with a full backup of an entire hard disk and continues with periodic incremental backups of just those files that have been created or altered since the last backup occurred.

- Troubleshooting your system can be as simple as restarting and as complex as tracking down a virus or a bad memory chip. A good rule of thumb is to do only what you feel comfortable doing and consult a professional technician at your local computer shop for other problems.

Go to **www.pearsonhighered.com/cayf** to review this chapter, answer the questions, and complete the exercises.

Key Terms and Concepts

account 147
antivirus software 161
archive 165
authentication 147
background application 148
backup software 159
bad sector 164
BIOS (basic input/output
   system) 145
boot disk (emergency disk) . . . 165
booting 145
cold boot 145
command-line user
   interfaces 153
desktop 151
dialog box 151
disk cleanup utilities 164
disk defragmentation
   program 164
disk scanning program 163
drive imaging software 160
driver 146
file compression utilities 164
file manager 162
foreground application 148
fragmented 164
full backup 160

graphical user interface
   (GUI) 151
icons 151
incremental backup 160
interrupt handlers 150
interrupt request (IRQ) 150
interrupts 150
IRQ conflict 150
kernel 145
Linux 156
load 145
login 147
Mac OS 155
menu-driven user
   interfaces 151
Microsoft Windows 153
Microsoft Windows
   Mobile 154
Microsoft Windows
   Server 2008 154
Microsoft Windows Vista . . . 153
MS-DOS (DOS) 157
multitasking operating
   systems 148
nonvolatile 146
open source software 156
operating system (OS) 144

pages 149
paging 149
platform 157
Plug-and-Play (PnP) 146
power-on self-test
   (POST) 146
preemptive multi-
   tasking 148
profile 147
registry 146
ROM (read-only memory) . . . 146
safe mode 166
search utility 163
setup program 146
single-tasking operating
   system 148
sleep 167
swap file 149
system software 144
system utilities (utility
   programs) 159
UNIX 155
user interface 151
virtual memory 149
volatile 145
warm boot 145
Windows Update 165

Go to **www.pearsonhighered.com/cayf** to review this chapter, answer the questions, and complete the exercises.

Matching

Match each key term in the left column with the most accurate definition in the right column.

_____ 1. virtual memory

_____ 2. kernel

_____ 3. bad sector

_____ 4. driver

_____ 5. interrupt request (IRQ) lines

_____ 6. profile

_____ 7. graphical user interface (GUI)

_____ 8. registry

_____ 9. load

_____ 10. preemptive multitasking

_____ 11. incremental backup

_____ 12. archive

_____ 13. sleep

_____ 14. file manager

_____ 15. full backup

a. these lines handle communications between input or output devices and the CPU

b. the process of transferring from storage to memory

c. a single file containing two or more files stored in a special format

d. the portion of the operating system that resides in memory at all times

e. only new or changed files are copied during this process

f. a process that copies all files and data

g. a utility program used by a peripheral device to function properly

h. stores configuration information for installed peripherals and software

i. ensures that all applications have fair access to the CPU and prevents them from monopolizing it

j. a system utility used to manage and organize data

k. used to create the desktop after the operating system loads

l. method whereby a computer's hard disk is used as an extension of RAM

m. a record of a specific user's preferences for the desktop theme, icons, and menu styles

n. the default shutdown method for Windows

o. caused by an irregularity on the hard disk surface

Go to **www.pearsonhighered.com/cayf** to review this chapter, answer the questions, and complete the exercises.

Multiple Choice

Circle the correct choice for each of the following.

1. Which operating system is specially designed for smartphones and PDAs?
   a. Windows XP
   b. Windows Vista
   c. Mac OS X
   d. Windows Mobile

2. Which of the following is *not* a feature of a command-line interface?
   a. commands are typed using keywords
   b. text-based menus provide user options
   c. syntax rules must be followed
   d. memorization is required

3. Which of the following is *not* an operating system function?
   a. creating documents and spreadsheets
   b. managing memory
   c. starting the computer
   d. providing the user interface

4. Which operating system is least likely to be used on a home computer?
   a. Windows Vista
   b. Windows Server 2008
   c. Linux
   d. Mac OS X

5. If RAM is full, what will happen?
   a. users will be authenticated
   b. an IRQ conflict will occur
   c. virtual memory will be used
   d. a power-on self-test will run

6. What happens when a warm boot is performed?
   a. a computer that is already on restarts
   b. a swap file is created
   c. a computer that is not already on starts up
   d. preemptive multitasking occurs

7. In virtual memory, what are program instructions and data divided into?
   a. drivers
   b. pages
   c. IRQs
   d. archives

8. Which of the following is *not* an example of a system utility?
   a. file compression tool
   b. disk defragmentation tool
   c. backup software
   d. menu-driven user interface

9. Which term describes all of the programs needed for a computer and its peripheral devices to function properly?
   a. operating system
   b. BIOS
   c. system utilities
   d. system software

10. Which tool creates a System Stability Chart to help diagnose performance problems in Windows Vista?
    a. Windows Update
    b. disk defragmentation tool
    c. Reliability Monitor
    d. Performance Monitor

Go to **www.pearsonhighered.com/cayf** to review this chapter, answer the questions, and complete the exercises.

Fill-In

In the blanks provided, write the correct answer for each of the following.

1. _____ _____ automatically installs fixes and service patches to maintain a computer's security and reliability.

2. Windows Explorer and Mac Finder are both examples of a(n) _____ _____ utility.

3. _____ is an example of a Microsoft operating system that uses a command-line user interface.

4. UNIX was the first operating system to use _____ _____, which helps keep the operating system running even if a program crashes.

5. A device _____ is a program that enables communication between the operating system and a peripheral device.

6. In a graphical user interface, a(n) _____ is used to represent computer resources such as programs and files.

7. The operating system function with the most impact on overall system quality is running and _____ applications.

8. The _____, or login, process verifies that the user is authorized to use the computer.

9. The first step in starting a computer is to load the _____.

10. The POST, or _____ _____, makes sure the computer and its peripherals are working correctly during the start-up process.

11. If memory is full, copies of pages are stored in a(n) _____ _____ on the hard disk.

12. A(n) _____ operating system permits users to work with more than one program at the same time.

13. A(n) _____ is determined by the combination of microprocessor chip and operating system used by a computer.

14. Linux makes its source code available for everyone to see and use. This is an example of _____ _____ software.

15. _____ _____ is an operating mode in which a minimal set of drivers is loaded, usually to help resolve configuration problems.

Short Answer

1. Explain the purpose of the power-on self-test (POST). In addition to a computer system, do you know of any other systems that perform a POST?

2. Visit **www.microsoft.com** and use the search box to search for the term "security." Visit one of the resulting sites. What is Microsoft doing to improve computer security?

3. What is the difference between shutting down your computer and putting it into sleep mode? What are the advantages to sleep mode? Are there any disadvantages?

4. What is the purpose of a device driver? Have you ever had to install a device driver when connecting a new peripheral device to a computer? If you did, what was the device? Was the driver supplied by the operating system or by the device's manufacturer?

5. Explain the differences between a full backup and an incremental backup. Have you ever lost important files because you did not back them up? If you have done a backup, did you copy the entire disk or just selected files? When was the last time you performed a backup?

Go to **www.pearsonhighered.com/cayf** to review this chapter, answer the questions, and complete the exercises.

Teamwork

1. Operating Systems

Your team is to research three of the operating systems presented in this chapter. What are the basic functions that need to be performed by an operating system? What future improvements in each operating system can you envision? If you have used several versions of the same operating system, what improvements have been incorporated into new versions? Go to **www.microsoft. com** and choose a link or search for "operating systems." Scroll around or search for Microsoft's operating system comparison section. Did you learn anything? How does the operating system you use stack up? Collaborate on a one- to two-page paper that summarizes your findings. Be sure to include information on Linux, Mac OS, and Windows.

2. Mac OS versus PC OS

Your team is to locate one or more labs on campus that have PCs and Macs. Experiment with both a Mac and a PC in determining the answers to the following questions. What version of each operating system did you use? Is it the latest release of the operating system? How are the two operating systems similar? Can you determine the strengths of each system? Which operating system do you prefer? Why? Write a paper that meets your professor's specifications.

3. Exploring UNIX

Despite its cryptic commands, UNIX has remained a popular operating system for about 30 years. Many educational institutions have computers running this operating system, and many Web servers run UNIX. Use the strengths of each member of your team to split the workload in answering the following questions. If you have used a UNIX computer, explain how and why you used it. Does your school have computers that use UNIX? If so, do you have an account? Can you get an account, or are the accounts restricted on these computers? Do you have an ISP? If you do, identify your provider and determine whether it uses UNIX to support customer Web sites. Write a one-page paper with your answers to these questions.

4. Using System Tools

Work as a team to determine the answers to the following questions. Each team member should use a different computer. To see how much you can learn about the Windows operating system, have each group member use a Windows-based PC to do the following. Choose Start, All Programs, Accessories, and System Tools. Now choose the System Information. How much memory is installed on the computer? How much virtual memory is defined? Now choose Start, Help and Support. Choose the Security and Maintenance area and have each team member investigate and write about two of the topics listed there.

5. Buying a Smartphone

You and your teammates are to consider the purchase of a smartphone. Split the following questions up among the team members. What companies manufacture smartphones? Some of these devices require special operating systems and application software. Go to a local mobile device store and take a smartphone out for a test drive. Specifically, try out the operating system. Do these devices use a special version of Windows? If they use Windows, what version and release is it? How does this operating system compare with those on desktop and notebook computers? How does it differ? Now that you have "kicked the keyboard" and taken a smartphone out for a spin, explain why you would or would not purchase one.

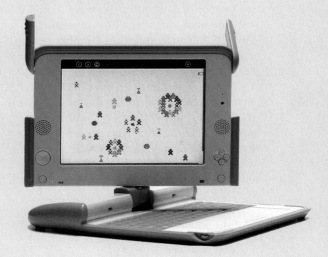

On the Web

1. File Compression

In this exercise, you'll examine a file compression tool. Write a one-page paper that summarizes your answers to these questions.

- Have you used a file compression program?
- If you have, identify the brand name and version of this software application. Which operating system were you using? Was the file compression program simple or complicated to use? Would you recommend this product to someone else? Why or why not?
- If you have not, visit the sites of two popular file compression programs, WinZip at **www.winzip.com** and StuffIt at **www.stuffit.com**. Which operating systems does each work with? What are the current versions and suggested retail prices for each? Are free or evaluation versions available? Would you purchase one of these products? Explain why or why not.

2. Antivirus Programs

In this exercise, you'll examine antivirus software. Write a one-page paper that summarizes your answers to the following questions.

- Have you ever had to disinfect a file that was infected by a virus?
- If you have, identify the brand name and version of the antivirus application you used and which operating system you were using. Were you able to disinfect the file successfully? Was the antivirus program simple or complicated to use? Would you recommend this product to someone else? Why or why not?
- If you have not, visit the sites of the two most popular antivirus applications, Norton AntiVirus at **www.symantec.com/norton/index.jsp** and McAfee VirusScan Plus at **www.mcafee.com**. Which operating systems does each work with? What are the current versions and suggested retail prices of each? Are free or evaluation versions available? Would you purchase one of these products? Explain why or why not.

3. Windows Vista

Visit **www.microsoft.com/windows/default.aspx** for information on the latest version of Windows.

Write a brief paper that summarizes your answers to the following questions.

- Why would users of Windows XP upgrade to Vista?
- What other types of users will benefit from Vista?
- What are the minimum hardware requirements for Vista?
- What are the purchase and upgrade prices for Vista?
- Would you consider purchasing or upgrading to Vista? Why or why not?

4. Using CNET

Go to **www.cnet.com**. Type "operating systems" into the search box. Review at least two articles about an operating system of your choice. Which operating system did you choose? What are three advantages and disadvantages to using this operating system? Would you consider using this operating system? Explain why or why not. Write a one-page paper that summarizes your findings.

5. Exploring Mac OS X

Visit the Mac OS X home page at **www.apple.com/macosx** to learn more about this operating system. Write a one-page paper that summarizes your answers to these questions.

- If the guided tour is available, take a few moments to view it. Did you find it helpful?
- What are some of the new features in this version of the operating system? Pick two features and describe them.
- What are some of the elements that make a Mac more secure than a PC ?
- What is the purpose of Boot Camp?
- What are the technical specifications for Mac OS X? Do some features have additional requirements?
- Name three utility programs included with Mac OS X and describe them.
- Spend some time exploring the remainder of the site. Explain why you would or would not purchase a Mac system.

Go to **www.pearsonhighered.com/cayf** to review this chapter, answer the questions, and complete the exercises.

Viruses: How to Tell if Your System Is Infected

Does your computer seem to have a mind of its own? Does it go to Web pages all by itself? Does it run really, really slowly at times? Do error messages fill your screen when your computer starts up? Is your computer doing something today that it wasn't doing yesterday? If so, you can be pretty sure that your computer has a virus. Computers infected by a virus often display symptoms in the same way that you do when you get sick. The following are some tips to help you keep your computer virus-free as well as some general guidelines for what to do in the event that your computer does get infected.

The best way to cure your computer of a virus is to not get one in the first place! Programs such as Symantec's Norton AntiVirus or McAfee's VirusScan Plus will help protect your computer from nearly all known viruses and should be the first program installed on any computer that will ever be connected to the Internet. Once installed, these programs should be regularly updated so they can protect you from the newest online threats. If you have a high-speed Internet connection, such as cable or DSL, then you can usually configure your antivirus software to perform these updates automatically. Most antivirus software comes with a year of free updates. After the year is up, you will have to pay a small service fee or upgrade to the newest version of the software to continue receiving essential updates. Anyone who has ever lost a lot of data because of a virus will tell you that this is definitely money and time well spent. Do not let your antivirus update subscription lapse. New threats are released onto the Internet every day, and old virus software is almost as bad as no virus software at all.

In addition to your antivirus software, you should keep your operating system updated with the latest security patches. Most viruses take advantage of systems that do not have the latest security enhancements installed. Windows users should ensure that their system is configured to automatically download and install the newest updates. Any items identified by Windows Update as "Critical Updates and Service Packs" should be installed as soon as possible to avoid compromising your computer.

In the event that your computer does become infected with a virus, the manufacturer of your antivirus software should provide you with a solution for cleansing your computer. You should check the manufacturer's Web site and the antivirus software user manual ahead of time so that you know where to find this information as well as the proper procedures to follow in the case of an emergency. Any damage from a virus infection can be further minimized by keeping backups of important files on removable media such as an external hard drive, CDs, or DVDs. You do back up your important files, right?

For a detailed list of ways to protect your computer from all types of threats, go to the "Home Computer Security" page of the CERT Coordination Center's Web site at **www.cert.org/homeusers/ HomeComputerSecurity**. The National Cyber Security Alliance (**www.staysafeonline.org**) is another useful resource for individuals, businesses, and educators (Figure 4.29).

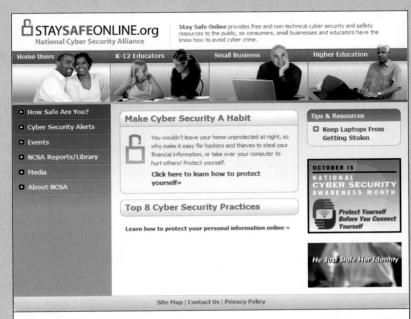

FIGURE 4.29 The National Cyber Security Alliance provides advice and resources for protecting your computer from online threats.

FILE MANAGEMENT

You've just finished your term paper—where should you save it?

You never know when you may need a writing sample for a graduate school or job application, so you'll want to keep it someplace safe. The secret to finding what you're looking for in the future is good file management now. Managing computer files is an essential skill for any computer user.

For most people, managing files is intuitive; it's simple once they learn the basics. You can think of managing computer files as being similar to the way you organize and store paper files and folders in a file cabinet (Figure 4A). You start with a storage device (the filing cabinet), divide it into definable sections (folders), and then fill the sections with specific items (documents) that fit the defined sections. Most people tend to organize the things in their lives, and the organizational principles used are the same ones used when managing computer files.

**Drive C: **

Fall Classes

Subfolders and Files

Winter Classes

THE BIG PICTURE: FILES, FOLDERS, AND PATHS

A **file** is a named unit of related data stored in a computer system. Your data (as well as the programs installed on your computer) is stored in files. Files store Word documents, music, photo images, Excel spreadsheets, applications, and a variety of other digital compilations. Every file that is stored has certain attributes. An **attribute** is a setting that provides information such as the file's date of creation, its size, and the date it was last modified.

You use **folders** (also called **directories**) to organize groups of files that have something in common. Many folders have **subfolders**—folders within folders—that enable you to organize your files even further. For example, you might create a folder called "Classes," and then create subfolders for your individual classes (Figure 4B).

All of the files and folders you create must reside on a storage device called a **drive**. The primary storage devices on desktop computers are the **hard drive**, the **CD** and **DVD drives**, the **external hard drives**, and **USB flash drives**. Older computers may also have a **floppy disk drive**. On PCs, these storage devices are designated by drive letters. A **drive letter** is simply a letter of the alphabet followed by a colon and a backslash character. If your computer has a floppy disk drive, it is typically referred to as A: \ . The hard drive is generally referred to as C: \ . The CD or DVD drive might

Figure 4A
You can organize files on your computer the same way you would organize documents in a filing cabinet.

177

be labeled drive D (D:\), and other drives are often labeled sequentially, so a USB flash drive might be labeled drive E (E:\). (On the Mac, drives are not labeled with letters. You'll see them as icons appearing on your screen.)

For the computer to access a particular file, it needs to know the path it should take to get to the file. A **path** is the sequence of directories that the computer must follow to locate a file. A typical path might look like this:

C:\Classes\Expository Writing 201\Homework#1_draft1.docx

In this case, the C:\ in the path indicates that the file is located on the C:\ drive. The **top-level folder**, "Classes," contains, as the name indicates, things that have to do with classes. The subfolder named "Expository Writing 201" is the subfolder for your writing class. The file at the end of the path, "Homework#1_draft1.docx," is the first draft of your first homework assignment. The .docx extension indicates that the file is a Microsoft Word 2007 document. We'll discuss filenames in greater depth shortly. Figure 4B illustrates what a hierarchical drive, folder, and file structure might look like.

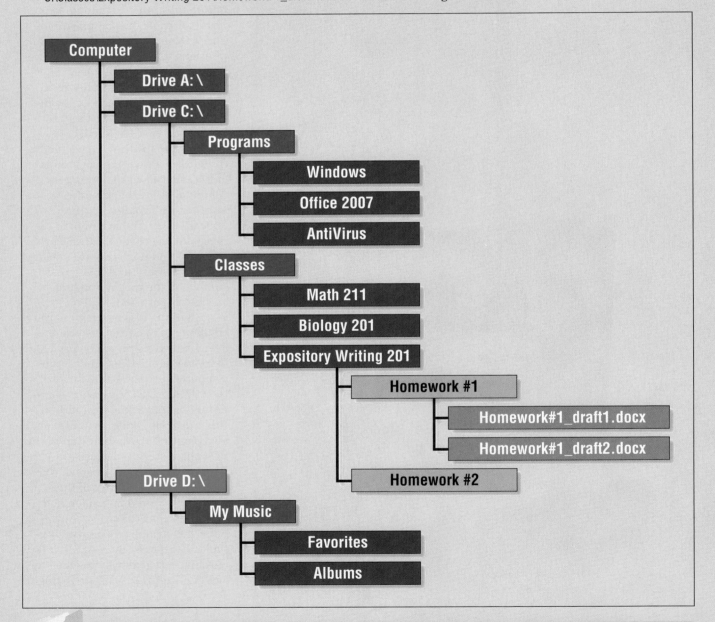

Figure 4B

The drive and folder structure is often referred to as a "tree" structure. The drive letters can be pictured as roots, the folders as branches, and the files as leaves.

FILE NAMING CONVENTIONS

To save a file, you need to know where you're going to store it—in other words, on which storage device and in which folder. In addition, each file needs a specific filename. The **filename** is the name that the storage device uses to identify each unique file, so the name must differ from all other filenames used within the same folder or directory. You may use the same name for different files, but they must exist on different drives or in different folders. Be careful to include enough detail in naming a file so that you will be able to recognize the filename when you need the file later. The name you use when you create a file is usually very obvious to you at the time—but the name may elude you when you try to remember it in the future.

Every filename on a PC has two parts that are separated by a period (read as "dot"). The first part, the part you're probably most familiar with, is called the **name**. The second part is called the **extension**, an addition to the filename typically three to five characters in length. In a file called Homework#1_draft1.docx, *Homework#1_draft1* is the name and *.docx* is the extension; together they make up the filename.

Typically, an extension is used to identify the type of data that the file contains (or the format it is stored in). Sometimes it indicates the application used to create the file. In Microsoft Windows, each application automatically assigns an extension to a file when you save it for the first time. For example, Microsoft Word automatically assigns the .docx extension. Workbooks created in Microsoft Excel use the .xlsx extension. When naming files, you never need to be concerned about typing in an extension, because all programs attach their extension to the filename by default.

Program files, also called application files, usually use the .exe extension, which stands for executable. The term *executable* is used because when you use an application, you execute, or run, the file. Figure 4C lists several of the most commonly used extensions and their file types. Note that when using Mac OS, extensions are not needed because Macintosh files contain a code representing the name of the application that created the file. However, it is generally recommended that Mac users add the appropriate extension to their filenames so that they can more easily exchange them with PC users and avoid conversion problems.

In Microsoft Windows, you can use up to 260 characters in a filename, including spaces. However, this length restriction includes the entire filepath name, therefore filenames actually need to be shorter than 260 characters to be valid. Windows filenames cannot include any of the following characters: forward slash (/), backslash (\), greater than sign (>), less than sign (<), asterisk (*), question mark (?), quotation mark ("), pipe symbol (|), colon (:), or semicolon (;). In Mac OS, you can use up to 255 characters in a filename,

Figure 4C
Commonly Used Filename Extensions

Extension	File Type
.exe	Program or application
.doc or .docx	Microsoft Word
.xls or .xlsx	Microsoft Excel
.ppt or .pptx	Microsoft PowerPoint
.mdb or .accdb	Microsoft Access
.pdf	Adobe Acrobat
.txt	ASCII text
.htm or .html	Web pages
.rtf	Files in Rich Text Format
.jpeg or .jpg	Picture or image format

including spaces, and all characters except the colon. Although you can use a large number of characters to create a filename, it is still best to keep filenames concise and meaningful. Longer filenames may be subject to automatic truncation (shortening), which can create file management difficulties.

Now that you understand the basics of paths, folders, and file-naming conventions, let's turn our attention to the business of managing files.

MANAGING FILES

Files can be managed in two ways: (1) with a file management utility such as Windows Explorer or (2) from within the programs that create them. In the following sections, we'll explore both methods.

FILE MANAGEMENT UTILITIES

Microsoft Windows uses the Windows Explorer program for file management. There are a number of ways that you can launch this program. The Start, All Programs, Accessories menu sequence is one method. Another method is to click Start and select one of the options shown on the top right side of the Start menu to view the contents of a specific folder (Figure 4D). The Start menu can also be used to access the Computer folder, which lets you view the disk drives and other hardware connected to your computer (Figure 4E).

The Windows Explorer program in Vista has a number of new features that make file management easier and more versatile. The Windows Explorer window includes navigation buttons, an address bar (also known as a breadcrumb bar), a search box, and a toolbar at the top of the window. The main body of the

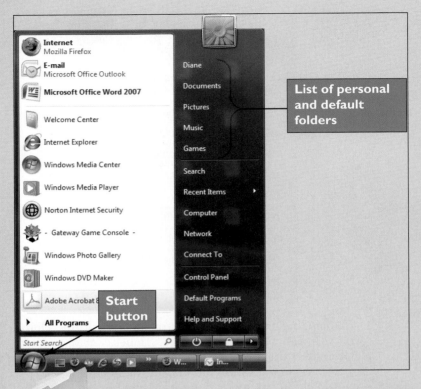

Figure 4D

The Start menu provides various options for viewing commonly accessed folders using Windows Explorer.

Figure 4E

The Computer window provides quick access to information about the disk drives and other hardware that is connected to your computer.

window is split into two panes—a navigation pane and a file list—with a detail pane displayed at the bottom of the window (Figure 4F). The **navigation pane** on the left allows you to navigate directly to specific folders listed in the Favorite Links area or access a prior search that you have saved by clicking on a desired folder. You can also add a shortcut to a frequently used folder by dragging the folder into the Favorite Links area of the navigation pane. At the bottom of the navigation pane is a Folders bar. Expanding this bar displays a hierarchical list of all folders and drives on the computer and also provides access to areas such as the Desktop, Control Panel, Computer, and Network.

The right pane, or **file list**, displays subfolders and files located within the selected folder. The column headings at the top of the file list can be used to change how the files are organized. New column headings can be added by right-clicking a heading and selecting one or more from the shortcut menu. As in previous versions of Windows Explorer, it is possible to sort the contents of a folder, but users can now also group, stack, and filter the items displayed in the right pane. To sort, simply click a column heading; click the column heading a second time to reverse the sort order. A sorted column displays a small triangle in the column heading; the direction of the triangle indicates whether the column has been sorted in ascending or descending order. If a folder contains subfolders and files, the subfolders are sorted separately from the files.

To access the group, stack, and filter options, click the drop-down arrow beside the column heading to reveal the submenu. The group option arranges files and folders within specified groups, depending on the column heading you've selected. In Figure 4G, the contents of the folder have been grouped by the dates they were modified. The stack option is similar to the group option, but rather than showing the contents of each group, a single icon is used to represent the entire collection of files (Figure 4H). To display the contents of a stack, just double-click it. When a folder's contents are filtered, only some of the contents are visible. The submenu of a column heading displays various criteria with check boxes. Placing a check in one or more of the check boxes will display only the folders that meet the selected criteria (Figure 4I). Windows

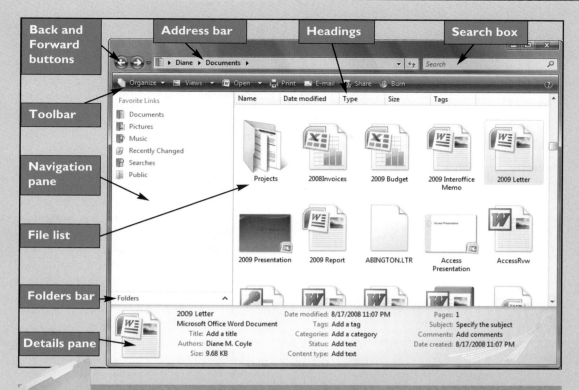

Back and Forward buttons
Address bar
Headings
Search box
Toolbar
Navigation pane
File list
Folders bar
Details pane

Figure 4F

Windows Explorer is a useful and versatile file management tool.

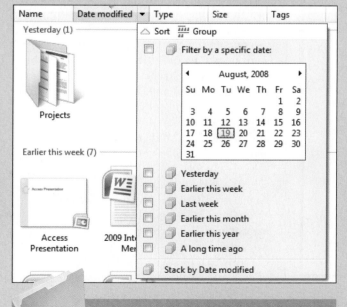

Figure 4G

Using the group option, files and folders can be grouped together according to specific criteria.

Explorer also displays a check next to the column heading to indicate that the folder's contents have been filtered and not all of the files or subfolders are displayed.

The **address bar** has also been updated. It is now possible to use it for breadcrumb navigation. The address bar displays the route you've taken to get to the current location. It may or may not correspond with a file's pathname. To view the actual pathname, click the icon on the left side of the address bar. The breadcrumbs can be used to easily move from one location to another—simply click the drop-down arrow to reveal a list of destinations (Figure 4J).

The **details pane** at the bottom of the window provides a thumbnail view and information about the selected file or folder. The details vary depending on the object that has been selected. Users can edit many of these items. Just click the item you wish to change, revise it, and press the Save button.

You can view the contents of the right pane in several ways. Seven different view options are accessible from the Views button on the toolbar. You can click the Views button to cycle through the choices or click the drop-down arrow next to the button to make a selection.

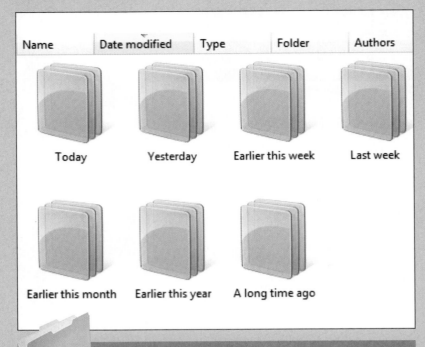

Figure 4H
The stack option groups files together, using a single icon to represent the entire group.

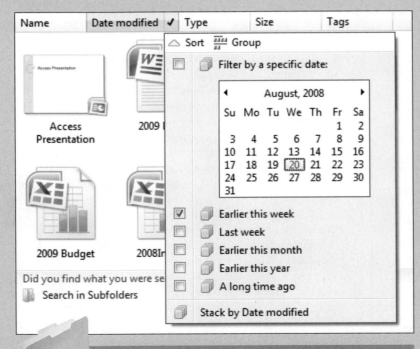

Figure 4I
In this example, the folder's contents have been filtered to display only those files that were modified within the current week.

The Tile view and various icon views are particularly helpful if you're searching through pictures and photographs, because they show you a small copy of the images you have in the folder—before you open them. The List view simply lists the names of the files, whereas the Details view offers you information regarding file size, file type, and the date a file was last modified.

Locating Files and Folders

Despite your best efforts, it's possible to forget where you've saved a file. The **Search box** in Windows Explorer can make this process less painful. Select one of the main folders, such as Documents, and begin typing a search term in the box. As you type, Windows Explorer searches the contents of the folder and its subfolders, immediately filtering the view to display any files that match the search term. Windows Explorer searches filenames, file properties, and file contents for the search term. If the search returns too many results, or you need to create a more complex search, the Advanced Search feature can help.

To open the Advanced Search pane you must have already begun a search. Scroll down to the end of your original search results and click the Advanced Search link or click Organize on the toolbar, then choose Layout, Search Pane, and click the Advanced Search button (Figure 4K). If you find that you are often searching for the same files, click the Save Search button on the toolbar. Assign a name for your search and, by default, the results will be stored in the Searches folder. Searches are **dynamic**, which means that the next time you open a saved search, the results are automatically refreshed—new files are added and files that no longer meet the search criteria are not included.

Creating Folders

Another way to manage your files effectively is to create a **folder**, or **directory**, **structure** (the terms *folder* and *directory* are synonymous)—an organized set of folders in which to save your files. The process of creating a folder structure is accomplished in two steps:

STEP I

Decide which drive, such as a USB flash drive, hard drive, or CD drive, you will create your folder on. To create a folder on your computer's hard disk drive, click the Start menu and select your personal folder—typically this folder will use your name and will appear at the top of the Start menu. Windows Explorer will open with a number of commonly used folders, such as Documents, Pictures, and Music, displayed in the right pane. If you prefer to

create your folder on a removable storage device, choose Computer from the Start menu instead and double-click the storage device you wish to use.

STEP 2

Select a folder, such as Documents, and double-click it. While pointing to the right pane, right-click and choose "New" and then "Folder" from the shortcut menus to create a folder within the selected folder. In other words, if you have selected the Documents folder, the new folder will be placed at the top level. See Figure 4L for an example of a new folder that has been created within the Documents folder.

You can repeat this process as many times as is necessary to create your desired folder structure. For example, if you're taking three classes, you might want to create three separate subfolders with the appropriate class names under a top-level folder called "Classes." That way, you'll know exactly where to save a file each time you create one, and you'll avoid having a cluttered and disorganized storage space.

Of course, creating a well-organized folder structure requires that you add, rename, and move folders as your needs change. For example, if you add a class to your schedule, you'll want to create a new subfolder in your top-level "Classes" folder. Next term, you'll create new subfolders for each of your classes.

One Windows method that is effective for managing, modifying, and creating folders, subfolders, and files is the use of the right-click mouse action. Right-clicking within the right pane of Windows Explorer, in a blank space, will cause a pop-up context-sensitive menu to appear. Right-clicking on a folder or file will provide a menu with different choices.

Transferring Files

When you've created a useful folder structure, you're ready to transfer files and folders that already exist. Whether you're working with files or folders, the same rules apply. Files and folders can be transferred in two ways: You can copy them or you can move them. The easiest way to accomplish these tasks is to *right-drag* the files you want to transfer to

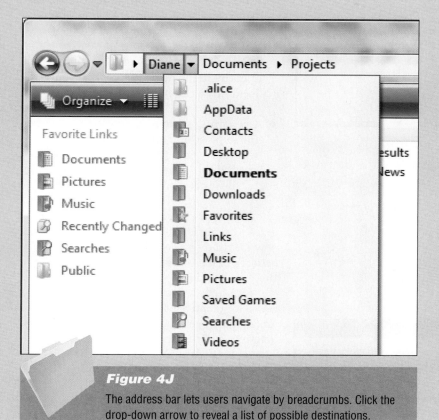

Figure 4J

The address bar lets users navigate by breadcrumbs. Click the drop-down arrow to reveal a list of possible destinations.

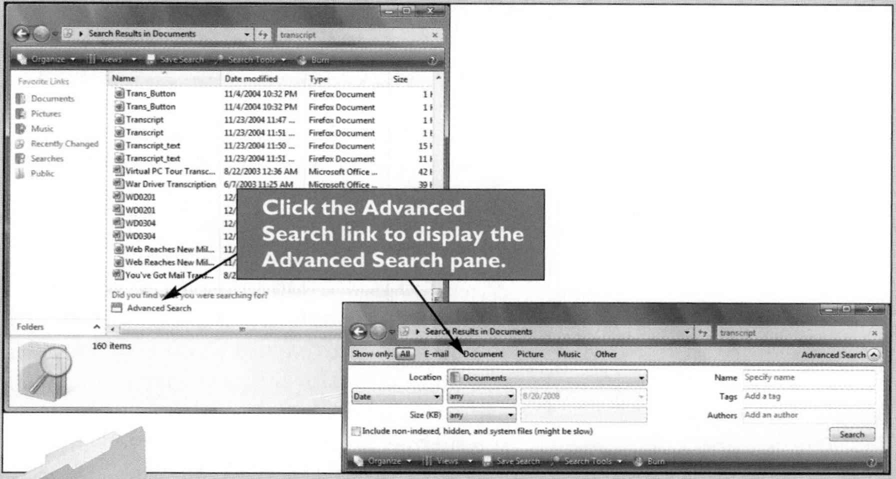

Figure 4K

The Advanced Search pane lets you fine-tune your searches for better results.

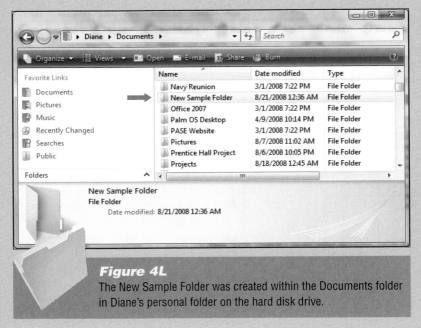

Figure 4L
The New Sample Folder was created within the Documents folder in Diane's personal folder on the hard disk drive.

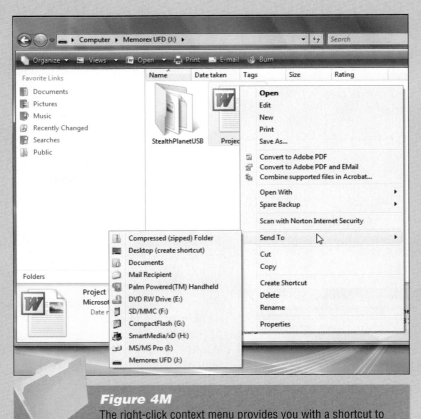

Figure 4M
The right-click context menu provides you with a shortcut to common tasks.

the new location. When you release the right mouse button, a context-sensitive menu appears, allowing you to choose the result of your right-drag. The choices on this menu are Copy Here, Move Here, Create Shortcuts Here, and Cancel.

- **Copying** creates a duplicate file at the new location and leaves the existing file as is.

- **Moving** is similar to cutting and pasting; the file is moved from its original location to the new location.

- **Creating a shortcut** leaves the original file in place and creates a pointer that will take you to the file for which you've created the shortcut. This action is handy for files that you access often.

If you *left-drag* a file *within the same drive*, the file is automatically moved to the new location on the drive. Left-dragging *between drives* creates a copy of the file in the new location.

Right-clicking a file invokes a context-sensitive menu that enables you to choose among many common tasks, such as copying, deleting, and renaming files and creating shortcuts (Figure 4M). You may also use the toolbar to accomplish these and other file management tasks.

Backing Up
You can create a backup copy of your files in several ways. The first, and easiest, way is to create intermediate copies as you work. You can do this by using the Save As menu sequence every 15 or 20 minutes. Name your intermediate copies by appending a number or letter to the filename. For example, Writing121_homework.docx would become Writing121_homework1.docx, then Writing121_homework2.docx, and so forth.

Additionally, you can use the Windows Explorer program to drag a copy of your file to a USB flash drive or CD/DVD drive. Backing up files to the same drive that the original copy is on risks losing both copies in a disk failure or other disaster, so you should always use a remote or portable medium for your backups.

A third way to be sure that you don't lose your work is to use backup software that is specifically designed to back up files.

Getting Help

If you need help when working within the Windows Explorer program, click the Get help button on the right side of the toolbar, and then type "managing files" into the Search box of the Windows Help and Support dialog box. This will bring up a variety of links to topics that will help you to further understand file management practices.

MANAGING FILES FROM WITHIN PROGRAMS

As mentioned earlier, all software applications use program-specific filename extensions. The advantage of using a default file extension is that both you and your computer will be able to easily associate the file with the program with which it was created. By using appropriate extensions, you can double-click a file in a file management utility such as Windows Explorer and the program will launch the appropriate application.

You can use an application to open a file or use a file to launch the application that created it. Let's say you create a document in Microsoft Word. You give the file the name "Letter Home," and Word assigns the extension ".docx" by default. Later, you use Windows Explorer to locate the file and then double-click the filename. The file will open in Word. Alternately, you could launch Word and then click the Office button and choose Open to locate the file and open it. The Open dialog box includes a button that allows you to decide which files to display—there are a number of options to choose from. Selecting All Files from the drop-down list will display all files in the current location, no matter what the file type might be. Choosing All Word Documents displays files created in any version of Word, whereas selecting Word Documents will show only Word 2007 files.

Choosing the File, Open menu sequence in many programs, or clicking the Office button and then choosing Open in Microsoft Office 2007 applications, also enables you to manage files. There are icons for creating new folders and for changing the current view, and there is an icon called *Organize* that enables you to copy, rename, and create shortcuts to files. Pointing to a file and pressing the right mouse button within the Open menu also invokes a file management menu with various tasks.

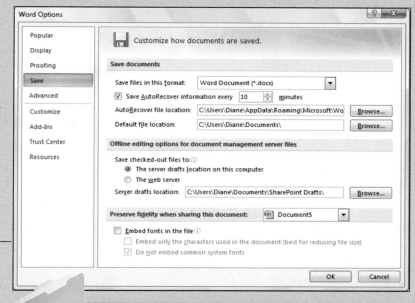

Figure 4N

To change the default location for saved files in Microsoft Office 2007, click the Office button, then click the Options button to access the dialog box.

SAVING FILES

Saving refers to the process of transferring a file from the computer's temporary memory, or RAM, to a permanent storage device, such as a hard disk. In Microsoft Windows, documents are saved by default to a folder called *Documents* unless you specify another folder from within the Tools, Options menu, or for Office 2007 applications, from within the program's Options menu, which can be found by clicking the Office button (Figure 4N). A critical decision you'll make when managing files is whether to use the Save or Save As command to save files.

Save or Save As?

Many computer users never figure out the difference between Save and Save As. It is actually quite simple. When you choose the Save command under the File menu (or Office button), the program takes what you've created or modified in memory and writes over, or replaces, it to the same storage device and folder, with the same filename that it had when it was opened in the application. When you first save a file, the initial Save menu sequence always invokes the Save As dialog box, because the drive, path, and filename must be designated the first time a file is saved. But when you're working with a previously saved file, you need to be more careful. The Save command doesn't allow you to designate a different drive, folder, or filename; it simply replaces what is stored with the contents of memory.

The Save As command, however, brings up a dialog box that offers all of the choices you had when you first saved a file. You may choose a different drive or a different folder or a different filename. Modifying the filename is a good way to save various versions of your work, just in case something happens to what is in memory and you need to go back to a previous version.

Once you've successfully saved a file, you can always save another copy elsewhere by using the Save As command, which enables you to save the file using a new location, a new filename, or both. You might also use the Save As command to save a copy of your finished work on a USB flash drive, CD, or DVD, or in an alternate folder as backup, just in case something happens to your original work.

If you're trying to find a message in a lengthy message list, remember that you can sort the mail in different ways. By default, your e-mail program probably sorts mail in the order the messages were received. You can also sort by sender or recipient; some programs give you more ways to sort. With Microsoft Outlook, you can quickly sort messages by clicking one of the buttons at the top of the message list. For example, to sort messages by date, click the Received button. Click it again to sort the list in the opposite order.

Still can't find a message? Most e-mail programs provide a Find or Search command, which enables you to search for information in the message header. The best programs enable you to search for text in the message body as well. To search for a message within Outlook, enter a search term in the Search box. Results begin to display as soon as you begin typing.

MANAGING E-MAIL

Many e-mail users quickly become overwhelmed by the number of messages they receive. It's not unusual to get dozens, or even hundreds, of messages every day. You can handle the deluge by organizing your messages into folders.

Most e-mail programs enable you to create your own mail folders. For example, you could create folders for each of the classes you're taking. In each folder, you can store mail from the teacher as well as from other students in the same class. You could create another folder to store mail from your family.

A FEW LAST REMINDERS

Good file management is the hallmark of a competent computer user. File management should not be an intimidating or frustrating task. Computers are tremendously complex and powerful devices, but the principles of managing your work are simple. Plan and construct folder structures that make sense to you. Name your files in such a way that you can easily find them. Always begin at the beginning. If something doesn't work, go back to when it did. Read the manual. Follow directions carefully. Make backup copies of your work. And if all else fails, don't be afraid to ask for help.

SPOTLIGHT EXERCISES

1. Launch Windows Explorer. Explore the Organize option on the toolbar. Write a brief paper that answers the following questions. What can you do with the Folder and Search Options? How can you adjust the layout of the Explorer window? Find out how to display the Menu and explore these options too. The Menu is hidden by default. Would you prefer to have the Menu visible all the time? Why or why not?

2. In this exercise, you will use the Windows Explorer program to build a folder structure within the Documents folder. Create a top-level folder named Junk that contains three subfolders and then right-drag two or more files from some other source into one of the three subfolders. Click the Junk folder in the address bar and then double-click on the subfolder that contains the files. Now press the Print Screen key that is at the top of the right side of your keyboard. Open a Word document and press Ctrl+V. Type your name below the picture on your screen and print out the file or e-mail it to your instructor.

3. Create a new folder in the Documents folder and name it "Junk." Launch your favorite Web browser and go to your favorite search engine's home page. Use the search engine's image search feature to locate a picture of your favorite vacation spot. After finding the picture, click on the image to go to the page on the Web where it resides. Write down the URL (address) of the Web site and note the day and time. Right-click on the image and save it to your Junk folder. Write a few paragraphs that describe what you've accomplished. Use good citation practices and be sure to include the information that identifies where and when you obtained the image.

4. In this exercise, you will practice changing the default folder icon image. From within Windows Explorer, right-click any folder name or icon. Choose Properties from the bottom of the menu. Choose the Customize tab at the top right of the window. At the bottom of the window are two choices for changing the appearance of the icon. The first choice is to add a picture to the folder icon by selecting the file you wish to use. To experiment with the different views, choose the View menu and observe how the folder looks using the various view choices. The second choice on the menu changes the default manila folder icon and provides a selection of alternative icons to use instead. Create a folder and name it "Junk." Create a subfolder within Junk and give it a name of your choosing. Now use the right-click, Properties sequence to change the image of each of these folders. When you are finished, display your subfolders in the right pane and then press the Print Screen key that is at the top of the right side of your keyboard. Open a Word document and press Ctrl+V. Type your name below the picture on your screen and print out the file or e-mail it to your instructor.

5. Open your e-mail program. Create a new folder using the File, New, Folder menu sequence (in Outlook—other mail readers will have a similar method). For the folder name, use the name and year of the term you are in now, such as Fall2009. Open your new folder and create a folder for each of your classes. Now practice dragging messages back and forth between your deleted files folder and your new folders. Feel free to delete these folders when you are through. Write a paragraph describing your experience.

6. Use your favorite Web browser to go to **www.worldstart.com/tips/cat-topics/7**. Browse the links to locate at least three that you find interesting. Use the Start, All Programs, Accessories menu sequence to find and launch Windows Explorer. Try the tips and tricks you learned at the Web site. Write a short paper describing where you went and what you learned.

What You'll Learn . . .

- Understand how system software supports application software.

- List the most popular types of general-purpose applications.

- Discuss the advantages and disadvantages of standalone programs, integrated programs, and software suites.

- Discuss the advantages of Web-hosted technology and file compatibility.

- Explain the concept of software versions and software upgrades.

- Understand how commercial software, shareware, freeware, and public domain software differ.

- Describe the essential concepts of application software and the skills needed to use it.

Application Software: Tools for Productivity

CHAPTER OUTLINE

General-Purpose Applications 190
    Personal Productivity Programs 190
    Multimedia and Graphics Software. 192
    Internet Programs. 197
    Home and Educational Programs 197

Tailor-Made Applications 198
    Custom versus Packaged Software. 199

Standalone Programs, Integrated Programs, &
    Software Suites 199
    Web-Hosted Technology: A New Way to Share Files 201

System Requirements & Software Versions 202
    Software Upgrades 202
    Distribution and Documentation 204

Software Licenses & Registration 204
    Commercial Software, Shareware, Freeware, and Public
        Domain Software. 205

Installing & Managing Application Software 206
    Installing Applications 206
    Launching Applications 208
    Choosing Options. 208
    Exiting Applications 209

Application software generally refers to all of the programs that enable you to use the computer for your work. In this sense, application software differs from system software, the programs that enable the computer to function properly. You use application software to work efficiently with the documents that are created in almost any line of work, such as invoices, letters, reports, proposals, presentations, customer lists, newsletters, tables, and flyers. Recalling our aquarium analogy, applications are the fish that swim in the water (the operating system). The operating system provides the environment in which the applications run. It supports the functions of input, processing, output, and storage, whereas the applications enable users to accomplish specific tasks. People use applications to create products, to communicate with others, and to store and find information. They also derive entertainment from certain types of applications.

In this chapter, you'll learn how to make sense of the world of application software. You'll read about the various types of application software and learn how to install, maintain, and upgrade the programs that you use each day.

General-Purpose Applications

General-purpose applications are applications used by many people to accomplish frequently performed tasks. These tasks include writing (word processing), working with numbers (spreadsheets), and keeping track of information (databases). General-purpose applications include productivity, multimedia and graphics, Internet, and home and educational programs. These applications are likely to be found on home and business users' personal computers. Figure 5.1 lists the various types of general-purpose application software.

PERSONAL PRODUCTIVITY PROGRAMS

The most popular general-purpose applications are **personal productivity programs**, which, as the name implies, help individuals do their work more effectively and efficiently. Productivity programs

---

FIGURE 5.1 General-Purpose Application Software

Personal Productivity Programs	Multimedia and Graphics Software	Internet Programs	Home and Educational Programs
Word processing	Desktop publishing and multimedia authoring programs	E-mail programs	Personal finance software
Spreadsheet		Web browsers	Tax preparation software
Database	Paint, drawing, and animation programs	Instant messaging software	Home design and landscaping software
Presentation graphics	Image-editing programs	Videoconferencing software	Computer-assisted tutorials
Personal information management	3-D rendering programs		Computerized reference information (e.g., encyclopedias street maps)
	Audio software		
	Video-editing software		Games

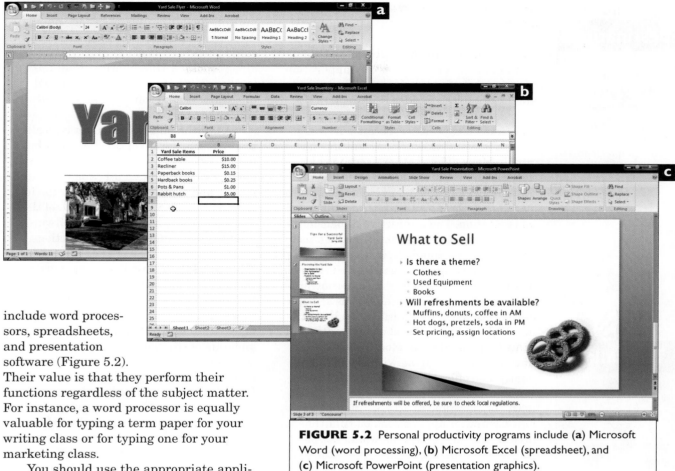

FIGURE 5.2 Personal productivity programs include (**a**) Microsoft Word (word processing), (**b**) Microsoft Excel (spreadsheet), and (**c**) Microsoft PowerPoint (presentation graphics).

include word processors, spreadsheets, and presentation software (Figure 5.2). Their value is that they perform their functions regardless of the subject matter. For instance, a word processor is equally valuable for typing a term paper for your writing class or for typing one for your marketing class.

You should use the appropriate application for the appropriate purpose. Excel can be used for a presentation, but it is much better to use PowerPoint and embed Excel spreadsheets and charts in it. In Word you can use tables to add numbers together, but Excel is much better suited to this task. One maxim you may have heard is that "You can drive a screw with a hammer—but a hammer is best used for driving nails and a screw should be set with a screwdriver." The same rule applies to using the right productivity program for the right job. You can increase your productivity by choosing an application such as Excel to manage numbers and an application such as Word to manage text.

Personal information managers, which offer electronic address books and scheduling tools, and database programs, which enable you to manage, track, report, and share information, are also considered personal productivity software. Outlook is an example of a personal information management program (Figure 5.3).

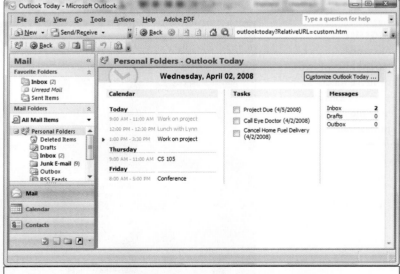

FIGURE 5.3 Outlook helps you manage your e-mail, contacts, calendar, and tasks.

Destinations

A great site to learn more about multimedia and graphics software is About's Web page "Graphics Software" at **http://graphicssoft .about.com**.

Techtalk

pixel
A *pixel*, short for "picture element," is a dot or point that represents color in a graphic image. Pixels are the smallest elements that a device, such as a monitor, can display.

MULTIMEDIA AND GRAPHICS SOFTWARE

What exactly is **multimedia**? The standard definition is that it is any application that involves two or more media, such as audio, graphics, or video (Figure 5.4). By this definition, any TV show or movie is a multimedia experience, because it uses both audio and video. Some multimedia applications offer another exciting characteristic: interactivity. For example, in an interactive multimedia presentation, users can choose their own path through the presentation. The interactive dimension makes computer-based multimedia a non-couch-potato technology; instead of sitting back and letting someone else determine the presentation's flow, you're in control.

One of the reasons the Web is so popular is because of its interactivity. In fact, the Web could be viewed as a gigantic multimedia presentation. Most Web pages include graphics along with the text, and many also offer animations, videos, and sounds. On some Web pages, you can click parts of a graphic to access different pages.

Computer applications use multimedia features where text alone would not be effective. Graphics, sounds, animations, and video can often do a more effective job of involving the user (and conveying information) than text alone.

Multimedia and graphics software includes professional desktop publishing programs (such as QuarkXPress) and multimedia authoring programs; paint, drawing, and animation programs; image-editing programs (such as Photoshop); three-dimensional (3-D) rendering programs (such as computer-aided design [CAD] programs); audio software; and video-editing programs.

A multimedia presentation typically involves some or all of the following: bit-mapped graphics, vector graphics, edited photographs, rendered 3-D images, edited videos, and synthesized sound. In the following sections, we'll discuss each of these and look briefly at some of the software used to create multimedia productions.

Compression and Decompression

Computers can work with art, photographs, videos, and sounds only when these multimedia resources are stored in digitized files, which require huge amounts of storage space. To use the space on your hard disk more efficiently and improve file transfer speeds over the Internet, most multimedia software programs reduce file size by using compression/decompression algorithms called **codecs**.

Codecs use two different approaches to compression: lossless compression and lossy compression. With **lossless compression**, the original file is compressed so that it can be completely restored, without flaw, when it is decompressed. With

FIGURE 5.4
Multimedia presentations involve two or more media. Such presentations are now the norm in professional settings.

lossy compression, the original file is processed so that some information is permanently removed from the file. Lossy compression techniques eliminate information that isn't perceived when people see pictures or hear sounds, such as frames from a video that are above the number needed to eliminate the flicker effect and very high musical notes.

Paint Programs

Paint programs are used to create **bit-mapped graphics** (also called **raster graphics**), which are composed of tiny dots, each corresponding to one pixel on the computer's display (Figure 5.5). You can use a professional paint program such as Corel Painter to create beautiful effects. Although paint programs enable artists to create pictures easily, the resulting bit-mapped image is difficult to edit. To do so, you must zoom the picture so that you can edit the individual pixels, and enlargement may produce an unattractive distortion called the *jaggies*.

Paint programs can save your work to the following standard formats:

- **Graphics Interchange Format (GIF**; pronounced "jiff" or "giff"). GIF is a 256-color file format that uses lossless compression to reduce file size. It's best for simple images with large areas of solid color. Because this file format is a Web standard, it's often used for Web pages.

- **Joint Photographic Experts Group (JPEG**; pronounced "jay-peg"). JPEG files can store up to 16.7 million colors and are best for complex images, such as photographs. This image format is also a Web standard. The JPEG file format uses lossy compression to reduce file size.

- **Portable Network Graphics (PNG**; pronounced "ping"). A patent-free alternative to GIF, PNG produces images that use lossless compression and are best suited to Web use only.

- **Windows Bitmap (BMP)**. BMP is a standard bit-mapped graphics format developed for Microsoft Windows. Compression is optional, so BMP files tend to be very large.

You can easily edit a picture to get just the part you need.

FIGURE 5.5 The program Paint is included in Microsoft Windows. Although not as full-featured as professional paint programs, it is possible to create your own bit-mapped graphics or edit existing images.

Drawing Programs

Drawing programs are used to create **vector graphics**, in which each on-screen object is stored as a complex mathematical description. What this means, in practice, is that every object in a vector graphic can be independently edited and resized without introducing edge distortion, the bane of bit-mapped graphics. To compose an image with a drawing program, you create independent lines and shapes; you can then add colors and textures to these shapes. Because the resulting image has no inherent resolution, it can be any size you want. The picture will be printed using the output device's highest resolution.

Professional drawing programs, such as CorelDRAW and Adobe Illustrator, save files by outputting instructions in PostScript, which is an automated page-description language. PostScript graphic files are saved to the Encapsulated PostScript (EPS) format, which combines the original PostScript document in a file that also contains a bit-mapped thumbnail image of the enclosed graphic. (The thumbnail image enables you to see the graphic on the screen.)

Drawing programs have been optimized to create art for the Web and mobile devices. Adobe Illustrator is tightly integrated with Adobe Flash, a program commonly used to create animated Web graphics.

Techtalk

page-description language (PDL)
A programming language capable of precisely describing the appearance of a printed page, including fonts and graphics. PostScript is an established PDL standard widely used in desktop publishing.

Three-Dimensional Rendering Programs

A 3-D rendering program adds three-dimensional effects to graphic objects. The results are strikingly realistic. Objects can be rotated in any direction to achieve just the result the artist is looking for.

In the past, rendering software required a high-powered engineering workstation, but today's top desktop computers are up to the task. One rendering technique, **ray tracing**, adds amazing realism to a simulated three-dimensional object by manipulating variations in color intensity that would be produced by light falling on the object from multiple directions (which is the norm in the real world).

Image Editors

Image editors are sophisticated versions of paint programs that are used to edit and transform—but not create—complex bit-mapped images, such as photographs. These programs make use of automated image-processing algorithms to add a variety of special effects to photographic images. They also enable skilled users to doctor photographs in ways that leave few traces behind. After using image editors to improve your photos, you can share them with friends and family at Web sites such as Flickr (Figure 5.6).

Professional design studios have used image editors such as Adobe Photoshop for years (Figure 5.7), but image editors have captured a wider market because of the popularity of digital cameras. Programs such as Adobe's Photoshop Elements are designed for beginners who want to perform the most common image-enhancement tasks quickly and easily and then print their pictures on a color printer. They can be used to remove red-eye from flash snapshots and adjust a picture's overall color cast.

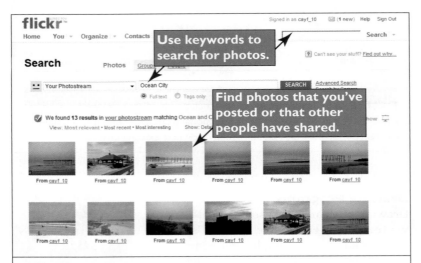

FIGURE 5.6 You can use Web-based photo communities such as Flickr (**www.flickr.com**) to upload photos and make them available to your friends and family at no charge.

Animation Programs

When you see a movie at a theater, you're actually looking at still images shown at a frame rate (images per second) that is fast enough to trick the eye into seeing continuous motion. Like a movie, an animation consists of the same thing: images that appear to move. Animators create each of the still images separately. In computer animation, the computer provides tools for creating the animation as well as for running it.

It's easy to create a simple animation using GIF, which enables programs to store more than one image in a GIF file. The file also stores a brief script that tells the application to play the images in a certain sequence and to display each image for a set time. Because Web browsers can

FIGURE 5.7 Adobe Photoshop is an image editor that has been used by professional design studios for years.

read GIF files and play the animations, GIF animations are common on the Web (Figure 5.8).

Professional animation programs provide more sophisticated tools for creating and controlling animations, but they create proprietary files. To view these files on the Web, you need a special plug-in program such as the Shockwave Player or Flash Player from Adobe (Figure 5.9).

Audio Software

A variety of programs are available for capturing and processing sound for multimedia presentations, including sound mixers, compression software, bass enhancers, synthesized stereo, and even on-screen music composition programs. You won't see any tape recorders in today's recording studios—just computers!

Sound files contain digitized data in the form of digital audio waveforms (recorded live sounds or music), which are saved in one of several standardized sound formats. These formats specify how sounds should be digitally represented and generally include some type of data compression that reduces the size of the file:

- **MP3**. MP3 is a sound file format that enables you to compress CD-quality digital audio by a ratio of 12:1 with no perceptible loss in sound quality (Figure 5.10).

- **Windows Media Audio (WMA)**. WMA is a Microsoft file format similar to the MP3 format, but it compresses files at a higher rate, creating a smaller file with the same audio quality. WMA is one of the most popular audio file formats.

- **WAV**. The default Microsoft Windows sound file format uses the .wav extension (short for "Wave Sounds"). It can be saved with a variety of quality levels, from low-fidelity mono to CD-quality stereo. WAV sounds usually aren't compressed, so they tend to take up a lot of disk space.

- **Ogg Vorbis**. An open source format that is an even faster format than MP3, Ogg files are also about 20 per-

cent smaller than MP3 files. You can fit more of them on your hard disk or MP3 player. See **www.vorbis.com**.

- **Musical Instrument Digital Interface (MIDI)**. MIDI files don't contain waveforms. They are text files that contain a text-based description that tells a synthesizer when and how to play individual musical notes.

Destinations

To learn more about some interesting 3-D rendering and modeling programs, visit **www.google.com/ Top/Computers/ Software/Graphics/ 3D/Rendering_and_ Modelling**.

FIGURE 5.8 Advanced GIF Animator (**www.gif-animator.com**) is an example of Web animation software.

FIGURE 5.9 To view animations on the Web, you need a special plug-in program such as Adobe's Flash Player or Shockwave Player.

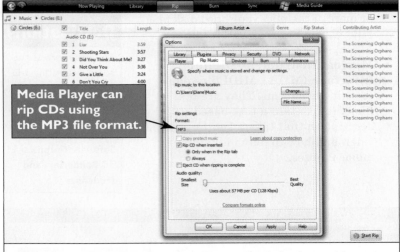

Media Player can rip CDs using the MP3 file format.

FIGURE 5.10 The Windows Media Player is handy for ripping (also known as burning) CDs and for creating MP3 files.

Streaming audio formats are available that enable Internet-accessed sounds to play almost immediately after the user clicks an audio link. The most popular streaming audio format, RealAudio, can deliver voice-quality audio over dial-up connections.

Video Editors

Video editors are programs that enable you to modify digitized videos. With a video editor, you can cut segments, resequence frames, add transitions, compress a file, and determine a video's frame rate (the number of still images displayed per second).

Video editors also enable you to save video files to some or all of the following video file formats:

- **Moving Picture Experts Group (MPEG)**. A family of video file formats and lossy compression standards for full-motion video, MPEG includes MPEG-2, the video format used by DVD-ROMs. MPEG-2 videos offer CD- and DVD-quality audio.

- **QuickTime**. A video file format developed by Apple Computer, QuickTime 7 Pro is the latest version. It plays full-screen, broadcast-quality video as well as CD- and DVD-quality audio. It is widely used in multimedia CD-ROM productions.

- **Video for Windows**. The native (or original format a program uses internally) video file format for Microsoft Windows, Video for Windows is often called AVI (Audio Video Interleave). This format is still widely used but is inferior to the new MPEG-4 standard.

Because a huge amount of data must be stored to create realistic-looking video on a computer, all video file formats use codec techniques. For the best playback, special video adapters are required. These adapters have hardware that decodes videos at high speed.

To make video available on the Internet, streaming video formats have been developed. These formats enable the video picture to start playing almost immediately after the user clicks the video link. (With nonstreaming video, users have to wait for the entire file to be transferred to their computer before it begins to play.) Streaming video formats rely on compression, low frame rates, and small image size to deliver video over the Internet, which does not have sufficient bandwidth (signal-carrying capacity) to disseminate broadcast-quality video. Other, competing streaming video formats are available; the most popular is RealNetworks' RealVideo format.

Multimedia Authoring Systems

Authoring tools are used to create multimedia presentations. These tools enable you to specify which multimedia objects to use (such as text, pictures, videos, or animations), how to display them in relation to each other, how long to display them, and how to enable the user to interact with the presentation. To take full advantage of an authoring tool's capabilities, it's often necessary to learn a scripting language (a simple programming language). A leading authoring package is Adobe Director.

Commercial authoring tools such as Adobe Director save output in proprietary file formats. To view Adobe presentations on a Web site, it's necessary to download and install a plug-in program (software that extends another program's capabilities). Some users do not like to download viewers, so the Web's standards-setting body, the World Wide Web Consortium (W3C), recently approved the Synchronized Multimedia Integration

FIGURE 5.11 You can easily build your own multimedia by using iMovie (part of Apple iLife) to combine audio, images, and video.

Language (SMIL), a simple multimedia scripting language designed for Web pages. SMIL enables Internet users to view multimedia without having to download plug-ins. However, multimedia presentations that use plug-ins (like Shockwave) are more widely used.

The Adobe Creative Suite media development kit is a powerful tool for developing multimedia Internet applications. If you are a Mac user, you'll most likely be interested in visiting **www.apple.com/ilife** to learn about Apple's multimedia iLife suite (Figure 5.11). With the iLife package, you can create music with GarageBand; integrate and organize your music, photos, and home videos with iTunes, iPhoto, and iMovie; and pull it all together on your own DVD with iDVD.

One thing to keep in mind is that multimedia authoring programs tend to use lots of disk space and often require extra memory to run efficiently. Be sure to read the program's system requirements, which are usually listed on the packaging or in the documentation, and realize that the numbers truly are minimums.

INTERNET PROGRAMS

Internet programs, such as e-mail clients, instant messaging programs, Web browsers, and videoconferencing software,

are general-purpose applications because they help us to communicate, learn, and interact.

HOME AND EDUCATIONAL PROGRAMS

General-purpose software also includes **home and educational programs**, such as personal finance and tax preparation software, home design and landscaping software, computerized reference information (such as encyclopedias, street maps, and computer-assisted tutorials), and games.

Hot sellers in the reference CD/DVD-ROM market include multimedia versions of dictionaries (which include recordings that tell you how to pronounce difficult words), encyclopedias (replete with sound and video clips from famous moments in history), and how-to guides (which use multimedia to show you how to do just about anything around the home; Figure 5.12).

Computer Games

By any standard, computer games are big business. In the United States, retail sales for gaming software, hardware, and accessories rose to almost $18 billion in 2007, and this trend is expected to continue.

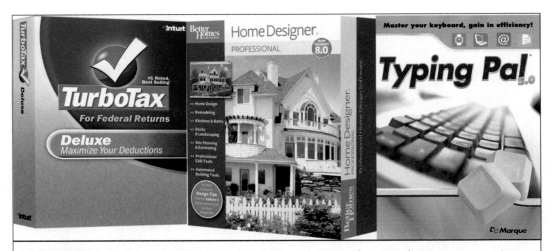

FIGURE 5.12 These personal finance, home design, and typing software applications represent just a few of the home and educational programs on the market today.

This highly profitable industry got its start in the 1970s, when the earliest computer video games (such as Pong) appeared in bars and gaming arcades. Video games then entered the living room with the advent of Atari, Nintendo, and Sega console game players, which are special-purpose computers designed to display their output on a TV screen. Games soon migrated to personal computers—and from there, to the Internet.

Multiplayer online gaming enables players to interact with characters who are controlled by other players rather than by the computer. Combining a rich graphical virtual environment with multiplayer thrills, these types of games are attracting increasing numbers of users. Role-playing games are a natural for Internet-connected computers, which enable players to participate even if they're not physically present in the same room. Originally, online role-playing games were known as **MUDs**, an acronym for **multiuser dungeons** (or **dimensions**). The name MUD is based on the noncomputerized Dungeons and Dragons role-playing game. Early MUDs and their various offshoots took place in a text-only environment and players used their imaginations to construct a persona and build their environment. They interacted with other players by means of text chatting, similar to talking in a chat room.

As the Internet and the Web have evolved over the years, Internet gaming has changed as well. Currently, **graphical MUDS (gMUDs)** bring the virtual environment to life in 3-D graphical environments, and **massively multiplayer online role-playing games (MMORPGs)** permit increasingly larger numbers of players to interact with one another in virtual worlds (Figure 5.13). These virtual worlds are often hosted and maintained by the software publisher, unlike other environments that end when the game is over. MMORPGs also encourage teambuilding—to progress to higher levels, it is frequently necessary to band with others whose skills and abilities complement those of your character.

Some MMORPGs are directly accessible online and do not require any special equipment other than a Web browser, whereas others require a locally installed game package to speed up processing. Examples of such games include EverQuest and Pirates of the Burning Sea. Players purchase the locally installed software and pay a monthly fee for online access.

If you can't find general-purpose applications to meet your computing needs, you might consider tailor-made applications.

Tailor-Made Applications

Tailor-made applications are designed for specialized fields or the business market. For example, programs are available to handle the billing needs of medical offices, to manage restaurants, and to track occupational injuries (Figure 5.14).

Tailor-made applications designed for professional and business use often cost much more than general-purpose applications. In fact, some of these programs cost $10,000 or more. The high price is due to the costs of developing the programs and the small size of most markets.

If the right application isn't available, programmers can create custom software to meet your specific needs.

CUSTOM VERSUS PACKAGED SOFTWARE

In the world of application software, a distinction can be made between custom software and packaged software. **Custom software** is developed by programmers and software engineers to meet the specific needs of an organization. Custom software can be quite expensive, but sometimes an organization's needs are so specialized that no alternative exists. An example of a custom software package might be the grade-tracking software that has been programmed to meet the needs of your college registrar's office. Custom software is almost always a tailor-made application.

Packaged software, in contrast, is aimed at a mass market that includes both home and business users. Although packaged software can be customized, it is designed to be immediately useful in a wide variety of contexts. An example of packaged software is the presentation software program your instructor may use to create class presentations. The payoff comes with the price: Packaged software is much cheaper than custom software.

In addition to the choices of custom or packaged software, users have three other options when purchasing software: standalone programs, integrated programs, and software suites.

Standalone Programs, Integrated Programs, & Software Suites

A **standalone program** is a program that is fully self-contained. Microsoft Word and Excel are examples of standalone

FIGURE 5.13 The 3-D graphical environments found in many MMORPGs, such as Pirates of the Burning Sea, continue to become more realistic and appeal to growing numbers of players.

programs. You can purchase and install them separately, and they function perfectly well all by themselves. However, standalone programs require a lot of storage space. For example, if you purchase Word and install it and then purchase Excel and install it, neither program would know about the other, nor would they share any resources, such as menus, drivers, graphics libraries, or tools. Obviously, this is a very inefficient way to install and use software when the programs have so many resources they could share.

Integrated programs offer all of the functions of the leading productivity programs in a single easy-to-use program. Integrated programs such as Microsoft Works are generally aimed at beginning users (Figure 5.15). They offer easy-to-learn and easy-to-use versions of basic productivity software. All of the functions, called

FIGURE 5.14 Medical offices often use tailor-made applications to manage their scheduling and billing.

FIGURE 5.15
Microsoft Works modules provide basic productivity tools that are helpful for new users.

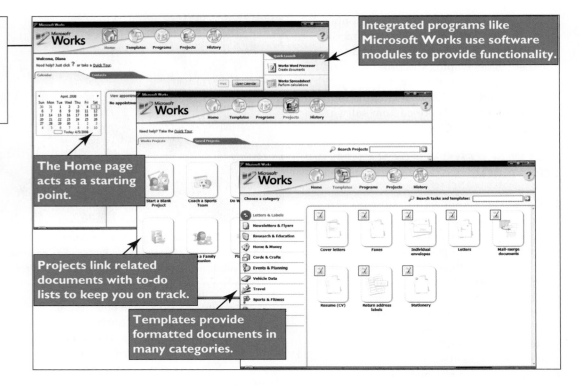

Integrated programs like Microsoft Works use software modules to provide functionality.

The Home page acts as a starting point.

Projects link related documents with to-do lists to keep you on track.

Templates provide formatted documents in many categories.

modules, share the same interface, and you can switch between them quickly. The individual modules, however, may be short on features compared with standalone programs or office suites. The lack of features may make these easy programs seem more difficult when you start exploring the program's more advanced capabilities.

Microsoft Works contains a word processor that is very similar to Word, a spreadsheet program that is very similar to Excel, a database program, a calendar, and other productivity tools. The modules of an integrated program are not available as standalone programs—you cannot purchase the spreadsheet program in Works as a standalone product.

A **software suite** (sometimes called an **office suite**) is an interconnected bundle of programs that share resources with each other and are designed to help workers accomplish the tasks they perform in a typical office environment. If Microsoft Windows is your operating system, then Microsoft Office is the set of tools that you typically use at work. A suite may include as many as five or more productivity applications. Today, most personal productivity software is sold in office suites, such as Corel WordPerfect Office, IBM Lotus

SmartSuite, and the market leader, Microsoft Office. Sun's StarOffice is another personal productivity software suite that has a small but loyal following.

The advantage of a software suite is that the individual applications share common program code, interface tools, drivers, and graphics libraries. For instance, if you purchased Word and Excel as standalone applications, each would require you to install a printer. Each would have its own dictionary, thesaurus, toolbars, and graphics library. When you use Word and Excel as a part of Microsoft Office, all of these features are shared.

Office suites typically include a full-featured version of leading word-processing, spreadsheet, presentation graphics, database, and personal information manager programs (Figure 5.16):

- **Word-processing programs** enable you to create, edit, and print your written work. They also offer commands that enable you to format your documents so that they have an attractive appearance. Although some people still prefer to use other writing tools, word-processing programs are the most often used office suite software.

FIGURE 5.16 Office Suites Available for Microsoft Windows

	Microsoft Office	WordPerfect Office	IBM Lotus SmartSuite
Word processing	Word	WordPerfect	Word Pro
Spreadsheet	Excel	Quattro Pro	Lotus 1-2-3
Database	Access	Paradox	Approach
Presentation graphics	PowerPoint	Presentations	Freelance Graphics
Personal information manager	Outlook	WordPerfect MAIL	Lotus Organizer

- **Spreadsheet programs** present users with a grid of rows and columns, the computer equivalent of an accountant's worksheet. By embedding formulas within the cells, you can create "live" worksheets, in which changing one of the values forces the entire spreadsheet to be recalculated. Spreadsheets are indispensable tools for anyone who works with numbers.

- **Presentation graphics programs** enable you to create transparencies, slides, and handouts for presentations.

- **Database programs** give you the tools to store data in an organized form and retrieve the data in such a way that it can be meaningfully summarized and displayed.

- **Personal information managers (PIMs)** provide calendars, contact managers, task reminders, and e-mail capabilities.

WEB-HOSTED TECHNOLOGY: A NEW WAY TO SHARE FILES

The new wave in office suites is **Web-hosted technology**, which for application software means the capability to upload files to an online site so they can be viewed and edited from another location. It is also possible to share your files with others, making group collaboration easier. Windows Office Live (**http://workspace.officelive.com**) and Google Docs (**http://docs.google.com**) are two examples of sites that offer these capabilities. Most of these services are free to use, but you do need to create an account and sign in.

Office Live provides storage space for your files and enables you to create separate areas called workspaces, some of which have themes and include sample files (Figure 5.17). You can share an individual document, an entire workspace, or even the screen you're currently working on by sending an e-mail invitation to one or more people. You can also set a

Destinations

To learn more about other office suites that offer Web integration, visit **www.wordperfect. com**, **www.openoffice .org**, and **www.sun .com/software/star/ staroffice.**

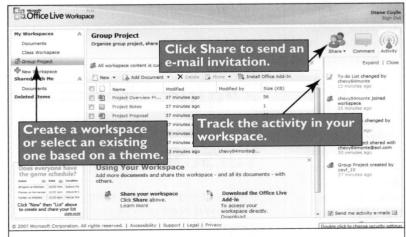

FIGURE 5.17 Web-hosted software suites like Microsoft's Office Live allow users to view and share documents over the Web.

person's access level by assigning viewing or editing rights. You can access and view all files online, even on computers that don't have Microsoft Office. However, to revise a file, it must be downloaded and edited using Microsoft Office and then uploaded to the site again.

Google Docs also provides file storage space and enables you to share your files with others. One advantage of Google Docs is the ability to open files directly within your Web browser and make basic editing and formatting changes—no additional software is required. It is also possible for more than one person to work on the same document at the same time, making real-time collaboration possible.

Web-hosted technology can help avoid file incompatibility problems that may arise when using traditional file sharing methods. Proprietary file formats can limit file usage to a specific vendor's software or computer model. For instance, if Microsoft Word is not installed on your system, you can't view a Word file unless you use a conversion program. Such problems can also arise when software publishers introduce new file formats in new versions to support new features. The ability to save a file to a Web-hosted software suite can eliminate file conversion costs, because the file can be read by anyone with a Web browser, not just those users who have installed the actual software.

Now that you are familiar with the many types of application software and how the software can be packaged, let's look at some other considerations to keep in mind when choosing application software.

System Requirements & Software Versions

When you buy software, your computer system will need to meet the program's **system requirements**, the minimal level of equipment that a program needs in order to run. For example, a given program may be designed to run on a PC with a

Pentium-class microprocessor, a CD or DVD drive, at least 512 MB of RAM, and 2 GB of free hard disk space. If you're shopping for software, you'll find the system requirements printed somewhere on the outside of the box or online through a link that is usually called "system requirements." Although a program will run on a system that meets the minimum requirements, it's better if your system exceeds them, especially when it comes to memory and disk space.

You've no doubt noticed that most program names include a number, such as 6.0, or a year, such as 2010. Software publishers often bring out new versions of their programs. These numbers help you determine whether you have the latest version. In a version number, the whole number (such as 6 in 6.0) indicates a major program revision. A decimal number indicates a **maintenance release** (a minor revision that corrects bugs or adds minor features). The year 2010 would indicate the year that the software was published; however, it does not indicate how many versions of the software there were previously. For example, Office 2003 is technically Office 11, whereas Office 2007 is Office 12.

Software publishers sometimes offer **time-limited trial versions** of commercial programs on the Internet, which expire or stop working when a set trial period (such as 60 or 90 days) ends. You can download, install, and use these programs for free, but after the time limit is up, you can no longer use them.

Beta versions of forthcoming programs are sometimes available for free. A **beta version** is a preliminary version of a program in the final phases of testing. Beta software is known to contain bugs (errors); it should be installed and used with caution.

SOFTWARE UPGRADES

Software upgrading describes the process of keeping your version of an application current with the marketplace. Some upgrades are small changes called *patches*; sometimes they are major fixes called *service releases* or *service packs*. Service releases keep the current version up to date. The ultimate upgrade is when you purchase and install the next version or release of a program. For instance, you

---

Green Tech Tip

A recent survey by Pricewaterhouse-Coopers revealed that 60 percent of technology manufacturers are developing green products and services, using recycled or recyclable materials, and creating packaging that meets or exceeds global environmental standards. For instance, Microsoft has eliminated the use of PVC in their packaging and McAfee encourages users to download their software, thereby eliminating the need for packaging. Want to do your part? If you have old copies of software on CD, stacks of obsolete floppy disks, or other unwanted computer accessories, GreenDisk (**www.greendisk. com**) will safely and responsibly dispose of them for you for a small fee.

IMPACTS

Safety and Security

What's Hiding on Your Computer? Spyware, Adware, and Pop-Ups

Right now, your hard drive probably holds some programs that you don't know about, didn't mean to install, and don't really want—and they're not viruses. Do you know what is hiding on your computer?

Spyware is Internet software that is installed on your computer without your knowledge or consent. It may monitor your computer or online activity, relay information about you to the spyware's source, or allow others to take control of your computer. Spyware usually enters your system through the Internet, sometimes when you open seemingly innocent e-mails and sometimes when you download software—especially shareware and freeware. Without knowing it, you may have agreed to install the spyware if you clicked Yes to accept the license agreement of the software you wanted to download. That's when the trouble begins.

Some types of spyware, known as keyloggers, can record every keystroke you type and every Internet address you visit. It can capture your login name and password, your credit card numbers, and anything else you input while the spyware is active. Other spyware programs look only at your Web browsing habits so they can arrange for ads keyed to your interests.

If you've ever downloaded software and then seen a banner or pop-up advertisement, you've downloaded a form of adware. Adware is like spyware, only it's created specifically by an advertising agency to collect information about your Internet habits. Although the practice is ethically questionable, shareware and freeware creators sometimes allow advertisers to tag along invisibly by bundling adware with their software. After you accept the license agreement and download the software, the adware is installed on your computer.

No matter how they get into your system, spyware and adware invade your privacy and present a serious security threat. How can you get rid of them? First, find out whether your ISP can help. Many ISPs provide built-in clean-up utilities that find and remove spyware and adware. Second, look into utilities from antivirus companies such as Symantec's Norton (**www.symantec.com**) and spyware specialists such as PC Tools' Spyware Doctor (**www.pctools.com**), and Webroot (**www.webroot.com**). These utilities scan your computer's memory, registry, and hard drive for known spyware and then safely eliminate these sneaky programs (Figure 5.18). Because new spyware is created all the time, remember to scan your system frequently (experts recommend at least once a week) so you can root out hidden programs.

Although newer browsers include tools to block pop-up windows, some still manage to get through. For extra protection, check out the Pop-Up Stopper software offered by Panicware (**www.panicware.com**). Be warned, however, that if you need to use pop-ups for online quizzes or other purposes, Panicware's utility can prevent such pop-ups from functioning properly. Often you can download free or trial versions of spyware, adware, and pop-up blocking software and then, for a small fee, upgrade to advanced versions with more options. In just a few minutes, you can turn the tables and protect yourself by spying on any intrusive software that may be hiding on your computer. Finally, before you download any software, read the fine print in the licensing agreement to find out whether you're saying yes to invisible extras you really don't want.

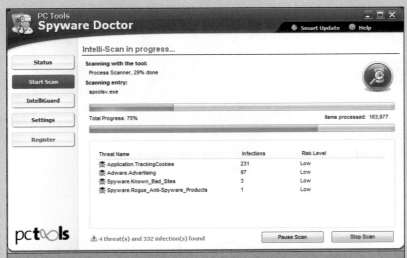

FIGURE 5.18 Programs such as Spyware Doctor help protect your system from spyware.

might have recently upgraded from Microsoft Office 2003 to Microsoft Office 2007.

So how do you know whether you should purchase the next version of a software application or whether there is a patch or fix available that will make your current version perform better? Well, when it comes to upgrading you should look at two things: Is your current version so out of date that you are having compatibility problems? Are there features in the newer version that you find attractive? As for patches, you should occasionally visit the software manufacturer's Web site to see if there are any service releases or patches. Microsoft software has a built-in capability to automatically check with Microsoft's Web site to determine whether updates are available.

DISTRIBUTION AND DOCUMENTATION

Before the Internet came along, most software was available only in shrink-wrapped packages that included floppy disks or CD-ROMs containing the program installation files. Now, many software publishers use the Internet to distribute programs and program updates. Doing so, rather than physically delivering a program in a box, is much cheaper for the company and often more convenient for the consumer.

If you buy software in a shrink-wrapped package, you typically get at least some printed **documentation** in the form of a brief tutorial to help you get started. Downloaded software contains Read Me files and help files. A Read Me file is a plain text document that is readable by any text-reading program. It contains information the software manufacturer thinks you'll find helpful. Many programs also have help screens that enable you to consult all or part of the documentation on screen (Figure 5.19). You may also find additional information at the software publisher's Web site.

Now that you've chosen the right application software version, considered upgrades, and looked over the documentation, let's look at some other considerations you might have when using application software.

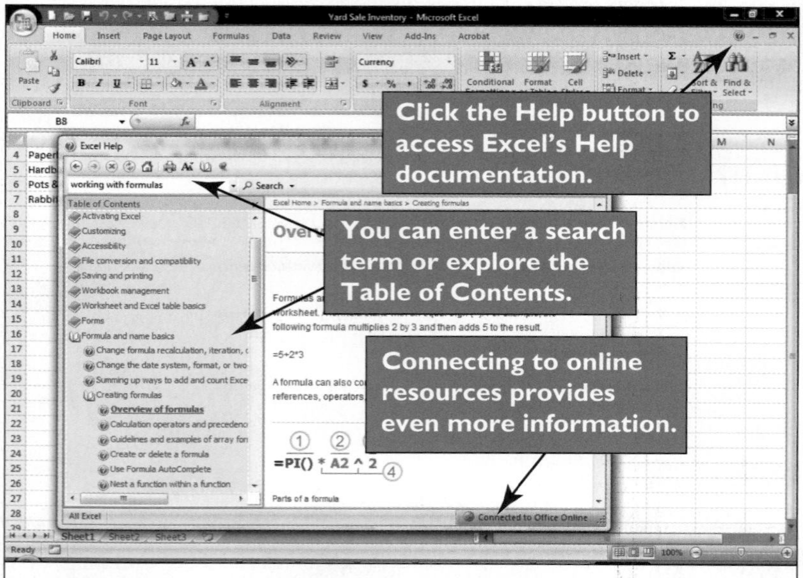

Software Licenses & Registration

A **software license** is a contract distributed with a program that gives you the right to install and use the program on one computer (Figure 5.20). Typically, to install a program on more than one computer, you must purchase additional licenses. However, some programs allow home users to install software on one or two additional computers. Always read the license to be sure.

Organizations such as colleges and universities often purchase **site licenses**, which are contracts with a software publisher that enable an organization to install copies of a program on a specified number of computers. Site licenses offer large organizations multiple software licenses at a slightly reduced cost.

In addition, when you own an original and legitimate copy of a program, you're entitled to certain warranties and guarantees. With regard to warranties, most software publishers will be happy to replace a defective CD or DVD, but that's it. The

Click the Help button to access Excel's Help documentation.

You can enter a search term or explore the Table of Contents.

Connecting to online resources provides even more information.

FIGURE 5.19 Instead of looking up information in a printed user's manual, you can use a program's Help feature to read documentation right on the computer.

software license expressly denies any liability on the publisher's part for any damages or losses suffered through the use of the software. If you buy a program that has bugs and if these bugs wipe out your data, it's your tough luck. At least that's what software companies would like you to believe. In the past, these licenses haven't stood up in court; judges and juries have agreed that the products were sold with an implied warranty of fitness for a particular use. Some unethical publishers may bundle spyware with their programs and actually include this information in their license. If you accept the license, they may claim you have no right to complain about the spyware! You should always carefully read any licensing agreement before installing software.

When you purchase a program, you may need to **validate** your software by providing a special code or product key before you can use it. Validation proves that you are using a legal copy, not a pirated version. You may also be asked to register your software. Doing so may provide you with product news or notifications about software upgrades. You may get the chance to upgrade to new versions at a lower price than the one offered to the general public. Registration may also qualify you for technical assistance or other forms of support.

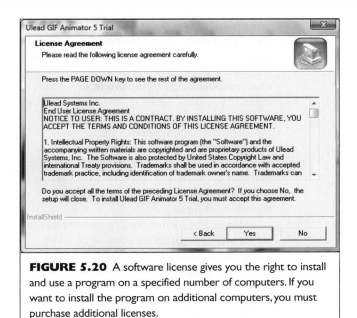

FIGURE 5.20 A software license gives you the right to install and use a program on a specified number of computers. If you want to install the program on additional computers, you must purchase additional licenses.

COMMERCIAL SOFTWARE, SHAREWARE, FREEWARE, AND PUBLIC DOMAIN SOFTWARE

The three types of copyrighted software are commercial software, shareware, and freeware. **Commercial software** is software you must pay for before using—such as Microsoft Office, Adobe Acrobat, and Apple iLife. **Shareware** refers to software that you can use on a "try before you buy" basis (Figure 5.21). If you like the program after using it for a specified trial period, you must pay a registration fee or you violate the copyright. **Freeware** refers to software given away for free, with the understanding that you can't turn around and sell it for profit. Included in the freeware category are programs distributed under the Free

Software Foundation's General Public License (GPL), such as the Linux operating system. There is one type of software that is not copyrighted. **Public domain software** is expressly free from copyright, and you can do anything you want with it, including modify it or sell it to others.

When a program includes some mechanism to ensure that you don't make unauthorized copies of it, it is called

Destinations

To learn more about software validation, visit the Genuine Microsoft Software site at **www.microsoft. com/genuine.**

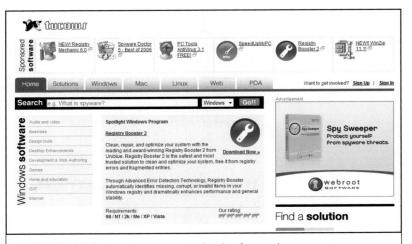

FIGURE 5.21 Shareware is copyrighted software that you can use on a "try before you buy" basis. Tucows, launched in 1993, is renowned for its large library of shareware.

copy-protected software. Examples of such software include Microsoft Office and some CDs and DVDs. Copy-protected software isn't popular with users because it often requires extra steps to install and usually requires a call to technical support if any program files become corrupted. Perhaps the loudest objection to copy-protected software, though, is that the copy-protection schemes are beginning to work. It is becoming difficult to "share" a copy of major software programs with friends and family.

Copyright or not, you're always better off owning a legitimate copy of the software you're using. It's the right thing to do, and it offers you the greatest opportunity to derive benefits from the software. You're entitled to full customer support services should anything go wrong and to add-ons or enhancements the company offers. You should also be sure that any shareware or freeware is from a reliable source.

Now that you know what to look for when you purchase application software, let's look at what to do with that software once you have it.

Installing & Managing Application Software

To use your computer successfully, you'll find it useful to understand the essential concepts and acquire the skills of using application software, including installing applications, launching and exiting applications, and choosing options. The following sections briefly outline these concepts and skills.

INSTALLING APPLICATIONS

Before you can use an application, you must install it on your computer. After you've purchased software, read the directions both before and during installation. When you purchase the right to use a software program, you are usually provided with CDs or DVDs that contain the program and an installation or setup utility. **Installing** an application involves more than transferring the software to your computer's hard disk. The program must also be configured properly to run on your system. Installation software makes sure that this configuration is performed properly.

To install an application on a computer running the Windows operating system, you insert the disk into the appropriate drive. The operating system automatically senses the insertion and attempts to locate and run an install or start-up file. You are then prompted for any necessary input as the program installs.

Should inserting the disk not invoke the installation program, you will need to click the Windows Start button and then type the drive letter designation for the drive (such as E:\) in the Start Search box. A list of the files on the disk will appear in the Start pane. Click the installation or start up file to begin the installation.

If the software was obtained from the Internet, you must first decompress it. Many programs from the Internet include decompression software; you simply open the file, and the decompression occurs automatically. Most programs are installed using a wizard. The installation wizard is a step-by-step process that installs the program in the correct location and may also provide some customization options. After the program has been installed, you will see its name in menus or on the desktop, and you can start using it.

You should know where the program is being installed, how to access it, and whether shortcuts have been created on the desktop. Shortcuts usually carry the name of the program and use the company logo for an icon. If you don't want these shortcuts on your desktop, delete them by right-clicking the icons and choosing Delete. This doesn't affect the program in any way, because a shortcut is just a pointer to a program or file. The program will still be available via the Start, Programs menu sequence.

If you later decide that you don't want to use an application, you shouldn't

Debates

Why Be a Beta Tester?

Should you be a beta tester? You may have noticed that a growing number of applications are being offered in beta versions. Users try out these preliminary versions and tell the publisher about any major bugs so they can be fixed before the applications are officially released. But there's more to it than just finding and fixing bugs. As users talk up the program to friends and colleagues, the publisher hopes more people will like what they hear and buy the program themselves (Figure 5.22).

Microsoft put Office 2007 through two rounds of beta testing, plus a "technical refresh" version for testers checking the first and second beta version's technical features. In all, more than 3.5 million testers participated, in addition to customers, partners, developers, and integrators. Sometimes Microsoft invites certain customers or partners to test a "private beta" version before it tests a "public beta" version. Like many software firms, Microsoft asks people to register and submit information about their computer systems so it can select beta testers for specific applications.

Beta testers like trying out new applications for four main reasons. First, many are power users who are extremely involved with a certain program and interested in seeing (and influencing) how it evolves. Second, testers want their voices to be heard when they give the publisher feedback about bugs, features, and functionality. Third, they really enjoy being on the cutting edge, being among the first people to try new versions. And finally, they may get the software for free or at a discount.

However, there's no guarantee that the beta version of any software will work as it should or that it will be compatible with your other software. Even though you know you'll find some bugs—after all, that's the reason for testing beta versions—you may encounter many more than you expect or have other, unexpected problems. You'll have to spend time learning the new software, which reduces your immediate productivity, and you could face security problems in the course of beta testing. To find out about upcoming beta tests, visit the BetaNews site (**www.betanews.com**), check individual software Web sites, or type "beta test" into your favorite search engine. Yes, beta testing is an important and exciting step in the development of sophisticated applications, but think carefully before you decide to participate.

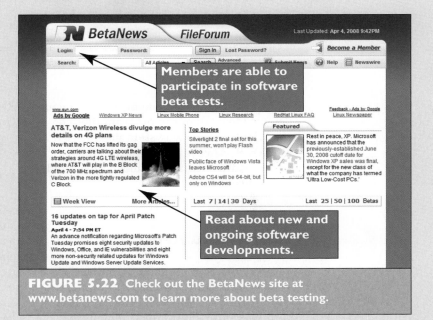

FIGURE 5.22 Check out the BetaNews site at www.betanews.com to learn more about beta testing.

just delete it from your hard disk. The proper way to remove, or uninstall, a program from your computer is to use the Windows Programs and Features utility located on the Control Panel, which is listed on the Start menu (Figure 5.23). **Uninstalling** removes the application's files from your hard disk. Choose the program that you wish to uninstall from the list of installed programs and then provide any input the uninstaller asks you for. Because most programs create library files and ancillary files in various directories, all of the files will not be removed if you simply delete the program icon or delete the program files from

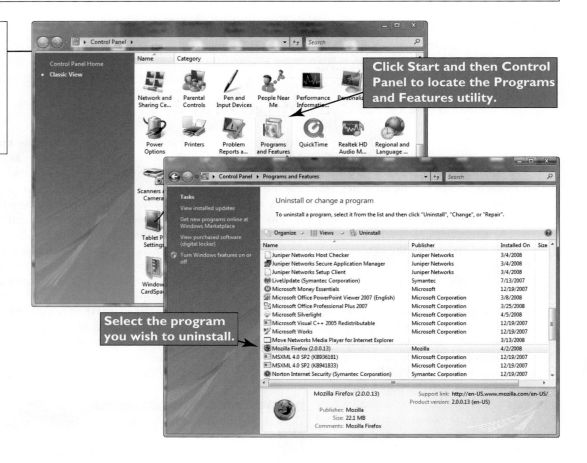

FIGURE 5.23
In Microsoft Windows, you should always use the Programs and Features utility to remove unwanted software.

Click Start and then Control Panel to locate the Programs and Features utility.

Select the program you wish to uninstall.

within the file management utility. If you don't remove all of the program files correctly, the operating system may not run efficiently. Always use the Programs and Features utility to remove unwanted programs.

LAUNCHING APPLICATIONS

After you have installed an application, you can launch it. **Launching** an application transfers the program code from your computer's hard disk to memory, and the application then appears on the screen. Programs can be launched in a number of ways. The two most reliable ways in Microsoft Windows are to click the Start menu, point to All Programs, and choose the application you want to launch or to type the program name in the Start Search text box (Figure 5.24). In the Mac OS, you locate the application's folder and double-click the application's icon. Application icons are also often available on the desktop, in the

System Tray on the taskbar, or on the Quick Launch toolbar.

CHOOSING OPTIONS

Applications typically enable you to choose **options** that specify how you want the program to operate. Your choices can change the program's **defaults**, which are the settings that are in effect unless you deliberately override them. For example, in Microsoft Word you can choose an option for displaying formatting marks on the screen—such as tabs, paragraph marks, and object anchors.

When you start working with a newly installed application, check the options menu for a setting—usually called **autosave** or **autorecover**—that automatically saves your work at a specified interval (Figure 5.25). With this option enabled, you'll ensure that you won't lose more than a few minutes' worth of work should the program fail for some reason.

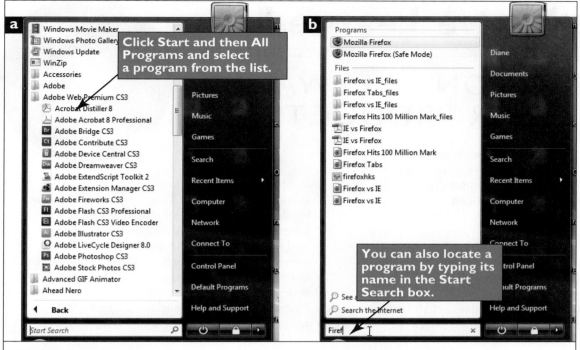

FIGURE 5.24 In Windows, (a) choose Start, All Programs to access the programs that are installed on your computer or (b) type the program's name in the Start Search box.

EXITING APPLICATIONS

When you've finished using an application, don't just switch off the computer. **Exiting** an application refers to quitting, or closing down, the program. You exit an application by choosing the Exit command from the File menu. By doing so, you ensure that the application will warn you if you've failed to save some of your work. In addition, you'll save any options you set while using the program.

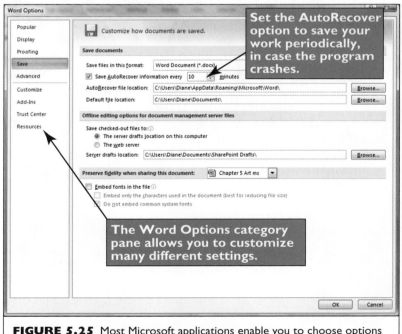

FIGURE 5.25 Most Microsoft applications enable you to choose options for program defaults by using the Office button at the top left corner of the application window.

What You've Learned

APPLICATION SOFTWARE: TOOLS FOR PRODUCTIVITY

- System software provides the environment in which application software performs tasks. Application software enables users to create, communicate, and be entertained.

- The most popular general-purpose applications are personal productivity programs, multimedia and graphics software, Internet programs, and home and educational programs.

- A standalone program provides just the software tool that you need, but it is often nearly as expensive as a complete office suite. Integrated programs are aimed at beginning users and may not include features that some users will want as they become more comfortable with the software. Most people who need personal productivity software purchase an office suite because they can save money by doing so. A potential downside is that suites tend to take up a lot of disk space and may include software that you don't need or want.

- Office suites that use Web-hosted technology are becoming popular. These programs can save data to HTML, eliminating file conversion costs, because HTML files can be read by anyone with a Web browser. The HTML format also enables the sharing of files that may otherwise be incompatible.

- Publishers often bring out new or updated versions of their software. In a version number, the whole number (such as 6 in 6.0) indicates a major program revision. A decimal number indicates a maintenance release. These numbers help you determine whether you have the latest version. Software upgrades enable you to keep your version of an application current with the marketplace by downloading and installing small changes called *patches* or major fixes called *service releases* or *service packs*.

- Commercial software is copyrighted software that you must pay for before using, such as Microsoft Office. Shareware is copyrighted but distributed on a "try before you buy" basis. You may use the program for a specified trial period without paying. Freeware is copyrighted but available for free, as long as you don't turn around and sell it. Public domain software is not copyrighted. You can do anything you want with it, including modifying it or selling it to others.

- To use your computer successfully, you need to learn the essential concepts and skills of using application software, including installing applications, launching applications, choosing options, and exiting applications.

Go to **www.pearsonhighered.com/cayf** to review this chapter, answer the questions, and complete the exercises.

Key Terms and Concepts

application software 190
autosave (autorecover) 208
beta version. 202
bit-mapped graphics
    (raster graphics). 193
codecs. 192
commercial software. 205
copy-protected software 206
custom software 199
defaults 208
documentation 204
exiting 209
freeware. 205
general-purpose
    applications 190
gMUDs (graphical
    MUDs). 198
home and educational
    programs. 197

image editors. 194
installing 206
integrated programs. 199
Internet programs 197
launching. 208
lossless compression 192
lossy compression 193
maintenance release. 202
massively multiplayer
    online role-playing
    games (MMORPGs) 198
modules 200
MUDs (multiuser dungeons
    or dimensions) 198
multimedia 192
multimedia and
    graphics software 192
options. 208
packaged software 199

personal productivity
    programs. 190
public domain software 205
ray tracing. 194
shareware 205
site licenses 204
software license. 204
software suite (office suite) . . 200
software upgrading. 202
sound files 195
standalone program 199
system requirements 202
tailor-made applications. 198
time-limited trial versions . . . 202
uninstalling. 207
validate 205
vector graphics 193
video editors 196
Web-hosted technology 201

Go to **www.pearsonhighered.com/cayf** to review this chapter, answer the questions, and complete the exercises.

Matching

Match each key term in the left column with the most accurate definition in the right column.

_____ 1. defaults

_____ 2. lossy compression

_____ 3. shareware

_____ 4. image editor

_____ 5. maintenance release

_____ 6. site license

_____ 7. lossless compression

_____ 8. video editor

_____ 9. codec

_____ 10. validate

_____ 11. module

_____ 12. MMORPG

_____ 13. MUD

_____ 14. multimedia

_____ 15. beta version

a. minor revision, indicated by a decimal number

b. function found in an integrated program

c. a contract between an organization and a software publisher permitting multiple installations

d. compression technique that permanently removes some data from the file

e. using a product key to verify the authenticity of a program

f. early versions took place in text-only environments

g. used to cut segments, sequence frames, add transitions, compress files, and determine frame rate

h. edits and transforms bit-mapped images

i. compression/decompression algorithm

j. an application involving two or more types of media, such as audio, video, or graphics

k. the software settings that are in effect until changed

l. preliminary version of a software program in the final testing phase

m. compression method that allows a file to be completely restored without any flaws

n. can be used for a specified trial period without payment

o. large groups of users work together in teams in virtual worlds hosted and maintained by the software publisher

Go to **www.pearsonhighered.com/cayf** to review this chapter, answer the questions, and complete the exercises.

Multiple Choice

Circle the correct choice for each of the following.

1. Which of the following describes transferring program code from the hard disk to memory?
   a. exiting
   b. launching
   c. defaulting
   d. autosaving

2. Copy-protected software:
   a. can be copied and shared.
   b. is known as open source software.
   c. resides in the public domain.
   d. uses a mechanism to prevent unauthorized copying.

3. Which of the following is *not* a feature of an integrated program?
   a. Modules can be purchased separately.
   b. It is targeted for beginning computer users.
   c. It is considered to be basic productivity software.
   d. Modules share the same interface.

4. Read Me files and help files are examples of which of the following?
   a. freeware
   b. documentation
   c. codecs
   d. packaged software

5. Which of the following is *not* an advantage of using Web-hosted technologies?
   a. collaboration capabilities
   b. online file storage
   c. ability to modify and share source code
   d. ability to track versions

6. Which of the following are examples of personal productivity software?
   a. word-processing and personal information management programs
   b. spreadsheets and Web browsers
   c. audio software and e-mail programs
   d. personal finance software and database programs

7. Which of the following is an example of home and education programs?
   a. presentation graphics
   b. paint, drawing, and animation programs
   c. tax preparation software
   d. videoconferencing software

8. Which of the following images can be edited and resized without edge distortion?
   a. bit-mapped graphic
   b. AVI file
   c. raster graphic
   d. vector graphic

9. WAV and MIDI files are examples of which of the following?
   a. animation files
   b. sound files
   c. video files
   d. graphic files

10. Adobe Director and Apple iLife are examples of which of the following?
    a. Internet programs
    b. multimedia authoring systems
    c. validation tools
    d. ray tracing software

Fill-In

In the blanks provided, write the correct answer for each of the following.

1. Videoconferencing, e-mail clients, and instant messaging programs are examples of _____ _____.

2. A virtual environment is brought to life in a(n) _____ MUD.

3. _____ _____ _____ is not copyrighted, is free to use, and can be used in any manner you wish.

4. The preferred method for _____ software is to use the Program and Features utility.

5. The AutoRecover feature is also known as _____.

6. To change an application's default settings, you would modify its _____ or settings.

7. _____ _____ represent the minimal level of equipment a computer needs for an application to run properly.

8. Quattro Pro and Lotus 1-2-3 are examples of _____ programs.

9. A(n) _____ _____ like Microsoft Word is fully self-contained.

10. An interconnected bundle of programs that share resources is known as a(n) _____ _____.

11. _____ _____ is a rendering technique that creates realistic 3-D images by manipulating color intensity.

12. _____ _____ are edited at the individual pixel level.

13. Targeted to a mass market, _____ _____ is designed to be immediately useful.

14. To ensure software has not been pirated, some companies require you to _____ your software by using a product key.

Short Answer

1. Visit the BetaNews site (**www.betanews.com**) and explore two of the beta programs you find. Be sure to check the reviews. Will the programs run on your operating system? Would you consider using either of the programs? Why or why not?

2. Visit **www.apple.com/support/downloads/** and choose a link to an update for application or system software. Write a paragraph that explains what the update accomplishes.

3. How do shareware, freeware, and public domain software differ? If you have ever used any of these types of software, identify the name of the product and the type of application. Describe your experience. If you have not used any of these programs, then use the Web to locate a program and report on what you learn.

4. Identify a software application you needed to uninstall, and explain why it was necessary to remove it. If the application did not uninstall completely, what directories or files still remained?

5. Visit Download.com (**www.download.com**) and locate two antispyware products. Write a report on each product's pros and cons.

Go to **www.pearsonhighered.com/cayf** to review this chapter, answer the questions, and complete the exercises.

Teamwork

1. Making Copies of Software

Have each team member answer the following questions on paper and then share your answers with each other. Have you ever made a copy of software that you've bought for yourself? Did you ever give a copy of it away? Although purchasers are permitted to make a backup copy of software that they have purchased, they are not allowed to make additional copies and distribute them to others. What are your feelings about software piracy, that is, making illegal copies of software? Originally, software applications were installed from a series of floppy disks. However, because most software is now downloaded from online or supplied on CD or DVD, copies must be burned. Do you own or have access to a burner? Write a one-page report that describes your group's findings.

2. Exploring Shareware

A full-function version of a shareware application can be downloaded, installed, and run on your computer for free for a specified period of time. After the time interval expires, your computer will not self-destruct, but the application will no longer function. Each team member should find and download at least one shareware program, try it out, and then uninstall it. As a consumer, what do you think about this method of distributing and selling software? Write a brief essay based on your findings.

3. Career-Specific Applications

For this exercise, each team member will interview a faculty member from his or her major or intended major department to find out what career-specific applications are used by professionals in that discipline. Alternatively, use the Web to find this information. Identify the discipline and the types of applications used. Explain how each application is used. Pull all of the interview material together and give a class presentation based on your findings.

4. The StarOffice Suite

Your team is to visit the StarOffice site at **www.sun.com/software/star/staroffice**. Divide the individual applications of the StarOffice suite among the team members. Each team member should learn as much as possible about his or her assigned application. How much does StarOffice cost? How would you compare the application you studied with an application you have used? For instance, compare the StarOffice word processor with the word processor you are currently using. Take a vote to determine how many team members would use StarOffice on their own computer. Write a brief report based on your findings.

5. Site Licenses

Businesses and institutions frequently use site licenses to purchase multiple copies of software applications. Your team is to contact your computing services center to find out whether your school uses this method to purchase software. If it does, identify the applications for which site licenses have been purchased. Is student home use of software applications included in the license? What is the primary advantage of purchasing site licenses for an application? If your university or college does not subscribe to site-licensed software, do research on the Web to see what you can learn about site licensing. Write a brief report based on your findings.

On the Web

1. Exploring Microsoft Office Features

Visit the Microsoft Office site at **www.office. microsoft.com** and research three links to Office features or applications that you find interesting. In a brief essay, explain to your professor what the link is, why you chose it, and what you learned.

2. Free Software

What is the difference between free software and open source software? What is public domain software? What is copyleft? Research these topics online, being sure to visit the Electronic Frontier Foundation (**www.eff.org**), the Free Software Foundation (**www.fsf.org**), and the Open Source Initiative (**www.opensource.org**). Present your findings to the class.

3. Finding Freeware

Do you want some free or inexpensive software? The Internet is frequently used to distribute shareware and freeware applications. Go to **www.yahoo.com** and type "freeware" in the Search box at the top of the window. Browse some of the more than 220 million sites returned by your search. Pick one or two to write about. Be sure that your description includes the product name, file size, function, and whatever caution you would exercise in using it.

4. Microsoft Office versus Microsoft Works

Microsoft offers two software packages that are aimed at productivity: Office for business and higher-education markets and Works for home and K–12 educational customers. Which, if either, of these products does your school use? Did you use either product when attending K–12 schools? Go to Microsoft's Works site at

www.microsoft.com/products/works to learn about this product. What is the current version of the Works suite? Name the applications that are included in this version. Which are already available as free downloads from Microsoft's Web site? What is the estimated retail price of the Works suite? Explain in a brief essay why you would or would not purchase this product.

5. Competitive Office Suites

The major competitors of Microsoft Office are Corel's WordPerfect Office, IBM's Lotus SmartSuite, and Sun's StarOffice.

- Visit the Corel Web site at **www.corel.com**. Identify the application areas and product names that are included in the professional version of Corel's office suite. What are the suggested full and upgrade prices? Are there different prices for digital and boxed versions? Is a free trial version available?
- Visit the IBM Lotus Software Web site at **www.lotus.com**. Identify the application areas and product names that are included in the professional version of the Lotus office suite. What are the suggested full and upgrade prices? Is a free trial version available?
- Visit the StarOffice site at **www.sun.com/ software/star/staroffice**. Identify the application areas and product names that are included in the professional version of the Sun office suite. What are the suggested full and upgrade prices? Are there different prices for digital and boxed versions? Is a free trial version available?

Explain in a brief essay why you would or would not purchase these products.

Capturing a Screenshot and Sending It as an E-mail Attachment

Have you ever tried to explain a weird computer problem to a technical support person or to a friend over the phone? A picture is not only worth a thousand words but also can lead to shorter technical support calls. All versions of Microsoft Windows have the built-in capability to capture a *screenshot*. A screenshot is a picture of the screen as it is displayed on your monitor. You can save a screenshot to a file that can then be printed, attached to an e-mail message, or published in a book like this one. Here are the steps for taking a screenshot and attaching the file to an e-mail message using the Web-based e-mail service Yahoo! Mail. The process of attaching a file to an e-mail message is similar for most Web-based e-mail services.

FIGURE 5.26 To take a screenshot of the entire desktop, press the Print Screen key one time.

CAPTURING A SCREENSHOT

1. When you have the screen or screens displayed on your monitor that you would like to capture, determine whether you need a screenshot of the entire desktop or just the active window. If you're trying to capture an error message, it is probably best that you take a screenshot of the entire desktop.

2. To take a screenshot of the entire desktop, press the Print Screen key one time (Figure 5.26). To capture just the currently selected window, press and hold down the Alt key and then press the Print Screen key. Nothing appears to happen, but the screenshot is copied to the Windows clipboard.

3. Launch your favorite word-processing or image-editing software, such as Microsoft Word, Microsoft Paint, or Corel WordPerfect. Because the screenshot was placed on the Windows clipboard, you will need to paste it into a document. If you're using Microsoft Word, go to the Edit menu and then choose the Paste option.

4. After the image has been pasted into a document, you can save or print the file.

ATTACHING A SCREENSHOT

1. Log on to your Yahoo! Mail account. Click the Compose button to create a mail message.

2. Enter the message text, a subject, and the e-mail address of the person who will be receiving the e-mail. It is usually good netiquette to briefly explain the contents of the attachment in the body of the e-mail message.

3. To attach a file, click the Attach Files button. You will be taken to a screen where you can attach files of up to 10 MB. To attach a file, click the Browse button next to the File 1 text input box. A standard Windows file system navigation window will appear. Locate the file you would like to attach and then click Open.

4. If you would like to attach more files, repeat the process in step 3 and choose the Browse button next to the input boxes for each file you wish to add. Click the Attach Files button, then click the Continue to Message button. When you have completed composing your message and attaching all of your screenshot files, click the Send button.

Many e-mail services limit the number and size of attachments that can be sent and received. Check to ensure that you are within the limits for e-mail attachments of screenshots.

SPOTLIGHT MICROSOFT OFFICE

Your boss asks you to create a presentation that she can deliver at the annual stockholders' meeting in two days. Although you know creating a professional presentation is a challenge, this is the opportunity you've been waiting for—you were hired, in part, because of your abilities to use productivity software programs.

You get started right away by using Microsoft Access to generate reports that are based on data that provides you with important information about your company's activities throughout the year. You then import some of the data from Access into Microsoft Excel, so that you can perform some statistical analyses and produce key charts and graphs for the stockholders. Now that you have the background materials covered, you open Microsoft Word. You paste the Excel charts and use the Report Merge feature to export reports from Access to Word using Access 2007's "Word (Export to RTF file)" button on the External Data tab in the Export group. You also type and format a meeting agenda that your boss will distribute to the attendees. Now comes the fun part: You open Microsoft PowerPoint and create a professional, visually appealing presentation using the Word, Excel, and Access documents you've already created. As you put the finishing touches on your presentation—embedding an MP3 file in the introduction slide—you realize you've finally been able to use the skills you worked so hard to acquire.

All of the programs you've used to create your presentation are components of a suite of software programs called Microsoft Office. This Spotlight explores the various programs, features, and uses of Microsoft Office (Figure 5A).

FIGURE 5A

Knowing how to use software programs, such as those in Microsoft Office, will help you gain a competitive edge in whatever career you choose.

INTRODUCING MICROSOFT OFFICE

If you intend to use a Microsoft operating system, then you will probably use the tools in the Microsoft Office suite to manage documents, spreadsheets, databases, presentations, and communications. Microsoft Office 2007 is available in eight versions. You are most likely going to use either the Home and Student edition, which includes Word, Excel, PowerPoint, and OneNote, or the Professional version, which also includes Access, Publisher, Outlook, and Accounting Express but omits OneNote. Released in early 2007, Office 2007 is the most recent version of Office for the PC on the market (Figure 5B). Office 2008 for Mac is the most current version for the Mac OS X operating environment.

In the following sections, we'll look more closely at how Office components can help you represent your thoughts, ideas, and solutions in a professional way.

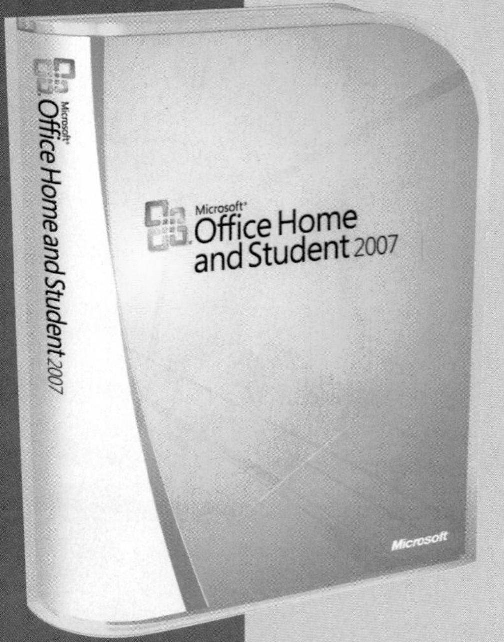

FIGURE 5B

Microsoft Office 2007 is the result of many generations of Office.

THE SHARED OFFICE INTERFACE AND TOOLS

Office applications use many interfaces that are similar to those of Windows. When an application is opened, you'll see some or all of the following features within the **application window**, the area that encloses and displays the application (Figure 5C).

The **application workspace** displays the document you are currently working on. In computing, a **document** is any type of product you create with the computer, including typewritten work, an electronic spreadsheet, or a graphic.

The topmost area of each program interface is called the **title bar**. It includes the name of the file you are working on and the name of the application. If you haven't yet saved the file, you'll see a generic file name, such as Untitled or Document1. Within the title bar, you'll also find three **window control** buttons. The left button enables you to **minimize**, or hide, the window so that it is cleared from the screen and reduced down to a button on the task bar. Simply click the task bar button to retrieve the document. The right button is used to **close** the window once you finish with the document. The middle button toggles between two functions, depending on whether the program is occupying the entire screen (known as full screen) or is a smaller size. If the window is full screen, the button is in the **restore down** mode, which means clicking it will cause the window to revert to a smaller size. If the window is not full screen, clicking this button enables you to **maximize**, or enlarge, the window so that it fills the whole screen.

In Microsoft applications, you can change the size of a window by dragging a vertical **window border** left or right or a horizontal border up or down. If you click and drag a window corner, you can size the window horizontally and vertically at the same time. Note that this process will work only if a window is not maximized.

The bottom part of the application interface, called the **status bar**, displays information about the application and the document, such as the current page number and the total number of pages.

Scroll bars are located at the right and bottom of a document. They allow you to see different parts of a document without moving your cursor or selection. You can use scroll bars and **scroll arrows** to move (scroll) through the document. Typically, you can click the scroll arrows to move line by line or drag the scroll bar to move longer distances faster.

At the top left of the application window is the **Office button**, which contains choices for creating new documents; opening existing documents; and printing, saving, and closing documents. The **Quick Access Toolbar** appears just to the right of the Office button. The Quick Access Toolbar displays a series of buttons used to perform common tasks, such as saving a document and undoing or redoing the last action. The Quick Access Toolbar is customizable, so you can add some of your favorite shortcuts to it. It remains available at all times, no matter which tab on the Ribbon is selected.

The shared interface also includes the **Ribbon** with tabs containing groups, which are positioned beneath the title bar. A **tab** contains categories of tasks you can accomplish within an application. The Ribbon enables you to manage and modify your documents. For instance, you might choose the Home tab and then in the Font group select the button for changing the font color.

Each application in Office has its own customized Ribbon of tabs. Office also has several advanced tabs, such as Add-Ins and Developer, that are not visible by default,

but can be turned on by clicking the Office button and then the Options button for that particular application at the bottom of the window. Some third-party programs, such as Adobe Acrobat, may also add helpful tabs to the Ribbon. However, the Ribbon in Word 2007 is representative of the Ribbons in other Office applications.

- **Home.** The Home tab includes many of the most frequently used features and is the default tab that appears when you open an Office program. On it you'll find groups for the clipboard, font management, paragraph settings, styles, and editing (find and replace, go to, etc).

- **Insert.** On the Insert tab, you'll find groups for working with pages, tables, illustrations, managing links, working

FIGURE 5C

These components are found in most of the Microsoft Office 2007 applications.

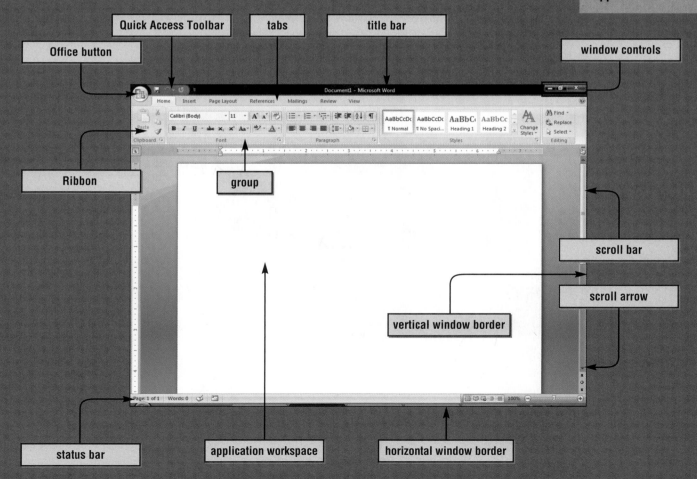

Quick Access Toolbar · tabs · title bar · Office button · window controls · Ribbon · group · scroll bar · scroll arrow · vertical window border · status bar · application workspace · horizontal window border

with headers and footers, manipulating text, and inserting symbols.

- **Page Layout.** The Page Layout tab contains groups for document themes, page setup, page background and borders, paragraph alignment, and object arrangement.

- **References.** The References tab contains groups for table of contents, footnotes, citations and bibliography, captions, indexing, and table of authorities.

- **Mailings.** The Mailings tab features groups for creating envelopes and labels, performing a mail merge, working with fields, previewing results, and finishing the merge.

- **Review.** The Review tab has groups for proofing a document, commenting, tracking changes, accepting or rejecting changes to tracking, comparing documents, and protecting documents.

- **View.** The View tab features groups for viewing a document in different ways, showing or hiding rulers and gridlines, zooming in to see different parts of a document, and window choices that allow you to work on more than one document simultaneously.

The Ribbon is a dynamic tool. Depending on what you are doing, other tabs may be displayed. For instance, if you insert a photo in a document, whenever the image is selected a Picture Tools tab appears. Such tabs are said to be **contextual** (Figure 5D).

Groups, which are located within the tabs, contain buttons and commands. The icon on each button provides a visual clue to the button's purpose. Clicking on a button causes the named action to occur. For instance, in Word, if you highlight any text and then select the Home tab, the Font group, and the Bold button (letter **B**), the highlighted text will be bolded (Figure 5E). Some groups also contain a

FIGURE 5D

Contextual tabs appear on the Ribbon to provide additional functionality when an object is inserted or selected.

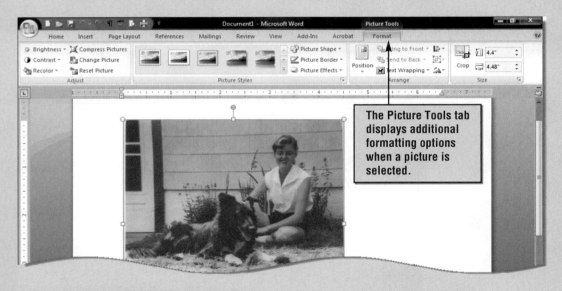

The Picture Tools tab displays additional formatting options when a picture is selected.

FIGURE 5E

Each group within a tab contains buttons and commands used to perform specific tasks.

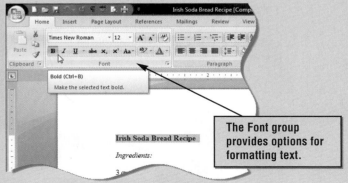

The Font group provides options for formatting text.

dialog launcher icon, which looks like a small arrow, in the bottom right corner. Clicking this icon will open a dialog box so you can make additional choices.

Office applications share a number of other resources, including the Clip Organizer and the Office Clipboard.

The **Clip Organizer** is a repository of clip art and images that can be inserted into a document or presentation (Figure 5F). You can access the Clip Organizer by selecting the Insert tab and then, from the Illustrations Group, choose the Clip Art button.

Office applications also share the Clipboard. The **Office Clipboard** temporarily stores in memory whatever you've cut or copied from a document and makes that cut or copied item available for use within any Office application. For example, you can create a financial summary in Excel, copy it to the Clipboard, and then paste it into Word.

Most Office applications also have smart tags. A **smart tag** is associated with text or data that has been entered in a document. Depending on the type of data, it may appear as a purple dotted underline or as a small icon or button. A smart tag is displayed when the program recognizes the location as a place where you might want to perform an additional task. When you click on a smart tag, an options menu appears (Figure 5G). For example, when you copy text from one place in a Word

document and paste it to another location, a Paste Options smart tag appears listing options for how the pasted text can be treated. The AutoCorrect Options smart

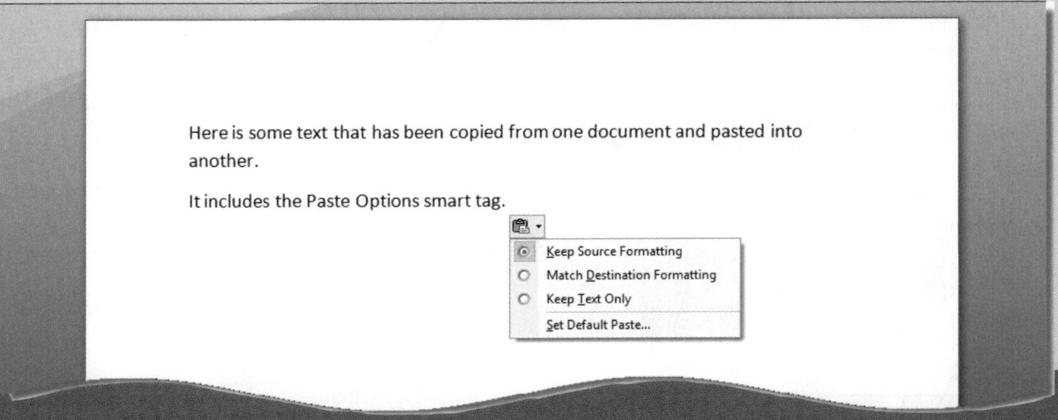

FIGURE 5F

The Clip Organizer is an efficient way to insert images into documents and presentations.

Here is some text that has been copied from one document and pasted into another.

It includes the Paste Options smart tag.

- Keep Source Formatting
- Match Destination Formatting
- Keep Text Only

Set Default Paste...

FIGURE 5G

Smart tags offer choices for completing common Office tasks and provide additional options.

tag lets you modify the program's AutoCorrect feature. Other tags such as those for dates, times, names, and addresses provide options for working with specific data.

Another feature common to Office applications is the ability to create a new document from a template. The templates vary depending on the application you are using. When you create a new document, you can start with a new blank document or a template (Figure 5H). **Templates** are document frameworks that are created once and then used many times. For example, word processing programs typically include templates for faxes, letters, memos, reports, resumes, brochures, and many more types of documents. The template may include text, formatting, graphics, and many other features.

To locate and use a template, click the Office button and select New. A New Document dialog box appears with three panes. The Template pane on the left shows the various types of template categories, including Blank and recent, Installed Templates, My templates, and New from existing. Below that is a list of categories for templates that can be downloaded from Microsoft Office Online. The middle pane displays the list of available templates within the category selected in the Template pane. The right pane shows a thumbnail view of the template selected in the middle pane. Once you've chosen the template you wish to use, click Create to open the template in a new document window. You can make any necessary changes to this document and save it. The original template will remain unchanged and will be available for use again later.

To **open** an existing document, you need to locate the document and load it into the application workspace. You can do this through the Open dialog box. Figure 5I shows the typical appearance of an Open dialog box. To open a document, select the folder that contains the document. Next, highlight the document's name. Click Open to transfer the document to the application workspace.

Now that you've gotten an overview of Office, let's explore each of the applications individually.

FIGURE 5H

Templates provide consistent background content and formatting for multiple documents.

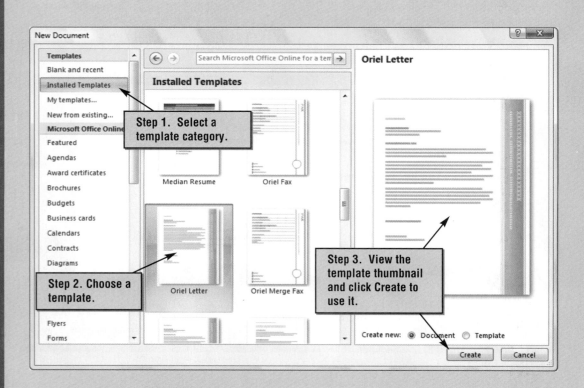

MICROSOFT WORD

Microsoft Word is a very powerful word processing program. As with other Office applications, its interface includes the title bar, the Office button, the Quick Access Toolbar, the Ribbon, and the groups of tasks that can be executed. The remainder of the screen is basically a blank sheet of paper on which you can create your documents.

Using Word at its most basic level to create short letters, memos, and faxes is extraordinarily simple; you just type text into the Word document, click the Office button, and click Print from the menu to send your document to the printer (Figure 5J). Word features automatic text wrapping, a Find and Replace utility, and the ability to cut, copy, and paste both within the document and between documents or other programs. To improve the presentation of your documents, you can use editing and formatting tools to insert headers and footers, page breaks, page numbers, and dates. Word also includes other features that can enhance your ability to present your thoughts in a formal way. For example, you can create lengthy reports and books that incorporate embedded pictures, graphics, charts, tables, and other objects. You can work with

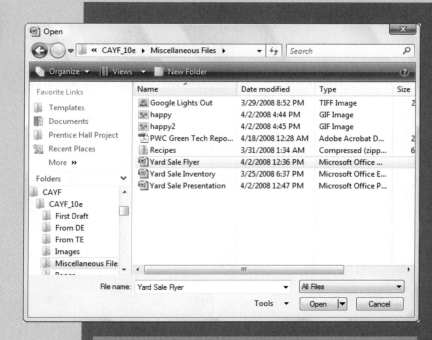

FIGURE 5I

To open a document, select the folder that contains the document, highlight the document's name, and then click Open.

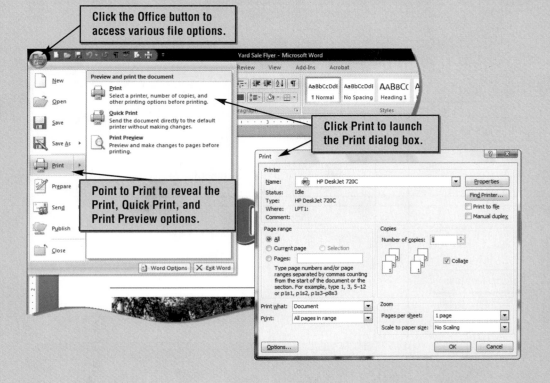

Click the Office button to access various file options.

Click Print to launch the Print dialog box.

Point to Print to reveal the Print, Quick Print, and Print Preview options.

FIGURE 5J

Use the Office button to view file options such as saving and printing.

columns and set tabs to align text. You can print your document in portrait (vertical) or landscape (horizontal) orientation. It's almost true that if you can imagine it, you can do it in Word.

If you're using a PC, the files that you create in Word 2007 include the .docx extension by default. Word can also save your documents as plain text (.txt), HTML (.htm), Rich Text Format (.rtf), or formats that can be read by previous versions of Word or by competing products, such as WordPerfect. You will learn about other Office program extensions as you continue reading this Spotlight.

Now that you have a basic understanding of what Word can do for you, you're ready to move on to other Office applications. The following section will introduce you to Excel.

MICROSOFT EXCEL

Microsoft Excel is the leading spreadsheet program for business and personal use. The primary function of a spreadsheet program is to store and manipulate numbers. You use a spreadsheet either to record things that have actually happened or to predict things that might happen through a method called **modeling**, or **what-if analysis**. Projected income statements are a good example of spreadsheet modeling. You plug in your assumed values, and the model provides the prediction. If your assumptions are correct, the model will closely match the actual outcome. If your assumptions are faulty, then you can learn from your experience and perhaps make better assumptions in the future.

Excel's user interface is very similar to that of Word. Like Word, Excel has a status bar at the bottom of the screen and scroll bars that enable you to move your view vertically and horizontally.

In Excel, each file is called a **workbook**. A workbook is made up of **worksheets**. Each worksheet is composed of **columns** and **rows**, the intersections of which are called **cells** (Figure 5K).

A cell is identified by its column letter and its row number—known as the **cell address**. The columns in a spreadsheet are identified by the letters of the alphabet; rows are represented by numbers. For example, A1, B3, and AC342 each represent an individual cell in column A, row 1; column B, row 3; and column AC, row 342, respectively.

A **range** of cells consists of two or more cells selected at the same time, and

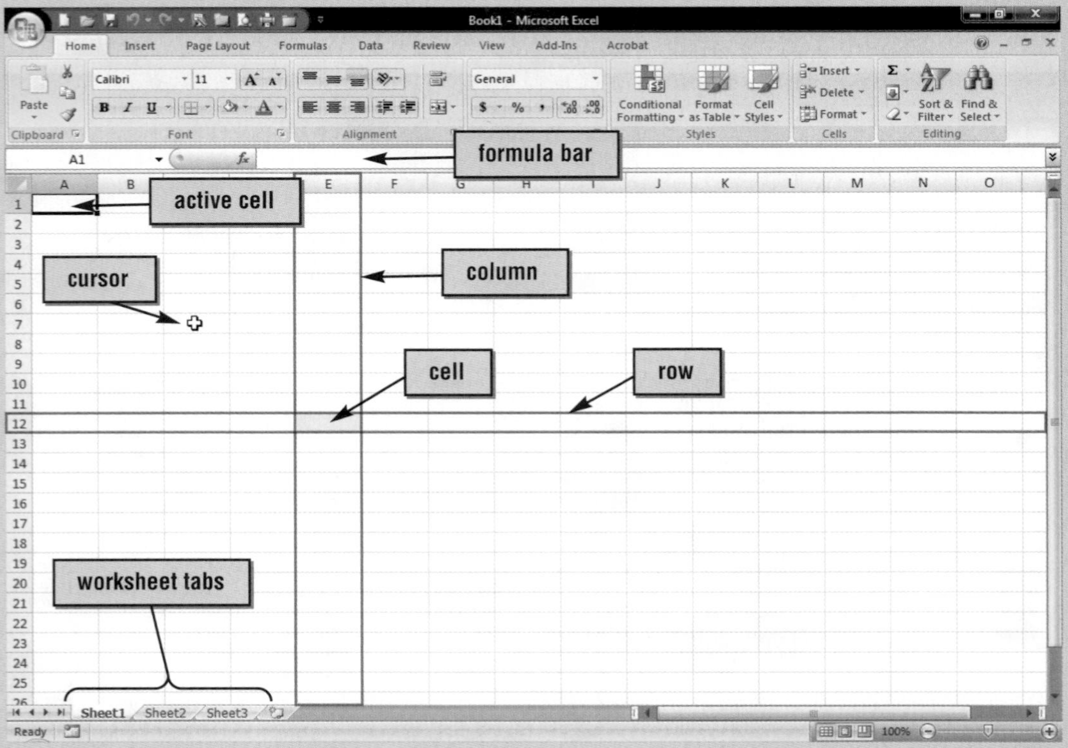

FIGURE 5K

By default, the Excel workbook includes three worksheets. Each worksheet is made up of columns and rows, the intersections of which are cells in which data can be entered.

is identified by the addresses of the top-left and bottom-right cells separated by a colon. For example, the range from cell A1 to cell D5 would be represented as A1:D5.

Cells store text, numbers, and formulas. Text entries, also referred to as **labels**, are used to identify numeric entries. For example, you might type the label "First month's rent" in cell A5 and then place the value "$650" next to it in cell B5. Labels are also used to identify typed-in numbers and the results of formulas.

A **formula** is a combination of a variety of elements, including numeric constants, cell references, arithmetic operators, or functions, that displays the result of a calculation. Excel interprets a cell entry as a formula if the entry is preceded by an equal sign (=). Formulas may be mathematical expressions or functions. In a **mathematical formula**, the mathematical order of operations is followed; that is, values in parentheses are acted on first, followed by exponentiation, multiplication and division, and then addition and subtraction. (You can remember this order of operations through the mnemonic Please Excuse My Dear Aunt Sally, or PEMDAS.) It is important to note that with PEMDAS order multiplication and division are the same rank, and addition and subtraction are also the same rank. You must evaluate from left to right for operations that are the same rank. For example, the formula =6*(4−2)/3+2 is equal to 6, because 4 minus 2 is 2, 6 times 2 is 12, 12 divided by 3 is 4, and 4 plus 2 is 6.

The other type of a formula is called a function. A **function** is a very powerful type of formula because it allows you to perform operations on multiple inputs. As an example, the payment function is able to take the rate of interest, time period, and amount borrowed to produce the payment amount on a loan. Like mathematical formulas, a function begins with the equal sign. However, it then lists the name of the function (such as PMT for calculating payments on a loan) and an argument set, which is placed within parentheses. An **argument set** contains the possible parameters or variables in a function. For example, when calculating loan payments, the argument set contains the rate of interest (6% divided by 12 monthly periods), the time period of the loan (4 years times 12 payments per year), and the amount borrowed ($18,000). For example, =PMT(6%/12,48,18000) would return the payment for a loan of $18,000 at an interest rate of 6 percent for 4 years.

Excel also has features for creating **charts**, which are a graphical representation of data (Figure 5L). Charts are based on data sets and the labels that identify

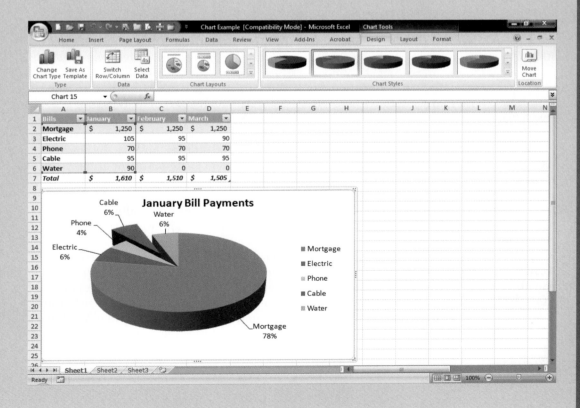

the data. There are 11 different categories of charts in Excel, and each category includes several different chart styles. The most commonly used charts are bar, column, pie, and area charts. Bar charts show the value of two or more items at the same point in time. They are good for depicting dramatic difference between positive and negative values. Column charts show two or more values side by side. Pie charts represent data as a percentage of the total. Area charts are good for depicting magnitude of change over time.

It's possible to create other types of useful charts with Excel too. Line charts illustrate trends over time. Doughnut charts have the appearance of a pie, but display more than one series. Radar charts depict frequency and change relative to a central point. Scatter charts depict two values and show relationships, usually independent of time. Surface charts present a 3-D surface that shows trends in values across two dimensions in a continuous curve. Stock charts require three series of values in the order of high, low, close. Bubble charts compare three sets of values. They are similar to scatter charts with the third value displayed as the size of a bubble. Various chart subtypes are available within each chart category. Depending on the type of chart selected, you may have the option to create 3-D charts or exploded charts, or to display data as cylinders, cones, or pyramids. Although these options can make your chart appear more interesting, it is important to make sure that your chart remains easy to read and that your data's perspective is not distorted.

Several other tools are also available for developing, managing, and assessing data. You can create pivot tables and charts (designed so that your data "pivots" about one field of interest) or sorted reports with subtotals. You can also use the database feature to extract information from your data set.

The files that you create in Excel 2007 include the .xlsx extension by default. Excel can also save your documents as plain text (.txt), HTML (.htm), eXtensible Markup Language (.xml), or in formats that can be read by previous versions of Excel.

To learn more about creating charts and reports in Excel, consult the online help at **www.microsoft.com** or use the Excel Help feature.

Next, we'll take a look at the Office application for managing databases.

MICROSOFT ACCESS

Microsoft Access is a database management system (DBMS), which is a software application designed to capture, store, manipulate, and report data and information.

The opening Access interface offers choices for opening an existing database, using a template to create a new database, or beginning a new blank database from scratch (Figure 5M). In Access, you must always work on an existing database or on a new database that you've named and saved to disk. Access does not offer a default blank database screen like the blank document in Word or the blank worksheet in Excel. Access must always work between storage and memory—you cannot work within the program without first establishing a file on disk.

Access uses objects to manage and present data. In Access, an **object** is a subprogram that manages one aspect of database management. For instance, you use the **Form object** to collect data, the **Table object** to store data, the **Query object** to ask questions of the database, and the **Report object** to present your data (Figure 5N). The functions of these four objects match your computer's input, storage, processing, and output functions. (The order is usually input, processing, output, and storage, but in a database management system, the input has to be stored before it can be processed.)

Access is capable of importing data from many sources, including Microsoft Excel. If data is not imported from an outside source, it can be entered directly into a table or by using a form. Entering data into a table is useful when you wish to see multiple records at one time. A **form** is a template with blank fields in which users input data one record at a time. You have filled out physical and electronic forms

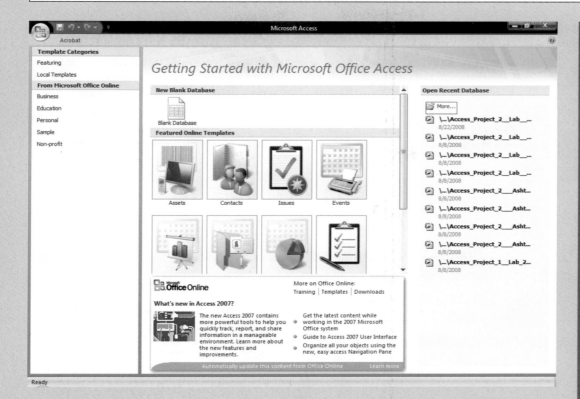

FIGURE 5M

The Access opening interface provides options for opening an existing database or creating a new database from scratch or from a selection of templates.

many times in your life. Forms should be organized so that the person who is typing in the data can easily move from one field to the next in a logical order.

To be useful, the data usually must be processed using the Query object. You can use the Query object to ask questions of a data set. A **data set** describes the contents of a table. Let's say you have a data set that includes the names and addresses of family, friends, and business associates. You want to send a mailing to your family to let them know how school has been going. To find the names and addresses of just your family members, you would run a query on your data set and set the filtering parameter to include only those names that have a field entry under the field name "family."

A **filter** uses one or more criteria to establish conditions an item must meet. Only the data that meets the conditions that have been set is allowed to pass through the filter. In this case, you are asking the Query object to provide you

with your family members and no one else. The filtering parameter is that the query will return only records where the field for "family" is checked.

When you use Access, you need to present the results of your query in a manner that is not only useful, but also professional in appearance—in short, you must design a report. We receive reports from databases all the time. Junk mail, utility bills, and credit card solicitations all come from reports that have been generated from massive data sets.

Access 2007 uses the .accdb file extension by default.

To learn more about how to use Access, visit the online help provided at **www.microsoft.com**. You can also use the Access wizards to create the objects that you'll need to manage whatever projects you may undertake.

Let's now look at a program that's a favorite among many college students: PowerPoint.

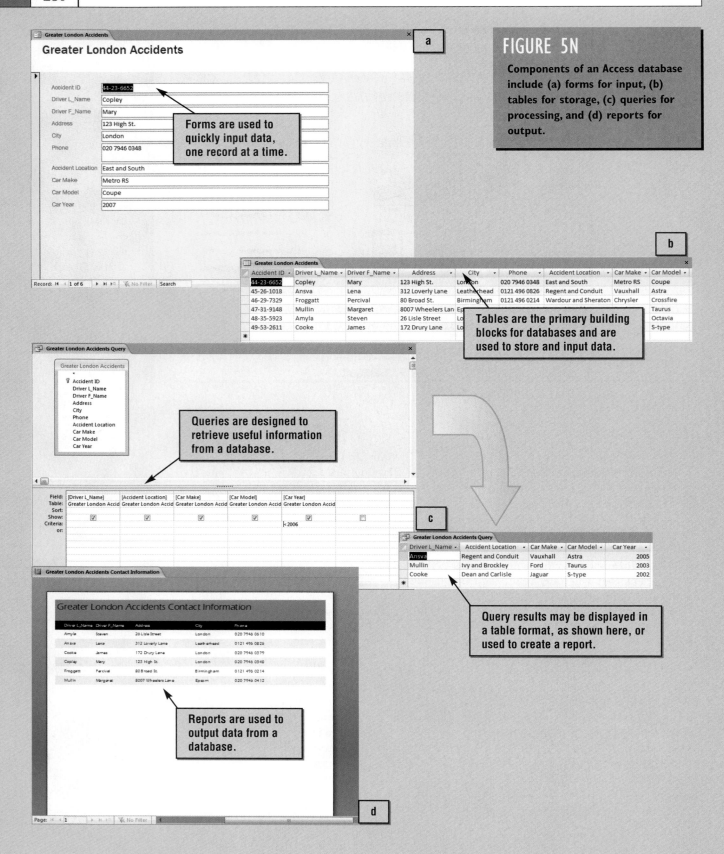

FIGURE 5N

Components of an Access database include (a) forms for input, (b) tables for storage, (c) queries for processing, and (d) reports for output.

a Forms are used to quickly input data, one record at a time.

b Tables are the primary building blocks for databases and are used to store and input data.

c Queries are designed to retrieve useful information from a database.

Query results may be displayed in a table format, as shown here, or used to create a report.

d Reports are used to output data from a database.

MICROSOFT POWERPOINT

Microsoft PowerPoint is a popular program used to create and deliver presentations. When you open PowerPoint, you are presented with a blank slide that is in the Title slide format (Figure 5O). A **slide** is the canvas on which you organize text boxes and graphics to represent your ideas or points. PowerPoint offers nine slide layouts. Each layout has text boxes for inserting text or graphics boxes for embedding graphics. These boxes are often referred to as placeholders. The various boxes are in a set position on the slide canvas, but you can modify the size or position of the placeholders by using your mouse or by selecting one and using the appropriate tools on the Ribbon. There are different layouts to choose from for each slide. For example, a Title slide has two text boxes. The top box is for the title of your presentation, and the bottom box is for a subtitle or your name. You might choose Title and

Text as the layout for your second slide, because it has a text box for the title at the top of the slide and a bulleted list text box for the major presentation points on the lower portion of the slide.

A PowerPoint template contains pre-formatted fonts, locations for text and graphics, and color schemes. **Design templates** are professionally created slide designs that can be applied to a presentation. You might create your slides in the blank presentation (black and white, with no special fonts or effects) and then apply various design templates until you achieve the desired effect (Figure 5P). Some of the templates are casual or festive, whereas others are appropriate for business purposes. As you create your presentation, keep in mind that the design template used should match the purpose and content of the presentation.

Click the Office button and then click New to open the New Presentation window. In the left pane, Microsoft Office Online includes presentation categories for home and business projects.

It is often helpful to create an outline for your topic (either by hand or with

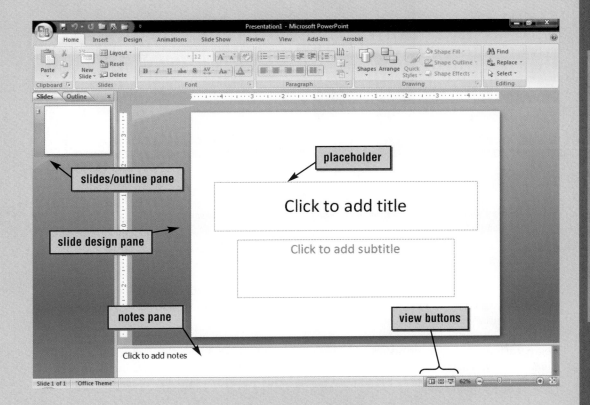

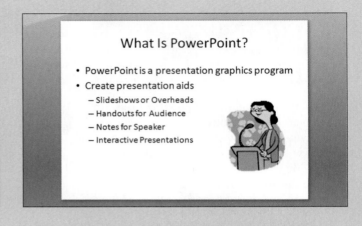

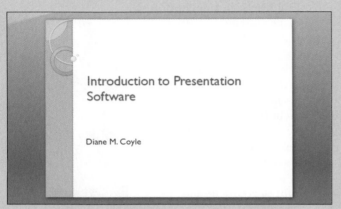

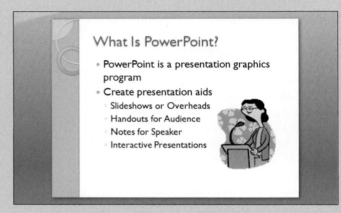

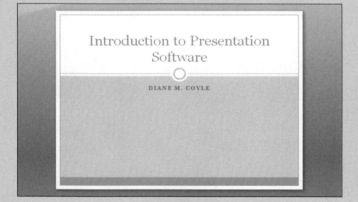

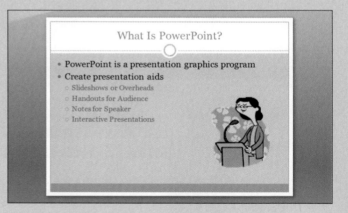

FIGURE 5P

Design templates provide a way to change the look and feel of your presentation to suit your audience.

Word) before starting PowerPoint. Once you've done so, you are ready to create your presentation. The easiest way to begin is with a blank presentation. If you begin with a blank presentation, you will perform an iterative process of typing in your text, choosing whether to include graphics, inserting a new slide that is based on a slide layout template, and then repeating.

It's very easy to get caught up in all the bells and whistles available in PowerPoint. Ultimately, though, *you* are the presenter, and therefore *you* must command your audience. A good PowerPoint slideshow should serve as a backdrop to your presentation; it shouldn't be the main feature (Figure 5Q).

Be forewarned: Presentations on a video projector almost never look the same as they do on your computer screen. With this in mind, it's a good idea to try out your presentation in the room where you'll give it. If you allow yourself plenty of time, you'll be able to change the design template to colors that will work best in the room.

PowerPoint 2007 applies the .pptx extension by default. PowerPoint can also save your documents as HTML (.htm); in various graphics formats, such as .jpg and .gif; or in formats that can be read by previous versions of PowerPoint.

Let's now move on to a program that will help you communicate with others and manage your busy schedule: Microsoft Outlook.

FIGURE 5Q

A PowerPoint slideshow should serve as an aid or supplement to a presentation—the presenter should be the primary focus of the audience.

MICROSOFT OUTLOOK

Microsoft Outlook is an e-mail and organizational communications tool that you can use to send and receive mail, maintain a personal calendar, schedule meetings with coworkers, and store information about your personal contacts. Figure 5R shows two aspects of the Outlook interface.

When you use the e-mail function of Outlook, you obviously need to know the recipient's e-mail address. An e-mail address might look like **student@college. edu**. Outlook has an autocomplete feature that suggests the completion of an address you've previously used as you type on the To: line. For example, if you begin typing **myfriend@yahoo.com** the autocomplete feature suggests the complete address when you type the first letter, m, in myfriend. If the suggestion is correct, press the Enter key to insert the address. If the suggestion is not the address you intend, then simply keep typing the correct address.

One feature of Outlook that is very helpful is the ability to create folders, which you can use to organize your saved e-mail messages. For example, you could create a Family folder for family mail, a separate folder for each of your classes, and perhaps a Friends folder for personal messages you've received from friends. Placing mail that you've read in these folders will then help you keep your inbox uncluttered.

You may find the Outlook calendar helpful in managing all of the activities associated with school, work, and socializing. The calendar is very easy to use and even includes an alarm to alert you 5, 10, 15, or 30 minutes, or some specified number of hours or days before a scheduled event.

The best way to learn how to use Outlook is to experiment with it. Also remember that you can use the Help program to learn how to use the various features Outlook includes. You'll be surprised at just how easy it is to manage Outlook.

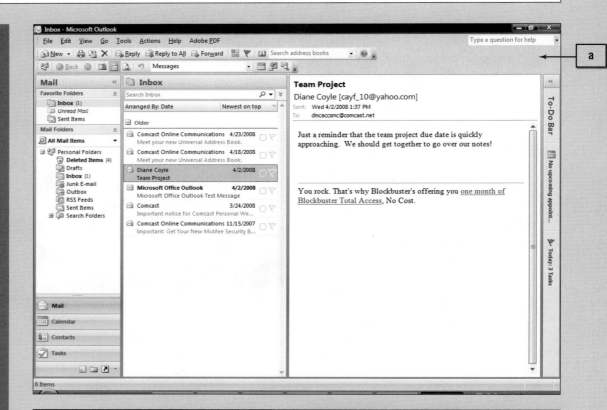

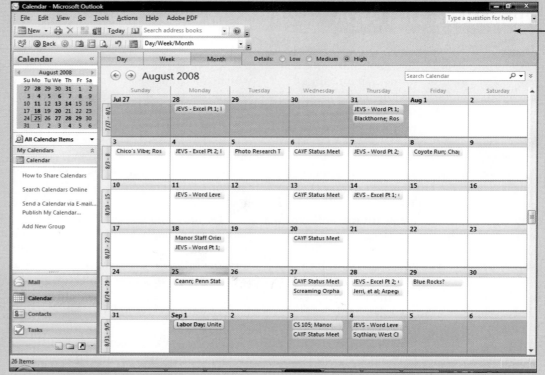

FIGURE 5R

Outlook helps you organize and manage your e-mail (a), and the calendar (b) is a good way to keep track of your college schedule and personal activities.

SPOTLIGHT EXERCISES

1. Open any Microsoft Office application from the Start, All Programs, Microsoft Office menu sequence. Click the Help button below the title bar. In the Help window, if the status bar displays Offline, click the Offline button and select Show content from Office Online. Find the links for What's new and Accessibility. Prepare a list that compares the minimum system requirements against the specifications of the computer you use most often. Be sure to list the version of Office that you are assessing.

2. Open Microsoft Word, click the Office button, and then click New to open the New Document window. In the left pane, under Microsoft Office Online, click the Featured category. In the middle pane, scroll down to locate the option or box that offers additional Microsoft Office Online information. Click the Templates link. Browse the site to learn about at least two templates. Write a short report that describes what you have learned.

3. Open Microsoft Excel from the Start, All Programs, Microsoft Office menu sequence. Click any cell to select it, type in "Cars," and then press the Enter key. Next, type in "Trucks," press Enter, and then type "Buses." Next, type a number next to each vehicle type. Select the Cars cell and hold down the left mouse button as you drag down through the vehicles and then over to the bottom number. Choose the Insert tab and then in the Charts group choose the column button. Use the mouse to move the chart around and resize it by clicking and dragging the sizing handles. Print the chart so that your professor can see what you've accomplished.

4. Open PowerPoint from the Start, All Programs, Microsoft Office menu sequence. Click the Office button, and then click New to open the New Presentation window. In the left pane, choose a category under Microsoft Office Online. Choose a subcategory in the middle pane, if necessary, and then double-click a template to download it. Fill the presentation with true or fictitious information. Have some fun with this—see if you can change the backgrounds or patterns. Hint: Click the Design tab. Click the Office button, point to the arrow to the right of the Print button, and then click Print. In the Print what drop-down list, select Handouts. In the Slides per page drop-down list, select 6. Staple the pages together and give them to your professor.

5. You can customize the Quick Access Toolbar by choosing the down pointing arrow at the right side of the toolbar. Experiment with adding and removing icons. Move the toolbar below the Ribbon. Write a short memo to your instructor that explores some of the pros and cons of adding buttons to the Quick Access Toolbar. Be sure to include your thoughts about how many icons you think would be enough and how many would be too many. Explain your reasoning.

What You'll Learn . . .

- Understand how computers represent data.

- Understand the measurements used to describe data transfer rates and data storage capacity.

- List the components found inside the system unit and explain their use.

- List the components found on the computer's motherboard and explain their role in the functioning of the computer's systems.

- Discuss (in general terms) how a CPU processes data.

- Explain the factors that determine a microprocessor's performance.

- List the various types of memory found in a computer system and explain the purpose of each.

- Describe the various physical connectors on the exterior of the system unit and explain their use.

Inside the System Unit

CHAPTER OUTLINE

How Computers Represent Data 238
    Representing Data as Numbers 238
    Representing Characters: Character Code 240

Introducing the System Unit 240

Inside the System Unit 240

What's on the Motherboard? 244
    The CPU: The Microprocessor 245
    The Chipset and the Input/Output Bus 251
    Memory. 251

What's on the Outside of the Box? 253
    The Front Panel. 253
    Connectors and Ports. 254

A computer performs four basic functions: inputting data, processing data, displaying the results using output devices, and storing the results for subsequent use. Computer hardware, especially the system unit, is involved in all of these functions.

The term **performance** refers to how fast a computer can obtain, process, display, and store data. To communicate knowledgeably with others about computer hardware capabilities, you need to know the terminology that's used to describe *how* computers represent data as well as *how much* data computers can transfer or store.

Computer performance is often equated with the speed of a computer's processor; however, the processor's capabilities are only part of the picture. Imagine that you have an engine that produces 500 horsepower. If you put this engine into your stock sedan and aggressively apply that horsepower, parts of the car will begin to break apart. The stock transmission, drive train, and axles are not designed to handle so much power. Your tires and wheels may not be able to handle the transfer of energy to the pavement. You will have an engine that you cannot fully use. It's the same with computers—all of the components need to be matched with regard to speed and performance.

In this chapter, you'll learn how computers represent data as well as how the components inside and outside the system unit process that data.

How Computers Represent Data

Computers can't do anything without data to work with. For a computer to work with data, the data must be represented by digits.

REPRESENTING DATA AS NUMBERS

We're all used to counting with decimal numbers, which consist of 10 digits (0, 1, 2, 3, 4, 5, 6, 7, 8, 9). Computers count with **binary numbers** (also called binary

digits, or bits for short), which consist of only two digits, 0 and 1. A **bit** is the smallest unit of information that a computer can work with (Figure 6.1).

You can think of a bit as being like a light switch: It has only two possible states, and it is always in one or the other. If you have one light switch, then the switch is either on or off. If you have two light switches, then you have four possibilities: both switches are on, both switches are off, the first switch is on and the second switch is off, or the first switch is off and the second switch is on. Three switches allow for eight possibilities, and so on, up to eight switches, which results in 256 possible combinations.

A **byte** consists of eight bits and represents one unit of storage. Because it takes eight bits (on/off switches) to make a byte, and eight bits results in 256 possible on/off combinations, you'll see the number 256 appearing behind the scenes in many computer functions and applications. A single byte usually represents one character of data, such as the essential numbers (0–9), the basic letters of the alphabet, and the most common punctuation symbols. For this reason, you can use the byte as a baseline for understanding just how much information a computer is storing. For example, a typical college essay contains 250 words per page, and each word contains (on average) 5.5 characters. Therefore, the page contains approximately 1,375 characters. In other words, you need about 1,375 bytes of storage for one page of a college paper.

Bits (1s and 0s) are commonly used for measuring the data transfer rate of computer communications devices such as modems. To describe rapid data transfer rates, the measurement units **kilobits**

Binary digit	0	1
Bit	○	●
Status	On	Off

FIGURE 6.1 A binary number is composed of binary digits, or bits for short. A bit is the smallest unit of information that a computer can work with.

FIGURE 6.2 Units of Data

Units	Abbreviation	Amount	Text
Bit	b		none
Kilobits per second	Kbps	1 thousand bits per second	125 characters
Megabits per second	Mbps	1 million bits per second	125 pages
Gigabits per second	Gbps	1 billion bits per second	125,000 pages
Byte	B	8 bits	one character
Kilobyte	KB	1 thousand bytes	one page
Megabyte	MB	1 million bytes	1,000 pages
Gigabyte	GB	1 billion bytes	1,000 books
Terabyte	TB	1 trillion bytes	1 million books

Techtalk

yottabytes
Because computers use binary numbers to store data, a kilobyte is not exactly 1,000 bytes. The exact measurement is 1,024 bytes (2^{10}). However, the exact amount is close enough that you can think in rounded, approximate terms (1 thousand, 1 million, or 1 billion) for most purposes. Terms that are becoming more prevalent are terabyte (1 trillion), petabyte (1 quadrillion), exabyte (1 quintillion), zettabyte (1 sextillion), and yottabyte (1 septillion). A yottabyte is 2^{80}—a very large number!

per second (**Kbps**), **megabits per second (Mbps)**, and **gigabits per second (Gbps)** are used. These respectively correspond (roughly) to 1 thousand, 1 million, and 1 billion bits per second. Remember that these terms refer to *bits* per second, not *bytes* per second.

Bytes are commonly used to measure data storage. The measurement units **kilobyte (KB)**, **megabyte (MB)**, **gigabyte (GB)**, and **terabyte (TB)** are used to describe the amount of data the computer is managing either in memory or in longer-term storage on disk. Figure 6.2 shows these units and the approximate equivalent of text data for each.

Binary numbers are difficult to work with because many digits are required to represent even a small number. For example, when you enter the decimal number 14 into your computer, the binary number representation is 1110. In addition, it's time-consuming for computers to translate binary numbers into their decimal equivalents. For these reasons, computers translate binary numbers into **hexadecimal (hex** for short) **numbers** using the numbers 0 through 9 and the letters A through F. For example, the letter K is represented as the lengthy binary number 01001011 and then quickly translated to 4B in hex (Figure 6.3).

FIGURE 6.3 Decimal, Binary, and Hexadecimal Numbers

Decimal Number	0	1	2	3	4	5	6	7	8	9	10	11	12	13	14	15
Binary Number	0	1	10	11	100	101	110	111	1000	1001	1010	1011	1100	1101	1110	1111
Hexadecimal Number	0	1	2	3	4	5	6	7	8	9	A	B	C	D	E	F

Representing Very Large and Very Small Numbers

To represent and process numbers that have fractional parts (such as 1.25) or are extremely large, computers use **floating-point notation**. The term *floating point* suggests how this notation system works: no fixed number of digits is before or after the decimal point, so the computer can work with very large as well as very small numbers. Floating-point notation requires special processing circuitry, which is generally provided by the floating-point unit (FPU). On modern computers, one or more FPUs are integrated with the CPU, but on older computers the FPU was sometimes a separate chip called the *math coprocessor*.

It would be difficult to use computers if they just spat out numbers at us. Fortunately, thanks to character code, we can understand computer output.

REPRESENTING CHARACTERS: CHARACTER CODE

Character code translates between the computer's numeric world and the letters, numbers, and symbols called **characters** that we're accustomed to using. Computers can recognize several different character codes.

ASCII, EBCDIC, and Unicode

The most widely used character code is **ASCII** (pronounced "ask-ee"), the **American Standard Code for Information Interchange**, which is used on minicomputers, personal computers, and computers that make information available over the Internet. IBM mainframe computers and some other systems use a different code, **EBCDIC** (pronounced "ebb-see-dic"), **Extended Binary Coded Decimal Interchange Code**.

Although ASCII and EBCDIC contain some foreign-language symbols, neither is sufficient in a global computer market. **Unicode** can represent many, if not most, of the world's languages.

Now that you understand bits, bytes, and how computers represent data, let's take a closer look at the system unit, where these concepts will come into play.

Introducing the System Unit

The **system unit** is a boxlike case that houses the computer's main hardware components (Figure 6.4). The system unit is more than just a case: it provides a sturdy frame for mounting internal components, including storage devices and connectors for input and output devices; it protects those components from physical damage; and it keeps them cool. A good case also provides room for system upgrades, such as additional disk drives.

System units come in a variety of styles. In some desktop computing systems, the system unit is a separate metal or plastic box. Originally, these cases were horizontal and sat on top of a desk, often with a monitor sitting on top, thus the name "desktop." To minimize the space it occupied, the case needed to have a small **footprint** (the amount of room taken up by the case on the desk). However, a small case didn't always allow enough room for add-on components. The **tower case**, a system unit case designed to sit on the floor next to a desk, provided the solution. The tower case has a vertical configuration, being tall and deep. A smaller version is called a **minitower case**.

In notebook computers and PDAs, the system unit contains all of the computer's components, including input components (such as a keyboard) and the display. All-in-one computers, such as Apple's iMac, contain the display within the system unit (Figure 6.5).

System units also vary in their form factor. A **form factor** is a specification for how internal components, such as the motherboard, are mounted in the system unit.

Now that you know what the system unit is, let's look at what's inside.

Inside the System Unit

Most computer users don't need to open their system unit; they receive their computer in a ready-to-use package. However, if you ever do need to open your system

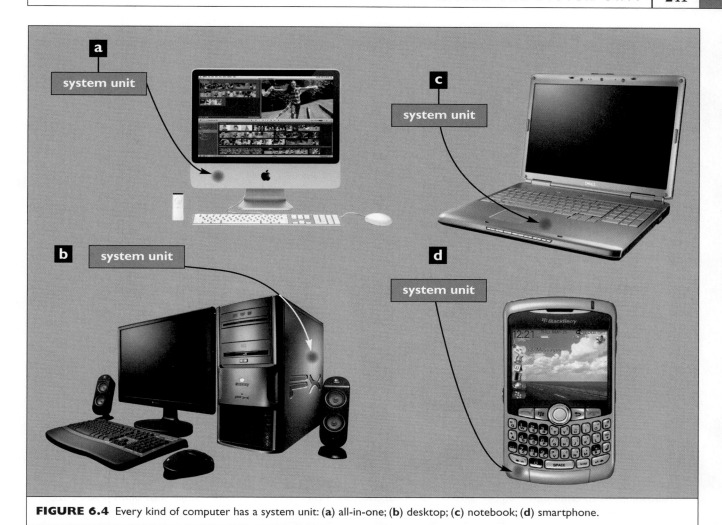

FIGURE 6.4 Every kind of computer has a system unit: (**a**) all-in-one; (**b**) desktop; (**c**) notebook; (**d**) smartphone.

FIGURE 6.5
(**a**) The Apple iMac's system unit sits on top of the desk and also contains the computer's display. (**b**) The Mac Pro has a tower case that sits on the floor next to the desk.

CURRENTS

Safety and Security

Playing It Really Safe

You might accidentally disclose your password or lose your smart card, but you can't easily change your fingerprints or your retina. That's the idea behind biometric authentication, verifying your identity by using hardware to check a unique personal characteristic before allowing access to a computer system. Characteristics may include facial geometry, ear shape, vein patterns, DNA recognition, voice recognition, or odor composition. In the future, you might carry your biometric data with you on a smart card or other chip-equipped token. To use an ATM or to pay for groceries, you would insert the token and look into the retinal scanner or put your finger on a sensor. The system would then check that the biometrics matched before allowing you to continue.

As individualized as biometric authentication may be, it can be fooled. Security experts have been able to lift fingerprints from a computer's previous user and reuse them to gain access. They have also duped face-recognition systems by showing the camera a color photo or a digital video of an authorized user. This is why researchers are working on new authentication methods, such as identifying users by the way they walk or taking fingerprints from three fingers before allowing access.

Even when fraud isn't involved, the environment around the authentication device can interfere with accuracy. Suppose you were on a crowded street corner trying to withdraw money from an ATM that controls access through voice recognition. If the noise level were too high or a police siren were wailing in the background, chances are you wouldn't be able to get into your account because the security system wouldn't be able to recognize your voice. Or say you were at an ATM that authenticates identity through facial geometry. If the light was too dim or part of your face was in shadow, the security system probably wouldn't get a clear enough picture to compare with the facial features in your file. Again, no access and no money.

Finally, a fingerprint or retinal scan that enabled your access to a computer system in the United States might not work if you tried to gain remote access when you were outside the country. The reason: No international standards exist for biometric authentication. This means you're either locked out of the system—you wouldn't be able to get money from an ATM in another country—or you would need a different way to verify your identity. Someday you may have to breathe on a special sensing device, insert a small token, and enter a password to gain access to a computer system. Setting up three levels of biometric authentication will not be cheap, but it will add another layer of security to keep sensitive data safe (Figure 6.6).

FIGURE 6.6 Biometric authentication devices such as this fingerprint reader help ensure access identification and security.

unit, bear in mind that the computer's components are sensitive to static electricity. If you touch certain components while you're charged with static electricity, you could destroy them. Always disconnect the power cord before opening your computer's case and discharge your personal static electricity by touching something that's well grounded. If it's one of those low-humidity days when you're getting shocked every time you touch a doorknob, don't work on your computer's internal components.

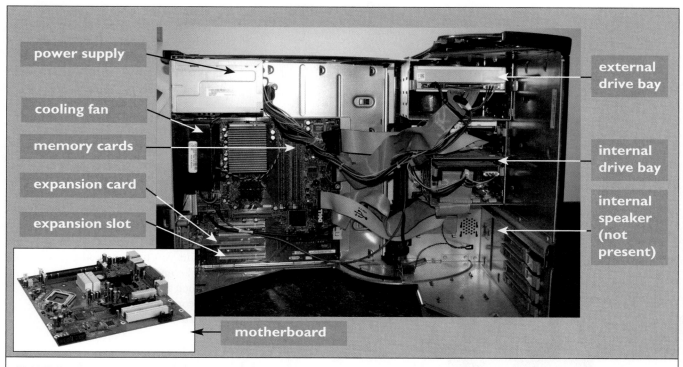

power supply

cooling fan

memory cards

expansion card

expansion slot

external drive bay

internal drive bay

internal speaker (not present)

motherboard

FIGURE 6.7 Inside the system unit, you'll find the motherboard, the power supply, a cooling fan, an internal speaker, internal drive bays, external drive bays, and various expansion cards (such as the sound card and network interface card).

If you do open your system unit, you'll see the following components (Figure 6.7):

- **Motherboard.** The **motherboard** contains the computer's CPU. You'll learn more about the motherboard and the CPU later in the chapter; for now, remember that the CPU is the computer in the strictest sense of the term; all other components (such as disk drives, monitors, and printers) are peripheral to, or outside of, the CPU.

- **Power supply.** A computer's **power supply** transforms the alternating current (AC) from standard wall outlets into the direct current (DC) needed for the computer's operation. It also steps the voltage down to the low level required by the motherboard. Power supplies are rated according to their peak output in watts. A 350-watt power supply is adequate for most desktop systems, but 500 watts provides sufficient voltage if you plan to add many additional components.

- **Cooling fan.** The computer's components can be damaged if heat accumulates within the system unit. A **cooling fan** keeps the system unit cool. The fan often is part of the power supply, although some high-powered systems include auxiliary fans to provide additional cooling.

- **Internal speaker.** The computer's **internal speaker** is useful only for the beeps you hear when the computer starts up or encounters an error. Current computers include a sound card and external speakers for better quality sound.

- **Drive bays. Drive bays** accommodate the computer's disk drives, such as the hard disk drive, CD or DVD drive, and portable drives. Internal drive bays are used for hard disks that are permanently contained within the drive's case. Therefore, they do not enable outside access. External drive bays mount drives that are accessible from the outside (a necessity if you need to

Green Tech Tip

The Climate Savers Computing Initiative (**www.climatesavers computing.org**), whose members include Intel and Google, along with more than 30 other organizations, is working to save energy and reduce greenhouse gas emissions. They hope to reach a 90 percent efficiency rate for computer power supplies by 2010, which could result in $5.5 billion or more in reduced energy costs. The corresponding reduction in greenhouse gases would be equivalent to removing more than 11 million cars from the road.

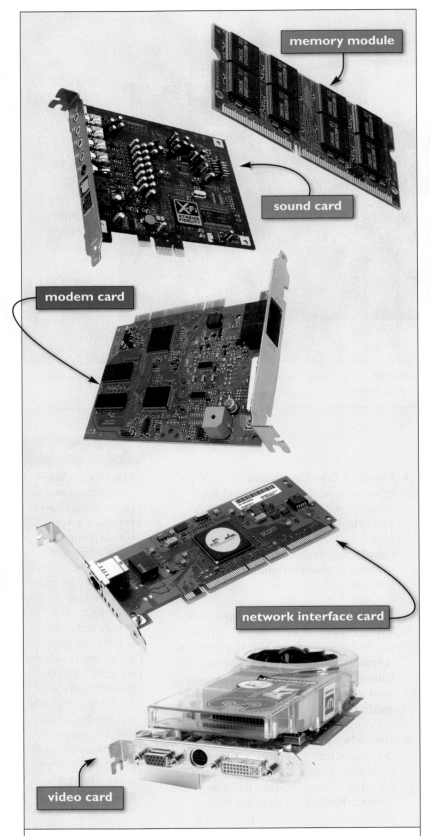

FIGURE 6.8 Expansion cards enable you to add enhancements to your system.

insert and remove disks from the drive). External drive bays vary in size. Some bays accommodate 5.25-inch drives (for CD or DVD drives), whereas others are designed for 3.5-inch drives (for older floppy or Zip drives).

- **Expansion slots.** The system unit also contains **expansion slots**, which are receptacles that accept additional circuit boards or expansion cards. Examples of expansion cards are memory modules, sound cards, modem cards, network interface cards (NICs), and video cards (Figure 6.8).

Now that you have a good overview of the internal components of the system unit, let's look more closely at the most important component: the computer's motherboard.

What's on the Motherboard?

The motherboard is a large printed circuit board, a flat piece of plastic or fiberglass that contains thousands of electrical circuits etched onto the board's surface (Figure 6.9). The circuits connect numerous plug-in receptacles, which accommodate the computer's most important components (such as the microprocessor). The motherboard provides the centralized physical and electrical connection point for the computer's most important components. Most of the components on the motherboard are integrated circuits. An **integrated circuit (IC)**, also called a **chip**, carries an electric current and contains millions of transistors. A **transistor** is an electronic switch (or gate) that controls the flow of electrical signals to the circuit. A computer uses such electronic switches to route data in different ways, according to the software's instructions. Encased in black plastic blocks or enclosures, most chips fit specially designed receptacles or slots on the motherboard's surface.

So what do these chips do? Let's look at some of the most important components you'll see on the motherboard: the CPU (or microprocessor), the system clock, the chipset, input/output buses, and memory.

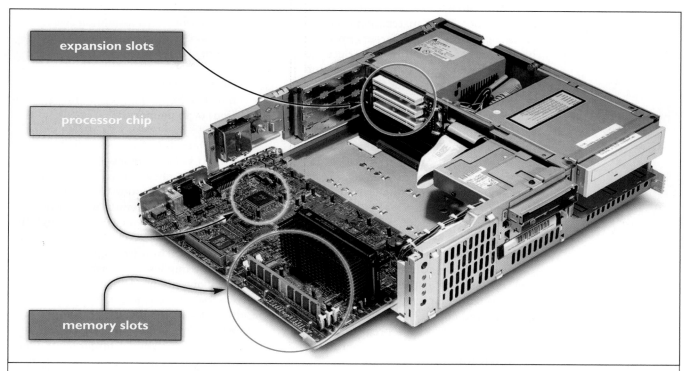

expansion slots

processor chip

memory slots

FIGURE 6.9 This example of a typical PC motherboard shows its processor chip and the expansion and memory slots.

THE CPU: THE MICROPROCESSOR

The **central processing unit (CPU)** is a **microprocessor** (or **processor** for short), an integrated circuit chip that is capable of processing electronic signals. It interprets instructions given by software and carries out those instructions by processing data and controlling the rest of the computer's components. Carefully inspect your environment and you'll find that processors are found in all kinds of electronic and mechanical devices such as cell phones, calculators, automobile engines, and even industrial and medical equipment. They process information so that humans can enjoy their effective and efficient operation. No other single element of a computer determines its overall performance as much as the CPU.

Although microprocessors are complex devices, the underlying ideas are easy to understand. When you're ready to buy a computer, you'll need to understand the capabilities and limitations of a given microprocessor.

Processor Slots and Sockets

An integrated circuit of fabulous complexity, a microprocessor plugs into a motherboard in much the same way that other integrated circuits do. However, special slots and sockets accommodate microprocessors. Part of the reason for this is that microprocessors are larger and have more pins than most other chips. In addition, microprocessors generate so much heat that they could destroy themselves or other system components. The microprocessor is generally covered by a **heat sink**, a heat-dissipating component that drains heat from the chip. To accomplish this, the heat sink may contain a small auxiliary cooling fan. The latest high-end microprocessors include their own built-in refrigeration systems, which are needed to keep these speedy processors cool.

The Instruction Set

Every processor can perform a fixed set of operations, such as retrieving a character from the computer's memory or comparing two numbers to see which is larger. Each of these operations has its own

Destinations

The Intel Museum (**www.intel.com/museum**) gives visitors a chance to see how chips are manufactured. For those who can't visit in person, Intel's "How Chips Are Made" feature (**www.intel.com/education/makingchips**) provides a nicely illustrated overview of the chip fabrication process.

unique number, called an instruction. A processor's list of instructions is called its **instruction set**. Different processors have different instruction sets. Because each processor has a unique instruction set, programs devised for one type of CPU won't run on another. For example, a program written for an Intel chip won't run on a Motorola chip. A program that can run on a given computer is said to be compatible with that computer's processor. Alternatively, if a program is compatible, it's said to be a native application for a given processor design.

The Control Unit and the Arithmetic-Logic Unit

CPUs contain two subcomponents: the control unit and the arithmetic-logic unit. The **control unit** extracts instructions from memory and decodes and executes them. Under the direction of a program, the control unit manages four basic operations (Figure 6.10):

- **Fetch.** Retrieves the next program instruction from the computer's memory.

- **Decode.** Determines what the program is telling the computer to do.

- **Execute.** Performs the requested instruction, such as adding two numbers or deciding which one of them is larger.

- **Store.** Stores the results to an internal register (a temporary storage location) or to memory.

This four-step process is called a **machine cycle**, or **processing cycle**, and consists of two phases: the **instruction cycle** (**fetch** and **decode**) and the **execution cycle** (**execute** and **store**). Today's microprocessors can go through this entire four-step process billions of times per second. The **arithmetic-logic unit** (**ALU**), as its name implies, can perform arithmetic or logical operations. **Arithmetic operations** include addition, subtraction, multiplication, and division. **Logical operations** involve comparing two data items to see which one is larger or smaller.

Some operations require the control unit to store data temporarily. **Registers** are temporary storage locations in the microprocessor that are designed for this purpose. For example, one type of register stores the memory location from which data was retrieved. Registers also store the results of intermediate calculations.

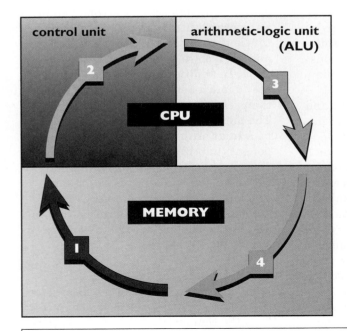

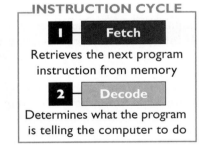

INSTRUCTION CYCLE

1 — Fetch
Retrieves the next program instruction from memory

2 — Decode
Determines what the program is telling the computer to do

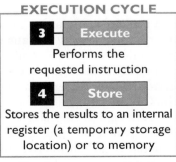

EXECUTION CYCLE

3 — Execute
Performs the requested instruction

4 — Store
Stores the results to an internal register (a temporary storage location) or to memory

FIGURE 6.10 The control unit manages four basic operations: fetch, decode, execute, and store.

Computer and Society
Power to the PC

It's not easy to be green when computers, especially notebooks, are power hogs. In fact, the higher the clock speed, the more power your microprocessor draws. The cooling fan inside the unit also drains the power supply. Imagine the number of kilowatts consumed if you keep your PC on 24/7 so you can check e-mail or open files at any time. Despite the convenience, this is a little like leaving a car parked with the engine running day and night—it wastes energy and puts stress on the internal components because of the constant heat. How can computers become greener without losing power or convenience?

The Environmental Protection Agency (EPA), technology manufacturers, and nonprofit organizations are all working on answers. If your computer bears the EPA's Energy Star logo, it already has the ability to save energy by going to "sleep," that is, powering down when not used for a certain amount of time. This boosts energy efficiency, but it also means that your computer needs a little time to resume normal operation after you press a key to wake it up. However, when you're really in a hurry, you may not want to wait even a fraction of a minute to get into a file or onto the Web, which is why many people disable the sleep function.

Experts at Intel, working with the Natural Resources Defense Council and several power-supply manufacturers, recently developed new specifications intended to reduce the electrical consumption of a computer's power supply by 25 percent or more. Equipping millions of PCs with this type of power supply is expected to save the United States an estimated 16 billion kilowatts per year, shrink electric bills by $1.25 billion annually, and reduce carbon emissions by

10 million tons. In addition to easing the burden on the nation's power grid, it is estimated that owners of such PCs can expect to save up to $50 in reduced electric bills over the course of three years.

Some manufacturers are experimenting with highly efficient fuel-cell power supplies for notebooks and other electronic items (Figure 6.11). Ideally, such fuel cells will use methanol to provide enough power to run a device for at least 24 hours. Although they are environmentally friendly, concerns over size, expense, and the by-products they produce have kept fuel cells from becoming commercially viable. However, research on fuel cells continues, so stay tuned.

FIGURE 6.11 Still in the prototype stage, methane-powered fuel cells may someday be used to run notebooks and other devices.

Microprocessor Performance

The number of transistors available has a huge effect on the performance of a processor. The greater their number and proximity to each other, the faster the processing speed. The data bus width and word size (discussed later), operations per microprocessor cycle, parallel processing, and the type of chip are also factors that contribute to microprocessor performance.

Data Bus Width and Word Size

The **data bus**, a highway of parallel wires, connects the internal components of the microprocessor. The bus is a pathway for the electronic impulses that form bytes. The more lanes this highway has, the faster data can travel. Data bus width is measured in bits (8, 16, 32, or 64).

The width of a CPU's data bus partly determines its **word size**, or the maximum number of bits the CPU can process

Destinations

To learn more about the 64-bit version of the Microsoft Windows operating system, visit **www. microsoft.com/ windows/products/ windowsvista/ editions/64bit.mspx**.

at once. Data bus width also affects the CPU's overall speed, because a CPU with a 32-bit data bus is capable of shuffling data around twice as fast as a CPU with a 16-bit data bus. The terms *8-bit CPU*, *16-bit CPU*, *32-bit CPU*, and *64-bit CPU* indicate the maximum number of bits a given CPU can handle at a time.

A CPU's word size is important because it determines which operating systems the CPU can use and which software it can run. Figure 6.12 lists the word-size requirements of past and current operating systems.

Today's PC market is dominated by 32-bit CPUs and 32-bit operating systems. However, 64-bit CPUs and 64-bit operating systems are beginning to enter the marketplace. Intel's 64-bit Itanium processor, introduced in 2001, brought 64-bit computing to the PC market for the first time. Linux was the first to make use of the 64-bit technology in 2001. In 2003, Apple released a 64-bit version of Mac OS X, and in 2005, Microsoft released Windows XP Professional x64. Windows Vista is available in both a 32-bit and a 64-bit version.

The System Clock Within the computer, events happen at a pace controlled by a tiny electronic "drummer" on the motherboard called the system clock. The **system clock** is an electronic circuit that generates pulses at a rapid rate and synchronizes the computer's internal activities. These electrical pulses are measured in billions of cycles per second (gigahertz, or GHz) and referred to as a processor's **clock speed**. Any computer you purchase today will have a clock speed of more than 1 GHz. Thus, a 3 GHz processor is capable of processing 3 billion cycles in 1 second. In general, the higher the processor's clock speed, the faster the computer. As a frame of reference, figure out how many seconds there are in the average human life span. The answer may surprise you (77 years × 365.25 days × 24 hours × 60 minutes × 60 seconds)!

Operations per Cycle The number of *operations* per clock tick (one pulse of the system clock) also affects microprocessor performance. You might think that a CPU can't perform more than one instruction per clock tick, but thanks to new technologies, that's no longer the case. **Superscalar architecture** refers to the design of any CPU that can execute more than one instruction per clock cycle. Today's fastest CPUs use superscalar architectures. Superscalar architectures often use **pipelining**, a processing technique that feeds a new instruction into the CPU at every step of the processing cycle so that four or more instructions are worked on simultaneously (Figure 6.13).

Pipelining resembles an auto assembly line in which more than one car is being worked on at once. Before the first instruction is finished, the next one is started. If the CPU needs the results of a completed instruction to process the next one, that condition is called **data dependency**. It can cause a pipeline stall in which the assembly line is held up until the results are known. To cope with this problem, advanced CPUs use a technique called **speculative execution** in which the processor executes and temporarily stores the next instruction in case it proves useful. CPUs also use a technique called **branch prediction** in which the processor tries to predict what will likely happen (with a surprisingly high degree of accuracy).

Parallel Processing Another way to improve CPU performance is by using **parallel processing**, a technique that uses more than one processor running simultaneously, in parallel (Figure 6.14). The idea is to speed up the execution of a program by dividing the program into multiple fragments that can execute simultaneously, each on its own processor. A program being executed across more than one processor will execute faster than it would by using a single processor.

Destinations

For the latest information on the hottest and fastest processors, take a look at the aptly named "Chip Geek" at www.geek.com/chips. You'll find the latest news on new, superfast processors as well as performance comparisons, reviews, and tips for putting together the ultimate high-speed system.

FIGURE 6.12 Word-Size Capacity (in bits) of Popular Operating Systems

Operating System	Word Size	When in Time?
MS-DOS	8	Past
Windows 3.1	16	Past
Windows 95/98/NT/2000/XP	32	Past
Windows Vista (all editions except Starter)	64	Current
Linux	64	Current
Mac OS X	64	Current

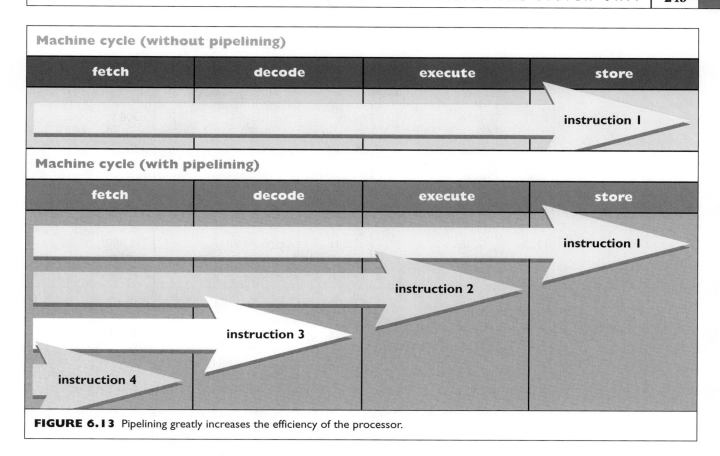

FIGURE 6.13 Pipelining greatly increases the efficiency of the processor.

Popular Microprocessors

The most commonly used microprocessors are those found in IBM-compatible computers and Macs. Most PCs are powered by chips produced by Intel; although AMD also makes IBM-compatible chips. Figure 6.15 shows how popular microprocessors for PCs have improved since the days of the first PC. In 2008, Intel released a version of the Core 2 Extreme

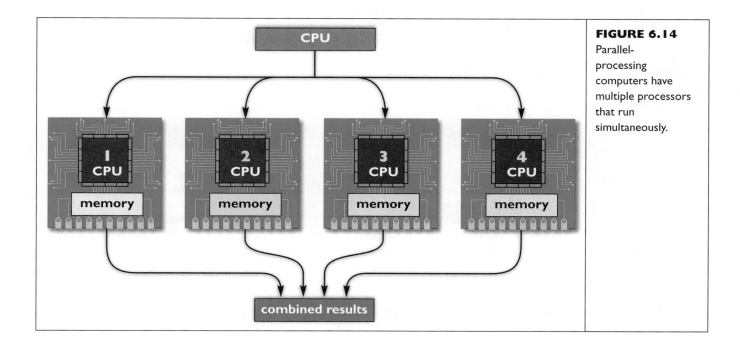

FIGURE 6.14
Parallel-processing computers have multiple processors that run simultaneously.

FIGURE 6.15 The Evolution of Intel Microprocessors

Year	Chip	Bus Width	Clock Speed	Transistors
1971	4004	4 bits	108 KHz	2,300
1974	8080	8 bits	2 MHz	6,000
1979	8088	8 bits	Up to 8 MHz	29,000
1982	80286	16 bits	Up to 12 MHz	134,000
1985	80386	32 bits	Up to 33 MHz	275,000
1989	Intel 486	32 bits	Up to 50 MHz	1.2 million
1993	Pentium	32 bits	Up to 66 MHz	3.1 million
1995	Pentium Pro	32 bits	Up to 200 MHz	5.5 million
1996	Pentium MMX	32 bits	Up to 200 MHz	4.5 million
1997	Pentium II	32 bits	Up to 300 MHz	7.5 million
1998	Xeon	32 bits	Up to 450 MHz	7.5 million
1998	Celeron	32 bits	Up to 300 MHz	7.5–19 million
1999	Pentium III	32 bits	Up to 600 MHz	9.5–28 million
2000	Pentium 4	32 bits	Up to 2 GHz	42 million
2001	Itanium	64 bits	Up to 800 MHz	25 million
2003	Pentium M	32 bits	Up to 1.7 GHz	77 million
2006	Core Duo	32 bits	Up to 2 GHz	151 million
2006	Dual Core Itanium 2	64 bits	Up to 1.60 GHz	1.72 billion
2006	Core 2 Duo	64 bits	Up to 2.66 GHz	291 million
2007	Core 2 Quad	64 bits	Up to 2.4 GHz	582 million

Ethics

Recycling—To Where?

People are becoming more responsible about recycling old computer equipment. But what happens to all that e-waste, estimated to be 400,000 tons annually? Often it is shipped overseas. But does this solve the problem or just move it? What impact does our e-waste have on other countries? What other options exist?

microprocessor with a clock speed of 3.20 GHz, the first commercially available chip to attain that speed (Figure 6.16). Since 2003, Intel has been concentrating on producing processors that are suited to certain computing needs—such as the release of the Centrino processor for mobile computing or the Core 2 Extreme for multimedia and gaming. Intel now rates their processors not only by cycles per second but also by features such as

architecture, cache, and bus type. The rating, then, is the power and usefulness of the processor—not just the clock speed.

For years, Motorola Corporation and IBM made the chips for Apple computers, producing the 68000 series and the PowerPC series. Apple gave its own name to the PowerPC chips: Motorola's 750 was the same as Apple's G3, Motorola's 7400 was the G4, and the 64-bit IBM chip was the G5. In January 2006, Apple began

FIGURE 6.16 The Core 2 Extreme quad-core processor (a) uses two pairs of processor cores (b) for parallel processing.

transitioning to Intel processors for the Mac, with all new Macs using Intel processors by August of that year.

THE CHIPSET AND THE INPUT/OUTPUT BUS

Another important motherboard component is the chipset. The **chipset** is a collection of chips that work together to provide the switching circuitry that the microprocessor needs to move data throughout the rest of the computer. One of the jobs handled by the chipset is linking the microprocessor with the computer's input/output buses.

An **input/output (I/O) bus** extends the computer's internal data pathways beyond the boundaries of the microprocessor to communicate with input and output devices. Typically, an I/O bus contains expansion slots to accommodate plug-in expansion cards.

Today's PCs and Macs use the **PCI (Peripheral Component Interconnect) bus**. Many motherboards still contain an Industry Standard Architecture (ISA) bus and have one or two ISA slots available. The Accelerated Graphics Port (AGP) is a bus designed for video and graphics display. I/O buses extend adapters.

The microprocessor is just one of several chips on the computer's motherboard. Among the other chips are those that provide the computer's memory.

MEMORY

The CPU needs to interact with multiple input/output requests at the same time. That's the job of the computer's memory. **Memory** refers to the chips that enable the computer to retain information. Memory chips store program instructions and data so that the CPU can access them quickly. As you'll see in this section, the computer's motherboard contains several different types of memory, each optimized for its intended use.

RAM

The large memory modules housed on the computer's motherboard contain the computer's RAM. **Random access memory (RAM)** stores information temporarily so that it's directly and speedily available to the microprocessor. This information includes software as well as the data to be processed by the software. RAM is volatile memory, which means its contents are erased when the computer's power is switched off. RAM is designed for fast operation; the processor acts directly on the information stored in RAM.

Why is it called *random access* memory? *Random access* doesn't imply that the memory stores data randomly. A better term would be *random address*, because each memory location has an address—just like a post office box. Using this address, called a **memory address**, the processor can store and retrieve data by

Destinations

To learn more about RAM, see Kingston Technology's "Ultimate Memory Guide" at **www. kingston.com/tools/ umg/default.asp**, which explains how memory works, what memory technologies are available, and how to select the best RAM chips for your computer system.

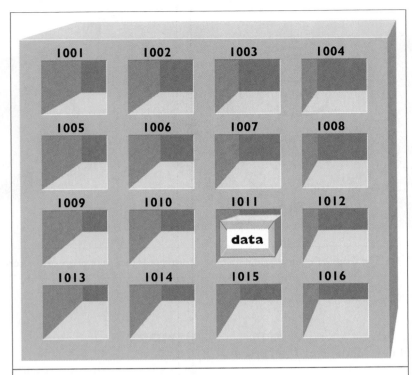

FIGURE 6.17 RAM stores data in specific, addressed locations for easy access and retrieval.

going directly to a single location in memory (Figure 6.17).

Of the various types of RAM available, today's newest and fastest PCs contain either DDR2 SDRAM (Double Data Rate 2 Synchronous Dynamic RAM) or DDR3 SDRAM (Double Data Rate 3 Synchronous Dynamic RAM). These types of RAM must have a constant power supply or they lose their contents.

How much RAM does a computer need? In general, the more memory the better. Windows Vista and Mac OS X theoretically require only 512 MB of RAM, but neither system functions very well with so little. For today's Microsoft Windows, Linux, and Macintosh operating systems, 1 GB of RAM is a practical working minimum. Often, these operating systems use virtual memory in addition to RAM. The computer uses virtual memory when RAM gets full (which can easily happen if you run two or more programs at once). Accessing data on a disk drive is much slower than RAM, so when virtual memory kicks in, the computer may seem to slow to a crawl. To avoid using virtual memory, you're better off with 2 GB of RAM, and increasingly, systems are sold with 3 GB of RAM or more.

ROM

If everything in RAM is erased when the power is turned off, how does the computer start up again? The answer is **read-only memory (ROM)**, a type of memory on which instructions have been prerecorded. The instructions to start the computer are stored in read-only memory chips. ROM allows these instructions to be only read; they cannot be erased. In contrast with RAM, ROM is nonvolatile memory, meaning it retains information even when the power is switched off.

Cache Memory

RAM is fast, but it isn't fast enough to support the processing speeds of today's superfast microprocessors, such as the Intel Core 2 Extreme or the AMD Phenom X4. These microprocessors use cache memory to function at maximum speed. **Cache memory** is a small unit of ultrafast memory built into the processor that stores frequently or recently accessed program instructions and data. Cache (pronounced "cash") memory is much faster than RAM, but it's also more expensive. Although relatively small (up to 12 MB) compared with RAM, cache memory greatly improves the computer system's overall performance.

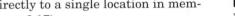

Techtalk

PROM, EPROM, EEPROM

PROM (programmable read-only memory) requires a special device to write instructions on a blank memory chip one time only. EPROM is erasable PROM that can be rewritten many times. EEPROM is electrically erasable PROM that can be overwritten without being removed from the computer.

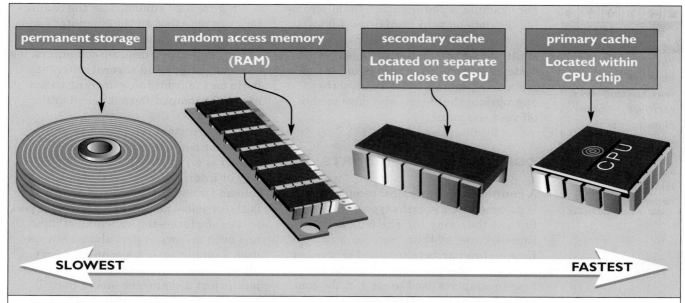

| permanent storage | random access memory (RAM) | secondary cache Located on separate chip close to CPU | primary cache Located within CPU chip |

SLOWEST ← → **FASTEST**

FIGURE 6.18 Primary cache is included in the microprocessor chip. Secondary cache is included on a separate printed circuit board. Keeping the secondary cache as close as possible to the processor improves performance.

Two types of cache memory are available. The first type, called **primary cache** or level 1 (L1) cache, is included in the microprocessor chip. The second type, called **secondary cache** or level 2 (L2) cache, is included on a separate printed circuit board. To improve secondary cache performance, the latest microprocessors are housed in plastic modules that provide a special type of secondary cache called **backside cache**. Keeping the secondary cache as close as possible to the processor improves performance (Figure 6.18).

The following sections explore what can be found on the outside of the system unit of a typical desktop computer.

What's on the Outside of the Box?

You'll find the following features on the outside of a typical desktop computer's system unit:

- the front panel with various buttons and lights

- the power switch

- connectors and ports for plugging in keyboards, mice, monitors, and other peripheral devices

THE FRONT PANEL

On the front panel of some computers, you'll find a **reset switch** (which enables you to restart your computer in the event of a failure), a **drive activity light** (which tells when your hard disk is accessing data), and a **power-on light** (which indicates whether the power is on). You may also find a key lock that you can use to prevent others from operating the machine. Do not press the reset switch unless you are certain that your computer is no longer responding to input. If your computer freezes up, always try pressing the Ctrl, Alt, and Del keys simultaneously to activate the Windows Task Manager and attempt to shut down your system normally. If you have any unsaved work when you press the reset switch, you will most likely lose it.

The **power switch** is usually located on the front of the computer. In earlier days, it was placed on the back of the system unit because of fears that users would accidentally press it and inadvertently shut down their systems. Computers don't handle sudden power losses well.

◤ ➡ ◥ ➡ ⬆ ➡

Destinations

To learn more about PC interfaces, see **www.howstuffworks. com**. Type the name of the port or the keywords "connectors and ports" in the search box that is located near the top of the screen.

For example, a power outage could scramble the data on your hard drive. Likewise, just turning off your computer instead of shutting it down properly can leave the system unstable and possibly unable to restart. You should always follow the appropriate shutdown procedure to shut off your computer.

CONNECTORS AND PORTS

A **connector** is a physical receptacle that is designed for a specific type of plug that fits into the connector. The plug is sometimes secured by thumbscrews. **Expansion cards** (also called expansion boards, adapter cards, or adapters) are plug-in adapters used to connect the computer with various peripherals. Connectors on the outside of the case enable you to connect peripheral devices, such as a printer, keyboard, or mouse (Figure 6.19). Connectors are described as being *male* (those with external pins) or *female* (those with receptacles for external pins).

Figure 6.20 summarizes the connectors you may find on the computer's case. Most of these connectors are on the back of the case, but on desktop computers, it's now common to find several different ports on the front too, providing easier access for many different peripheral devices.

It's important to remember that a connector isn't the same thing as a port. A **port** is an electronically defined pathway or interface for getting information into and out of the computer. A connector is the physical device—the plug-in. A port is the interface—the matching of input and output flows. A port almost always uses a connector, but a connector isn't always a port. For example, a telephone jack is just a connector—not a port. To function, a port must be linked to a specific receptacle. This linking is done by the computer system's start-up and configuration software.

In the following section, *port* is used as if it were synonymous with *connector*, in line with everyday usage; however, it's important to keep the distinction in mind. Let's now look at the types of ports found on the exterior of a typical computer system's case.

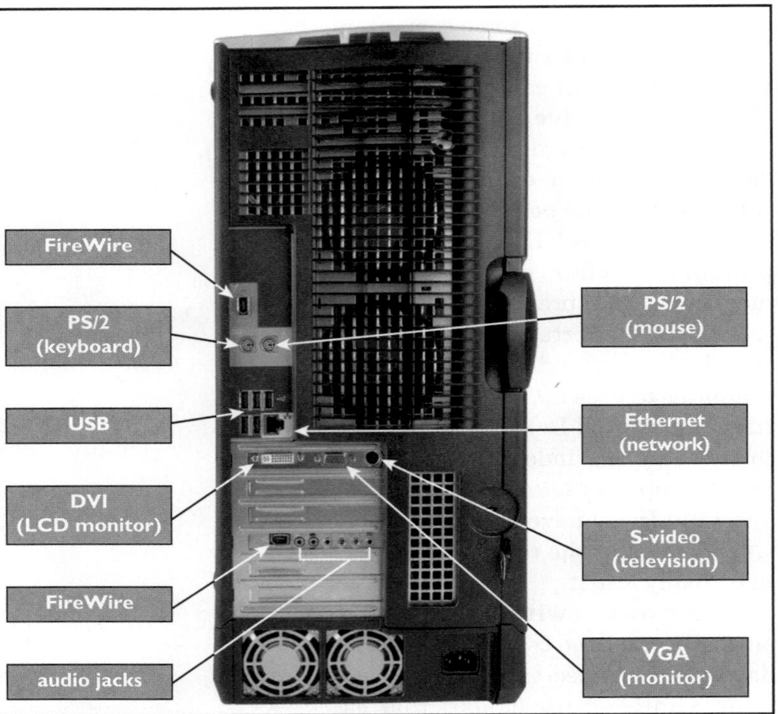

USB Ports

USB (Universal Serial Bus) ports can connect a variety of devices, including keyboards, mice, printers, and digital cameras, and were designed to replace older parallel and serial ports. A single USB port can connect up to 127 peripheral devices, eliminating the need for special ports that only work with specific devices (Figure 6.21). Although introduced in 1995, USB didn't become widespread until the release of the best-selling iMac in 1998. The current standard, USB 2.0 (High-speed USB), replaced USB 1.1 and was released in April 2000. USB 2.0 is fully compatible with USB 1.1 products, cables, and connectors.

USB 2.0 ports use an external bus standard that supports data transfer rates of 480 Mbps (480 million bits per second) between the computer and its peripheral devices—but they do not transfer data between devices within the system. Some advantages include **hot swapping** and support for **Plug-and-Play (PnP)**. Hot

FireWire
PS/2 (keyboard)
USB
DVI (LCD monitor)
FireWire
audio jacks

PS/2 (mouse)
Ethernet (network)
S-video (television)
VGA (monitor)

FIGURE 6.19 The connectors on the outside of a system unit enable you to connect peripherals such as a printer, a keyboard, or a mouse.

FIGURE 6.20 Most of these connectors are on the back of the computer's case, but some of them may be in front.

Connector	Use
Current Technologies	
 **USB**	many devices including mice, keyboards, printers, external hard drives, digital cameras, and USB drives
 **FireWire**	digital cameras and digital video camcorders
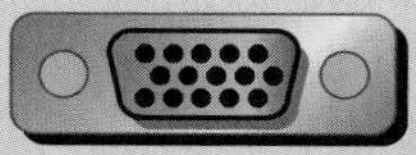 **VGA**	analog video and CRT monitors
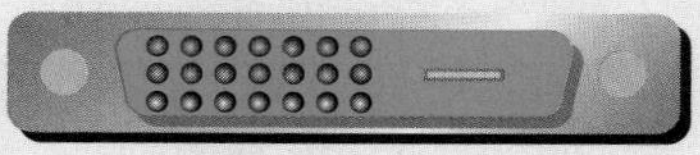 **DVI**	digital video and LCD monitors
 **S-Video**	analog video for TVs
 **RJ-11**	phone line
 **Ethernet/RJ-45**	network connections and cable modems
 **Audio/Video**	microphones, speakers, or headphones
Legacy Technologies	
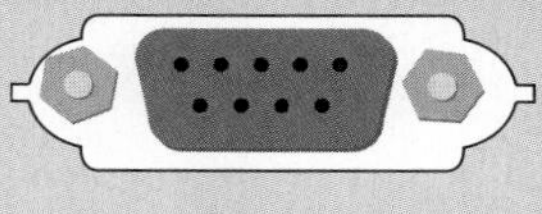 **Serial**	dial-up modems, mice, scanners, or printers
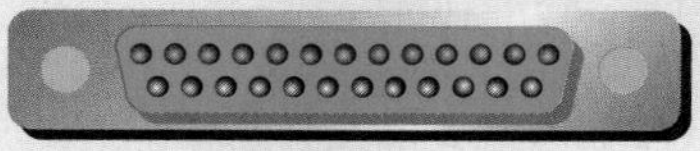 **Parallel**	printers, external storage devices, or scanners
 **PS/2**	mice and keyboards

swapping is the ability to connect and disconnect devices without shutting down your computer. This is convenient when you're using devices that you want to disconnect often, such as a digital camera. With PnP, the computer automatically detects the brand, model, and characteristics of a device when you plug it in and configures the system accordingly.

Computer manufacturers have been installing increasing numbers of USB ports, because of their convenience and versatility. Many systems now have six or more. Ports on the back of a computer are typically used for peripherals that won't be removed often, like a printer or keyboard, whereas front ports are ideal for syncing a handheld device or MP3 player. If your computer doesn't have enough USB ports, it is possible to obtain a USB hub—a device that plugs into an existing USB port and contains four or more additional ports (Figure 6.22).

Up next on the horizon is USB 3.0, known as *SuperSpeed USB*. USB 3.0 is expected to use a fiber-optic link to attain a data transfer rate of 4.8 Gbps—up to 10 times faster than USB 2.0. Additionally, USB 3.0 will be compatible with older versions, providing the same benefits while consuming less power.

1394 Ports (FireWire)

In 1995 Apple introduced **FireWire**, an interface Apple created and standardized as the IEEE 1394 High Performance Serial Bus specification. It is also known as *Sony i.Link* or *IEEE 1394*, the official name for the standard. FireWire is very similar to USB in that it offers a high-speed connection for dozens of peripheral devices (up to 63 of them). It is especially well-suited for the transmission of digital video and digital audio data (Figure 6.23).

On non-Apple systems, this port is called a **1394 port**, after the international standard that defines it. Like USB, FireWire enables hot swapping and PnP. However, it is more expensive than USB and is used only for certain high-speed peripherals, such as digital video cameras,

FIGURE 6.21 USB ports and connectors will be the standard for years to come.

you'll find a standard **VGA (Video Graphics Array) connector**, a 15-pin male connector that works with standard monitor cables. VGA connectors transmit analog video signals and are traditionally used for CRT monitors.

Many LCD monitors can receive analog or digital video signals. A **DVI (Digital Visual Interface) port** enables LCD monitors to use digital signals. However, unless you have a keen eye or are doing professional video editing, the difference between analog and video signals is not that noticeable.

On some computers, the video circuitry is built into the motherboard. This type of video circuitry is called **on-board video**. On such systems, the video connector is found on the back of the case.

Additional Ports and Connectors

You may find the following additional ports and connectors on the exterior of a computer's case or on one of the computer's expansion cards:

that need greater throughput (data transfer capacity) than USB provides.

FireWire 400 has a data transfer rate of 400 Mbps; for FireWire 800, it's 800 Mbps. The next generation, FireWire S3200, is expected to transfer data at a rate of 3.2 Gbps. Although some experts consider FireWire to be technologically superior to USB, the popularity and affordability of USB 2.0, coupled with the promise of an even faster USB interface in the future, lead most to believe that the 1394 FireWire standard will most likely fade away.

Video Connectors

Most computers use a video adapter (also called a video card) to generate the output that is displayed on the computer's screen or monitor. On the back of the adapter,

- **Telephone connector.** The standard modem interface, the telephone connector (called RJ-11) is a standard modular telephone jack that will work with an ordinary telephone cord.

- **Network connector.** Provided with networking adapters, the network connector (called RJ-45 or Ethernet port) looks like a standard telephone jack, but it's bigger and capable of much faster data transfer.

FIGURE 6.22 If your computer needs more USB ports, a USB hub can expand your options.

FIGURE 6.23 FireWire cables are used with FireWire ports to transmit digital video or audio files at high rates of speed.

- **PC card slots.** On notebook computers, one or more PC card slots are provided for plugging in PC cards or ExpressCards. Like USB devices, these cards can be inserted or removed while the computer is running.

- **Sound card connectors.** PCs equipped with a sound card (an adapter that provides stereo sound and sound synthesis) as well as Macs with built-in sound offer two or more sound connectors. These connectors, also called jacks, accept the same stereo miniplug used by portable CD players. Most sound cards provide four connectors: Mic (microphone input), Line In (accepts input from other audio devices), Line Out (sends output to other audio devices), and Speaker (sends output to external speakers).

- **Game card.** Game cards provide a connector for high-speed access to the CPU and RAM for graphics-intensive interaction.

- **TV/sound capture board connectors.** If your computer is equipped with TV and video capabilities, you'll see additional connectors that look like those found on a television monitor. These include a connector for a coaxial cable, which can be connected to a video camera or cable TV system.

Legacy Technology

Legacy technology is used to describe an older technology, device, or application that is being phased out in favor of new advances in technology. Although legacy technology may still work, it may not be available on newer computer systems. The following types of ports are all considered to be legacy technology.

Parallel ports were commonly used to connect a PC to a printer but have been replaced by USB ports and Ethernet ports. Many newer computers no longer include a parallel port. Parallel ports could send and receive data eight bits at a time over eight separate wires. Data transfer was fast, but an eight-wire cable was bulky. Later versions were capable of two-way communication between the printer and computer, allowing the printer to send information, such as error messages, back to the computer.

Serial ports were one of the earliest types of ports and were often used with dial-up modems to achieve two-way communications. Although they are still in use on servers, many newer computers no longer include a serial port, opting to use USB ports instead. Serial ports sent and received data one bit at a time, using three separate wires—one to send, one to receive, and a common signal ground wire. A serial port took eight times as long as a parallel port to transfer data, but cables were smaller and less expensive.

SCSI (pronounced "scuzzy"; short for **Small Computer System Interface) ports** were a type of parallel interface. Unlike a standard parallel port, a SCSI port enabled users to connect up to eight SCSI-compatible devices, such as printers, scanners, and digital cameras, in a daisy-chain series. SCSI ports are seldom found on newer systems, having been replaced by technologies like serial ATA (SATA).

PS/2 ports were typically used for mice and keyboards but were not interchangeable. Only one port could be used by each device, and ports were often color coded to prevent users from plugging in the wrong device. USB ports don't have these limitations.

Some of these older ports are becoming obsolete because many of the newer ports provide a greater degree of flexibility and faster data transfer rates.

Techtalk

ExpressCard
The ExpressCard is the newest standard for the PC card, originally known as the PCMCIA card (short for Personal Computer Memory Card International Association). Mostly used in notebook computers, the ExpressCard can also be used with desktops. The ExpressCard is a credit-card–sized adapter that fits into a designated slot to provide expanded capabilities such as wired or wireless communications, additional memory, multimedia, or security features.

What You've Learned

INSIDE THE SYSTEM UNIT

- For a computer to work with data, the data must be represented by digits inside the computer. The basic unit of information in a computer is the bit, a single-digit binary number (either 1 or 0). An eight-bit sequence of numbers, called a byte, is sufficient to represent the basic letters, numbers, and punctuation marks of languages that use the Latin alphabet, such as English and European languages.

- Data transfer rates of communications devices, such as modems, are measured in bits per second (bps), as well as Kbps (approximately 1,000 bits per second), Mbps (approximately 1 million bits per second), and Gbps (approximately 1 billion bits per second). Data storage capacity is measured in bytes, such as kilobyte (KB, approximately 1,000 bytes), megabyte (MB, approximately 1 million bytes), gigabyte (GB, approximately 1 billion bytes), and terabyte (TB, approximately 1 trillion bytes).

- The system unit contains the motherboard, which acts as the central connector for the processor, memory, and circuits within the computer. It also contains the power supply, which converts AC power to DC; a cooling fan, which keeps the processor and circuits cool; and an internal speaker, which emits beeps and a few basic tones. Additionally, the system unit holds drive bays for storage devices and expansion cards for additional memory, a modem, sound, video, and games.

- The computer's motherboard contains the microprocessor (the CPU—the "brains" of the computer), the system clock (which generates pulses to synchronize the computer's activities), the chipset (chips that help the processor move data around), and memory modules. Expansion slots give expansion cards access to the computer's input/output (I/O) bus, which provides access to the CPU and other system services to devices such as modems, sound cards, game controllers, and more.

- A computer's central processing unit (CPU) processes data in a four-step cycle called a machine cycle using two components: the control unit and the arithmetic-logic unit (ALU). The control unit follows a program's instructions and manages four basic operations: fetch, decode, execute, and store. The ALU can perform arithmetic operations and logical operations.

- Factors that affect a microprocessor's performance include the data bus width (how many bits it can process at once), clock speed (the number of operations the chip can execute per clock cycle), pipelining (a processing technique that feeds a new instruction into the CPU at every step of the processing cycle), and parallel processing (using multiple processors running in parallel).

- The computer's main memory, random access memory (RAM), holds programs, data, and instructions for quick use by the processor. Read-only memory (ROM) holds prerecorded start-up operating instructions. Primary and secondary cache memory operate at very high speeds and keep frequently accessed data available to the processor.

- Most computers have several USB ports (for peripherals such as digital cameras or printers), a video port, input and output audio jacks for microphones and speakers, a telephone connector, and a network connector. They may also have a FireWire (1394) port (for peripherals such as digital video cameras). Some computers may also include legacy ports such as serial ports (for mice or external modems), parallel ports (mainly for printers), PS/2 ports (for mice and keyboards), and possibly a SCSI port (for SCSI devices such as scanners).

Go to **www.pearsonhighered.com/cayf** to review this chapter, answer the questions, and complete the exercises.

Key Terms and Concepts

1394 port 255
arithmetic-logic unit
    (ALU) 246
arithmetic operations 246
ASCII (American Standard
    Code for Information
    Interchange) 240
backside cache 253
binary numbers. 238
bit. 238
branch prediction 248
byte 238
cache memory 252
central processing unit
    (CPU; microprocessor
    or processor) 245
character code 240
characters 240
chipset 251
clock speed. 248
connector 254
control unit 246
cooling fan 243
data bus. 247
data dependency 248
drive activity light 253
drive bays 243
DVI (Digital Visual
    Interface) port 256
EBCDIC (Extended
    Binary Coded Decimal
    Interchange Code) 240
execution cycle
    (execute, store) 246
expansion cards 254

expansion slots 244
FireWire 255
floating-point notation 240
footprint. 240
form factor. 240
gigabits per second (Gbps) . . . 239
gigabyte (GB) 239
heat sink 245
hexadecimal (hex)
    numbers 239
hot swapping. 254
input/output (I/O) bus. 251
instruction cycle
    (fetch, decode). 246
instruction set. 246
integrated circuit
    (IC or chip) 244
internal speaker 243
kilobits per second
    (Kbps) 238
kilobyte (KB). 239
legacy technology 257
logical operations 246
machine cycle
    (processing cycle) 246
megabits per second
    (Mbps). 239
megabyte (MB) 239
memory 251
memory address 251
minitower case 240
motherboard 243
on-board video. 256
parallel ports. 257
parallel processing 248

PCI (Peripheral
    Component
    Interconnect) bus 251
performance 238
pipelining 248
Plug-and-Play (PnP). 254
port 254
power-on light 253
power supply 243
power switch 253
primary cache 253
PS/2 port 257
random access memory
    (RAM) 251
read-only memory
    (ROM). 252
registers. 246
reset switch 253
SCSI (Small Computer
    System Interface) ports . . . 257
secondary cache 253
serial ports 257
speculative execution 248
superscalar architecture. 248
system clock 248
system unit 240
terabyte (TB). 239
tower case 240
transistor. 244
Unicode 240
USB (Universal Serial
    Bus) port. 254
VGA (Video Graphics
    Array) connector. 256
word size 247

Matching

Match each key term in the left column with the most accurate definition in the right column.

_____ 1. port

_____ 2. chipset

_____ 3. motherboard

_____ 4. register

_____ 5. bit

_____ 6. form factor

_____ 7. transistor

_____ 8. DVI port

_____ 9. volatile

_____ 10. character

_____ 11. byte

_____ 12. gigabits per second

_____ 13. superscalar architecture

_____ 14. serial port

_____ 15. connector

a. smallest unit of information a computer can work with

b. includes letters, numbers, and symbols

c. legacy technology used to connect a dial-up modem or mouse

d. provides the switching circuitry needed by the microprocessor to move data through the computer

e. provides a digital signal to an LCD monitor

f. usually represents one character of data

g. temporary storage location used by the control unit

h. unit of measure for data transmission rate

i. an electronic switch that controls the flow of electrical signals to a circuit

j. physical receptacle designed for a plug

k. an electronically defined pathway for getting information into or out of a computer

l. provides a centralized physical and electrical connection point for a computer's components

m. describes memory that is erased when the power is turned off

n. describes a CPU designed to process more than one instruction per clock cycle

o. specification for placement of internal components in a system unit

Multiple Choice

Circle the correct choice for each of the following.

1. Which of the following is *not* an example of a legacy port?
   a. serial
   b. parallel
   c. RJ-45
   d. SCSI

2. ROM is an example of which of the following?
   a. nonvolatile memory
   b. cache memory
   c. volatile memory
   d. secondary memory

3. Which of the following is listed in order from smallest to largest?
   a. KB, GB, MB, TB
   b. KB, MB, TB, GB
   c. MB, KB, GB, TB
   d. KB, MB, GB, TB

4. Which of the following statements is true?
   a. A hexadecimal is the smallest unit of information a computer can work with.
   b. Hexadecimals use 0 through 9 and A through F.
   c. Hexadecimals use floating-point notation.
   d. Ten hexadecimals equals one decimal.

5. Which of the following is *not* a microprocessor manufacturer?
   a. Microsoft
   b. Intel
   c. Motorola
   d. AMD

6. Which of the following character codes can represent many languages?
   a. ASCII
   b. Unicode
   c. PCI
   d. EBCDIC

7. What does the control unit do?
   a. Creates a native application for a processor.
   b. Performs arithmetic or logical operations.
   c. Extracts instructions from memory, decodes them, and executes them.
   d. Drains heat away from the microprocessor.

8. What is a footprint?
   a. a device that measures distance
   b. the size of a hexadecimal number
   c. the amount of space required by the system unit
   d. an expansion slot

9. Which of the following is *not* a component found within the system unit?
   a. motherboard
   b. PS/2
   c. cooling fan
   d. drive bay

10. What does the drive activity light indicate?
    a. the computer is turned on
    b. there is insufficient ROM
    c. the I/O bus is malfunctioning
    d. the hard disk is accessing data

Fill-In

In the blanks provided, write the correct answer for each of the following.

1. _____ is a processing technique that provides a new instruction to the CPU at each step of the processing cycle.

2. The maximum number of bits a CPU can process at once is its _____ _____.

3. CPUs use a process known as _____ _____ to try to determine what will happen next.

4. The electronic circuit that generates pulses and synchronizes the computer's internal activities is the _____ _____.

5. The four basic steps of the machine cycle are _____, _____, _____, and _____.

6. The motherboard is composed of many _____ _____ also known as chips, that carry electric currents and contain millions of transistors.

7. Requiring a fingerprint or retinal scan to access a computer is an example of _____ authentication.

8. The computer's _____ _____ converts current from AC to DC.

9. A(n) _____ _____ covers a microprocessor and may contain a small cooling fan.

10. One Gbps is equal to one _____ bits per second.

11. A(n) _____ port can connect up to 127 peripheral devices and can transfer data at 480 Mbps.

12. Serial ports, parallel ports, and SCSI ports are all examples of _____ technology.

13. The instructions to start up a computer have been prerecorded and are stored in _____.

14. _____ _____ improves CPU performance by running more than one processor at the same time.

15. The ALU performs _____ operations that compare two data items to determine which is larger.

Short Answer

1. Explain the difference between RAM and ROM. Why are both types of memory used in a computer?

2. What is a drive bay and how does it work?

3. What factors affect the performance of a computer?

4. What is the difference between a VGA port and a DVI port?

5. How does the control unit work? Describe the control unit's four basic operations. What is the purpose of the arithmetic-logic unit (ALU)?

Teamwork

1. Exploring Ports

You have read about a variety of ports, so now let's look at some actual computers to see which ones are installed. Divide your team into two groups. Each group should locate at least three different computers. You may use your own computers or campus computers. Determine the number and types of ports that are available and identify the external devices that are connected to each port. Write a one-page report that describes each brand of computer and the configuration of external devices and ports found on each brand.

2. Pipelining and Parallel Processing

As a team, work together to answer the following questions and then write a one-page summary based on your findings. Most of the newer processors use pipelining. Explain how pipelining enhances overall processing speed. Give a noncomputer example of pipelining (that is, an activity that you have personally performed that requires multiple steps to complete and in which you can begin the next step before the current one is completed). Explain parallel processing. Compare parallel processing and pipelining.

3. Working with Cache

Your team is to research the purpose of cache memory. Explain the difference between level 1 (L1) and level 2 (L2) cache. Although it was not discussed in the chapter, there is a third level of cache memory called L3. See what information you can find about this additional level of cache. Prepare a group presentation that includes a diagram showing how each level of cache memory relates to the processor.

4. Buses for Data

As processor size and speed have improved, system bus improvements have not been as dramatic as those for processors. The size of data buses in the first generation of personal computers was eight bits, and they operated at a speed of 2 or 4 MHz. Your team is to work together to find the current size and speed of the Intel Core 2 Extreme and the AMD Phenom X4 data buses. How do the bus speeds compare with the processor speeds? Construct a table (or a chart) that shows the processors and speeds. Embed this table within a one-page document that explains why data bus size and speed are important.

5. Biometric Security

As a group, compile a list of different ways that biometrics can be used to enforce security. Have each group member research one of the items on the list. Get together to discuss your findings. Each team member should then write two to three paragraphs based on his or her research. Combine these paragraphs into a single paper.

On the Web

1. Speeding Processors

Because technology changes rapidly, some of the information printed in this textbook may no longer be up to date. Currently, the fastest Intel processor for a personal computer is the Core 2 Extreme with a clock speed of 3.2 GHz and the fastest AMD processor is the Phenom X4 with a clock speed of more than 2.5 GHz. Visit Intel at **www.intel.com** and AMD at **www.amd.com** to find their fastest processors (type "processor" into each home page's search box). Use other sites or research tools to find additional information on these processors. Which computer system would you purchase if you used speed as the deciding factor? (Remember that processor speed alone does not determine the overall speed of the computer.)

2. The Cost of Storage

Unlike today's computers, in which memory chips are located on the motherboard, memory for the first microcomputers (circa 1978) was located on separate expansion cards and 4 KB (not 4 MB) cost $295! Warm up your calculator and divide the cost by the number of bytes to determine the cost per byte of storage. Visit **www.cnet.com** and use the on-screen search box to find the current price for 1 GB of RAM. Again, divide the cost by the number of bytes to determine the cost per byte. Using 1978 prices, how much would 1 GB of RAM cost today?

3. Discovering USB Ports

USB ports enable you to connect a mouse, cameras, external DVD drives, and lots of other devices to your computer. Visit **http://computer.howstuffworks.com/usb.htm** to learn more about how USB ports work and what they can do for you. Write a short paper that describes how USB 1.1 and USB 2.0 differ. What are the benefits of the new USB 3.0 standard?

4. Motherboard Functions

Go to **http://computer.howstuffworks.com/motherboard.htm** to see what else you can learn about motherboards. Look for some of the key terms that you learned in this chapter. Write a short paper that clearly explains what the motherboard does and how it performs at least one function within the system unit. For instance, the motherboard acts as the connection point for electrical circuits within the system unit.

5. Managing Memory

Go to **www.kingston.com/tools/umg/default.asp** to learn how computers use memory. Browse at least three of the links that you find there. Develop three questions that you think someone might have about memory and then provide detailed answers. You cannot copy your information from the Web site; you must paraphrase your answers. Your document should be roughly two pages, double spaced.

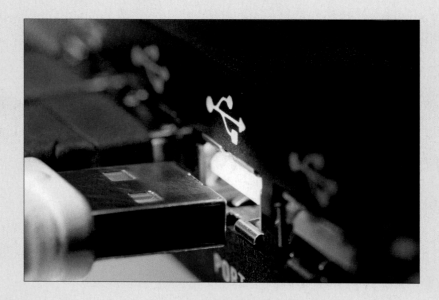

CPUs—What's the Difference?

Although many factors affect the overall performance of a computer, the one feature that is most often touted by manufacturers is the speed of the computer's main processor, or CPU. Years of advertising have convinced most people that a faster processor is always a better processor. If faster is always better, then why aren't there more people driving around in Ferraris? Because of price!

When purchasing a new PC, it is important that you balance your computing needs with your bank account. This can be a difficult task, because most companies that manufacture CPUs produce several product families that are targeted at various price and performance levels. How can you decide which CPU is right for you? The following are some tips to help you choose.

First, make a list of everything you plan to do with your computer. Will you use your computer for tasks such as composing e-mails, doing your taxes, and surfing the Web? Or will you perform more advanced tasks such as editing video or designing graphics? Be sure to write down everything that you might use your computer for over the next few years.

After you have identified exactly how you would like to use your computer, you will need to match those needs with the appropriate type of processor. Most computers today come with CPUs manufactured by Intel. You will likely encounter at least three different families of Intel processors when you look for a new computer (Figure 6.24):

- **Intel Celeron.** The Celeron provides a good mix of performance and value. It is geared more toward those who use their computers for basic tasks such as word processing, Web surfing, and buying and listening to music online.

- **Intel Pentium Core 2.** The Pentium Core 2 is the current workhorse of Intel's consumer processor line and is geared toward advanced applications such as gaming, video editing, and advanced digital photography. The increase in performance also comes with an increase in price.

- **Intel Atom.** The Atom is one of the newest processors from Intel and is made specifically for

FIGURE 6.24 Three of the different families of Intel processors are (**a**) Celeron, (**b**) Pentium Core 2, and (**c**) Pentium Atom.

handheld devices and small mobile Internet devices (MIDs). The Atom is Intel's smallest processor and also contains the world's smallest transistors.

Once you have matched your needs with a particular type of processor, you will need to determine what processor speed is appropriate for you. Processor speeds are measured in gigahertz (GHz); the higher the number, the faster the processor. But when comparing speeds be sure to compare only processors in the same family. A 3.2 GHz Celeron processor will almost always be slower than a 3.2 GHz Pentium Core 2 because of how they are designed. It is also important to realize that you will probably not gain much in performance by paying extra for a computer with a 3.6 GHz processor versus a 3.2 GHz processor. When it comes to incremental speed differences, do some research to determine if the increase in processing speed is worth the extra money. A great resource for detailed information on a large variety of processors and other computer hardware is **www.tomshardware.com/cpu**.

HT
Buying and Upgrading Your Computer System

When buying a computer, you need to know a lot to make a good decision. But buying a computer doesn't have to be intimidating! Many students successfully purchase and maintain their own computers. In fact, at a typical state university, 95 percent of students own a computer.

By having your own PC, you can type term papers, create slide presentations, and in many cases, use a high-speed network connection right in your own dorm room. Many schools encourage students to purchase a computer before they arrive on campus. Even though schools still provide computer labs, with your own computer you can work when you want and, in the case of notebooks, where you want. This Spotlight will guide you step by step through the process of buying your own computer. Read on to learn how to choose the equipment you'll need at the best prices on today's market.

GETTING STARTED THE RIGHT WAY

There's a right way and a wrong way to select a computer system. The right way involves understanding the terminology and the relative value of computer system components. You then determine your software needs and choose the computer that runs this software in the most robust way. What's the wrong way? Buying a computer system based only on price, being influenced by sales hype, or purchasing a system you know nothing about. First we'll discuss how to select the best type of computer for your needs.

NOTEBOOK OR DESKTOP?

Deciding whether to buy a notebook or a desktop computer is often one of the hardest decisions you'll have to make when considering which computer to buy (Figure 6A). Today's notebook computers rival the power of desktop machines. The best of them are truly awesome machines, with big (17-inch or larger) displays and fast processors.

The main advantages of a notebook computer are portability and size. Because notebooks are portable, you can take them to class in a specially designed carrying case (Figure 6B). Once in class, you can easily fit a notebook on your desk to type notes. As you're probably well aware, campus housing or shared rental units often have a limited amount of desk space, which makes notebooks even more appealing.

On the downside, notebook computers cost more than comparable desktop models. You also should consider that notebooks can be easily lost or stolen. And if your notebook goes missing, your precious data will go

FIGURE 6A The notebook has become the computer of choice for students on many college campuses.

along with it. More than 12,000 notebooks are lost every week in U.S. airports, and the FBI reports that every 53 seconds a notebook is stolen. Sadly, 97 percent of these notebooks are never recovered. Thieves also target college campuses, making safety another important factor when considering a notebook.

In the end, the decision most often hinges on convenience versus expense. It's a good idea to speak with friends, family, and instructors about their experiences with different computers. Additionally, many computer sites like **www.pcmag.com** or **www.cnet.com** regularly review and rate products from many different

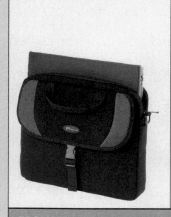

FIGURE 6B Notebook computer bags come in a variety of sizes and styles designed to protect your computer and hold your work too.

manufacturers. Besides choosing a notebook or desktop model, another decision you'll need to make is which platform you want to work on: Mac or PC.

MAC OR PC?

There are two main computer system platforms: Windows (PC) and Mac (Figure 6C). If you ask around, you'll find that some users prefer the Mac, whereas others prefer Windows. Each thinks their platform is the best, and rarely do they cross platforms. How do you know which platform is best for you?

Today's top-of-the-line Macs and PCs are virtually indistinguishable in terms of features and performance. Although the market share for Macs is only about 7.5 percent, they have been gaining on PCs in recent years. This has been attributed to Macs now using Intel processors and being capable of running the Microsoft Windows operating system and Windows-based software. In addition, the dissatisfaction that many people have expressed regarding the Windows Vista operating system has helped the Mac's market share grow. So how do you decide? First, you need to know some of the differences between Macs and PCs that can become major issues for some people.

One difference between Macs and PCs is software availability. More than 90 percent of the computers in use today are PCs, and developers are more inclined to develop software for the broadest market. The most noticeable gap is within the gaming software industry, which is primarily Windows-based.

Some software publishers have discontinued some of their Mac products altogether. For example, Autodesk, publisher of the top-selling computer-aided design (CAD) program AutoCAD, dropped its sluggish-selling Mac version to focus on its Windows products, but it still produces other applications for Macs. Even software publishers that continue to support the Mac typically bring out the Mac versions later and may not include as many features. However, many of the most popular software packages, including Microsoft Office, are available for Macs as well as PCs. And if you choose to run Windows on your Mac, you will be able to use Windows-based software too.

In the past, file compatibility between Macs and PCs was a problem, but that's no longer true. Not only can users easily share files between Macs and PCs, but they can also attach both types of computers to a network and share printers, Internet access, and other resources.

So does software availability really make a difference? If you're planning to use your computer only for basic applications, such as word processing, spreadsheets, databases, presentation graphics, e-mail, and Web browsing, the Mac-versus-PC issue really isn't important. Excellent software for all of these important applications is available for both platforms. But look down the road. What if you declare a major a couple of years from now only to find that your professors want you to use special-purpose programs that run on the platform that you don't have?

Thus, when deciding whether to buy a PC or a Mac, it's important that you anticipate your future software needs. Find out which programs students in your major field of study are using, as well as which programs are used by graduates working in the career you're planning to pursue. To find out what type of computer is preferred by people working in your chosen career, interview appropriate professionals. In general, Macs have a strong niche market in artistic fields, such as publishing, music, graphics, illustration, and Web site design. PCs figure prominently on the desktops of engineers and businesspeople. The classic stereotype is that the successful artist has a Mac, but her accountant uses a PC. But like all stereotypes, this is not always the case. For example, you might think that scientists would use PCs, but that's not necessarily true. In the "wet" sciences (chemistry and biology), Macs have many adherents because these sciences involve visual representation, an area in which Macs excel.

FIGURE 6C **(a)** PCs figure prominently on the desktops of engineers and businesspeople. **(b)** Macs have a strong niche market in artistic fields, such as publishing, music, graphics, illustration, and Web site design.

If you're on a budget, consider cost, too. Although the price gap is narrowing, Macs and Mac peripherals and software are somewhat more expensive than comparable PC equipment. Macs used to be easier to set up and use, but thanks to improvements in Microsoft Windows, Macs and PCs are now about even.

Now that you've determined whether your notebook or desktop computer will be a Mac or a PC, we'll discuss how to select the right hardware.

CHOOSING THE RIGHT HARDWARE

You'll need to understand and evaluate the following hardware components when buying your computer:

- Processors
- Memory
- Hard disks
- Internal and external drives
- Monitors and video cards
- Printers
- Speakers and sound cards
- Modems and network cards
- Keyboards and mice
- Uninterruptible power supplies

The following sections examine each of these components.

PROCESSORS

One of the most important choices you'll make when buying a computer is the microprocessor (also known as the processor or CPU). This decision may seem overwhelming. Not only do you have to compare brands— Intel versus AMD—and each brand's models, you also need to consider features such as clock speed, number of cores, and power consumption. With the advent of multi-core processing, a processor's performance isn't defined solely by its clock speed (typically measured in GHz). In most modern applications, a dual-core CPU can outperform a single-core CPU, even if the single-core has a higher clock speed. Using this reasoning, you might think that a quad-core CPU would be even better, but many applications are unable to take advantage of the quad-core's power. Using a quad-core processor for ordinary computer tasks such as word processing and surfing the Internet is a bit like taking a Formula One race car around the block to the minimarket! When it comes to measuring performance, a dual-core processor is about 50 percent faster than a single-core processor. A quad-core processor is only about 25 percent faster than a dual-core processor. Visit the Intel (**www.intel.com**) and AMD (**www.amd.com**) sites to compare the different types of processors each company manufactures. Many sites, such as PassMark Software (**www.cpubenchmark.net**), rigorously test processors. Known as benchmarking, these tests provide a good way to compare overall processor performance results (Figure 6D). Keep these results in mind as you compare computer systems. Each system will have its strengths and weaknesses; however, the processor is the heart of the machine and often dictates the robustness of the rest of the components. It's important that the processor be a good match for the rest of the system. You don't want to put a high-performance processor on a low-end machine or use an underperforming processor on a high-end system.

When researching different processors, keep in mind that you'll pay a premium if you buy the newest, most powerful processor available. One approach is to buy the second-best processor on the market. That way you'll get plenty of processing power without paying a penalty for being the first to have the most. You only need enough processing power to handle the work or play you intend to accomplish. If you're a heavy game user, you may need a lot of processing power, but if you will use your computer only to surf the Web, play audio files, and communicate using e-mail and instant messaging, a mid-speed processor should suit your needs just fine.

MEMORY

The next item to consider when buying a computer is how much memory you need. Two important issues are the amount of RAM and whether the system has cache memory. You really can't have too much memory; a good rule of thumb is to buy as much as you can afford.

RAM
To maximize your computer's performance, you should seriously consider purchasing at least 2 GB of RAM; 4 GB would be even better. The operating system uses RAM for temporary storage. Increasing the amount of available memory allows the CPU to process more instructions and permits more applications to be run simultaneously. Computers with sufficient amounts of RAM are quicker and more responsive than computers with inadequate amounts.

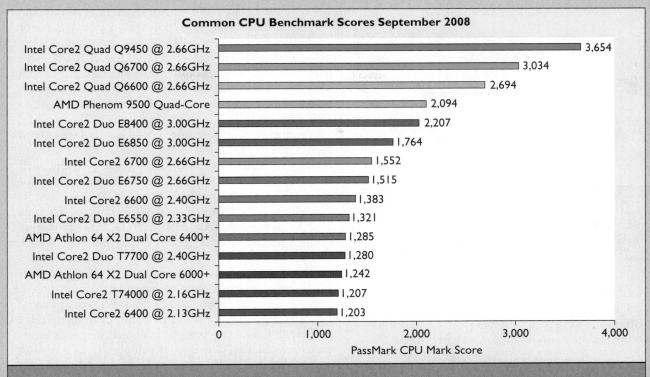

Common CPU Benchmark Scores September 2008

CPU	PassMark CPU Mark Score
Intel Core2 Quad Q9450 @ 2.66GHz	3,654
Intel Core2 Quad Q6700 @ 2.66GHz	3,034
Intel Core2 Quad Q6600 @ 2.66GHz	2,694
AMD Phenom 9500 Quad-Core	2,094
Intel Core2 Duo E8400 @ 3.00GHz	2,207
Intel Core2 Duo E6850 @ 3.00GHz	1,764
Intel Core2 6700 @ 2.66GHz	1,552
Intel Core2 Duo E6750 @ 2.66GHz	1,515
Intel Core2 6600 @ 2.40GHz	1,383
Intel Core2 Duo E6550 @ 2.33GHz	1,321
AMD Athlon 64 X2 Dual Core 6400+	1,285
Intel Core2 Duo T7700 @ 2.40GHz	1,280
AMD Athlon 64 X2 Dual Core 6000+	1,242
Intel Core2 T74000 @ 2.16GHz	1,207
Intel Core2 6400 @ 2.13GHz	1,203

FIGURE 6D PassMark Software (**www.cpubenchmark.net**) provides benchmark test results for more than 300 CPU models and updates its results daily.

When purchasing a new computer, ask if the memory can be upgraded and what the maximum amount of memory is for the system. You never know what your future use will demand. You may find that you already own a perfectly good system that just needs more memory to be effective and efficient.

Secondary Cache

When researching cache memory, keep in mind that systems with cache memory tend to be faster than systems without it. Secondary cache, also known as L2 cache, provides an additional location for memory storage that can be quickly accessed by the processor. It may be located on the processor's architecture or very close to it. If a CPU already includes L2 cache, another level, known as L3 cache, may be located close to the processor.

HARD DISKS

A common mistake made by first-time buyers is underestimating the amount of disk storage they'll need. Today, a 350 GB hard drive may sound like quite a lot, but you won't believe how easy it is to fill it up. (For example, 500 high-resolution photos take up approximately 1 GB of storage.) A good rule of thumb is to never use more than 75 percent of available disk space. Many entry-level systems on the market today come with hard drives that store anywhere from 160 GB to more than 1 TB. Yes, that's correct—1 trillion bytes! Storage has become very inexpensive, so purchase as much as you can.

INTERNAL AND EXTERNAL DRIVES

A **drive** is a connected storage device. Drives can be internal (installed within the system unit) or external (attached to the system unit by a cable connected to a port). For instance, to install new software from a DVD or CD, you'll need a drive that is capable of reading these discs. Although it is possible to have individual DVD and CD drives installed internally or attached as standalone devices, most new computers include a combination DVD±RW/CD-RW drive that is capable of reading and writing both DVDs and CDs. Not only will you be able to read CDs, but you'll also be able to view movies on DVDs and save files to either storage medium. The latest optical disc format is Blu-ray Disc, which was developed to enable recording and viewing of high-definition video (Figure 6E). Blu-ray also enables you to store large amounts of data. Up to 5 GB of data can be stored on a single-layer disc and up to

FIGURE 6E Blu-ray Disc drives are used for recording and playing high-definition video and storing large quantities of data.

50 GB can be stored on a dual-layer disc. Currently only available on high-end systems or as an external drive, Blu-ray is expected to become more popular as high-definition material becomes more prevalent.

MONITORS AND VIDEO CARDS

Monitors are categorized by the technology used to generate images, the colors they display, their screen size, and additional performance characteristics.

In the past few years, as LCD monitor pricing has dropped, CRT monitors have become obsolete and are now considered legacy technology. LCD monitors have become popular because they consume less electricity, have a slimmer design, and weigh less than older CRT monitors. LCD monitors are sometimes referred to as flat-screen or flat-panel monitors because they are very thin, usually no more than 2 inches deep. The flat screen also causes less distortion, which results in decreased eye strain—which is critical for people who spend long stretches of time working on a computer.

The quality and resolution of the display you see on your monitor is determined by the computer's **video card**. Display standards vary depending on whether you have a standard monitor with a 4:3 aspect ratio or a widescreen monitor with a 16:10 aspect ratio. Aspect ratios are determined by dividing a monitor's width by its height. Standard 17- and 19-inch monitors typically use **Super Extended Graphics Array** (**SXGA**) with a resolution of 1280 × 1024. Widescreen standards include **Widescreen Extended Graphics Array +** (**WXGA+**) for 19-inch monitors with a 1440 × 900 resolution, **Widescreen Super Extended Graphics Array +** (**WSXGA+**) for 20-inch monitors with a 1680 × 1050 resolution, and **Widescreen Ultra Extended Graphics Array** (**WUXGA**) for 24-inch monitors with a 1920 × 1200 resolution. The higher

the resolution, the more memory that is required. To display 2560 × 1600 resolution with a color palette of 16.7 million colors, for example, you need to equip your video card with 512 MB of **video RAM** (**VRAM**), which is memory that's set aside for video processing. Generally, video cards made before 2006 are unable to support widescreen monitors and standard monitors larger than 19 inches.

To increase performance speed, video data is transferred directly from the video graphics card to the motherboard. The interface used by the graphics card is determined by the motherboard. Older systems used the **Accelerated Graphics Port** (**AGP**) interface; however, AGP is being phased out in favor of the faster **PCI Express** interface. Most current video cards from manufacturers like ATI and NVIDIA use PCI Express (Figure 6F).

Monitors are available in different sizes. You can purchase anything from a 17-inch to a 26-inch monitor, but the larger the monitor, the higher the cost. The industry standard for desktop monitors ranges from 19 to 22 inches, and the typical notebook computer screen measures 15.4 to 17 inches. If you plan to do any desktop publishing or CAD work, you may want to upgrade to a 24-inch monitor.

The monitor's dot pitch is also an important factor. **Dot pitch** (also called aperture grill) is a physical characteristic that determines the smallest dot the screen can display. Don't buy a monitor with a dot pitch larger than 0.28 mm—the smaller the dot pitch, the better your display.

PRINTERS

Printers fall into four basic categories: color inkjet printers, monochrome laser printers, color laser printers, and multifunction devices that fax and scan as well as print. The difference in print quality between inkjets and laser printers is virtually

FIGURE 6F Current video graphics cards use PCI Express technology for improved performance.

indistinguishable. Color inkjets and monochrome laser printers are popular and affordable choices for college students. However, the pricing for color lasers and multifunction devices is becoming more competitive, making these viable options too.

You should also consider the cost of supplies such as ink or toner for your printer. Toner for laser printers is often more expensive than the ink used by inkjet printers, but it also lasts longer. When shopping for a new printer, be sure to research a printer's cost-per-page, not just the purchase price.

Speed matters, too. The slowest laser printers are faster than the fastest inkjet printers, and the slowest inkjet printers operate at a glacial pace. High-end laser printers can print as many as 60 ppm (pages per minute). Still, the best inkjet printers churn out black-and-white pages at a peppy pace—as many as 35 ppm. If you go the inkjet route, look for a printer that can print at least 15 ppm.

Stay with a major brand name, and you'll be served well. It's always a good idea to purchase an extra print cartridge and stash it away with 30 or 40 sheets of paper. This way, Murphy's law won't catch you at 2 a.m. trying to finish an assignment without ink or paper.

SPEAKERS AND SOUND CARDS

To take full advantage of the Internet's multimedia capabilities, you will need speakers and a sound card. On Macs, the sound is built in; however, you'll need external speakers to hear stereo sound. Windows PCs require a sound card. For the richest sound, equip your system with a subwoofer, which reproduces bass notes realistically.

Be aware that many computers, especially the lowest-priced systems, come with cheap speakers. If sound matters a lot to you—and it does to many college students—consider upgrading to a higher-quality, name-brand speaker system.

MODEMS AND NETWORK CARDS

If you plan to log on to the campus network, you'll need a modem or a **Network Interface Card (NIC)**, or both. Check with your campus computer center to find out how to connect to your school's system, which modem protocols are supported, and what kind of network card you need. Most colleges run 100-Mbps (100Base-T) Ethernet networks, but some require you to get a 1000-Mbps (1000Base-T) network card.

Macs have built-in support for Ethernet networks. On Windows PCs, you'll need an Ethernet card, which is usually integrated into the motherboard.

FIGURE 6G A wheel mouse includes a scrolling wheel and programmable buttons.

KEYBOARDS AND MICE

Most computers come with standard keyboards. If you use your computer keyboard a lot and you're worried about carpal tunnel syndrome, consider upgrading to an ergonomic keyboard, such as the Microsoft Natural Keyboard.

Most systems also come with a basic mouse, but you can ask for an upgrade. With Windows PCs, there's good reason to do so, thanks to the improved mouse support built into the Windows operating system. Any mouse that supports Microsoft's IntelliMouse standard includes a wheel that enables you to scroll through documents with ease. Wheel mice also include programmable buttons to tailor your mouse usage to the software application you're using (Figure 6G).

To choose a good keyboard and mouse, go to a local store that sells computers and try some out. The button placement and action vary from model to model. You'll be using these input devices a lot, so be sure to make an informed decision.

UNINTERRUPTIBLE POWER SUPPLIES

"I'm sorry I don't have my paper. I finished it, and then a power outage wiped out my work." If this excuse sounds familiar, you may want to purchase an **uninterruptible power supply (UPS)**, a device that provides power to a computer system for a short time if electrical power is lost (Figure 6H). With the comparatively low price of today's UPSes—you can get one with surge protection for less than $50—consider buying one for your computer, especially if you experience frequent power outages where you live or work. A UPS gives you enough time to save your work and shut down your computer properly until the power is back on.

Now that you understand your choices for a computer system's physical components, let's look at some other decisions you will have to make when shopping for your new system.

FIGURE 6H A UPS device can easily justify its purchase price by saving your data in an unexpected power outage.

SHOPPING WISELY

As you get ready to buy a computer, it's important to shop wisely. Should you buy a top-of-the-line model or a bargain-bin special? Is it better to buy at a local store or through a mail-order company? What about refurbished or used computers or a name-brand versus a generic PC? Let's take a look at some of these issues.

TOP-OF-THE-LINE MODELS VERSUS BARGAIN-BIN SPECIALS

A good argument for getting the best system you can afford is that you don't want it to become obsolete before you graduate. Inexpensive systems often cut corners by using less powerful CPUs, providing the bare minimum of RAM, and including an operating system with fewer features and capabilities. In your senior year, do you want to spend time upgrading your hard drive when you should be focusing on your studies? In addition, every time you open the computer's cover and change something, you risk damaging one of the internal components.

The most important consideration is the type of software you plan to run. If you'll be using basic applications such as word processing, you don't need the most powerful computer available. In this situation, a bargain-bin special may be okay, as long as you exercise caution when making such a purchase. But what if you decide to declare a major in mechanical engineering? You might want to run a CAD package, which demands a fast system with lots of memory. In that case, you'd be better off paying extra to get the memory you need up front, rather than settling for a bargain-bin special that may end up being inadequate later.

LOCAL STORES VERSUS MAIL-ORDER AND ONLINE COMPANIES

Whether you're looking for a Windows PC or a Mac, you need to consider whether to purchase your system locally or from a mail-order or online company. If you buy locally, you can resolve problems quickly by going back to the store (Figure 6I). With a system from a mail-order or online company, you'll have to call the company's technical support line.

If you're considering ordering through the mail or online, look for companies that have been in business a long time—and particularly those that offer a no-questions-asked return policy for the first 30 days. Without such a policy, you could get stuck with a lemon that even the manufacturer won't be able to repair. Be aware that the lowest price isn't always the best deal—particularly if the item isn't in stock and will take weeks to reach you. Also, don't forget about shipping and handling charges, which could add considerably to the price of a system purchased online or through the mail.

In addition, make sure you're not comparing apples and oranges. Some quoted prices include accessories such as modems and monitors; others do not. To establish a level playing field for comparison, use the shopping comparison worksheet in Figure 6J. For the

FIGURE 6I If you buy a computer at a local retail store, you can evaluate different models and speak with a salesperson to obtain additional information.

Shopping Comparison Worksheet

VENDOR _____   Date _____

  Brand Name _____

  Model _____

  Real Price _____ (including selected components)

PROCESSOR

  Brand _____

  Model _____

  Speed _____ MHz

RAM

  Type _____

  Amount _____ MB

HARD DRIVE

  Capacity _____ GB   Seek time _____ ns

  Speed _____ rpm   Interface _____

MONITOR

  Size _____ x _____ pixels   Dot pitch _____ mm

VIDEO CARD

  Memory _____ MB   Max. resolution _____ x _____ pixels

  Accelerated? .... ☐ yes ☐ no

REMOVABLE DRIVE

  Type _____

  Location .... ☐ internal ☐ external

DVD DRIVE

  Speed _____

DVD BURNER

  Included? .... ☐ yes ☐ no

BLU-RAY DISC DRIVE

  Included? .... ☐ yes ☐ no

SPEAKERS

  Included? .... ☐ yes ☐ no

  Upgraded? .... ☐ yes ☐ no

SUBWOOFER

  Included? .... ☐ yes ☐ no

NETWORK CARD

  Included? .... ☐ yes ☐ no

  Speed (100/1000) _____

KEYBOARD

  Upgraded? .... ☐ yes ☐ no

  Model _____

MOUSE

  Included? .... ☐ yes ☐ no

  Upgraded? .... ☐ yes ☐ no

UPS

  Included? .... ☐ yes ☐ no

SOFTWARE

_____

_____

WARRANTY _____

  Service location _____

  Typical service turnaround time _____

FIGURE 6J

Shopping Comparison Worksheet

system's actual price, get a quote that includes all of the accessories you want, such as a modem, a monitor, and a UPS.

You should also consider warranties and service agreements. Most computers come with a one-year warranty for parts and service. Make sure you read the warranty carefully. Some companies offer service agreements for varying lengths of time that will cover anything that goes wrong with your system—for a price. In the vast majority of cases, a computer will fail within the first few weeks or months. You should be covered for as much as you feel comfortable with during the first year. Be aware, though, that extra warranty coverage and service contracts can add significantly to the cost of your system.

BUYING USED OR REFURBISHED

What about buying a used system? It's risky. If you're buying from an individual, chances are the system is priced too high. People just can't believe how quickly computers lose their value. They think their systems are worth a lot more than they actually are. Try finding some ads for used computers in your local newspaper and then see how much it would cost to buy the same system new, right now, if it's still on the market. Chances are the new system is cheaper than the used one.

A number of computer manufacturers and reputable businesses refurbish and upgrade systems for resale. National chains such as TigerDirect.com or Newegg.com have standards to ensure that their systems are "as good as new" when you make a purchase. As always, check out the storefront and stay away from establishments that don't look or feel right. And most important, your refurbished machine should come with a warranty.

NAME-BRAND VERSUS GENERIC PCS

Name-brand PC manufacturers, such as Hewlett-Packard, Dell, and Gateway, offer high-quality systems at competitive prices. You can buy some of these systems from retail or mail-order stores, but some are available only by contacting the vendor directly.

If you're buying extended warranty protection that includes on-site service, make sure the on-site service really is available where you live; you may find out that the service is available only in major metropolitan areas. Make sure you get 24-hour technical support; sometimes your problems don't occur between 8 a.m. and 5 p.m.

If something breaks down, you might have only one repair option: Return the computer to the manufacturer. And after the warranty has expired, you may end up paying a premium price for parts and repairs.

Fortunately, this is becoming less and less of an issue. Almost all of today's name-brand computers run well right out of the box, and in-service failure rates are declining.

What about generic PCs? In most cities, you'll find local computer stores that assemble their own systems using off-the-shelf components. These systems are often just as fast (and just as reliable) as name-brand systems. You save because you don't pay for the name-brand company's marketing and distribution costs. Because of their smaller client base, the staff at local computer stores have a better chance of knowing their customers personally and thus may provide more personalized service. Their phones are not nearly as busy, and if something goes wrong with your computer, you won't have to ship it halfway across the country. Ask the technician about his or her training background and experience. Another thing to consider is that the industry's profit margin is razor thin; if the local company goes bankrupt, your warranty may not mean much.

What if you don't need an entire new computer system, but just want to improve your current system's performance? That's when you should consider upgrading.

UPGRADING YOUR SYSTEM

You may want to upgrade your system for a variety of reasons. You may have purchased new software that requires more memory to run properly. You may decide to add a game controller. You could decide that a new monitor and printer will enhance your computing experience. Many computer owners improve their system's performance and utility by adding new hardware, such as modems, sound cards, and additional memory. This section discusses the two most common hardware upgrades: adding expansion boards and adding memory.

Before you decide to upgrade your computer on your own, be aware that doing so may violate your computer's warranty. Read the warranty to find out. You may need to take your computer to an authorized service center to get an upgrade. Also, although it can be relatively simple to install new components, it can be risky. If you aren't absolutely certain of what you're doing—don't do it! Also consider whether it may be more cost-effective to purchase a new computer than to upgrade your existing one.

REMOVING THE COVER

To upgrade your system, begin by unplugging the power cord and removing all of the cables attached to the back of the system unit. Make a note of which cable went where so that you can correctly plug the cables back in later. With most systems, you can remove the cover by removing the screws on the back of the case. If you don't know how to remove the cover, consult your computer manual. Keep the screws in a cup or bowl so they'll be handy when you reassemble the computer.

ADDING EXPANSION BOARDS

To add an expansion board to your system, identify the correct type of expansion slot (ISA, PCI, or AGP) and unscrew the metal insert that blocks the slot's access hole. Save the screw, but discard the insert. Gently but firmly press the board into the slot. Don't try to force it, though, and stop pressing if the motherboard flexes. If the motherboard flexes, it is not properly supported, and you should take your computer to the dealer to have it inspected. When you've pressed the new expansion board fully into place, screw it down using the screw you removed from the metal insert. Before replacing the cover, carefully check that the board is fully inserted.

UPGRADING MEMORY

Many users find that their systems run faster when they add more memory. With additional memory, it's less likely that the operating system will need to use virtual memory, which slows the computer down. To successfully upgrade your computer's memory, visit a leading memory site like Kingston (**www.kingston.com**) or Crucial (**www.crucial.com**). There are several different kinds of memory, but only one type will work with your computer. Both of these sites include tools to help you determine what type of memory your computer requires. Crucial also includes a system scanner that will tell you how much memory is currently installed in your computer. Both sites will tell you the maximum amount of memory your system can use, what type of memory is compatible with your system, and whether you need to buy the memory modules singly or in pairs. You can purchase the specified memory directly from the site or use this information to check pricing and shop around.

When you purchase memory modules, a knowledgeable salesperson might help you determine which type of module you need and how much memory you can install. But in most cases the salesperson won't know any more about installing memory than you do.

Before you install memory modules, be aware that memory chips are easily destroyed by static electricity. Do not attempt to install memory chips without wearing a **grounding strap**, a wrist-attached device that grounds your body so that you can't zap the chips. Remember, don't try to force the memory

modules into their receptacles; they're supposed to snap in gently. If they won't go in, you don't have the module aligned correctly or you may have the wrong type of module.

REPLACING THE COVER

When you have checked your work and you're satisfied that the new hardware is correctly installed, replace the cover and screw it down firmly. Replace the cables and then restart your system. If you added PnP devices, you'll see on-screen instructions that will help you configure your computer to use your new hardware.

If you're thinking about upgrading your system or if you want to understand what a particular component does, the Internet is a great resource. Sites like CNET (**www.cnet.com**) and PCMag.com (**www.pcmag.com**) can be used to learn about the newest products and read expert reviews. Other sites like HowStuffWorks (**www.howstuffworks.com**) can provide details and explanations for various components. Using a search engine for specific questions can also turn up valuable information.

Whether your computer system is brand new or merely upgraded, you need to know how to properly maintain your system's components.

CARING FOR YOUR COMPUTER SYSTEM

After your computer is running smoothly, chances are it will run flawlessly for years if you take a few precautions:

X *Equip your system with a surge protector, a device that will protect all system components from power surges caused by lightning or other power irregularities (Figure 6K).*

X *Consider purchasing a UPS. These devices protect your system if the computer loses power.*

X *Don't plug your dorm refrigerator into the same outlet as your computer. A refrigerator can cause fluctuations in power, and a consistent power supply is critical to the performance and longevity of your computer.*

X *There should be sufficient air circulation around the components. Don't block air intake grilles by pushing them flush against walls or other barriers. Heat and humidity can harm your equipment. Your computer should not be in direct sunlight or too close to a source of moisture.*

FIGURE 6K Surge protectors prevent costly damage to delicate circuitry and components.

✗ Before connecting or disconnecting any cables, make sure your computer is turned off.

✗ Cables shouldn't be stretched or mashed by furniture. If your cables become damaged, your peripherals and computer might not communicate effectively.

✗ Clean your computer and printer with a damp, soft, lint-free cloth.

✗ To clean your monitor, use a soft, lint-free cloth and gently wipe the surface clean. If the monitor is very dirty, unplug it and wipe it with a cloth slightly dampened with distilled water. Never apply any liquids directly to the surface, and don't press too hard on it.

✗ Avoid eating or drinking near your computer. Crumbs can gum up your mouse or keyboard, and spilled liquids (even small amounts) can ruin an entire system.

✗ To clean your keyboard, disconnect it from the system unit and gently shake out any dust or crumbs. You can also use cans of compressed air to clear dust or crumbs from underneath the keys. Vacuums specially designed for keyboards also are on the market. Never use a regular vacuum cleaner on your keyboard; the suction is too strong and may damage the keys.

✗ To keep your hard disk running smoothly, run a disk defragmentation program regularly. This program ensures that related data is stored as a unit, increasing retrieval speed.

✗ Get antivirus and antispyware software and run it frequently. Don't install and run any software, or open any files, that you receive from anyone until you check it for viruses and spyware.

SOME FINAL ADVICE

Conducting research before you buy a computer is fairly painless and very powerful. To prepare for buying a computer, peruse newspaper and magazine ads listing computer systems for sale. Another great source is the Web, which makes side-by-side comparison easy. For instance, typing "PC comparison shopping" (including the quotes) into the Google search engine returns more than 2 million links. It's also a good idea to visit a comparison site, such as CNET, PCMag.com, Yahoo! AOL, or PCWorld. To research particular computer manufacturers (such as Apple, Dell, Sony, Toshiba, Lenovo, Gateway, and so on), simply type the manufacturer's name in the address bar of your Web browser and add the .com extension. Use as many resources as you can, and then remember that no matter how happy or unhappy you are with the result, you'll most likely be doing it all again within three to five years.

SPOTLIGHT EXERCISES

1. Have you considered purchasing a used or refurbished computer? Just as with automobiles, you can purchase a computer from a company or from an individual. What are some of the advantages and disadvantages of purchasing a used or refurbished computer from a company or individual? Visit **www.tigerdirect.com** or **www.newegg.com** and search for refurbished computers. Select a specific notebook computer. Identify the computer, its specifications, and its cost. Review this Spotlight and then write a short paper that shows that you understand at least six key terms from the Spotlight as they apply to purchasing a used computer.

2. Create a table in a word processor or use a spreadsheet program to replicate Figure 6J. Save your file without filling in the blank fields. Research the purchase of a new notebook computer and determine the specifications of at least three different models or manufacturers. Fill in the details in your checklist, creating a new file for each computer. Write a cover sheet that includes a paragraph that explains why you would purchase one system over the others. Use key terms from the Spotlight to support your argument.

3. Use your favorite browser to go to **www2.shopping.com/xPP-Monitors**. Locate and compare two 19-inch monitors—one standard monitor (4:3) and one widescreen monitor (16:10). Use key terms from the "Monitors and Video Cards" section of this Spotlight as a basis for comparing the two. Write a paper that includes a table that compares the monitors on at least four points and that explains why you would purchase one monitor type over the other.

4. Research comparable notebook and desktop computers. Your task is to make an argument as to why one would suit your needs better than the other. Consider such things as cost, speed, output quality (monitor size), flexibility, connectivity, and reliability. You may even wish to use the checklist in Figure 6J as a guide. Write a paper that explains why you would be more likely to purchase either a notebook or a desktop.

5. Compare online shopping with in-store shopping. Pick any online computer sales vendor and build a system of your choice. Write down or print out the details and specifications of the computer you've built, including the price and shipping costs. Visit a store that sells computers, such as Wal-Mart, Best Buy, Circuit City, or a local shop, duplicating what you accomplished online. (If you do not have a computer store in your area, use newspaper or magazine advertisements). Write at least two paragraphs about each experience. Which did you prefer? What are the advantages and disadvantages of each? Would you rather buy online or in person? Why?

6. Use the Start, All Programs, Accessories, System Tools menu sequence to access the System Information utility. Write a short paper that includes a table with the values for the following components: the operating system, processor, total physical memory, available physical memory, total virtual memory, and available virtual memory. Using what you learned in the sections on processing, memory, and RAM, is your system current with today's standards? Should you upgrade your computer? Why or why not?

What You'll Learn . . .

- Explain the purpose of the special keys on the keyboard and list the most frequently used pointing devices.

- List the types of monitors and the characteristics that determine a monitor's quality.

- Identify the two major types of printers and indicate the advantages and disadvantages of each.

- Distinguish between memory and storage.

- Discuss how storage media and devices are categorized.

- List factors that affect hard disk performance.

- Explain how data is stored on hard disks and flash drives.

- List and compare the various optical storage media and devices available for personal computers.

- Describe solid-state storage devices and compare them with other types of storage devices.

Input/Output
& Storage

CHAPTER OUTLINE

Input Devices: Giving Commands. 282
    Keyboards 282
    The Mouse and Other Pointing Devices 285
    Additional Input Devices. 287

Output Devices: Engaging Our Senses. 288
    Monitors 288
    Printers 291
    Additional Output Devices. 292

Storage: Holding Data for Future Use 293
    Memory versus Storage 293
    Hard Disk Drives 295
    Flash Drives and Storage. 298
    CD and DVD Technologies. 300
    Solid-State Storage Devices 302
    Storage Horizons 303

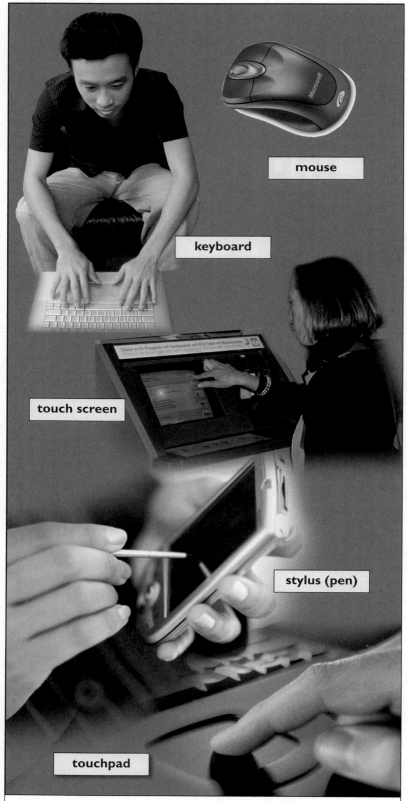

mouse

keyboard

touch screen

stylus (pen)

touchpad

FIGURE 7.1 Input devices enable you to get data, programs, commands, and responses into the computer's memory.

Now that you've learned about hardware and software, let's take a look at the practical effect of inputting data and commands, receiving audio and visual output, and storing your work. When using a computer, your attention is focused on the input and output devices, typically a keyboard, a mouse, and a monitor. Input devices enable you to direct the computer's activity. Output devices transform processed digital information into forms that make sense to humans. They engage our senses—eyes, ears, even touch—with the data that has been processed. Finally, storage devices provide nonvolatile (permanent) storage for the programs and data you work with.

In this chapter, you'll learn about input devices, output devices, the importance of storage, and the types of devices used to store your data.

Input Devices: Giving Commands

Input refers to any data or instructions that you enter into the computer. This section discusses **input devices**, the hardware components that enable you to get data and instructions into the computer's memory (Figure 7.1).

KEYBOARDS

Despite all of the high-tech input devices on the market, the keyboard is still the most common way to get data into the computer. A **keyboard** is an input device that provides a set of keys representing letters, numbers, punctuation marks, and symbols, as well as cursor-movement, toggle, function, and modifier keys.

How do keyboards work? When you press a key, the keyboard sends a digital impulse through a cable (usually a USB cable) to the computer. When the computer receives the impulse, it displays the corresponding character on the screen. The character appears at the on-screen location of the **cursor** (also called the

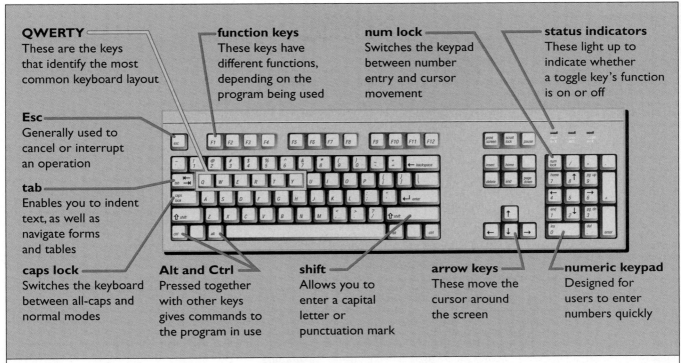

FIGURE 7.2 Most computers use the standard QWERTY keyboard layout. (QWERTY layout is named after the first six letters at the upper left of the letter area.) This enhanced QWERTY keyboard also includes a number of special keys and a numeric keypad.

insertion point), which shows where text will appear when you type. The cursor may be a blinking vertical line, a blinking underscore, or a highlighted box.

Using a Keyboard

All keyboards include keys that enable you to type letters, punctuation marks, and numbers. The keyboard has an assortment of other special keys that enable you to backspace over or delete characters, use a 10-key number pad, navigate software programs, and give commands to the operating system. Desktop PCs typically come equipped with an enhanced keyboard, which has 101 keys (Figures 7.2 and 7.3). The Macintosh equivalent, called the *extended keyboard*, has almost exactly the same keyboard layout.

Let's look at some of the special keys on the keyboard. To reposition the cursor, you can use the mouse or the **cursor-movement keys** (also called **arrow keys**) to move it to another location.

A **toggle key** is a key named after a type of electrical switch that has only two positions: on and off. For example, the

Caps Lock key functions as a toggle key. It switches the Caps Lock mode on and off. When the Caps Lock mode is engaged, you do not have to press the Shift key to enter capital letters. To turn off the Caps Lock mode, just press the Caps Lock key again.

Above the letters and numbers on the keyboard, you'll find **function keys** (labeled F1 through F12 or F15), which provide different commands, depending on the program in use. Near the function keys, you'll also notice the Esc (short for Escape) key. The Esc key's function also depends on which program you're using, but it's generally used to interrupt or cancel an operation.

Some keys have no effect unless you hold them down and press a second key. These are called **modifier keys**, because they modify the meaning of the next key you press. You'll use modifier keys for keyboard shortcuts, which provide quick keyboard access to menu commands.

Using Alternative Keyboards

Although most desktop computers come equipped with a keyboard that is connected by a keyboard cable, some

Destinations

For a list of keyboard shortcuts for many Microsoft products, see Microsoft's "Keyboard Assistance and Shortcuts" at **www.microsoft.com/ enable/products/ keyboard.aspx**. You can find the Mac shortcuts at **http:// docs.info.apple.com/ article.html?artnum= 75459**.

FIGURE 7.3 Special Keys on the PC Enhanced Keyboard

Key Name	Typical Function
Alt	In combination with another key, enters a command (example: Alt + F = file menu).
Backspace	Deletes the character to the left of the cursor.
Caps Lock	Toggles Caps Lock mode on or off.
Ctrl	In combination with another key, enters a command (example: Ctrl + C = copy).
Delete	Deletes the character to the right of the cursor.
Down arrow	Moves the cursor down, one line at a time.
End	Moves the cursor to the end of the current line.
Esc	Cancels the current operation or closes a dialog box.
F1	Displays on-screen help.
Home	Moves the cursor to the beginning of the current line.
Insert	Toggles between insert and overwrite mode, if these modes are available in the program you're using.
Left arrow	Moves the cursor to the left, one character at a time.
Num Lock	Toggles the numeric keypads Num Lock mode between number entry and cursor movement.
Page Down	Moves down one full screen or one page.
Page Up	Moves up one full screen or one page.
Pause/Break	Suspends a program. (This key is not used by most applications.)
Menu key	Displays context-sensitive menu (instead of right-clicking).
Print Screen	Captures the screen image and places it in memory.
Right arrow	Moves the cursor to the right, one character at a time.
Up arrow	Moves the cursor up, one line at a time.
Windows key	Displays the Start menu in Microsoft Windows.

computers are equipped with a radio frequency (RF) receiver that enables them to use a wireless keyboard (also called a cordless keyboard). These keyboards use radio waves to send signals to the computer.

As media center PCs become an integral part of home theaters, the need for a stylish, unobtrusive keyboard takes on greater importance. Small, wireless keyboards combining a cursor control pad with a mini-keyboard let you control your PC entertainment center from the comfort of your own couch (Figure 7.4).

Now that we've discussed the basics of using keyboards, let's move on to another piece of equipment commonly used for input: pointing devices.

FIGURE 7.4 Keyboards for PC home entertainment systems are compact and allow users to control various media components by keyboard or touchpad.

THE MOUSE AND OTHER POINTING DEVICES

A **pointing device** gives you control over the movements of the on-screen pointer. The **pointer** is an on-screen symbol that signifies the type of command, input, or response you can give. Pointing devices such as a mouse also enable you to initiate actions, such as clicking, double-clicking, selecting, and dragging. By these actions, you can give commands and responses to whatever program the computer is running. Pointing devices can also be used to provide input (Figure 7.5). For example, pointing devices can be used in graphics programs to draw and paint on the screen, just as if you were using a pencil or brush.

The most widely used pointing device is the mouse, which is a standard piece of equipment with today's computer systems. A **mouse** is a palm-size pointing device designed to move about on a clean, flat surface. Although older roller-ball mice needed a mouse pad for traction, newer optical mice do not. As you move the mouse, its movements are mirrored by the on-screen pointer. You initiate actions by using the mouse buttons.

Developed by Microsoft, the **wheel mouse** includes a rotating wheel that can be used to scroll text vertically within a document or on a Web page (Figure 7.6). Another type of mouse, the wireless mouse (also called a cordless mouse), uses radio

FIGURE 7.5 Pointing devices come in a variety of shapes and styles.

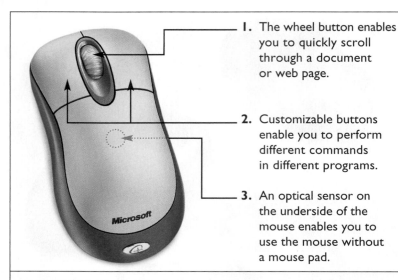

1. The wheel button enables you to quickly scroll through a document or web page.

2. Customizable buttons enable you to perform different commands in different programs.

3. An optical sensor on the underside of the mouse enables you to use the mouse without a mouse pad.

FIGURE 7.6 The optical wheel mouse is a commonly used pointing device.

waves to communicate with a transceiver on the computer.

Mouse Alternatives

Although the mouse is by far the most popular pointing device, some people prefer alternative devices, such as trackballs, pointing sticks, or touch pads. These alternatives are especially attractive when desktop space is limited or nonexistent (as is often the case when using a notebook computer). Additional input devices, such as joysticks, touch screens, and styluses,

are also available for special purposes, such as playing games, using ATMs, and managing handheld devices.

A **trackball** is basically a mouse flipped on its back. Instead of moving the mouse, you move the rotating ball. Trackballs usually come with one or more buttons that work in the same way as mouse buttons.

A **pointing stick** is a small, stubby nub that protrudes from the computer's keyboard. Pointing sticks are pressure sensitive; you use the stick by pushing it in various directions with your finger. Separate buttons initiate clicking and dragging motions in conjunction with the pointing stick.

Most notebook computers use a touchpad for a pointing device. A **touchpad** (also called a **trackpad**) is a pressure-sensitive device that responds to your finger's movement over the pad's surface.

A **joystick** is an input device with a large vertical lever that can be moved in any direction. Although you can use joysticks as pointing devices, they're most often used to control the motion of an on-screen object in a computer game or training simulator.

A **touch screen** is a pressure-sensitive panel that detects where a user has tapped the display screen with a fingertip. Because touch screens are reliable, easy to use, and virtually impossible to steal, they are often used in kiosks. A **kiosk** is a booth that provides a computer service of some type, such as an ATM. In addition to banks, touch screen kiosks can be found in places such as airports, department stores, movie theaters, pharmacies, and convenience stores, allowing people to bypass clerks and quickly place orders, access gift registries, apply for jobs, or look up information (Figure 7.7).

Because human fingers are much bigger than an on-screen pointer, software designers must provide fewer options and larger on-screen buttons on touch screens. These characteristics of touch screens make them best suited to simple, special-purpose programs.

A **stylus**, which looks like an ordinary pen except that the tip is dry and semi-blunt, is commonly used with various handheld devices. Styluses are often used along with a pressure-sensitive graphics tablet in CAD applications and other graphics applications to create designs or draw objects, such as cars, buildings, medical devices, and robots. You may have also used a stylus to create your digital

FIGURE 7.7 Self-service kiosks using touch screen technology can be found in many locations.

signature when using your credit card or accepting a package from a delivery person.

ADDITIONAL INPUT DEVICES

Though keyboards and pointing devices are most commonly used to input data, a number of specialized input devices are also available. This section introduces some of these alternative input devices and their uses.

Speech recognition, also called **voice recognition**, is a type of input in which the computer recognizes spoken words. To accept speech, a computer must have a microphone. A **microphone** is an input device that converts sound waves into electrical signals that the computer can process. All modern computers are equipped with a sound card, which is an expansion board designed to record and play back sound files.

Dragon NaturallySpeaking is a popular stand-alone voice recognition software package. Microsoft's new Vista operating system also enables you to use speech recognition with any software package. Vista's speech-recognition capability enables you to control software by issuing menu commands such as "Open file" or perform tasks such as dictating a letter in Microsoft Word, simply by speaking into a microphone (Figure 7.8).

To use speech-recognition software, you first have to "train" the software to understand how you speak and how to translate this speech into typed words. You do this by dictating a number of prepared passages into the computer through a microphone so that the software can "learn" how you speak—your accent, enunciation, and pronunciation. The more you train the software, the better it becomes at correctly recognizing your words. If the computer doesn't know which word you have spoken (for example, if it hears "to" but isn't sure if it's "to," "too," or "two"), it will figure out which word is correct based on the context in which it is found.

Early speech-recognition systems used discrete speech recognition—you had to speak each word separately. In contrast, today's continuous speech-recognition software enables users to speak without pausing between words.

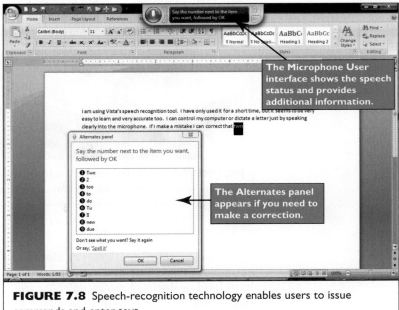

FIGURE 7.8 Speech-recognition technology enables users to issue commands and enter text.

Although many people use speech recognition as a simple dictation device, speech-recognition software not only improves productivity, relieving tired and overused hands, but it also provides an alternative input option for people who are not able to use a keyboard.

A **scanner** copies anything that's printed on a sheet of paper, including artwork, handwriting, and typed or printed documents, and converts the input into a digital file. Most scanners use **optical character recognition** (**OCR**) software to automatically convert scanned text into a text file. This technology has improved so much that most printed or typed documents can be scanned into text files, eliminating the need to retype such documents to get them into the computer.

Flatbed scanners copy items placed on a stationary glass surface (Figure 7.9a). They are good for books or other bulky objects and are also useful for photos and other documents that shouldn't be bent. Sheet-fed scanners use a roller mechanism to draw in multiple sheets of paper, one sheet at a time, and are useful for high-volume scanning. Handheld scanners are similar to sheet-fed scanners, in that the item to be copied must pass through the scanner, but are smaller and portable. They are often used to copy business cards, magazine articles, small photos, or business documents (Figure 7.9b).

Destinations

Speech recognition has improved over the years, but is still not perfect. Read about some of the weaknesses and flaws of speech recognition software at **http://electronics. howstuffworks.com/ speech-recognition3. htm**.

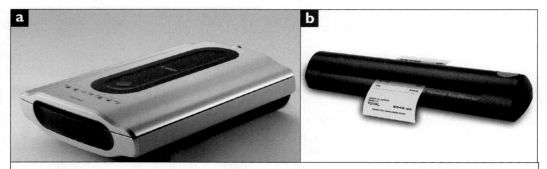

FIGURE 7.9 (a) Flatbed scanners scan a single piece of paper at a time. (b) Handheld scanners are more portable and flexible and are often used to scan business cards, small photos, or documents.

In many retail and grocery stores, employees use a **bar code reader**, a handheld or desktop-mounted scanning device that reads an item's universal product code (UPC). The UPC is a pattern of bars printed on merchandise that the store's computer system uses to retrieve information about an item and its price. Today, bar codes are used to update inventory and ensure correct pricing. For example, FedEx uses a bar code system to identify and track packages.

In class, every time you take a test on a Scantron form, you're creating input suitable for an optical mark reader. An **optical mark reader** (**OMR**) is a scanning device that senses the magnetized marks from your #2 pencil to determine which responses are marked. Almost any type of questionnaire can be designed for OMR devices, making it helpful to researchers who need to tabulate responses to large surveys.

Now that we know how to get our data into a computer system, let's look at how output devices are used to send the data back to us.

Output Devices: Engaging Our Senses

Output devices enable people to see, hear, and even feel the results of processing operations. The most widely used output devices are monitors and printers.

MONITORS

Monitors (also called **displays**) display output. The on-screen display enables you to see your processed data. It's important to remember that the screen display isn't a permanent record. To drive home this point, screen output is sometimes called *soft copy*, as opposed to *hard copy* (printed output). To make permanent copies of your work, you should save it to a storage device or print it.

The big, bulky monitors that are often connected to older desktop computers are **cathode-ray tube (CRT) monitors** (Figure 7.10). In a CRT monitor, three light "guns" (corresponding to the colors red, green, and blue) are combined in

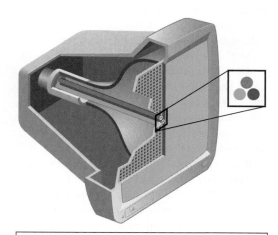

FIGURE 7.10 Most cathode-ray tube (CRT) monitors display color output.

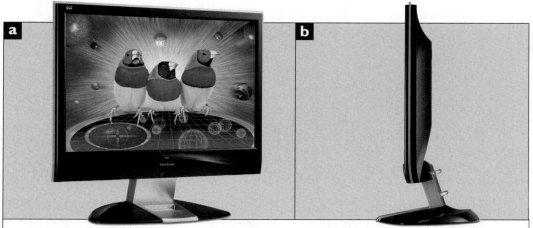

FIGURE 7.11 This 28-inch widescreen LCD monitor (a) from ViewSonic includes built-in speakers and HDMI input for high-definition video, and (b) has an incredibly thin profile.

varying intensities to produce on-screen colors.

The thinner monitors used with notebooks and newer desktop computers are known as **liquid crystal displays (LCDs)** or **flat-panel displays** and are rapidly replacing CRT monitors. The least expensive LCDs are called passive-matrix LCDs (also called dual scans). These monitors may generate image flaws and are too slow for full-motion video. **Active-matrix**, or **Thin Film Transistor (TFT)**, technology is used in most current LCD monitors. Active-matrix LCDs use transistors to control the color of each on-screen pixel (Figure 7.11).

Other flat-panel display technologies include gas-plasma displays and field-emission displays (FEDs). Still under development, FEDs look like LCDs, except that a tiny carbon nanotube produces each on-screen pixel.

LCD monitors are ideal for portable computers, including notebooks, PDAs, and Web-enabled devices, such as smartphones (Figure 7.12).

Screen Size

The size of a monitor is determined by measuring it diagonally. This is fairly straightforward for LCD monitors. However, for CRT monitors it's a bit trickier because there are two different measurements. The **quoted size** is the diagonal measurement of the CRT screen, but because part of the screen is

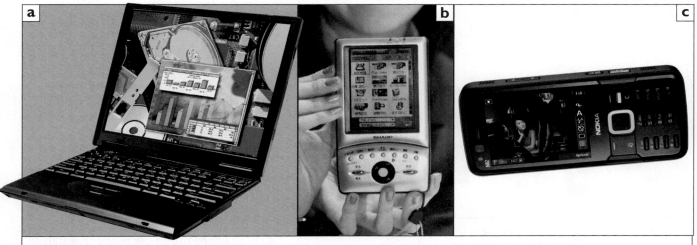

FIGURE 7.12 LCD monitors are ideal for portable devices such as (**a**) notebooks, (**b**) PDAs, and (**c**) smartphones.

FIGURE 7.13 Common PC Monitor Resolutions

640 × 480	VGA	Video Graphics Array
800 × 600	SVGA	Super Video Graphics Array
1,024 × 768	XGA	Extended Graphics Array
1,280 × 1,024	SXGA	Super Extended Graphics Array
1,600 × 1,200	UXGA	Ultra Extended Graphics Array

obscured by its housing, the actual **viewable area** is somewhat smaller. Both of these sizes must be disclosed by the manufacturer.

Typical desktop PC monitors range from 17 to 21 inches, whereas notebook computers measure 12 to 17 inches. Larger monitors, such as the 28-inch ViewSonic monitor shown in Figure 7.11, are popular with gamers, graphic designers, and others who need to display two documents side by side. In fact, a recent study found that larger monitors can improve productivity—individuals using a 24-inch monitor completed their work almost twice as fast as those using a smaller monitor!

Resolution

The term **resolution** generally refers to the sharpness of an image. Video adapters conform to standard resolutions that are expressed as the number of dots (pixels) that can be displayed. For example, a resolution of 1,024 × 768 means 1,024 horizontal pixels by 768 vertical pixels. Figure 7.13 lists common PC monitor resolutions.

For color graphics displays, **Video Graphics Array** (**VGA**) is the lowest-resolution standard (640 × 480). Most of today's monitors are equipped with at least **Super VGA** (1,024 × 768). The newest models sport Super and Ultra Extended Graphics Array video adapters—allowing for an amazing 1,600 pixels per line and 1,200 lines of pixels per screen!

Refresh Rate

Another important measurement of video adapter quality is the refresh rate generated at a given resolution. The **refresh rate** refers to the frequency at which the screen image is updated, and it's measured in hertz (Hz), or cycles per second. Below 60 Hz, most people notice an annoying, eye-straining flicker. Very few people notice flicker when the refresh rate exceeds 72 Hz.

Televisions as Monitors

To the casual observer, there doesn't seem to be much difference between an LCD monitor and an LCD TV, so why not hook up your PC to your TV for an even bigger computer screen? **High-definition television** (**HDTV**), a digital television standard that provides extremely high-quality video and audio, makes this a possibility. You'll need to have a video card with a DVI or HDMI port on your PC and the corresponding input on the TV (Figure 7.14). One possible limitation has to do with resolution. The resolution on older TVs was much lower than PCs, so the viewing results were less than optimal. However, newer HDTVs have higher resolutions, typically 1920 × 1080 or better, making this less of a problem.

If you'd rather watch live TV on your PC, you can do that too. Install a TV tuner card in your PC and get ready to watch or record your favorite shows.

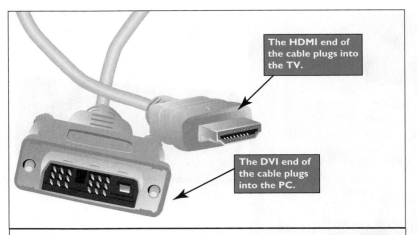

The HDMI end of the cable plugs into the TV.

The DVI end of the cable plugs into the PC.

FIGURE 7.14 If your PC doesn't have an HDMI port, an HDMI-DVI cable can be used to connect the PC to the TV.

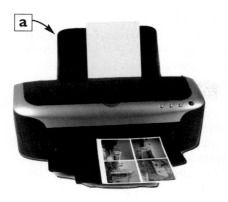

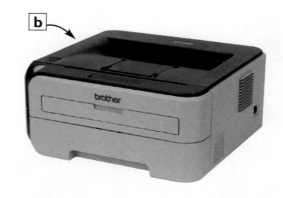

FIGURE 7.15 Inkjet printers (**a**) produce high-quality color output. Black and white laser printers (**b**) provide quick output at affordable prices.

Now that we've discussed monitors and soft copy, let's move on to devices that produce hard-copy output: printers.

PRINTERS

Printers produce a permanent version, or *hard copy*, of the output on the computer's display screen. Some of the most popular printers are inkjet printers and laser printers (Figure 7.15).

Inkjet printers are relatively inexpensive and produce excellent color output, which makes them popular choices for home users. Inkjet printers form an image that is composed of tiny dots. The printout is difficult to distinguish from the fully formed characters printed by laser printers. Inkjet printers are relatively slow compared with laser printers, and per-page printing costs can be high owing to the high cost of ink cartridges.

A **laser printer** is a high-resolution printer that uses an electrostatic reproductive technology similar to that used by copiers. Under the printer's computerized control, a laser beam creates electrical charges on a rotating print drum. These charges attract toner, which is transferred to the paper and fused to its surface by a heat process. Laser printers print faster than inkjets; some laser printers can crank out 60 or more pages per minute. Black and white laser printers are becoming more affordable and generally have a lower per-page print cost than inkjet printers; however, color laser printers are still more expensive to buy.

Dot-matrix printers (also known as impact printers) were once the most popular type of printer but are declining in use. Although they are capable of printing 3,000 lines per minute, their print quality is lower than other printers and they are noisy. Dot-matrix printers are mainly used for printing backup copies or for printing multipart forms, such as invoices or purchase orders.

Thermal-transfer printers use a heat process to transfer colored dyes or inks to the paper's surface and are often used for industrial applications. The best thermal-transfer printers are called dye sublimation printers. These printers are slow and expensive, but they produce results that are difficult to distinguish from high-quality color photographs.

Photo printers, when used with good-quality photo paper, can produce pictures that are as good as those from commercial photo processors. Photo printers are often inkjets, but they can also be color lasers. The best photo printers use at least six colors of special ink. Many allow you to bypass your computer to print directly from a digital camera or memory card.

A **plotter** is a printer that produces high-quality images by physically moving ink pens over the surface of the paper. A continuous-curve plotter draws maps from stored data (Figure 7.16). Computer-generated maps, such as those used by cartographers and weather analysts, can be retrieved and plotted or used to show changes over time.

> ### Green Tech Tip
>
> More than 700 million inkjet and laser toner cartridges are sold every year. What happens when they are empty? Although many organizations and retail stores have recycling programs, every second nearly eight used cartridges are thrown away in the United States—approximately 875 million pounds of environmental waste! So what can you do? Take advantage of your local recycling program. Some programs will even pay you for your old cartridges, because they can be recycled and sold again. Keeping them out of the waste stream reduces toxicity levels and saves landfill space. Plus, half a gallon of oil is conserved for every toner cartridge you recycle!

FIGURE 7.16 Plotters are useful for printing oversized output such as maps, charts, and blueprints.

ADDITIONAL OUTPUT DEVICES

Speakers are needed to listen to computer-generated sound, such as music and synthesized speech, and are standard equipment on new computer systems. Like microphones, speakers also require a sound card to function. Sound cards play the contents of digitized recordings, such as music recorded in WAV and MP3 sound file formats. Some sound cards do this job better than others. Quality enters into the picture most noticeably when the sound card reproduces MIDI files. MIDI files play over **synthesizers**, electronic devices that produce music by generating musical tones. Sound cards have built-in synthesizers. Better sound cards use wavetable synthesis, whereby the sound card generates sounds using ROM-based recordings of actual musical instruments. The latest sound cards include surround-sound effects.

Data projectors display a computer's video output on a screen for an audience to view. They range from small, light-weight devices used for business or class presentations and home theaters, to larger, more expensive models suitable for use in auditoriums or stadiums. Individuals and businesses often use LCD or DLP projectors. In an **LCD projector**, an image is formed by passing light through three colored panels—red, green, and blue. LCD projectors produce sharp, accurate color images; however, they are subject to pixelation and have less contrast than a DLP projector. **DLP (digital light-processing) projectors** project light onto a chip made up of millions of microscopic mirrors. DLP projectors (Figure 7.17a) are often smaller and lighter than LCD projectors and have better contrast; but in some models, the reflected light can create a rainbow effect that causes eyestrain for some people.

Computers equipped with a fax modem and fax software can receive incoming faxes. The incoming document is displayed on the screen, and it can be printed or saved.

Computers can also send faxes as output. To send a fax using your computer, you must save your document using a special format that is compatible with the fax program. The fax program can then send the document through the telephone system to a distant fax machine. This output function is helpful because you don't have to print the document to send it as a fax (Figure 7.17b).

FIGURE 7.17 The ViewSonic PJ260D (a) is a powerful portable DLP projector. A fax machine (b) performs both input and output functions.

Multifunction devices combine inkjet or laser printers with a scanner, a fax machine and a copier, enabling home office users to obtain all of these devices without spending a great deal of money (Figure 7.18).

Now that you've learned about a variety of output devices, let's look at how you can store data for later use.

Storage: Holding Data for Future Use

Storage (also called **mass storage** or **auxiliary storage**) refers to the ways a computer system can store software and data. Storage relies on two components— storage media and storage devices. **Storage media** includes hard disks, floppy disks, flash memory, CDs, and DVDs that run on storage devices. A **storage device** is computer hardware that is capable of retaining data even when electrical power is switched off. In other words, storage devices are the various drives (hard drive, floppy drive, USB flash drive, and so on) that enable the disks to operate.

Organizations increasingly turn to computer storage systems to store all of their computer software, data, and information. The reason? Storing information on paper is expensive and offers no opportunity for electronic manipulation and sharing. As you'll learn in this section, a simple storage device can store the amount of information that would cost $10,000 to store on paper for less than $10 per giga-byte. In fact, storage devices are increasing in capacity to the point that they can hold an entire library's worth of information. Read on to learn why storage is necessary, what kinds of storage devices and media are out there, and which will best fit your computing needs.

MEMORY VERSUS STORAGE

To understand the distinction between memory and storage, think of the last time you worked at your desk. In your file

FIGURE 7.18 A multifunction device combines an inkjet or laser printer with a scanner, a fax machine, and a copier.

drawer, you store all of your personal items and papers, such as your checking account statements. The file drawer is good for long-term storage. When you decide to work on one or more of these items, you take it out of storage and put it on your desk. The desktop is a good place to keep the items you're working with; they're close at hand and available for use right away. Your desktop can be thought of as mem-ory—the place where you temporarily store things that you are working on.

Computers work the same way. When you want to work with the contents of a file, the computer transfers the file to a temporary workplace: the computer's memory. Memory is a form of storage, but it is temporary. Why don't computers just use memory to hold all of those files? Here are some reasons:

- **Storage devices retain data when the current is switched off.** The computer's RAM is volatile. This means that when you switch off the computer's power, all of the information in RAM is irretrievably lost. In contrast, storage devices are non-volatile. They do not lose data when the power goes off.

- **Storage devices are cheaper than memory.** RAM operates very quickly to keep up with the computer's CPU. For this reason, RAM is expensive— much more expensive than storage. In fact, most computers are equipped with just enough RAM to accommodate all of the programs a user wants to run

↖ → ↘ → ↑ →

Destinations

Looking for the latest news and information concerning storage media? SearchStorage. com at **http://searchstorage. techtarget.com** offers a wealth of informa-tion about storage technologies, including product reviews, background informa-tion, storage-related software, online discussions, and troubleshooting tips.

CURRENTS

Emerging Technologies

Wearables: The Fashion of Technology

After getting dressed in the morning, you head down the street in your "wearables." As you walk to the library, you use your wrist pad to e-mail a friend, asking her to meet you for lunch later. At the library, the network automatically recognizes you by your ring. You search your pocket for your stylus, find it, point at a library computer screen, and the computer acknowledges you. You use your monocle to access your documents. You open one and jot notes by waving your pen in the air. As you leave the library, you call three of your friends and visually chat with them through your monocle and earpiece until your next class. Your wearables seamlessly connect you to a network throughout your day.

Sound intriguing but unbelievable? Some of these technologies already exist. Just think about the number of people walking around with an MP3 player clipped to their jacket, using a Bluetooth headset for a hands-free phone conversation, while carrying more than 1 GB of files on their USB-drive key ring. Although many wearable technology concepts remain rather futuristic, some are taking on more practical applications, especially in industrial and health care fields. Most wearable technologies have been incorporated into headsets and glasses; backpacks and fanny packs; rings, watches, wristbands; and multipocket pants, jackets, and vests.

Honda's experimental walking assist device uses some of the same technology that their ASIMO robot does and is designed to improve mobility for the elderly and disabled. Meanwhile, CSIRO is developing a Flexible Integrated Energy Device (FIED) to be incorporated into clothing. Energy generated by the wearer's movements will be stored by the FIED and used to charge batteries or supply power to other portable devices.

Already on the market, Voltaic solar bags are made of recycled materials and include solar panels to recharge your devices (Figure 7.19). Their newest offering, the Generator, is powerful enough to charge a notebook computer. Not bad, considering the Consumer Electronics Association estimates that 5 percent of an individual's energy usage is devoted to powering mobile devices.

Wearable technology may not be mainstream yet, but the chances of one day finding it in your closet are getting closer!

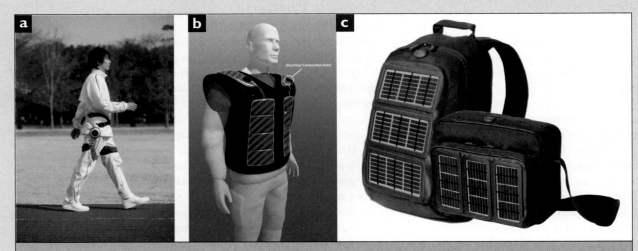

FIGURE 7.19 Honda's walking assist device (a) and CSIRO's flexible integrated energy device (b) are still in development, but some wearable technology, like the Voltaic solar bags (c), are already in use.

at once. In contrast, a computer system's storage devices hold much more data and software than the computer's memory does. Today, you can buy a storage device capable of storing more than 300 GB of software and data for about the same amount you would pay for 2 GB of RAM (Figure 7.20).

FIGURE 7.20 Memory versus Storage

		Access Speed	Cost per MB	Storage Capacity
Memory	Cache memory	Fastest	Highest	2 MB
	RAM	Fast	High	4 GB
Storage	Hard disk	Medium	Medium	1 TB
	CD-R disc	Slow	Low	700 MB

- **Storage devices play an essential role in system start-up operations.** When you start your computer, the BIOS reads essential programs into the computer's RAM, including one that begins loading essential system software from the computer's hard disk.

- **Storage devices are needed for output.** When you've finished working, you use the computer's storage system as an output device to save a file. When you save a file, the computer transfers your work from the computer's memory to a storage device. If you forget to save your work, it will be lost when you switch off the computer's power. Remember, the computer's RAM is volatile!

For all of these reasons, demand for storage capacity is soaring. Storage capacity is measured in bytes (KB, MB, GB, and TB). Capacities range from the flash drive's 2 GB (and up) to huge room-filling arrays of storage devices capable of storing terabytes or even petabytes of data. To provide this much storage with print-based media, you'd need to cut down several million trees. According to one estimate, the need for digital storage is increasing 60 percent each year, and the pace shows no signs of slowing down.

Now that you understand the importance of storage, let's look at the devices and media used to hold data.

HARD DISK DRIVES

On almost all computers, the hard disk drive is by far the most important storage device. A **hard disk drive** (or simply **hard**

disk) is a high-capacity, high-speed storage device that usually consists of several fixed, rapidly rotating disks called **platters**.

The computer's hard disk is also referred to as secondary storage. The computer's memory is considered primary storage. **Secondary storage** (also called **online** or **fixed storage**) consists of the storage devices that are actively available to the computer system and that do not require any action on the part of the user. Hard disks can also be categorized as random access or magnetic storage devices. A **random access storage device** can go directly to the requested data without having to go through a linear search sequence. **Magnetic storage devices** use disks that are coated with magnetically sensitive material.

With magnetic storage devices, an electromagnet called a **read/write head** moves across the surface of a disk and records information by transforming electrical impulses into a varying magnetic field. As the magnetic materials pass beneath the read/write head, this varying field forces the particles to rearrange themselves in a meaningful pattern of positive and negative magnetic indicators. This operation is called *writing*. When *reading*, the read/write head senses the recorded pattern and transforms this pattern into electrical impulses.

A hard disk contains two or more vertically stacked platters, each with two read/write heads (one for each side of the disk). The platters spin so rapidly that the read/write head floats on a thin cushion of air, at a distance one three-hundredth the width of a human hair. To protect the platter's surface, hard disks are enclosed in a sealed container.

How does the read/write head know where to look for data? To answer this question, you need to know a little about how stored data is organized on a disk. Like a vinyl record, disks contain circular bands called **tracks**. Each track is divided into pie-shaped wedges called **sectors**. Two or more sectors combine to form a **cluster** (Figure 7.21).

To keep track of where specific files are located, the computer's operating system records a table of information on the disk. This table contains the name of each file and the file's exact location on the disk. Older versions of Microsoft Windows called this the **file allocation table**, or **FAT**; however, the current system is known as **NTFS** (**new technology file system**).

Hard disks can be divided into partitions. A **partition** is a section of a disk set aside as if it were a physically separate disk. Partitions are often used to enable computers to work with more than one operating system. For example, Linux users often create one partition for Linux and another for Microsoft Windows. In this way, they can work with programs developed for either operating system.

To communicate with the CPU, hard disks require a hard disk controller. A **hard disk controller** is an electronic circuit board that provides an interface between the CPU and the hard disk's electronics. The controller may be located on the computer's motherboard, on an expansion card, or within the hard disk.

Network Attached Storage (NAS)

As demands for data storage have increased, **network attached storage** (**NAS**) devices are becoming more popular. NAS devices are comprised primarily of hard drives or other media used for data storage and are attached directly to a network. The network connection permits each computer on the network to access the NAS to save or retrieve data.

Some external hard drives sold for the home market can function as NAS devices. The advantage is that one device can be used to coordinate and store backup files for all PCs connected to the home network.

Remote Storage

Remote storage, sometimes referred to as an **Internet hard drive**, is storage space on a server that is accessible from the Internet. In most cases, a computer user subscribes to the storage service and agrees to rent a block of storage space for a specific period of time. Instead of sending e-mail attachments to share with family and friends, you might simply post the files to the remote storage site and then allow them to be viewed or retrieved by

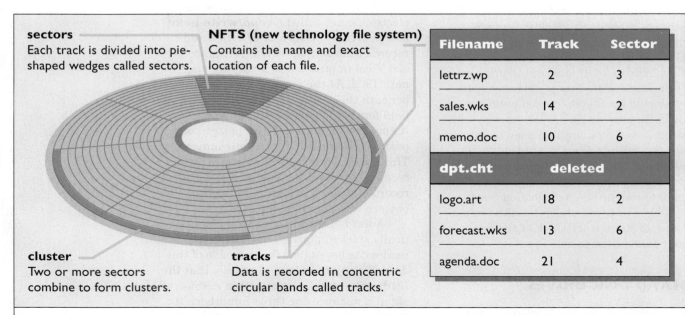

sectors
Each track is divided into pie-shaped wedges called sectors.

NFTS (new technology file system)
Contains the name and exact location of each file.

Filename	Track	Sector
lettrz.wp	2	3
sales.wks	14	2
memo.doc	10	6
dpt.cht	**deleted**	
logo.art	18	2
forecast.wks	13	6
agenda.doc	21	4

cluster
Two or more sectors combine to form clusters.

tracks
Data is recorded in concentric circular bands called tracks.

FIGURE 7.21 Disks contain circular bands called tracks, which are divided into sectors. Two or more sectors combine to form a cluster.

others. You might save backup copies of critical files or all the data on your hard disk to your Internet hard drive.

The key advantage of this type of remote storage is the ability to access data from multiple locations. You can access your files from any device that can connect with the Internet, so everything you store on the site is available to you at any time. Some disadvantages are that your data may not be secure; the storage device might become corrupt, causing you to lose your data; and the company offering the Internet storage may go out of business.

Factors Affecting Hard Disk Performance

If a hard disk develops a defect or a read/write head encounters an obstacle, such as a dust or smoke particle, the head bounces on the disk surface, preventing the computer from reading or writing data to one or more sectors of the disk. Hard disks can absorb minor jostling without suffering damage, but a major jolt—such as one caused by dropping the computer while the drive is running—could cause a head crash to occur. Head crashes are one of the causes of **bad sectors**—areas of the disk that have become damaged and that can no

longer reliably hold data. If you see an on-screen message indicating that a disk has a bad sector, try to copy the data off the disk and don't use it to store new data.

A storage device's most important performance characteristic is the speed at which it retrieves desired data. The amount of time it takes for the device to begin reading data is its **access time**. For disk drives, the access time includes the **seek time**, the time it takes the read/write head to locate the data before reading begins. **Positioning performance** refers to how quickly the drive positions the read/write head to begin transferring data and is measured by seek time.

Transfer performance refers to how quickly the disk transfers data from the disk to memory. One way disk manufacturers improve transfer performance is to increase the speed at which the disk spins, which makes data available more quickly to the read/write heads. Another way is to improve the spacing of data on the disk so that the heads can retrieve several blocks of data on each revolution.

Another way to improve hard disk performance is with a type of cache memory called disk cache (Figure 7.22). A **disk cache** is a type of RAM that stores the

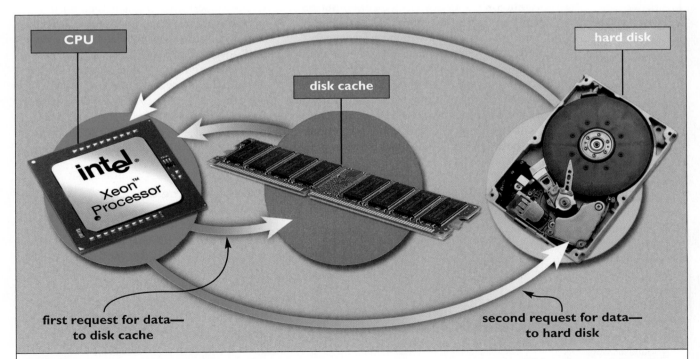

FIGURE 7.22 Disk cache, a type of RAM, dramatically improves hard disk performance. When the CPU needs to get information, it looks in the disk cache first.

program instructions and data you are working with. When the CPU needs to get information, it looks in the disk cache first. If it doesn't find the information it needs, it retrieves the information from the hard disk.

Although hard disks are currently the most important storage media, the disks explored in the next section are examples of portable storage, which means that you can remove a disk from one computer and insert it into another.

FLASH DRIVES AND STORAGE

A **flash drive** is a type of storage device that uses solid-state circuitry and has no moving parts (Figure 7.23). Flash drives are also known as **solid-state drives** (**SSDs**) and use **flash memory**, which is nonvolatile, electronic memory. Flash memory stores data electronically on a chip in sections known as **blocks**. Rather than erasing data byte by byte, flash memory uses an electrical charge to delete all of the data on the chip or just the data contained in a specific block, which is a much quicker method than other types of storage use. Flash memory is limited to 100,000 write cycles. This means information can be written and erased 100,000 times to each block, which could conceivably take years to occur. Because of their lack of moving parts, lower power consumption, and lighter weight, flash drives are becoming an alternative to hard disk drives, especially in notebook computing. Lenovo's ThinkPad and Apple's MacBook Air both offer a 64 GB flash drive in place

of a traditional hard disk drive. Flash drives are also found in some MP3 players, smartphones, and digital cameras. Although flash drives are more expensive and have less storage capacity than hard disk drives, these differences are expected to erode over time. Additionally, some hard disk drives are incorporating flash technology, creating **hybrid hard drives** (**HHDs**) that use flash memory to speed up the boot process.

Another form of flash storage is the USB flash drive. **USB flash drives**, also known as memory sticks, thumb drives, or jump drives, are popular **portable**, or **removable**, **storage** devices. Because of their small size and universal ease of use, they have supplanted floppy disks and Zip disks as the removable storage medium of choice. Both floppy disks and Zip disks are now considered legacy technologies. USB flash drives work with both the PC and the Mac, and no device driver is required—just plug it into a USB port and it's ready to read and write. USB flash drives are made of plastic and are shock-proof, moisture-proof, and magnetization-proof. Many USB flash drives include security and encryption software to help protect your data in case you lose it. Some devices have a retractable USB connector, eliminating the need for a protective cap, which is often misplaced, and others are available in different colors and novelty shapes (Figure 7.25). One interesting characteristic is that the drives get their power supply from the device they are plugged into. Capacities range from 1 GB to 16 GB, and they can read and write at speeds up to 30 Mbps. Watch for capacities to go up and prices to come down.

Protecting the Data on Your USB Drive

Because your USB drive has no moving parts, it can be difficult to tell when it is working. Usually, if the contents of a USB drive are being accessed, a small LED light on the drive will flash. It is very important not to disconnect the flash drive when a file is being saved or accessed, because this can corrupt the data. Make sure any files on your USB drive are closed, then look for the Safely Remove Hardware icon in the System Tray on the bottom right side of the

FIGURE 7.23 Flash drives provide a durable, lightweight alternative to hard disks.

Ethics

USB flash drives are incredibly popular, but many experts worry that they pose a great security risk too. Some companies are so concerned about corporate espionage that they disable USB ports to prevent the unauthorized copying of data. Even so, many people carry a lot of critical or personal data on their flash drives. What are the implications if the device is lost? Should USB drive manufacturers be required to provide a means of securing these devices? What actions should individuals take to safeguard their data? Have you ever found a USB drive? What did you do with it?

IMPACTS

Milestones

Storage 100 Times More Efficient Is on the Way!

Flash memory and hard drives are the main storage devices in today's computing devices. But the designers of storage devices constantly face these challenges:

1. making data storage more cost effective
2. reducing the size of storage devices
3. decreasing the power consumption of storage devices

These issues are extremely critical for mobile devices. Hard drives and flash memory may eventually be replaced by a new technology called "racetrack" memory, which is under development by Stuart Parkin and his colleagues at IBM's Almaden Research Center (Figure 7.24).

Racetrack memory uses the spin of electrons to store information. This allows the memory to operate at much higher speeds than today's storage media, which is a boon for transferring and retrieving data. In addition, it is anticipated that racetrack memory will consume much less power and that mobile devices may be able to run for as long as several weeks on a single charge. After the memory is rolled out for the mass market, it should be even cheaper to produce than flash memory.

A current limitation of flash memory is that it can only be written to (store data) several thousand times before it wears out. Racetrack memory will not suffer from this limitation and will have no moving parts, making it much less susceptible to breakage than conventional hard drives. The capacity of racetrack memory could allow iPods to store 500,000 songs instead of the 40,000 that the largest units can handle today.

The principles of physics being used to develop racetrack memory might help break the barrier that Moore's Law is quickly approaching. Gordon Moore, one of the founders of Intel Corporation, observed in 1965 that computing speed (related to CPUs) would double roughly every two years. This concept was dubbed Moore's law. As chip technologies improved, the time frame was updated to 18 months. But scientists are reaching the limits for the number of transistors they can put on a silicon wafer using conventional methods. In fact, Gordon Moore recently stated that by 2020 the laws of physics might prevent Moore's law from being true any longer. However, IBM's research on racetrack memory might also have applications in transistor applications and may eventually provide a solution to the Moore's law barrier.

The ability to carry mobile computing devices loaded with tons of information that can be retrieved very quickly with processors that operate at extremely high speeds should lead to the development of devices that we haven't even dreamed about yet. Perhaps we will eventually be able to carry around the entire contents of the Internet in a mobile device!

FIGURE 7.24 IBM scientists like Stuart Parkin (shown in the lead car) are researching racetrack memory, which may enable electronic devices to store much more data in the same amount of space with much faster access times.

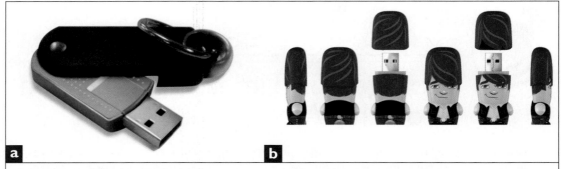

FIGURE 7.25 Many USB flash drives retract to protect the USB connector (**a**), whereas others (**b**) take a more unique approach to data storage.

screen. Double-click the icon to open the dialog box, then select USB Mass Storage Device and click the Stop button. Another box may appear with a list of USB devices—if it does, click the device name that matches the USB flash drive, then click OK. You can unplug the flash drive when the message appears indicating that it is safe to do so.

CD AND DVD TECHNOLOGIES

Because most software, music, and movies are distributed on CDs and DVDs, CD and DVD drives are standard and necessary equipment on today's personal computers (Figure 7.26). **CD-ROM** (short for **compact disc read-only memory**) and **DVD-ROM** (**digital video** [or **versatile**] **disc read-only memory**) are

FIGURE 7.26 CD and DVD drives, which run the most popular and least expensive optical discs, are standard on today's personal computers.

the most popular and least expensive types of optical disc standards. These discs are read-only discs, which means that the data recorded on them can be read many times, but it cannot be changed.

A **CD drive** and a **DVD drive** are read-only disk drives that read data encoded on CDs and DVDs and transfer this data to a computer. These drives are referred to as optical storage devices. **Optical storage devices** use tightly focused laser beams to read microscopic patterns of data encoded on the surface of plastic discs (Figure 7.27). Microscopic indentations called **pits** scatter the laser's light in certain areas. The drive's light-sensing device receives no light from these areas, so it sends a signal to the computer that corresponds to a 0 in the computer's binary numbering system. Flat reflective areas called **lands** bounce the light back to a light-sensing device, which sends a signal equivalent to a binary 1.

CD-ROMs are capable of storing up to 700 MB of data. DVD-ROMs can store up to 17 GB of data—enough for an entire digitized movie. Whereas CD drives can transfer data at speeds of up to 150 Kbps, DVD drives can transfer data at even higher speeds (up to 12 Mbps; comparable to the data transfer rates of hard drives). DVD drives read CD-ROMs as well as DVD-ROMs.

CD-R, CD-RW, DVD-R, and DVD+RW Discs and Recorders
Several types of optical read/write media and devices are available.

Many PCs now include a combination drive that can read and write CDs and DVDs. For this reason, these read/write discs are a popular, cost-effective alternative medium for archival and storage purposes.

CD-R (short for **compact disc–recordable**) is a "write-once" technology. After you've saved data to the disc, you can't erase or write over it. An advantage of CD-Rs is that they are relatively inexpensive. **CD-RW** (short for **compact disc–rewritable**), which is more expensive than CD-R, allows data that has been saved to be erased and rewritten. **CD-RW drives**, also known as **burners** or **CD burners**, provide full read/write capabilities.

DVDs come in two standards. The first is the DVD+ (DVD plus) standard. This standard employs two types of discs, DVD+R and the DVD+RW. **DVD+R** is a recordable format that enables the disc to be written to one time and read many times. The **DVD+RW** is a recordable format that enables the disc to be rewritten to many times.

The second format is the DVD- (DVD dash) standard. **DVD-R** operates the same way as CD-R; you can write to the disc once and read from it many times. With **DVD-RW**, you can write to, erase, and read from the disc many times.

One of the newest forms of optical storage is Blu-ray. **Blu-ray Disc (BD)** technology was developed for the management of high-definition video and for storing large amounts of data. The name is derived from the blue-violet laser beams (blue rays) used to read and write data. Single-layer Blu-ray discs can hold up to 25 GB of data, and dual-layer Blu-ray discs can store up to 50 GB—the equivalent of 9 hours of high-definition video or 23 hours of standard definition (SD) video. Multilayer discs capable of even more storage are under development. **BD-ROM** discs are a read-only format used for video or data distribution. **BD-R** is a recordable disc useful for HD video or PC data storage, and **BD-RE** is the rewritable format, allowing data or video to be recorded and erased as needed. Currently, a dedicated Blu-ray player or recorder is required to use this new technology; however, there are plans to create a hybrid Blu-ray

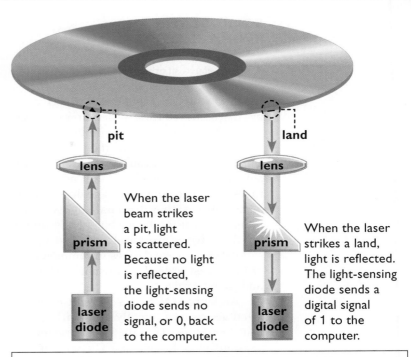

FIGURE 7.27 In optical storage devices such as CD and DVD drives, a tightly focused laser beam reads data encoded on the disc's surface. Some optical devices can write data as well as read it.

Disc/DVD that can be used in Blu-ray or DVD players. And, it is expected that Blu-ray will eventually replace DVDs, especially when HDTVs become more commonplace.

Protecting the Data on Your Discs

As with disks, it's important that you handle CDs and DVDs carefully. The following are a few things to remember when caring for discs:

● Do not expose discs to excessive heat or sunlight.

● Do not touch the underside of discs. Hold them by their edges.

● Do not write on the label side of discs with a hard instrument, such as a ballpoint pen.

● To avoid scratches, do not stack discs.

● Store discs in jewel boxes (plastic protective cases) when they are not being used.

Techtalk

disk or *disc*?
If the subject is magnetic media, the correct spelling is *disk*. *Disc* is used to describe optical media.

SOLID-STATE STORAGE DEVICES

A **solid-state storage device** consists of nonvolatile memory chips, which retain the data stored in them even if the chips are disconnected from a computer or other device. The term *solid state* indicates that these devices have no moving parts; they consist only of semiconductors. Solid-state storage devices have important advantages over mechanical storage devices such as disk drives: they are small, lightweight, highly reliable, and portable. In addition to the flash drives discussed earlier, some solid-state storage devices in common use are ExpressCards, flash memory cards, and smart cards.

An **ExpressCard** is a credit-card-sized accessory typically used with notebook computers (Figure 7.28). Previous versions were known as **PC cards** or **PCMCIA cards**. ExpressCards can serve a variety of functions. For example, some ExpressCards are modems, others are network adapters, and still others provide additional memory or storage capacity.

When used as storage devices, ExpressCards are most commonly used to transfer data from one computer to another. (However, each computer must have an ExpressCard slot.) For example, a notebook computer user can store documents created on a business trip on a solid-state memory card and then transfer the documents to a desktop computer.

ExpressCards follow standards set by the Personal Computer Memory Card International Association (PCMCIA), a consortium of industry vendors. As a result, a notebook computer equipped with

FIGURE 7.28 ExpressCards are about the size of a credit card and fit into ExpressCard slots, which are standard in most notebooks.

an ExpressCard slot can use ExpressCards from any ExpressCard vendor.

Increasingly popular are flash memory cards, which use nonvolatile flash memory chips (Figure 7.29). **Flash memory cards** are wafer-thin, highly portable solid-state storage systems that are capable of storing as much as 32 GB of data. Flash memory cards are also used with smartphones, MP3 players, digital video cameras, and other portable digital devices. To use a flash memory card, the device must have a compatible **flash memory reader**—a slot or compartment into which the flash memory card is inserted (Figure 7.30).

The SmartMedia flash memory card was one of the first examples of this technology. Many others, in various sizes and storage capacities, soon followed, including CompactFlash, Secure

FIGURE 7.30 A flash memory reader can be used to transfer the contents of a memory card to your PC.

FIGURE 7.29 Flash memory cards are thin, portable solid-state storage systems.

Digital, Memory Stick, miniSD, and microSD. It is important to know what type of memory card a specific device requires, because they are not interchangeable.

A **smart card**, also known as a **chip card** or an **integrated circuit card** (**ICC**), is a credit-card-sized device that combines flash memory with a tiny microprocessor, enabling the card to process as well as store information. Such cards provide an additional level of security for the user and may include a hologram to help prevent counterfeiting. Smart cards also promote quicker transactions with little need for personal interaction. If you've ever waved your card at the gas pump to pay for your gas or used a specially encoded student ID card to pay in the dining hall or unlock your dorm room, you've used a smart card (Figure 7.31).

Many applications for smart cards already exist, and more are on the way. **Digital cash systems**, which are widespread in Europe and Asia, enable users to purchase a prepaid amount of electronically stored money to pay the small amounts required for parking, bridge tolls, transport fares, museum entrance fees, and similar charges.

STORAGE HORIZONS

In response to the explosive demand for more storage capacity, designers are creating storage media and devices that store larger amounts of data and retrieve it more quickly. Exemplifying these trends are holographic storage and wireless flash memory cards.

Holographic Storage

Holographic storage uses two laser beams to create a pattern on photosensitive media, resulting in a three-dimensional image similar to the holograms you can buy in a novelty shop.

It is anticipated that this 3-D approach will enable much higher-density storage capacities and is being promoted for its archiving capabilities. Although still under development, experts predict that holographic storage may enable us to store terabytes of data in a space no thicker than the width of several CDs. Or to put it another way, imagine storing 50,000 music files on an object the size of a postage stamp!

Wireless Memory Cards

The Eye-Fi **wireless memory card** takes all the storage features of a regular flash memory card and combines it with wireless circuitry so it can connect with your PC via a wireless network or send pictures directly from your digital camera to your favorite online photo site. The Eye-Fi card can store up to 2 GB of pictures and works like a traditional memory card if you are out of wireless range. Digital photography is the only application this wireless memory card is currently marketed for, but new uses are being explored.

FIGURE 7.31
Smart cards can be used for quick transactions, to identify the user, or to access electronically controlled doors.

What You've Learned

INPUT/OUTPUT & STORAGE

- The computer keyboard's special keys include cursor-movement keys (arrow keys and additional keys such as Home and End), the numeric keypad (for entering numerical data), toggle keys (for switching keyboard modes on and off, such as Num Lock and Caps Lock), function keys (defined for different purposes by different applications), modifier keys (such as Ctrl and Alt for use with keyboard shortcuts), and special keys for use with Microsoft Windows. The most frequently used pointing device is the mouse. Other pointing devices include trackballs, pointing sticks, touchpads, joysticks, touch screens, and styluses.

- The large monitors that look like older television screens are cathode-ray tube (CRT) monitors. The thinner monitors used on notebook and newer desktop computers are known as liquid crystal displays (LCDs) or flat-panel displays. Among factors determining a monitor's quality are the disc's size and viewable area (the larger, the better), resolution, and refresh rate (72 Hz or higher).

- Printers use either inkjet or laser technology. Inkjet printers produce excellent-quality text and images for a reasonable price. However, they are slow and ink cartridges may be expensive. Laser printers are faster and produce excellent-quality text and graphics, but color models are expensive.

- Memory uses costly, high-speed components to make software and data available to the CPU. Memory must have enough capacity to hold the software and data that are currently in use. RAM is volatile and doesn't retain information when the computer is switched off. In contrast, storage is slower and less costly, but it offers far greater capacity. Storage devices are nonvolatile; they retain information even when the power is switched off. Storage devices play important input and output roles by transferring information into memory and saving and storing your work.

- Storage media and devices can be categorized as read only or read/write; random access; magnetic, flash, or optical; and secondary (online or fixed), external, or portable (or removable).

- Several factors can affect a hard disk's performance. Head crashes can damage an area of the disk, creating bad sectors that are unable to hold data reliably. Positioning performance measures how quickly the drive positions the read/write head, whereas transfer performance measures how quickly the drive sends the information once the head has reached the correct position. Disk cache stores program instructions and data that is in use, so the CPU doesn't need to access the hard disk.

- Disks store data in circular bands called tracks, which are divided into pie-shaped wedges called sectors. Combined sectors, called clusters, provide the basic unit of data storage. To access data on the drive, the read/write head moves to the track containing the desired data. Hard disks store data magnetically on multiple platters.

- CD-ROM and DVD-ROM drives are standard equipment in today's computer systems, largely because most software, music, and movies are now distributed on discs. CD-R, DVD-R, and DVD+R are read-only technologies. CD-R discs can record once; CD-RW, DVD-RW, and DVD+RW discs can be rewritten to multiple times.

- Flash drives, USB flash drives, and memory cards all use solid-state technology to electronically store data. Their lack of moving parts, lighter weight, and durability make them a popular storage alternative.

Key Terms and Concepts

access time 297
active-matrix (Thin Film
   Transistor [TFT]) 289
arrow keys. 283
bad sectors. 297
bar code reader 288
BD-R 301
BD-RE 301
BD-ROM 301
blocks. 298
Blu-ray Disc (BD) 301
cathode-ray tube (CRT)
   monitors 288
CD drive 300
CD-R (compact
   disc–recordable) 301
CD-ROM (compact disc
   read-only memory) 300
CD-RW (compact
   disc–rewritable) 301
CD-RW drives (burners
   or CD burners) 301
cluster 296
cursor (insertion point) 282
cursor-movement keys
   (arrow keys) 283
digital cash systems 303
disk cache 297
DLP projector (digital
   light-processing projector) . . 292
DVD drive 300
DVD-R 301
DVD-ROM (digital video
   [or versatile] disc
   read-only memory) 300
DVD-RW 301
DVD+R 301
DVD+RW. 301
ExpressCard 302
file allocation table (FAT) 296
flash drive 298
flash memory 298
flash memory cards 302
flash memory reader. 302
function keys. 283

hard disk controller 296
hard disk drive
   (hard disk) 295
high-definition television
   (HDTV) 290
holographic storage 303
hybrid hard drives
   (HHDs) 298
inkjet printers. 291
input 282
input devices. 282
Internet hard drive. 296
joystick 286
keyboard 282
kiosk 286
lands 300
laser printer 291
LCD projector 292
liquid crystal
   displays (LCD)
   (flat-panel displays) 289
magnetic storage devices 295
microphone 287
modifier keys. 283
monitors (displays) 288
mouse 285
multifunction devices 292
network attached
   storage (NAS) 296
NTFS (new technology
   file system) 296
optical character
   recognition (OCR). 287
optical mark reader (OMR) . . 288
optical storage devices 300
output devices. 288
partition 296
PC card (PCMCIA card) 302
photo printers 291
pits. 300
platters 295
plotter 291
pointer 285
pointing device 285
pointing stick 286

portable (removable) storage . 298
positioning performance. 297
printers 291
quoted size. 289
random access storage
   device 295
read/write head. 295
refresh rate 290
remote storage 296
resolution 290
scanner 287
secondary storage
   (online storage,
   fixed storage) 295
sectors 296
seek time. 297
smart card (chip card,
   integrated circuit
   card [ICC]) 303
solid-state drive (SSD) 298
solid-state storage
   device 302
speakers 292
speech recognition (voice
   recognition). 287
storage (mass storage
   or auxiliary storage). 293
storage device 293
storage media 293
stylus. 286
Super VGA 290
synthesizers 292
thermal-transfer
   printers. 291
toggle key 283
touch screen 286
touchpad (trackpad) 286
trackball 286
tracks. 296
transfer performance 297
USB flash drives. 298
Video Graphics Array (VGA) . 290
viewable area 290
wheel mouse 285
wireless memory card. 303

Matching

Match each key term in the left column with the most accurate definition in the right column.

_____ 1. cluster

_____ 2. positioning performance

_____ 3. inkjet printer

_____ 4. ExpressCard

_____ 5. remote storage

_____ 6. optical character recognition

_____ 7. hybrid hard drive

_____ 8. NTFS

_____ 9. resolution

_____ 10. DLP projector

_____ 11. refresh rate

_____ 12. Blu-ray Disc

_____ 13. transfer performance

_____ 14. disk cache

_____ 15. hard disk controller

a. can provide additional storage and follows standards set by the PCMCIA

b. measures the time required to retrieve data from a storage device

c. a magnetic storage device that uses flash memory to improve boot up speed

d. creates an image using light reflected from a chip containing microscopic mirrors

e. a combination of two or more sectors

f. accessed via the Internet, also known as an Internet hard drive

g. measure of image sharpness for monitors

h. optical storage media for high-definition video

i. an electronic circuit board providing the interface between the CPU and the hard disk's electronics

j. measures the seek time required by the read/write head

k. software used by scanners to convert scanned text to a text file

l. RAM used to store program instructions and data needed by the CPU

m. system used to track file names and locations

n. advantages include affordability and excellent color output

o. measured in hertz (Hz), lower settings may produce flicker and cause eye strain

Multiple Choice

Circle the correct choice for each of the following.

1. Which of the following optical media contains data that *cannot* be changed?
   a. BD-RE
   b. CD-RW
   c. DVD-ROM
   d. DVD+R

2. Which of the following is an input device?
   a. Video Graphics Array
   b. microphone
   c. Internet hard drive
   d. plotter

3. Optical storage devices use which of the following to record data?
   a. laser beams
   b. magnetic particles
   c. solid-state circuitry
   d. wireless signals

4. Hard disk drives store data in circular bands and pie-shaped wedges called:
   a. platters and partitions
   b. tracks and sectors
   c. clusters and partitions
   d. tracks and FAT

5. Which of the following storage devices stores data in blocks?
   a. Blu-ray Disc
   b. hard disk drive
   c. holographic storage
   d. USB flash drive

6. Which of the following methods uses three-dimensional technology to store data?
   a. optical
   b. magnetic
   c. holographic
   d. flash

7. The Eye-Fi combines flash memory with special circuitry and is an example of a(n):
   a. ExpressCard
   b. wireless memory card
   c. hybrid hard drive
   d. high-definition storage device

8. Which of the following is *not* considered a pointing device?
   a. trackball
   b. touchpad
   c. toggle key
   d. stylus

9. A USB flash drive is an example of:
   a. portable storage
   b. volatile storage
   c. holographic storage
   d. remote storage

10. Which of the following statements about Blu-ray Discs is *not* true?
    a. They are used to store large amounts of data.
    b. They are used to manage high-definition video.
    c. Single-layer discs can hold up to 50 GB of data.
    d. A special blue-violet laser is used to read and write data.

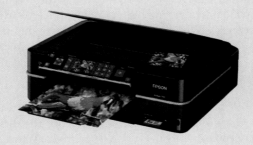

Fill-In

In the blanks provided, write the correct answer for each of the following.

1. A hard disk drive usually contains several fixed, rapidly rotating disks called _____.

2. A(n) _____ _____ is an electromagnet that moves across the surface of a hard disk to record or retrieve data.

3. Flash drives are also known as _____ _____ drives because of the circuitry they use.

4. A(n) _____ device often combines a printer, scanner, and copier.

5. A(n) _____ is an electronic device that produces music and plays MIDI files.

6. Copiers and _____ _____ use an electrostatic reproduction technology.

7. _____ - _____, also known as Thin Film Transistor, technology uses transistors to control the color of each onscreen pixel for LCD monitors.

8. Typically used to scan an item's UPC, a(n) _____ _____ _____ is an input device.

9. A(n) _____ is a booth that provides some type of computer service, such as a gift registry or ATM.

10. Often found above the top row of numbers on a keyboard, the _____ _____ are labeled F1 through F12 and provide different commands.

11. The Caps Lock and Num Lock keys are examples of _____ _____ and switch between on and off modes.

12. A(n) _____ _____ forms an image by passing light through three colored panels.

13. Scanners, joysticks, and touch screens are all examples of _____ devices.

14. A wireless mouse or keyboard uses _____ _____ to send signals to the computer.

15. Optical storage devices use laser beams to read data patterns formed by indented _____ and flat _____.

Short Answer

1. If you have used a notebook computer, which of the various pointing devices—trackball, touchpad, or pointing stick—have you used? Which input device do you prefer? Explain why. Would you consider using an auxiliary mouse (a regular mouse that you plug into a notebook)? Why or why not?

2. What is the difference between memory and storage?

3. Many instructors use blackboards, whiteboards, or overhead projectors to display course materials. Do any of your instructors use data projectors to complement the presentation of their lectures or labs? If so, are they LCD or DLP projectors? What types of software do they use? What are your thoughts about using this technology to deliver classroom instruction?

4. What is the difference between a flash storage device and an optical storage device? Give an example of each.

5. Explain the difference between inkjet and laser printers. What are the pros and cons of each?

Go to **www.pearsonhighered.com/cayf** to review this chapter, answer the questions, and complete the exercises.

Teamwork

1. Long-Term Storage

The ability to store data for long periods is extremely important. For example, how long does your school need to store student transcripts? Your team is to discuss the inability of computers to store data permanently. Use material in this chapter and other resources to describe the two major hindrances of using computers to store and access data "forever." Give a thoughtful and detailed example of each barrier. Is paper a good storage medium? Why or why not? Write a short paper summarizing your findings.

2. Understanding Disk Capacity

When hard disks first became available, their storage capacities were around 5 MB. At the time, this seemed like an enormous amount of storage. Because many applications and some data files now use many megabytes of storage, current personal computers come with hard disks that are measured in gigabytes. Your team is to split up the following tasks and then collaborate in writing a one- or two-page paper that clearly describes the answers in detail.

Select any brand of personal computer and determine the hard disk capacity for both the least and the most expensive computer models. Do you think that you would ever fill the hard disk on even the least expensive model? Why or why not?

Use the Internet to find the storage requirements for the following popular applications:

- Any version of Microsoft Office
- Adobe Photoshop
- Mozilla Firefox

Certain data files also require large amounts of storage. What types of files do you think would require several megabytes of storage?

3. Wireless Input Devices

Until Apple released the first Mac in 1984, a mouse was just a rodent that ate cheese. With the advent of wireless technology, users of mice (and keyboards) are no longer tethered to their computers. Explain how wireless mice and keyboards work. Check newspaper advertisements or call or visit a local vendor and compare the purchase prices of conventional mice and keyboards with the prices of wireless ones. On the basis of cost and convenience, explain why you would or would not upgrade to a wireless mouse or keyboard or purchase one with a new computer. Write a short paper that describes your findings.

4. Portable Memory

As a team, research portable memory devices. Be sure to research memory sticks, memory cards (used in digital cameras), and USB flash drives. What is the storage capacity of each type of device and how much does it cost? Construct tables to show the different amounts of memory the cards hold, their total cost, and the cost per megabyte. Write a paragraph or two that describes your prediction of the future of portable memory devices. Also discuss how you think such devices will be used in the future.

5. Comparing Printers

Work together or split up the tasks in this exercise and then write a one-page paper that provides the answers to the following questions. Visit your school's or department's computer facilities to determine the types of printers available for student use. Do students have access to dot-matrix, inkjet, or laser printers? Which, if any, of the printers are capable of color output? Are printing services free? If not, what are the printing costs? Do you have a printer at home? If so, what type of printer is it? Explain why you prefer to use your own or your school's printers.

Go to **wwwpearsonhighered.com/cayf** to review this chapter, answer the questions, and complete the exercises.

On the Web

1. Portable Storage

Although Iomega was not the first company to market removable high-capacity disks, it has been the most successful. Visit Iomega's Web site at **http://iomega.com/na/landing.jsp** to learn more about its products. Compare and contrast the storage capacity of the older, legacy technology Zip and floppy disks with the new external hard drives and network attached storage devices Iomega offers. Determine the cost per megabyte for each and write a one-page paper presenting your findings. Which of these products would you consider using, and why?

2. The DVD Revolution

Because a DVD-ROM can store up to 14 times the amount of information that a CD-ROM can, DVD drives have replaced CD drives on many new computers. Visit CNET's DVD site at **http://shopper.cnet.com** (type "DVD drives" into the search box) and find the best price on the fastest DVD drive available. In addition to video, what other types of information can be stored on a DVD? Explain why you would or would not purchase a new computer with a DVD drive or upgrade your present CD drive to a DVD. Write a short paper that describes your findings.

3. Internet Storage

One method for increasing your storage capacity is to use an Internet hard drive. Have you ever considered using an Internet hard drive? Visit the Xdrive site at **www.xdrive.com** to learn more about an Internet storage site. Perform a Web search to determine which two major ISPs also offer Internet storage. List at least one advantage and one disadvantage of using Internet storage. In addition to storage, what other services do ISPs provide? Some sites provide free storage, whereas others charge a fee. Select a site that offers free storage and describe the following:

- the registration process
- the amount of free storage space
- additional services provided

Would you consider using this site? Explain why or why not. Write a one- to two-page paper that discusses your findings.

4. Computer Voice Commands

Tired of entering input with a keyboard? One of the features of Microsoft Vista is speech recognition. Go to your favorite search engine and type in the keywords "Vista Speech Recognition" to learn about this novel method of entering input. Go to the Microsoft site (**www.microsoft.com**) and enter the same keywords in the search box there. On the basis of your research, what three actions can speech recognition help users perform? What types of users will benefit from this technology? In addition to voice-recognition training, what are two suggestions for minimizing speech-recognition errors?

Although most computer systems include a sound card and speakers, a microphone may not be supplied. If you have a computer, was a microphone included in the purchase price? What are the names and costs of the microphone and headset combinations that Microsoft suggests to use with Windows Vista? In a short paper, answer these questions and explain why you would or would not consider using speech-recognition technology.

5. Surround Sound

Use your favorite browser and search engine to find information on surround-sound systems for PCs. What is the range of costs for such systems? What components are required? Is it acceptable to buy at the low end, or is there a mid-range point that will ensure a good result? Is there much to install? Can a nontechnical person install a surround-sound system? Based on your research, which system would you recommend? (Include a list of the components and the cost.) Why? Construct a one-page summary of these questions aimed at the novice user. The paper should help the reader understand surround-sound systems.

Backing Up
Your Data

When it comes to the data stored on your computer, it is not a matter of if it will be lost but rather a matter of when. A comprehensive backup strategy is not just a good idea, it's a necessity. Consider the following when preparing a backup plan for your data.

1. **The amount and type of data that you want to back up.** Do you only want to back up a few files or directories? Or do you want to back up your entire hard disk, including the operating system and your important data files? If your hard disk crashes, it may be easier to restore your computer's operating system and applications manually, as long as you have your original system restore disks. However, this can be time-consuming, depending on the number of applications you had installed and need to restore. You also should ask yourself if you really want to back up all of your data. Large music or photo collections should be backed up because it could be time-consuming to restore your music files and might be impossible to re-create your photos.

2. **Backup frequency.** Should you back up your data every day? Every week? To determine the backup schedule that is appropriate for you, ask yourself one question: if my computer goes down, how much data am I willing to lose or re-create? If your answer is none, then everyday backups are probably best. On the other hand, if you don't use your computer every day, then maybe your data files don't change often enough to warrant such a frequent backup schedule. However, with today's inexpensive external hard drives it is easy to have your system make backups of files right after you create them!

3. **The capacity of your storage device or medium.** The capacity of your storage device or medium obviously determines the amount of data you can back up. Although you could back up data to CDs, DVDs, or flash drives, the storage capacity and affordability of external hard drives make them a sensible and convenient choice. However, if you need to back up only a few files, flash drives or CDs are probably the best option.

FIGURE 7.32 Products such as the Seagate FreeAgent Pro external hard drive include software that allows you to back up files as you create them.

If you have only a small number of files or directories to back up infrequently, then manually backing up files is probably OK. *Manual backup* means copying or dragging and dropping your files to the storage medium. If you need to regularly back up large amounts of data (such as the operating system), you should consider purchasing an external hard drive (such as the Seagate FreeAgent Pro; Figure 7.32) that includes backup software. With the FreeAgent Pro you can back up files as you create them and also back up your entire Windows system in case you need to restore it. Additionally, you can schedule periodic backups of files or directories to ensure that your data is always safely duplicated on the external hard drive. External hard drives are available in sizes of 1 TB or higher, making it possible to back up even the largest digital photo, music, and video collections.

If you really want your data to be 100 percent secure, you should consider keeping your important backup files somewhere safe, such as a bank safety deposit box, a friend's house, or any trusted location that is physically separated from your home. Nobody wants to think about a disaster occurring, but the reality is that your backups are useless if they are destroyed in the same fire that destroys your computer. Your computer can be replaced; the data stored on it cannot.

SPOTLIGHT

MULTIMEDIA
DEVICES

Multimedia has been around for a long time, but now

because of computer and Internet technologies it's much easier to implement. Multimedia is one of the reasons that the Web is so popular. Simply put, **multimedia** can be defined as *multisensory stimulators*, or things that stimulate our senses of sight, sound, touch, smell, or taste. For our purposes, we'll consider multimedia that stimulates the senses of sight, sound, and touch.

Just a few years ago, most personal computers needed additional equipment to run multimedia applications. Today, such equipment—sound cards, CD or DVD drives, and speakers—is standard issue. However, for advanced multimedia applications, you may still need additional equipment, such as a pen-based graphics tablet, a stereo microphone, a digital camera, or a video adapter. If you enjoy playing games, you'll want a 3D video accelerator, which is an add-on video adapter that works with your current video card. For surround sound, you'll need a sound card capable of producing the surround effect. And you'll probably want to pick up a few extra speakers and a subwoofer.

FIGURE 7A Self-service kiosks using touch screen technology can be found in many locations.

Multimedia is part of computer games of all kinds, but it is also being used more and more in computer-based education (CBE), distance learning, and computer-based training (CBT). Businesses use it in multimedia presentations using PowerPoint and other software. It's also finding its way into **information kiosks**, which are automated presentation systems used to provide information to the public or employee training (Figure 7A).

What if you want your multimedia files to travel with you? Today, a number of portable multimedia devices are available, from MP3 players and digital cameras to Web-enabled devices such as smartphones and PDAs. In this Spotlight, you'll learn about a variety of multimedia devices, both mobile ones and those used with desktop computers.

AUDIO: MP3 PLAYERS AND VOICE RECORDERS

Unlike previous forms of push technology (products marketed by industries to consumers), such as cassette tapes and CDs, the MP3 movement has been largely fueled by music lovers' use of the Internet to compile and share libraries of digitized music files. Files are created and shared by the users—without industry involvement. An MP3 file is a compressed audio format that is usually used for music files. The term MP3 is derived from the acronym MPEG, which stands for the Motion Picture Experts Group; the "3" refers to audio layer 3.

Without losing any noticeable sound quality, the MP3 format reduces the size of sound files by eliminating frequencies and sounds the human ear cannot hear. A song on a typical music CD takes up approximately 32 MB. The same song in MP3 format takes up 3 MB.

MP3 works like this: A CD has a sample rate of 44,100 times per second. Each sample is two bytes in size, and separate samples are taken for the left and right speakers. Thus, the sample rate in bits per second is $44,100 \times 8$ bits per byte $\times 2$ bytes $\times 2$ channels, which is 1,411,200 bits per second. This equals a sample rate of 176,400 bytes per second $\times 180$ seconds in an average song, or roughly 32 MB per song. As a result, an MP3 file is 1/10 the size of an uncompressed sound file.

You can record, store, and play MP3 files on your computer. You can legally copy music from CDs that you own, or you can purchase files from Web sites such as **www.apple.com/itunes**, **www.zune.net**, and **www.mp3.com**. Windows-based PCs come with the Windows Media Player already installed (Figure 7B). Other systems may have a different default player or you may need to download one, such as Winamp, from the Internet. You can find a list of players at **www.superwarehouse.com/ mp3_players/c2b/2387**.

MP3 files also can be stored on portable players. Portable players come in many shapes and sizes (Figure 7C). When purchasing an MP3 player, make sure to consider the battery life and storage capacity of the device. Over 3.5 million MP3 players were shipped in 2003. As of September 2007, six years after releasing the iPod, Apple has sold more than 150 million MP3 players, making it the best-selling digital audio player in history.

MP3 players have several components: a data port that is used to upload files, memory, a processor, a display screen, playback controls, an audio port for output, an amplifier, and a power

FIGURE 7B You can use the Windows Media Player to copy, record, and play audio files.

supply. When you select a file to listen to on your MP3 player, the device's processor pulls the file from storage and decompresses the MP3 encoding. The decompressed bytes are converted from digital to analog, amplified, and then sent to the audio port for your enjoyment. MP3 players plug into your computer by way of a USB or FireWire port. Most players have solid-state memory, but some use a microdrive (a tiny hard drive) to store files. MP3 players are usually very small, portable, and battery-powered.

You can use a digital voice recorder to record voice and sound that can later be retrieved from the device or downloaded to your computer. The device captures sound through a built-in microphone and then stores it on a memory chip. Several companies make these devices (Figure 7D). Two things to consider when purchasing a digital voice recorder are the amount of storage offered and the price.

FIGURE 7C You can use a portable MP3 player to take your music with you.

FIGURE 7D Digital voice recorders provide advanced recording and playback features.

VISUAL: E-BOOKS, DIGITAL CAMERAS, AND CAMCORDERS

E-books have the potential to provide a richness that is not possible in a printed book. An **e-book** is a book that has been digitized and distributed by means of a digital storage medium (such as flash memory or a CD disc). An **e-book reader** is a book-size device that displays e-books. E-book readers may be devices that are built solely for reading e-books or they may be PDAs, handheld devices, or other computing devices that have a processor and display screen (Figure 7E).

Someday you may read an e-book that provides background music for each page or scenario. You may find hot links on the page that will take you to pictures that support the scene. Or better yet, you may find a link to a video of the scene. All of this extra material can be easily stored on a flash memory card along with the text of the story. It may not be long before you can use your cell phone as an e-book reader!

DIGITAL CAMERAS

It seems as though it was just yesterday that computer technology was so difficult to use that only computer scientists were able to use it. But today's digital technology is so easy to use that you can even digitize your family photo album!

FIGURE 7E E-book readers share the market with PDAs and other computing devices.

One of the hottest products on today's consumer market is the digital camera (Figure 7F). Approximately 76 percent of households owned a digital camera by the end of 2008. A **digital camera** uses digital technology to store and display images instead of recording them on film. When you take a photo with a digital camera, the shot is stored in the camera until it is transferred to a computer for long-term storage or printing.

Like traditional cameras, digital cameras have a lens, a shutter, and an optical viewfinder. What sets digital cameras apart from traditional cameras is their inner workings—specifically, how an image is saved. With digital cameras, the captured image's light falls on a charge-coupled device (CCD), a photosensitive computer chip that transforms light patterns into pixels (individual dots). A CCD consists of a grid made up of light-sensitive elements. Each element converts the incoming light into a voltage that is proportional to the light's brightness. The digital camera's picture quality is determined by how many elements the CCD has. Each CCD element corresponds to one pixel, or dot, on a computer display or printout; the more elements, the sharper the picture.

A 1-megapixel digital camera has a CCD consisting of at least 1 million elements; such a camera can produce a reasonably sharp snapshot-size image. With at least 2 million elements, 2-megapixel cameras can take higher-resolution pictures; you can expect to get near-photographic quality prints at sizes of up to 5 × 7 inches with such a camera. Three- and 4-megapixel cameras can produce images that can print at sizes of 8 by 10 inches or even 11 by 14 inches. Today's 5- to 10-megapixel cameras produce high-quality photographs that can be greatly enlarged without loss of quality.

Because digital cameras do not have film, any photos you take are stored in the camera until you transfer them to a computer for long-term storage or printing. The two most popular methods of storing images in the camera are **CompactFlash** and **SmartMedia** (Figure 7G). Both use flash memory technologies to store anywhere from 64 MB to 16 GB of image data. About 12 MB of flash memory is the equivalent of a standard 12-exposure film roll. However, most cameras enable you to select from a variety of resolutions, so the number of shots you get will vary depending on the resolution you choose. If you need more "film," you need only carry more flash memory cards. Digital cameras enable you to preview the shots you've taken on a small LCD screen, so you can create more room on the flash memory cards by erasing pictures that you don't like.

In most cases, you'll need to download the image data to a computer for safekeeping and printing. Some cameras are designed to connect to a computer by means of a serial or USB cable. Others can transfer data into your computer by means of an infrared port. If you're using a digital camera that stores images on flash memory cards, you can obtain a PC card that contains a flash memory card reader. This type of PC card enables the computer to read the images from the flash memory card as if it were a disk drive. Also available are standalone flash memory readers, which serve the same purpose. Once you've transferred the images to the computer for safekeeping and printing, you can erase the flash memory card and reuse it, just as if you had purchased a fresh roll of film.

Once the images are transferred to the computer, you can use a **photo-editing**

FIGURE 7F Digital cameras are among today's hottest products.

FIGURE 7G Flash memory can store hundreds of high-quality photos.

program to enhance, edit, crop, or resize the images. Photo-editing programs also can be used to print the images to a color printer. Some specially designed printers called **photo printers** have flash memory card readers that enable you to bypass the computer completely (Figure 7H).

How good are digital cameras? With the exception of a few expensive high-end digital cameras, most digital cameras are the equivalent of the point-and-shoot 35-mm cameras that dominate the traditional (film-based) camera market. They take pictures that are good enough for family photo albums, Web publishing, and business use (such as a real estate agent's snapshots of homes for sale); however, they are not good enough for professional photography. A color printer or a photo printer can make prints from digital camera images that closely resemble the snapshots you used to get from the drugstore, but only if you choose the highest print resolution and use glossy photo paper. Getting

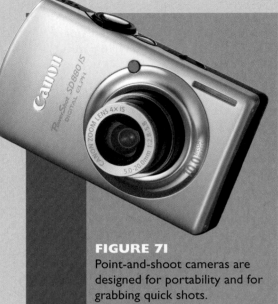

FIGURE 7I
Point-and-shoot cameras are designed for portability and for grabbing quick shots.

good printout results takes time—most consumer-oriented printers will require several minutes to print an image at the printer's highest possible resolution—and it costs money, too. The best photo-printing papers cost as little as 50 cents per sheet.

But printing is only one of the distribution options that are open to you when you use a digital camera—and that's exactly why so many people love digital photography. In addition to printing snapshots for the family album, you can copy the images onto CDs or DVDs, send them to friends and family via e-mail, and even display them on the Internet.

Point-and-shoot digital cameras are designed so that anyone can take good pictures (Figure 7I). Their features typically include automatic focus, automatic exposure, built-in automatic electronic flash with red-eye reduction, and optical zoom lenses with digital enhancement. Most point-and-shoot cameras come with a built-in LCD viewfinder, so you can preview the shot to make sure it comes out right.

Single-lens reflex (SLR) digital cameras are much more expensive than point-and-shoot cameras, but they offer the

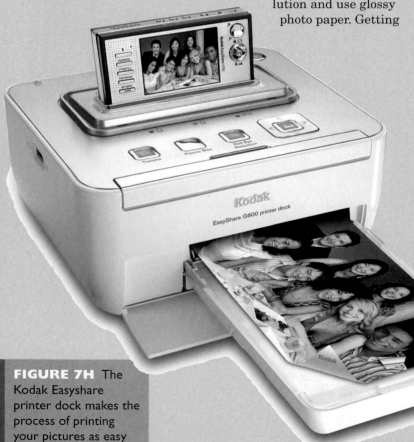

FIGURE 7H The Kodak Easyshare printer dock makes the process of printing your pictures as easy as a plug and a click.

features that professional photographers demand, such as interchangeable lenses, through-the-lens image previewing, and the ability to override the automatic focus and exposure settings (Figure 7J).

DIGITAL CAMCORDERS

Just as digital cameras are revolutionizing still photography, indications are that **digital video** is poised to do the same for full-motion images—animations, videos, and movies.

In the past, most full-motion images were captured and stored by means of analog techniques. A video-capture board is a device that inputs analog video into a computer. A video-capture board (also called a video-capture card) transforms an analog video into its digital counterpart. Because a digital video file for even a short video requires a great deal of storage space, most video-capture boards are equipped to perform on-the-fly data compression to reduce file size using one of several **codecs** (compression/decompression standards), such as MPEG, Apple's QuickTime, or Microsoft's AVI. Three-dimensional games have driven computer video card manufacturers to new feats of technical innovation; today's 3D video cards offer sophisticated, ultrafast graphics processing that only a few years ago would have required a supercomputer.

Video-capture boards enable computers to display and process full-motion video—a "movie" that gives the illusion of smooth, continuous action. Like actual movies, digitized video consists of a series of still photographs called **frames** that are flashed on the screen at a rapid rate. The frame-flashing speed—the **frame rate**—indicates how successfully a given video can create the illusion of smooth, unbroken movement. A rate of at least 24 frames per second (fps) is needed to produce an illusion of smooth, continuous action. What can you "capture" with a video-capture board? You can use just about any video source, including TV broadcasts,

FIGURE 7J The Nikon D700 is Nikon's new professional model SLR digital camera.

FIGURE 7K JVC's line of Everio camcorders combines hard disk storage and high resolution still images.

taped video, or live video from video cameras.

Increasingly popular are **digital video cameras**, which use digital rather than analog technologies to store recorded video images. Like digital cameras, digital video cameras can connect to a computer, often by means of a USB port. Because the signal produced by a digital video camera conforms to the computer's digital method of representing data, a video-capture board is not necessary. Most digital video cameras can take still images as well as movies (Figure 7K).

For reviews, comparisons, and price information for digital cameras, see the "Digital Camera Buyer's Guide: Summer 2008" at **www.digitalcamerareview.com/default.asp?newsID=3439**.

FIGURE 7L The Apple iPhone 3G features phone, iPod, and Internet capabilities.

FIGURE 7M The Samsung Instinct features phone, audio, video, and Internet capabilities.

COMMUNICATION AND ENTERTAINMENT DEVICES

Multimedia devices continue to transform ordinary devices and expand their capabilities. A phone is no longer just a device used to speak with another person. Many are sophisticated, wireless devices that enable you to surf the Web, send text messages, take photos, and listen to music—and you can still call your friends too!

The most notable of these is the Apple iPhone 3G (Figure 7L). The original iPhone was first sold in July 2007, and later that year it was named *Time* magazine's invention of the year. The 3G version was released a year later and works with fast 3G cellular and Wi-Fi networks worldwide, contains integrated GPS technology, and is controlled by a multitouch interface. The iPhone 3G combines three products in one—a phone, a widescreen iPod, and an Internet device with HTML e-mail capability and a Web browser. It is a small device (4.5 by 2.4 by 0.48 inches, and weighing only 4.7 ounces) yet has a 3.5-inch display screen with a screen resolution of 480×320 pixels. To function as a phone, it requires a broadband connection with AT&T. Additionally, it has 802.11b/g and Bluetooth 2.0 wireless compatibilities. With an iPod player, you can scroll through songs, artists, albums, and playlists, browse the music library by album artwork, and view song lyrics that have been added to the library in iTunes. The video feature enables you to watch TV shows and movies from the iTunes Store. When you connect your iPhone to your computer you can use iTunes to sync the audio and video files from your computer's iTunes library to your iPhone.

A possible contender to the iPhone's popularity is the Samsung Instinct (Figure 7M). It was first sold in June 2008. It works with fast 3G cellular networks, but it does not support Wi-Fi. It contains GPS technology and is also controlled by a multitouch interface. The Instinct is a phone, an audio and video player, and an Internet device with e-mail capability and a Web browser. It is a small device (4.57 by 2.17 by 0.49 inches, and weighing only 4.4 ounces) yet has a 3.1-inch display screen with a screen resolution of 432×240 pixels. To function as a phone, it requires a broadband connection with Sprint. You can get streaming media from more than 30 channels—music, videos, sporting news—streamed to your phone. The Instinct is Sprint TV Enabled, which allows you to watch live TV and video-on-demand with full-motion video and sound. As with Apple's iTunes store, you can use Sprint's Music Store to download stereo-quality tracks to your wireless phone or PC.

DIGITAL VIDEO RECORDERS

Digital video recorders (DVRs) are similar to VCRs, but instead of using tape to store video they use a hard disk. Hard disk storage is digital, thus the user can quickly move through video data, fast-forwarding through commercials. You can use a DVR just like a VCR or you can subscribe to a DVR-management service. One service provider, TiVo, can record up to 180 hours of your favorite shows automatically to a DVR every time they're on (Figure 7N). This way, all of your entertainment is ready for you to watch whenever you are. Just buy a DVR, activate the TiVo service, and you can enjoy television viewing your way. Many cable television companies and satellite broadcasters also offer DVR service. In some instances, the DVR is part of the cable box so you don't have to find room for another component. Newer DVRs are capable of recording high-definition television and may even be able to record two shows at the same time.

COMPUTER GAMING DEVICES

Computer game consoles such as Sony's PlayStation, Nintendo's Wii, and Microsoft's Xbox are popular

FIGURE 7N You can use a DVR and a service such as TiVo to capture your favorite shows and watch them at your convenience.

multimedia devices. You can use these devices to load and play interactive games using a television or computer screen as the display device (Figure 7O). You also can go online and play games against a diverse population of players. Gaming accessories are available, such as game consoles, specialized backpacks, wireless support, and cable accessory packs.

Game consoles are similar to computers. A game console has a processor, a graphics driver, an audio driver, memory, and an operating system. It reads input from a storage device, such as a CD or memory card, processes that input into sounds and animation, and then stores user input for further processing as the game progresses.

Gamers can use portable handheld game consoles such as Nintendo's popular Game Boy to take their games with them. Sony released the newest version of its

FIGURE 7O The Nintendo Wii brings a new level of interactivity to computer games.

FIGURE 7P Headsets help the wearer to become totally immersed in virtual 3D worlds.

popular PlayStation console in December 2007. Called the PSP-2000, the device is much smaller than the bulky, older PlayStation console.

HEADSETS

Perhaps the ultimate multimedia device is the headset. A **headset** (also called a **head-mounted display**) is a wearable device that includes twin LCD panels. When used with special applications that generate stereo output, headsets can create the illusion that an individual is walking through a 3D environment (Figure 7P). Although headsets have yet to become a commercial success, Apple and Motorola both applied for patents in 2008. Apple's patent relies on lasers, while Motorola's is meant to be used with mobile phone technology.

Gaming enthusiasts can use the **Cave Automated Virtual Environment** (**CAVE**) to dispense with the headsets in favor of 3-D glasses. In the CAVE, the walls, ceiling, and floor display projected 3-D images. More than 50 CAVEs exist, primarily at universities and research centers. Researchers use CAVEs to study topics as diverse as the human heart and the next generation of sports cars.

SPOTLIGHT EXERCISES

1. To learn about MP3 files, software, and portable players, visit the MP3 site at **www.mp3.com**. Explore the MP3 Players link and choose which MP3 player you might purchase, and explain why. Although illegal MP3 copies of copyrighted music are available, why would an artist choose to place free copies of his or her work on the Internet? Write a short paper that includes the answers to these questions and that includes a summary paragraph of what you've learned.

2. Have you used a digital video recorder? Visit the TiVo site at **www.tivo.com** to explore this technology. Write your answers to the following questions:

- What is needed to use the TiVo service?
- What are the manufacturer's suggested retail prices for the DVRs? Explain which, if any, you would purchase and why.
- What are the available service plans? Explain which, if any, you would purchase and why.

3. Use your favorite search engine and the World Wide Web to research digital cameras. How many pixels will suffice for your picture-taking needs? What is the price range for such cameras? What is the difference between optical zoom and digital zoom? How much optical zoom would be acceptable for your personal use? What is the storage medium of your chosen camera? How many pictures can you store on a 16-MB disk? How much storage capacity will you buy? What will it cost? Write a brief paper describing what you've learned.

4. Do some research on multifunction camcorder devices. Compare the features of an entry-level product with those of a top-of-the-line model. Pick one that you might purchase for yourself and describe it in a one-page paper that clearly explains why you would choose this camera for your video recording needs.

5. Want to take your TV show with you? Sling Media uses "placeshifting" technology that sends your television, DVR, digital cable, satellite receiver, or DVD player signal to you anywhere in the world. Its Slingbox is a set-top box that connects to your TV and streams the signal to another machine in real time—there is no recording involved. This other machine might be your computer in your home, in which case your home network is used. If you are away from home, you can connect your notebook or cell phone using a high-speed Internet connection. Slingbox works with the SlingPlayer software you install on your computer. After installing the software, you can control the video source from your computer just as you can from the remote that came with your TV. Visit **www.slingmedia.com** to watch the videos, compare the three Slingbox versions, and check the minimum PC or Mac requirements. If you had the necessary funds, explain which model you would purchase, the reasons for your choice, and how you would use the Slingbox. Use the Internet to find the best price. Where and at what price would you buy your Slingbox?

6. Use your favorite browser and the World Wide Web to learn more about Sony's PSP-2000 or PSP Slim. In addition to visiting the Sony Web site, visit other sites, such as CNET or PCWorld, to see what else you can learn. Write a one-page summary of your findings.

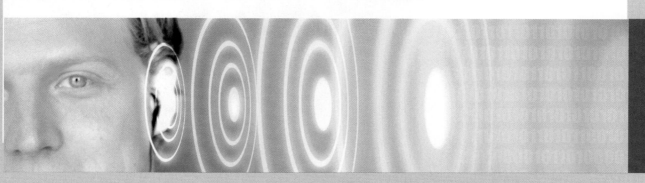

What You'll Learn . . .

- **Understand basic networking concepts.**

- **Discuss the advantages and disadvantages of networks.**

- **Distinguish between peer-to-peer and client/server local area networks (LANs).**

- **Define topology and understand how the three LAN topologies differ.**

- **Explain the importance of network protocols.**

- **Name the most widely used LAN protocol and its versions.**

- **Identify the special components of a wide area network (WAN) that differentiate it from a LAN.**

- **Contrast circuit-switching and packet-switching networks and explain their respective strengths and weaknesses.**

Networks: Communicating & Sharing Resources

CHAPTER OUTLINE

Network Fundamentals 326

Advantages & Disadvantages of Networking 329

Local Area Networks 330
    Peer-to-Peer Networks 331
    Client/Server Networks 331
    LAN Topologies. 333
    LAN Protocols 334

Wide Area Networks 339
    Point of Presence 339
    Backbones 339
    WAN Protocols 340
    WAN Applications 342

Fast forward a few years and imagine that you are building a house. Everyone in your five-person family wants a computer, a printer, and an Internet connection. You could pay for five computers, five printers, and five Internet accounts. Or you could pay for five computers, one really good printer, one Internet account, and inexpensive network hardware so that everyone can share the printer and the Internet connection. If you think the second option makes sense, you've just joined the huge and growing number of people who've discovered the benefits of networking.

Businesses of all sizes are already convinced that networking is a great idea. They're spending billions of dollars annually on networking equipment. The benefits of networking go far beyond saving money on shared peripherals. Networks enable organizations to create massive, centralized pools of information, which are vital to performing their mission. In addition, networks enable people to communicate and collaborate in ways that were not possible before computers could be connected to each other (Figure 8.1).

As an informed and literate computer user, you need to know enough about networking to understand the benefits and possibilities of connecting computers. In addition, learning about networking is a good idea for anyone looking for a job these days; employers like to hire workers who understand basic networking concepts. This chapter presents essential networking concepts and explains the basic networking terms you'll need to know to discuss the subject intelligently.

Network Fundamentals

Computer networking is essential to businesses and has become popular with many home users too. The concepts behind computer networking are easy to understand: Computer networking is all about getting connected.

A **network** is a group of two or more computer systems linked together to exchange data and share resources, including expensive peripherals such as high-performance laser printers (Figure 8.2).

Computer networks fall into two categories: local area networks and wide area networks. A **local area network (LAN)** uses cables, radio waves, or infrared signals to link computers or peripherals, such as printers, within a small geographic

FIGURE 8.1
Businesses use networks to create common pools of data that employees can access to obtain the information they need.

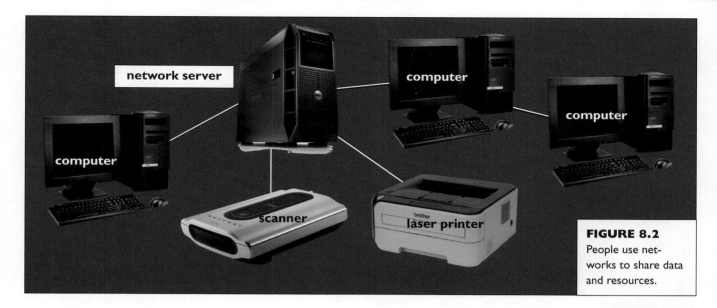

network server

computer

computer

computer

scanner

laser printer

FIGURE 8.2
People use networks to share data and resources.

area, such as a building or a group of buildings. A **wide area network (WAN)** uses long-distance transmission media to link computers separated by a few miles or even thousands of miles. The Internet is the largest WAN—it connects millions of LANs all over the globe.

A network needs communications devices to convert data into signals that can travel over a physical (wired) or wireless medium. **Communications devices** include computers, modems, routers, switches, wireless access points, and network interface cards. These devices transform data from analog to digital signals and back again, determine efficient data-transfer pathways, boost signal strength, and facilitate digital communication (Figure 8.3).

When a computer is connected to a network, it is referred to as a **client**, or **node**. The term *node* can describe any computer or peripheral device (printer, scanner, modem, etc.) that is connected to the network. Every node on the network has a unique name that is visible to users as well as a unique numeric network address.

A computer needs a network interface card to connect to a network. **Network interface cards (NICs)** are expansion boards that fit into a computer's expansion slots. They provide the electronic connection between a computer and the network (Figure 8.4). Today's desktop computers usually include NICs, and most notebook computers have wireless NICs.

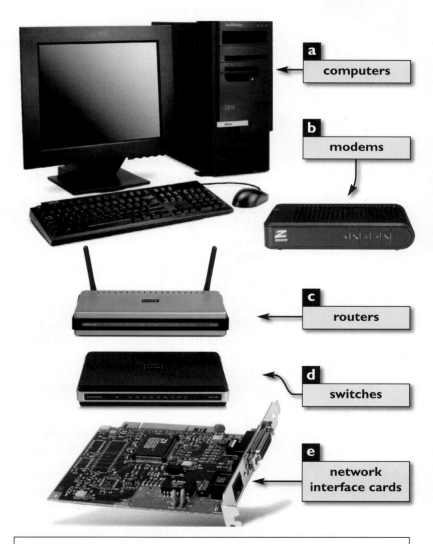

a computers

b modems

c routers

d switches

e network interface cards

FIGURE 8.3 Communications devices include (**a**) computers, (**b**) modems, (**c**) routers, (**d**) switches, and (**e**) network interface cards.

FIGURE 8.4
A network interface card (NIC) provides the electronic connection between a computer and a network.

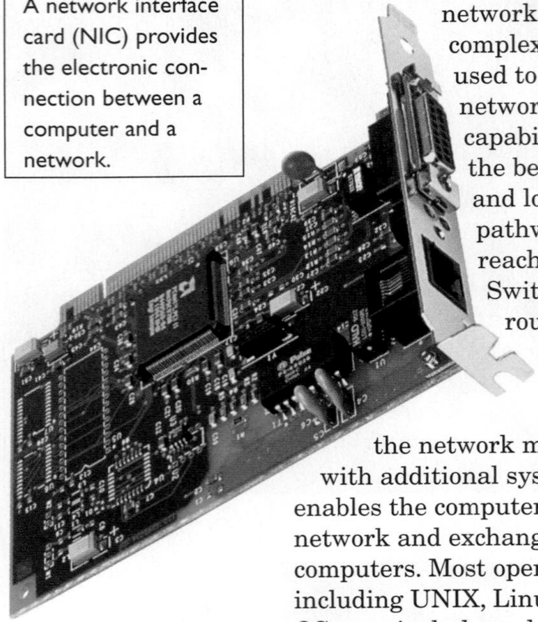

Routers, switches, and wireless access points provide similar functions in a network. **Routers** are complex devices that are used to connect two or more networks. Routers have the capability to determine the best path to route data and locate alternative pathways so that the data reaches its destination. Switches are similar to routers but are used only to move data within one network. Each computer on the network must also be equipped with additional system software that enables the computer to connect to the network and exchange data with other computers. Most operating systems, including UNIX, Linux, Windows, and Mac OS, now include such software in their standard installations.

Most business networks also typically include a **file server**, which is a high-capacity, high-speed computer with a large hard disk. The file server contains network versions of programs and large data files. The file server also contains the **network operating system (NOS)**, the software required to run the network. A network operating system, such as Novell SUSE or Microsoft Windows Server 2008, is a complex program that requires skilled technicians to install and manage it. A network operating system provides the following:

- File directories that make it easy to locate files and resources on the LAN

- Automated distribution of software updates to the desktop computers on the LAN

- Support for Internet services such as access to the World Wide Web and e-mail

In addition to a network's special hardware and software, people are also necessary for the proper functioning of a network. **Network administrators** (sometimes called *network engineers*) install, maintain, and support computer networks (Figure 8.5). They interact with users, handle security, and troubleshoot problems.

A network administrator's most important task is granting access to the network. In most cases, a network user provides a user name and a password to gain access to the network. When logged in, the user has access to his or her folders that reside on the server. In some cases, the user may be able to access other people's folders that the user has permission to see or use. The user also gains access to peripheral devices on the network, such as printers, and to the Internet.

As you read through this chapter, note that some of the concepts discussed apply to local networking, in which all of the computers and peripherals are locally connected, whereas others apply to networks that are made up of computers and peripherals that may be tens or hundreds of miles apart.

What's the point of having a computer network instead of many standalone

FIGURE 8.5 Network administrators are essential to the efficient management of networks.

computers and peripherals? Let's look at some of the benefits as well as the risks of networking.

Advantages & Disadvantages of Networking

When you connect two or more computers, you see gains in every aspect of computing, especially with regard to efficiency and costs:

- **Reduced hardware costs.** Networks reduce costs because users can share expensive equipment. For example, dozens of users on a network can share a high-capacity printer, storage devices, and a common connection to the Internet.

- **Application sharing.** Networks enable users to share software. Network versions of applications installed on a file server can be used by more than one user at a time. For example, companies that have implemented server-based order-tracking programs that enable their sales representatives to upload orders from their notebook computers have found that the salespeople gained up to 20 percent more time to focus on their customers' needs.

- **Sharing information resources.** Organizations can use networks to create common pools of data that employees can access. At publisher Pearson Education, for example, book designers can use the network to access a vast archive of illustrations, greatly reducing the amount of time spent tracking down appropriate photographs for textbooks and other publishing projects.

- **Centralized data management.** Data stored on a network can be accessed by multiple users. Organizations can ensure the security and integrity of the data on the network with security software and password protection. Centralized storage also makes it easier to maintain consistent backup procedures.

- **Connecting people.** Networks create powerful new ways for people to work together. For example, workers can use groupware applications to create a shared calendar for scheduling purposes. Team members can instantly see who's available at a given day and time. What's more, these people don't have to work in the same building. They can be located at various places around the world and still function effectively as a team.

The advantages of networks are offset by some disadvantages:

- **Loss of autonomy.** When you become a part of a network, you become a part of a community of users. Sometimes this means that you have to give up personal freedoms for the good of the group. For example, a network administrator may impose restrictions on what software you can load onto network computers.

- **Lack of privacy.** Network membership can threaten your privacy. Network administrators can access your files and may monitor your network and Internet activities.

- **Security threats.** Because some personal information is inevitably stored on network servers, it is possible that others may gain unauthorized access to your files, user names, and even your passwords.

- **Loss of productivity.** As powerful as networks are, they still fail. Access to resources is sometimes restricted or unavailable because of viruses, hacking, sabotage, or a simple breakdown. Data loss can be minimized by good backup practices, but waiting for your data to be restored is an inconvenience, or worse yet, a direct threat to your ability to produce work on time.

Destinations

To learn more about computer networks, visit **http://en. wikipedia.org/wiki/ Computer_network**. For more specific information about home networks, visit **http://compnetworking .about.com/cs/ homenetworking/a/ homenetguide.htm**.

Now that you know the benefits and risks of using networks, let's look at the specific types of networks.

Destination

To learn more about how a home network works, go to **http://computer.how stuffworks.com/home-network.htm**.

Local Area Networks

Have you ever walked into your dorm, your school's computer lab, or your office at work and wondered how all of the separate computers in each room, seat, or office are able to work at the same time? The answer is through a local area network. A home network is also an example of a LAN. It comprises two or more computers that communicate with each other and with peripheral devices such as a printer or cable modem (Figure 8.6).

LANs transform hardware into what appears to be one gigantic computer system. From any computer on the LAN, you can access any data, software, or peripherals (such as fax machines, printers, or scanners) that are on the network.

With a **wireless LAN**, users access the network through radio waves instead of wires. Wireless LANs come in handy when users need to move around in or near a building. In Veterans Administration hospitals, for example, wireless LANs help hospital personnel track the distribution of controlled substances, a job that's both time-consuming and prone to error without a computer's help. Nurses use bedside computers that are connected to the network through wireless signals to track the use of these controlled substances. Most colleges have installed wireless LANs to serve students seamlessly as they move around the campus.

Most wireless LANs ensure security with a radio transmission technique that spreads signals over a seemingly random series of frequencies. Only the receiving device knows the series, so it isn't easy to eavesdrop on the signals. Radio-based wireless LAN signals have an effective range of between 125 and 300 feet.

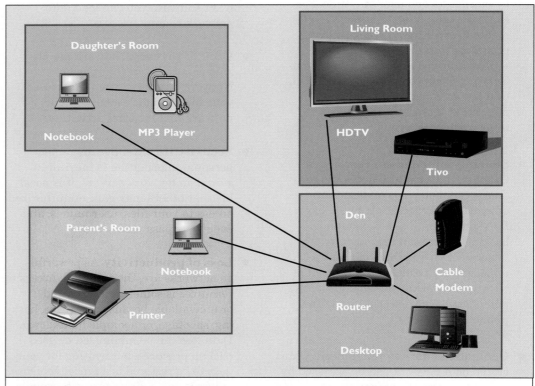

FIGURE 8.6 Setting up a LAN for the home enables everyone to use the available resources.

Whether wired or wireless, LANs can be differentiated by the networking model they use: peer-to-peer or client/server.

PEER-TO-PEER NETWORKS

In a **peer-to-peer (P2P) network**, all of the computers on the network are equals, or peers—that's where the term *peer-to-peer* comes from—and there's no file server. But there is file sharing, in which each computer user decides which, if any, files will be accessible to other users on the network. Users also may choose to share entire directories or even entire disks. They also can choose to share peripherals, such as printers and scanners.

Peer-to-peer networks are easy to set up; people who aren't networking experts do it all the time, generally to share an expensive laser printer or to provide Internet access to all of the computers on the LAN (Figure 8.7). P2P networks are often used for home networks or small businesses. They tend to slow down as the number of users increases, and keeping track of all of the shared files and peripherals can quickly become confusing. For this reason, peer-to-peer LANs are best used for simple networks connecting no more than 10 computers.

CLIENT/SERVER NETWORKS

The typical corporate or university LAN is a **client/server network**, which includes one or more file servers as well as clients (Figure 8.8). Clients can be any type of computer: PCs, Macs, desktops, notebooks, or even handheld devices. Clients send requests to the server. They can connect via modem, dedicated physical connection, or wireless connection. The client/server model works with any size or physical layout of LAN and doesn't tend to slow down with heavy use.

Techtalk

virtual private network

Many businesses use a virtual private network (VPN) to provide their employees and customers with quick, secure access to corporate information. A VPN operates as a private network over the Internet, making data accessible to authorized users in remote locations through the use of secure, encrypted connections and special software.

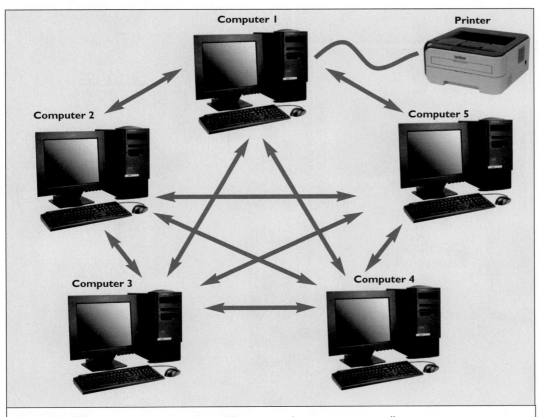

FIGURE 8.7 Peer-to-peer networks enable users to share resources equally.

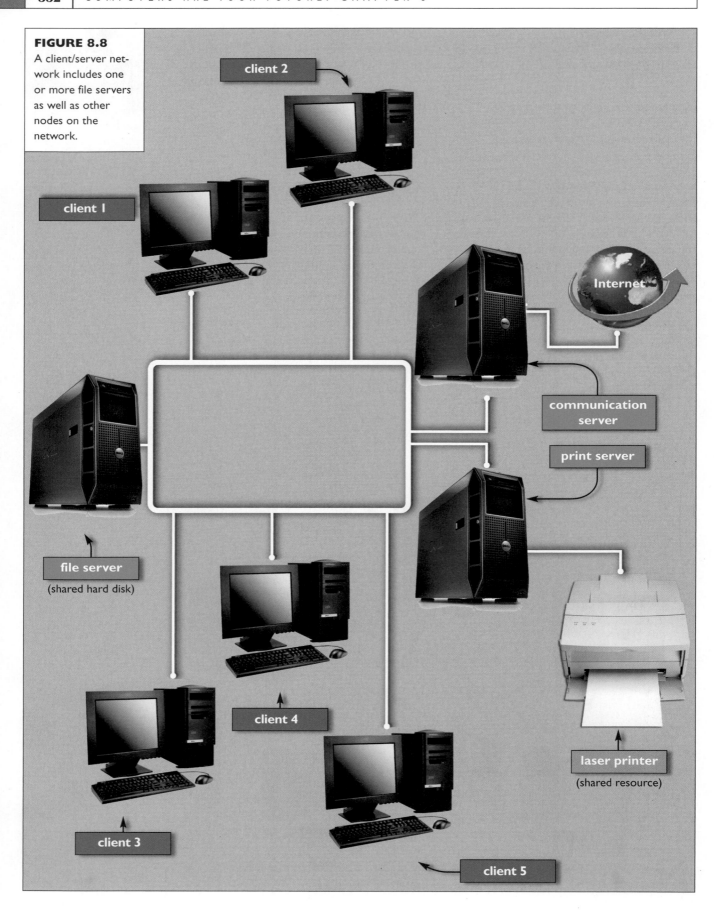

FIGURE 8.8
A client/server network includes one or more file servers as well as other nodes on the network.

client 2

client 1

Internet

communication server

print server

file server
(shared hard disk)

client 4

client 3

client 5

laser printer
(shared resource)

Now that you've learned about the different types of LANs, let's look at their various physical layouts.

LAN TOPOLOGIES

Consider the typical college dorm or corporate office. Each separate room, office, or cubicle contains a computer. How does data travel across the network when you are in your dorm room working on your computer at the same time as your neighbor across the hall and your neighbor next door? How can you all use the same Internet connection and the printer in the common area down the hall at the same time? It all depends on the type of network topology in place. The physical layout of a LAN is called its **network topology**. A topology isn't just the arrangement of computers in a particular space; a topology provides a solution to the problem of **contention**, which occurs when two computers try to access the LAN at the same time. Contention sometimes results in **collisions**, the corruption of network data caused when two computers transmit simultaneously.

With a **bus topology**, the network cable forms a single bus, or line; every node, whether it is a computer or peripheral device, is attached to that bus (Figure 8.9a). At the ends of the bus, special connectors called **terminators** signify the end of the circuit. With a bus topology, only one node can transmit at a time. Other limitations of a bus topology include length restrictions because of the loss of signal strength and practical limits as to the number of nodes attached because of increases in contention caused by each added node. On the plus side, bus networks are simple, reliable, and easy to expand. The bus topology is practical in a relatively small environment such as a home or small office.

To resolve the contention problem, bus networks use some type of **contention management**, a technique that specifies what happens when a collision occurs. A common contention-management technique is to abandon any data that could have been corrupted by a collision.

A **star topology** solves the expansion problems of the bus topology with a central wiring device called a **switch** (Figure 8.9b). Adding users is simple; you

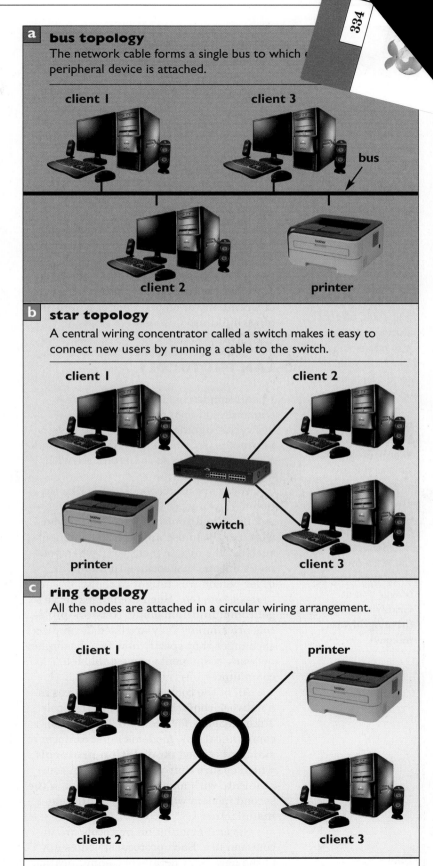

a **bus topology**
The network cable forms a single bus to which peripheral device is attached.

client 1   client 3

bus

client 2   printer

b **star topology**
A central wiring concentrator called a switch makes it easy to connect new users by running a cable to the switch.

client 1   client 2

switch

printer   client 3

c **ring topology**
All the nodes are attached in a circular wiring arrangement.

client 1   printer

client 2   client 3

FIGURE 8.9 Most networks use **(a)** bus, **(b)** star, or **(c)** ring topology.

Green Tech Tip

Thanks to networking, smart homes and appliances that communicate with one another are closer to reality than ever. Many people can already program some appliances to run only when needed or during off-peak energy times to save money and resources. But what if the power grid could talk back? During times of high power usage, it could ask your air conditioner to turn up the thermostat a few degrees or turn off your water heater to conserve energy. Programs such as this are already being tested in Toronto and may be rolled out to Baltimore and Boulder soon. You can learn more about managing the power grid at GridWise at PNNL (**http://gridwise. pnl.gov**).

just run a cable to the switch and plug the new user into a vacant connector. Star networks also generally use contention management to deal with collisions. The star topology is ideal for office buildings, computer labs, and WANs.

With a **ring topology**, all of the nodes are attached in a circular wiring arrangement. This topology provides a unique way to prevent collisions (Figure 8.9c). A special unit of data called a **token** travels around the ring. A node can transmit only when it possesses the token. Although ring networks are circular in that the token travels a circular path, they look more like star networks because all of the wiring is routed to a central switch. The ring topology is well suited for use within a division of a company or on one floor of a multifloor office building.

LAN PROTOCOLS

In addition to the physical or wireless transmission media that carry the network's signals, a network also uses **protocols** (standards) that enable network-connected devices to communicate with each other.

What are protocols? They're like the manners you were taught when you were a child. When you were growing up, you were taught to use appropriate comments, such as "It's nice to meet you," when you met someone in a social situation. The other person was taught to reply, "It's nice to meet you, too." Such exchanges serve to get communication going. Network protocols are similar. They are fixed, formalized exchanges that specify how two dissimilar network components can establish a communication.

All of the communications devices in a network conform to different protocols. Take modems, for example. To establish communications, modems must conform to standards called **modulation protocols**, which ensure that your modem can communicate with another modem, even if the second modem was made by a different manufacturer.

Several modulation protocols are in common use. Each protocol specifies all of the necessary details of communication, including the data transfer rate—the rate at which two modems can exchange data.

The protocol also includes standards for data compression and error checking.

Two modems can communicate only if both follow the same modulation protocol. When a modem attempts to establish a connection, it automatically negotiates with the modem on the other end. The two modems try to establish which protocols they share and the fastest data transfer rate that each is capable of. When that is established, data will be transferred at the fastest speed the slower modem is capable of.

A single network may use dozens of protocols. The complete package of protocols that specify how a specific network functions is called the network's **protocol suite**. Collectively, a protocol suite specifies how the network functions, or its **network architecture**. The term *architecture* may sound daunting, but in the next section you'll learn that the basic idea isn't much more complicated than a layer cake.

Network Layers

Because they're complex systems, networks use a network architecture that is divided into separate **network layers**. Each network layer has a function that can be isolated and treated separately from other layers. Because each layer's protocols precisely define how each layer passes data to another layer, it's possible to make changes within a layer without having to rebuild the entire network.

How do layers work? To understand the layer concept, it's helpful to remember that protocols are like manners, which enable people to get communication going. Let's look at an example.

Suppose you're sending an e-mail message. Now imagine that each protocol is a person, and each person has an office on a separate floor of a multistory office building. You're on the top floor, and the network connection is in the basement. When you send your message, your e-mail client software calls the person on the next floor down, "Excuse me, but would you please translate this message into a form the server can process?" The person on the floor below replies, "Sure, no problem." That person then calls the person on the next floor down, "If it isn't too much trouble, would you please put this translated

IMPACTS

Debates

Peer-to-Peer Networks: The Controversy Continues

Remember Napster? Once known for offering free peer-to-peer music file sharing and then attacked in court for copyright infringement, the company has a new owner and now sells unlimited music downloads for a monthly subscription fee. Even though Napster has gone mainstream, the controversy over P2P is far from over. Other file sharing sites, such as Kazaa and Lime Wire, have lost similar battles with the entertainment industry. Individuals who have shared copyrighted files have also been successfully sued, and proposed legislation seeks to make universities responsible for monitoring students' downloads or forfeit financial aid funds. Similarly, ISPs are in contention with sites like BitTorrent because of the large amounts of bandwidth taken up by users sharing videos.

However, not everybody wants to stop P2P music swapping. Some artists offer free downloads in hopes that fans will share the files with friends and buy more songs. Some companies are even sponsoring music downloads that link their products with promising new groups and build goodwill as the groups' music files move from computer to computer. And P2P networks are good for sharing more than music. Legitimate companies such as Skype (**www.skype .com**) or Joost (**www.joost.com**) use the power of P2P technology to provide Voice over IP (VoIP) phone service and streaming television content to their users (Figure 8.10).

If you decide to join a P2P network, give some thought to privacy and security. Unless you read all the fine print before you download free versions of programs such as Kazaa, you may not realize that you're also getting adware, spyware, and other files. And keep your antivirus software up to date to avoid getting a nasty surprise in the form of infected files from another computer on the P2P network.

Some of the biggest P2P security threats come from Trojan horses and other malware designed to hijack infected PCs. Hackers can use these backdoor programs to convert your PC to a zombie and add it to their botnet. As a zombie, your computer is then used to send out spam, conduct denial of service attacks, threaten other systems, and perform other illegal tasks. Here, P2P networking's strengths—not having a central file server and not needing technical expertise to set up the network—can actually make you vulnerable, because the rogue programs spread quickly and automatically from one PC to another. Clearly, the controversy over P2P networks will continue for some time.

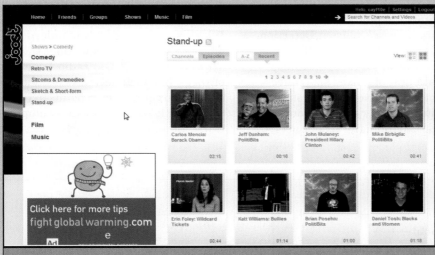

FIGURE 8.10 Sites such as Joost use P2P technology to legally distribute high-bandwidth video content to their subscribers.

Destinations

To learn more about Ethernet, check out Charles Spurgeon's Ethernet Web site at **www.ethermanage. com/ethernet/ ethernet.html**. The site covers all of the Ethernet technologies in use today and includes a practical guide for do-it-yourselfers.

message in an envelope and address it to such-and-such computer?" And so it goes, until the message finally reaches the physical transmission medium that connects the computers in the network.

At the receiving computer, precisely the opposite happens. The message is received in the basement and is sent up. It's taken out of its envelope, translated, and handed up to the top floor, where it's acted on.

To summarize, a network message starts at the top of a stack of layers and moves down through the various layers until it reaches the bottom (the physical medium). Because the layers are arranged vertically like the floors in an office building, and because each is governed by its own protocols, the layers are called a **protocol stack**. On the receiving end, the process is reversed: the received message goes up the protocol stack. First, the network's data envelope is opened, and the data is translated until it can be used by the receiving application. Figure 8.11 illustrates this concept.

LAN Technologies

By far the most popular LAN standard for large and small businesses is **Ethernet**. The various versions of Ethernet are used by approximately 90 percent of all LANs.

Ethernet uses a protocol called Carrier Sense Multiple Access/Collision Detection, or CSMA/CD. Using the CSMA/CD protocol, a computer looks for an opportunity to place a data unit of a fixed size called a **packet** onto the network and then sends it on its way. Every time a packet reaches its destination, the sender gets

confirmation, and the computer waits for a gap to open to shoot off another packet. Devices along the way read the address and pass the packet along to the next device, routing it toward its destination. Occasionally, two devices send a packet into the same gap at the same time, resulting in a collision and the loss of both packets, but only for the moment. When packets collide, the computers that sent them are instantly notified, and each chooses a random interval to wait before it resends the packet. This approach helps prevent network gridlock.

Although early versions of Ethernet (called 10Base2 and 10Base5) used coaxial cable in bus networks, the most popular versions today are Ethernet star networks that use switches and twisted-pair wire. Currently, three versions of Ethernet are in use: 10Base-T (10 Mbps), Fast Ethernet (100 Mbps, also called 100Base-T), and Gigabit Ethernet. The newest version, Gigabit Ethernet is not as widely implemented as the other two versions. Gigabit Ethernet sends data at 1 Gbps; a 10-Gbps version is on the horizon. These superfast connections are often used to create large networks because they prevent data bottlenecks. Several popular LAN protocols are listed in Figure 8.12.

Wi-Fi

Wi-Fi is a wireless LAN standard that offers Ethernet speeds without the wires. Wi-Fi networking uses radio waves instead of wires, but such networks still need a central server or access point. In other words, with Wi-Fi technology computers can communicate with each other, but to

FIGURE 8.11

A message starts at the top of a stack of layers and moves down through the various layers (protocol stack) until it reaches the bottom, or physical medium. On the receiving end, the process is reversed.

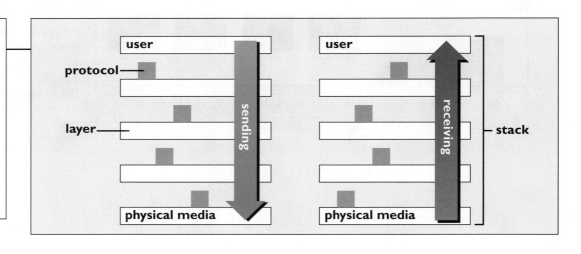

FIGURE 8.12 Popular LAN Protocols

Protocol Name	Data Transfer Rate	Physical Media	Topology
Ethernet (10Base-T)	10 Mbps	Twisted-pair cable	Star
Fast Ethernet (100Base-T)	100 Mbps	Twisted-pair or fiber-optic cable	Star
Gigabit Ethernet	1,000 Mbps	Fiber-optic cable	Star
Token Ring Network	4–16 Mbps	Twisted-pair cable	Star

access the Internet or to communicate across distances a central access point is required. Wireless routers sold for home use contain a wireless access point inside the router. The router also has an omnidirectional antenna to receive the data transmitted by wireless transceivers. External Wi-Fi transceivers connect to desktop computers through USB connections, whereas most notebooks are equipped with built-in wireless network adapters.

Wi-Fi uses the 802.11 wireless networking standard and transmits on the 2.4 GHz or 5 GHz radio frequency band. There are currently four 802.11 standards (Figure 8.13). The 802.11g standard is the most common, while 802.11n is the newest standard and is expected to be ratified in 2009. Wireless products using the 802.11n draft standard are already available and should work when the standard is finalized.

Although Wi-Fi is convenient, there are some security risks. Wired networks require a computer or other device to be physically connected, but wireless networks broadcast radio waves that can be picked up by anyone using the correct configuration. These signals can extend beyond the walls of your home or office, so it is important to properly

FIGURE 8.13 Popular Wireless Networking Standards

Standard	Frequency	Transmission Speed	Comments
802.11a	5 GHz	Up to 54 Mbps	Fast, low interference, short range, doesn't work well indoors
802.11b	2.4 GHz	Up to 11 Mbps	Low cost, replaced by faster standards
802.11g	2.4 GHz	Up to 54 Mbps	Fast, backward compatible with 802.11b
802.11n (draft)	2.4 GHz and/or 5 GHz	Up to 300 Mbps	Improved speed and range, operates on both frequencies, backward compatible with 802.11a/b/g, standards ratification expected in 2009
802.15	2.4 GHz	Up to 55 Mbps	Used for Bluetooth technology, very short range (up to 10 meters)
802.16	2–11 GHz	Up to 70 Mbps	WiMax, provides high-speed wireless Internet access over long distances (more than 30 miles)

CURRENTS

Computers and Society

Make a Difference: Lend Your Computer to Science

You can help save the planet, save lives, or find new life in space by offering your computer's idle time to science. Distributed computing, in which networked computers work on small pieces of large complex tasks, is revolutionizing research in a number of areas. Nearly 5 million computer users are already lending their computing power to a variety of diverse projects. Climateprediction.net (**http://climateprediction. net**) is attempting to forecast the climate for the 21st century. The Folding@home (**http://folding. stanford.edu**) project studies the behavior of human proteins, and SETI@home (**http://setiathome. berkeley.edu**) analyzes radio signals in the search for extraterrestrial life (Figure 8.14). The combined power of these networked computers is equivalent to years of super-computer time—an enormous help to non-profits with limited resources but ambitious goals.

To volunteer your computer, you will need to download and install a special screensaver program. If this software detects that your computer is on and not busy with something else, it uses your Internet connection to reach the research center's server, downloads numbers to crunch or data to sift, and then submits the results to the server. At the other end, the research center's computer assembles all of these bite-size answers to complete one task and then parcels out pieces of the next task. Your computer's spare computing power may be used dozen of times daily or just a few days a week, depending on what the scientists are working on at that time. To see how much computing time your computer has contributed, you can check the screensaver or the project's Web site.

Many of these research projects use the Berkeley Open Infrastructure for Network Computing (BOINC, **http://boinc.berkeley.edu**) as their software platform, which means that your computer can work on multiple projects by using just a single screen saver. If you decide to get involved, you will need to update your security program regularly to protect against hackers. Is distributed computing in your future?

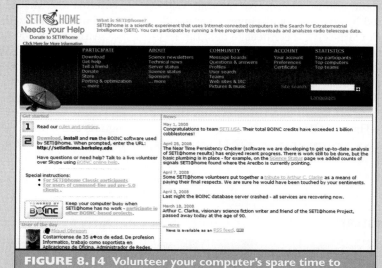

FIGURE 8.14 Volunteer your computer's spare time to help with the SETI project and search for signs of extraterrestrial life.

secure your network and data. To safeguard your network do the following:

- Always use a firewall and updated antivirus and antispyware software.

- Change the router's default network name, also known as an SSID, and the default password.

- If possible, turn off SSID broadcasting to avoid detection by hackers.

- Ensure your router's software has been upgraded to the most recent version.

- Turn on WEP (Wired Equivalent Privacy) or WPA (Wi-Fi Protected Access) to enable encryption. WPA provides stronger protection.

- Turn on MAC (Media Access Control) address filtering so only authorized devices can obtain access.

Similarly, when using a public wireless access location, known as a **hotspot**, you should take the following precautions:

- Be aware of your surroundings— ensure no one is watching over your shoulder for logon and password information.

- Be sure to log on to the correct wireless network, not a look-alike or so-called *Evil Twin* network.

- Disable file and printer sharing.

- Don't transmit confidential data—if you must, be sure to use encryption.

- Turn off your wireless access when it is not in use.

Whether wired or wireless, LANs enable an organization to share computing resources in a single building or across a group of buildings. However, a LAN's geographic limitations pose a problem. Today, many organizations need to share computing resources with distant branch offices, employees who are traveling, and even people outside the organization, including suppliers and customers. This is what wide area networks (WANs) are used for—to link computers separated by even thousands of miles.

Wide Area Networks

Like LANs, WANs have all of the basic network components—cabling, protocols, and devices—for routing information to the correct destination. WANs are like long-distance telephone systems. In fact, much WAN traffic is carried by long-distance voice communication providers and cable companies. So you can picture a WAN as a LAN that has long-distance communications needs among its servers, computers, and peripherals. Let's look at the special components of WANs that

differentiate them from LANs: a point of presence and backbones.

POINT OF PRESENCE

To carry computer data over the long haul, a WAN must be locally accessible. Like long-distance phone carriers or ISPs, WANs have what amounts to a local access number, called a point of presence. A **point of presence (POP)** is a WAN network connection point that enables users to access the WAN by a local analog telephone call (using a modem) or a direct digital hookup that enables a continuous, direct connection. For this reason, WANs have a POP in as many towns and cities as needed.

BACKBONES

The LANs and WANs that make up the Internet are connected to the Internet backbone. **Backbones** are the high-capacity transmission lines that carry WAN traffic. Some backbones are regional, connecting towns and cities in a region such as Southern California or New England. Others are continental, or even transcontinental, in scope (Figure 8.15).

Whatever their scope, backbones are designed to carry huge amounts of data traffic. Cross-country Internet backbones, for example, can handle up to 13 Gbps, and much higher speeds are on the way.

To understand how data travels over a WAN, it helps to understand how data travels over the Internet. This journey can be compared to an interstate car trip. When you connect to the Internet and request access to a Web page, your request travels by local connections—the city streets—to your ISP's local POP. From there, your ISP relays your request to the regional backbone—a highway. Your request then goes to a network access point—a highway on-ramp— where regional backbones connect with national backbone networks. And from there, the message gets on the national backbone network—the interstate. When your request nears its destination, your message gets off the national backbone network and travels regional and local networks until it reaches its destination.

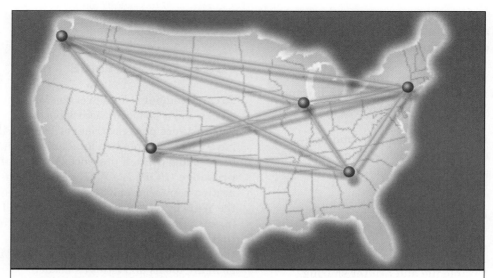

FIGURE 8.15 Some backbones are regional, connecting towns and cities in a region such as Southern California or New England. Others are continental, or even transcontinental, in scope.

WAN PROTOCOLS

Like any computer network, WANs use protocols. For example, the Internet uses more than 100 protocols that specify every aspect of Internet usage, such as how to retrieve documents through the Web or send e-mail to a distant computer. Internet data can travel over any type of WAN because of Internet protocols.

The Internet Protocols

The Internet protocols, collectively called **TCP/IP**, are open protocols that define how the Internet works. TCP/IP is an abbreviation for Transmission Control Protocol (TCP)/Internet Protocol (IP). However, more than 100 protocols make up the entire Internet protocol suite.

Of all of the Internet protocols, the most fundamental one is the **Internet Protocol (IP)** because it defines the Internet's addressing scheme, which enables any Internet-connected computer to be uniquely identified. IP is a connectionless protocol. This means that with IP, two computers don't have to be online at the same time to exchange data. The sending computer just keeps trying until the message gets through.

Because IP enables direct and immediate contact with any other computer on the network, the Internet bears some similarity to the telephone system (although the Internet works on different principles). Every computer on the Internet has an **Internet address**, or **IP address** (similar to a phone number). A computer can exchange data with any other Internet-connected computer by "dialing" the other computer's address. An IP address has four parts, which are separated by periods (such as 128.254.108.7).

The **Transmission Control Protocol (TCP)** defines how one Internet-connected computer can contact another to exchange control and confirmation messages. You can see TCP in action when you use the Web; just watch your browser's status bar. You'll see messages such as "Contacting server," "Receiving data," and "Closing connection."

Circuit and Packet Switching

WAN protocols are based on either circuit- or packet-switching network technology, but most use packet switching. The Internet uses packet switching, whereas the public switched telephone network (PSTN) uses circuit switching. Still, the Internet does for computers what the telephone system does for phones: It enables any Internet-connected

Techtalk

gigaPoP

A gigaPoP (gigabits per second points of presence) is a POP that provides access to a backbone service capable of data transfer rates exceeding 1 Gbps (1 billion bits per second). These network connection points link to high-speed networks that have been developed by federal agencies.

computer to connect almost instantly and effortlessly with any other Internet-connected computer anywhere in the world.

With **circuit switching**, data is sent over a physical end-to-end circuit between the sending and receiving computers. Circuit switching works best when avoiding delivery delays is essential. In a circuit-switching network, high-speed electronic switches handle the job of establishing and maintaining the connection.

With **packet switching**, the sending computer's outgoing message is divided into packets (Figure 8.16). Each packet is numbered and addressed to the destination computer. The packets then travel to a router, which examines each packet it detects. After reading the packet's address, the router consults a table of possible pathways that the packet can take to get to its destination. If more than one path exists, the router sends the packet along the path that is most free of congestion. The packets may not arrive in the order they were sent, but that's not a problem. On the receiving computer, protocols put the packets in the correct order and decode the message they contain. If any packets are missing, the receiving computer sends a message requesting retransmission of the missing packet.

So which type of switching is best? Compared with circuit switching, packet switching has many advantages. It's more efficient and less expensive than circuit switching. What's more, packet-switching networks are more reliable. A packet-switching network can function even if portions of the network aren't working.

However, packet switching does have some drawbacks. When a router examines a packet, it delays the packet's progress by a tiny fraction of a second. In a huge packet-switching network—such as the Internet—a given packet may be examined by many routers, which introduces a noticeable delay called **latency**. If the network experiences **congestion** (overloading), some of the packets may be further delayed, and the message can't be decoded until all of its packets are received.

The oldest packet-switching protocol for WAN usage, **X.25**, is optimized for dial-up connections over noisy telephone lines and is still in widespread use. Local connections generally offer speeds of 9.6 to 64 Kbps. X.25 is best used to create a point-to-point connection with a single computer. A point-to-point connection is a single line that connects one communications device to one computer. It is widely used with ATMs and credit card authorization devices. New protocols designed for 100 percent digital lines, such as Switched Multimegabit Data Service (SMDS) and Asynchronous Transfer Mode (ATM), enable much faster data transfer rates (up to 155 Mbps).

Now that you understand how WANs work, let's explore how they are used.

WAN APPLICATIONS

WANs enable companies to use many of the same applications that you use, such as e-mail, conferencing, document exchange, and remote database access. Some WANs are created to serve the public, such as those maintained by online service providers such as AOL and MSN. Other WANs are created and maintained for the sole purpose of meeting an organization's internal needs.

LAN-to-LAN Connections
In corporations and universities, WANs are often used to connect LANs at two or more geographically separate locations. This use of WANs overcomes the major limitation of a LAN—its inability to link computers separated by more than a few thousand feet. Companies can connect their LANs over their ISP connection, which often provides bandwidth that far exceeds capabilities of internal networks. With these connections, users get the impression that they're using one huge LAN that connects the entire company and all of its branch offices.

Transaction Acquisition
When you make a purchase at a retail store, information about your transaction is instantly relayed to the company's central computers through its WAN.

Destinations

To learn more about WAN protocols, visit Cisco's WAN documentation site at **www.cisco.com/ en/US/docs/ internetworking/ technology/handbook/ Intro-to-WAN.html**.

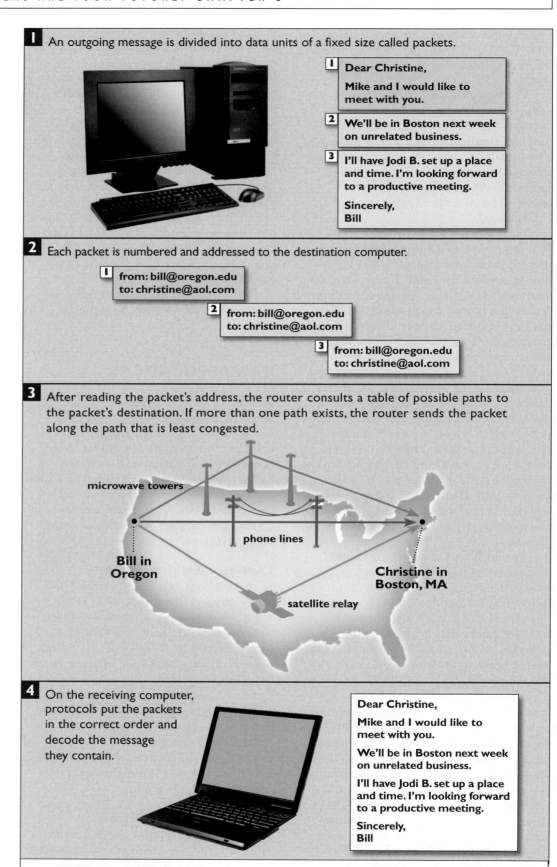

1 An outgoing message is divided into data units of a fixed size called packets.

1 Dear Christine,

Mike and I would like to meet with you.

2 We'll be in Boston next week on unrelated business.

3 I'll have Jodi B. set up a place and time. I'm looking forward to a productive meeting.

Sincerely,
Bill

2 Each packet is numbered and addressed to the destination computer.

1 from: bill@oregon.edu
to: christine@aol.com

2 from: bill@oregon.edu
to: christine@aol.com

3 from: bill@oregon.edu
to: christine@aol.com

3 After reading the packet's address, the router consults a table of possible paths to the packet's destination. If more than one path exists, the router sends the packet along the path that is least congested.

microwave towers

phone lines

Bill in Oregon

Christine in Boston, MA

satellite relay

4 On the receiving computer, protocols put the packets in the correct order and decode the message they contain.

Dear Christine,

Mike and I would like to meet with you.

We'll be in Boston next week on unrelated business.

I'll have Jodi B. set up a place and time. I'm looking forward to a productive meeting.

Sincerely,
Bill

FIGURE 8.16 Packet Switching

FIGURE 8.17 POS terminals instantly relay information about transactions to the company's central computers through its WAN.

That's because the cash register the clerk uses is actually a computer, a point-of-sale (POS) terminal, that's linked to a data communications network (Figure 8.17). The acquired data is collected for accounting purposes and analyzed to see if a store's sales patterns have changed.

As you've seen, networking is a powerful tool, allowing users to communicate, share resources, and exchange data.

What You've Learned

NETWORKS: COMMUNICATING & SHARING RESOURCES

- Computer networks link two or more computers so that they can exchange data and share resources, such as printers, scanners, and an Internet connection. Networks are of two primary types: local area networks (LANs), which serve a building or a small geographic area, and wide area networks (WANs), which can span buildings, cities, states, and nations. Networks consist of special hardware, software, and people. For example, most networks have nodes (which can be computers, printers, communications devices, or file servers), network interface cards (NICs), network operating systems, and network administrators.

- Computer networks can reduce hardware costs, enable application sharing, create a means of pooling an organization's mission-critical data, and foster teamwork and collaboration. Disadvantages of computer networks include loss of autonomy, threats to security and privacy, and potential productivity losses due to network outages.

- A peer-to-peer LAN doesn't use a file server. It is most appropriate for small networks of fewer than 10 computers. Client/server networks include one or more file servers as well as clients such as desktops, notebooks, and handheld devices. The client/server model works with any size or physical layout of LAN and doesn't slow down with heavy use.

- The physical layout of a LAN is called its network topology. A topology isn't just the arrangement of computers in a particular space; a topology provides a solution to the problem of contention, which occurs when two nodes try to access the LAN at the same time. The three different LAN topologies are bus (single connections to a central line), star (all connections to a central switch), and ring (tokens carry messages around a ring).

- Protocols define how network devices can communicate with each other. A network requires many protocols to function smoothly. When a computer sends a message over the network, the application hands the message down the protocol stack, where a series of protocols prepares the message for transmission through the network. At the other end, the message goes up a similar stack.

- The most widely used LAN protocol is Ethernet, which is available in two versions that use switches and twisted pair wiring: 10Base-T (10 Mbps) and 100Base-T (or Fast Ethernet; 100 Mbps). The newest version, Gigabit Ethernet, can transfer data at the rate of 1,000 Mbps, or 1 Gbps.

- The special components that distinguish a WAN from a LAN are a point of presence and backbones. A point of presence (POP) is a WAN network connection point that enables users to access the WAN by a local analog telephone call (using a modem) or a direct digital hookup that enables a continuous, direct connection. Backbones are the high-capacity transmission lines that carry WAN traffic.

- Circuit switching creates a permanent end-to-end circuit that is optimal for voice and real-time data. Circuit switching is not as efficient or reliable as packet switching; it is also more expensive. Packet switching does not require a permanent switched circuit. A packet-switched network can funnel more data through a medium with a given data transfer capacity. However, packet switching introduces slight delays that make the technology less than optimal for voice or real-time data.

Go to **www.pearsonhighered.com/cayf** to review this chapter, answer the questions, and complete the exercises.

Key Terms and Concepts

backbones 339
bus topology 333
circuit switching 340
client 327
client/server network 331
collisions 333
communications devices 327
congestion 341
contention 333
contention management 333
Ethernet 336
file server 328
hotspot 339
Internet address (IP address) 340
Internet Protocol (IP) 340
latency 341

local area network (LAN) 329
modulation protocols 334
network 326
network administrators 328
network architecture 334
network interface cards
  (NICs) 327
network layers 334
network operating system
  (NOS) 328
network topology 333
node 327
packet 336
packet switching 340
peer-to-peer (P2P) network . . 331
point of presence (POP) 339

protocol stack 336
protocol suite 334
protocols 334
ring topology 334
routers 328
star topology 333
switch 333
TCP/IP 340
terminators 333
token 334
Transmission Control
  Protocol (TCP) 340
wide area network (WAN) . . . 327
Wi-Fi 336
wireless LAN 330
X.25 341

Go to **www.pearsonhighered.com/cayf** to review this chapter, answer the questions, and complete the exercises.

Matching

Match each key term in the left column with the most accurate definition in the right column.

_____ 1. terminator

_____ 2. packet

_____ 3. router

_____ 4. backbone

_____ 5. hotspot

_____ 6. latency

_____ 7. network operating system

_____ 8. circuit switching

_____ 9. protocols

_____ 10. LAN

_____ 11. TCP

_____ 12. IP

_____ 13. modulation protocol

_____ 14. switch

_____ 15. network architecture

a. avoids delivery delays but can't function if portions of the network aren't working

b. a public wireless access point

c. a unit of data transferred over the Ethernet

d. defined by network protocol and divided into layers

e. enables modems to communicate with one another, regardless of the manufacturer

f. uses cable, radio waves, or infrared signals to link devices within a building

g. a fundamental, connectionless protocol

h. a device used to move data between two or more networks

i. used to define the way Internet-connected computers communicate

j. a special connector located at the end of a bus

k. central wiring device that enables network expansion

l. delay caused by the examination of a packet by multiple routers

m. designed to carry high amounts of data traffic

n. installed on the server and managed by a network administrator

o. standards that enable devices on a network to communicate

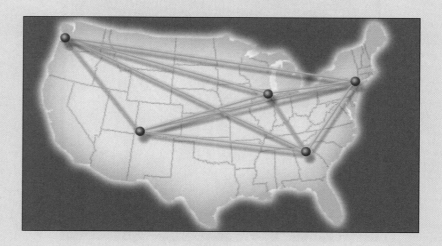

Multiple Choice

Circle the correct choice for each of the following.

1. Which of the following statements about packet switching is not true?
   a. It is used by WAN protocols.
   b. Packets are examined by routers.
   c. Packets must be received in the same order in which they were sent.
   d. Missing packets must be retransmitted.

2. A protocol suite:
   a. includes all the standards that specify how a network functions.
   b. determines how nodes are connected to a network.
   c. is the process by which a message moves through network layers.
   d. consists of nodes and physical media.

3. Which type of network topology uses a token?
   a. P2P
   b. star
   c. bus
   d. ring

4. Which of the following is a WAN network connection point?
   a. TCP
   b. IP
   c. NOS
   d. POP

5. Which of the following statements about client/server networks is *not* true?
   a. They can be wired or wireless.
   b. They require at least one server.
   c. They can be used for peer-to-peer computing.
   d. Servers receive requests from clients.

6. A device that is connected to a network is known as a:
   a. packet
   b. node
   c. token
   d. circuit

7. Which of the following can cause network data to become corrupted because of simultaneous transmission?
   a. collision
   b. congestion
   c. collusion
   d. contention

8. Which of the following is a common contention-management technique?
   a. abandon data corrupted by a collision
   b. retransmit unreceived packets
   c. generate a new token
   d. add terminators to minimize signal loss

9. NIC is short for:
   a. network information client
   b. node interface circuit
   c. network interface card
   d. network interval circuit

10. Which wireless standard operates on the 2.4 GHz frequency and is capable of transmitting data at speeds up to 54 Mbps?
    a. 802.11a
    b. 802.11g
    c. 802.11n
    d. 802.16

Go to **www.pearsonhighered.com/cayf** to review this chapter, answer the questions, and complete the exercises.

Fill-In

In the blanks provided, write the correct answer for each of the following.

1. The newest wireless networking standard, capable of operating on either 2.4 GHz or 5 GHz frequency, is _____.

2. A network allows two or more computer systems to exchange data or share _____ such as printers and Internet connections.

3. A computer that is connected to a network is known as a node or a(n) _____.

4. The expansion board used to connect a computer to a network is known as a(n) _____ _____ _____.

5. A(n) _____ is used to move data within only one network.

6. A high-speed, high-capacity computer containing the network operating system, network applications, and data files is a(n) _____ _____.

7. A(n) _____ _____ is assigned to every computer on the Internet to facilitate the exchange of data.

8. For safer wireless connections, WEP or WPA should be used to enable _____.

9. _____ Ethernet uses fiber-optic cable to transfer data at 1,000 Mbps.

10. Network _____ is specified by the network's protocol suite.

11. _____ _____ is a physical layout that uses a switch to facilitate network expansion.

12. In a _____ - _____ - _____ network, all of the computers are equals and there is no file server.

13. A wireless LAN uses _____ _____ instead of wires to transmit data.

14. Novell's SUSE and Windows Server 2008 are both examples of a(n) _____ _____ _____.

15. Modems, switches, and wireless access points are all examples of _____ devices.

Short Answer

1. Describe a protocol stack and then draw a diagram that shows what you have described.

2. Explain the difference between peer-to-peer and client/server networks.

3. How do LANs and WANs differ?

4. Name three types of LAN topologies and describe how each works.

5. What is the difference between contention and congestion?

6. How do circuit switching and packet switching differ? What are the advantages of each method?

Teamwork

1. Finding IP Addresses

Frequently, the IP addresses of an organization's Internet-connected computers begin with the same several digits. For example, all of the computers at Buffalo State College have an IP address of the form 136.183.xxx.xxx. The last two sets of numbers usually denote the campus building and the individual computer. Have one of your team members stop by your school's computing services center and find out if your institution has a common set of IP addresses for its computers. If it does, what are the common digits? Have each team member access your school's Windows-based networked computers to determine their IP addresses by visiting the What Is My IP Address Web site (**http://whatismyipaddress.com**). What is the IP address of each computer? Do they begin with a common set of digits? Write a short paper that describes your findings.

2. Computer Lab Topologies

Have each team member visit campus computer labs and determine the network topology used. In addition to computers, what other devices are connected to each network? What types of physical media are used to connect the computers and the peripherals in each lab? How does your school connect to the Internet? Write a short paper that describes your findings.

3. Designing a Network

If you were responsible for setting up a network for a company that had offices in five different states, how would you do it? What part would the Internet play in your plans? Assume that each office is on one floor of a building and has three divisions, each having six employees. Each division needs access to a printer and an Internet connection. All divisions at all five locations need to have 24/7 access to each other. As a team, collaborate on a paper that describes the network (including a schematic of the network and one division). Be sure to use several of the key terms from this chapter.

4. Researching Routers

The number of households that have more than one computer is increasing, and families want to share resources among them. One of these resources is the Internet connection. Although newer versions of Microsoft Windows offer software that enables two computers to share an Internet connection, consumers with high-speed connections such as cable or DSL also can use a router to share Internet access. Your team is to go to a local computer store and investigate both cable and DSL routers. How many ports do these devices have? How much do they cost? What physical medium is used to connect the devices to the router? Can a printer be shared using a router? What type of network topology is used? What additional hardware is needed to network the computers to the router? Be sure to explore wireless routers also. Do you use a router now? Why or why not?

5. Wireless Networks

Your team is to go to a local computer store and investigate wireless access points. What are the prices for these devices? How do wireless connection speeds compare with wired ones? What type of network topology is used? What additional hardware is needed to network computers to the wireless access point? If you had a home network, would you consider this networking alternative? Why or why not? Write a paper that answers these questions and describes your experience at the computer store.

On the Web

1. Establishing a Wired Home Network

Visit CNET at **www.cnet.com** to learn more about establishing a home network. Although you may find information on wireless networking, restrict your research to wired networks. Assume that you have two computers, a printer, and a scanner that you wish to network. What hardware and software will you need to purchase? How much will your network cost? Will you connect to the Internet? If so, how and at what cost? If not, why not?

2. Researching Fast Ethernet

The text discussed Gigabit Ethernet technology that enables LAN connection speeds of up to 1 Gbps. Go to Charles Spurgeon's Ethernet Web Site (**www.ethermanage.com**) to learn more about an even faster technology—10 Gigabit Ethernet. What does 10 GEA stand for? When was it formed? Name three of the founding organizations. When was the 10 GEA dissolved? When was 10 Gigabit Ethernet ratified? What types of companies, organizations, or institutions do you think will use this technology?

3. Exploring NICs

Assume that you have both a desktop and a notebook and you want to network them. To do this, each computer needs a NIC. Go to **www.pricegrabber.com** to find the best prices for NICs for a desktop and a notebook computer. What are the prices for each? Why do you think notebook cards are more expensive? Many desktops and notebooks now have automatic built-in network connectivity. Locate and name specific desktop and notebook models that have internal networking capabilities. If you currently have a desktop or notebook, does your computer have internal networking capabilities?

4. A Smartphone for You

Because of their small size, smartphones are popular mobile computing devices. Do you own or have you considered buying a smartphone? Go to Tiger Direct (**www.tigerdirect.com**) and search for "smartphone" to find information on smartphones. What are the most popular methods for networking a smartphone to a desktop computer? Which of these methods require additional PC hardware? Is the use of the word *networking* correct? Explain why or why not.

5. Novell Network Operating Systems

One of the oldest and most widely used network operating systems is Novell's NetWare. Visit the Novell site at **www.novell.com**. What is replacing NetWare? In addition to LAN software, what Internet features does this new OS support? What are the initial purchase and upgrade costs for a small system that supports a server and five client computers? What products qualify for competitive upgrades? In addition to English, name three other languages in which the new OS is available. Does the new OS support Mac and UNIX-based computers? Does your school use any Novell networking software?

Choosing an ISP

Your ISP is your lifeline to the online world. Every month you spend your hard-earned money to maintain that connection. Depending on the speed and type of Internet connection, you can spend anywhere from $10 to $60 or more each month to read your e-mail, surf the Web, and trade files with your friends (legally, of course). That monthly fee can quickly add up over the course of a year! Before you pay your next ISP bill, you should ask yourself exactly what you get in return for your monthly service fee. Speed is important, but it shouldn't be the only determining factor when choosing an ISP. Here are some tips to help you determine if you and your ISP are a good match as well as some ideas on how to get the most bang for your buck each month.

CHOOSING AN ISP

How much time do you spend online each month? Do you need unlimited access, or do you only occasionally check your e-mail and visit Web sites? Many dial-up ISPs provide a discounted service for users who don't go over a specific number of hours per month. Why pay for unlimited access if you don't need it?

Do you really need a high-speed connection? The difference in price between dial-up and cable or DSL access can be significant. You'll need to determine if the price is worth the extra money. If you rarely download large files and you spend a limited amount of time online each month, then you may want to consider using a dial-up service at home and using computers at school or your local library for those few times when speed really does matter. (Be sure to check in advance if this is an acceptable use of computing resources wherever you choose to download files.)

What else do you get for your money? Services such as AOL charge a premium for access to their custom content and features. (AOL also is a great choice if you are new to the Internet and all the Internet has to offer.) Some other questions you should ask yourself include the following: Do you need an e-mail address for each member of your family? Would you like to host a Web site? Do you need parental controls? It is important to create a list and prioritize everything you would like from your ISP before you start to shop around.

Web sites such as The List (**www.thelist.com**) can be helpful when shopping for an ISP. Alternatively, type "ISP" into your favorite search engine.

GETTING THE MOST FOR YOUR MONEY

Find out how many e-mail accounts are available to you and use them all. Have separate e-mail accounts for activities such as online purchases, correspondence with friends and family, work, Web site memberships, and so on.

If your ISP provides you with storage space to host a Web site, then what are you waiting for? A variety of Web resources are available to help you learn HTML, and it isn't very difficult to create a basic Web site. Many ISPs will even provide you with an automated tool to help you create and manage your Web pages. Who knows, you and your Web site may even be famous someday!

If you pay for a broadband connection, you should download, download, download! Many sites sell downloadable music, books, and movies. Instead of taking a trip in your car to rent a movie, the next time you're bored why not try downloading and playing a movie from the Web? If your computer has the appropriate connections, you can even watch the movies using your TV. If you're paying for a lot of bandwidth, use it!

SPOTLIGHT
EMERGING

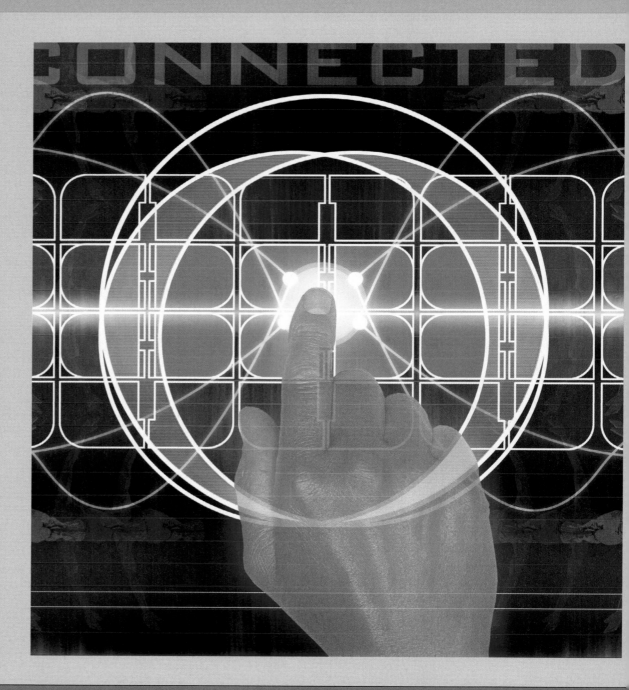

CONNECTED

TECHNOLOGIES

It's easy to predict the future, the hard part is getting it right, particularly where technology is concerned. Past attempts offer examples of just how difficult it can be to predict technology. For example, in 1876, a Western Union official said, "The telephone has too many shortcomings to be seriously considered as a means of communication. The device is inherently of no value." A century later, the chairman of IBM stated that there was no reason why anyone would want a computer in his or her home.

No one can accurately predict the future of technology. However, you can keep abreast of news and learn to recognize emerging technology trends. This Spotlight looks at the trends driving contemporary computing and the potential impact of artificial intelligence as computer designers work toward creating a truly intelligent machine.

TOMORROW'S HARDWARE: SMALLER, FASTER, CHEAPER, AND CONNECTED

In the early days of computing, room-size noisy machines read punched cards to perform their calculations. Today, many computers are smaller than the palm of your hand and can accomplish a wide array of tasks. But what will computers be like in the future?

NANOTECHNOLOGY AND BIOCHIPS

What would you say if someone told you that someday various products will be able to manufacture themselves or that computers will work billions of times faster than they do now? And that it will be possible to use computers to end famine and disease or to bring extinct animals and plants back to life? Or that computers will be used to make distant, uninhabitable planets more Earthlike? All of these things and more may one day be possible with nanotechnology (Figure 8A).

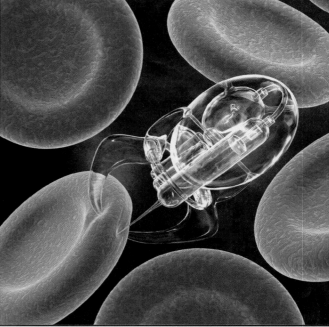

FIGURE 8A

Someday a nanoinjector may travel through your bloodstream, carrying out its mission to cure an illness or enhance your life in some way.

Merriam-Webster's Collegiate Dictionary, 11th edition, defines **nanotechnology** as "the art of manipulating materials on an atomic or molecular scale especially to build microscopic devices." Nanotechnology is based on a unit of measure called a nanometer, which is a billionth of a meter. Today, nanotechnologists manipulate atoms and molecules to perform certain limited tasks, but someday, nanotechnology will be used to perform an array of tasks. And because of the small size of atoms and molecules, we'll be able to use them to do things we never before thought possible.

The tie between medical and corporate research in nanotechnology is already strong (Figure 8B). In fact, the first breakthroughs in nanotechnology will probably be in nanomedicine and the use of medical nanorobots. For instance, medical nanorobots may one day be able to destroy fatty deposits in the bloodstream or organize cells to restore artery walls, thereby preventing heart attacks. Nanorobots may also one day improve our immune system by disabling or ridding viruses from our bodies. Someday, doctors may use nanorobots to deliver cancer-treatment drugs to specific areas of the body.

Meanwhile, NASA has funded research to create nanoparticles and nanocapsules. Although this research will be invaluable to medical researchers, NASA hopes to use nanotechnology applications for space travel and for long-term space habitation. One of NASA's concerns is the effect of radiation on astronauts. NASA thinks that nanomedicine could perhaps be used to provide radiation protection to astronauts, to enable the self-diagnosis of disease while in space, and to deliver medication during long space missions, among other things. Nanotechnology may also be able to alter the properties of known materials, making them lighter and stronger for lengthy space flights.

Perhaps the most interesting practical use of nanotechnology is the development of the **biochip** (Figure 8C). Think of a biochip as being similar to a microprocessor, or a computer chip, with one main difference. A computer chip processes millions of computer instructions per second, whereas a biochip processes biological instructions, such as determining the number of genes in a strand of DNA.

Because the silicon-based microprocessors we know today are limited as to how fast and small they can become, researchers are looking at biochips to produce faster computing speeds. Chip makers are hoping that they will be able to integrate DNA into a computer chip to create a so-called DNA computer that will be capable of storing billions of times more data than your personal computer. Scientists are using genetic material to create nanocomputers that may someday take the place of silicon-based computers.

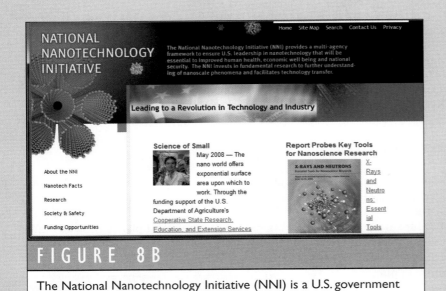

FIGURE 8B

The National Nanotechnology Initiative (NNI) is a U.S. government program that coordinates research and development in nanotechnology.

FIGURE 8C

Researchers at Argonne National Laboratory are using biochip technology to study and identify infectious diseases.

Nanotechnology sounds complex, and it is, but its possibilities and implications are truly endless. In fact, some say that nanotechnology is the most important technological breakthrough since steam power. With corporate and medical research and development on parallel "nanopaths," there may be high demand for nanotechnicians in your lifetime.

Besides shrinking components through the use of nanotechnology and biochips, tomorrow's computers are affected by two laws of technology and economics: Moore's Law and Metcalfe's Law.

MOORE'S LAW AND METCALFE'S LAW

Moore's Law, formulated more than 40 years ago by Intel Corporation chairman Gordon Moore, states that microprocessors and other miniature circuits double in circuit density (and therefore in processing power) every 18 to 24 months. If Moore's Law remains true until the middle of this century, computers will be 10 billion times more powerful than today's fastest machines. Storage technology shows a similar trend: steep increases in capacity and steep declines in cost.

Metcalfe's Law, formulated by Ethernet inventor Bob Metcalfe, states that the value of a computer network grows in proportion to the square of the number of people connected to it. A telephone line that connects two people is of limited value, but a telephone system that connects an entire city becomes an indispensable resource. Using Metcalfe's Law, a network connecting two people has a value of 4, but a network connecting four people has a value of 16. According to some predictions, the Internet will ultimately connect 1 billion users worldwide.

If you put these two laws together, you get a potent mixture: The computer industry is now giving us *networked* machines that double in power every 18 to 24 months.

As computers become smaller, faster, cheaper, and more interconnected, new technology will encourage the trend toward the digitization of all of the world's information and knowledge—the entire storehouse of accumulated human experience (Figure 8D).

Over the next several years, you'll see both Moore's and Metcalfe's Laws at work. Figure 8E lists the characteristics of a 2008 personal computer, characteristics

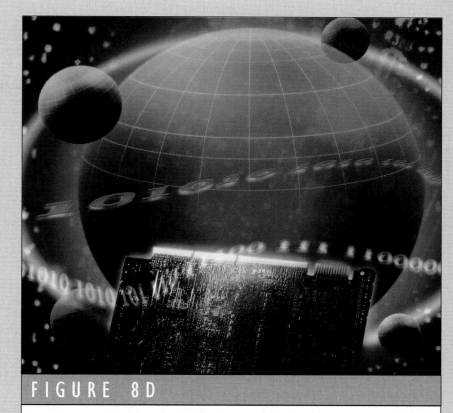

FIGURE 8D

As computers become smaller, faster, cheaper, and more interconnected, new technology will encourage the trend toward the digitization of all of the world's information and knowledge.

FIGURE 8E The Predicted 2008 Computer versus an Actual 2008 Computer

Component	1999	Predicted 2008	Actual 2008
RAM	64 MB	4 GB	4–8 GB
Processor speed (instructions per second)	400 million	9.6 billion	3.2 billion (with multiple processors)
Circuit density (number of transistors)	7.5 million	250 million	460 million
Hard disk capacity	8 GB	600 GB	1000 GB
Average Internet connection speed (bps)	56,000	6 million	8 million

predicted in 1999 on the basis of Moore's Law. Compare an actual 2008 personal computer with the computer of 1999—the difference is astounding.

Moore's Law predicts that by 2020 all of the components of unbelievably powerful computers will be accommodated on just one tiny mass-produced silicon chip. These chips will hold superfast processors (capable of performing a trillion instructions per second), huge amounts of RAM, video circuitry—the works. And they could cost less than $500!

COMPUTERS EVERYWHERE

In light of these trends toward lower cost and miniaturization, some computer scientists are beginning to speak of ubiquitous computing (*ubiquitous* means "everywhere"). With **ubiquitous computing**, computers are everywhere, even in the background, providing computer-based intelligence all around us. The realms of business, industry, science, and entertainment are employing ubiquitous computing in a number of ways.

Automated Highway Systems

Imagine that you're cruising down the freeway at 120 mph. It's foggy, and the driver of the vehicle in the next lane over has apparently fallen asleep. But you're not concerned. In fact, you're not even watching the road. Instead, you're watching television. Sound crazy? Actually, you're quite safe. You're driving a computer-equipped smart car on the next century's Automated Highway System (AHS), which, according to its proponents, will eliminate 1.2 million crashes per year, save thousands of lives, and save $150 billion in annual economic losses due to car crashes.

As you probably know, today's cars are already equipped with onboard computers that control braking and other systems. With the AHS, information will be passed between vehicles and highways via various devices and sensors that will prevent automobile collisions by electronically controlling an automobile's guidance, brakes, and steering.

According to the U.S. Department of Transportation (USDOT), there were 42,636 highway deaths in the United States in 2004. In addition, traffic and congestion on American highways equals lost time and money. In response, the USDOT has launched an Intelligent Transportation Systems (ITS) program to improve traffic flow and safety on America's roads.

The USDOT's ITS program has been around for 20 years. Its initiatives cover all areas of road transportation, including equipping new cars with integrated safety systems, working with state and local transportation organizations to install roadside sensor systems, and developing a national network to share data concerning weather conditions.

But could AHS actually make traffic worse in the long run? AHS is being designed to relieve congestion by moving more vehicles down existing roads in a tight, platoonlike formation. In this sense, AHS is like adding more lanes to a freeway. But adding more freeway lanes solves traffic problems only temporarily. As transportation officials in crowded urban areas have learned to their dismay, if you build more road capacity, more people drive—and they take longer trips. If AHS brings a massive expansion of road capacity, traffic will soon increase to fill this capacity, and we'll be right back to the same problem we have now: too much congestion.

Some futurists foresee a day when you'll be able to ride in an intelligent car on an intelligent highway and enjoy a safe ride with no worries about traffic jams or multivehicle pileups (Figure 8F). Although this may not happen for 20 or 30 years, cars and highways will continue to become safer and more efficient due to the power of automated systems.

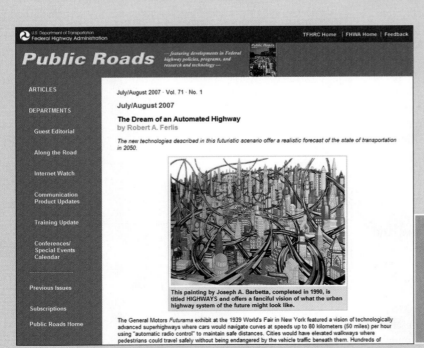

U.S. Department of Transportation
Federal Highway Administration

TFHRC Home | FHWA Home | Feedback

Public Roads

—featuring developments in Federal highway policies, programs, and research and technology—

ARTICLES

DEPARTMENTS

Guest Editorial

Along the Road

Internet Watch

Communication Product Updates

Training Update

Conferences/ Special Events Calendar

Previous Issues

Subscriptions

Public Roads Home

July/August 2007 · Vol. 71 · No. 1

July/August 2007

The Dream of an Automated Highway
by Robert A. Ferlis

The new technologies described in this futuristic scenario offer a realistic forecast of the state of transportation in 2050.

This painting by Joseph A. Barbetta, completed in 1990, is titled HIGHWAYS and offers a fanciful vision of what the urban highway system of the future might look like.

The General Motors *Futurama* exhibit at the 1939 World's Fair in New York featured a vision of technologically advanced superhighways where cars would navigate curves at speeds up to 80 kilometers (50 miles) per hour using "automatic radio control" to maintain safe distances. Cities would have elevated walkways where pedestrians could travel safely without being endangered by the vehicle traffic beneath them. Hundreds of

FIGURE 8F

The U.S. Department of Transportation continues its research on the Automated Highway System, which some experts believe could be implemented within the next 30 years.

Digital Forensics

Because computers are everywhere, they are often used to commit crimes. A new science called **digital forensics** has emerged that uses computers to fight cybercrime and computer crime. After a network or other type of attack, investigators use digital forensics tools to determine what occurred, what resources were affected, and who was responsible (Figure 8G).

In fact, digital forensics is such a hot area that a number of colleges and universities offer courses, programs, and degrees in the field. Students who take digital forensics study computer and networking technology, criminal justice, and other related fields.

Information Technology Laboratory
Computer Forensics Tool Testing Program

NIST
National Institute of Standards and Technology

We look for things; we find them

COMPUTER FORENSIC TOOL TESTING
NIST

CFTT Methodology Overview

The testing methodology developed by NIST is functionality driven. The activities of forensic investigations are separated into discrete functions or categories, such as hard disk write protection, disk imaging, string searching, etc. A test methodology is then developed for each category. Currently we have developed a methodology for disk imaging tools and are developing a methodology for software hard disk write blocking tools. Deleted file recovery tools will be the next category for development of a test methodology.

The CFTT testing process is directed by a steering committee composed of representatives of the law enforcement community. Included are the FBI, DoD, NIJ (representing state and local agencies), NIST/OLES and other agencies. Currently the steering selects tool categories for investigation and tools within a category for actual testing by CFTT staff. A vendor may request testing of a tool, however the steering committee makes the decision about which tools to test.

HOME

GENERAL INFORMATION

FIGURE 8G

The National Institute of Standards and Technology is attempting to bring proven methods and standards to digital forensics with its Computer Forensics Tool Testing program.

Biological Feedback Devices

Biological feedback devices translate eye movements, body movements, and even brain waves into computer input. Using **eye-gaze response systems** (also called **vision technology**), quadriplegics can use this technology to control a computer by focusing their eyes on different parts of the screen. A special camera tracks the person's eye movements and moves the cursor in response.

Microsoft researchers are working on vision technology computer programs that enable computers to "see" and respond to a user's physical presence, gestures, and even certain facial expressions. Of course, Microsoft is not the only company working on this technology. Research labs around the world are trying to develop new ways for people to interact with computers that do not rely on standard input devices, such as keyboards.

In fact, vision technology is part of a larger category of research (called *perceptual user interfaces* at Microsoft) that focuses not just on vision technology, but also on speech recognition, gesture recognition, and machines that "learn."

Gesture-recognition research focuses on enabling computers to understand hand movements. As you might imagine, gesture recognition would have an obvious benefit if it could be used with American Sign Language. It will also one day play a large role in making entertainment applications, including games, more entertaining. Many hope that perceptual user interfaces will one day help physically challenged computer users control their computers with facial expressions and eye gazes. Already on the market, VisualMouse translates a user's head motions into mouse movements, allowing users to control a mouse without using their hands.

Virtual Reality

Virtual reality (VR) refers to immersive, 3D environments that are generated by a computer. With virtual reality, you can actually go in and explore a virtual environment (see Figure 8H).

FIGURE 8H

Where *are* you when you experience virtual reality?

Helmets and sensor-equipped gloves enable users to experience virtual reality programs. The helmet or **head-mounted display** (**HMD**), which is a helmetlike contraption or a pair of goggles, contains two miniature television screens that display the world in what appears to be three dimensions (Figure 8I). In addition to the dual monitors that display three-dimensional images, a head tracker adjusts images when you move your head to the left or right. If you turn your head, your view of the world moves accordingly. Users can use **data gloves** to touch and manipulate simulated objects. You can also use navigation controls to walk around—or fly, if you prefer—in the simulated world. You can physically explore what appears to be a complex virtual environment, even though you're really walking around a big, empty room.

The most advanced (and expensive) immersive technology to date is the **Cave Automated Virtual Environment** (**CAVE**), which projects stereoscopic images onto walls to give the illusion of a virtual environment. To create the illusion of objects in the virtual environment, users wear special shutter glasses that alternately block the left and right eyes in synchrony with the projection sequence, which similarly alternates between the left and right stereo vision seen from the person's location. The resulting effect is so realistic that users can't tell the difference between real and simulated objects in the room unless they touch them.

On the Web, **Virtual Reality Modeling Language** (**VRML**, pronounced "vir-mal") can be used to create virtual environments online. Programmers can use VRML to define the characteristics of Web-accessible, 3D worlds. To visit a VRML site on the Web, you'll need to equip your Web browser with a VRML plug-in, such as the Microsoft VRML Viewer for Internet Explorer or the Cosmo Player, a VRML plug-in for Firefox, Opera, Safari, and Chrome. After installing the plug-in and accessing a VRML "world" (a Web site with a .wrl extension), you can walk or fly through the 3D construct.

What's the point of virtual reality? For consumers, the answer is simple: Games. Almost all of the top-selling computer games offer 3D virtual realities. But virtual reality isn't all fun and games. The military uses virtual reality systems to train fighter pilots and combat soldiers. Architects use virtual reality

FIGURE 8I

Virtual reality refers to immersive, 3D environments that are generated by computers. The Navy's VR Parachute Trainer teaches aircraft personnel how to handle a parachute in different weather conditions and during equipment malfunctions.

simulations to enable clients to preview and walk through a design. Surgeons can use virtual reality to learn and practice delicate and dangerous surgical techniques (Figure 8J). Manufacturers use virtual reality to analyze the manufacturing costs and design of complex, 3D structures.

Wearable virtual reality devices could even affect the lives of maintenance workers. A computer on a belt could easily be connected with a display monitor concealed in an ordinary pair of eyeglasses. As the worker looks at the inside of a piece of equipment, the computer could supply a schematic. The schematic, shown on the inside of the eyeglass lens, could then be positioned over the piece of equipment. This would enable the worker to quickly pinpoint the name, purpose, and condition of each of the item's components.

This blending of virtual reality with the real world, known as **augmented reality**, is not science fiction. It's already being used by some large corporations. Taken to the next level, the schematics shown in the worker's field of vision could be interfaced with motion and position sensors so that when the worker moves his or her head, the schematics projected by the computer change to reflect the worker's field of view.

New uses for augmented reality are being discovered all the time. For instance, agents for the U.S. Customs and Border Protection have special wearable computers that use voice-recognition software and full-color monitors. When looking for stolen vehicles, the agents can use the computers to recall the license number of any vehicle in the United States as they stroll through parking lots or drive through traffic.

Chemical Detectors

The human nose can detect remarkably minute traces of airborne chemicals. And increasingly, so can computers. If you've visited an airport recently, you may already have been "sniffed" by a computer device designed to detect minute traces of explosives. Some travelers are asked to step into special booths that use air jets to dislodge chemicals from clothes and hands. The air is then sucked through a chemical sensor that can identify many types of explosives. A computer screen displays the results of the test and tells the operator if explosives are detected.

Tactile Displays

You've seen how computers engage our eyes and ears. What about our sense of touch? If researchers in a new field called **haptics** have their way, you'll soon be able to feel with computers as well. (The term *haptics* refers to the sense of touch.) Haptics researchers are developing a variety of technologies, including **tactile displays** that stimulate the skin to generate a sensation of contact. Stimulation techniques include vibration,

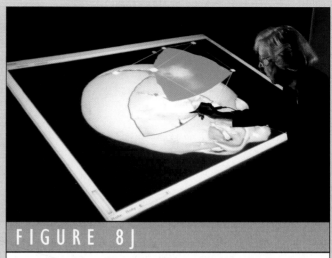

FIGURE 8J

In medicine, surgeons can use virtual reality to learn and practice new techniques.

pressure, and temperature changes. When used in virtual reality environments, these technologies enhance the sense of "being there" and physically interacting with displayed virtual objects.

It's unclear when perceptual interfaces will hit computer store shelves. But one thing is clear: Someday it will be possible for people to interact with electronic devices using every one of their senses.

What if we put all of these capabilities together to develop a machine endowed with human intelligence, giving it the ability to reason, to converse in natural language (ordinary human speech), and to formulate a plan or strategy? One branch of technology is moving in that direction—artificial intelligence.

ARTIFICIAL INTELLIGENCE: TOWARD THE SMART MACHINE?

The goal of **artificial intelligence** (**AI**) is to endow computers with humanlike intelligence. AI specialists have succeeded in creating special-purpose programs that exhibit some aspects of human intelligence, but these programs are still unable to function intelligently outside the context for which they were designed. Computer scientists are sharply divided between optimists who believe that these problems will be overcome and pessimists who believe that the underlying problems are so difficult that they're impossible to solve. So let's start with an easy question: just what *is* intelligence?

Intelligence has many components:

- Learning and retaining knowledge

- Reasoning on the basis of this knowledge

- Adapting to new circumstances

- Planning (developing strategies)

- Communicating

- Recognizing patterns

However, there's no scientific consensus as to what constitutes intelligence. So how do we answer the question of whether a computer is more intelligent than the human brain?

THE COMPUTER VERSUS THE HUMAN BRAIN

How does the human brain compare with a computer? Some speculative estimates are shown in Figure 8K. Compared with computers, the human brain accepts voluminous amounts of input and stores an unbelievable amount of data. In terms of processing, the human brain excels at pattern recognition (for example, recognizing faces and understanding speech), but it's a slow calculator. In contrast, computers accept much smaller amounts of input and do a poor job of recognizing patterns, but they can calculate rapidly and produce output much faster than humans can.

So how can we tell if a computer is intelligent? British computer scientist Alan Turing created the Turing Test to measure artificial intelligence (Figure 8L). During a Turing Test, a person sits at a computer and types questions. The computer is connected to two hidden computers. At one of the hidden computers, a person reads the questions and types responses. The other hidden computer runs a program that also gives answers. If the person typing the questions can't tell the difference between the person's answers and the computer's answers, Turing says that the computer is intelligent.

By Turing's standard, computers have already passed the test of artificial intelligence. In the mid-1960s, Joseph Weizenbaum, a computer scientist at the Massachusetts Institute of Technology (MIT), wrote a simple program called ELIZA. This program mimics a human therapist. If you type "I'm worried about my girlfriend," the program responds with "Tell me more about your girlfriend." The program is actually very simple. If the user types a word that matches one on the program's list, such as girlfriend, father, guilt, or problem, the program copies this word and puts it into the response. Even so, some people were fooled into thinking that they were conversing with a real therapist.

ELIZA doesn't fool many people for long, but today's programs are much larger and more resourceful. Many of these programs have been displayed at the Loebner Prize Competition, an annual event designed to implement the Turing Test and award a prize to the most "human" computer. In 2000, 2002, and 2004 Richard Wallace won the prize for his work on ALICE. Short for Artificial Linguistic Internet Computer Entity, ALICE uses AI case-based reasoning to formulate replies to comments. However, the program is unable to pass the Turing Test.

Neural Networks

Neuroscientists know that the brain contains billions of interconnected brain cells called neurons (Figure 8M). One type of AI involves creating computers that mimic the structure of the human brain. Called **neural networks** (or neural nets), these computers are composed of hundreds

FIGURE 8K	The Human Brain as a CPU (Speculative Estimates)
Operation	**Estimated Speed or Capacity**
Input	Fast (1 gigabit per second); the human retina can achieve a resolution of approximately 127 million "pixels"
Processing	Fast for pattern recognition (10 billion instructions per second); slow for calculations (2 to 100 per second)
Output	Slow (speech: 100 bits per second)
Storage	Very large (10 terabytes), but retrieval can be uncertain

FIGURE 8L

British computer scientist Alan Turing. According to most psychologists, the Turing test's type-and-response method is too simplistic.

of thousands of tiny processors that are interconnected, just like the neurons in the human brain.

Neural nets aren't programmed; they're trained. A neural net learns by trial and error, just as humans do. An incorrect guess weakens a particular pattern of connections; a correct guess reinforces a pattern. After the training is finished, the neural net knows how to do something, such as operate a robot.

Neural nets behave much the way that brains do. In fact, neural nets exhibit electromagnetic waves that are surprisingly similar to human brain waves. None of today's neural nets approach the complexity of even a farm animal's brain, but more complex neural nets are being developed.

Ordinary computers are good at solving problems that require linear thinking, logical rules, and step-by-step instructions. Neural nets are good at recognizing patterns, dealing with complexity, and learning from experience. As a result of these abilities, neural nets are emerging from laboratories and finding their way into commercial applications. Right now, banks are using neural nets to compare a customer's signature made at the bank counter with a stored signature. Neural nets can also be used to monitor aircraft engines and to predict stock market trends.

FIGURE 8M

The brain contains billions of neurons. Just as the brain connects these neurons, a neural net connects thousands of computer processing units in multiple ways.

PATTERN RECOGNITION

Imagine a computer that can see beyond the digitized image that it's recording. Computers equipped with digital cameras and **pattern-recognition software** can process digital images and draw connections between the patterns they perceive and patterns stored in a database. Pattern-recognizing computers are already used for security. For example, a new type of video surveillance camera can detect shoppers with suspicious patterns of movement and alert security personnel. The U.S. Department of State operates one of the largest face recognition systems in the world, with over 75 million photographs, which it uses for visa processing. Pattern-recognition software is also playing an important role in data mining, discovering previously unnoticed trends in massive amounts of transaction data.

INTELLIGENT AGENTS

You may not realize it, but you already have a helper inside your computer, one that can converse with you, understand your needs, and offer assistance. These helpers, called **intelligent agents**, can monitor conversations in newsgroups and recommend items of interest, locate human experts who can solve specific problems, help you negotiate the best price for a purchase, or scout ahead for Web pages based on your interests.

If you used Microsoft Office before the release of Office 2007, you may have been familiar with an intelligent agent: the Office Assistant. The Office Assistant was linked to Office's Help feature, so the Office Assistant could suggest formatting options and shortcuts or help find topics in the Help library. The online Help feature in Office 2007 has been completely redesigned and does not include the Office Assistant. You can download agents to help your Web ventures. One source of such agents is Agentland (**www.agentland.com**; Figure 8N).

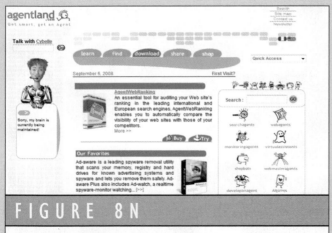

FIGURE 8N

Agentland (**www.agentland.com**) has a variety of agents and shopbots that you can download.

FIGURE 8O

Believe it or not, the Franklin TGA-490 translates 450,000 words and phrases and speaks 115,000 words in 12 languages!

TRANSLATION TECHNOLOGY

In the 1960s, experts confidently predicted that **machine translation**—the use of computers to translate foreign language text automatically—could be achieved quite easily. However, many problems emerged, including how to resolve ambiguity. For example, compare the word *pen* in the following two sentences: "My pen is in my pocket" and "Charlie is doing 25 to life in the pen." After many years of work, automatic translation software is coming closer to the dream of machine translation. The software is fast—one program can translate 300,000 words per hour—but the results can be riddled with errors. Still, the results are good enough to provide a working draft to human translators; some systems make only three to five errors for every 100 words translated.

Today, computer-aided translation (CAT) software can be used to translate text from one language to another. CAT technology is being used in international business to stand in when a human translator is not available. Even professional translators can use CAT tools to improve their skills.

Three major categories of CAT tools are currently available: terminology managers to handle basic word translations, automatic or machine translation (MT) tools to provide computer-aided translations, and machine-assisted human translation (MAHT) to aid professional translators. In addition to these programs, portable handheld translation devices, some as small as a credit card, help international travelers translate conversations from English to French, Spanish, German, Russian, Chinese, Japanese, and many more languages. (Figure 8O). As more-sophisticated translation technology emerges, someday people may be able to use CAT tools to communicate with anyone using any language.

GENETIC ALGORITHMS

Intelligence is a product of evolution through natural selection. So why not try to create artificial intelligence by creating laboratory conditions in which the most intelligent programs survive? That's the object of research on **genetic algorithms**, defined as automated program development environments in which various approaches compete to solve a problem.

According to evolutionary theory, an organism's goal is to survive and reproduce. Occasional errors in the genetic code introduce mutations, which lead to changes. Sometimes these changes are advantageous and give the organism a better chance of surviving and reproducing. Organisms with an advantageous genetic code dominate because they have more opportunities to reproduce.

Genetic algorithm research mimics nature by imitating this competition for survival. For example, researchers place a number of algorithms into a computer environment and allow them to mutate in random ways. All of the algorithms compete to try to solve a problem. Over time, one algorithm emerges as the best at tackling the problem. Where's the AI connection here? AI requires the creation of algorithms that can mimic the behavior of intelligent beings, and genetic algorithm techniques offer a new way to discover these algorithms.

STRONG AI

Although these piecemeal advances in artificial intelligence are transforming the computers and software we use every day, the decades-old dream of creating a truly intelligent computer seems as far away as ever. What's been achieved so far is a semblance of intelligence within only highly restricted areas of knowledge, such as routing parts through a factory or making airline reservations. Is the dream of true machine intelligence still alive? Proponents of **strong AI**, an area of research based on the conviction that computers will achieve an intelligence equal to that of humans, believe that it is, and that the achievement of true artificial intelligence is only decades away.

What is needed to achieve true artificial intelligence? Everyone agrees that an intelligent computer would need a high proportion of the knowledge that people carry around in their heads every day, such as that Philadelphia is a city on the East Coast, and that East Coast cities can be almost unbearably hot in the summer. You use this type of knowledge constantly. If someone tells you, "My friend went to work in Philadelphia for the summer," you can respond, "She must not mind the heat!" But there's considerable disagreement about how this knowledge can be provided to a computer. Should humans provide such knowledge or should computers learn it on their own? One AI project, Cyc, illustrates the first approach to knowledge acquisition.

CYC

In Austin, Texas, computer scientist Douglas B. Lenat and the Cycorp company are programming a computer called Cyc (pronounced "sike," from *encyclopedia*) with basic facts about the world that everyone knows, such as "mountain climbing is dangerous" and "birds have feathers." The goal is to create a computer that knows as much as a 12-year-old. The challenge is that 12-year-olds know a great deal. Lenat's staff has spent more than 20 years feeding basic knowledge into Cyc—the computer now stores nearly 200,000 terms and hundreds of thousands of rules, and they're still many years away from achieving their goal. Eventual goals for Cyc are to provide text and speech understanding, translation, expert systems, training simulations, games, and online advice. It will also be capable of integrating databases and spreadsheets, providing an encyclopedia, and answering questions as well as searching for documents and photos (Figure 8P).

Cyc's designers say that someday the computer will be able to learn on its own, reading material from the Internet and asking questions when it can't understand something. Already, companies are using Cyc in various capacities, and the U.S. military has invested millions of dollars in Cyc in hopes of using the computer as a military intelligence tool.

Cog, Kismet, and Nexi

MIT professor Rodney A. Brooks takes a different approach to computer learning, one that is based on the natural world. For example, in the natural world, intelligence evolved as organisms needed information to survive and reproduce. The path to artificial intelligence, Brooks argues, lies in creating robots that have minimal preprogrammed knowledge. The robots will then gather information on their own using massive sensory input (sight, hearing, and touch) and have artificially programmed "desires." For Brooks, intelligence isn't reasoning but rather a set of behaviors acquired as organisms interact with their environment.

Brooks and his students constructed a series of robots that learned how to crawl across fields strewn with boulders. Their projects were Cog, a humanoid robot that has a torso, a head, and two arms, and Kismet, a "sociable humanoid robot" that elicited emotional responses and was able to learn from and interact with humans. A current project of MIT's Personal Robots Group is Nexi, a mobile-dexterous-social (MDS) robot. The purpose of this group is "to support research and education goals in human-robot interaction, teaming,

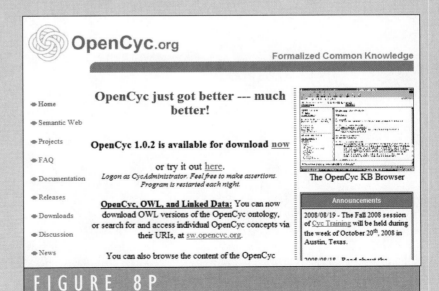

FIGURE 8P

The objective of the Cyc project is to program a computer with basic common sense facts.

and social learning." Visit the Personal Robots Group's Web site **http://robotic.media.mit.edu/projects/robots/mds/overview/overview.html** for information and videos about Nexi.

ROBOTS

Late at night, Dottie cleans the floors in a Richmond, Virginia, office building. The work is dull and repetitive, but she doesn't mind. She's never late to work, doesn't call in sick, and doesn't even receive a salary. Dottie is a robot, created by CyberClean, a company that's going after a $50 billion industrial cleaning market. A **robot** is a computer-based device programmed to perform motions that can accomplish useful tasks. But can robots function safely? Using video sensors, Dottie observes simple rules to avoid doing any damage, such as stopping and waiting if somebody walks in front of her. When her work is finished, she returns to her charging station.

Dottie and robots like her are at the cutting edge of **robotics**, a division of the computer science field that is devoted to improving the performance and capabilities of robots. Robots are taking the place of humans in industry in many ways. In 2001, IBM conducted an experiment in which robots participated in simulated trading of commodities such as pork bellies and gold. By using specially designed algorithms, the robots performed the same tasks as human commodity brokers—

and made 7 percent more money than their human counterparts!

More than 1 million industrial robots are in operation throughout the world. The United States is second only to Japan in robot use. Increasingly, robots are performing tasks such as assembly, welding, material handling, and material transport (Figure 8Q). Once found only in scientific labs, today robots paint cars for auto manufacturers, help surgeons conduct surgery, and make trips to outer space. Rock-steady surgical robots are saving lives where natural hand tremors in human surgeons could lead to fatal consequences. Robots are also exploring hazardous environments, such as the radioactive ruins of the Chernobyl Unit 4 nuclear power plant.

Need help at home or at work? Honda's ASIMO (Advanced Step in Innovative Mobility) humanoid robot may be able to assist you. Launched in 2000, ASIMO remains the world's most advanced bipedal humanoid robot. It can run 4 miles per hour, climb stairs, grasp objects, carry trays, and evade moving obstacles. With its AI capabilities for improved human interaction, it can comprehend simple voice commands and recognize a familiar face. ASIMO visited children who had experienced the Sichuan earthquake and entertained them with games such as rock, paper, scissors and balancing on one foot.

Another robot is the Japanese-made PaPeRo (short for **pa**rtner-type **pe**rsonal **ro**bot; Figure 8R). PaPeRo's colorful, rounded canister shape may not look huggable at first, but when treated with kindness, it's irresistible. PaPeRo can welcome you home after a long day, and when you're away, it wanders around looking for human companionship. If it doesn't find any, it takes a nap. PaPeRo even has the ability to recognize voice patterns; if these patterns are unfriendly, it runs away.

So where's the all-in-one personal robot that will someday mow the lawn, clean the house, and shampoo the carpets? Most experts agree that such personal robots are a decade or so away. These robots are just too expensive for consumers right now, but that will change as technology advances and market demand grows.

Researchers are also working on a robot that changes its shape to accomplish a specific task. The shape-changing robot has pieces that are moved

FIGURE 8Q

Increasingly, robots are performing tasks such as assembly, welding, material handling, and material transport.

FIGURE 8R

Robots such as ASIMO and PaPeRo are the cutting edge of the robotics field. As seen in this picture, ASIMO is leading the Detroit Symphony Orchestra.

around by a computer-managed algorithm. Such shape-changing robots will one day walk, crawl, carry tools, and fit into tight spaces where humans cannot.

THE FUTURE OF EMERGING TECHNOLOGY

What will the computers of the future be like? We know that they'll be fast and will have tremendous storage capacity. We are at the very beginning of an age: the information age. The one distinguishing feature about this age is that we know we're in it. Just think of what might have happened if people had known that they were at the beginning of the Industrial Revolution and could envision the fantastic advances to come. Think what they could have accomplished had they only known what was to happen!

Today, we know we are at the dawn of a new age. So *think*. Think about the new possibilities *every day*. Computers are your future, and they'll provide you with the means for a successful and satisfying life. Enjoy the ride!

SPOTLIGHT EXERCISES

1. Because of the enormous growth in the amount of available information, intelligent software agents have been developed to help users gather and analyze information. Visit Agentland's Web site at **www.agentland.com** to learn about this type of software. Interact with Cybelle. Find and download any of the agents that interest you. Spend at least 30 minutes exploring the site. Write a one-page paper that highlights your experience.

2. It has been over 15 years since the Intermodal Surface Transportation Efficiency Act of 1991 specified the development of "an automated highway and vehicle prototype from which future fully automated intelligent vehicle-highway systems can be developed." Read two articles from 1994 about the system at **www.tfhrc.gov/pubrds/summer94/p94su1.htm** and **ttp://findarticles.com/p/articles/mi_m3724/is_n1_v58/ai_16112768/pg_1?tag=artBody;col1**, familiarize yourself with the Automated Highway System (AHS), and use the phrase "automated highway systems" to search for other information sources. Identify products, technologies, and concepts underlying AHS that currently exist or are under development. Find the current state of AHS development, and write a brief report based on your findings.

3. Investigators are using digital forensics to fight computer crime and cybercrime. Type "digital forensics" into your favorite search engine and browse at least three of the links provided. Write a one-page paper that describes what you've learned.

4. Virtual reality is a hot topic. Search the Web to learn more about virtual reality games. Is any special hardware needed? Describe your recommendations for computer components that would provide an optimal gaming experience (monitor size, video memory requirements, processor speed, and so on). Write a one-page paper that describes a virtual reality game and the ideal computer system for playing it.

5. Visit iRobot's Web site (**www.irobot.com**) to learn about the home and tactical robotic products they manufacture. Check out the five home products and watch the videos. Briefly describe the products, features, and prices. Check out the four tactical products, watch the videos, and briefly describe the products and their features.

What You'll Learn . . .

- **Understand how technological developments are eroding privacy and anonymity.**

- **List the types of computer crime and cybercrime.**

- **List the types of computer criminals.**

- **Understand computer system security risks.**

- **Describe how to protect your computer system and yourself.**

- **Define *encryption* and explain how it makes online information secure.**

- **Describe the issues the government faces when balancing the need to access encrypted data and the public's right to privacy.**

Privacy, Crime, & Security

CHAPTER OUTLINE

Privacy in Cyberspace **368**
    The Problem: Collection of Information Without Consent. 368
    Technology and Anonymity. 369
    Protecting Your Privacy. 372

Computer Crime & Cybercrime **377**
    Types of Computer Crime 377
    Meet the Attackers 384

Security **387**
    Security Risks 387
    Protecting Your Computer System. 389

The Encryption Debate **392**
    Encryption Basics 393
    Public Key Encryption. 393
    Encryption and Public Security Issues 394

The public nature of the Internet raises privacy issues as more and more corporations and private citizens conduct business online. Just as stores in your neighborhood lock their doors at night to protect merchandise and equipment, electronic businesses employ a variety of security measures to protect their interests and your privacy from cybercriminals. In this chapter, you will explore how being online can threaten your privacy, personal safety, and computer system and learn how to protect yourself from online threats.

Privacy in Cyberspace

Of all the social and ethical issues raised by the spread of widely available Internet-linked computers, threats to privacy and anonymity are among the most contentious (Figure 9.1).

Defined by U.S. Supreme Court Justice Louis Brandeis in 1928 as "the right to be left alone," **privacy** refers to an individual's ability to restrict or eliminate the collection, use, and sale of confidential personal information. Some people say that privacy isn't a concern unless you have something to hide. However, this view ignores the fact that individuals, governments, and corporations sometimes collect and use information in ways that may harm people unnecessarily.

THE PROBLEM: COLLECTION OF INFORMATION WITHOUT CONSENT

Many people are willing to divulge information when asked for their consent and when they see a need for doing so. When you apply for a loan, for example, the bank can reasonably ask you to list your other creditors to determine whether you'll be able to repay your loan.

Much information is collected from public agencies, many of which are under a legal obligation to make their records available to the public upon request (public institutions of higher education, departments of motor vehicles, county clerks, tax assessors, and so on). This information finds its way into computerized

FIGURE 9.1 The ability to use the Internet anonymously and keep personal information private is important to many people.

databases—thousands of them—that track virtually every conceivable type of information about individuals. You are probably aware of credit reporting databases that track your credit history (Figure 9.2). Other databases include information such as your current and former addresses and employers, other names you've used (and your previous name, if you're married and use a different name now), current and former spouses, bankruptcies, lawsuits, property ownership, driver's license information, criminal records, purchasing habits, and medical prescriptions.

Most of the companies that maintain these databases claim that they sell information only to bona fide customers such as lending institutions, prospective employers, marketing firms, and licensed private investigators. They maintain that their databases don't pose a threat to the privacy of individuals because they are highly ethical firms that would not release this information to the general public.

According to privacy activists, the problem is what happens to information after it's sold. The Internet has made it much easier and much cheaper for ordinary individuals to gain access to sensitive personal information. If you search the Web for "Social Security numbers," you'll find dozens of Web sites run by private investigators who offer to find someone's Social Security number for a small fee, which can easily be charged to your credit card. Sites such as InfoUSA (**www.infousa. com**) provide sales leads and mailing lists for businesses, but the personal information they offer on more than 210 million consumers can easily be misused (Figure 9.3).

TECHNOLOGY AND ANONYMITY

Marketing firms, snoops, and government officials can use computers and the Internet to collect information in ways that are hidden from users. The same technology also makes it increasingly difficult for citizens to engage in anonymous speech. **Anonymity** refers to the ability to convey a message without disclosing your name or identity.

FIGURE 9.2 Credit reporting agencies such as Equifax, Experian, and TransUnion collect and store data about your credit history.

FIGURE 9.3 Web sites can sell your Social Security number or other personal information to anyone they please. In the United States, you have no legal recourse against those who collect and sell sensitive personal information.

Anonymity can be abused because it frees people from accountability. As a result, people may abuse the privilege of anonymous speech. Still, the U.S. Supreme Court recently held that anonymity—despite its unpalatable aspects—must be preserved. In a democracy, it is essential that citizens have access to the full range of possible ideas to make decisions for themselves. Freeing authors from accountability for anonymous works, the Court argued, raises the potential that false or misleading ideas will be brought before the public,

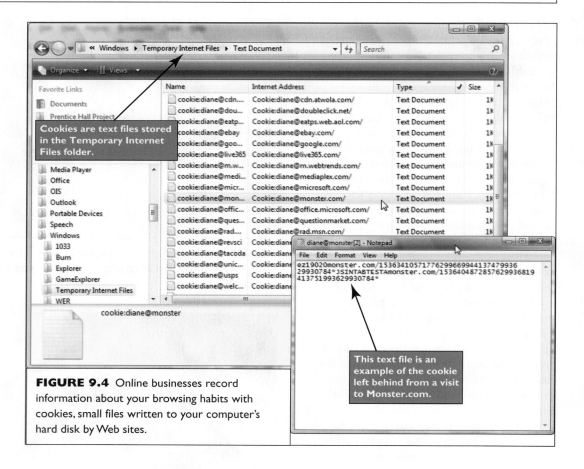

FIGURE 9.4 Online businesses record information about your browsing habits with cookies, small files written to your computer's hard disk by Web sites.

but this risk is necessary to maintain a free society.

Examples of technologies that threaten online anonymity include cookies, global unique identifiers, ubiquitous computing, and radio frequency identification.

Cookies

A **cookie** is a small plain-text file that is written to your computer's hard disk by many of the Web sites you visit (Figure 9.4). In many cases, cookies are used for legitimate purposes. For example, online retail sites use cookies to implement "shopping carts," which enable you to make selections that will stay in your cart so that you can return later to the online store for more browsing and shopping. What troubles privacy advocates is the use of tracking cookies to gather data on Web users' browsing and shopping habits without their consent.

Several Internet ad networks, such as DoubleClick, use cookies to track users' browsing actions across thousands of the most popular Internet sites. When you visit a Web site that has contracted with one of these ad networks, a cookie containing a unique identification number is deposited on your computer's hard drive. This cookie tracks your browsing habits and preferences as you move among the hundreds of sites that contract with the ad network. When you visit another site, the cookie is detected, read, and matched with a profile of your previous browsing activity. On this basis, the ad network selects and displays a **banner ad**, which often appears at the top of a Web page but can appear in other locations as well. A banner ad is not actually part of the Web page you are viewing but an ad supplied separately by the ad network.

In response to concerns that their tracking violates Internet users' privacy, ad network companies claim that they do not link the collected information with users' names and addresses. However, current technology would enable these firms to do so—and privacy advocates fear that some of them already have. Internet ad networks such as DoubleClick can collect the following:

- Your e-mail address

- Your full name

- Your mailing address (street, city, state, and zip code)

- Your phone number

- Transactional data (names of products purchased online, details of plane ticket reservations, and search phrases used with search engines)

Internet marketing firms explain that by collecting such information, they can provide a "richer" marketing experience, one that's more closely tailored to an individual's interests. Privacy advocates reply that once collected, this information could become valuable to others. These kinds of debates ensure that cookies and the information they collect will remain on the forefront of the privacy controversy for years to come.

Global Unique Identifiers
A **global unique identifier (GUID)** is an identification number that is generated by a hardware component or a program. Privacy advocates discovered GUIDs in several popular computer components and programs, such as Intel's Pentium III chip and Microsoft's Word 97 and Excel 97. The GUIDs can be read by Web servers or embedded in various documents, inadvertently making it more difficult to use the Internet anonymously. Although the use of GUIDs does not seem to be as prevalent as it was earlier this decade, a similar concept has been discovered in color laser printers. The Electronic Frontier Foundation (**www.eff.org**) has reported that many color laser printers embed printer tracking dots—nearly invisible yellow dots—on every page that is printed, at the urging of the U.S. government. These dots can identify the serial number and manufacturing code of the printer, as well as the time and date the document was printed. Officially, the tracking dots are designed to track counterfeiters,

but privacy advocates are concerned because there is no law to prevent this information from being used by U.S. government agencies, foreign governments, or individuals to identify materials printed and distributed by private citizens.

Companies that introduce GUIDs into their products generally conceal this information from the public. When forced to admit to using GUIDs, the firms typically remove the GUID-implanting code or enable users to opt out of their data collection systems. Advocates of online anonymity insist that these companies are missing the basic point: Users, not corporations, should determine when and how personal information is divulged to third parties.

Ubiquitous Computing
Ubiquitous computing describes an emerging trend in which individuals no longer interact with one computer at a time but instead with multiple networked devices that are often small or embedded in everyday objects. Digital music players and smartphones are good examples of this, as is the technology that allows your desktop PC to act as a media center for your entire home. Not only do these devices transmit data about us, they also search for data about others. Privacy can be compromised when smaller devices are lost or stolen. Most devices maintain some form of log, such as a playlist, records of incoming or outgoing calls, or a list of recently viewed media, which can be retrieved and exploited. As users become accustomed to using such technology, privacy advocates are concerned that society has become more willing to tolerate lower levels of privacy in favor of convenience.

Radio Frequency Identification
Radio frequency identification (RFID) uses radio waves to track a chip or tag placed in or on an object (Figure 9.5). RFID tags are often used as a means of inventory control in the retail environment. However, if the tag is not deactivated, the object's movements can continue to be tracked indefinitely. This technology

Destinations

To learn more about how cookies work and their pros and cons, visit the HowStuffWorks Web site at **http://computer. howstuffworks.com/ cookie.htm**. For information about how to delete cookies when using Internet Explorer, visit Microsoft's Help and Support site at **http://support.micro soft.com/kb/278835**. If you are using Firefox, visit **http:// support.mozilla .com/en-US/kb/ Clearing+private+ data**.

is also used when microchips are inserted in pets and other livestock, and has even been used for people. The RFID chip can include contact information and health records for the individual or animal, or other personal details. Privacy advocates have been concerned about the use of encrypted, passive RFID tags in U.S. passports for several years. The tag contains the same information included on the actual passport—name, nationality, gender, date of birth, and place of birth of the passport holder, as well as a digitized signature and photograph of that person. The government asserts that the RFID tag does not broadcast a signal and can only be read within close proximity of special scanning devices. However, a new passport card approved in 2008 as part of the Western Hemisphere Travel Initiative for travel to Mexico, Canada, Bermuda, and the Caribbean will use an unencrypted chip that can be read from up to 30 feet away, raising serious concerns that a passport holder's identity could easily be stolen or their location tracked without their consent or awareness. So far, these scenarios remain hypothetical, but the concept is disturbing to many.

Now that you've read about some of the privacy threats posed by the Internet, let's discuss how you can protect your privacy.

PROTECTING YOUR PRIVACY

How should governments protect the privacy of their citizens? Privacy advocates agree that the key lies in giving citizens the right to be informed when personal information is being collected as well as the right to refuse to provide this information.

In the European Union (EU), a basic human rights declaration gives all citizens the following privacy rights:

- Consumers must be informed exactly what information is being collected and how it will be used.

- Consumers must be allowed to choose whether they want to divulge the requested information and how collected information will be used.

- Consumers must be allowed to request that information about themselves be removed from marketing and other databases.

Protecting the privacy rights of U.S. citizens has been a controversial area for years. Most of us agree that our rights need to be protected, but our definition of acceptable levels of protection varies

FIGURE 9.5 RFID tags are often used as antitheft devices or to track merchandise, but concerns arise when we use the same technology for personal items or individuals.

widely. Some of the legislation currently in place includes the Fair Credit Reporting Act, which provides limited privacy protection for credit information; the Health Insurance Portability and Privacy Act (HIPAA), which establishes standards for the transmission of electronic health care data and the security and privacy of this information; and the Family Educational Rights and Privacy Act (FERPA), which protects the privacy of student education records. However, there is no comprehensive federal law governing the overall privacy rights of U.S. citizens. Instead, privacy is protected by a patchwork of limited federal and state laws and regulations. Most of these laws regulate what government agencies can do. Except in limited areas covered by these laws, little exists to stop people and companies from acquiring and selling your personal information (Figure 9.6).

Marketing industry spokespeople and lobbyists argue that the U.S. government should not impose laws or regulations to protect consumers' privacy. They argue that the industry should regulate itself. Privacy advocates counter that technology has outpaced the industry's capability to regulate itself, as evidenced by the widespread availability of highly personal information on the Internet.

The Direct Marketing Association (DMA) claims to enforce a basic code of ethics among its member organizations. However, many of the most aggressive Internet-based marketing firms have no ties to or previous experience with the DMA. The DMA takes steps to ensure that confidential information doesn't fall into the wrong hands and that consumers can opt out of marketing campaigns if they wish. However, opt-out systems on the Internet are already used for fraudulent purposes. For example, e-mail spammers typically claim that recipients can opt out of mass e-mail marketing campaigns. But recipients who respond to such messages succeed only in validating their e-mail addresses, and the result is often a major increase in the volume of unsolicited e-mail. A recent report from

Techtalk

Web beacon

A Web beacon, sometimes called a Web bug, is a tiny, all-but-invisible graphic, typically only one pixel in size, that is included on a Web page so that a third party can monitor "hits" on that page. Combined with HTML code, the graphic can send a third party—such as an Internet ad network—the contents of an identification cookie. Web beacons also can be included in HTML-formatted e-mail messages to reveal the recipient's address and notify the sender when the recipient opens the e-mail message.

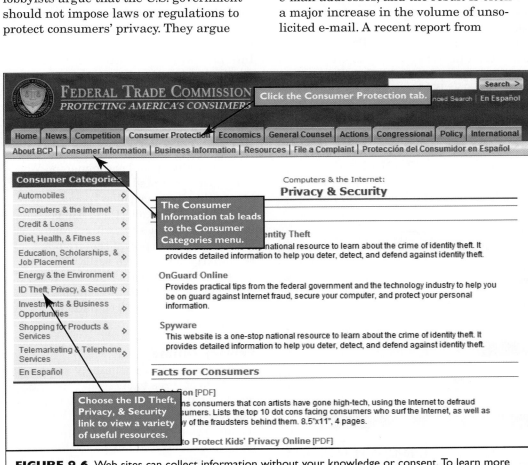

FIGURE 9.6 Web sites can collect information without your knowledge or consent. To learn more about this and other privacy issues, visit the Federal Trade Commission's Consumer Information site at **www.ftc.gov/bcp/menus/consumer/data/privacy.shtm**.

security firm SophosLabs revealed that spam accounted for more than 92 percent of all e-mail sent during the first quarter of 2008. The majority of spam is sent from Asia and Europe. Spam from Russia more than doubled from 2007 to 2008, but the United States still sent more spam than any other individual country (Figure 9.7).

In the United States, the CAN-SPAM Act of 2004 gave ISPs the tools to combat spammers. The Federal Trade Commission (FTC) and the Department of Justice have primary jurisdiction over spammers, but other agencies, including states and ISPs, can also prosecute them. The legislation has been criticized because it prevents states from enacting tougher laws, prevents individuals from suing spammers, and does not require e-mailers to request permission before sending messages. Additionally, it may be ineffective against foreign spammers who are outside U.S. jurisdiction. Although many contend that any drop in spam is most likely due to changing technology, the monetary threat the CAN-SPAM Act poses can't hurt. In 2008 MySpace successfully sued the so-called "Spam King" Sanford Wallace and a business partner for violations of the CAN-SPAM Act. A federal judge awarded MySpace close to $230 million, although it is doubtful the money will ever be collected. At one time a National Do Not Email Registry (similar to the National Do Not Call list to combat telemarketers) was

considered but discarded because of the potential for misuse and the inability to provide effective enforcement. States are also enacting their own laws, within the parameters of the CAN-SPAM Act, and other types of legislation, such as the Anti-Phishing Consumer Protection Act of 2008, are being debated. Private lawsuits have not been effective yet, but they may be a bright spot on the horizon. The threat of monetary penalties may be the only thing that can thwart the growth of the spam industry.

Although some individuals may be discouraged from participating in e-commerce activities because of privacy concerns and fears regarding the use of information collected by Web sites, the Internet retail sector continues to thrive. Census Bureau records show that online revenue has increased from $7.4 billion in the third quarter of 2000 to $34.7 billion in the third quarter of 2007. According to a 2008 survey by the Pew Internet and American Life Project, 66 percent of Americans who use the Internet have made purchases online, despite the fact that 75 percent of online users are concerned about providing personal and financial information online. The survey results also indicate that if privacy concerns are addressed, Internet sales would increase by at least 7 percent. Most popular commercial Web sites have attempted to allay these fears by creating "privacy policy" pages that explain how they collect and use personal information about site visitors. Many also display an approval seal from a third-party vendor such as TRUSTe or the Better Business Bureau to indicate that they comply with the vendor's privacy standards and regulations (Figure 9.8).

Privacy Online

Internet users overwhelmingly agree—by a ratio of three to one—that the U.S. government needs to adopt laws that will safeguard basic privacy rights. Until then, it's up to you to safeguard your privacy on the Internet. To do so, follow these suggestions:

- Surf the Web anonymously by using software products such as Anonymizer's

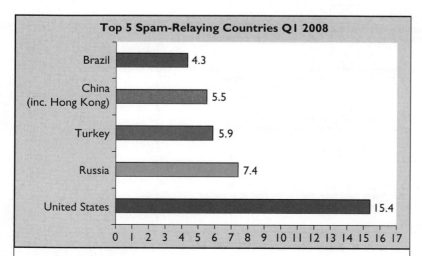

FIGURE 9.7 Almost 40 percent of all spam sent during the first quarter of 2008 was sent by just five countries.

FIGURE 9.8 Many third-party vendors provide privacy seals that can be displayed by sites that meet their program's standards for privacy and good business practices.

Anonymous Surfing (**www.anonymizer.com**) or devices such as the IronKey Secure USB flash drive (**www.ironkey.com**), which includes special security software to protect your data and encrypt your online communications (Figure 9.9).

- Use a "throwaway" e-mail address from a free Web-based service such as Google's Gmail (**www.google.com**) for the e-mail address you place on Web pages, mailing lists, chat rooms, or other public Internet spaces that are scanned by e-mail spammers.

- Tell children not to divulge any personal information online without first asking a parent or teacher for permission.

- Don't fill out site registration forms unless you see a privacy policy statement indicating that the information you supply won't be sold to third parties.

Privacy at Home

Are you aware that all new cell phones in the United States must have GPS awareness? This means that your phone can be located, usually within 30 feet, by law enforcement and emergency services personnel when you dial 911. Some services, such as uLocate and Wherify, provide the exact location of a cell phone. This can come in handy when a parent is trying to keep track of a child, but it can be intrusive when an employer uses it to track an employee using a company cell phone.

Some software is so powerful that it will send a notification to the home unit whenever the cell phone leaves a designated geographic area. MIT students recently developed programs using GPS capabilities for the upcoming Android mobile OS by Google. One program lets you change your phone's settings as your location changes, so it will be silent in the movie theater or classroom but will ring when you're outdoors. Another program will remind you that you need to pick up milk as you pass by the store! This location-aware tracking software is already in use by the criminal justice system to keep track of offenders who are sentenced to home detention. The subject is fitted with an ankle or wrist bracelet, and then

FIGURE 9.9 Devices like the IronKey Secure USB flash drive include special security software and services to allow you to surf the Web privately and securely, while protecting your identity and data.

Destinations

If you believe you've been a victim of a cybercrime, the Internet Crime Complaint Center (IC3) may be able to help. The IC3 is a partnership between the FBI, the National White Collar Crime Center, and the Bureau of Justice Assistance. Law enforcement agencies and individuals can make reports at **www.ic3.gov**.

the software is set to trigger an alarm if the wearer strays from the designated area. These bracelets also are being used to keep track of Alzheimer's patients.

Privacy at Work

In the United States, more than three-quarters of large employers routinely engage in **employee monitoring**, observing employees' phone calls, e-mails, Web browsing habits, and computer files. One program, Spector, provides employers with a report of everything employees do online by taking hundreds of screen snapshots per hour (Figure 9.10). About one company in four has fired an employee based on what it has found.

Such monitoring is direct and invasive, but it will continue until laws are passed against it. Why do companies monitor their employees? Companies are concerned about employees who may offer trade secrets to competitors in hopes of landing an attractive job offer. Another concern is sexual harassment lawsuits. Employees who access pornographic Web sites or circulate offensive jokes via e-mail may be creating a hostile environment for other employees—and that could result in a huge lawsuit against the company.

To protect your privacy at work, remember the following rules:

- Unless you have specific permission, don't use your employer's telephone system for personal calls. Make all such calls from a pay phone or from your personal cell phone.

- Never use your e-mail account at work for personal purposes. Send and receive all personal mail from your home computer.

- Assume that everything you do while you're at work—whether it's talking on the phone, using your computer, taking a break, or chatting with coworkers—may be monitored and recorded.

Now that you've learned about some important privacy issues, let's take a look at some intentional invasions of your privacy—computer crime.

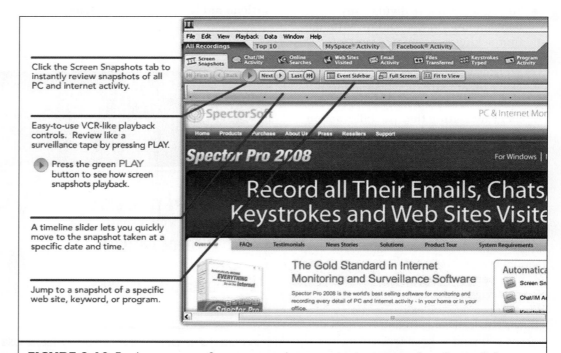

FIGURE 9.10 Employers can use Spector, an employee-monitoring program from SpectorSoft, to track everything employees do online.

Computer Crime & Cybercrime

Privacy issues, such as collecting personal information and employee monitoring, should be distinguished from **computer crimes**, which are actions that violate state or federal laws. **Cybercrime** describes crimes carried out by means of the Internet. A new legal field—**cyberlaw**—is emerging to track and combat computer-related crime.

In 2006 the United States ratified the Convention on Cybercrime. Developed by the Council of Europe, this is the first international treaty to address the issues and concerns surrounding cyber-crime. Its goal is to provide guidelines for consistent cybercrime legislation that is compatible with other member countries and to encourage international cooperation in these areas. Many government agencies, such as the Department of Justice (**www.cybercrime. gov**) and the FBI (**www.fbi.gov/cyberinvest/ cyberhome.htm**) have set up special sites to provide information and assistance to help combat cybercrime. The FTC's OnGuard Online site (**http:// onguardonline.gov**) has collaborated with government agencies and technology organizations to provide tutorials and activities to educate consumers about the threats and risks posed by cybercriminals (Figure 9.11).

TYPES OF COMPUTER CRIME

Anyone who wants to invade or harm a computer system can use a variety of tools and tricks. Pay close attention; you'll learn several facts that could help you avoid becoming a victim.

Identity Theft

The phone rings and it's a collection agency demanding immediate payment for a bill for a $5,000 stereo system that's past due. You can't believe what you're hearing—you always pay your bills on time, and you haven't purchased any stereo equipment lately. What's going on?

It's identity theft, one of the fastest-growing crimes in the United States and Canada. With **identity theft**, a criminal obtains enough personal information to impersonate you. With a few key pieces of information, such as your address and Social Security number, and possibly a credit card or bank account number, they can open a credit account, apply for a driver's license, access your bank account, open accounts for utilities or cell phones,

FIGURE 9.11 The FTC's OnGuard Online site provides many resources to help educate the public about various types of cybercrime. Visitors can view tutorials, explore topics, or file a complaint if they've been a victim.

or apply for a loan or mortgage—all in your name! Although some laws may limit your liability for fraudulent charges, victims of identity theft have found themselves saddled with years of agony. The bad marks on their credit reports can prevent them from buying homes, obtaining telephone service, and even getting jobs. Although some reports show a slight decline in identity theft in the United States, total identity theft losses in 2007 were estimated at $45 billion, with the average victim spending more than 40 hours to resolve each case.

How do criminals get this information? Most identity theft doesn't even involve computers. Disgruntled employees may steal information from their company, thieves may steal your mail or wallet, or they may go through your trash or a company's trash. But, information can also be stolen by criminals if computer data is not properly secured, if you respond to spam or phishing attacks, or if you have malware on your computer. And unfortunately, many Web sites and spammers sell individuals' Social Security numbers.

In a **phishing** attack, a "phisher" poses as a legitimate company in an e-mail or on a Web site in an attempt to obtain personal information such as your Social Security number, user name, password, and account numbers. For example, you might receive an e-mail that appears to come from XYZ Company asking you to confirm your e-identity (user name and password). Because the communication looks legitimate, you comply. The phisher can now gain access to your accounts.

Malware

The term **malware** is short for *malicious software* and describes software designed to damage or infiltrate a computer system without the owner's consent or knowledge. Malware is used to commit fraud, send spam, and steal your personal data. It includes spyware and computer viruses, as well as other rogue programs like worms and Trojan horses. McAfee Labs estimates malware will increase by 54 percent in 2008, with online ads being responsible for more than 80 percent of the malicious code. Even worse, a 2007 study by McAfee and the National Cyber Security Alliance (**http://staysafeonline.org**)

indicates that fewer than one in four Americans is fully protected against malware.

Spyware is software that collects your personal information, monitors your Web surfing habits, and distributes this information to a third party, often leading to identity theft. Some spyware, such as **adware**, generates pop-up ads and targeted banner ads and is usually considered a nuisance rather than malicious. However, **keyloggers**, which can record all the keystrokes you type—such as passwords, account numbers, or conversations—and relay them to others, pose a more dangerous security threat.

Spyware is often distributed when you download free software or infected files. File-sharing sites are notorious for this. However, clicking on a pop-up ad can also install spyware and visiting an infected Web site can also trigger a "drive-by" download.

Most spyware is not designed to disable your computer, but you might find that your computer seems sluggish or crashes more frequently. Other signs of infection include an increase in pop-up ads, unauthorized changes to your home or search pages, and the appearance of new browser toolbars.

Your best defense is to install antispyware software and update it frequently. Many experts recommend using at least two products, because one may catch something the other missed. Other safe practices include using a firewall, avoiding questionable Web sites, never clicking on pop-up ads, and downloading software only from reputable sources.

A **computer virus** is hidden code within a program that may damage or destroy the infected files. Like living viruses, computer viruses require a host (such as a program file), and they're designed to make copies of themselves.

Typically, virus infections spread when an infected file or program is downloaded onto a computer. Opening the file or running the program executes the virus, allowing it to perform its designated tasks. Most viruses act as **file infectors** by attaching themselves to a program file. When the program is executed, the virus spreads to other programs on the user's hard disk. If you copy a file on your computer to a USB drive, CD, or DVD and give

CURRENTS

Ethical Debates

Software Piracy: It Can Get You into Big Trouble

There's one important thing to know about software piracy: It's illegal. Thanks to the Internet, trafficking in illegally duplicated software and files is rampant and rapidly increasing. According to the Business Software Alliance, an anti-piracy industry group, the global piracy rate rose to 38 percent in 2007, amounting to nearly $48 billion in losses. So where does the United States rank? At 20 percent, the United States had the lowest piracy rate of the 108 countries studied (Figure 9.12). But, this still represents an $8 billion loss. Reducing piracy by 10 percentage points over the next four years could result in billions of dollars in economic growth and hundreds of thousands of new jobs.

Much software piracy takes place on file-sharing sites like LimeWire or BitTorrent or on online auction sites. It's difficult, but not impossible, to trace the actions of individuals. And when software pirates are found, it is becoming more likely that they will be prosecuted. In fact, the first criminal lawsuit against a member of a piracy group has resulted in a guilty verdict in federal court. Barry Gitarts hosted and maintained a server for the Apocalypse Production Crew that traded hundreds of thousands of pirated copies of movies, music, games, and software. He is facing up to five years in prison for conspiracy to commit criminal copyright infringement, a $250,000 fine, and three years of supervised release, and he must make full restitution. Gitarts may be the first person to go to jail for illegally uploading files to the Internet.

New legislation is being debated that would make piracy penalties even tougher. If passed, the Prioritizing Resources and Organization for Intellectual Property (Pro-IP) Act will strengthen civil and criminal penalties for copyright and trademark infringement, substantially increasing fines and allowing officials to confiscate equipment. What about sharing programs without money changing hands? That's illegal, too—and subject to similar penalties: Under the No Electronic Theft (NET) Act, profit does not need to be a motive in cases of criminal copyright infringement.

Law enforcement officials are fighting piracy through cross-border cooperation with initiatives like Operation Fastlink. More than 200 search warrants have been executed in 15 countries, resulting in 56 convictions. Hundreds of computers and related equipment have been confiscated, and more than $100 million worth of illegally copied copyrighted files has been removed from illicit distribution channels. Although the battle never lets up, new laws and new technology are improving the odds that people who sell or trade software illegally will be caught.

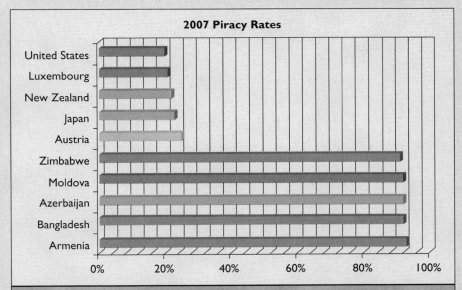

2007 Piracy Rates

(Countries listed, top to bottom: United States, Luxembourg, New Zealand, Japan, Austria, Zimbabwe, Moldova, Azerbaijan, Bangladesh, Armenia; horizontal axis: 0%, 20%, 40%, 60%, 80%, 100%)

FIGURE 9.12 The Fifth Annual Global Software Piracy Study details the five countries with the lowest piracy rates and the five countries with the highest piracy rates, as reported in 2007.

it to someone, the infection spreads even further (Figure 9.13).

Many computer viruses are spread by e-mail attachments. When you open an e-mail, you may see a dialog box asking whether you want to open an attachment. Don't open it unless you're sure the attachment is safe.

Consider the following scenario. A professor with a large lecture section of 100 students receives an e-mail from a former student with an attachment named "Spring Break" that apparently contains a picture from the student's spring break. The professor opens the attachment, which appears to do nothing, and the professor moves on to the next e-mail. The attachment, however, is doing something. It is sending a copy of itself to everyone in the professor's e-mail address box—including each of the 100 students in the class. As students open the attachment, the virus will continue to propagate to the addresses in each of their contact lists. The attachment is received by parents, friends, other professors, and fellow students. Many open the attachment, and the process accelerates very rapidly.

Executable file attachments pose the most serious risk. You can tell an executable file by its extension. In Microsoft Windows, the extension is .exe, but executable files also can be named .vbs, .com, .bin, or .bat. However, you can't be sure that a file is executable by its extension alone. You should also be wary of opening Microsoft Office documents, such as Microsoft Word and Microsoft Excel files. The best policy is to always check attachment files with an antivirus program before you open them.

Although some viruses are best categorized as nuisances or pranks, others can corrupt or erase data or completely disable a computer. All of them consume system memory and slow the computer's processing speed. In the prank category is the Wazzu virus, which randomly relocates a word in a Microsoft Word document and sometimes inserts "wazzu" into the text. Still others, such as Disk Killer, are far more malicious: Disk Killer wipes out all of the data on your hard drive.

A far more serious type of virus is a boot sector virus. A **boot sector virus** also propagates by an infected program, but it

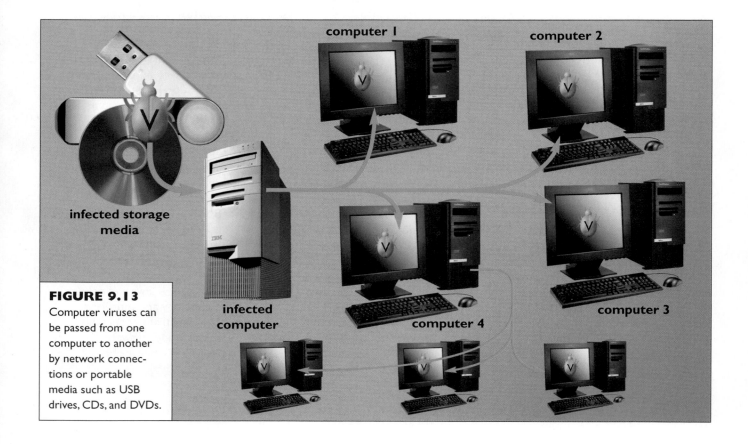

FIGURE 9.13
Computer viruses can be passed from one computer to another by network connections or portable media such as USB drives, CDs, and DVDs.

installs itself on the beginning tracks of a hard drive, where code is stored that automatically executes every time you start the computer. Unlike file infectors, boot sector viruses don't require you to start a specific program to infect your computer; starting your system is sufficient. Boot sector viruses also may lead to the destruction of all the data stored on your hard drive.

A **macro virus** takes advantage of the automatic command execution capabilities (called **macros**) of productivity software, such as word processing and spreadsheet programs. Macro viruses infect data files, which contain the data created with an application such as Microsoft Word. When these files are shared with others, the virus infects their computers. By default, macros are disabled in newer versions of Microsoft Office, but users can adjust security settings to allow them. Files containing macros should always be scanned by antivirus software.

Security experts expect the number of viruses and Trojan horses to exceed 1 million by 2009, with more being written every day. In fact, during the first quarter of 2008 one newly infected Web page was found every 5 seconds, compared with one page every 14 seconds in 2007.

Malware has spread beyond computers. During the 2007 holiday season, many shoppers found that their new digital photo frames came from the factory with a preinstalled virus. Fortunately, it was an old virus and consumers using up-to-date antivirus software were protected. However, other devices, such as GPS units and digital music players, have had similar experiences. Mobile devices are also at risk. A spam text message, known as **spim**, was sent to more than 200 million mobile phone users in China during just one day in March 2008. Luckily, the spim did not include any malicious code, but it's a very real possibility. And contrary to popular belief, Mac and Linux computers are also vulnerable. Although not as prevalent, malware designed for these systems can also infect them, with the same negative results.

Computer virus authors are trying to "improve" their programs. Some new viruses are self-modifying; each new copy, known as a **variant**, is slightly different from the previous one, making it difficult to protect your computer. Sites such as Snopes.com and Vmyths.com can help you determine whether the latest news about a virus is real or a hoax.

More Rogue Programs

Spyware and viruses aren't the only types of rogue programs. Other destructive programs include time bombs, worms, zombies, Trojan horses, and botnets.

A **time bomb**, also called a **logic bomb**, is a virus that sits harmlessly on a system until a certain event or set of circumstances causes the program to become active. For example, before leaving a Texas firm, a fired programmer planted a time bomb program that ran two days after he was fired and wiped out 168,000 critical financial records.

A **worm** is a program that resembles a computer virus in that it can spread from one computer to another. Unlike a virus, however, a worm can propagate over a computer network, and it doesn't require an unsuspecting user to execute a program or macro file. It takes control of affected computers and uses their resources to attack other network-connected systems. Some worms such as Sasser and Slammer exploit vulnerabilities found in Microsoft Windows and quickly propagate. Newer worms have begun infecting social networking sites such as MySpace and Facebook, retrieving user information and passwords, and directing users to phishing sites. Although patches are usually released quickly, if your computer isn't updated, it remains vulnerable. Even if you don't think your personal information is worth protecting, worms compromise the security of a computer, making it accessible to cybercriminals who can then use it for their own purposes.

Another type of threat is a denial of service attack. With a **denial of service (DoS) attack** (also called **syn flooding** owing to technical details of the attack method), an attacker bombards an Internet server with a huge number of requests so that the server becomes overloaded and unable to function. Because network administrators can easily block data from specific IP addresses, hackers must commandeer as many computers as possible to launch their attack. When multiple computer systems are involved, it becomes a **distributed denial of service (DDoS) attack**. The commandeered computers form a **botnet**, and the individual computers are called

zombies because they simply do what the hacker's DoS program tells them to do. In 2008, botnets numbered close to 3,000—twice as many as the year before. Each botnet consists of thousands of zombie computers. Some security experts believe that millions of computers have been infected, with more than 250,000 new infections being found every day!

A **Trojan horse** is a rogue program disguised as a useful program, but it contains hidden instructions to perform a malicious task instead. Sometimes a Trojan horse is disguised as a game or a utility program that users will find appealing. Then, when users begin running the game, they discover that they have loaded another program entirely. A Trojan horse may erase the data on your hard disk or cause other irreparable damage. More frequently, Trojan horses are used to install malware or to open a port for easy access by hackers. The Storm Trojan, which is frequently delivered via holiday-themed or weather-related e-mails, has more than 50,000 variants and has infected millions of computers. These infected computers then send out more Storm-infected spam in an endless cycle. At one point, it was responsible for one in every six e-mails that were sent.

Fraud and Theft

When computer intruders make off with sensitive personal information, the potential for fraud multiplies. For example, the Hannaford supermarket chain recently experienced a data breach that exposed credit and debit card numbers for more than 4 million customers, resulting in more than 2,000 cases of fraud.

Physical theft of computer equipment is a growing problem as well (Figure 9.14). An estimated 85 percent of computer thefts are inside jobs, leaving no signs of forced physical entry. In addition, it's difficult to trace components after they've been taken out of a computer and reassembled. Particularly valuable are the microprocessor chips that drive computers. **Memory shaving**, in which knowledgeable thieves remove some of a computer's RAM chips but leave enough to start the computer, is harder to detect. Such a crime might go unnoticed for weeks.

Tricks for Obtaining Passwords

The most publicized computer crimes involve unauthorized access, in which an intruder gains entry to a supposedly secure computer system. Typically, computer systems use some type of authentication technique—usually plain-text passwords—to protect the system from uninvited guests. Many techniques are used to guess or obtain a password (Figure 9.15). Another widely used technique involves exploiting well-known holes in obsolete e-mail programs, which can be manipulated to disclose a user's password.

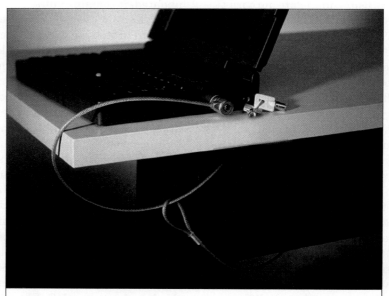

FIGURE 9.14 To prevent theft, users should lock their doors and turn off their computers. In some cases, it may be wise to secure hardware to desks.

FIGURE 9.15 Techniques Used to Obtain Passwords

Password guessing	Computer users too often choose a password that is easily guessed, such as password. " Other popular passwords are "qwerty" (the first six letters of the keyboard), obscene words, personal names, birthdays, celebrity names, movie characters such as Frodo or Gandalf, and cartoon characters such as Garfield.
Shoulder surfing	In a crowded computer lab, it's easy to peek over someone's shoulder, look at their keyboard, and obtain their password. Watch out for shoulder surfing when using an ATM machine, too.
Packet sniffing	A program called a packet sniffer examines all of the traffic on a section of a network and looks for passwords, credit card numbers, and other valuable information.
Dumpster diving	Intruders go through an organization's trash hoping to find documents that contain lists of user IDs and even passwords. It's wise to use a shredder!
Social engineering	This is a form of deception to get people to divulge sensitive information. You might get a call or an e-mail from a person who claims, "We have a problem and need your password right now to save your e-mail." If you comply, you might give an intruder entry to a secure system.
Superuser status	Enables system administrators to access and modify virtually any file on a network. If intruders gain superuser status, they can obtain the passwords of everyone using the system.

Salami Shaving and Data Diddling

With **salami shaving**, a programmer alters a program to subtract a very small amount of money from an account— say, two cents—and diverts the funds to the embezzler's account. Ideally, the sum is so small that it's never noticed. In a business that handles thousands of accounts, an insider could skim tens of thousands of dollars per year using this method.

With **data diddling**, insiders modify data by altering accounts or database records so that it's difficult or impossible to tell that they've stolen funds or equipment. A Colorado supermarket chain recently discovered it was the victim of data diddling when it found nearly $2 million in unaccounted losses.

Forgery

Knowledgeable users can make Internet data appear to come from one place when it's really coming from another. Third-party remailer sites and programs strip the sender's tracking data from a message and then resend the message.

Forged messages and Web pages can cause embarrassment and worse. A university professor in Texas was attacked with thousands of e-mail messages and Usenet postings after someone forged a racist Usenet article in his name. In Beijing, a student almost lost an $18,000 scholarship when a jealous rival forged an e-mail message to the University of Michigan turning down the scholarship. Fortunately, the forgery was discovered and the scholarship was reinstated, but only after a lengthy delay.

Blackmail

According to one estimate, more than 40 percent of all computer crimes go unreported. Why? Suppose you're running a bank. You've lost $1 million because of computer theft. What's going to cost you more, covering the loss or telling the world that depositors' money isn't safe?

According to news reports, adverse publicity fears have been used to blackmail financial institutions. In London, computer attackers have reportedly extorted nearly $650 million from banks in the past few years after demonstrating to senior executives that they could completely wipe out the banks' computer systems.

Now that you've learned about the types of computer crime and cybercrime, let's discuss the kinds of computer criminals you may run into on the Web.

Techtalk

IP spoofing

Hackers send a message with an IP address disguised as an incoming message from a trusted source to a computer. The hacker must first locate and modify the message packet headers of a trusted source (called a port) and then manipulate the hacker's own communication so that it appears to come from the trusted port.

Ethics

Several medical-device security researchers recently hacked a combination pacemaker and heart defibrillator, causing it to stop. They accessed the device wirelessly, obtained patient information stored on it, and were able to reprogram it to shock the person on command. They published their exploits and how to fix the device, on their Web site. How do you feel about this type of research? What are the advantages? What are the disadvantages? Should this type of information be freely distributed on the Internet?

MEET THE ATTACKERS

A surprising variety of people can cause security problems, ranging from pranksters to hardened criminals, such as the Russian intruders who recently made off with $10 million from Citibank. Motives vary, too. Some attackers are out for ego gratification and don't intend any harm. Others are out for money or on a misguided crusade; some are just plain malicious.

Hackers, Crackers, Cybergangs, and Virus Authors

To the general public a hacker is a criminal who illegally accesses computer systems. Within the computing community, several terms are used to describe various types of hacking. However, it is important to note that accessing someone's computer without authorization is illegal, no matter what the motivation might be. The most celebrated intruders are computer hobbyists and computer experts for whom unauthorized access is something of an irresistible intellectual game. **Hackers** are computer hobbyists who enjoy pushing computer systems (and themselves) to their limits. They experiment with programs to try to discover capabilities that aren't mentioned in the software manuals. They modify systems to obtain the maximum possible performance. And sometimes they try to track down all of the weaknesses and loopholes in a system's security. When hackers attempt unauthorized access, they rarely damage data or steal assets. Hackers generally subscribe to an unwritten code of conduct, called the **hacker ethic**, which forbids the destruction of data. Hackers form communities. Such communities have a pecking order that is defined in terms of an individual's reputation for hacking prowess. **Cybergangs** are groups of hackers or crackers working together to coordinate attacks or post online graffiti, as well as other malicious conduct.

Crackers (also called **black hats**) are hackers who become obsessed (often uncontrollably) with gaining entry to highly secure computer systems. The frequency and sophistication of their attacks can cause major headaches for system administrators. Many U.S. government sites are constant targets for hackers, but they are usually able to divert them. However, in June 2007, Chinese hackers were able to breach an unclassified e-mail system in the Department of Defense, affecting more than 1,500 users and shutting down the network for more than a week. A recent attack on the Epilepsy Foundation's forums caused actual headaches, and much worse, for their viewers. Hackers posted hundreds of pictures and links to flashing animations that caused severe migraines and seizures in some visitors.

Like hackers, crackers are often obsessed with their reputations in the hacking and cracking communities. To document their feats, they often leave calling cards, such as a prank message, on the systems they penetrate. Sometimes these traces enable law enforcement personnel to track them down.

Hackers and crackers should be distinguished from criminals who seek to use unauthorized access to steal money or valuable data. Keep in mind, however, that anyone who tries to gain unauthorized access to a computer system is probably breaking one or more laws. However, more than a few hackers and crackers have turned pro, offering their services to companies hoping to use hacker expertise to shore up their computer systems' defenses. Those who undertake this type of hacking are called **ethical hackers**, or **white hats**.

Computer virus authors create viruses and other types of malware to vandalize computer systems. Originally, authors were usually teenage boys, interested in pushing the boundaries of antivirus software and seeking to prove their authoring skills over those of their competitors. These days, virus authoring has become big business, and many authors are involved with organized crime. If caught and convicted, virus authors face prison and heavy fines. David L. Smith, the 33-year-old programmer who created the Melissa virus, was sentenced to 20 months in jail and a $5,000 fine in 2002, and in 2004 a 19-year-old female hacker known as Gigabyte faced up to three years in jail and almost $200,000 in fines. More recently, Li Jun, the 25-year-old creator of the Fujack, or Panda, worm, was sentenced by a Chinese court to four years in prison. Hackers and other cybercriminals can no longer be stereotyped—their members include all ages, both sexes, and many nationalities (Figure 9.16).

Swindlers

Swindlers typically perpetuate bogus work-at-home opportunities, illegal pyramid schemes, chain letters, risky business opportunities, bogus franchises, phony goods that won't be delivered, overpriced scholarship searches, and get-rich-quick scams. Today, the distribution media of choice include e-mail, Internet chat rooms, and Web sites.

Estimates of the scope of the problem vary, especially because many cases of fraud are never reported. According to the 2007 Internet Crime Report, consumers reported losses of more than $239 million on a variety of Internet scams—and the figure is growing by leaps and bounds (Figure 9.17).

Shills

Internet auction sites such as eBay attract online versions of the same scams long perpetrated at live auctions. A **shill** is a secret operative who bids on another seller's item to drive up the price. In a recent case, an online jewelry store was charged with illegally bidding on its own merchandise. The store allegedly made more than 200,000 bids totaling more than $5 million and drove up auction prices by as much as 20 percent. In a settlement with the New York attorney general's office, the jeweler has agreed to pay $400,000 in restitution and is banned from online auctions for four years.

FIGURE 9.16 Can you identify the hacker in this group? Although often stereotyped as young male "computer geeks," hackers can be young or old, male or female, and of any ethnicity.

Cyberstalkers, Sexual Predators, and Cyberbullying

One of the newest and fastest growing of all crimes is **cyberstalking**, or using the Internet, social networking sites, e-mail, or other electronic communications to repeatedly harass or threaten a person. For example, one San Diego university student terrorized five female classmates for more than a year, sending them hundreds of violent and threatening e-mail messages. Kathy Sierra was a well-known technology blogger and author who began receiving offensive comments on her blog,

Destinations

To learn more about the history of hacking, the types of vulnerabilities hackers look for, and what motivates hackers, check out Kaspersky Lab's Viruslist site at **www.viruslist.com/ en/hackers/info**.

FIGURE 9.17 Internet Scams	
Rip and tear	A Seattle man posted ads for Barbie dolls and other goods on eBay, collected more than $32,000 in orders, and never delivered any goods. Swindlers move to a new state once their activities are uncovered. The perpetrators believe that law enforcement won't be concerned with the relatively small amounts involved in each transaction.
Pumping and dumping	Crooks use Internet stock trading sites, chat rooms, and e-mail to sing the praises of worthless companies in which they hold stock. Then, after the share prices go up, they dump the stocks and make a hefty profit.
Bogus goods	Two Miami residents were indicted on charges of mail and wire fraud after selling hundreds of "Go-boxes," which purported to turn red traffic lights to green. The boxes which were actually nothing more than strobe lights, sold for between $69 and $150.

Creating Passionate Users. These comments included disturbingly edited images of Sierra and violent, sexual threats that finally escalated to death threats from several sources. The posts also appeared on other blogs. Because of their seriousness, Sierra cancelled plans to make a presentation at a technology conference, claiming she feared for her life, and she eventually suspended her blog. Although several people were linked to the comments, no one was ever prosecuted.

Cyberstalking has one thing in common with traditional stalking: Most perpetrators are men, and most victims are women, particularly women in college. One in every eight women attending college has been followed, watched, phoned, written, or e-mailed in ways that they found obsessive and frightening.

Concerns about online sexual predators and the risk they pose to children have continued to grow. The Crimes Against Children Research Center (CCRC) reports that 1 in 25 children has received an aggressive sexual solicitation that included an attempt to contact the child offline. Additionally, 1 in 25 youths was asked to take sexual photos of himself or herself, and 1 in 25 reported being extremely upset or distressed because of these solicitations. Some online predators may pose as children, but the CCRC reports that many predators admit that they are older and manipulate their victims by appealing to them in other ways. They attempt to develop friendships and often flatter or seduce their victims. Although there have been situations that have ended in kidnapping or murder, violence has occurred in only 5 percent of reported cases. In the majority of cases, the victims have gone with the predator willingly, expected to have a sexual relationship, and often met with the predator on multiple occasions.

Online predators also look for new victims on cyberdating sites. Most cyberdating sites use profiling to match potential dates. The downside is that it is difficult to check someone's cyberidentity against his or her actual identity. Although some sites indicate that they perform background checks, it is doubtful that they are as comprehensive as necessary (Figure 9.18). Most are based on user provided information – usually a credit card and birthdate. An effective background check more detailed information, such as a Social Security number, home address and possibly finger prints. And this information would apply only to paying customers – it would not apply to free social networking sites. Some sites have been effective in blocking convicted felons and sex offenders from their sites by screening someone's cyberidentity against public and private background screening databases. These screenings are based on user – provided information – usually a name, credit card, and birthdate. More detailed background checks may be more comprehensive when checking additional information, such as Social Security numbers, home address and possible finger prints.

Cyberbullying involves situations in which one or more minors harass or threaten another minor using the Internet or other forms of digital technology. Cyberbullying can include sending threatening e-mail or text messages or assuming someone else's online identity for the purpose of humiliating or misrepresenting him or her. In a recent case, a group of eight Florida

TRUE Prosecutes Felons and Marrieds

We can't guarantee that criminals won't get on our site, but we can guarantee that they'll be sorry they did.

Email TRUE about this information

We turn away tens of thousands of felons and marrieds who, despite our warnings, try to communicate with our TRUE members. At TRUE, we take our members' safety seriously. We don't want felons or marrieds on our website, period.

If you are a criminal or married, DO NOT use our website. Consider this to be fair warning: Our Member Safety team vigorously pursues individuals who misrepresent themselves on our website. We report violators to appropriate federal, state and local authorities, including parole boards. We also actively pursue prosecution of these offenders in other ways. For example, we recently took the unprecedented step of filing a lawsuit in federal court against a convicted felony sex offender from California who applied for membership with TRUE and accessed TRUE's database in violation of TRUE's policies. The dispute was resolved by agreement, the terms of which require the sex offender to: (1) cancel his existing memberships and refrain from using TRUE.com and other companies in the online dating and relationship industry; (2) complete a community service obligation; and (3) pay damages to TRUE.

WARNING: Married People and Criminals Will Be Prosecuted

If you are married and representing yourself as single, or if you are a convicted criminal, be aware that you could be guilty of fraud and subject to civil and criminal penalties under U.S. federal and state law. For example, Title 18, Section 1343 of the U.S. Code authorizes fines of up to $250,000 and jail sentences of up to five years for each offense. TRUE reserves the right to report violators to appropriate law enforcement authorities and seek prosecution or civil redress to the fullest extent of the law. **If you are married or a convicted criminal, please close your browser.**

FIGURE 9.18 To protect site users from unscrupulous predators, True.com conducts criminal and marital status checks on its communicating members and requires all site users to agree to a member code of ethics.

teenagers viciously beat up an unsuspecting friend while filming it to post on YouTube. The victim suffered a concussion and eye injuries. The eight so-called friends were charged with false imprisonment and battery. Preventing cyberbullying can be just as difficult as preventing real-time bullying. Parents and schools need to make children aware of the dangers and provide them with the knowledge and confidence they need to stand up to bullies.

Now that you understand the types of perpetrators who pose a risk to your online privacy and safety, let's look closer at the growing risks to equipment and data security.

Security

As our entire economy and infrastructure move to networked computer systems, breaches of computer security can be costly. Even when no actual harm has occurred, fixing the breach and checking to ensure that no damage has occurred requires time, resources, and money. It's no wonder that security currently accounts for an estimated 10 to 20 percent of all corporate expenditures on computer systems.

SECURITY RISKS

Not all of the dangers posed to computer systems are caused by malicious, conscious intent. A **computer security risk** is any event, action, or situation—intentional or not—that could lead to the loss or destruction of computer systems or the data they contain. Some research indicates that security breaches may cost individuals and industry billions of dollars per year because of their impact on customer service, worker productivity, and so on.

Wireless Networks

Wireless LANs pose challenges to security, especially hotspots that are designed for open access. Unlike wired networks, which send traffic over private dedicated lines, wireless LANs send their traffic across shared space—airwaves. Because no one owns the space that airwaves travel across, the opportunity for interference from other traffic is great and the need for additional security is paramount.

To break into a wireless network, you must be within the proximity limits of the wireless signal. In a process called **wardriving**, an individual drives around with a wireless device, such as a notebook computer or smartphone, to look for wireless networks. Some people do this as a hobby and map out different wireless networks, whereas hackers look for wireless networks to break into. It is fairly easy to break into an unsecured wireless network and obtain confidential information. Wardriving applications carry names such as NetStumbler, MiniStumbler, Kismet, and MacStumbler and are readily available for download from the Internet.

Security methods for wireless networks include **WEP (Wired Equivalent Privacy)**, **WPA (Wi-Fi Protected Access)**, and **WPA2**. WEP was the earliest of the three and has several well-known weaknesses, but it may be the only option for some devices or older equipment. WPA was developed to provide a stronger level of security, and WPA2 improves on WPA's abilities. WPA2 provides confidentiality and data integrity and is far superior to WEP, because it uses AES (Advanced Encryption Standard) to provide government-grade security. The need for wireless security is great, and more powerful security systems continue to be developed. Wireless network owners should implement the security that is currently available so their systems are at least protected from the casual hacker.

Corporate Espionage

Corporate computer systems contain a great deal of information that could be valuable to competitors, including product development plans and specifications, customer contact lists, manufacturing process knowledge, cost data, and strategic plans. According to computer security experts, **corporate espionage**, the unauthorized access of corporate information, usually to the benefit of a competitor, is on the rise—so sharply that it may soon eclipse all other sources of unauthorized access (Figure 9.19). The perpetrators are often ex-employees who have been hired by a competing firm precisely because of their knowledge of the computer system at their previous place of employment.

According to one estimate, 80 percent of all data loss is caused by company insiders. Unlike intruders, employees

FIGURE 9.19 Corporate espionage may soon eclipse all other sources of unauthorized access to computer systems.

have many opportunities to sabotage a company's computer system, often in ways that are difficult to trace. Although incoming e-mail is routinely scanned for threats, outgoing mail is often overlooked, allowing employees to easily transfer data. Similarly, employees can easily copy sensitive data to USB drives, iPods, or other small storage devices in an activity known as **podslurping**. They may discover or deliberately create security holes called **trap doors** that they can exploit after leaving the firm. They can then divulge the former employer's trade secrets to a competitor or destroy crucial data.

The espionage threat goes beyond national borders. Nations bent on acquiring trade secrets and new technologies also are trying to break into corporate computer systems. According to a recent estimate, the governments of more than 125 countries are actively involved in industrial espionage.

Information Warfare

Information warfare is the use of information technologies to corrupt or destroy an enemy's information and industrial infrastructure. A concerted enemy attack would include electronic warfare (using electronic devices to destroy or damage computer systems), network warfare (hackerlike attacks on a nation's network infrastructure, including the electronic banking system), and structural sabotage (attacks

on computer systems that support transportation, finance, energy, and telecommunications). However, we shouldn't overlook old-fashioned explosives directed at computer centers. According to one expert, a well-coordinated bombing of only 100 key computer installations could bring the U.S. economy to a grinding halt.

According to experts, defenses against such attacks are sorely lacking, as the country of Estonia learned in the spring of 2007. Estonia is a small country, but it is on the leading edge of technology, with most of its population relying on the Internet for news, communication, and finance. When a Soviet-era war monument was relocated, against the wishes of the Russian government, several days of civil unrest ensued. Once the rioting ended, the cyber attacks began. Estonian sites, including government agencies, ISPs, financial networks, and media outlets, suffered massive DoS attacks originating from botnets controlling nearly 1 million computers. Incoming Internet traffic, primarily from Russia but also from other countries, rose to thousands of times above normal, disrupting commerce and communications for several weeks. Although allegations were made against the Russian government, nothing was ever proven. Many believe the attacks were conducted by activist hackers rather than by a specific government agency. Many also fear that the attack against Estonia was just a test—a way of demonstrating the power of those who control the botnets and a warning to other countries.

The U.S. Department of Homeland Security (DHS) reports that in 2007 there was an 81 percent increase in hacking attacks on banks. The U.S. Computer Emergency Readiness Team (US-CERT) is a national cyber watch and warning center that coordinates activities with the private sector and handled more than 37,000 incidents in 2007. It also oversees EINSTEIN, an early-warning system that looks for malicious or irregular activity on the Internet. Once every two years, the DHS and US-CERT coordinate a national simulation known as Cyber Storm to assess the ability of the U.S. to identify and respond to a critical cyber attack. Cyber Storm II, held in March 2008, involved 18 government agencies, 5 countries, 9 states, 40 companies, and 10 information-sharing and analysis centers. The exercise simulated an attack on telecommunication centers, the Internet, and control systems. Preliminary results emphasize the need for improved communications between the public and the private sectors before, during, and after an attack.

Even if no enemy nation mounts an all-out information war on the United States, information terrorism is increasingly likely. Thanks to the worldwide distribution of powerful but inexpensive microprocessors, virtually anyone can construct electronic warfare weapons from widely available materials. These weapons include high-energy radio frequency (HERF) guns and electromagnetic pulse transformer (EMPT) bombs, which can damage or destroy computer systems up to a quarter mile away.

If this scenario sounds frightening, remember that information technology is a double-edged sword. Information technology gives despots a potent weapon of war, but it also undermines their power by giving citizens a way to organize democratic resistance. In Russia, for example, e-mail and fax machines played a major role in the failure of the 1989 military coup. In the United States, we have learned more about the importance of redundant data backup systems and the resiliency of the U.S. monetary system since the September 11 attacks, but we're still vulnerable and must develop ways to protect our computer systems and infrastructure.

Security Loophole Detection Programs

Intruders can use a variety of programs that automatically search for unprotected or poorly protected computer systems and notify them when a target is found. They can also use SATAN, a security loophole detection program used by system administrators. In the wrong hands, the program can help an intruder figure out how to get into a poorly secured system.

Public Safety

Perhaps the greatest threat posed by security breaches is the threat to human life; computers are increasingly part of safety-critical systems, such as air-traffic control. By paralyzing transportation and power infrastructures, attackers could completely disrupt the distribution of electricity, food, water, and medical supplies (Figure 9.20).

FIGURE 9.20 Cyberterrorism could affect key targets in a country's infrastructure.

This threat nearly became a reality when a 14-year-old hacker knocked out phone and radio service to a regional airport's communications tower. Although the hacker didn't realize he had accessed an airport computer and meant no harm, his actions paralyzed the airport's computer system and forced air-traffic controllers to rely on cellular phones and battery-powered radios to direct airplanes until the system was back up and running.

Terrorism

Perhaps the brightest spot in the war on terror is the identification of persons of interest using special security software programs. One program that attempts to find such people is IBM's Real-Time Collaborative Criminal Investigation and Analysis tool. It quickly analyzes data to discover similarities and links between individuals and determine if they are connected with unsavory characters. The SOMA Terror Organization Portal (STOP) permits analysts to network with other analysts to pool their knowledge and resources about the behavior of terrorist organizations and to forecast potential terrorist behavior. The downside of these methods is the potential for violating individual privacy rights and mistakenly targeting innocent people.

PROTECTING YOUR COMPUTER SYSTEM

Several measures can safeguard computer systems, but none of them can make a computer system 100 percent secure. A trade-off exists between security and usability: The more restrictions imposed by security tools, the less useful the system becomes.

Power-Related Problems

Power surges, which are often caused by lightning storms or fluctuations in electrical currents, and power outages can destroy sensitive electronic components and carry the threat of data loss. To safeguard your equipment and data, you should always use a surge protector. Additionally, some applications offer an autosave feature, which backs up your work at a specified interval (such as every 10 minutes). You can also equip your system with an **uninterruptible power supply (UPS)**, a battery-powered device that provides power to your computer for a limited time when it detects an outage or critical voltage drop (Figure 9.21). Many companies have electric generators to run large-scale computer systems when the power fails.

Controlling Access

Because many security problems originate with purloined passwords, password authentication is crucial to controlling authorized access to computer systems. Typically, users select their own passwords—and that is the source of a serious computer security risk. If an intruder can guess your password, the intruder can gain access to the computer system. Any damage that results will appear to have been perpetrated by you, not the intruder. What's a good password? The best passwords contain at least eight characters, combine upper- and lowercase letters, and include one or more numbers. Xa98MsoZ is an example of a good password.

In addition to password authentication, **know-and-have authentication** requires using tokens, which are handheld electronic devices that generate a logon code. Increasingly popular are smart cards, devices the size of a credit card with their own internal memories. In tandem with a supplied personal identification number (PIN), a smart card can reliably establish that the person trying to gain access has the authorization to do so.

However, when used with digital cash systems, smart cards pose a significant threat to personal privacy. Because every smart card transaction, no matter how minute, is recorded, a person's purchases can

FIGURE 9.21 A UPS is a battery-powered device that provides power to your computer for a limited time during a power outage.

be assembled and scrutinized. An investigator could put together a list of the magazines and newspapers you purchase and read, where and when you paid bridge tolls and subway fares, and what you had for lunch.

The most secure authentication approach is **biometric authentication**, which uses a variety of techniques, including voice recognition, retinal scans, fingerprint scans, and face and hand recognition (Figure 9.22). For example, Gateway now offers a built-in biometric fingerprint sensor on its latest notebook that locks access to the computer unless the correct fingerprint is matched. In an experiment in Barcelona, Spain, a soccer club used a database of ticket barcodes matched with fans' photographs to verify the tickets of more than 100,000 ticket holders as they entered the stadium. If the ticket holder's face did not match the face in the database, the person was not admitted to the stadium.

Firewalls

A **firewall** is a computer program or device that permits an organization's internal computer users to access the external Internet but severely limits the ability of outsiders to

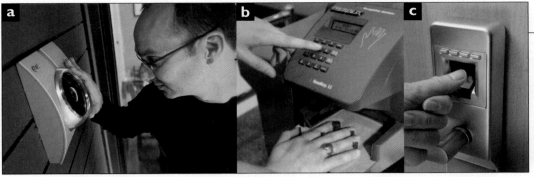

FIGURE 9.22
Biometric authentication devices such as (**a**) retinal scanners, (**b**) hand-geometry readers, and (**c**) fingerprint scanners are often used to provide access to restricted locations.

access internal data (Figure 9.23). A firewall can be implemented through software, hardware, or a combination of both. Firewalls are a necessity, but they provide no protection against insider pilferage.

Home users opting for "always on" broadband connections, such as those offered by cable modems or DSL, face a number of computer security risks. **Personal firewalls** are programs or devices that protect home computers from unauthorized access.

Avoiding Scams

To avoid being scammed on the Internet, follow these tips:

- Do business with established companies that you know and trust.

- Read the fine print. If you're ordering something, make sure it's in stock and that the company promises to deliver within 30 days.

- Don't provide financial or other personal information or passwords to anyone, even if the request sounds legitimate.

- Be skeptical when somebody in an Internet chat room tells you about a great new company or stock.

Preventing Cyberstalking

To protect yourself against cyberstalking, follow these tips:

- Don't share any personal information, such as your real name, in chat rooms. Use a name that is gender- and age-neutral. Do not post a user profile.

Destinations

Personal firewalls are an excellent way to protect your computer from unauthorized access. For more information about firewalls, go to **http:// computer. howstuffworks.com/ firewall.htm** or **www. microsoft.com/protect/ computer/firewall/ choosing.mspx**. To find out if your firewall is configured properly, use the free ShieldsUp! service found at **www. grc.com**.

FIGURE 9.23
A firewall permits an organization's internal computer users to access the Internet but limits the ability of outsiders to access internal data.

your organizations PCs

corporate network

firewall

Internet

IMPACTS

Safety and Security
Tracking an Intruder

If you've ever visited the Kennedy Space Center in Florida, where the National Aeronautics and Space Administration (NASA) launches space shuttles, you know that unless you have top-security clearance, getting closer than a binocular view of a space shuttle is impossible. A few years ago, however, a hacker known as "RaFa" was able to get a much closer view of NASA space shuttles—without even leaving his computer. The 23-year-old hacker downloaded about 43 MB of data from a top-security NASA server, including a 15-slide PowerPoint presentation of a future shuttle design.

RaFa supposedly used an anonymous FTP vulnerability in the NASA computer system to hack the design plans. He then sent the plans to a *ComputerWorld* reporter as proof that the NASA system was not secure. Although NASA didn't experience any direct financial loss from RaFa's activities, many companies do lose money because of hacker attacks—as much as $1 million can be lost from a single security incident.

However, a lot more is at stake than just money. What if terrorists or foreign agents could hack the U.S. government's computers and read, change, or steal sensitive documents? What if hackers could disrupt the networks that support vital national infrastructures such as finance, energy, and transportation?

Recognizing the danger, the federal government, through US-CERT, has emergency-response teams ready to fend off attacks on critical systems. Internationally, a group of security specialists is using "honeypots"—computers baited with fake data and purposely left vulnerable—to study how intruders operate and prepare stronger defenses (Figure 9.24).

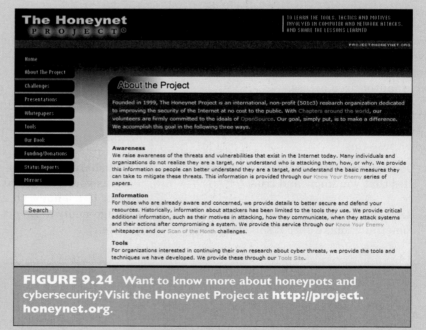

FIGURE 9.24 Want to know more about honeypots and cybersecurity? Visit the Honeynet Project at **http://project. honeynet.org**.

● Be extremely cautious about meeting anyone you've contacted online. If you do, meet in a public place and bring friends along.

● If a situation you've encountered online makes you uncomfortable or afraid, contact the police immediately. Save all the communications you've received.

Now that you've learned some ways to protect your security, let's discuss one of the major security measures used to keep information safe on the Internet: encryption.

The Encryption Debate

Cryptography is the study of transforming information into an encoded or scrambled format. Individuals who practice in this field are known as **cryptographers**. **Encryption** refers to a coding or scrambling process that renders a message unreadable by anyone except the intended recipient. Until recently, encryption was used only by intelligence services, banks, and the military.

E-commerce requires strong, unbreakable encryption; otherwise, money could not be safely exchanged over the Internet. But now, powerful encryption software is available to the public, and U.S. law enforcement officials and defense agencies aren't happy about it. Criminals, including drug dealers and terrorists, can use encryption to hide their activities. In the aftermath of the September 11 terrorist attacks, U.S. officials revealed that the terrorist network had used encrypted e-mail to keep their plans and activities secret.

ENCRYPTION BASICS

To understand encryption, try this simple exercise: Consider a short message such as "I love you." Before it is encrypted, a readable message such as this one is in **plaintext**. To encrypt the message, for each character substitute the letter that is 13 positions to the right in the 26-letter alphabet. (When you reach the end of the alphabet, start counting from the beginning.) This is an example of an **encryption key**, a formula that makes a plaintext message unreadable. After applying the key, you get the coded message, which is now in **ciphertext**. The ciphertext version of the original message looks like this:

```
V YBIR LBH
```

It looks like gibberish, doesn't it? That's the idea. No one who intercepts this message will know what it means. Your intended recipient, however, can tell what the message means if you give him or her the decoding key: in this case, counting 13 characters down (Figure 9.25). When your recipient gets the message and decrypts it, your message reappears:

```
I LOVE YOU
```

With **symmetric key encryption**, the recipient must possess the key to decrypt the message. Some of the keys used by banks and military agencies are so complex that the world's most powerful computer would have to analyze the ciphertext for several hundred years to discover the key. However, there is one way to defeat symmetric key encryption: stealing the key, or **key interception**. Banks deliver decryption keys using trusted courier services; the military uses trusted personnel or agents. These methods provide opportunities for key theft.

PUBLIC KEY ENCRYPTION

Public key encryption is considered one of the greatest (and most troubling) scientific achievements of the twentieth century. In brief, **public key encryption** uses two different keys: an encryption key (the **public key**) and a decryption key (the **private key**). People who want to receive secret messages publish their public key, for example, by placing it on a Web page or sending it to those with whom they wish to communicate. When the public key is used to encrypt a message, the message becomes unreadable. The message becomes readable only when the recipient applies his or her private key, which nobody else knows (Figure 9.26).

Public key encryption is essential for e-commerce. When you visit a secure site on the Web, for example, your Web browser provides your public key to the Web server; in turn, the Web server provides the site's public key to your Web browser. Once a secure communication channel has been created, your browser displays a distinctive icon, such as a lock in the address bar, or the address bar may turn green. You can now supply confidential information, such as your credit card number, with a reasonable degree of confidence that this information will not be intercepted while it is traveling across the Internet.

Digital Signatures and Certificates
Public key encryption can be used to implement **digital signatures**, a technique that guarantees a message has not been tampered with. Digital signatures are important to e-commerce because they enable computers to determine whether a received message or document is authentic and in its original form. For instance, a digital signature would provide an assurance that an order was authentic and not

A	1
B	2
C	3
D	4
E	5
F	6
G	7
H	8
I	9
J	10
K	11
L	12
M	13
N	14
O	15
P	16
Q	17
R	18
S	19
T	20
U	21
V	22
W	23
X	24
Y	25
Z	26

FIGURE 9.25
This is the decoding key for "I love you."

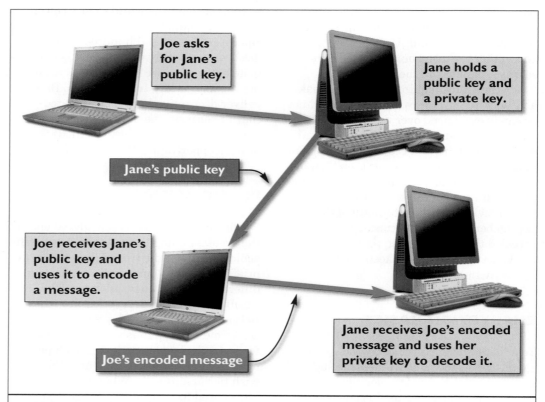

Joe asks for Jane's public key.

Jane holds a public key and a private key.

Jane's public key

Joe receives Jane's public key and uses it to encode a message.

Jane receives Joe's encoded message and uses her private key to decode it.

Joe's encoded message

FIGURE 9.26 Jane's private key ensures that no one else can decipher Joe's message.

the result of a hacker who was trying to disrupt a business transaction.

Public key encryption also enables **digital certificates**, which validate your identity in a manner similar to showing your driver's license when you cash a check. For example, to protect both merchants and customers from online credit card fraud, Visa, MasterCard, and American Express collaborated to create an online shopping security standard for merchants and customers called **Secure Electronic Transaction (SET)** that uses digital certificates. They enable parties engaged in Internet-mediated transactions to confirm each other's identity.

Toward a Public Key Infrastructure

A **public key infrastructure (PKI)** is a uniform set of encryption standards that specify how public key encryption, digital signatures, and digital certificates should be implemented in computer systems and on the Internet. Although there are numerous contenders, no dominant PKI has emerged.

One reason for the slow development of a PKI involves the fear, shared by many

private citizens and businesses alike, that a single, dominant firm will monopolize the PKI and impose unreasonable fees on the public. This was a concern when Microsoft introduced their Windows Live ID system, which implements a Microsoft-developed PKI (Figure 9.27). Originally devised as a single sign-on service for e-commerce sites, consumers and businesses feared it might be used to drive Microsoft's competitors out of business and impose artificially high costs on e-commerce, but Live ID has failed to gain popular acceptance in the marketplace and those fears have proved unfounded. Another concern involving the implementation of a PKI is that governments may step in to regulate public key encryption—or at the extreme, outlaw its use entirely.

ENCRYPTION AND PUBLIC SECURITY ISSUES

Just one year before the September 11 terrorist attacks on the World Trade Center and Pentagon, FBI Director Louis Freeh told the U.S. Congress that "the widespread use of robust unbreakable encryption ultimately will devastate our ability to fight crime and prevent terrorism. Unbreakable encryption will allow drug lords, spies, terrorists, and even violent gangs to communicate about their crimes and their conspiracies with impunity." In light of the terrorists' use of public key encryption—specifically, Pretty Good Privacy (PGP)—Freeh's warning now seems prophetic. Soon after the attacks, there were calls in the U.S. Congress to outlaw public key encryption.

However, recognizing that public key encryption is vital to the electronic economy, U.S. law enforcement and security agencies have not recommended that public key encryption be outlawed entirely. Instead, they advise that the U.S. Congress pass laws requiring a public key algorithm or a PKI that would enable investigators to eavesdrop on encrypted communications. U.S. government agencies have proposed some possibilities.

The government's need to know often conflicts with the public's right to privacy. Recently, the government released a new random-number standard, a critical component of encryption methods. It consisted of four random-number generators, one of which was included at the request of the National Security Agency (NSA). Upon examination, it was discovered that the NSA's random-number generator included a **backdoor**, a vulnerability that could enable someone to crack the code, compromising the security of this encryption tool. Experts are still debating the ramifications of this discovery. In another instance, Sebastian Boucher was arrested at the U.S.-Canada border when his notebook computer was found to contain child pornography. When authorities tried to examine his computer several days later, they found his data was encrypted by PGP

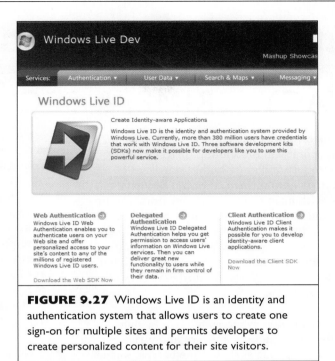

FIGURE 9.27 Windows Live ID is an identity and authentication system that allows users to create one sign-on for multiple sites and permits developers to create personalized content for their site visitors.

and they were unable to access it without the password. The government has tried to force Boucher to reveal the password, but his attorneys successfully argued that this was in violation of his Fifth Amendment rights, which protect him against self-incrimination. Further appeals are expected and privacy experts are carefully watching the outcome.

The government doesn't dispute the importance of encrypting data. The theft of a government employee's notebook computer containing the names and Social Security numbers of more than 26.5 million veterans and military personnel resulted in the federal Data at Rest Encryption program, which is mandatory for all military agencies and optional for civilian agencies. The software is available for all notebooks and other portable or handheld devices. It's obvious that there is a fine line between security and privacy, and the debate is far from resolved.

Destinations

For more information concerning cryptography, visit the SSH Communications Security "Cryptography A–Z" page at **www.ssh.com/support/cryptography**.

What You've Learned

PRIVACY, CRIME, & SECURITY

- Because no comprehensive federal regulations exist that protect an individual's privacy, many Web sites collect and store highly sensitive personal information, such as Social Security numbers, without informing their visitors. Public agencies and online merchants use computerized databases to track information about individuals. Other personal information, such as browsing habits, is often captured in cookies and by global unique identifiers (GUIDs) in hardware components and programs.

- Computer crime and cybercrime include identity theft; malware, including spyware and viruses; other rogue programs such as time bombs, worms, zombies, and Trojan horses; fraud and theft; password theft; salami shaving and data diddling; forgery; and blackmail.

- Computer criminals include crackers, members of cybergangs, virus authors, swindlers, shills, cyberstalkers, and sexual predators.

- A computer security risk is any event, action, or situation—intentional or not—that could lead to the loss or destruction of computer systems or the data they contain. Threats include corporate espionage, information warfare, security loophole detection programs, and attacks on safety-critical systems, such as air-traffic control.

- No computer system is totally secure, but you can do several things to cut down on security risks. Use an uninterruptible power supply (UPS) to combat power-related problems. Use good passwords, know-and-have authentication, biometric authentication, and firewalls to control access to computer systems. Avoid scams and cyberstalking by doing business with well-known companies and by guarding your identity online.

- Encryption refers to a coding or scrambling process by which a message is rendered unreadable by anyone except the intended recipient. Encryption can be used to guard privacy online through public key encryption schemes.

- The U.S. government continues to look for ways to balance the government's need to know with the public's right to privacy. The inclusion of backdoors in encryption standards creates unacceptable vulnerabilities, and legal issues surround attempts to force people to divulge their passwords.

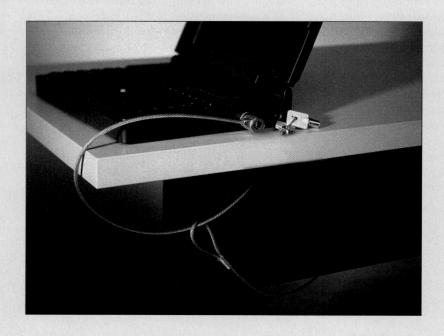

Key Terms and Concepts

adware 378
anonymity 369
backdoor 395
banner ad 370
biometric authentication 390
boot sector virus 380
botnet 382
ciphertext 393
computer crimes 377
computer security risk 387
computer virus 378
cookie 370
corporate espionage 387
crackers (black hats) 384
cryptographer 392
cryptography 392
cyberbullying 386
cybercrime 377
cybergangs 384
cyberlaw 377
cyberstalking 384
data diddling 383
denial of service (DoS)
    attack (syn flooding) 381
digital certificates 394
digital signatures 393
distributed denial of service
    (DDoS) attack 382

employee monitoring 376
encryption 392
encryption key 393
ethical hackers
    (white hats) 384
file infectors 378
firewall 390
global unique identifier
    (GUID) 371
hacker ethic 384
hackers 377
identity theft 377
information warfare 388
key interception 393
keyloggers 378
know-and-have
    authentication 390
macro 381
macro virus 381
malware 378
memory shaving 382
personal firewalls 391
phishing 378
plaintext 393
podslurping 388
privacy 395
private key 393
public key 393

public key encryption 393
public key infrastructure
    (PKI) 394
radio frequency
    identification (RFID) 371
salami shaving 383
Secure Electronic
    Transaction (SET) 394
shill 385
spim 381
spyware 378
symmetric key encryption . . . 393
time bomb (logic bomb) 381
trap doors 388
Trojan horse 382
ubiquitous computing 371
uninterruptible power
    supply (UPS) 390
variant 381
wardriving 387
WEP (Wired Equivalent
    Privacy) 387
worm 381
WPA (Wi-Fi Protected
    Access) 387
WPA2 387
zombie 382

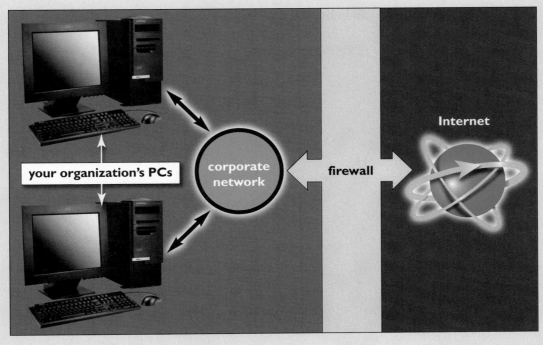

your organization's PCs

corporate network

firewall

Internet

Go to **www.pearsonhighered.com/cayf** to review this chapter, answer the questions, and complete the exercises.

Matching

Match each key term in the left column with the most accurate definition in the right column.

_____ 1. podslurping

_____ 2. cracker

_____ 3. biometric authentication

_____ 4. file infector

_____ 5. worm

_____ 6. wardriving

_____ 7. variant

_____ 8. backdoor

_____ 9. digital signature

_____ 10. cyberlaw

_____ 11. botnet

_____ 12. private key

_____ 13. memory shaving

_____ 14. salami shaving

_____ 15. macro

a. a slightly modified copy of a virus

b. a rogue program that propagates over a network without user assistance

c. embezzling technique in which small amounts of money are diverted into another account by altering a program

d. used to determine the authenticity of a message or document

e. secure method used to identify individuals and provide access

f. a collection of zombies used to launch DoS attacks and distribute spam or malware

g. a virus that attaches itself to a program

h. a type of physical theft involving RAM chips

i. automatic command execution capability found in productivity software

j. the process of searching for an unsecured wireless network

k. the act of copying sensitive data to a small, removable storage device

l. the field that tracks and combats computer-related crimes

m. used to decrypt messages

n. an individual who attempts to gain illegal access to computer systems

o. a vulnerability that may compromise an encryption code

Multiple Choice

Circle the correct choice for each of the following.

1. An individual who studies the process of transforming information into an encoded state is known as a(n):
   a. variant.
   b. phisher.
   c. cryptographer.
   d. anonymizer.

2. Which of the following is *not* a rogue program?
   a. cyberstalker
   b. Trojan horse
   c. logic bomb
   d. worm

3. Unwanted text messages are known as:
   a. DoS.
   b. ciphertext.
   c. GUID.
   d. spim.

4. When the recipient must possess the key to decrypt a message, this is known as:
   a. symmetric key encryption.
   b. public key encryption.
   c. public key infrastructure.
   d. Secure Electronic Transaction.

5. A trend that involves the interaction of people with multiple small networked devices is called:
   a. radio frequency identification.
   b. ubiquitous computing.
   c. biometric authentication.
   d. know-and-have authentication.

6. Which of the following is an example of malware?
   a. wardriving
   b. phishing
   c. boot sector virus
   d. podslurping

7. The ability to convey a message without disclosing your name or identity is known as:
   a. private key encryption.
   b. public key encryption.
   c. memory shaving.
   d. anonymity.

8. A deliberately created security hole used for corporate espionage is called a:
   a. shill.
   b. spim.
   c. key interception.
   d. trap door.

9. Which of the following is used to validate identity and engage in Internet-mediated transactions?
   a. cookie
   b. digital certificate
   c. plaintext
   d. global unique identifier

10. Which of the following is one of the earliest wireless security standards with several well-known weaknesses but may be the only option for older devices?
    a. 802.11n
    b. WPA
    c. GUID
    d. WEP

Fill-In

In the blanks provided, write the correct answer for each of the following.

1. The use of a fingerprint or retinal scanner to access a system is an example of _____ _____.

2. Applications such as NetStumbler or Kismet are often used in _____ to locate wireless networks.

3. _____ is the act of harassing or threatening a minor repeatedly through the use of electronic communications.

4. _____ _____ is a uniform set of encryption standards specifying how various encryption tools should be implemented online and in computer systems.

5. Pretty Good Privacy is an example of _____ _____ _____.

6. Various credit card companies worked together to create _____ _____ _____, an online shopping security standard that uses digital certificates.

7. Unlawful acts carried out by means of the Internet are described as _____.

8. _____ _____ is a legal form of privacy invasion conducted in the workplace.

9. A(n) _____ _____ is a tiny graphic that allows Web site or e-mail monitoring by third parties.

10. Often used for inventory tracking, a(n) _____ _____ _____ tag can also pose privacy risks if it is not deactivated.

11. In a(n) _____ _____ _____ attack, also known as syn flooding, an attacker bombards an Internet server with an overwhelming number of requests until it can no longer function.

12. Commandeered computers known as _____ are often used by botnets to distribute spam and malware.

13. A(n) _____ _____ is designed to reproduce itself and requires a host or program file to spread.

14. _____ _____ is one way to defeat symmetric key encryption.

15. A(n) _____ _____ _____ is an identification number generated by a hardware component or software program.

Short Answer

1. What are the different cookie settings on the browser that you use most often? (Hint: If you're not sure, click the browser's Help button and enter "cookies.") Describe how to switch the cookie settings. What cookie setting do you prefer? Explain why.

2. What is a digital signature? What is a digital certificate? How do they differ?

3. How do time bombs, worms, and Trojan horses differ?

4. Name some of the common types of passwords that users choose. Why are these poor choices?

5. Do you believe that the online marketing industry can adequately and effectively regulate itself? If not, who should regulate it?

Teamwork

1. Computer Security

Your group is to investigate how individuals and institutions protect their computers. Interview fellow students or a professor, asking the following questions. If you own a computer, especially a notebook, what measures do you take to protect it from theft while on campus or when traveling? Is your computer covered by homeowner's or renter's insurance? If it is covered, what is the deductible? Compile your answers. Split the following questions among the various team members. How does your school secure public computers and computer components against theft? Do the computer labs have any special security provisions in place? How are faculty and staff office computers protected? Check with campus security and find out whether any computers have been stolen in the past month. Do you feel that the laboratory and office computers and components are adequately protected from theft? Collaborate on a paper that answers these questions.

2. Password Requirements

Have each team member find the answers to the following questions and then collaborate on a paper that provides an overview of password security at your institution. How do students at your school obtain computer accounts? How are passwords initially assigned? How do users change them? Does your computer system prohibit using common words as passwords? What is the minimum number of characters required in a password? What are some of the tricks intruders can use to obtain passwords? Have any unauthorized persons gained access to your computer account? If they did, do you know how they obtained your password? Did they alter or destroy any of your files? Were you able to learn the identity of the intruders?

3. Encryption Standards

Strong encryption is required to prevent certain types of attacks. Both Internet Explorer and Mozilla Firefox provide 128-bit encryption versions for domestic use. However, under the International Traffic in Arms Regulations Act, U.S. encryption technologies are considered munitions. Consequently, only 56-bit versions of software browsers are generally available for international users. Currently, the U.S. Department of Commerce grants export permits for programs that contain 56-bit encryption tools, but only if the company promises to develop key recovery tools for domestic surveillance. Have each member of your group identify which browser and version of that browser they use most often. Explain how your browser indicates that you have connected to a secure site. This is especially important when making an online purchase with a credit card. Have you ever made purchases online? Were they always at secure sites? Collaborate on a paper that summarizes your findings and discusses the necessity of using secure sites for online purchases.

4. Fighting Spam

Have each group member compile a short list of the individuals and companies from which he or she has received unsolicited e-mail or spam and then answer the following questions. Have you received any messages that provide an option to cancel all further mailings? Did you reply that you wished to be removed from future mailings? If you did reply, did you notice an increase in unsolicited e-mail? What do you think can be done about spam? Should the government be involved? Why or why not? Collaborate on writing a paper that discusses your findings and your views on how to stop unsolicited e-mail.

5. Big Brother Is Watching

A recent newspaper article reported that a customer was fined by a car rental company for speeding. Although he was not cited for a speeding violation by any police agencies, his credit card was charged a penalty. His rental car was equipped with a GPS system that reports the location of the vehicle. This feature allowed the company to determine the speed at which the driver was traveling. This type of system is also used by some long-distance trucking companies to monitor the movements of their trucks. Divide your group into two and then have one subgroup take the company viewpoint and the other the consumer viewpoint. Debate the following: Should this type of monitoring be allowed? From a privacy standpoint, what are your feelings about these systems? What are the advantages of using these systems? Disadvantages? Write two papers: one that affirms the use of such systems and one that argues against their use.

Go to **www.pearsonhighered.com/cayf** to review this chapter, answer the questions, and complete the exercises.

On the Web

1. Personal Firewalls

Two of the leading antivirus applications, McAfee Internet Security Suite and Norton Internet Security, include personal firewall software and are designed for personal computers running various Windows operating systems. Visit the McAfee Web site at **http://us.mcafee.com** and the Symantec Web site at **www.symantec.com/index.jsp**. According to these sites, why should you use firewall software? What are the costs associated with each of these products? Are they superior to the firewall that is included in the Windows operating system? Look for a stand-alone firewall product. How does it compare with the others? Write a short paper that describes your findings.

2. The Enigma Machine

During World War II, the German military used Enigma encoding machines. It appeared that the Allies were unable to break the code generated by these machines. Visit PBS's *NOVA* Web site at **www.pbs.org/wgbh/nova** to learn the truth about these cipher machines (type "cipher machine" in the search window). Write a short paper that answers the following questions. For how many years did the breaking of the Enigma machine code remain a classified secret? Enigma machines were mechanical devices that used wheels and rings that could be easily changed. What made code breaking so difficult was the sheer number of combinations of wheel orders and ring settings. What were the number of wheel orders and ring settings? How many pairings did these produce?

3. Monitoring Software

SpectorSoft produces software that monitors and records all of the activities that take place on a personal computer. Visit the company's Web site at **www.spectorsoft.com** and answer the following questions. In addition to employees, this software monitors the activities of what two other groups? Identify the products that SpectorSoft distributes, explain how they differ, and identify their prices. Some people are easily offended by the use of this software, so explain why someone would purchase and use it.

4. Web Beacons

What is a Web beacon? They are sometimes referred to as Web bugs. Help stamp out bugs by visiting the Bugnosis Web site at **www.bugnosis.org**. From which foundation does Bugnosis get its support? What browser and versions is the bug detection software limited to? What is the cost of this software? Select the Documentation/FAQ link to learn more about Web beacons. Write a short paper that answers the preceding questions and explains why Web beacons are a potential privacy threat.

5. Electronic Privacy

Visit the Electronic Privacy Information Center at **www.epic.org**. Choose an article from the Latest News list and write a summary of the article for your instructor.

Safer Surfing

Not long ago, the only way to avoid pop-up ads was to install blocking software or add an extension, such as the Google toolbar (**http://toolbar.google.com**), to your browser. These options still exist, but the two main browsers, Internet Explorer (IE) (**www.microsoft.com/windows/products/winfamily/ie/default.mspx**) and Mozilla Firefox (**http://en-us.www.mozilla.com/en-US/firefox**), now include pop-up blocking features. Although some pop-ups may be able to evade the browsers, most are blocked and a yellow information bar will appear at the top of the browser. It's important to read the message on the information bar—it usually gives you options about how to handle the incident it is reporting. For instance, if you need the blocked pop-up window, the information bar allows you to temporarily disable the pop-up blocker so the window can appear. If you regularly use a site that requires a pop-up window, simply add it to a list of exceptions and the browser will automatically allow it to open.

Both browsers also offer built-in antiphishing features to help protect you from known phishing sites. The lists of phishing sites are regularly updated. Firefox will display a warning dialog box when you attempt to access a phishing site (Figure 9.28a), and IE uses a color-coded Security Status bar (Figure 9.28b). IE uses the familiar stoplight color code—green indicates a site that is using a new High Assurance identity verification certificate, yellow indicates a site that may be suspicious, and red is used for known phishing sites or sites whose identification does not match their encryption certificate. A white status bar simply means that no identity information is available. However, the lack of a warning color or dialog box does not guarantee that a site is safe. It is still important to practice safe surfing methods:

- Don't click on pop-up windows.

- Don't reply to e-mails from people you don't know.

- Don't click on links in an e-mail, instant message, or chat if you don't think it is legitimate.

- Don't provide personal or financial information by completing an e-mail form.

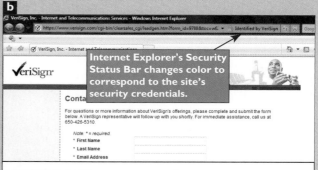

FIGURE 9.28 Both (**a**) Mozilla Firefox and (**b**) Microsoft Internet Explorer provide antiphishing features for safer Web surfing.

- Be sure you're using a secure Web site when submitting passwords or credit information.

- Carefully examine the URL to be sure you're at the correct site.

- Be sure you have updated your antivirus and antispyware software and that all security patches have been installed.

To get the most from your browser, be sure to investigate the Tools area and research its features on the developer's Web site. If you would like to explore alternative Web browsers, a good place to start is the Opera Web browser (**www.opera.com**). Mac users looking for an alternative to Safari (**www.apple.com/safari**) may be interested in the free Camino open source browser (**http://caminobrowser.org**).

Acronym Finder

NOTE: SEE GLOSSARY FOR DEFINITIONS

ADSL Asymmetric Digital Subscriber Line
AGP Accelerated Graphics Port
AI artificial intelligence
ALU arithmetic-logic unit
ASCII American Standard Code for Information Interchange
ASP application service provider
AUP acceptable use policy
BIOS basic input/output system
BLOB binary large object
BMP Windows Bitmap
BPR business process reengineering
bps bits per second
CASE computer-aided software engineering
cat-5 category 5
CAVE Cave Automated Virtual Environment
CBT computer-based training
CD-R compact disc-recordable
CD-ROM compact disc read-only memory or CD-ROM drive
CD-RW compact disc-rewritable
CMOS complementary metal-oxide semiconductor
COM Component Object Model
CORBA Common Object Request Broker Architecture
CPU central processing unit
CRM customer relationship management
CRT cathode ray tube
CS computer science
CTS carpal tunnel syndrome
DBS Direct Broadcast Satellite
DDoS distributed denial of service attack
DNS domain name system
DoS denial of service attack
DRAM dynamic random access memory
DSL Digital Subscriber Line
DSS decision support system
DVD digital video disc
DVD-RAM digital video disc-RAM
DVD-ROM digital video disc-ROM
DVI Digital Video Interface Port
EAI enterprise application integration
EBCDIC Extended Binary Coded Decimal Interchange Code
EDI electronic data interchange
EE electrical engineering
EIS executive information system
ERD entity-relationship diagram
ESS executive support system
FAT file allocation table
FED field emission display
FiOS fiber-optic service
GB gigabyte
GIF Graphics Interchange Format
GPL General Public License
GPS Global Positioning System

GUI graphical user interface
HHD hybrid hard drive
HMD head-mounted display
HTML Hypertext Markup Language
HTTP Hypertext Transfer Protocol
IC integrated circuit
IM instant messaging
IP Internet Protocol
IS information systems
ISDN Integrated Services Digital Network
ISP Internet service provider
IT information technology
ITS Intelligent Transportation System
ITU International Telecommunications Union
JAD joint application development
JPEG Joint Photographic Experts Group
KB kilobyte
L2 level 2
LAN local area network
LCD liquid crystal display
MB megabyte
MICR magnetic-ink character recognition
MIDI Musical Instrument Digital Interface
MIS management information system
MMPORG massively multiplayer online role-playing game
MP3 MPEG Audio Layer 3
MPEG Moving Picture Experts Group
MSC mobile switching center
MUD multiuser dungeon
NAS network attached storage
NC network computer
NIC network interface card
NOS network operating system
NTFS new technology file system
OCR optical character recognition
OLAP online analytical processing
OMR optical mark reader
OO object-oriented
OOP object-oriented programming
OS operating system
OSS operational support system
P2P peer-to-peer network
PAN Personal Area Network
PC personal computer
PCI Peripheral Component Interconnect
PCS Personal Communication Service
PDA personal digital assistant
PDL page description language
PDLC program development life cycle
PIM personal information manager
PNG Portable Network Graphics
PnP Plug-and-Play
PoP point of presence
POS point-of-sale
POTS Plain Old Telephone Service

PSTN public switched telephone network
RAD rapid application development
RAID redundant array of independent disks
RAM random access memory
RDBMS relational database management system
RFID Radio Frequency Identification Device
RFP request for proposal
RFQ request for quotation
ROI return on investment
ROM read-only memory
SaaS software as a service
SCSI Small Computer System Interface
SDLC systems development life cycle
SDRAM synchronous DRAM
SET secure electronic transfer
SFA sales force automation
SOHO small office/home office
SONET Synchronous Optical Network
SPOF single point of failure
SQL Structured Query Language
SSD solid state drive
SVGA Super Video Graphics Array
TB terabyte
TCP Transmission Control Protocol
TFT active matrix (Thin Film Transistor)
TLD top-level domain
TPS transaction processing system
UPC universal product code
UPS uninterruptible power supply
URL uniform resource locator
USB universal serial bus
VAN value-added network
VAR value-added reseller
VB Visual Basic
VoIP Voice over Internet Protocol
VPN virtual private network
VR virtual reality
W3C World Wide Web Consortium
WAN wide area network
WBT Web-based training
WEP Wired Equivalent Privacy
WLAN wireless LAN
WPA Wi-Fi Protected Access
WSXGA+ Widescreen Super Extended Graphics Array +
WUXGA Widescreen Ultra Extended Graphics Array
WWW World Wide Web
WXGA+ Widescreen Extended Graphics Array +
XHTML eXtensible Hypertext Markup Language
XBRL Extensible Business Reporting Language
XML Extensible Markup Language

Glossary

DEFINITIONS

@ In an e-mail address, a symbol used to separate the user name from the name of the computer on which the user's mailbox is stored (for example, frodo@bagend.org). Pronounced "at."

10baseT An Ethernet local area network capable of transmitting 10 megabits of data per second through twisted-pair cabling

100baseT See Fast Ethernet

1394 port See FireWire port

2G Second-generation cellular technology that quickly replaced most analog cellular services

3G Third-generation cellular technology that uses radio signals to transmit voice, text, images, and video data

4G Fourth-generation cellular technology that supports much higher numbers of data and voice customers and provides higher data transfer rates

A

Accelerated Graphics Port (AGP) A port specification developed by Intel Corporation to support high-speed, high-resolution graphics, including 3D graphics

acceptable use policy (AUP) An Internet service provider (ISP) policy that indicates which types of uses are permissible. Also used by universities and public entities

acceptance testing In information systems development, the examination of programs by users

access point See network access point

access speed time The amount of time that lapses between a request for information from memory and the delivery of the information. Also called access time

account On a multiuser computer system, a user information profile that includes the user's name, password, and home directory location. Unlike a profile on a consumer-oriented operating system, an account provides basic security features that prevent users from accessing or overwriting each others' files

active matrix (Thin Film Transistor) A technology that is used in most current LCD monitors. Active-matrix LCDs use transistors to control the color of each on-screen pixel

active monitoring In online banking, a security measure in which a security team constantly monitors the system that holds account information for the telltale signs of unauthorized access

ActiveX control A small program that can be downloaded from a Web page and used to add functionality to a Web browser. ActiveX controls require Microsoft Windows and Microsoft Internet Explorer and are usually written in Visual Basic (VB)

Ada A programming language that incorporates modular programming principles, named after Augusta Ada Byron

adapter 1. A circuit board that plugs into an expansion slot in a computer, giving the computer additional capabilities. Synonymous with card. Popular adapters for personal computers include video adapters that produce video output, memory expansion boards, internal modems, and sound boards. 2. A transformer that enables a computer or peripheral to work with line voltage that differs from its electrical requirements

Add or Remove Programs An icon in a computer operating system's control panel that allows for proper installation and uninstallation of programs

address bar The top bar in a Windows Explorer window that displays the route you've taken to get to the current location

ADSL (Asymmetric Digital Subscriber Line) A type of Digital Subscriber Line (DSL) service for Internet access. ADSL enables download speeds of up to 1.5 Mbps

adware A type of Internet spyware created by advertising agencies to collect information about computer users' Internet habits

algorithm A mathematical or logical procedure for solving a problem

all-in-one computer A system unit that contains all of the computer's components, including input components and the display

alphabetic check Ensures that only alphabetical data (the letters of the alphabet) are entered into a field

analog signal A signal sent via continuous waves that vary in strength and quality, such as those that phones and phone lines send and receive

anonymity On the Internet, the ability to post a message or visit Web sites without divulging one's identity. Anonymity is much more difficult to obtain than most Internet users realize

anonymous FTP An Internet service that enables you to contact a distant computer system to which you have no access rights, log on to its public directories, and transfer files from that computer to your own

antivirus software A utility that checks for and removes computer viruses from memory and disks

applet 1. A small- to medium-sized computer program that provides a specific function, such as emulating a calculator. 2. In Java, a mini-program embedded in a Web document that, when downloaded, is executed by the browser. Leading browsers can execute Java applets

application service provider (ASP) A third-party commercial firm, nonprofit, or government entity that provides software-based services and solutions to companies that want to outsource some or almost all of their information technology needs

application software Programs that enable you to do something useful with the computer, such as writing or accounting (as opposed to utilities, which are programs that help you maintain the computer)

application testing In information systems development, the examination of programs individually, and then further examination of the programs as they function together

application window The area on-screen that encloses and displays a launched application

application workspace The area within an application window that displays the document

archive A file that contains two or more files that have been stored together for convenient archiving or network transmission in a special format. An archive is useful for storage and file-exchange purposes

argument set In spreadsheet programs such as Microsoft Excel, the part of a mathematical function that contains its passable parameters or variables

arithmetic-logic unit (ALU) The portion of the central processing unit (CPU) that makes all the decisions for the microprocessor, based on the mathematical computations and logic functions that it performs

arithmetic operations One of the two groups of operations performed by the arithmetic-logic unit (ALU). The arithmetic operations are addition, subtraction, multiplication, and division

arrow keys See cursor-movement keys

artificial intelligence (AI) A computer science field that tries to improve computers by endowing them with some of the characteristics associated with human intelligence, such as the capability to understand natural language and to reason under conditions of uncertainty

artificial system A collection of components constructed by people and organized into a functioning whole to accomplish a goal

ASCII (American Standard Code for Information Interchange) A standard computer character set consisting of 96 uppercase and lowercase letters along with 32 nonprinting control characters. Developed in 1963, ASCII was the first computer industry standard

assembler A program that transforms source code in assembly language into machine language readable by a computer

assembly language A low-level programming language in which each program statement corresponds to an instruction that the microprocessor can carry out

authentication In computer security, a method of preventing unauthorized users from accessing a computer system, usually by requesting a password

automation The replacement of human workers by machines

autosave A software feature that backs up open documents at a user-specified interval

auxiliary storage See storage

B

backbone In a wide area network (WAN), such as the Internet, a high-speed, high-capacity medium that transfers data over hundreds or thousands of miles. A variety of physical media are used for backbone services, including microwave relay, satellites, and dedicated telephone lines

backdoor A secret vulnerability that enables investigators to decrypt messages without first having to obtain a private key, compromising message security

background application In a multitasking operating system, any inactive application

backside cache See secondary cache

backup software A program that copies data from a secondary storage device (most commonly a hard disk) to a backup medium, such as a CD or DVD

bad sector In magnetic storage media such as hard drives, a portion of the disk's surface that is physically damaged to the point that it can no longer store data safely

bandwidth The amount of data that can be transmitted through a given communications channel, such as a computer network

banner ad On the World Wide Web, a paid advertisement—often rectangular in shape, like a banner—that contains a hyperlink to the advertiser's page

bar code reader An input device that scans bar codes and, with special software, converts the bar code into readable data

BASIC Acronym for Beginner's All-Purpose Symbolic Instruction Code. An easy-to-use high-level programming language developed in 1964 for instruction

basic input/output system (BIOS) Read-only memory (ROM) built into the computer's memory that contains the instructions needed to start the computer and work with input and output devices

batch processing A mode of computer operation in which program instructions are executed one after the other without user intervention. Batch processing uses computer resources efficiently but is less convenient than interactive processing, in which you see the results of your commands on-screen so that you can correct errors and make necessary adjustments before completing the operation

BD-R Blu-ray discs that can record HD video or PC data storage

BD-RE Blu-ray discs that can record and erase HD video or PC data storage

BD-ROM Blu-ray discs that are in read-only format used for video or data distribution

beta version In software testing, a preliminary version of a program that is widely distributed before commercial release to users who test the program by operating it under realistic conditions

binary digit See bit

binary numbers A number system with a base (radix) of 2, unlike the number systems most of us use, which have bases of 10 (decimal numbers), 12 (feet and inches), and 60 (time). Binary numbers are preferred for computers for precision and economy. Building an

electronic circuit that can detect the difference between two states (high current and low current, or 0 and 1) is easy and inexpensive; building a circuit that detects the difference among 10 states (0 through 9) is much more difficult and expensive. The word bit derives from the phrase binary digit

biological feedback device A device that translates eye movements, body movements, and brain waves into computer input

biometric authentication A method of authentication that requires a biological scan of some sort, such as a retinal scan or voice recognition

bit Short for binary digit, the basic unit of information in a binary numbering system

bit-mapped graphics Images formed by a pattern of tiny dots, each of which corresponds to a pixel on the computer's display. Also called raster graphics

bits per second (bps) a measurement of data transmission speed. In personal computing, bps rates frequently are used to measure the performance of modems and serial ports

black hat See cracker

BLOB (binary large object) In databases, a data type for very large objects, such as an entire spreadsheet file or a picture file, that may be several megabytes or more in size

blocks Sections on a chip in which flash memory stores data electronically

Blu-ray Disc (BD) A form of optical storage, this technology was developed for the management of high-definition video and for storing large amounts of data. The name is derived from the blue-violet laser beams (blue rays) used to read and write data

Bluetooth A trademarked personal area network (PAN) technology, conceived by cell phone giant Ericsson and named after a 10th-century Viking, that allows computers, mobile phones, printers, and other devices within a certain range of each other to communicate automatically and wirelessly

Boolean search A database or Web search that uses the logical operators AND, OR, and NOT to specify the logical relationship between search concepts

boot To start the computer. See cold boot and warm boot

booting The process of loading the operating system to memory

boot disk See emergency disk

boot sector virus A computer virus that copies itself to the beginning of a hard drive, where it is automatically executed when the computer is turned on

botnet The group of commandeered computers that hackers take over during a distributed denial of service (DDoS) attack

bps (bits per second) rate The rate used to measure data exchange

branch control structure See selection control structure

branch prediction A technique used by advanced CPUs to prevent a pipeline stall. The processor tries to predict what is likely to happen

broadband Refers to any transmission medium that transports high volumes of data at high speeds, typically greater than 1 Mbps

broken link On the World Wide Web, a hyperlink that refers to a resource (such as a sound or a Web page) that has been moved or deleted. See dead link

browser See Web browser

bubble-jet printer See inkjet printer

bug A syntax or logic-based programming error that causes a program or a computer system to perform erratically, produce incorrect results, or crash

build-or-buy decision In the development of information systems, the choice of building a new system within the organization or purchasing it from an outside vendor

burner See CD-RW drive

bus See data bus

bus topology The physical layout of a local area network that does not use a central or host computer. Instead, each node manages part of the network, and information is transmitted directly from one computer to another

business process management (BPM) The use of information technology to improve business processes and optimize assets by effectively and efficiently managing the entire life cycle of these business processes

business process reengineering (BPR) The use of information technology to bring about major changes and cost savings in an organization's structure

business processes Activities that have an identifiable output and value to the organization's customers

business skills Skills such as teamwork, project management skills, communication skills, and business savvy

business-to-business (B2B) e-commerce A type of e-commerce where one business provides another business with the materials and supplies it needs to conduct its operations

byte Eight bits grouped to represent a character (a letter, a number, or a symbol)

C

C A high-level programming language developed by Bell Labs in the 1970s. C combines the virtues of high-level programming with the efficiency of assembly language but is somewhat difficult to learn

C++ A flexible high-level programming language derived from C that supports object-oriented programming but does not require programmers to adhere to the object-oriented model

cable modem A device that enables a computer to access the Internet by means of a cable TV connection. Some cable modems enable downloading only; you need an analog (POTS) phone line and an analog modem to upload data. The best cable modems enable two-way communications through the cable TV system and do not require a phone line. Cable modems enable Internet access speeds of up to 1.5 Mbps, although most users typically experience slower speeds due to network congestion

cache memory A small unit of ultra-fast memory used to store recently accessed or frequently accessed data, increasing a computer system's overall performance

call center A computer-based telephone routing system that automatically connects credit card authorization systems to authorization services

carpal tunnel syndrome (CTS) A painful swelling of the tendons and the sheaths around them in the wrist due to injury caused by motions repeated thousands of times daily (such as mouse movements or keystrokes)

case control structure In structured programming, a logical construction of programming commands that contains a set of possible conditions and instructions that are executed if those conditions are true

category 5 (cat-5) A type of twisted-pair cable used for high-performance digital telephone and computer network wiring

cathode ray tube (CRT) A monitor type in which a vacuum tube that uses an electron gun to emit a beam of electrons to illuminate phosphorus on-screen as the beam sweeps across the screen repeatedly

Cave Automated Virtual Environment (CAVE) A virtual reality environment that replaces headsets with 3D glasses and uses the walls, ceiling, and floor to display projected three-dimensional images

CD burner See CD-RW drive

CD drive Read only disk drive that reads data encoded on a CD and transfers it to the computer

CD/DVD Jukebox An enterprise storage device that offers multiple DVD-ROM and CD-ROM drives to store and give users network access to all of an enterprise's digital content

CD-R Compact disc-recordable storage media that cannot be erased or written over once data has been saved; they're relatively inexpensive

CD-R drives Compact disc-recordable devices that can read standard CD-ROM discs and write data to CD-R discs

CD-ROM See compact disc read-only memory

CD-ROM drive A read-only disk drive that reads data encoded on compact discs and transfers this data to a computer

CD-RW Compact disc-rewritable storage media that allows data that has been saved to be erased or written over

CD-RW drive A compact disc-rewritable drive that provides full read/write capabilities using erasable CD-RWs

cell 1. In a spreadsheet, a rectangle formed by the intersection of a row and a column in which you enter information in the form of text (a label) or numbers (a value). 2. In telecommunications, a limited geographical area in which a signal can be broadcast

cell address The colum letter and row number that identifies a cell

cell site In a cellular telephone network, an area in which a transmitting station repeats the system's broadcast signals so that the signal remains strong even though

the user may move from one cell site to another

cellular telephone A radio-based telephone system that provides widespread coverage through the use of repeating transmitters placed in zones (called cells). The zones are close enough so that signal strength is maintained throughout the calling area

centralized structure When technology management is centered in the IT department, and everyone within the organization works with standardized technology solutions in their everyday work

central processing unit (CPU) The computer's processing and control circuitry, including the arithmetic-logic unit (ALU) and the control unit

certification An endorsement of professional competence that is awarded on successful completion of a rigorous test

channel In Internet Relay Chat (IRC), a chat group in which as many as several dozen people carry on a text-based conversation on a specific topic

character Any letter, number, punctuation mark, or symbol produced on-screen by the press of a key or a key combination

character code An algorithm used to translate between the numerical language of the computer and characters readable by humans

check-screening system A computer system used in point-of-sale (POS) terminals that reads a check's account number and accesses a database of delinquent accounts

chip An integrated circuit (IC) that can emulate thousands or millions of transistors

chip card See smart card

chipset A collection of supporting components that are all designed to work together smoothly on a computer motherboard

ciphertext The result of applying an encryption key to a message

circuit switching A type of telecommunications network in which high-speed electronic switches create a direct connection between two communicating devices. The telephone system is a circuit-switching network

citing sources Providing enough information about the source of information you are using so that an interested or critical reader can locate this source without difficulty

class In object-oriented (OO) programming, a category of objects that performs a certain function. The class defines the properties of an object, including definitions of the object's variables and the procedures that need to be followed to get the object to do something

click-and-brick In electronic commerce, a retail strategy in which a Web retail site is paired with a chain of local retail stores. Customers prefer this strategy because they can return or exchange unwanted goods more easily

clickstream The trail of links left behind to reach a particular Web site

client 1. In a client/server network, a program that runs on users' computers and enables them to access a certain type of data. 2. On a computer network, a computer

that is capable of contacting the server and obtaining needed information

client/server network A method of organizing software use on a computer network that divides programs into servers (programs that make information available) and clients (programs that enable users to access a certain type of data)

client/server network A computer network in which some computers are dedicated to function as servers, making information available to client programs running on users' computers

Clip Organizer In Microsoft Office, a repository of clip art and images that can be inserted into a document or presentation

clock speed The speed of the internal clock of a microprocessor that sets the pace at which operations proceed in the computer's internal processing circuitry

cluster On a magnetic disk, a storage unit that consists of two or more sectors

CMOS (complementary metal-oxide semiconductor) A special type of nonvolatile memory used to store essential startup configuration options

coaxial cable A high-bandwidth connecting cable in which an insulated wire runs through the middle of the cable

COBOL (Common Business-Oriented Language) An early, high-level programming language for business applications

code The written computer instructions that programmers create

code of conduct A set of ethical principles developed by a professional association, such as the Association for Computing Machinery (ACM)

codec Short for compression/decompression standard. A standard for compressing and decompressing video information to reduce the size of digitized multimedia files. Popular codecs include MPEG (an acronym for Motion Picture Experts Group), Apple's QuickTime, and Microsoft's AVI

cold boot A system start that involves powering up the computer

collision In local area networks (LANs), a garbled transmission that results when two or more workstations transmit to the same network cable at exactly the same time. Networks have means of preventing collisions

command A user-initiated instruction that tells a program which task to perform

command-line user interface In an operating system, a variety of user interface that requires users to type commands one line at a time

commercial software Copyrighted software that must be paid for before it can be used

Common Object Request Broker Architecture (CORBA) In object-oriented (OO) programming, a leading standard that defines how objects can communicate with each other across a network

communications The high-speed movement of data within and between computers

communications channel (also referred to as links) In communications, the path through which messages are passed from one location to the next

communications device Any hardware device that is capable of moving data into or out of the computer

compact disc read-only memory (CD-ROM) A standard for storing read-only computer data on optical compact discs (CDs), which can be read by CD-ROM drives

compact disc-recordable (CD-R) A "write-once" optical storage. Once you've recorded on the disc, you can't erase the stored data or write over the disc again. You can play the recorded CD on most CD-ROM drives

compact disc-rewritable (CD-RW) A read/ write optical storage technology that uses a CD-R drive to record data on CD-RW discs. You can erase the recorded data and write new data as you please. Most CD-ROM drives can read the recorded data. CD-RW drives can also write to CD-R discs, but you can write to CD-R discs only once

CompactFlash A popular flash memory storage device that can store up to 128 MB of digital camera images

compatible The capability to function with or substitute for a given make and model of computer, device, or program

compatible computers Computer systems capable of using the same programs and peripherals

competitive advantage A condition that gives an organization a superior position over the companies it competes with

compiler A program that translates source code in a third-generation programming language into machine code readable by a computer

completeness check Determines whether a required field has been left empty. If so, the database prompts the user to fill in the needed data

Component Object Model (COM) In object-oriented (OO) programming, a standard developed by Microsoft Corporation that is used to define how objects communicate with each other over networks

computer A machine that can physically represent data, process this data by following a set of instructions, store the results of the processing, and display the results so that people can use them

computer crimes Computer-related actions that violate state or federal laws

computer ethics A new branch of philosophy dealing with computing-related moral dilemmas

computer network See network

computer science (CS) A scientific discipline that focuses on the theoretical aspects of improving computers and computer software

computer security risk Any event, action, or situation—intentional or not—that could lead to the loss or destruction of computer systems or the data they contain

computer system A collection of related computer components that have all been designed to work smoothly together

computer virus A program, designed as a prank or as sabotage, that replicates itself by attaching to other programs and carrying out unwanted and sometimes dangerous operations

computer-aided software engineering (CASE) Software that provides tools to help with every phase of systems development and enables developers to create data flow diagrams, data dictionary entries, and structure charts

computer-based training (CBT) The use of computer-assisted instruction (CAI) programs to educate adults

conditional control structure See selection control structure

congestion In a packet switching network, a performance interruption that occurs when a segment of the network experiences overload

connectivity The ability to link various media and devices, thereby enhancing communication and improving access to information

connector A component that enables users or technicians to connect a cable securely to the computer's case. A male connector contains pins or plugs that fit into the corresponding female connector

consistency check Examines the data entered into two different fields to determine whether an error has been made

contention In a computer network, a problem that arises when two or more computers try to access the network at the same time. Contention can result in collisions, which can destroy data

contention management In a computer network, the use of one of several techniques for managing contention and preventing collisions

control module In a program design tool called a structure chart, the top module or box that oversees the transfer of control to the other modules

control structure In structured programming, a logical element that governs program instruction execution

control unit A component of the central processing unit (CPU) that obtains program instructions and sends signals to carry out those instructions

convergence The coming together of information technologies (computer, consumer electronics, telecommunications) and gadgets (PC, TV, telephone), leading to a culmination of the digital revolution in which all types of digital information (voice, video, data) will travel over the same network

cookie A text file that is deposited on a Web user's computer system, without the user's knowledge or consent, that may contain identifying information. This information is used for a variety of purposes, such as retaining the user's preferences or compiling information about the user's Web browsing behavior

cooling fan A part of the system unit that prevents components from being damaged by heat

copy-protected software Computer programs that include some type of

measure to prevent users from making unauthorized copies

copyright infringement The act of using material from a copyrighted source without getting permission to do so

copyright protection scheme A method used by software manufacturers to ensure that users cannot produce unauthorized copies of copyrighted software

corporate espionage The unauthorized access of corporate information, usually to the benefit of one of the corporation's competitors

cost/benefit analysis An examination of the losses and gains, both tangible and intangible, related to a project

cracker A computer user obsessed with gaining entry into highly secure computer systems

crash An abnormal termination of program execution

crash conversion See direct conversion

cross-platform programming language A programming language that can create programs capable of running on many different types of computers

cryptographer An individual who practices cryptography

cryptography The study of transforming information into an encoded or scrambled format

cursor A flashing bar, an underline character, or a box that indicates where keystrokes will appear when typed. Also called insertion point

cursor-movement keys A set of keys on the keyboard that move the location of the cursor on the screen. The numeric keypad can also move the cursor when in the appropriate mode. Also called arrow keys

customer relationship management (CRM) Enterprise software that keeps track of an organization's interactions with its customers and focuses on retaining those customers

custom software Application software designed for a company by a professional programmer or programming team. Custom software is usually very expensive

cybercrime Crime carried out by means of the Internet

cyberbullying A situation in which minors harass another minor using the Internet and other digital technologies

cybergang A group of computer hackers and crackers working together to coordinate attacks, post online graffiti, or conduct other malicious acts

cyberlaw A new legal field designed to track developments in cybercrime

cyberspace Territory that isn't an actual, physical space and is accessible only with computers

cyberstalking A form of harassment in which an individual is repeatedly subjected to unwanted electronic mail or advances in chat rooms

D

data The raw material of computing: facts, words, numbers, images, and/or sounds information represented for computer processing

data bus A high-speed freeway of parallel connections that enables the CPU to communicate at high speeds with memory

data dependency A microprocessor performance problem in which a CPU is slowed in its functioning by the need to wait for the results of one set of instructions before moving on to process the next ones

data dictionary In information systems development, a collection of definitions of all data types that may be input into the system, including field name, data types, and validation settings

data diddling A computer crime in which data is modified to conceal theft or embezzlement

data exchange rate The rate at which two modems can exchange data

data file A named unit of information storage that contains data rather than program instructions

data flow diagram A graphical representation of the flow of data through an information system

data glove A device that translates hand and arm movements into computer input

data independence In a database, the storage of data in such a way that it is not locked into use by a particular application

data integrity In a database, the validity of the stored data; specifically, its freedom from error due to improper data entry, hardware malfunctions, or transmission errors

data maintenance Includes procedures for adding, updating, and deleting records for the purpose of keeping a database in optimal shape

data mart A large database that contains all the data used by one of the divisions of an organization

data mining The analysis of data stored in data warehouses to search for previously unknown patterns

data processing system See transaction processing system

data redundancy In a database, a design error in which the same data appears more than once, creating opportunities for discrepant data entry and increasing the chance that the data will be processed incorrectly

data security Ensuring that the data stored in a database isn't accessible to people who might misuse it, particularly when the collected data are sensitive

data table See data file

data transfer rate 1. In secondary storage devices, the maximum number of bits per second that can be sent from the hard disk to the computer. The rate is determined by the drive interface. 2. The speed, expressed in bits per second (bps), at which a modem can transfer, or is transferring, data over a telephone line

data type In a database or spreadsheet program, a particular type of information, such as a date, a time, or a name

data validation In a database, a method of increasing the validity of data by defining acceptable input ranges for each field in the record

data warehouse A very large database, containing as many as a trillion data records, that stores all of a firm's data and makes this data available for exploratory analysis (called data mining)

database A collection of information stored in an organized way

database management system (DBMS) An application that enables users to create databases that contain links from several files. Database management systems are usually more expensive than file management programs

database program An application that stores data so that needed information can be quickly located, organized, and displayed

database server software In a client/server database system, software that runs on a LAN and responds to remote users' requests for information

dead link On the World Wide Web, a hyperlink that refers to a resource (such as a sound or a Web page) that has been moved or deleted

debugging In programming, the process of finding and correcting errors, or bugs, in the source code of a computer program

decision support system (DSS) A program that helps management analyze data to make decisions on semistructured problems

decode One of four basic operations carried out by the control unit of a microprocessor. The decode operation involves determining what the program is telling the computer to do

default In a computer program, a fallback setting or configuration value that is used unless the user specifically chooses a different one

default value The setting in a database field that is automatically selected unless another value is provided

deliverable In the development of an information system, the outcome of a particular phase of the systems development life cycle (SDLC)

denial of service (DoS) attack A form of network vandalism that attempts to make a service unavailable to other users, generally by flooding the service with meaningless data. Also called syn flooding

desktop The portion of the graphical user interface (GUI) that appears after the operating system finishes loading into memory

desktop computer A personal computer designed for an individual's use. Desktop computers are increasingly used to gain access to the resources of computer networks

details pane The pane at the bottom of the Windows Explorer window that provides a thumbnail view and information about the selected file or folder

device driver A program file that contains specific information needed by the operating system so that a specific brand or model of device will function

dialog box In a graphical user interface (GUI), an on-screen message box used to request information from the user

digital camera A camera that records an image by means of a digital imaging system, such as a charged-coupled device (CCD), and stores the image in memory or on a disk

digital cash system A method for using smart cards and prepaid amounts of electronically stored money to pay for small charges such as parking and tolls

digital certificate A form of digital ID used to obtain access to a computer system or prove one's identity while shopping on the Web. Certificates are issued by independent, third-party organizations called certificate authorities (CA)

digital divide The racial and/or income disparity in computer ownership and Internet access

digital light processing (DLP) projector A computer projection device that employs millions of microscopic mirrors, embedded in a microchip, to produce a brilliant, sharp image

digital modem See ISDN adapter

digital signal A signal sent via discontinuous pulses, in which the presence or absence of electronic pulses represents 1s and 0s, such as computers send and receive. See analog signal

digital signatures A technique used to guarantee that a message has not been tampered with

digital telephony Telephone systems using all-digital protocols and transmission, offering the advantage over analog telephony of noise-free transmission and high-quality audio

digital video camera Camera that uses digital rather than analog technologies to store recorded video images

digital video disc (DVD) The newest optical disc format, DVD is capable of storing an entire digitized movie. DVD discs are designed to work with DVD video players and televisions

digital video disc-RAM (DVD-RAM) A digital video disc (DVD) format that enables users to record up to 2.6 GB of data

digital video disc-ROM (DVD-ROM) A digital optical disc format capable of storing up to 17 GB on a single disc, enough for a feature-length movie. DVD is designed to be used with a video player and a television. DVD discs can be read also by DVD-ROM drives

Digital Video Interface (DVI) port A port that enables LCD monitors to use digital signals

digitization The transformation of data such as voice, text, graphics, audio, and video into digital form, thereby allowing various technologies to transmit computer data through telephone lines, cables, or air and space

Direct Broadcast Satellite (DBS) A consumer satellite technology that offers cable channels and one-way Internet access.

To use DBS for an Internet connection, a modem and phone line are required to upload data

direct conversion In the development of an information system, the termination of the current system and the immediate institution of the new system throughout the whole organization

disaster recovery plan A written plan, with detailed instructions, specifying an alternative computing facility to use for emergency processing until a destroyed computer can be replaced

disintermediation The process of removing an intermediary, such as a car salesperson, by providing a customer with direct access to rich information and warehouse-size selection and stock

disc A portable storage optical media, such as CD-ROM

disk A portable storage magnetic media, such as floppy disks, that provides personal computer users with convenient, near-online storage

disk cache A small amount of memory (up to 512 KB), usually built into the electronics of a disk drive, used to store frequently accessed data. Disk caches can significantly improve the performance of a disk drive

disk cleanup utility A utility program that removes unneeded temporary files

disk defragmentation program A program used to read all the files on a disk and rewrite them so that files are all stored in a contiguous manner. This process almost always improves disk performance by some degree

disk drive A secondary storage mechanism that stores and retrieves information on a disk by using a read/write head. Disk drives are random-access devices

disk scanning program A utility program that can detect and resolve a variety of physical and logical problems related to file storage

display See monitor

distributed denial of service (DDoS) attack A computer attack on multiple systems by a hacker who bombards an Internet server with a huge number of requests so that the server becomes overloaded and unable to function.

distributed hypermedia system A network-based content development system in which individuals connected to the network can each make a small contribution by developing content related to their area of expertise. The Web is a distributed hypermedia system

distributed structure When technology management is decentralized and users are able to customize their technology tools to suit their individual needs and wants

DLP (digital light processing) Projector A device that projects light onto a chip made up of millions of microscopic mirrors. It is often smaller and lighter than LCD projectors and has better contrast

document A file created with an application program, such as a word processing or spreadsheet program

documentation 1. With software, tutorials and instructions on how to use the software. 2. In information systems development, the recording of all information pertinent to the development of an information system, usually in a project notebook

domain name On the Internet, a readable computer address (such as www.microsoft.com) that identifies the location of a computer on the network

domain name registration On the Internet, a process by which individuals and companies can obtain a domain name (such as www.c34.org) and link this name to a specific Internet address (IP address)

Domain Name System (DNS) The conceptual system, standards, and names that make up the hierarchical organization of the Internet

dot-com The universe of Internet sites, especially those doing electronic commerce, with the suffix com appended to their names

dot pitch On a monitor, the space (measured in millimeters) between each physical dot on the screen

double data rate (DDR) SDRAM A type of SDRAM that can both send and receive data within a single clock cycle

download To transfer a file from another computer to your computer by means of a modem and a telephone line. See upload

downsizing In corporate management, a cost-reduction strategy involving layoffs to make a firm leaner and more competitive. Downsizing often accompanies technology-driven restructuring that theoretically enables fewer employees to do the same or more work

drawing program An application program used to create, edit, and display vector graphics

drill-down A technique used by managers to view information in a data warehouse. By drilling down to lower levels of the database, the manager can focus on sales regions, offices, and then individual salespeople, and view summaries at each level

drive activity light A light on the front panel of most computers that signals when the hard disk is accessing data

drive bay A receptacle or opening into which you can install a floppy drive, a CD-ROM or DVD-ROM drive, or a removable drive

drive imaging software A type of software that creates a mirror image of the entire hard disk—including the operating system, applications, and all other files and data

driver A utility program that is needed to make a peripheral device function correctly

DSL (Digital Subscriber Line) A general term for several technologies that enable high-speed Internet access through twisted-pair telephone lines. Also called xDSL. See ADSL (Asymmetric Digital Subscriber Line)

DSL modem Similar to a traditional telephone modem in that it modulates and demodulates analog and digital signals for transmission over communications channels, but does so using signaling methods based on broadband technology for much higher transfer speeds

dumpster diving A technique used to gain unauthorized access to computer systems by retrieving user IDs and passwords from an organization's trash

DVD drive A read-only disk drive that reads data encoded on a CD or DVD and transfers the data to the computer

DVD-R Digital video disc-recordable optical storage media that, like CD-R discs, cannot be erased or written over once data has been saved

DVD-ROM Optical storage media that can hold up to 17 GB of data

DVD-ROM drive A read-only disk drive that reads the data encoded on DVD-ROM discs and transfers this data to a computer

DVD+R A recordable optical storage media that enables the disc to be written to one time and read many times

DVD+RW discs Digital video disc-read/write optical storage media that allow you to write, erase, and read from the disc many times

DVD-RW Optical storage media on which you can write, erase, and read from the disc many times

DVI port See Digital Video Interface (DVI) port

dynamic A term used to describe searches in Windows Explorer, which are automatically refreshed every time you open up a saved search. New files are added and old files that no longer meet the criteria are deleted

dynamic random access memory (DRAM) A random access memory chip that must be refreshed periodically; otherwise, the data in the memory will be lost

E

e-book A book that has been digitized and distributed by means of a digital storage medium

e-book reader A book-sized device that displays an e-book

EBCDIC (Extended Binary Coded Decimal Interchange Code) The code used by IBM mainframe computers and some other systems

e-commerce See electronic commerce

ECMA Script (Java Script) A scripting language for Web publishing, developed by Netscape Communications, that enables Web authors to embed simple Java-like programming instructions in the HTML text of their Web pages

economic feasibility Capable of being accomplished with available fiscal resources. This is usually determined by a cost-benefit analysis

e-learning The use of computers and computer programs to replace teachers and the time–place specificity of learning

electrical engineering (EE) An engineering discipline that is concerned with the design and improvement of electrical and electronic circuits

electronic commerce The use of the Internet and other wide area networks (WANs) for business-to-business and business-to-consumer transactions. Also called e-commerce

electronic data interchange (EDI) A communications standard for the electronic exchange of financial information through information services

electronic mail See e-mail

electronic mailing list Similar to newsgroups and forums, electronic mailing lists automatically broadcast messages via e-mail to those on the list

electronic vault In online banking, a mainframe computer that stores account holders' information

element In HTML, a distinctive component of a document's structure, such as a title, heading, or list. HTML divides elements into two categories: head elements (such as the document's title) and body elements (headings, paragraphs, links, and text)

e-mail Electronic mail; messages sent and received through the use of a computer network

e-mail address A series of characters that precisely identifies the location of a person's electronic mailbox. On the Internet, e-mail addresses consist of a mailbox name (such as jsmith) followed by an at sign (@) and the computer's domain name (as in jsmith@hummer.virginia.edu)

e-mail attachment A computer file that is included with an e-mail message

emergency disk A disk that can be used to start the computer in case the operating system becomes unusable for some reason

employee monitoring When large employers routinely engage in observing employees' phone calls, e-mails, Web browsing habits, and computer files

encapsulation In object-oriented programming, the hiding of all internal information of objects from other objects

encryption The process of converting a message into ciphertext (an encrypted message) by using a key, so that the message appears to be nothing but gibberish. The intended recipient, however, can apply the key to decrypt and read the message

encryption key A formula that is used to make a plaintext message unreadable

enterprise A business organization or any large computer-using organization, which can include universities and government agencies

enterprise application integration (EAI) A combination of processes, software, standards, and hardware that results in the integration of two or more enterprise systems

enterprise computing The use of technology, information systems, and computers within an organization or a business

enterprise resource planning (ERP) Enterprise software that brings together various enterprise functions, such as manufacturing, sales, marketing, and finance, into a single computer system

enterprise storage system The collection of storage within an organization. The system typically makes use of servers connected to hard disks or massive RAID systems

enterprise systems Information systems that integrate an organization's information and applications across all of the organization's functional divisions

entity-relationship diagram (ERD) In the design of information systems, a diagram that shows all the entities (organizations, departments, users, programs, and data) that play roles in the system, as well as the relationships between those entities

ergonomic Describes a product that matches the best posture and functionality of the human body

Ethernet A set of standards that defines local area networks (LANs) capable of operating at data transfer rates of 10 Mbps to 1 Gbps. About 80 percent of all LANs use one of several Ethernet standards

Ethernet card A network interface card (NIC) designed to work with Ethernet local area networks (LANs)

ethical hacker (white hat) Hackers and crackers who have turned pro, offering their services to companies hoping to use hacker expertise to shore up their computer systems' defenses

ethical principle A principle that defines the justification for considering an act or a rule to be morally right or wrong. Ethical principles can help people find their way through moral dilemmas

event-driven programming language In programming, a program design method that structures the program around a continuous loop, which cycles until an event occurs (such as the user clicking the mouse)

e-waste Obsolete computer equipment

exception report In a transaction processing system (TPS), a document that alerts someone of unexpected developments, such as high demand for a product

exclusion operator In database and Internet searching, a symbol or a word that tells the software to exclude records or documents containing a certain word or phrase

executable file A file containing a script or program that can execute instructions on the computer. Program files usually use the .exe extension in the filename

execute One of four basic operations carried out by the control unit of a microprocessor. The execute operation involves performing a requested action, such as adding or comparing two numbers

execution cycle In a machine cycle, a phase consisting of the execute and storage write-back operations

executive information system (EIS) A system that supports management's strategic planning function

executive support system (ESS) A type of decision support system designed to provide high-level executives with information summarizing the overall performance of their organization on the most general level

Exiting Quitting or closing down an application or program

expansion board A circuit board that provides additional capabilities for a computer

expansion bus An electrical pathway that connects the microprocessor to the expansion slots. Also called I/O bus

expansion card See expansion board

expansion slot A receptacle connected to the computer's expansion bus that accepts an expansion board

expert system In artificial intelligence (AI), a program that relies on a database of if-then rules to draw inferences, in much the same way a human expert does

express card A credit-card size accessory that is typically used with notebook computers. Previous versions were known as PC cards or PCMCIA cards. Amongst other things, express cards can function as modems, network adapters, and provide additional memory or storage capacity

Extended Binary Coded Decimal Interchange Code (EBCDIC) See EBCDIC

Extensible Business Reporting Language (XBRL) Similar to XML, a language that uses standardized formatting that allows enterprises to publish and share financial information, including net revenue, annual and quarterly reports, and SEC filings, with each other and industry analysts across all computer platforms and the Internet

eXtensible Hypertext Markup Language A newer version of HTML, this language uses XML to produce Web pages that are easily accessible by devices such as PDAs, notebooks, and desktops

Extensible Markup Language (XML) A set of rules for creating markup languages that enables Web authors to capture specific types of data by creating their own elements. XML can be used in HTML documents

extension A three-letter suffix added to a DOS filename. The extension is often supplied by the application and indicates the type of application that created the file

external drive bay In a computer case, a receptacle designed for mounting storage devices that is accessible from the outside of the case

external hard drive

external modem A modem with its own case, cables, and power supply that plugs into the serial port of a computer

extranet A corporate intranet that has been opened to external access by selected outside partners, including customers, research labs, and suppliers

eye-gaze response system A biological feedback device that enables quadriplegics to control computers by moving their eyes around the screen

F

facsimile transmission (fax) The sending and receiving of printed pages between two locations, using a telephone line and fax devices that digitize the page's image

fair use An exception to copyright laws made to facilitate education, commentary, analysis, and scholarly research

Fast Ethernet An Ethernet standard for local area networks (LANs) that enables data transfer rates of 100 Mbps using twisted-pair cable; also called 100baseT

fault tolerance The ability to continue working even if one or more components fail, such as is found in a redundant array of independent disks

fax modem A modem that also functions as a fax machine, giving the computer user the capability of sending word processing documents and other files as faxes

fetch One of four basic operations carried out by the control unit of a microprocessor. The fetch operation retrieves the next program instruction from the computer's memory

fiber-optic cable A network cable made from tiny strands of glasslike material that transmit light pulses with very high efficiency and can carry massive amounts of data

fiber-optic service (FiOS) Fiberoptic lines that run directly to the home and provide users with incredibly fast Internet access, easily surpassing other methods

field In a database, an area for storing a certain type of information

field emission display (FED) A flat-panel display technology that uses tiny CRTs to produce each on-screen pixel

field name Describes the type of data that should be entered into the field

file A document or other collection of information stored on a disk and identified as a unit by a unique name

file allocation table (FAT) On older versions of Microsoft operating systems, it's a hidden on-disk table that keeps vital records concerning exactly where the various components of a given file are stored. The file allocation table is created at the conclusion of the formatting process

file compression The reduction of a file's size so that the file can be stored without taking up as much storage space and can be transferred more quickly over a computer network

file compression utility A program to reduce the size of files without harming the data

file infector A computer virus that attaches to a program file and, when that program is executed, spreads to other program files

file list The right pane in a Windows Explorer window that displays subfolders and files located within the selected folder

file management program An application that enables users to create customized databases and store in and retrieve data from those databases

file manager (Windows Explorer in Windows, File Manager in Mac OS X, and various file management utilities in Linux) A utility program that enables you to organize and manage the data stored on your disk

file menu In a graphical user interface (GUI), a pull-down menu that contains standard file-management commands, such as Save and Save As

file server In client/server computing, a computer that has been set aside (dedicated) to make program and data files available to client programs on the network

File Transfer Protocol (FTP) An Internet standard for the exchange of files between two computers connected to the Internet. With an FTP client, you can upload or download files from a computer that is running an FTP server. Normally, you need a user name and password to upload or download files from an FTP server, but some FTP servers provide a service called anonymous FTP, which enables anyone to download the files made available for public use

filename A unique name given to a stored file

filter In e-mail, a rule that specifies the destination folder of messages conforming to certain criteria

firewall A program that permits an organization's internal computer users to access the Internet but places severe limits on the ability of outsiders to access internal data

FireWire port An input-output port that combines high-speed performance (up to 400 Mbps) with the ability to guarantee data delivery at a specified speed, making the port ideal for use with real-time devices such as digital video cameras. Synonymous with 1394 port. FireWire is Apple Computer's name for 1394 port technology

fixed storage See secondary storage

flame In Usenet and e-mail, a message that contains abusive, threatening, obscene, or inflammatory language

flash drive A type of storage device that uses solid-state circuitry and has no moving parts

flash memory A special type of read-only memory (ROM) that enables users to upgrade information contained in memory chips. Also called flash BIOS

flash memory card Wafer-thin, highly portable solid state storage system that is capable of storing as much as 1 gigabyte of data. Used with some digital cameras, the card stores digitized photographs without requiring electrical power to maintain the data

flash memory reader A slot or compartment in digital cameras and other devices into which a flash memory card is inserted

flat file A type of file generated by a file management program. Flat files can be accessed in many different ways but cannot be linked to data in other files

flatbed scanner A device that copies an image (text or graphics) from one side of a sheet of paper and translates it into a digital image

flat-panel display A low-power, lightweight display used with notebook computers (and increasingly with desktop computers)

floating-point notation A method for storing and calculating numbers so that the location of the decimal point isn't fixed but floats. This allows the computer to work with very small and very large numbers

floppy disk drive A mechanism that enables a computer to read and write information on a removable medium that provides a convenient way to move data from one computer to another

flowchart In structured programming, a diagram that shows the logic of a program

folder A graphical representation of a directory. Most major operating systems display directories as though they were file folders

folder structure An organized set of primary and secondary folders within which to save your files

footprint The amount of room taken up by the case on the desk

foreground application In a multitasking operating system, the active application

Form In the Microsoft Access database management system, the object used to collect data

form factor A specification for mounting internal components, such as the motherboard

format 1. A file storage standard used to write a certain type of data to a magnetic disk (also called file format). 2. To prepare a magnetic disk for first use. 3. In word processing, to choose the alignment, emphasis, or other presentation options so that the document will print with an attractive appearance

format menu In a graphical user interface (GUI), a pull-down menu that allows you to modify such features as font style and paragraph settings

formatting The process of modifying a document's appearance so that it looks good when printed

Formatting toolbar In Microsoft Office, a default-loaded toolbar that includes icons for various functions, including choosing document font size and style

formula In a spreadsheet program, a mathematical expression embedded in a cell that can include cell references. The cell displays the formula's result

formula bar In a spreadsheet program, an area above the worksheet that displays the contents of the active cell. The formula bar enables the user to work with formulas, which normally do not appear in the cell

Fortran An early third-generation language that enabled scientists and engineers to write simple programs for solving mathematical equations

fourth-generation language (4GL) A programming language that does not force the programmer to consider the procedure that must be followed to obtain the desired result

fragmentation A process in which the various components of a file are separated by normal reading and writing operations so that these components are not stored close together. The result is slower disk operation. A defragmentation utility can improve a disk's performance by placing these file components closer together

fragmented A disk with portions of files scattered here and there

frames In a video or animation, the series of still images flashed on-screen at a rapid rate

frame rate In a video or animation, a measurement of the number of still images shown per second

freeware Copyrighted software that can be freely copied but not sold

front panel An area on the front of most computers containing various indicator lights and controls

full backup The process of copying all files from a secondary storage device (most commonly a hard disk) to a backup medium, such as a CD or DVD

function In spreadsheet programs such as Microsoft Excel, one of the two basic types of formulas (along with mathematic expressions). In a function, operations can be performed on multiple inputs

function keys A row of keys positioned along the top of the keyboard, labeled F1 through F12, to which programs can assign various commands

G

Gantt chart A bar chart that summarizes a project's schedule by showing how various activities proceed over time

GB Abbreviation for gigabyte, approximately one billion (one thousand million) bytes or characters

Gbps A data transfer rate of approximately one billion bits per second

General Public License (GPL) A freeware software license, devised by the Open Software Foundation (OSF), stipulating that a given program can be obtained, used, and even modified, as long as the user agrees to not sell the software and to make the source code for any modifications available

general-purpose application A software program used by many people to accomplish frequently performed tasks such as writing (word processing), working with numbers (spreadsheets), and keeping track of information (databases)

genetic algorithm An automated program development environment in which various alternative approaches to solving a problem are introduced; each is allowed to mutate periodically through the introduction of random changes. The various approaches compete in an effort to solve a specific problem. After a period of time, one approach may prove to be clearly superior to the others

geosynchronous orbit A circular path around the Earth in which a communications satellite, for example, has a velocity exactly matching the Earth's speed of rotation, allowing the satellite to be permanently positioned with respect to the ground

GIF (Graphics Interchange Format) A bitmapped color graphics file format capable of storing images with 256 colors. GIF incorporates a compression technique that reduces file size, making it ideal for use on a network. GIF is best used for images that have areas of solid color

GIF animation A graphics file that contains more than one image stored using the GIF graphics file format. Also stored in the file is a brief script that indicates the sequence of images, and how long to display each image

gigabit A unit of measurement approximately equal to one billion bits

Gigabit Ethernet An Ethernet local area network (LAN) that is capable of achieving data transfer rates of 1 Gbps (one billion bits per second) using fiber-optic cable

gigabit per second (Gbps) A data transfer measurement equivalent to one billion bits per second

gigabits per second points of presence (gigaPoPs) In Internet II, a high-speed testbed for the development of next-generation Internet protocols, a point of presence (PoP) that provides access to a backbone service capable of data transfer rates in excess of 1 Gbps (one billion bits per second)

gigabyte (GB) A unit of measurement commonly used to state the capacity of memory or storage devices; equal to 1,024 megabytes, or approximately one billion bytes or characters

globalization Conducting business internationally where the transaction of goods and services is transparent to the consumer

Global Positioning System (GPS) A satellite-based system that enables portable GPS receivers to determine their location with an accuracy of 100 meters or less

global unique identifier (GUID) A uniquely identifying serial number that is generated by some popular computer components and programs that can be used by Web servers to identify the computer accessing a Web site

Graphical MUD A multiuser dungeon (MUD) that uses graphics instead of text to represent the interaction of characters in a virtual environment

graphical user interface (GUI) An interface between the operating system and the user that takes advantage of the computer's graphics capabilities. Graphical user interfaces are the most popular of all user interfaces but also require the most system resources

graphics accelerator A display adapter (video card) that contains its own dedicated processing circuitry and video memory (VRAM), enabling faster display of complex graphics images

graphics file A file that stores the information needed to display a graphic. Popular graphics file formats include BMP (Windows Bitmap), JPEG, and GIF

groupware The software that provides computerized support for the information needs of individuals networked into workgroups

H

hacker Traditionally, a computer user who enjoys pushing his or her computer capabilities to the limit, especially by using clever or novel approaches to solving problems. In the press, the term *hacker* has become synonymous with criminals who attempt unauthorized access to computer systems for criminal purposes, such as sabotage or theft. The computing community considers this usage inaccurate

hacker ethic A set of moral principles common to the first-generation hacker community (roughly 1965–1982), described by Steven Levy in *Hackers* (1984). According to the hacker ethic, all technical information should, in principle, be freely available to all. Therefore, gaining entry to a system to explore data and increase knowledge is never unethical. Destroying, altering, or moving data in such a way that could cause injury or expense to others, however, is always unethical. In increasingly more states, unauthorized computer access is against the law

handheld computer See personal digital assistant

haptics A field of research in developing output devices that stimulate the sense of touch

hard copy Printed computer output, differing from the data stored on disk or in memory

hard disk A secondary storage medium that uses several rigid disks (platters) coated with a magnetically sensitive material and housed in a hermetically sealed mechanism. In almost all modern computers, the hard disk is by far the most important storage medium. Also called hard disk drive

hard disk controller An electronic circuit that provides an interface between a hard disk and the computer's CPU

hard disk drive See hard disk

hardware The physical components, such as circuit boards, disk drives, displays, and printers, that make up a computer system

head crash In a hard disk, the collision of a read/write head with the surface of the disk, generally caused by a sharp jolt to the computer's case. Head crashes can damage the read/write head, as well as create bad sectors

header In e-mail or a Usenet news article, the beginning of a message. The header contains important information about the sender's address, the subject of the message, and other information

head-mounted display (HMD) See headset

headset A wearable output device with twin LCD panels for creating the illusion that an individual is experiencing a three-dimensional, simulated environment

heat sink A heat-dissipating component that drains heat away from semiconductor devices, which can generate enough heat in the course of their operation to destroy themselves. Heat sinks are often used in combination with fans to cool semiconductor components

help menu In a graphical user interface (GUI), a pull-down menu that provides access to interactive help utilities

help screen In commercial software, information that appears on-screen that can provide assistance with using a particular program

help utilities Programs, such as a table of contents of frequently requested items, offered on most graphical user interface (GUI) applications

hexadecimal number A number that uses a base 16 number system rather than a decimal (or base 10) number system. It uses the numbers 0 through 9 and letters A through F

hierarchy chart See structure chart

High Definition Television (HDTV) The name given to several standards for digital television displays

high-level programming language A programming language that eliminates the need for programmers to understand the intimate details of how the computer processes data

history list In a Web browser, a window that shows all the Web sites that the browser has accessed during a given period, such as the last 30 days

Holographic Storage A type of storage that uses two laser beams to create a pattern on photosensitive media, resulting in a three-dimensional image, similar to the holograms you can buy in a novelty shop

home and educational programs General-purpose software programs for personal finance, home design and landscaping, encyclopedias and other computerized reference information, and games

home page 1. In any hypertext system, including the Web, a document intended to serve as an initial point of entry to a web of related documents. Also called an index page, a home page contains general introductory information, as well as hyperlinks to related resources. A well-designed home page contains internal navigation buttons that help users find their way among the various documents that the home page makes available. 2. The start page that is automatically displayed when you start a Web browser or click the program's Home button. 3. A personal page listing an individual's contact information, and favorite links, and (generally) some information—ranging from cryptic to voluminous—about the individual's perspective on life

home phone-line network A linked personal communications system that works off a home's existing phone wiring, thus being easy to install, inexpensive, and fast

home power-line network A linked personal communications system that works by connecting computers to one another through the same electrical power outlet, thus providing the convenience of not having to locate each computer in the home next to a phone jack

Home Wi-Fi networks Wireless networks in which each computer on the network broadcasts its information to another using radio signals

host name The name of the group or institution hosting a Web site

hotspot A public wireless access location:

hot swapping Connecting and disconnecting peripherals while the computer is running

hub In a local area network (LAN), a device that connects several workstations and enables them to exchange data

hybrid hard drive A drive that uses flash memory to speed up the boot process in a hard disk drive

hyperlink In a hypertext system, an underlined or otherwise emphasized word or phrase that, when clicked, displays another document

hypermedia A hypertext system that uses various multimedia resources, such as sounds, animations, and videos, as a means of navigation as well as decoration

hypermedia system A hypertext system that uses various multimedia resources, such as sounds, movies, and text, as a means of navigation as well as illustration

hypertext A method of preparing and publishing text, ideally suited to the computer, in which readers can choose their own paths through the material. To prepare hypertext, you first "chunk" the information into small, manageable units, such as single pages of text. These units are called nodes. You then embed hyperlinks in the text. When the reader clicks a hyperlink, the hypertext software displays a different node.

The process of navigating among the nodes linked in this way is called browsing. A collection of nodes interconnected by hyperlinks is called a web. The Web is a hypertext system on a global scale

Hypertext Markup Language (HTML) A language for marking the portions of a document (called elements) so that, when accessed by a program called a Web browser, each portion appears with a distinctive format. HTML is the markup language behind the appearance of documents on the Web. HTML is standardized by means of a document type definition in the Standard Generalized Markup Language (SGML). HTML includes capabilities that enable authors to insert hyperlinks, which when clicked display another HTML document. The agency responsible for standardizing HTML is the World Wide Web Consortium (W3C)

Hypertext Transfer Protocol (HTTP) The Internet standard that supports the exchange of information on the Web. By defining uniform resource locators (URLs) and how they can be used to retrieve resources anywhere on the Internet, HTTP enables Web authors to embed hyperlinks in Web documents. HTTP defines the process by which a Web client, called a browser, originates a request for information and sends it to a Web server, a program that responds to HTTP requests and provides the desired information

I

I/O bus An electrical pathway that connects the microprocessor to the expansion slots

I/O device Generic term for any input or output device

icon In a graphical user interface (GUI), a small picture that represents a program, a data file, or some other computer entity or function

identify theft A form of fraud in which a thief obtains someone's Social Security number and other personal information, and then uses this information to obtain credit fraudulently

image editor A sophisticated paint program for editing and transforming complex bitmapped images, such as photographs

image processing system A filing system in which incoming documents are scanned and stored digitally

inbox In e-mail, a default folder that contains any new mail messages, as well as older messages that have not been moved or deleted

inclusion operator In database or Web searching, a symbol or keyword that instructs the search software to make sure that any retrieved records or documents contain a certain word or phrase

incremental backup The process of copying files that have changed since the last full backup to a backup medium, such as a CD or DVD

index page See home page

information Processed data

information hiding A modular programming technique in which information inside a module remains hidden with respect to other modules

information kiosk An automated presentation system used for public information or employee training

information overload A condition of confusion, stress, and indecision brought about by being inundated with information of variable value

information processing cycle A complete sequence of operations involving data input, processing, storage, and output

information system A purposefully designed system that brings data, computers, procedures, and people together to manage information important to an organization's mission

information systems (IS) department In a complex organization, the division responsible for designing, installing, and maintaining the organization's information systems

information technology (IT) professionals Businesspeople who work with information technology in all its various forms (hardware, software, networks) and functions (management, development, maintenance)

information technology steering committee Within an organization, the group, which generally includes representatives from senior management, information systems personnel, users, and middle managers, that reviews requests for systems development and decides whether or not to move forward with a project

information warfare The use of information technology to corrupt or destroy an enemy's information and industrial infrastructure

infrared A data transmission medium that uses the same signaling technology used in TV remote controls

inheritance In object-oriented (OO) programming, the capacity of an object to pass its characteristics to subclasses

inkjet printer A nonimpact printer that forms an image by spraying ink from a matrix of tiny jets

input The information entered into a computer for processing

input device Any device that is capable of entering data into the computer for processing

input/output (I/O) bus See expansion bus

insertion point See cursor

install To set up a program so that it is ready to function on a given computer system. The installation process may involve creating additional directories, making changes to system files, and other technical tasks. For this reason, most programs come with setup programs that handle the installation process automatically

instant messaging (IM) system Software program that lets you know when a friend or business associate is online. You can then contact this person and exchange messages and attachments in real time

instruction A unique number assigned to an operation performed by a processor

instruction cycle In a machine cycle, a phase consisting of the fetch and decode operations

instruction set A list of specific instructions that a given brand and model of processor can perform

intangible benefits Gains that have no fixed dollar value, such as access to improved information or increased sales due to improved customer services

integrated circuit (IC) A semiconductor circuit containing more than one transistor and other electronic components; often referred to as a chip

integrated circuit card (ICC) See smart card

integrated program A program that combines three or more productivity software functions, including word processing, database management, and a spreadsheet

intelligent agent An automatic program that is designed to operate on the user's behalf, performing a specific function in the background. When the agent has achieved its goal, it reports to the user

Intelligent Transportation System (ITS) A system, partly funded by the U.S. government, to develop smart streets and smart cars. Such a system could warn travelers of congestion and suggest alternative routes

interactive multimedia A presentation involving two or more media, such as text, graphics, or sound, and providing users with the ability to choose their own path through the information

interface A means of connecting two dissimilar computer devices. An interface has two components, a physical component and a communications standard, called a protocol. The physical component provides the physical means for making a connection, while the protocol enables designers to design the devices so that they can exchange data with each other. The computer's standard parallel port is an example of an interface that has both a distinctive physical connector and a defining, standard protocol

internal drive bay In a computer's case, a receptacle for mounting a storage device that is not easily accessible from outside the computer's case. Internal drive bays are typically used to mount nonremovable hard drives

internal modem A modem that fits into the expansion bus of a personal computer. See also external modem

internal speaker One of the components inside a computer's system unit, typically for emitting beeps and other low-fidelity sounds

International Telecommunications Union (ITU) A branch organization of the United Nations that sets international telecommunications standards

Internet An enormous and rapidly growing system of linked computer networks, worldwide in scope, that facilitates data communication services such as remote logon, file transfer, electronic mail, the World Wide Web, and newsgroups. Relying on TCP/IP, the Internet assigns every connected computer a unique Internet address (called an IP address) so that any two connected computers can locate each other on the network and exchange data

Internet 2 The next-generation Internet, still under development

Internet address The unique, 32-bit address assigned to a computer that is connected to the Internet, represented in dotted decimal notation (for example, 128.117.38.5). Synonymous with IP address

Internet appliance A device that provides much of a personal computer's functionality but at a much lower price, connects to a network, such as the Internet, and has limited memory, disk storage, and processing power

Internet hard drive Storage space on a server that is accessible from the Internet

Internet programs General-purpose software programs for e-mailing, instant messaging, Web browsing, and videoconferencing

Internet Protocol (IP) One of the two core Internet standards (the other is the Transmission Control Protocol, TCP). IP defines the standard that describes how an Internet-connected computer should break data down into packets for transmission across the network, and how those packets should be addressed so that they arrive at their destination. IP is the connectionless part of the TCP/IP protocols

Internet Relay Chat (IRC) A real-time, Internet-based chat service, in which one can find "live" participants from the world over. IRC requires the use of an IRC client program, which displays a list of the current IRC channels. After joining a channel, you can see what other participants are typing on-screen, and you can type your own repartee

Internet service A set of communication standards (protocols) and software (clients and servers) that defines how to access and exchange a certain type of information on the Internet. Examples of Internet services are e-mail, FTP, Gopher, IRC, and Web

Internet Service Provider (ISP) A company that provides Internet accounts and connections to individuals and businesses. Most ISPs offer a range of connection options, ranging from dial-up modem connections to high-speed ISDN and ADSL. Also provided are e-mail, Usenet, and Web hosting

Internet telephony The use of the Internet (or of nonpublic networks based on Internet technology) for the transmission of real-time voice data

InterNIC A consortium of two organizations that provide networking information services to the Internet community, under contract to the National Science Foundation (NSF). Currently, AT&T provides directory and database services, while Network Solutions, Inc., provides registration services for new domain names and IP addresses

interoperability The ability to work with computers and operating systems of differing types and brands

interpreter In programming, a translator that converts each instruction into machine-readable code and executes it one line at a time. Interpreters are often used for learning and debugging, due to their slow speed

interrupt handlers Miniprograms in an operating system that kick in when an interrupt occurs

interrupt request (IRQ) Lines that handle the communication between input or output devices and the computer's CPU

interrupts Signals generated by input and output devices that inform the operating system that something has happened, such as a document has finished printing

intranet A computer network based on Internet technology (TCP/IP) that meets the internal needs of a single organization or company. Not necessarily open to the external Internet and almost certainly not accessible from the outside, an intranet enables organizations to make internal resources available using familiar Internet tools. See also extranet

IP address A 32-bit binary number that uniquely and precisely identifies the location of a particular computer on the Internet. Every computer that is directly connected to the Internet must have an IP address. Because binary numbers are so hard to read, IP addresses are given in four-part decimal numbers, each part representing 8 bits of the 32-bit address (for example, 128.143.7.226)

IrDA port A port housed on the exterior of a computer's case that is capable of sending and receiving computer data by means of infrared signals. The standards that define these signals are maintained by the Infrared Data Association (IrDA). IrDA ports are commonly found on notebook computers and personal digital assistants (PDAs)

IRQ conflict A serious system failure that results if two devices are configured to use the same IRQ but are not designed to share an IRQ line

ISDN (Integrated Services Digital Network) A worldwide standard for the delivery of digital telephone and data services to homes, schools, and offices using existing twisted-pair wiring

ISDN adapter An internal or external accessory that enables a computer to connect to remote computer networks or the Internet by means of ISDN. (Inaccurately called an digital modem.)

IT industry The industry that consists of organizations focused on the development and implementation of technology and applications

iteration control structure See repetition control structure

J

Java A cross-platform programming language created by Sun Microsystems that enables programmers to write a program that will execute on any computer capable of running a Java interpreter (which is built into today's leading Web browsers). Java is an object-oriented programming (OOP) language similar to C++, except that it eliminates some features of C++ that programmers find tedious and time-consuming. Java programs are compiled into applets (small programs executed by a browser) or applications (larger, standalone programs that require a Java interpreter to be present on the user's computer), but the compiled code contains no machine code. Instead, the output of the compiler is bytecode, an intermediary between source code and machine code that can be transmitted by computer networks, including the Internet

Java Virtual Machine (VM) A Java interpreter and runtime environment for Java applets and Java applications. This environment is called a virtual machine because, no matter what kind of computer it is running on, it creates a simulated computer that provides the correct platform for executing Java programs. In addition, this approach insulates the computer's file system from rogue applications. Java VMs are available for most computers

joint application development (JAD) In information systems development, a method of system design that involves users at all stages of system development

joystick An input device commonly used for games

JPEG (Joint Photographic Experts Group) A graphics file format, named after the group that designed it. JPEG graphics can display up to 16.7 million colors and use lossy compression to reduce file size. JPEG is best used for complex graphics such as photographs

K

KB Abbreviation for kilobyte, approximately one thousand bytes or characters

Kbps A data transfer rate of approximately one thousand bits per second

kernel The essential, core portion of the operating system that is loaded into random access memory (RAM) when the computer is turned on and stays in RAM for the duration of the operating session. Also called supervisor program

key field See primary key

key interception The act of stealing an encryption key

keyboard An input device providing a set of alphabetic, numeric, punctuation, symbolic, and control keys

keyloggers Programs that can record all the keystrokes you type, including passwords and account numbers

keyword In a command-line interface, words that tell the operating system what to do (such as "format" or "copy")

kilobits per second (Kbps) A data transfer rate of approximately one thousand bits of computer data per second

kilobyte (KB) The basic unit of measurement for computer memory and disk capacity, equal to 1,024 bytes or characters

kiosk A booth that provides a computer service of some type

know-and-have authentication A type of computer security that requires using tokens, which are handheld electronic devices that generate a logon code

knowledge base A database of represented knowledge

knowledge management system An information system that captures knowledge created by employees and makes it available to an organization

L

lands Flat reflective areas on an optical disc

laser printer A popular nonimpact, high-resolution printer that uses a version of the electrostatic reproduction technology of copying machines

last-mile problem The lack of local network systems for high-bandwidth multimedia communications that can accommodate the Information Superhighway

last-mile technologies Digital telecommunications services and standards, such as coaxial cable and ISDN, that serve as interim solutions to the limitations associated with the twisted pair analog phone wiring still common in many homes and businesses

latency In a packet-switching network, a signal delay that is introduced by the time network routers consume as they route packets to their destination

launching Starting an application program

layer In a computer network, a level of network functionality governed by specific network protocols. For example, the physical layer has protocols concerned with the transmission of signals over a specific type of cable

LCD monitors The thinner monitors used on notebooks and some desktop computers

LCD projector An output device that projects a computer's screen display on a screen similar to those used with slide projectors

leased line A permanently connected and specially conditioned telephone line that provides wide area network (WAN) connectivity to an organization or a business

left pane In the My Computer primary file management utility for PCs, one of two main default windows. It displays links to system tasks, such as viewing system information. See also right pane

legacy system A technically obsolete information system that remains in use, often because it performs its job adequately or is too expensive to replace

legacy technology Devices, such as floppy disk drives or Zip drives, that are found on older systems and are quickly becoming obsolete

level 2 (L2) cache See secondary cache

libel A form of defamation that occurs in writing

life cycle In information systems, the birth, development, use, and eventual abandonment of the system

link See hyperlink

Linux A freeware open source operating system closely resembling UNIX developed for IBM-compatible PCs but also available for other platforms, including Macintosh

liquid crystal display (LCD) A small, flat-screen monitor that uses electrical current to control tiny crystals and form an image

listserv An automatic mailing list server developed by Eric Thomas for BITNET in 1986

load To transfer program instructions from storage to memory

local area network (LAN) A computer network that connects computers in a limited geographical area (typically less than one mile) so that users can exchange information and share hardware, software, and data resources

local exchange switch A telephone system device, based on digital technology and capable of handling thousands of calls, located in the local telephone company's central office

local loop In the public switched telephone network (PSTN), the last segment of service delivery, typically consisting of analog connections from neighborhood distribution points

location (position) awareness A technology that uses GPS-enabled chips to pinpoint the location of a cell phone (and its user)

login The process of authenticating yourself as a user with a valid account and usage privileges on a multiuser computer system or a computer network. To login, you supply your user name and password

logic bomb A flaw concealed in an otherwise usable computer program that can be triggered to destroy or corrupt data. See time bomb

logic error In programming, a mistake made by the programmer in designing the program. Logic errors will not surface by themselves during program execution because they are not errors in the structure of the statements and commands

logical data type A data type that allows only a yes or no answer

logical operations One of two groups of operations performed by the arithmetic-logic unit (ALU). The logical operations involve such operations as comparing two data items to see which one is larger or smaller

looping See repetition control structure

lossless compression In data compression, a method used to reduce the size of a file that enables the file to be restored to its original size without introducing errors. Most lossless compression techniques reduce file size by replacing lengthy but frequently occurring data sequences with short codes; to decompress the file, the compression software reverses this process and restores the lengthy data sequences to their original form

lossy compression In data compression, a method of reducing the size of multimedia files by eliminating information that is not normally perceived by human beings

low-level language One step up from machine language, a language using more than just numbers. Assembly language, a low-level language, uses basic structures and commands to tell the CPU what to do

M

MB Abbreviation for megabyte, approximately one million bytes or characters of information

Mac OS Operating system and user interface developed by Apple Computer for

Macintosh computers; introduced the first graphical user interface

machine cycle A four-step process followed by the control unit that involves the fetch, decode, execute, and write-back operations. Also called processing cycle

machine dependent The dependence of a given computer program or component on a specific brand or type of computer equipment

machine language The native binary language consisting of 0s and 1s that is recognized and executed by a computer's central processing unit

machine translation Language translation performed by the computer without human aid

macro In application software, a user-defined command sequence that can be saved and executed to perform a complex action

macro virus A computer virus that uses the automatic command execution capabilities of productivity software to spread itself and often to cause harm to computer data

magnetic storage device In computer storage systems, any storage device that retains data using a magnetically sensitive material, such as the magnetic coating found on floppy disks or the platters of the hard drive

mainframe A multiuser computer system that meets the computing needs of a large organization

maintenance release A minor revision to a software program, indicated by the decimal in the version number, that corrects bugs or adds minor features

malware Short for *malicious software*, it describes software designed to damage or infiltrate a computer system without the owner's consent or knowledge

management information system (MIS) 1. A computer-based system that supports the information needs of management. 2. Typically found in a business school, a department focusing on the practical application of information systems and technology in businesses

markup language In text processing, a system of codes for marking the format of a unit of text that indicates only that a particular unit of text is a certain part of the document, such as an abstract, a title, or an author's name and affiliation. The actual formatting of the document part is left to another program, called a viewer, which displays the marked document and gives each document part a distinctive format (fonts, spacing, and so on). HTML is a markup language

mass storage See storage

massively multiplayer online role-playing game (MMORPG) An online game that permits increasingly larger numbers of players to interact with one another in virtual worlds. These virtual worlds are often hosted and maintained by the software publisher, unlike other environments that end when the game is over

math coprocessor A separate chip that frees the main processor from performing

mathematical operations, usually operations involving floating-point notation

mathematic formula In spreadsheet programs such as Microsoft Excel, one of the two basic types of formulas (along with functions). In a mathematic formula, or expression, the mathematic order of operation is followed

maximize To enlarge a window so that it fits the entire screen

mechanical mouse A type of mouse that uses a rotating ball to generate information about the mouse's position

megabits per second (Mbps) In networking, a data transfer rate of approximately one million bits per second

megabyte (MB) A measurement of storage capacity equal to 1,024 kilobytes, or approximately one million bytes or characters

megapixel Type of digital camera that has a charge-coupled device with at least one million elements

memo In databases, a data type used for large units of text

memory Circuitry that stores information temporarily so that it is readily available to the central processing unit (CPU)

memory address A code number that specifies a specific location in memory

memory shaving A type of computer crime in which knowledgeable thieves remove some of a computer's RAM chips but leave enough to start the computers

menu The list of words, such as file, edit, and view, signifying categories of tasks that can be accomplished within an application

menu bar In a graphical user interface (GUI), a rectangular bar (generally positioned near the top of the application window) that provides access to pull-down menus. On the Macintosh, an active application's menu bar is always positioned at the top of the screen

menu-driven user interface An interface between the operating system and the user in which text-based menus show options, rather than requiring the user to memorize the commands and type them in

Metcalfe's Law A prediction formulated by Bob Metcalfe, creator of Ethernet, that the value of a network increases in proportion to the square of the number of people connected to the network

method In object-oriented programming, a procedure or operation that processes or manipulates data

microcomputer A computer that uses a microprocessor as its CPU

microphone An input device that converts sound into electrical signals that can be processed by a computer

microprocessor See central processing unit (CPU)

Microsoft Windows Generic name for the various operating systems in the Microsoft Windows family, including, but not limited to, Microsoft Windows 2000/ME, Microsoft Windows XP, and Microsoft Windows Vista. Microsoft Windows 98, and Microsoft Windows NT

Microsoft Windows Mobile A user interface designed for smartphones and PDAs

Microsoft Windows Server An operating systems designed to support client/server computing systems. The current version is 2008

Microsoft Windows Vista The latest version of Microsoft's operating systems, it replaced the Windows XP. It's designed for home and professional use. Vista is available in five different versions—Basic, Home Premium, Business, Ultimate, and Enterprise. Vista features a new interface called Windows Aero (unavailable in the Basic version) that features translucent windows, three-dimensional animation, and live taskbar thumbnails

microwave An electromagnetic radio wave with a very short frequency

middleware In object-oriented programming, standards that define how programs find objects and determine what kind of information they contain

MIDI (Musical Instrument Digital Interface) A standard that specifies how musical sounds can be described in text files so that a MIDI-compatible synthesizer can reproduce the sounds. MIDI files are small, so they're often used to provide music that starts playing automatically when a Web page is accessed. To hear MIDI sounds, your computer needs a sound card. MIDI sounds best with wavetable synthesis sound cards, which include sound samples from real musical instruments

minicomputer (mid-range servers) A multiuser computer that meets the needs of a small organization or a department in a large organization

minimize To reduce the size of a window so that it appears only as an icon or an item on the taskbar

minitower case A smaller version of a system unit case designed to sit on the floor next to a desk

mnemonic In programming, an abbreviation or a word that makes it easier to remember a complex instruction

mobile switching center (MSC) The part of a cellular network that handles communications within a group of cells. Each cell tower reports signal strength to the MSC, which then switches your signal to whatever cell tower will provide the clearest connection for your conversation

mobile telephone switching office (MTSO) In a cellular telephone system, the switching office that connects all of the individual cell towers to the central office and the public switched telephone network

modeling (what-if analysis) A method by which spreadsheet programs are able to predict future outcomes

modem Short for modulator/demodulator, a communications device that enables the computer to access the Internet via telephone lines, cable, satellite, and even wireless connections by converting digital signals to analog, and vice versa. The speed at which a modem transmits data is measured in units called bits per second, or bps

modifier keys Keys that are pressed to modify the meaning of the next key that's pressed

modular programming A programming style that breaks down program functions into modules, each of which accomplishes one function and contains all the source code and variables needed to accomplish that function

modulation protocol In modems, the communications standard that governs how the modem translates between the computer's digital signals and the analog tones used to convey computer data over the Internet. Modulation protocols are defined by ITU standards

module A part of a software program; independently developed modules are combined to compile the final program

monitor A television-like device that produces an on-screen image

Moore's Law A prediction by Intel Corp. cofounder Gordon Moore that integrated circuit technology advancements would enable the semiconductor industry to double the number of components on a chip every 18 to 24 months

motherboard A large circuit board containing the computer's central processing unit, support chips, random access memory, and expansion slots

mouse A palm-sized input device, with a ball built into the bottom, that is used to move a pointer on-screen to draw, select options from a menu, modify or move text, and issue commands

MPEG (Moving Pictures Experts Group) A set of standards for audio and video file formats and lossless compression, named after the group that created it

MPEG Audio Layer 3 (MP3) A sound compression standard that can store a single song from an audio CD in a 3M file. MP3 files are easily shared over the Internet and are costing recording companies billions of dollars in lost royalties due to piracy

MS-DOS An operating system for IBM-compatible PCs that uses a command-line user interface

multifunction devices Machines that combine printing, scanning, faxing, and copying

multimedia operating systems The presentation of information using graphics, video, sound, animation, and text

multimedia and graphics software General-purpose software programs for professional desktop publishing, image editing, three-dimensional rendering, and video editing

multiplexing A technique that enables more than one signal to be conveyed on a physical transmission medium

multitasking In operating systems, the capability to execute more than one application at a time. Multitasking shouldn't be confused with multiple program loading, in which two or more applications are present in random access memory (RAM) but only one executes at a time

multiuser dungeon (MUD) A text-based environment in which multiple players can assume online personas and interact with each other by means of text chatting

N

nanotechnology Manipulating materials on an atomic or molecular scale in order to build microscopic devices

native application A program that runs on a particular brand and model of processor or in a particular operating system

natural language A human language, such as English or Japanese

navigation pane The left pane in a Windows explorer window that allows you to navigate directly to specific folders listed in the Favorite Links area or access a prior search that you have saved by clicking on a desired folder

nest In structured programming, to embed one control structure inside another

nesting Using parentheses in a Boolean search to embed expressions. The search engine evaluates the expression from left to right and searches for the content within the parentheses first. It then uses the other keywords and operators to search these results and provide the final results

netiquette Short for network etiquette. A set of rules that reflect long-standing experience about getting along harmoniously in the electronic environment (e-mail and newsgroups)

network A group of two or more computer systems linked together to enable communications by exchanging data and sharing resources

network access point (NAP) A special communications device that sends and receives data between computers that contain wireless adapters

network administrator Computer professionals who install, maintain, and support computer networks, interact with users, handle security, and troubleshoot problems. Sometimes called network engineers

network architecture The overall design of a computer network that specifies its functionality at every level by means of protocols

network attached storage (NAS) devices High-performance devices that provide shared data to clients and other servers on a local area network

network computer (NC) A computer that provides much of a PC's functionality at a lower price. Network computers don't have disk drives because they get their software from the computer network

network engineer See network administrator

network interface card (NIC) An adapter that enables a user to connect a network cable to a computer

network layers Separate divisions within a network architecture with specific functions and protocols, allowing engineers to make changes within a layer without having to redesign the entire network

network operating system (NOS) The software needed to enable data transfer and application usage over a network

network topology The physical layout of a local area network (LAN), such as a bus, star, or ring topology, that determines what happens when, for example, two workstations try to access the LAN or transmit data simultaneously

neural network In artificial intelligence, a computer architecture that attempts to mimic the structure of the human brain. Neural nets "learn" by trial and error and are good at recognizing patterns and dealing with complexity

newsgroup In Usenet, a discussion group devoted to a single topic. Users post messages to the group, and those reading the discussion send reply messages to the author individually or post replies that can be read by the group as a whole

new technology file system (NTFS) On newer versions of Microsoft operation systems, it's a table that keeps vital records concerning exactly where the various components of a given file are stored. The NTFS is created at the conclusion of the formatting process

node In a LAN, a connection point that can create, receive, or repeat a message

nonprocedural Not tied down to step-by-step procedures. In programming, a nonprocedural programming language does not force the programmer to consider the procedure that must be followed to obtain the desired result

nonvolatile With respect to memory, ROM or read-only memory that is permanent and unchanging

notebook computer A portable computer that is small enough to fit into an average-size briefcase but includes nearly all peripherals commonly found on desktop computers

numeric check Ensures that numbers are entered into a field

O

object 1. In object-oriented programming (OOP), a unit of computer information that contains data and all the procedures or operations that can process or manipulate the data. 2. Nontextual data. Examples of objects include pictures, sounds, or videos

object code In programming, the machine-readable instructions created by a compiler from source code

object-oriented database The newest type of database structure, well suited for multimedia applications, in which the result of a retrieval operation is an object of some kind, such as a document. Within this object are miniprograms that enable the object to perform tasks such as displaying graphics. Object-oriented databases can incorporate sound, video, text, and graphics into a single database record

object-oriented (OO) programming A type of database that creates generic building blocks of a program (the objects). The user then assembles different sets of objects as needed to solve specific problems. Also called OOP, for object-oriented programming

Office button The button at the top left of a Microsoft Office application. It contains choices for creating new documents; opening existing documents; and printing, saving, and closing documents of the Office button

Office Clipboard In Microsoft Office, a feature that temporarily stores in memory whatever has been cut or copied from a document, allowing for those items to be used within any Office application

office suite See software suite

offshoring The transfer of labor from workers in one country to workers in other countries

off-the-shelf software See packaged software

on-board video Video circuitry that comes built into a computer's motherboard

online Directly connected to the network

online analytical processing (OLAP) In a decision support system (DSS), a method of providing rich, up-to-the-minute data from transaction databases

online banking The use of a Web browser to access bank accounts, balance checkbooks, transfer funds, and pay bills

online processing The processing of data immediately after it has been input by a user, as opposed to waiting until a predetermined time, as in batch processing

online service A for-profit firm that makes current news, stock quotes, and other information available to its subscribers over standard telephone lines. Popular services include supervised chat rooms for text chatting and forums for topical discussion. Online services also provide Internet access

online stock trading The purchase or sale of stock through the Internet

online storage See secondary storage

online travel reservations A rapidly growing area of e-commerce that allows consumers to use the Internet to research, book, and purchase airline flights, hotel rooms, and rental cars

open To transfer an existing document from storage to memory

open source software Software in which the source code is made available to the program's users

operating system (OS) A program that integrates and controls the computer's internal functions and provides a user interface

operational decisions Management decisions concerning localized issues (such as an inventory shortage) that need immediate action

operational support system (OSS) A suite of programs that supports an enterprise's network operations

operational system See transaction processing system

operational feasibility Capable of being accomplished with an organization's available resources

optical character recognition (OCR) Software that automatically decodes imaged text into a text file. Most scanners come with OCR software

optical mark reader (OMR) A reader that senses magnetized marks made by the magnetic particles in lead from a pencil

optical storage A storage system in which a storage device retains data using surface patterns that are physically encoded on the surface of plastic discs. The patterns can be detected by a laser beam

optical storage device A computer storage device that retains data in microscopic patterns, detectable by a laser beam, encoded on the surface of plastic discs

options Choices within an application that allow users to change defaults and to specify how they want the program to operate

output The results of processing information, typically shown on a monitor or a printer

output devices Monitors, printers, and other machines that enable people to see, hear, and even feel the results of processing operations

outsourcing The transfer of a project to an external contractor

P

packaged software Ready-to-use software that is sold through mass-market channels and contains features useful to the largest possible user base. Synonymous with off-the-shelf software and shrink-wrapped software

packet In a packet-switching network, a unit of data of a fixed size—not exceeding the network's maximum transmission unit (MTU) size—that has been prepared for network transmission. Each packet contains a header that indicates its origin and its destination. See also packet switching

packet sniffer In computer security, a device that examines all traffic on a network and retrieves valuable information such as passwords and credit card numbers

packet switching One of two fundamental architectures for a wide area network (WAN); the other is a circuit-switching network. In a packet-switching network such as the Internet, no effort is made to establish a single electrical circuit between two computing devices; for this reason, packet-switching networks are often called connectionless. Instead, the sending computer divides a message into packets, each of which contains the address of the destination computer, and dumps them onto the network. They are intercepted by devices called routers, which send the packets in the appropriate direction. The receiving computer assembles the packets, puts them in order, and delivers the received message to the appropriate application. Packet-switching networks are highly reliable and efficient, but they are not suited to the delivery of real-time voice and video

page In virtual memory, a fixed size of program instructions and data that can be stored on the hard disk to free up random access memory

page description language (PDL) A programming language capable of precisely describing the appearance of a printed page, including fonts and graphics

paging An operating system's transference of files from storage to memory and back

paint program A program that enables the user to paint the screen by specifying the color of the individual pixels that make up the screen display

parallel conversion In the development of an information system, the operation of both the new and old information systems at the same time to ensure the compatibility and reliability of the new system

parallel port An interface that uses several side-by-side wires so that one or more bytes of computer data can travel in unison and arrive simultaneously. Parallel ports offer faster performance than serial ports, in which each bit of data must travel in a line, one after the other. Considered legacy technology

parallel processing The use of more than one processor to run two or more portions of a program simultaneously

partition A section of a storage device, such as a hard disk, that is prepared so that it can be treated as if it were a completely separate device for data storage and maintenance

Pascal A high-level programming language that encourages programmers to write well-structured programs, named after seventeenth-century mathematician Blaise Pascal

passive matrix LCD An inexpensive liquid crystal display (LCD) that sometimes generates image flaws and is too slow for full-motion video. Also called dual scan LCD

password A unique word that a user types to log on to a system. Passwords should not be obvious and should be changed frequently

password guessing In computer security, a method of defeating password authentication by guessing common passwords, such as personal names, obscene words, and the word "password."

path The sequence of directories that the computer must follow to locate a file

pattern recognition In artificial intelligence, the use of a computer system to recognize patterns, such as thumbprints, and associate these patterns with stored data or instructions

PC 100 SDRAM A type of SDRAM capable of keeping up with motherboards that have bus speeds of 100 MHz

PC card Synonymous with PCMCIA card. A computer accessory (such as a modem or network interface card) that is designed to fit into a compatible PC card slot mounted on the computer's case. PC cards and slots are commonly used on notebook computers because they offer system expandability while consuming a small fraction of the space required for expansion cards

peer-to-peer network (P2P) A computer network design in which all the computers can access the public files located on other computers in a network

performance How fast a computer can obtain, process, display, and store data

peripheral A device connected to and controlled by a computer, but external to the computer's central processing unit

PCI (Peripheral Component Interconnect) bus A type of expansion bus used with Macs and PCs to communicate with input and output devices, containing expansion slots to accommodate plug-in expansion cards

PCI Express A faster interface than AGP used to support high-speed, high-resolution graphics, including 3-D graphic

Personal Area Network (PAN) Also known as a piconet, it's a network that enables all kinds of devices—desktop computers, mobile phones, printers, pagers, PDAs, and more—within 30 feet of each other to communicate

Personal Communication Service (PCS) A digital cellular phone service that is rapidly replacing analog cellular phones. Also referred to as 2G technology

personal computer (PC) A computer system that meets the computing needs of an individual. The term PC usually refers to an IBM-compatible personal computer

Personal Computer Memory Card International Association (PCMCIA) card See PC card

personal computing Any situation or setup where one person controls and uses a PC for personal or business activities

personal digital assistant (PDA) A small, handheld computer that accepts input written on-screen with a stylus. Most include built-in software for appointments, scheduling, and e-mail

personal firewall A program or device that is designed to protect home computer users from unauthorized access

personal information manager (PIM) A program that stores and retrieves a variety of personal information, such as appointments. PIMs have been slow to gain acceptance due to their lack of convenience and portability

personal productivity program Application software, such as word processing software or a spreadsheet program, that assists individuals in doing their work more effectively and efficiently

phased conversion In the development of an information system, the implementation of the new system in different time periods, one part at a time

phishing Posing as a legitimate company in an e-mail or on a Web site in an attempt to learn personal information such as your Social Security number, user name, password, and account numbers

photo checkout systems Used with POS terminals, a security check that accesses a database of customer photos and displays the customer's picture when a credit card is used

photo-editing program A program that enables images to be enhanced, edited, cropped, or sized. The same program can be used to print the images on a color printer

photo printer A printer with six or more ink colors used to print photos with high quality results. Typically an inkjet printer

phrase searching In database and Web searching, a search that retrieves only documents that contain the entire phrase

piconet See Personal Area Network (PAN)

picture messaging A mobile service that allows you to send full-color pictures, backgrounds, and even picture caller IDs on your cell phone

pilot conversion In the development of an information system, the institution of the new system in only one part of an organization. When that portion of the organization is satisfied with the system, the rest of the organization then starts using it

pipelining A processing technique that feeds a new instruction to the CPU at every step of the processing cycle, so that four or more instructions are processed simultaneously

pit A microscopic indentation in the surface of an optical disc that absorbs the light of the optical drive's laser, corresponding to a 0 in the computer's binary number system

pixel Short for picture element, the smallest element that a device can display and out of which the displayed image is constructed

plagiarism The presentation of somebody else's work as if it were one's own

Plain Old Telephone Service (POTS) A term used to describe the standard analog telephone service

plaintext A readable message before it is encrypted

platform A distinct type of computer that uses a certain type of processor and operating system, such as a Macintosh or an Intel-based Windows PC

platter In a hard drive, a fixed, rapidly rotating disk that is coated with a magnetically sensitive material. High-capacity hard drives typically have two or more platters

plotter A printer that produces high-quality output by moving ink pens over the surface of the paper

Plug-and-Play (PnP) A set of standards that enables users of Microsoft Windows–based PCs to configure new hardware devices automatically. Operating systems equipped with plug-and-play capabilities can automatically detect new PnP-compatible peripherals that may have been installed while the power was switched off

Plug-in Softwares Programs that allow you to derive the full benefits of a Web site, such as sound or video

podslurping An activity in which employees easily copy sensitive data to USB drives, iPods, or other small storage devices

point of presence (PoP) A locality in which it is possible to obtain dialup access to the network by means of a local telephone call. Internet service providers (ISPs) provide PoPs in towns and cities, but many rural areas are without local PoPs

point-and-shoot digital cameras Digital cameras that typically include automatic focus, automatic exposure, built-in automatic electronic flash with red eye reduction, and optical zoom lenses with digital enhancement

point-of-sale (POS) terminal A computer-based cash register that enables transaction data to be captured at the checkout stand. Such terminals can automatically adjust inventory databases and enable managers to analyze sales patterns

pointer An on-screen symbol, usually an arrow, that shows the current position of the mouse

pointing device Any input device that is capable of moving the on-screen pointer in a graphical user interface (GUI), such as a mouse or trackball

pointing stick A pointing device introduced by IBM that enables users to move the pointer around the screen by manipulating a small, stubby stick that protrudes slightly from the surface of the keyboard

popup menu A menu that appears at the mouse pointer's position when you click the right mouse button

port An interface that controls the flow of data between the central processing unit and external devices such as printers and monitors

Portable Network Graphics (PNG) A graphics file format closely resembling the GIF format but lacking GIF's proprietary compression technique (which forces publishers of GIF-enabled graphics software to pay a licensing fee)

Portable Storage A type of storage that is small in size, is easy to carry around and use, and can be easily plugged into any computer

portal On the Web, a page that attempts to provide an attractive starting point for Web sessions. Typically included are links to breaking news, weather forecasts, stock quotes, free e-mail service, sports scores, and a subject guide to information available on the Web. Leading portals include AOL (www.aol.com), Yahoo! (www.yahoo.com), and Snap! (www.snap.com)

positioning performance A measure of how much time elapses from the initiation of drive activity until the hard disk has positioned the read/write head so that it can begin transferring data

post-implementation system review In the development of an information system, the ongoing evaluation of the information system to determine whether it has met its goals

power-on light A light on the front panel of most computers that signals whether the power is on

power-on self test (POST) The series of system integrity tests that a computer goes through every time it is started (cold boot) or restarted (warm boot). These tests verify that vital system components, such as the memory, are functioning properly

power supply A device that supplies power to a computer system by converting AC current to DC current and lowering the voltage

power surge A sudden and sometimes destructive increase in the amount of voltage delivered through a power line

power switch A switch that turns the computer on and off. Often located on the front of a computer

preemptive multitasking In operating systems, a method of running more than one application at a time. Unlike cooperative multitasking, preemptive multitasking allows other applications to continue running if one application crashes

presentation graphics A software package used to make presentations visually attractive and easy to understand

primary cache A small unit (8 KB to 32 KB) of ultra-fast memory included with a microprocessor and used to store frequently accessed data and improve overall system performance

printed circuit board A flat piece of plastic or fiberglass on which complex patterns of copper pathways have been created by means of etching. These paths link integrated circuits and other electrical components

printer An output device that prints computer-generated text or graphics onto paper or another physical medium

privacy The right to live your life without undue intrusions into your personal affairs by government agencies or corporate marketers

private key A decryption key

problem A state of difficulty that needs to be resolved; the underlying cause of a symptom

procedural language A programming language that tells the computer what to do and how to do it

procedure The steps that must be followed to accomplish a specific computer-related task

processing The execution of arithmetic or comparison operations on data to data into information

processing cycle See machine cycle

processor See central processing unit (CPU)

professional organizations (associations) IT organizations that can help you keep up with your area of interest as well as provide valuable career contacts

professional workstation A very powerful computer system for engineers, financial analysts, and other professionals who need exceptionally powerful processing and output capabilities. Professional workstations are very expensive

profile In a consumer-oriented operating system, such as Windows 98, a record of a user's preferences that is associated with a user name and password. If you set up two or more profiles, users see their own preferences. However, profiles do not prevent users from accessing and overwriting each others' files

program A list of instructions telling the computer what to do

program development life cycle (PDLC) A step-by-step procedure used to develop software for information systems

program maintenance In phase 6 of the PDLC, the process in which the programming team fixes program errors discovered by users

program specification In software development, a technical description of the software needed by the information system.

The program specification precisely defines input data, the processing that occurs, the output format, and the user interface

programmer A person skilled in the use of one or more programming languages. Although most programmers have college degrees in computer science, certification is an increasingly popular way to demonstrate one's programming expertise

programming The process used to create the software applications you use every day

programming language An artificial language composed of a fixed vocabulary and a set of rules used to create instructions for a computer to follow

project dictionary In the development of information systems, a compilation of all terminology relevant to the project

project notebook In the development of an information system, a place where documentation of information regarding system development is stored

project plan A specification of the goals, scope, and individual activities that make up a project

project proposal In phase 1 of the SDLC, a document that introduces the nature of the existing system's problem, explains the proposed solution and its benefits, details the proposed project plan, and concludes with a recommendation

protocol In data communications and networking, a standard specifying the format of data and the rules to be followed. Networks could not be easily or efficiently designed or maintained without protocols; a protocol specifies how a program should prepare data so that it can be sent to the next stage in the communication process. For example, e-mail programs prepare messages so that they conform to prevailing Internet mail standards, which are recognized by every program involved in the transmission of mail over the network

protocol stack In a computer network, a means of conceptualizing network architecture in which the various layers of network functionality are viewed as a vertical stack, like the layers of a layer cake, in computers linked to the network. When one computer sends a message to the network, the message goes down the stack and then traverses the network; on the receiving computer, the message goes up the stack

protocol suite In a computer network, the collection of network protocols that defines the network's functionality

prototyping In information systems development, the creation of a working system model that is functional enough to draw feedback from users. Also called joint application development (RAD)

PS/2 port A type of port that was typically used for mice and keyboards but was not interchangeable. Only one of these ports could be used by each device, and these ports were often color coded to prevent users from plugging in the wrong device. Considered legacy technology

pseudocode In structured programming, a stylized form of writing used as an alternative to flowcharts to describe the logic of a program

public domain software Noncopyrighted software that anyone may copy and use without charge and without acknowledging the source

public key In public key cryptography, the encoding key, which you make public so that others can send you encrypted messages. The message can be encoded with the public key, but it cannot be decoded without the private key, which you alone possess

public key cryptography In cryptography, a revolutionary new method of encryption that does not require the message's receiver to have received the decoding key in a separate transmission. The need to send the key, required to decode the message, is the chief vulnerability of previous encryption techniques. Public key cryptography has two keys: a public one and a private one. The public key is used for encryption, and the private key is used for decryption

public key encryption A computer security process in which an encryption (or private) key and a decryption (or public) key are used to safeguard data

public key infrastructure (PKI) A uniform set of encryption standards that specify how public key encryption, digital signatures, and digital certificates should be implemented in computer systems and on the Internet

public switched telephone network (PSTN) The world telephone system, a massive network used for data communication as well as voice

pull-down menu In a graphical user interface (GUI), a named item on the menu bar that, when clicked, displays an on-screen menu of commands and options

pumping and dumping An illegal stock price manipulation tactic that involves purchasing shares of a worthless corporation and then driving the price up by making unsubstantiated claims about the company's value in Internet newsgroups and chat rooms. The perpetrator sells the shares after the stock price goes up but before other investors wise up to the ploy

Q

query In the Microsoft Access database management system, the object used to ask questions of the database

query language A retrieval and data-editing language for composing simple or complex requests for data

Quick Access Toolbar A toolbar in Microsoft Office that appears just to the right of the Office button. It displays a series of buttons used to perform common tasks, such as saving a document and undoing or redoing the last action. The Quick Access Toolbar is customizable, so you can add some of your favorite shortcuts to it

quoted size The front surface measured diagonally on a cathode-ray tube monitor, a figure that is greater than the viewable area, since some of the surface is hidden and unavailable for display purposes

QWERTY keyboard A keyboard that uses the standard keyboard layout in which the first six letters on the left of the top row spell "QWERTY."

R

radio A wireless signaling technology that sends data by means of electromagnetic waves that travel through air and space between separate or combined transmitting and receiving devices

radio frequency Identification Device (RFID) A device that uses radio waves to track a chip or tag placed in or on an object

RAID (redundant array of independent disks) A storage device that groups two or more hard disks containing exactly the same data

Rambus DRAM Type of RAM that uses a narrow but very fast bus to connect to the microprocessor

random access An information storage and retrieval technique in which the computer can access information directly, without having to go through a sequence of locations

random access memory (RAM) Another name for the computer's main working memory, where program instructions and data are stored to be easily accessed by the central processing unit through the processor's high-speed data bus. When a computer is turned off, all data in RAM is lost

random access storage device A storage device that can begin reading data directly without having to go through a lengthy sequence of data

range check Verifies that the entered data falls within an acceptable range

rapid application development (RAD) In object-oriented programming, a method of program development in which a small-scale mock-up, or prototype, of the system is developed and shown to users

raster graphics See bitmapped graphics

ray tracing A 3-D rendering technique in which color intensity on a graphic object is varied to simulate light falling on the object from multiple directions

read To retrieve data or program instructions from a storage device such as a hard or floppy disk

read/write The capability of a primary or secondary storage device to record (write) data and to play back (read) data previously recorded or saved

read/write head In a hard or floppy disk, the magnetic recording and playback device that travels back and forth across the surface of the disk, storing and retrieving data

read-only Capable of being displayed or used but not altered or deleted

read-only memory (ROM) The part of a computer's primary storage that contains essential computer instructions and doesn't lose its contents when the power is turned off. Information in read-only memory cannot be erased by the computer

record In a database, a group of one or more fields that contains information about something

refresh rate The frequency with which the screen is updated. The refresh rate determines whether the display appears to flicker

register 1. In a microprocessor, a memory location used to store values and external

memory addresses while the microprocessor performs logical and arithmetic operations on them. 2. In commercial software and shareware, to contact the software vendor and submit a form that includes personal information such as the user's name and address. Registering allows the software vendor to inform the user of important information and software updates

registration fee An amount of money that must be paid to the author of a piece of shareware to continue using it beyond the duration of the evaluation period

registry 1. A database that contains information about installed peripherals and software. 2. In Microsoft Windows, an important system file that contains configuration settings that Windows requires in order to operate

relational database management system (RDBMS) A type of database software that uses the contents of a particular field as an index to reference particular records

remote storage Sometimes referred to as an Internet hard drive, this is a type of storage space on a server that is accessible from the Internet

removable storage See portable storage

repetition control structure In structured programming, a logical construction of commands repeated over and over. Also called looping or iteration control structure

Report In the Microsoft Access database management system, the object used to present data

report generator In programming, a programming language for printing database reports. One of four parts of a database management system (DBMS) that helps the user design and generate reports and graphs in hard copy form

request for proposal (RFP) In the development of information systems, a request to an outside vendor to write a proposal for the design, installation, and configuration of an information system

request for quotation (RFQ) In the development of information systems, a request to an outside vendor or value-added reseller (VAR) to quote a price for specific information components

requirements analysis A process in phase 1 of the SDLC that determines the requirements of the system by analyzing how the system will meet the needs of end users

reset switch A switch on the front panel of most computers that can restart the computer in the event of a failure

resolution A measurement, usually expressed in linear dots per inch (dpi) both horizontally and vertically, of the sharpness of an image generated by an output device such as a monitor or a printer

restore To return a window to its size and position before it was maximized

return on investment (ROI) The overall financial yield of a project at the end of its lifetime. ROI is often used by managers to decide whether a project is a good investment

right pane In the My Computer primary file management utility for PCs, one of two main default windows. It displays the various files and drives you can choose from. See also left pane

ring topology The physical layout of a local network in which all nodes are attached in a circle, without a central host computer

robot A computer-based device that is programmed to perform useful motions

robotics A division of computer science that is devoted to improving the performance and capabilities of robots

router In a packet-switching network such as the Internet, one of two basic devices (the other is a host). A router is an electronic device that examines each packet of data it receives and then decides which way to send it toward its destination

routine A section of code that executes a specific task in a program. Also referred to as procedure, function, or subroutine.

row In a spreadsheet, a block of cells going across the screen

S

safe mode An operating mode in which Windows loads a minimal set of drivers that are known to function correctly

salami shaving A computer crime in which a program is altered so that it transfers a small amount of money from a large number of accounts to make a large profit

sales force automation (SFA) Enterprise Software that automates many of the business processes involved with sales, including processing and tracking orders, managing customers and other contacts, monitoring and controlling inventory, and analyzing sales forecasts

satellite In data communications, a communications reflector placed in a geosynchronous (stationary) orbit

satellite radio A type of communications technology that broadcasts radio signals back and forth between satellites orbiting more than 22,000 miles above the Earth and radio receivers on Earth

save To transfer data from the computer's memory to a storage device for safekeeping

save as A command that enables the user to store a document with a new name or to a new location

saving In an application software program, the process of transferring a document from the computer's temporary memory to a permanent storage device, such as a hard disk, for safekeeping

scalability

A hardware or software system's ability to continue functioning effectively as demands and use increase

scanner A device that copies the image (text or graphic) on a sheet of paper and translates it into a digital image. Scanners use charge-coupled devices to digitize the image

script A short program written in a scripting language to control any action or feedback on a Web site

scripting language A simple Web-based programming language that enables users to create useful programs (scripts) quickly. VBScript is one example of a scripting language

scroll To bring hidden parts of a document into view within the application workspace

scroll arrow An arrow appearing within the scroll bar that enables the user to scroll up or down (or, in a horizontal scroll bar, left and right) by small increments

scroll bar A vertical or horizontal bar that contains scroll arrows and a scroll box. The scroll bar enables the user to bring hidden portions of a document into view within the application workspace

search box A box in a Windows Explorer window that allows you to find files. Select one of the main folders, such as Documents and begin typing a search term in the box. As you type, Windows Explorer searches the contents of the folder and subfolders, immediately filtering the view to display any files that match the search term

search engine Any program that locates needed information in a database, but especially an Internet-accessible search service (such as Yahoo!, AltaVista or Google) that enables you to search for information on the Internet

search operator In a database or a Web search engine, a word or a symbol that enables you to specify your search with precision

search utility A utility program which enables you to search an entire hard disk for a file (in Microsoft Windows it is called the Instant Search in Mac OS it is called Spotlight)

secondary cache A small unit (256 K to 1 MB) of ultra-fast memory used to store frequently accessed data and improve overall system performance. The secondary cache is usually located on a separate circuit board from the microprocessor, although backside cache memory is located on the processor. Also called level 2 (L2) cache

secondary storage Also called online or fixed storage, it consists of the storage devices that are actively available to the computer system and that do not require any action on the part of the user

sector A pie-shaped wedge of the concentric tracks encoded on a disk during formatting. Two or more sectors combine to form a cluster

secure electronic transfer (SET) An online shopping security standard for merchants and customers that uses digital certificates

secure mode In a Web browser, a mode of operation in which all communication to and from the server is encrypted

seek time In a secondary storage device, the time it takes for the read/write head to reach the correct location on the disk. Seek times are often used with rotational speed to compare the performance of hard drives

selection control structure In structured programming, a method of handling a program branch by using an IF-THEN-ELSE structure. This is more efficient than using a GOTO statement. Also called conditional or branch control structure

sequence control structure In structured programming, a logical construction of programming commands executed in the order in which they appear

sequential storage device A storage device that cannot begin reading data until the device has moved through a sequence of data in order to locate the desired beginning point

serial port An input/output (I/O) interface that is designed to convey data in a bit-by-bit stream. Compare with parallel port

server A computer dedicated to providing information in response to external requests

setup program A utility program provided by a computer's manufacturer that enables users to specify basic system configuration settings, such as the correct time and date and the type of hard disk that is installed in the system. Setup programs are accessible by pressing a special key (such as Delete) during the computer's power-on self test (POST)

shareware Copyrighted software that may be tried without expense but requires the payment of a registration fee if you decide to use it after a specified trial period

sheets In Microsoft Excel workbook files, the 255 sets of columns and rows intersecting at cells

shill In an auction, an accomplice of the seller who drives up prices by bidding for an item that the shill has no intention of buying

shoulder surfing In computer security, a method of defeating password authentication by peeking over a user's shoulder and watching the keyboard as the user inputs his or her password

signature capture A computer system that captures a customer's signature digitally, so that the store can prove that a purchase was made

single-lens reflex (SLR) digital camera Expensive digital camera that offers features such as interchangeable lenses, through-the-lens image previewing, and the ability to override the automatic focus and exposure settings

single point of failure (SPOF) Any system component, such as hardware or software, that causes the entire system to malfunction when it fails

single—tasking operating system Capable of running only one application at a time

site license An agreement with a software publisher that allows multiple copies of the software to be made for use within an organization

slide In a presentation graphics program, an on-screen image sized in proportion to a 35mm slide

sleep A low-power state that allows the computer to return to full power without completing a full boot

Small Computer System Interface (SCSI) A bus standard for connecting peripheral devices to personal computers, including hard disks, CD-ROM discs, and scanners. Considered legacy technology

small office/home office (SOHO) Small businesses run out of homes or small offices—a rapidly growing market segment

Smalltalk An early object-oriented programming language that many OO promoters believe is still the only pure OO language

smart card A card that resembles a credit card but has a microprocessor and memory chip, enabling the card to process as well as store information

smartphone Handheld devices that have many of a PDA's characteristics, while integrating mobile phone capability and Web access

smart tags In Microsoft Office, icons attached to items, allowing various choices for how text is treated when pasted within an application or between applications

social networking A method of creating and expanding online communities. For example, sites such as MySpace or Facebook, allow users to create online profiles, invite friends and acquaintances to join their network, and invite their friends to join too

soft copy A temporary form of output, as in a monitor display

software One of two basic components of a computer system (the other is hardware). Software includes all the instructions that tell the computer what to do

software engineering A new field that applies the principles of mainstream engineering to software production

software license An agreement included with most commercial software that stipulates what the user may and may not do with the software

software piracy Unauthorized duplication of copyrighted software

software suite A collection of full-featured, standalone programs that usually share a common command structure and have similar interfaces

software upgrading The process of keeping a version of an application current with the marketplace, whether through patches, service releases, or new versions

solid state drive (SSD) A drive that consists of nonvolatile memory chips, which retain the data stored in them even if the chips are disconnected from a computer or other device. The term solid state indicates that these devices have no moving parts; they consist only of semiconductors

solid state storage device This device consists of nonvolatile memory chips, which retain the data stored in them even if the chips are disconnected from their current source

sound board See sound card

sound card An adapter that adds digital sound reproduction capabilities to an IBM-compatible PC. Also called a sound board

sound file A file containing digitized sound that can be played back if a computer is equipped with multimedia

sound format A specification of how a sound should be digitally represented. Sound formats usually include some type of data compression to reduce the size of sound files

source code The program instructions that people write. The program is then translated into machine instructions that the computer can execute

spaghetti code In programming, source code that contains numerous GOTO statements and is, in consequence, difficult to understand and prone to error

spam Unsolicited e-mail or newsgroup advertising

speaker A device that plays the computer's audio output

specialized search engines Web location programs that index particular types of information, such as job advertisements

speculative execution A technique used by advanced CPUs to prevent a pipeline stall. The processor executes and temporarily stores the next instruction in case it proves useful

speech recognition The use of a computer system to detect the words spoken by a human being into a microphone, and translate these words into text that appears on-screen. Compare with speech synthesis

spim A spam text message

spreadsheet A program that processes information in the form of tables. Table cells can hold values or mathematical formulas

spreadsheet programs The computer equivalent of an accountant's worksheet

spyware Internet software that is placed on a computer without the user's awareness, usually during a shareware or freeware download

SQL See abbreviation for Structured Query Language

standalone program An application sold individually

standard toolbar In Microsoft Office, a default-loaded toolbar that includes icons for various functions, including opening, closing, and printing files

star topology The physical layout of a local network in which a host computer manages the network

status bar An area within a typical application's window that is reserved for the program's messages to the user

storage A general term for computer components that offer nonvolatile retention of computer data and program instructions

storage area network (SAN) Links high capacity storage devices to all of an organization's servers, which makes any of the storage devices accessible from any of the servers

storage device A hardware component that is capable of retaining data even when electrical power is switched off. An example of a storage device is a hard disk

storage media A collective term used to describe all types of storage devices

store One of four basic operations carried out by the control unit of a microprocessor that involves writing the results of previous operations to an internal register

strategic decisions Executive decisions concerning the organization's overall goals and direction

streaming audio An Internet sound delivery technology that sends audio data as

a continuous, compressed stream that is played back on the fly

streaming video An Internet video delivery technology that sends video data as a continuous, compressed stream that is played back on the fly. Like streaming audio, streaming video begins playing almost immediately. A high-speed modem is required. Quality is marginal; the video appears in a small, on-screen window, and motion is jerky

strong AI In artificial intelligence, a research focus based on the conviction that computers will achieve the ultimate goal of artificial intelligence, namely, rivaling the intelligence of humans

structural unemployment Unemployment caused by advancing technology that makes an entire job or job category obsolete

structure chart In structured programming, a program planning chart that shows the top-down design of the program and the relationship between program modules

structured programming A set of quality standards that make programs more verbose but more readable, more reliable, and more easily maintained. A program is broken up into manageable components, each of which contributes to the overall goal of the program. Also called top-down program design

stylus A pen-shaped instrument used to draw on a graphics tablet or to input commands and handwriting to a personal digital assistant (PDA)

subdirectory A directory created in another directory. A subdirectory can contain files and additional subdirectories

subfolder A folder within a folder, usually created to allow for better file organization. Also known as secondary folder

subject guide On the World Wide Web, an information discovery service that contains hyperlinks classified by subjects in broad categories and multiple levels of subcategories

subnotebook A portable computer that omits some components (such as a CD-ROM drive) to cut down on weight and size

subscriber loop carrier (SLC) A small, waist-high curbside installation of the public switched telephone network that transforms local home and business analog calls into digital signals and routes them through high-capacity cables to the local exchange switch

summary report In a transaction processing system (TPS), a document that provides a quick overview of an organization's performance

Super Extended Graphics Array (SXGA) A resolution of 1280 × 1024 typically found on standard 17- and 19-inch monitors

Super Video Graphics Array (SVGA) A resolution of 1024 × 768. Most current monitors have at least this resolution

supercomputer A sophisticated, expensive computer that executes complex calculations at the maximum speed permitted by state-of-the-art technology. Supercomputers are used mostly by the government and for scientific research

superscalar architecture A design that lets the microprocessor take a sequential

instruction and send several instructions at a time to separate execution units so that the processor can execute multiple instructions per cycle

surge protector An inexpensive electrical device that prevents high-voltage surges from reaching a computer and damaging its circuitry

swap file In virtual memory, a file on the hard disk used to store pages of virtual memory information

swapping In virtual memory, the operation of exchanging program instructions and data between the swap file (located on the hard disk) and random access memory (RAM)

switch Similar to routers, these are used only to move data within one network

symmetric key encryption Encryption techniques that use the same key for encryption and decryption

symptom An indication or a sign of something; an unacceptable or undesirable result

syn flooding See denial of service (DoS) attack

synchronous DRAM (SDRAM) The fastest available memory chip technology

Synchronous Optical Network (SONET) A standard for high-performance networks using optical fiber that provides transfer rates between 52 Mbps and 1 Gbps

syntax The rules governing the structure of commands, statements, or instructions given to a computer

syntax error In programming, a flaw in the structure of commands, statements, or instructions

synthesizer An audio component that uses FM (frequency modulation), wavetable, or waveguide technology to create sounds imitative of actual musical instruments

system A collection of components purposefully organized into a functioning whole to accomplish a goal

system clock An electronic circuit in the computer that emits pulses at regular intervals, enabling the computer's internal components to operate in synchrony

system requirements The stated minimum system performance capabilities required to run an application program, including the minimum amount of disk space, memory, and processor capacity

system software All the software used to operate and maintain a computer system, including the operating system and utility programs

system unit A boxlike case that houses the computer's main hardware components and provides a sturdy frame for mounting and protecting internal devices, connectors, and drives

system utilities Programs such as speaker volume control and antivirus software that are loaded by the operating system

systems analysis A discipline devoted to the rational and organized planning, development, and implementation of artificial systems, including information systems

systems analyst A computer professional who helps plan, develop, and implement information systems

systems development life cycle (SDLC) An organized way of planning and building information systems

systems engineering A field of engineering devoted to creating and maintaining quality systems

system utilities Programs, such as file management and file finder, that provide a necessary addition to an operating system's basic system-management tools

T

T1 A high-bandwidth telephone trunk line capable of transferring 1.544 megabits per second (Mbps) of data

T3 A high-bandwidth fiber-optic line capable of handling 44.7 megabits per second (Mbps) of computer data

tabbed browsing A type of internet browsing that enables a user to quickly switch between Web sites. You can customize your home page by adding tabs for sites that you frequently access

table In the Microsoft Access database management system, the object used to store data

tablet PC A type of notebook computer that has an LCD screen that the user can write on using a special-purpose pen or stylus

tactical decisions Middle management decisions about how to best organize resources to achieve their division's goals

tactile display A display that stimulates the sense of touch using vibration, pressure, and temperature changes

tailor-made applications Software designed for specialized fields or the consumer market, such as programs that handle the billing needs of medical offices, manage restaurants, and track occupational injuries

tangible benefits In a cost-benefit analysis, benefits such as increased sales, faster response time, and decreased complaints that can be easily measured

task pane In Microsoft Office, a feature that usually appears on the right side of an opened application window and that provides various options, such as for opening or formatting work

TCP/IP The two most important Internet protocols. See Transmission Control Protocol and Internet Protocol

technical skills Skills such as knowledge and experience in networking, Microsoft Windows XP, UNIX, C++, and Internet-related technologies

teamware See groupware

technical feasibility Able to be accomplished with respect to existing, proven technology

telecommuting Performing work at home while linked to the office by means of a telecommunications-equipped computer system

teleconferencing A simple and secure wired voice communications application in

which more than two distant people conduct business by conference call

terabyte (TB) A unit of measurement commonly used to state the capacity of memory or storage devices; equal to 1,024 gigabytes, or approximately one trillion bytes or characters

terminal An input/output device consisting of a keyboard and a video display that is commonly used with mainframe and minicomputer systems

terminator Special connectors that signify the end of a circuit in bus topology

text messaging A mobile service, similar to using your phone for instant messaging or as a receiver and transmitter for brief e-mail messages

thermal transfer printer A printer that uses a heat process to transfer colored dyes or inks to the paper's surface. Although thermal transfer printers are the best color printers currently available, they are very expensive

Thin Film Transistor (TFT) See active matrix

third-generation language (3GL) A programming language that tells the computer what to do and how to do it but eliminates the need for understanding the intimate details of how the computer works

thread 1. In multithreading, a single type of task that can be executed simultaneously with other tasks. 2. In Usenet, a series of articles on the same specific subject

throughput This is the actual amount of data that can be sent through a specific transmission medium at one time (usually per second). Throughput is almost always lower than bandwidth, especially with wireless communications

time bomb A destructive program that sits harmlessly until a certain event or set of circumstances makes the program active

time-limited trial versions Internet-offered commercial programs capable of being used on a trial basis for a period of time, after which the software is unusable

title bar In a graphical user interface (GUI), the top bar of an application window. The title bar typically contains the name of the application, the name of the document, and window controls

toggle key A key on a keyboard that functions like a switch. When pressed, the function is turned on, and when pressed again, the function is turned off

toolbar In a graphical user interface (GUI), a bar near the top of the window that contains a row of graphical buttons. These buttons provide quick access to the most frequently used program commands

tools menu In a graphical user interface (GUI), a menu that provides access to special program features and utilities, such as spell-checking

top-down program design See structured programming

top-level domain (TLD) name The last part of an Internet computer address. For computers located in the United States, it indicates the type of organization in which the computer is located, such as commercial businesses (com), educational institutions

(edu), and government agencies (gov)

top-level folder See primary folder

topology See network topology

touch screen A touch-sensitive display that enables users to input choices by touching a region of the screen

touchpad An input device for notebook computers that moves the pointer. The touchpad is a small pad in front of the keyboard that moves the pointer when the user moves a finger on the pad

tower case A tall and deep system unit case designed to sit on the floor next to a desk and easily accommodate add-on components

track One of several concentric circular bands on computer disks where data is recorded, similar to the grooves on a phonographic record. Tracks are created during formatting and are divided into sectors

trackball An input device, similar to the mouse, that moves the pointer. The trackball looks something like an inverted mouse and does not require the desk space that a mouse does

trackpad See touchpad

trackpoint An input device on some notebook computers that resembles a tiny pencil eraser; you move the cursor by pushing the tip of the trackpoint

trade show A periodic meeting in which computer product manufacturers, designers, and dealers display their products

tracks The concentric circular bands on a hard disk. Data is recorded in the tracks, which are divided into sectors to help keep track of where specific files are located

traditional organizational structure In an organization, a method used to distribute the core functions of the organization into divisions such as finance, human resources, and operations

training seminars Computer-related training sessions, typically presented by the developer of a new hardware or software product or by a company specializing in training IT professionals in a new technology

transaction processing system (TPS) A system that handles the day-to-day operations of a company; examples include sales, purchases, orders, and returns

transfer performance A measure of how quickly read/write heads are able to transfer data from a hard disk to memory

transistor A device invented in 1947 by Bell Laboratories that controls the flow of electricity. Due to their small size, reduced power consumption, and lower heat output, transistors replaced vacuum tubes in the second generation of computers

Transmission Control Protocol (TCP) One of two basic Internet protocols (the other is Internet Protocol, IP). TCP is the protocol (standard) that permits two Internet-connected computers to establish a reliable connection. TCP ensures reliable data delivery with a method known as Positive Acknowledgment with Re-transmission (PAR). The computer that sends the data continues to do so until it receives a confirmation from the receiving computer that the data has been received intact

trap door In computer security, a security hole created on purpose that can be exploited at a later time

Trojan horse An application disguised as a useful program but containing instructions to perform a malicious task

truncation Using symbols such as ? and * , in a search engine, to take the place of zero or more characters. It allows you to search for various word endings and spellings simultaneously

Turing test A test developed by Alan Turing and used to determine whether a computer could be called intelligent. In a Turing test, judges are asked to determine whether the output they see on computer displays is produced by a computer or a human being. If a computer program succeeds in tricking the judges into believing that only a human could have generated that output, the program is said to have passed the Turing test

twisted pair An inexpensive copper cable used for telephone and data communications. The term *twisted pair* refers to the braiding of the paired wires, a practice that reduces interference from electrical fields

two-megapixel Type of digital camera that can produce sharp images at higher enlargements such as 8 by 10 inches

U

ubiquitous computing A scenario for future computing in which computers are so numerous that they fade into the background, providing intelligence for virtually every aspect of daily life

ultraportables Also known as subnotebooks, these are notebook computers that omit some components (such as a CD or DVD drive) so as to cut down on weight and size

unicode A type of code that can represent many, if not most, of the world's languages

uninstall Removing a program from a computer system by using a special utility

uninterruptible power supply (UPS) A device that provides power to a computer system for a short period of time if electrical power is lost

universal product code (UPC) A label with a series of bars that can be either keyed in or read by a scanner to identify an item and determine its cost. UPC scanners are often found in point-of-sale (POS) terminals

universal serial bus (USB) An external bus architecture that connects peripherals such as keyboards, mice, and digital cameras. USB offers many benefits over older serial architectures, such as support for 127 devices on a single port, Plug and Play, and higher transfer rates

UNIX A 32-bit operating system that features multiuser access, preemptive multitasking, multiprocessing, and other sophisticated features. UNIX is widely used for file servers in client/server networks

upload To send a file to another computer by means of a computer network

URL (uniform resource locator) In the World Wide Web, one of two basic kinds of Universal Resource Identifiers (URI), a string of characters that precisely identifies an Internet resource's type and location. For example, the fictitious URL http://www.wolverine.virginia.edu/ ~toros/winerefs/merlot.html identifies a World Wide Web document (http://), indicates the domain name of the computer on which it is stored (www.wolverine.virginia.edu), fully describes the document's location in the directory structure (~toros/sports/), and includes the document's name and extension (lacrosse.html)

USB Flash Drive A type of flash storage, also known as memory sticks, thumb drives, or jump drives, that are popular portable storage devices. USB flash drives work with both the PC and the Mac, and no device driver is required—just plug it into a USB port and it's ready to read and write

Usenet A worldwide computer-based discussion system that uses the Internet and other networks for transmission media. Discussion is channeled into more than 50,000 topically named newsgroups, which contain original contributions called articles, as well as commentaries on these articles called follow-up posts. As follow-up posts continue to appear on a given subject, a thread of discussion emerges; a threaded newsreader collates these articles together so readers can see the flow of the discussion

user A person who uses a computer and its applications to perform tasks and produce results

user ID A word or name that uniquely identifies a computer user. Synonymous with user name

user interface The part of system software that interacts with the user

user name A unique name that a system administrator assigns to you that you use as initial identification. You must type this name and also your password to gain access to the system

utilities See system utilities

utility programs See system utilities

V

validate After purchasing a software program, it is the process of providing a special code or product key before you can use it. Validation proves that you are using a legal copy, not a pirated version

value-added network (VAN) A public data network that provides value-added services for corporate customers, including end-to-end dedicated lines with guaranteed security. VANs, however, also charge an expensive per-byte fee

value-added reseller (VAR) An independent company that selects system components and assembles them into a functioning system

variant A type of virus that is self-modifying and creates a new copy that is slightly different from the previous one, making it difficult to protect your computer

VBScript A scripting language used to write short programs (scripts) that can be embedded in Web pages

vector graphic An image composed of distinct objects, such as lines or shapes, that may be moved or edited independently. Each object is described by a complex mathematical formula

vendor A company that sells goods or services

VGA connector A physical connector that is designed to connect a VGA monitor to a video adapter

video adapter Video circuitry that fits into an expansion bus and determines the quality of the display and resolution of your monitor. Also called display adapter

video capture board See video capture card

video capture card An expansion board that accepts analog or digital video signals, which are then compressed and stored

video card See video adapter

video editor A program that enables you to view and edit a digitized video and to select special effects

Video Graphics Array (VGA) A display standard that can display 16 colors at a maximum resolution of 640 pixels by 480 pixels

video RAM (VRAM) A random access memory chip that maximizes the performance of video adapters

videoconferencing A technology enabling two or more people to have a face-to-face meeting even though they're geographically separated

view menu In a graphical user interface (GUI), a menu that provides access to document viewing options, including normal layout, print layout, and document magnification (zoom) options

viewable area The front surface on a cathode-ray tube monitor actually available for viewing, which is less than the quoted size. See quoted size

virtual memory A means of increasing the size of a computer's random access memory (RAM) by using part of the hard disk as an extension of RAM

virtual private network (VPN) A method of connecting two physically separate local area networks (LANs) by using the Internet. Strong encryption is used to ensure privacy

virtual reality (VR) A computer-generated illusion of three-dimensional space. On the Web, virtual reality sites enable Web users to explore three-dimensional virtual reality worlds by means of VR plug-in programs. These programs enable you to walk or "fly" through the three-dimensional space that these worlds offer

Virtual Reality Modeling Language (VRML) A scripting language that enables programmers to specify the characteristics of a three-dimensional world that is accessible on the Internet. VRML worlds can contain sounds, hyperlinks, videos, and animations as well as three-dimensional spaces, which can be explored by using a VRML plug-in

virus See computer virus

Visual Basic (VB) An event driven programming language programming language developed by Microsoft based on the BASIC programming language. Visual Basic is one of the world's most widely used program development packages

Visual Studio .NET A suite of products that contains Visual Basic .NET, which enables programmers to work with complex objects; Visual C++, which is based upon C++; and Visual C# (pronounced "C sharp"), which is a less complex version of C++ that is used for rapid application development of Web programs

Voice over Internet Protocol (VoIP) A type of internet telephony that uses the Internet for real-time voice communication

voice recognition See speech recognition

volatile Related to memory, it is memory that is lost when the computer loses power or is turned off

W

wardriving A process in which an individual drives around with a wireless device, such as a notebook or smartphone, to look for wireless networks to break into

warm boot To restart a computer that is already operating

waterfall model A method in information systems development that returns the focus of the systems development project to a previous phase if an error is discovered in it

waveform A type of digitized audio format used to record live sounds or music

Web See World Wide Web (WWW)

Web 2.0 The next generation of the Web that provides even more opportunities for individuals to collaborate, interact with one another, and create new content by using applications such as blogs, wikis, and podcasts

Web-based training (WBT) Computer-based training implemented via the Internet or an intranet

Web Beacon A graphic that alerts senders when a message has been opened

Web browser A program that runs on an Internet-connected computer and provides access to information on the World Wide Web (WWW)

Webcam A low-cost video camera used for low-resolution videoconferencing on the Internet

Web-database integration The latest trend in database software, techniques that make information stored in databases available through Internet connections

Web-enabled devices Devices that have the ability to connect to the Internet and e-book readers

Web page A document you create to share with others on the Web. A Web page can include text, graphics, sound, animation, and video

Web portal (portal) A Web site that provides multiple online services; a jumping off place that provides an organized way to go to other places on the Web

Web server On the Web, a program that accepts requests for information framed according to the Hypertext Transfer Protocol (HTTP). The server processes these requests and sends the requested document

Web site A computer location that is accessible to the public Internet and is running a server program that makes Web pages available

Web-hosted technology A new wave in office suites that offers the capability to upload files to an online site so they can be viewed and edited from another location. It is also possible to share files with others, making group collaboration easier

wheel mouse A type of mouse that has a dial that can be used to scroll through data on-screen

whistleblowing Reporting illegal or unethical actions of a company to a regulatory agency or the press

white hat See ethical hackers

whiteboard A separate area of a videoconferencing screen enabling participants to create a shared workspace. Participants can write or draw in this space as if they were using a chalkboard in a meeting

wide area network (WAN) A commercial data network that provides data communications services for businesses and government agencies. Most WANs use the X.25 protocols, which overcome problems related to noisy analog telephone lines

Widescreen Extended Graphics Array + (WXGA+) Widescreen computer display standards for 19-inch monitors with a 1440 × 900 resolution

Widescreen Super Extended Graphics Array + (WSXGA+) Widescreen computer display standards for 20-inch monitors with a 1680 × 1050 resolution

Widescreen Ultra Extended Graphics Array (WUXGA) Widescreen computer display standards for 24-inch monitors with a 1920 x 1200 resolution

Wi-Fi A collection of wireless transmission standards for wireless networks

WiFi Protected Access (WPA) This is a security method for wireless networks that was developed to provide stronger security than WEP

wildcard A symbol that stands for any character or any group of characters

WiMAX An up-and-coming technology to deliver high-speed access using microwaves over long distances

window border The outer edge of a window on a graphical user interface (GUI); in Microsoft Windows it can be dragged to change the size of the window

window controls In a graphical user interface (GUI), a group of window management controls that enable the user to minimize, maximize, restore, or close the window

Windows Bitmap (BMP) A bitmapped graphics format developed for Microsoft Windows

Windows Update Microsoft operating system update service that keeps your operating system up-to-date with any fixes (service patches) or protections against external environment changes

Wired Equivalent Privacy (WEP) One of the earliest security methods for wireless networks, WEP has several well-known weaknesses, but it may be the only option for some devices or older equipment

wired Connected by a physical medium

wireless Connected through the air or space

wireless LANs (WLANs) Local area networks that use a radio signal spread over a seemingly random series of frequencies for greater security

wireless memory card A card that has all the storage features of a regular flash memory card and combines it with wireless circuitry. It can connect with your PC via a wireless network or send pictures directly from your digital camera to your favorite online photo site

wizard In a graphical user interface (GUI), a series of dialog boxes that guide the user through a complex process, such as importing data into an application

word-processing program An office application that enables the user to create, edit, format, and print textual documents

word size The number of bits a computer can work with at one time

word wrapping A word processing feature that automatically moves words down to the beginning of the next line if they extend beyond the right margin

workbook In a spreadsheet program, a file that can contain two or more spreadsheets, each of which has its own page in the workbook

workflow automation An information system in which documents are automatically sent to the people who need to see them

workgroup A collection of individuals working together on a task

workgroup computing Any situation in which all of the members of a workgroup have specific hardware, software, and networking equipment that enables them to connect, communicate, and collaborate

worksheet In MIcrosoft Excel, a single tab of a workbook

World Wide Web (WWW) A global hypertext system that uses the Internet as its transport mechanism. In a hypertext system, you navigate by clicking hyperlinks, which display another document (which also contains hyperlinks). Most Web documents are created using HTML, a markup language that is easy to learn and that will soon be supplanted by automated tools. Incorporating hypermedia (graphics, sounds, animations, and video), the Web has become the ideal medium for publishing information on the Internet

World Wide Web Consortium (W3C) An independent standards body made up of university researchers and industry practitioners devoted to setting effective standards to promote the orderly growth of the World Wide Web. Housed at the Massachusetts Institute of Technology (MIT), W3C sets standards for HTML and many other aspects of Web usage

WPA See WiFi Protected Access

WPA2 A security method for wireless networks that improves on WPA's abilities. WPA2 provides confidentiality and data integrity and is far superior to WEP, because it uses AES (Advanced Encryption Standard) to provide government-grade security

worm A program resembling a computer virus that can spread over networks

WWW See World Wide Web (WWW)

X

X.25 A packet-switching network protocol optimized for use on noisy analog telephone lines

xDSL See DSL (Digital Subscriber Line)

Z

Zero configuration (Zeroconf) A method for networking devices via an Ethernet cable that does not require configuration and administration

zombie A computer commandeered by a hacker to do what the hacker's program tells it to do

Illustration Credits

CHAPTER I **Chapter Opener** Photoshot **Figure 1.1a** Photoshot **Figure 1.1b** Asiaimages\Photoshot **Figure 1.1c** Photoshot **Figure 1.1d** OJO Images\Photoshot **Figure 1.1e** David Young Wolff\PhotoEdit Inc. **Figure 1.1f** Fred Prouser/Reuters/Landov Media **Figure 1.1g** Rolf Haid/dpa/Landov Media **Figure 1.1h** George Frey/Bloomberg News/Landov Media **Figure 1.2** © Jose Luis Pelaez; Inc./CORBIS. All Rights Reserved. **Figure 1.3a** Michael Jarrett\Gateway Inc. **Figure 1.3b** Courtesy of Apple **Figure 1.3c** Courtesy of Research In Motion (RIM). Research In Motion, the RIM logo, BlackBerry, the BlackBerry logo, and SureType are registered with the U.S. Patent and Trademark Office and may be pending or registered in other countries—these and other marks of Research In Motion Limited are used under license. **Figure 1.3d** © 2009 Dell Inc. All rights reserved. The Dell logo is a trademark of Dell Inc. **Figure 1.3e** Used by permission of Sony Electronics, Inc. **Figure 1.4** © 2006 Lexar Media, Inc. All Rights Reserved. Used with Permission. **Figure 1.5g** Susan Van Etten\PhotoEdit Inc. **Figure 1.5i** © Greg Nicholas/Courtesy of **www.istockphoto.com** **Figure 1.5j** Motorola, Inc. **Figure 1.5k** Courtesy of Cisco **Figure 1.6** Photographer's Choice\Superstock Royalty Free **Figure 1.7a** Reprinted with permission from Microsoft Corporation. **Figure 1.7b** Reprinted with permission from Microsoft Corporation. **Figure 1.8** Intel Corporation Pressroom Photo Archives **Figure 1.9a** Courtesy of IBM Archives. Unauthorized use not permitted. **Figure 1.10a** Alan Klehr\Churchill & Klehr Photography **Figure 1.10b** Getty Images, Inc.-Photodisc **Figure 1.10c** Eyewire, Inc./Getty Images **Figure 1.11a** Zefa Collection\Corbis Zefa Collection **Figure 1.11d** Nick Koudis\Getty Images, Inc. - Photodisc **Figure 1.13** Michael Jarrett\Gateway Inc. **Figure 1.13a** © Dell Inc. All Rights Reserved. The Dell logo is a trademark of Dell Inc. **Figure 1.13b** Toshiba America Information Systems, Inc. **Figure 1.13c** Courtesy of Apple **Figure 1.14a** Courtesy of IBM Archives. Unauthorized use not permitted. **Figure 1.14b** Sun Microsystems, Inc. **Figure 1.14c** Courtesy of IBM Archives. Unauthorized use not permitted. **Figure 1.14d** Courtesy of International Business Machines Corporation. Unauthorized use not permitted. **Figure 1.15a** Comstock Complete **Figure 1.15b** Comstock Complete **Figure 1.15c** © Artiga Photo/CORBIS. All Rights Reserved. **Figure 1.15d** © Meeke/zefa/CORBIS. All Rights Reserved. **Figure 1.15e** © Don Mason/CORBIS. All Rights Reserved. **Figure 1.15f** Corbis Royalty Free\Inmagine Corporation LLC **Figure 1.17** Photodisc/Getty Images **Figure 1.18** © Images.com/Corbis **Figure 1.20** Lockheed Martin Corporation **Figure 1.21** Gravitonus, Inc. **Figure 1.22** Corbis/Reuters America LLC **Figure 1.23** H. David Seawell/Corbis Edge **Figure 1.24** Johner Bildbyra AB/Getty Images-Johner Images Royalty Free **Figure 1.25** Courtesy Western Digital Corporation

SPOTLIGHT I **Chapter Opener** © Alan Schein Photography/CORBIS. All Rights Reserved. **Figure 1A** Blend Images\Inmagine Corporation LLC **Figure 1C** Courtesy of **www.istockphoto.com** **Figure 1E** © Roger Ressmeyer/CORBIS. All Rights Reserved. **Figure 1G** © Jim Criagmyle/CORBIS. All Rights Reserved. **Figure 1H** © Jose Luis Pelaez, Inc./CORBIS. All Rights Reserved. **Figure 1I** The Software & Information Industry Association **Figure 1.1** Al Riccio\Getty Images, Inc.-Photodisc.

CHAPTER 2 **Chapter Opener** Hunt, Steven\Getty Images Inc.-Image Bank **Figure 2.1a** All content copyright Librarian's Internet Index **Figure 2.3a** Polkadot royalty free\Inmagine Corporation LLC **Figure 2.3b** Polkadot royalty free\Inmagine Corporation LLC **Figure 2.3c** Polkadot royalty free\Inmagine Corporation LLC **Figure 2.3d** © R. Nyberg. Courtesy USAID. **Figure 2.6** Imageclub Royalty Free\Inmagine Corporation LLC **Figure 2.17** All content copyright Librarian's Internet Index **Figure 2.24** Getty Images

SPOTLIGHT 2 **Chapter Opener** Jim Arbogast/Getty Images/Digital Vision **Figure 2B** Dana Neely/Getty Images—Taxi **Figure 2J** Froemel Kapitza/Getty Images—Stone **Figure 2O** Neil Selkirk/Getty Images—Stone **Figure 2P-b** Photos courtesy of Glazier Photography. Web design and hosting provided by SkilTech, Inc.

CHAPTER 3 **Chapter Opener** Jose Luis Pelaez/Getty Images, Inc.-Blend Images **Figure 3.0** Palm, Treo, Zire, Tungsten, logos, stylizations, and design marks associated with all the preceding, and trade dress associated with Palm Inc.'s products, are among the trademarks or registered trademarks owned by or licensed to Palm, Inc. **Figure 3.3** Michael Jarrett/Gateway Inc. **Figure 3.5** © Digital Art/Surf/CORBIS. All Rights Reserved. **Figure 3.6** Digital Art\Corbis Edge **Figure 3.7** Cables Unlimited **Figure 3.8** © Bluetooth SIG 2008 **Figure 3.9** Ambient Images/Creative Eye/MIRA.com **Figure 3.10** © Louis R. Bostwick/CORBIS. All Rights Reserved. **Figure 3.13a** Courtesy of IBM Archives. Unauthorized use not permitted. **Figure 3.13c** MOTOROLA, stylized M Logo, and SURFboard are registered in the US Patent & Trademark Office. All other product or service names are the property of their respective owners. © Motorola, Inc. 2008. All rights reserved.

Figure 3.14a Courtesy of Research In Motion (RIM). Research In Motion, the RIM logo, BlackBerry, the BlackBerry logo and SureType are registered with the U.S. Patent and Trademark Office and may be pending or registered in other countries - these and other marks of Research In Motion Limited are used under license. **Figure 3.14b** Oqo, Inc. **Figure 3.15** © choicegraphx/ Courtesy of **www.istockphoto.com Figure 3.17a** Nokia **Figure 3.17b** Nokia **Figure 3.20** Steve Chen\Corbis Edge **Figure 3.21** © 2008 Logitech. All rights reserved. Used with permission from Logitech. **Figure 3.25** Reprinted courtesy of HowStuffWorks.com **Figure 3.26** AP Wide World Photos **Figure 3.28** Getty Images Inc.-Photographer's Choice Royalty Free **Figure 3.28-**Cheryl Raulo/Corbis/Reuters America LLC **Figure 3.29** Nokia

SPOTLIGHT 3 Chapter Opener Neil Hendrickson/Getty Images/Digital Vision **Figure 3A-1** A. Chederros/ONOKY/Getty Images **Figure 3A-2** Getty Images Inc-Image Source Royalty Free **Figure 3A-3** Sky Bonillo-IPhotoEdit Inc. **Figure 3D** Apple Computer, Inc. **Figure 3F-1** Courtesy of Linksys, A Division of Cisco **Figure 3F-2** Courtesy of Cisco **Figure 3F-3** Courtesy of Cisco **Figure 3G** Courtesy of Cisco **Figure 3H** Netgear, Inc.

CHAPTER 4 Figure 4.3 Dave Graham **Figure 4.7b** Thomas Brummett\Getty Images Inc.–PhotoDisc **Figure 4.9** Copyright American Megatrends, Inc. This image is protected by copyright laws, and may not be reproduced, republished, distributed, transmitted, displayed, broadcast, or otherwise exploited in any manner without the express prior written permission of American Megatrends, Inc. **Figure 4.14** Courtesy of Verizon Wireless **Figure 4.16** Sun Microsystems, Inc. **Figure 4.18a** © One Laptop Per Child **Figure 4.18b** Everex, Inc. **Figure 4.29** National Cyber Security Alliance

CHAPTER 5 Chapter Opener PhotoDisc/Getty Images **Figure 5.4** John Madere/Surf/CORBIS. All Rights Reserved. **Figure 5.11** Apple Computer, Inc. **Figure 5.12a** Intuit, Inc. **Figure 5.12b** Better Homes & Gardens Home Designer Products **Figure 5.12c** De Marque, Inc. **Figure 5.13** Flying Lab Software **Figure 5.14** Darrin Klimek\Inmagine Corporation LLC **Figure 5.26** Reprinted courtesy of Microsoft Corporation

SPOTLIGHT 5 Chapter Opener © Devan\Corbis Zefa Collection **Figure 5B** Reprinted with permission from Microsoft Corporation. **Figure 5Q** © Helen King/CORBIS. All Rights Reserved.

CHAPTER 6 Chapter Opener Banagan, John W/Getty Images Inc.-Image Bank **Figure 6.5** Apple Computer, Inc. **Figure 6.6** Lenovo, Inc. **Figure 6.7a** Alan Evans\Diane M. Coyle **Figure 6.7b** Intel Corporation Pressroom Photo Archives **Figure 6.8b** Creative Labs, Inc. **Figure 6.8c** ©US Robotics **Figure 6.8d** © 3Com Corporation **Figure 6.8e** Manic

Photos\Alamy Images **Figure 6.9** Courtesy of IBM Archives. Unauthorized use not permitted. **Figure 6.11** © PolyFuel. Courtesy of Roeder-Johnson Corporation. **Figure 6.16a** Intel Corporation Pressroom Photo Archives **Figure 6.16b** Intel Corporation Pressroom Photo Archives **Figure 6.19** © Carolina K. Smith, M.D./Courtesy of **www.istockphoto.com Figure 6.21** © Mark M. Lawrence/CORBIS. All Rights Reserved. **Figure 6.22** Lewis-Global Public Relations **Figure 6.23** Goodshot\Corbis Royalty Free **Figure 6.24a** Intel Corporation Pressroom Photo Archives **Figure 6.24b** Intel Corporation Pressroom Photo Archives **Figure 6.24c** Intel Corporation Pressroom Photo Archives

SPOTLIGHT 6 Chapter Opener 1 © 2008 XFXForce.com **Chapter Opener 2** ©Fabrik, Inc. and Simple Tech Inc. **Figure 6A** Getty Images, Inc.-Stockbyte Royalty Free **Figure 6B-a** Targus, Inc. **Figure 6B-b** Targus, Inc. **Figure 6B-c** Photoalto Royalty-free\Inmagine Corporation LLC **Figure 6I** Peter Cade/Image Bank/Getty Images **Figure 6E** Pioneer North America, Inc. **Figure 6F** XFX – USA **Figure 6G** Reprinted with permission from Microsoft Corporation. **Figure 6K** Mark Scott/Taxi/Getty Images

CHAPTER 7 Figure 7.1 Getty Images, Inc.-Stockbyte Royalty Free **Figure 7.4** © 2008 Logitech. All rights reserved. Used with permission from Logitech. **Figure 7.5** © Hank Drew/Stock this Way/CORBIS. All Rights Reserved. **Figure 7.5a** Reprinted with permission from Microsoft Corporation. **Figure 7.5b** Logitech Inc. **Figure 7.5c** Courtesy of IBM Archives. Unauthorized use not permitted. **Figure 7.5d** Courtesy of IBM Archives. Unauthorized use not permitted. **Figure 7.5e** © Kim Kulish/COR-BIS. All Rights Reserved. **Figure 7.6** Reprinted with permission from Microsoft Corporation. **Figure 7.7** mediacolor's\Alamy Images **Figure 7.9a** Courtesy of Canon USA. The Canon logo is a trademark of Canon Inc. All rights reserved. **Figure 7.9b** Visioneer Inc. **Figure 7.11a** ViewSonic Corporation **Figure 7.11b** ViewSonic Corporation **Figure 7.12a** Courtesy of IBM Archives. Unauthorized use not permitted. **Figure 7.12c** AP Wide World Photos **Figure 7.15b** Brother International Corporation **Figure 7.16** Photo courtesy of XEROX Corporate Public Relations. **Figure 7.17a** ViewSonic Corporation **Figure 7.17b** Panasonic Corporation of North America **Figure 7.18** Courtesy of Epson pressroom **Figure 7.19a** American Honda Motor Co. Inc. **Figure 7.19b** CSIRO Publishing **Figure 7.19c** Voltaic Systems, Inc. **Figure 7.19d** Voltaic Systems, Inc. **Figure 7.22a** Intel Corporation Pressroom Photo Archives **Figure 7.22b** Courtesy of IBM Archives. Unauthorized use not permitted. **Figure 7.23** Samsung Electronics America, Inc. **Figure 7.24** IBM Research, Almaden Research Center **Figure 7.25a** Imation Corp. **Figure 7.25c** Copyright 2008 Mimoco and Lucasfilm Ltd. **Figure 7.25b**

Copyright 2008 Mimoco. COURTESY OF LUCAS-FILM LTD. TM & (c) Lucasfilm Ltd. All rights reserved. Used under authorization. Unauthorized duplication is a violation of applicable law. **Figure 7.26** © Michael Keller Studio/CORBIS. All Rights Reserved. **Figure 7.28** ExpressCard – PCMCIA **Figure 7.29a** SanDisk Corporation **Figure 7.29b** SanDisk Corporation **Figure 7.29c** Lexar Media, USA **Figure 7.30** SanDisk Corporation **Figure 7.31** © William Whitehurst/CORBIS. All Rights Reserved. **Figure 7.32** Seagate Technology, Inc.

SPOTLIGHT 7 Chapter Opener Jason Reed/Ryan McVay/Getty Images – Digital Vision **Figure 7Ca** Reprinted with permission of Microsoft Corporation **Figure 7Cb** SanDisk Corporation **Figure 7Cc** Creative Labs, Inc. **Figure 7Cd** Apple Computer, Inc. **Figure 7D** Stuart O'Sullivan/Getty Images – Digital Vision **Figure 7E** ZUMA Press/Newscom **Figure 7F** Casio, Inc. **Figure 7G** SanDisk Corporation **Figure 7I** Canon U.S.A., Inc. **Figure 7J** Nikon **Figure 7K** JVC Americas Corp. **Figure 7L** Apple Computer, Inc. **Figure 7M** MWW Group **Figure 7N** TiVo **Figure 7O** Tim Robberts/Image Bank/Getty Images **Figure 7P** © Ausloeser/Zefa/Corbis

CHAPTER 8 Chapter Opener Getty Images, Inc.-Stockbyte Royalty Free **Figure 8.1** LWA/Stone/Getty Images **Figure 8.2** Copyright 2008 Dell, Inc. All rights reserved. The Dell logo is a trademark of Dell Inc. **Figure 8.3a** Courtesy of IBM Archives. Unauthorized use not permitted. **Figure 8.3b** ZOOM Telephonics, Inc. **Figure 8.3c** D-Link Systems, Inc. **Figure 8.3d** D-Link Systems, Inc. **Figure 8.5** © Darren Modricker/Flirt/CORBIS. All Rights Reserved. **Figure 8.17** © Gabe Palmer/CORBIS. All Rights Reserved.

SPOTLIGHT 8 Figure 8A J. Cantly\Photo Researchers, Inc. **Figure 8D** © Al Francekevich/CORBIS. All Rights Reserved. **Figure 8H** Blake Little\Getty Images Inc.-Stone Allstock **Figure 8J** NASA/Getty Images, Inc. **Figure 8L** Courtesy of The Computer History Museum **Figure 8M** © John Martin/Images.com/Corbis **Figure 8O** Courtesy of Franklin Electronic Publishers, Inc. **Figure 8Q** © George Steinmetz/Corbis **Figure 8R1** Issei Kato/Corbis/Reuters America LLC **Figure 8R2** Personal Robot PaPeRo. Courtesy of NEC Corporation, http://www.nec.co.jp/robot/

CHAPTER 9 Chapter Opener Laurence Dutton/Getty Images, Inc. **Chapter Opener Inset** Photo courtesy of Toshiba America Information Systems **Figure 9.1** Pulp Photography/Getty Images, Inc. **Figure 9.2** Chemistry/Photographer's Choice/Getty Images **Figure 9.3** Mel Yates/Getty Images—Taxi **Figure 9.5** Photodisc/Alamy Images Royalty Free **Figure 9.8a** TRUSTe **Figure 9.8b** Council of Better Business Bureau, Inc. **Figure 9.13** Courtesy of Kensington Technology Group **Figure 9.15** Digital Vision\Inmagine Corporation LLC **Figure 9.18** CORBIS Images.com **Figure 9.19** Lester Lefkowitz/Stone/Getty Images **Figure 9.20** American Power Conversion Corporation **Figure 9.21a** Jim Wilson/The New York Times/Redux Pictures **Figure 9.21c** GSO Images/Photographer's Choice/Getty Images

Index

SYMBOLS

( ) (search operator), 66, 67
- (exclusion operator), 66–67, 78
// (forward slash marks), 58
+ (inclusion operator), 66, 78
* (wildcards), 66, 67
" " (*quotation marks* search operator), 66

A

Acceleration Watch, 356
acceptable use policy
   in organizations, 39
   in schools, 36
Access (Microsoft), 228–230
   objects, 228, 230
access points, 107, 137, 141
access time, 297
account, 147
ACCS. *See* Alternative Computer Control
      System
ACM (Association for Computing
      Machinery), 40–41
   www.acm.org, 40
active monitoring, 96
Active-matrix, 289
adapter cards, wireless, 138, 139
Ad-Aware, 161
address bar, 181
addresses
   e-mail, 70
      throwaway, 375
   IP, 57, 340
   Web, 57–60
Adobe Creative Suite media development
      kit, 197
Adobe Director, 196
Adobe Flash Player, 71, 195
Adobe Illustrator, 193
Adobe Photoshop, 194
Adobe Reader, 71
Adobe Shockwave Player, 71, 195
AdSense, 92
ADSL (asymmetric digital subscriber
      line), 111
Advanced GIF Animator, 195
Advanced Step in Innovative Mobility
      (ASIMO) robot, 23, 364, 365
Adventure GPS, 132
adware, 203, 378
.aero, 59
AFIS. *See* Automated Fingerprint
      Identification System
Agentland (www.agentland.com), 361,
      362, 365
AHS (Automated Highway System), 356, 365
AI. *See* artificial intelligence
AIM (AOL), 71, 74, 545

air traffic control systems, 21, 41
Albertsons.com, 91
www.albion.com/netiquette, 37
algorithms, 10
   genetic, 362
A.L.I.C.E. (Artificial Linguistic Internet
      Computer Entity), 360
all-in-one computers, 13, 15
   system unit in, 241
alt newsgroups, 77
Alternative Computer Control System
      (ACCS), 22
ALU (arithmetic-logic unit), 246
Amazon Marketplace, 88
Amazon.com, 91
AMD processors, 249
American Standard Code for Information
      Interchange. *See* ASCII
Americans with Disabilities Act of 1990,
      22
Ameritrade, 97
'An Atlas of Cyberspaces,' 51
analog signals, 102
analog technology, 108
AND operator, 66, 67
Android mobile OS, 375
animation programs, 194–195
anonymity, 369–372. *See also* privacy
   privacy and, 369–370
   threats to, 369
      cookies, 370–371
      GUIDs, 371
      RFID, 372
      ubiquitous computing, 371–372
Anonymizer's Anonymous Surfing, 374,
      375
anonymous FTP, 75, 76
Anonymous Surfing, 374, 375
Anti-Phishing Consumer Protection Act,
      374
anti-phishing features, Internet
      Explorer/Firefox, 403. *See also*
      phishing attacks
antispyware, 375
antivirus software, 161–162, 174, 203
AOL, 51
   AIM, 71, 74
   Mail, 71
   search engine, 63, 64
   TV, 320
Apocalypse Production Crew, 379
Apple
   iLife suite, 197
   iMac, system unit in, 241
   iMovie, 197
   iPhone 3G, 320–321
   Mac OS X, 155, 174
   Mac Pro, 241

   Macs, 6, 13, 31
      PCs v., 157, 159, 269–270
      PCs v. Linux v., 157, 159
   QuickTime Player, 71
   Software Update, 165
appliances
   Internet, 15, 320
   set-top, 15, 320
   smart, 140, 334
application software, 9, 188–217. *See also*
      specific programs
   automatic translation, 362
   beta versions of, 207
   CAT, 362
   commercial, 205, 210
   copy-protected, 206
   custom, 199
   database. *See* database programs
   defined, 190
   distribution of, 204
   documentation for, 204
   exiting, 209
   general-purpose, 190–198, 210
   home and educational, 197–198
   installing, 206–208
   integrated, 199–200
   launching, 208
   managing, 208–209
      OS and, 147–148
   multimedia and graphics, 192–197
   office suites (software suites), 200–202,
      210, 216
   options/settings for, 208
   packaged, 199
   pattern-recognition, 361
   personal productivity, 190–191
   public domain, 205
   registration of, 205
   shareware, 43, 205, 215
   sharing, networks and, 329
   software licenses for, 204–206
   software upgrades for, 202, 204
   speech-recognition, 287, 310, 357
   standalone, 199, 210
   system requirements, 202
   system software v., 210
   tailor-made, 198–199
   uninstalling, 207–208
application window, 220
application workspace, 220
applications. *See* application software
aquarium, computer system as, 9
architecture, network, 334, 336
archive, 165
argument set, 227
arithmetic operations, 246
arithmetic-logic unit (ALU), 246
arrow keys, 283

artificial intelligence (AI), 359
  brain *v.* computer, 360–361
  CYC project, 363
  genetic algorithms and, 362
  intelligence and, 359–360
  learning machines, 357
  pattern recognition and, 361
  robots, 364–365
    ASIMO, 23, 364, 365
    automation and, 24
    Cog, 363
    computer-guided, 23, 24
    defined, 364
    www.irobot.com, 365
    Kismet, 363
    MDS, 363
    nano-, 354
    Nexi, 363
    PaPeRo, 364, 365
    Personal Robots Group and, 364
    worldwide usage of, 24
  strong, 363
  translation technology and, 362
Artificial Linguistic Internet Computer
    Entity (A.L.I.C.E.), 360
ASCII (American Standard Code for
    Information Interchange), 75, 240
ASIMO (Advanced Step in Innovative
    Mobility) robot, 23, 364, 365
Ask (search engine), 63, 64
Ask Dr.Tech, 167
Association for Computing Machinery.
    See ACM
asymmetric digital subscriber line
    (ADSL), 111
Asynchronous Transfer Mode (ATM), 341
ATM (Asynchronous Transfer Mode), 341
Atom, 62
attachments (e-mail), 70
  screenshots as, 217
  viruses and, 380
attackers. *See also* computer crimes;
        cybercrime
  crackers, 384
  cyberbullying, 77, 386
  cybergangs, 384
  cyberstalking, 74, 77, 385–386,
        391–392
  hackers, 384–385, 389
  shills, 385
  swindlers, 385
  virus authors, 384
attacks
  DDoS, 382
  DoS, 382
  phishing, 378
  September 11th, 388, 394, 395
  spear phishing, 386
attribute, 177
auction sites, 88. *See also* eBay
AuctionFinder, Pay Pal, 98
audio software, 195–196

augmented reality, 359. *See also* virtual
        reality
authentication, 147
  biometric, 242, 390, 391
  know-and-have, 390
authoring systems, 196–197
authoritative online sources, 68
Automated Fingerprint Identification
        System (AFIS), 18
Automated Highway System (AHS), 356,
        365
automatic translation software, 362
automation, 24
autorecover, 208
autosave, 208
auxiliary storage, 293. *See also* storage

B

B2B e-commerce. *See* business-to-
        business e-commerce
B2C e-commerce. *See* business-to-
        consumer e-commerce
backbones, 339, 340, 344
backdoor, 395
back-end reports, 94
background application, 148
Backseat TV, 121
backside cache, 253
backup software, 159–161
backups, 33, 183–184, 311. *See also*
        storage devices
  complete, 33
  full, 160
  incremental, 160
  in organizations, 39
  remote, 33
  storage devices and, 10–11
bad sectors, 164, 297
bandwidth, 102–103, 126
  stealing, 110
  throughput *v.,* 102
banking (online), 95–96
  Microsoft Money Plus and, 96
  Quicken and, 96
  security and, 96
  Web-based, 96
Bankrate.com, 96
banner ads, 370, 371
bar code readers, 288
bargain-bin specials *v.* top-of-the-line
        computer systems, 274
The Bargainist, 89
base unit. *See* system unit
Basic Input/Output System. *See* BIOS
BD. *See* Blu-ray Discs
BD-R, 301
BD-RE, 301
BD-ROM, 301
beacons, Web, 73, 373, 402
Berkeley Open Infrastructure for
        Network Computing (BOINC), 338
beta versions (software), 207

BetaNews site, 207
Better Business Bureau, 374, 375
binary mode, 75
binary numbers, 238, 239
biochips, 353–355
biological feedback devices, 357
biometric authentication, 242, 390, 391
biometrics, 263
BIOS (Basic Input/Output System),
        145–146
bitmapped graphics, 193
BITNET, 77
bits, 239
BitTorrent, 331, 335, 379
.biz, 59
biz newsgroups, 77
black hats, 384
BlackBerry Curve 8320, 113
BlackBerry devices, 117
blackmail, 383
blocks, 298
blogs (Weblogs), 62
Bluetooth, 106–107, 125, 132
Blu-ray Discs (BD), 33, 271–272, 301
  BD-R discs, 301
  BD-RE discs, 301
  BD-ROM discs, 301
  data protection, 301
  drives, 272, 301
BMP (Windows Bitmap), 193
bogus goods, 385
BOINC (Berkeley Open Infrastructure for
        Network Computing), 338
Bookmarks, 61
Boolean searches, 66, 67, 78
  AND operator, 66, 67
  NOT operator, 66, 67
  OR operator, 66, 67
  parentheses ( ), 66, 67
boot disk, 165–166
boot sector viruses, 380–381
booting, 145
botnets, 382
box, computer. *See* system unit
Bplans, 92
bps rate, 104
brain, computer *v.,* 360–361
branch prediction, 248
broadband, 102–103, 126. *See also* cable;
        DSL; fiber-optic cables
broken links, 55
brokerages, online trading and, 97
Brookings Institution, Computer Ethics
        Institute of, 37
browsers, 55–57
  cached files and, 56
  Camino, 403
  defined, 55, 78
  first, 55
  Internet Explorer, 55, 57
    anti-phishing feature in, 403
    customizing, 58

encryption and, 401
Favorites, 61
features of, 57
pop-up blocker and, 403
micro-, 117
Mosaic, 55
Mozilla Firefox, 55, 57
anti-phishing feature in, 403
Bookmarks, 61
encryption and, 401
pop-up blocker and, 403
Netscape Navigator, 55
Opera, 56, 403
Safari, 70, 403
secure mode for, 96
types, 55, 56
Web connection via, 56
browsing
tabbed, 60
the Web, 60–62
BSA. *See* Business Software Alliance
Bsafe Online, 77
bugs, 21. *See also* debugging; errors
beta testing and, 207
bus topology, 333
Business Software Alliance (BSA), 14, 39
businesses (online), 92–94
back-end reports and, 94
business plan for, 92–93
credit cards and, 93–94
Homestead and, 94
naming, 93
search engines and, 93
Web hosting services for, 93
Web page development for, 93
business-to-business (B2B) e-commerce, 88
business-to-consumer (B2C) e-commerce, 89–98
banking and, 95–96
dot-com phenomenon and, 91–94
nonretail services and, 97
risks in, 97–98
shopping and, 89–91
stock trading and, 96–97
travel reservations and, 94–95
buying. *See* shopping
bytes, 239

C

C2C e-commerce. *See* consumer-to-consumer e-commerce
C3B Center (Clemson University), 354
cable (Internet access/television service), 8, 51, 52, 78, 111, 112, 141
cable routers, 141
cache, 263
backside, 253
disk, 297
primary, 253
secondary, 253

cache memory, 252–253
cached files, browsers and, 56
camcorders, digital, 319
cameras (digital), 317–319. *See also* cell phones
Webcams, 118, 119
Logitech Quickcam Pro 9000, 119
online information for, 120
in public locations, 119
Camino open source browser, 403
CAN-SPAM act, 73, 374
capturing screenshots, 217
caring, for computer systems, 277–278
carpal tunnel syndrome, 20
Carrier Sense Multiple Access/Collision Detection (CSMA/CD), 336
case/box, computer. *See* system unit
cash systems, digital, 303
CAT (computer-aided translation) software, 362
cat-5 cable, 105, 136
cat-6 cable, 136
cathode-ray tube (CRT) monitors, 288–289, 304
CAVE (Cave Automated Virtual Environment), 322, 358
Cave Automated Virtual Environment (CAVE), 322, 358
CCRC (Crimes Against Children Research Center), 386
CD (compact disc) technologies. *See also* DVD technologies
CD drives, 8, 10, 11, 300, 301
DVD-RW/CD-RW, 271, 301
rewritable, 33
CD-ROMs, 300, 304
CDs
CD-Rs, 301
CD-RWs, 301
data protection, 301
cell address, 226
cell phones, 114–116. *See also specific cell phones*
BlackBerry Curve 8320, 113
cameras in, 124–125
computers *v.,* 114
convergence and, 114–116
donating, 114
etiquette for, 115, 116
4G, 116, 132
holes and, 115
iPhone 3G, 320–321
location awareness and, 125, 375
MSCs and, 114–115
Nokia E90 Communicator, 116
Nokia N82, 125
phone number portability and, 113
picture messaging, 124–125
recycling, 114, 115–116
replacing, 131
Samsung Instinct, 321
2G, 116

services, evaluation of, 131
smartphones. *See* smartphones
teen usage of, 122, 124
text messaging. *See* text messaging
3G, 114
cell sites, 114
cells, 114, 226
central office (CO), 108, 109
central processing units (CPUs), 10, 245–251. *See also* microprocessors
64-bit, 247, 248
certificates, digital, 394
channels, 74
character code, 240
charts, Excel, 227–228
chat groups, 74. *See also* instant messaging; Internet Relay Chat
CheapTickets, 94
checkout stands, POS terminals as, 343
chemical detectors, 359
child pornography, 45, 77, 395
Children's Internet Safety Program, 77
children's security
Bsafe Online and, 77
Crimes Against Children Research Center and, 386
Crossing the Digital Divide and, 77
CyberAngels and, 77
myspaceWatch and, 77
Net Nanny and, 77
Online Safety Institute and, 77
Stop Cyberbullying and, 77
chip, 244
chip cards, 303
Chip Geek, 248
chipset, 251
ChoiceMail, 72
choosing. *See* selecting
ciphertext, 393
circuit switching, 340–341, 344
Cisco's WAN documentation, 341
citing online sources, 68
Clemson University's C3B Center, 354
click-and-brick stores, 91–92
clickstream, 63
clients, 15, 327
client/server networks, 15, 331–332
wireless, 137
Climate Savers Computing Initiative, 243
http://climateprediction.net, 338
Clip Organizer, 223
Cloudmark, 72
clusters, 296, 304
CMOS (complementary metal-oxide semiconductor), 146
CNET, 174
www.cnet.com, 25, 350
CO. *See* central office
coaxial cable, 104–105, 112
code
mission-critical/safety-critical, 21, 40–41
in software programs, 21

Code of Ethics of the Institute for Certification of Computing Professionals, excerpt from, 40
codecs, 192, 319
codes of conduct, 36, 40
  ACM, 40–41
Cog robot, 363
cold boot, 145
Collective-Good, 114
collisions, 333
Columbine High School tragedy, 38
columns, 226
.com, 59
Comcast, 51
command-line user interfaces, 153
commerce, 87. *See also* e-commerce
commercial application software, 205, 210
communications, 11, 102–133. *See also* networks
  data movement in, 102–104
    bandwidth and, 102–103
    modems and, 103–104
  defined, 102
  wired, 102
    transmission media, 104–105
  wireless, 102
    transmission media, 105–108
communications channels, 102
communications devices, 11, 327
Comp newsgroups, 76
compact disc read-only memory (CD-ROMs), 300, 304
compact disc technologies. *See* CD technologies
compact disc-recordables (CD-Rs), 301
CompactFlash, 317
complementary metal-oxide semiconductor (CMOS), 146
compression
  lossless, 192
  lossy, 193
compression utilities, 164–165
computer(s)
  advantages of, 17–19
  all-in-one, 13, 15, 241
  Apple. *See* Apple
  box. *See* system unit
  brain *v.,* 360–361
  categories of, 12, 26
  cell phones *v.,* 114
  cover. *See also* system unit
    removing, 276–277
    replacing, 277
  data and, 238–240. *See also* data
  definition of, 7, 26
  desktop, 13, 31, 241, 268–269
  development timeline (online), 7
  disabilities and, 22
  disadvantages of, 18–19
  DNA, 354
  donating, 25
  employment and, 5, 23–24, 26

ethics. *See* ethics
handheld, 15
hardware. *See* hardware
health care
  nanomedicine, 354
  VR and, 360
IBM-compatible, 13
for individuals, 12, 13, 15, 26
information and, 17
information-processing cycle, 7, 9–12, 26
informed choices and, 4–6
interoperability and, 48, 50, 51, 78
Mac. *See* Apple
micro, 13
mini, 16
Moore's Law and, 355–356
multicomputer families, 141
network, 15
notebook, 6, 13, 15, 31, 241, 268–269
OQO Model 02, 113
for organizations, 12–13, 15–16, 26
outside components of. *See* system unit
overusage of, 25, 26
ownership inequities and, 174
personal, 6, 13, 15
pervasiveness of, 4, 5
power-related problems and, 390
professional workstations, 15
responsible usage of, 24–25, 26
robots. *See* robots
role of, 17–18
shutting down, 167
society impacted by, 22
software. *See* software
starting, OS and, 145–147
super, 16, 32
system unit. *See* system unit
types of, 12–16
  online information, 15
viruses. *See* viruses
zombie, 335, 382
Computer Almanac site, 84
computer crimes, 377–387. *See also* cybercrime
  attackers in, 384–387
  blackmail and, 383
  data diddling, 383
  forgery, 383
  fraud, 88, 97, 382
  identity theft, 97, 377–378
  malware. *See* malware
  memory shaving, 382
  password obtaining, 382–383
  privacy threats *v.,* 377
  salami shaving, 383
  theft, 382
  unauthorized access, 382–383
computer ethics. *See* ethics
Computer Ethics Institute of the Brookings Institution, 37
computer gaming. *See* gaming

computer professionals, 40–41
computer systems, 7, 26. *See also* hardware; software
  as aquarium, 9
  buying, 267–276, 278, 279
  caring for, 277–278
  environment, safety in, 19–20
  protecting, 389–392
  recycling, 25
  refurbished, 276
  selecting, 268–274
  upgrading, 276–277
  used, 276
computer use policy, 36
Computer window, 180
computer-aided translation (CAT) software, 362
computer-guided robots, 23, 24
computer-to-phone service, 118
computing
  distributed, 338
  emerging technologies in, 352–365
  ubiquitous, 356–360
    AHS and, 356, 365
    biological feedback devices, 357
    chemical detectors and, 359
    digital forensics and, 357, 365
    privacy threats and, 371–372
    tactile displays and, 359
    VR and, 357–359, 365
concepts. *See key terms/concepts*
congestion, 341
connectivity, 102
connectors, 254–257. *See also specific connectors*
Consumer Information site, FTC, 373
consumer-to-consumer (C2C) e-commerce, 88–89
contention, 333
contention management, 333
contextual tabs, 222
control, of Internet/Web, 53
control structures, nesting, 67
control unit, 246
Convention on Cybercrime, 377
convergence, 113–117, 126, 131
  cell phones and, 114–116
  digitization and, 113, 126, 355
  home networking and, 140
  media, 113
  PDAs and, 117
  Web-enabled devices and, 117
convertible notebooks, 15
cookies, 370–371
cooling fans, 243
.coop, 59
copying, illegal. *See* piracy
copy-protected application software, 206
copyrights
  infringement, 42, 67, 379
  protection schemes, 43
  software, 43

violations, 67
www.copyright.gov, 67
www.eff.org, 67, 371
Core 2 Extreme, 250, 251, 264
CorelDRAW, 193
corporate espionage, 387–388
cover, computer. *See also* system unit
removing, 276–277
replacing, 277
CPUs. *See* central processing units
craigslist, 88
credit cards
online businesses and, 93–94
security and, 97–98
credit reporting agencies, 369
Equifax, 369
Experian, 369
TransUnion, 369
credit reports, 97
crimes. *See* computer crimes; cybercrime
Crimes Against Children Research Center
(CCRC), 386
Crossing the Digital Divide, 77
CRT (cathode-ray tube) monitors,
288–289, 304
cryptographers, 392
cryptography, 392, 395. *See also*
encryption
CSMA/CD (Carrier Sense Multiple
Access/Collision Detection), 336
cursor, 282
custom application software, 199
Cybelle, 365
CyberAngels, 77
CyberAngels Global Community
Web site, 77
cyberbullying, 77, 386
cybercrime, 377–387
attackers in, 384–387
government agencies and, 377
scams, 97, 385
bogus goods, 385
pumping and dumping, 385
rip and tear, 385
www.cybergeography.org/atlas/atlas
.html, 51
cyberlaw, 377
cyberspace, 48. *See also* Internet
cyberstalking, 74, 77, 385–386, 391–392
cyberterrorism, 388, 389
CYC project, 363

D

data, 9. *See also* files; information
backing up. *See* backups
character code as, 240
computers and, 238–240
misuse, 39
moving. *See* communications
numbers as, 238–240
privacy, 39

protection, discs and, 301
sharing, 44
storing. *See* backups
transporting, 33
data bus, 247
data communications. *See*
communications
data dependency, 248
data diddling, 383
data files (tables), 228, 230
data gloves, 358
data set, 229
data transfer rate, 104
database management systems (DBMSs),
software, Access 2007, 228–230
database programs, 201
dating services, 97, 98
day trading, 97
DBS. *See* direct broadcast satellite
DDoS (distributed denial of service)
attacks, 382
dead links, 55
debugging, bugs, 21
decimal numbers, 239
defragmentation programs, 164
demodulation, 103, 126
denial of service (DoS) attacks, 382
Department of Homeland Security. *See*
U.S. Department of Homeland
Security
design templates, 231, 232
desktop, 151
desktop computers, 13, 31
notebooks *v.*, 268–269
system unit in, 241
details pane, 181
Device Manager, 150
DHS. *See* U.S. Department of Homeland
Security
dialog box, 151, 152
dial-up Internet access, 51, 52, 78
dictionary, programs, 197
digital camcorders, 319
digital cameras, 317–319. *See also* cell
phones
point-and-shoot, 318
SLR, 318–319
Webcams, 118, 119
Logitech Quickcam Pro 9000, 119
online information for, 120
in public locations, 119
digital cash systems, 303
digital certificates, 394
digital divide, 17
digital forensics, 357, 365
digital light-processing (DLP) projectors,
292
digital modems, 111
digital piracy. *See* piracy
digital service line. *See* DSL
digital signals, 102, 103
digital signatures, 393–394

digital telephony, 108–109, 127. *See also*
last-mile technologies
digital video, 319
digital video cameras, 319
digital video recorders (DVRs), 321–322
digital video/versatile disc read-only
memory (DVD-ROMs), 300, 304
digital video/versatile disc technologies.
See DVD technologies
Digital Visual Interface port. *See* DVI port
digitization, 113, 126, 355. *See also*
convergence
direct broadcast satellite (DBS), 107
Direct Marketing Association (DMA),
73, 373
Director, Adobe, 196
directories, 177, 182–183
DIRECTTV, 107
disabilities
ACCS and, 22
Americans with Disabilities Act of
1990, 22
computers and, 22
discs. *See also* Blu-ray Discs; CD
technologies; DVD technologies
data protection on, 301
disks *v.*, 301
as optical storage devices, 300, 301
discussion forums, netiquette for, 37
discussion threads, 75
disintermediation, 92
disk cache, 297
disk cleanup utilities, 164
disk defragmentation programs, 164
Disk Killer virus, 380
disk operating system. *See* DOS
disk scanning programs, 163–164
disks. *See also* discs; floppy disks; hard
disks
boot, 165–166
discs *v.*, 301
emergency, 165–166
fragmented, 164
displays. *See* monitors
distributed computing, 338
distributed denial of service (DDoS)
attacks, 382
distributed hypermedia system, 54
distribution of application software, 204
DLP (digital light-processing) projectors,
292
DMA. *See* Direct Marketing Association
DNA computers, 354
DNS. *See* Domain Name System
documentation
Cisco's WAN, 341
software, 204
documents, 220
.docx, 226
Dogpile (search engine), 66
domain name registration, 59, 84
Domain Name System (DNS), 59

domain names, 58–59
online information for, 60
top-level, 59
donations
cell phone, 114
computer, 25
lending computers to science, 338
DoS (denial of service) attacks, 382
DOS (disk operating system), 157
dot pitch, 272
dot-com phenomenon, 91–94
double layer DVDs, 33
Download.com, 161
downloading, 61
Dragon NaturallySpeaking, 287
drawing programs, 193
drive activity light, 253
drive bays, 243
drive imaging software, 160
drivers, 146
drives, 177
Blu-ray Disc, 272, 301
CD, 8, 10, 11
rewritable, 33
defined, 271
DVD, 8, 10, 11
rewritable, 33
DVD-RW/CD-RW, 271
external, 271–272
flash, 298, 302
USB, 11, 33, 298–300
floppy disk, 10, 33, 177
internal, 271–272
Zip, 10
DSL (digital service line), 8, 78, 111–112
DSL routers, 141
dumpster diving, 383
DVD (digital video/versatile disc)
technologies
Blu-ray Discs, 33, 271–272, 301
DVD drives, 8, 10, 11, 300, 301
DVD-RW/CD-RW, 271
rewritable, 33
DVD-ROMs, 300, 304
DVDs
data protection, 301
double layer, 33
DVD+ standard, 301
DVD- standard, 301
DVD+R, 301
DVD-R, 301
DVD+RW, 301
formats for, 33
DVI (Digital Visual Interface) port, 255, 256
DVRs (digital video recorders), 321–322
dynamic searches, 182

E

Easter Egg Archive, 32
eBay, 88, 89, 99
EBCDIC (Extended Binary Coded
Decimal Interchange Code), 240

e-books, 316
EBSCOhost, 68
Echelon, 122
e-commerce (electronic commerce), 86–99
B2B, 88
B2C, 89–98
C2C, 88–89
eCoupons, 89
.edu, 59
educational and home programs, 197–198
EEPROM, 252
www.eff.org, 67, 371
Egencia, 95
802.11a standard, 138, 337
802.11b standard, 138, 337
802.11g standard, 138, 337
802.11n standard, 138, 337
802.15 standard, 337
802.16 standard, 337
EINSTEIN, 388
e-learning, 22
electromagnetic pulse transformer
(EMPT) bombs, 389
electronic commerce. See e-commerce
Electronic Frontier Foundation
(www.eff.org), 67, 371
electronic mail. See e-mail
electronic mailing lists, 77
Electronic Privacy Information Center
(EPIC), 368, 402
electronic vault, 96
electronic voting, 123
ELIZA, 360
e-mail (electronic mail), 70, 72–73
addresses, 70
throwaway, 375
advantages/disadvantages, 70
attachments, 70
screenshots as, 217
viruses in, 380
electronic mailing lists and, 77
fax-to-mail technology, 120
filtering, 72–73, 85
free, 83
managing, 185–186
netiquette, 37–38
programs
AOL Mail, 71
Gmail, 71
Hotmail, 71
Mozilla Thunderbird, 71
Outlook, 71
Windows Mail, 71
Yahoo! Mail, 71
spam. See spam
text messaging and, 70
usage amounts, 72
emergency disk, 165–166
emerging/new computing technologies,
352–365
employee monitoring, 376
employment

computers' impact on, 5, 23–24, 26
Internet search for, 83
outsourcing and, 31
structural unemployment and, 24
EMPT (electromagnetic pulse
transformer) bombs, 389
encryption, 392–395
basics, 393
cryptography and, 392, 395
defined, 393
56-bit, 401
Internet Explorer and, 401
Mozilla Firefox and, 401
128-bit, 401
PGP Corporation and, 395
PKI and, 394
public key, 393–394
public security issues and, 394–395
symmetric key, 393
WEP, 133, 387
encryption keys, 393
Energy Star logo, 247
Enigma machines, 402
Environmental Protection Agency site, 25
www.epa.gov, 25
EPIC (Electronic Privacy Information
Center), 368, 402
EPROM, 252
Equifax, 369
ergonomic keyboards, 20, 304
ergonomics, 20
Ericsson, 106
errors, in software programs, 20–21, 26
espionage
corporate, 388–389
international, 388
e-tailers, 86
Ethernet, 136, 336, 337, 344
cat-5 cable, 105, 136
cat-6 cable, 136
Fast Ethernet (100Base-T), 136, 336,
337, 350
gigabit Ethernet (1000Base-T), 136,
336, 337
home network, 136–137
Metcalfe and, 355
network adapters (NICs), 8, 11, 136,
273, 327, 328
10Base-T, 336, 337
ethical hackers, 384
ethical principles, 36
ethics (computer), 21–22, 35–45
codes of conduct, 36, 40
ACM, 40–41
for computer professionals, 40–41
copyrights
infringement, 42, 67, 379
protection schemes, 43
software, 43
violations, 67
crime and. See cybercrime
defined, 21, 35

gaming and, 38, 197
GPS and, 122
illegal actions and
   file sharing, 44
   libel, 42
   piracy, 14, 39, 43–44
   plagiarism, 41–42
   unethical v., 35
Internet and, 22
netiquette and, 37–38
for organizations, 39
piggybacking and, 110, 339
privacy and. See privacy
respect and, 36
safety-critical software programs and,
   21, 40–41
smartphones and, 15
spotlight on, 35–45
Ten Commandments for Computer
   Ethics, 37
etiquette
   cell phone, 115, 116
   Internet. See netiquette
E*TRADE, 97, 99
e-trading. See stock trading
EverQuest, 198
e-waste, 25
exabytes, 239
Excel (Microsoft), 226–228
exclusion operators (-), 66–67, 78
executable file attachments, viruses and,
   380
execution cycle, 246
exercises. See fill-in; matching; multiple
   choice; on the Web; short answer;
   spotlight; teamwork
exiting application software, 209
expansion cards, 243, 244, 277. See also
   memory; modems; network
   interface cards; sound cards; video
   cards
Expedia, 94, 95
Experian, 369
ExpressCards, 257, 302
Extended Binary Coded Decimal
   Interchange Code. See EBCDIC
extensions, 59, 179
external drives, 271–272
external hard disks, 33
external modems, 104
external peripheral devices, 11
eye-gaze response systems, 357

F

face recognition systems, 361
Facebook, 74, 75
facsimile transmissions. See faxes
Fair Credit Reporting Act, 373
fair use doctrine, 42, 132
Family Educational Rights and Privacy
   Act (FERPA), 373

fans, cooling, 243
FAQs (frequently asked questions), 37
Fast Ethernet (100Base-T), 136, 336,
   337, 350
FAT (file allocation table), 296
Favorites, 61
fax machines, 120
fax modems, 120
faxes (facsimile transmissions), 120,
   121, 131
fax-to-mail technology, 120
Federal Trade Commission (FTC)
   Consumer Information site, 373
   OnGuard Online site, 377
   spam site (www.ftc.gov/spam), 73
FERPA (Family Educational Rights and
   Privacy Act), 373
fiber-optic cables, 105
   T1 lines, 112
   T3 lines, 112
fiber-optic service (FiOS), 51, 52, 78
56-bit encryption, 401
file allocation table (FAT), 296
file compression utilities, 164–165, 174
file infectors, 378. See also viruses
file list, 180
file management, 176–187
   e-mail, 185–186
   from within programs, 184–185
   Windows Explorer and. See Windows
      Explorer
file manager, 162–163
file servers, 328. See also networks
File Transfer Protocol. See FTP
filenames, 179
file-naming conventions, 179
files. See also data; information
   data. See data files
   defined, 177
   saving, 185
   sharing, 44
   transferring, 183
   transporting, 33
fill-in
   chapter 1, 30
   chapter 2, 82
   chapter 3, 130
   chapter 4, 172
   chapter 5, 214
   chapter 6, 262
   chapter 7, 308
   chapter 8, 348
   chapter 9, 400
filter, 229
filtering
   content on Internet, 77
   e-mail, 72–73, 85. See also spam
FindSounds (search engine), 66
FiOS. See fiber-optic service
Firefox. See Mozilla Firefox
firewalls, 390–391
   hardware, 141

home networks and, 139, 140
   personal, 139, 140, 391, 402
   software, 139, 140, 141
FireWire cables, 257
FireWire (1394) ports, 255–256
flames, 77
flash drives, 298, 302, 304
   USB, 11, 33, 298, 300, 304
      IronKey Secure, 375
flash memory cards, 11, 302–303, 304
flash memory readers, 302
Flash Player, Adobe, 71, 195
Flickr, 194
floating point notation and, 240
floppy disks, 10, 33, 177. See also hard
   disks
folders, 177
   creating, 182–183
   sub, 177
   top-level, 178
folding@home project
   (http://folding.stanford.edu), 338
footprint, 240
foreground application, 148
forgery, 383
form factor, 240
Form object, 228
forms, 228, 230
formulas, 227
forward slash marks (//), 58
fourth generation cell phones. See 4G cell
   phones
4G cell phones, 116, 132
fragmented disk, 164
frame rate, 319
frames, 319
Franklin TGA-490 (language translator),
   362
fraud, 88, 97, 382
free e-mail, 83
free software, 159, 205, 216. See also open
   source software
freeware, 205, 216
frequently asked questions. See FAQs
front panel, 253–254
FTC. See Federal Trade Commission
www.ftc.gov/spam, 73
FTP (File Transfer Protocol), 58, 78
   anonymous, 75, 76
   site access, Windows Explorer and, 75, 76
   WS_FTP Home and, 75
fuel cells, methane-powered, 247
Fujack worm, 384
full backups, 160
function keys, 283
functions, 227

G

gadgets, 154
game cards, 257
gaming (online), 84, 197–198
   devices for, 322

gaming *(continued)*
    ethics and, 38
        multimedia and, 313–314
        violence and, 38
gateway mobile switching center
        (GMSC), 114
GB (gigabytes), 239
General Public License (GPL), 43, 205
general-purpose application software,
        190–198, 210
generic *v.* name-brand PCs, 276
genetic algorithms, 362
gesture recognition, 357
GIF (Graphics Interchange Format),
        193, 194
gigabit Ethernet (1000Base-T), 136,
        336, 337
gigabits per second, 239
gigabytes (GB), 239
Gitarts, Barry, 379
Global Positioning System. *See* GPS
global unique identifiers (GUIDs), 371
globalization, 24
gloves, data, 358
Gmail, 71
GMSC (gateway mobile switching
        center), 114
GoDaddy, 93
going online, 51–53
Goodwin, Doris Kearns, 42
Google
    AdSense, 92
    Android mobile OS, 375
    Gmail, 71
    image search site, 132
    toolbar, 403
    as top search engine, 63, 64
Google Docs, 202
Google Groups, 77
Google Scholar, 68, 69
Google Talk, 71
.gov, 59
GPL. *See* General Public License
GPS (Global Positioning System), 121–122
    Adventure GPS site, 132
    ethics/privacy and, 122
    location awareness and, 125, 375
    OnStar and, 122
    receivers, 107, 121–122
    rental cars and, 401
graphical MUDs, 198
graphical user interfaces (GUIs), 151
graphics and multimedia software,
        192–197
Graphics Interchange Format (GIF), 193,
        194
Gravitonus, 22
Green Maven (search engine), 64
GreenDisk, 202
GridWise at PNNL, 334
grocery shopping (online), 89–91
groups, 222–223

Guardian Angels, 77
GUIDs (global unique identifiers), 371
GUIs (graphical user interfaces), 151

H

hacking/hackers, 384–385
    black hats, 384
    ethical, 384
    history of, 385
    information warfare and, 388
    IP spoofing and, 384
    NASA and, 392
    public safety and, 389
    RaFa, 392
    stereotypes, 385
    white hats, 384
handheld computers, 15
hard copy, 291
hard disks, 10, 11, 295–298. *See also*
        drives
    external, 33
    HHD, 298
    Internet, 296–297
    magnetic, 295, 301
    memory *v.,* 295
    NAS, 296
    partitions, 296
    performance, 297–298, 304
    random access, 295
    remote storage, 296–297
    as secondary storage, 295
    selecting, 271
hardware, 7–8. *See also* input devices;
        output devices; storage devices
    firewalls, 141
    intimidation and, 19
    recycling, 25
    safety and, 19–20
HDTV (high-definition television), 290
head-mounted display (HMD), 322, 358
headsets
    with microphone, 8
    as multimedia devices, 322
health care
    nanomedicine, 354
    VR and, 360
Health Insurance Portability and Privacy
        Act (HIPAA), 373
heat sink, 245
HelloDirect, 109
Help and Support utility, 167
HERF (high-energy radio frequency)
        guns, 389
hex (hexadecimal) numbers, 239
hexadecimal (hex) numbers, 239
HHDs (hybrid hard drives), 298
High-definition television (HDTV), 290
high-energy radio frequency (HERF)
        guns, 389
HIPAA (Health Insurance Portability and
        Privacy Act), 373

history (online)
    of computers, 7
    of hacking, 385
    of Internet, 48
history list, 60
HMD (head-mounted display), 322, 358
hoaxes, virus, 381
holes, 115
holographic storage devices, 303
home and educational programs, 197–198
home design programs, 198
home directory, 147
home networks, 134–141. *See also*
        LANs
    convergence and, 140
    defined, 136
    future of, 140
    maintenance/support for, 140
    Network and Sharing Center
        and, 140
    Network Setup Wizard, 140
    setting up, 138–140
        configuration, 139–140
        online information, 139
        planning, 138–139
    wired, 136–137
        Ethernet, 136–137
        home power-line network, 137
    wireless, 137–138
        advantages/disadvantages, 138
        client/server, 137
        peer-to-peer, 137
home page (index page), 53
home power-line networks, 137
Home tab, 221
Homestead (www.homestead.com), 94
Honda's ASIMO robot, 23, 364, 365
Honeynet Project, 392
honeypots, 392
HopeLine project, 114
Hopper, Grace Murray, 21
host name, 59
hosting services, 93
    GoDaddy, 93
    1&1, 93
    Yahoo!, 93
hot swapping, 254
Hotmail, Windows Live, 71
HotSpot Haven, 133
hotspots, 110, 133, 339
www.howstuffworks.com, 32, 254
HTML (Hypertext Markup Language), 54
HTTP (Hypertext Transfer Protocol), 58
https, 98
HughesNet, 122, 124
human brain, computer *v.,* 360–361
hybrid hard drives (HHDs), 298
hyperlinks (links), 54, 60
    broken, 55
    dead, 55
hypermedia system, distributed, 54
hypertext, 54–55, 78

Hypertext Markup Language. *See* HTML
Hypertext Transfer Protocol. *See* HTTP

I

I2 project. *See* Internet2 project
IAB. *See* Internet Architecture Board
IBM 'Roadrunner' supercomputer, 16
IBM-compatible computers, 13
IC (integrated circuit), 244
IC3 (Internet Crime Complaint
        Center), 376
ICANN. *See* Internet Corporation for
        Assigned Names and Numbers
ICQ, 71
identity theft, 97, 377–378
IETF (Internet Engineering Task
        Force), 54
iLife suite, 197
illegal actions. *See also* cybercrime; ethics
    fair use doctrine and, 42, 132
    file sharing, 44
    libel, 42
    piracy, 14, 31, 39, 43–44
    plagiarism, 41–42
    stealing bandwidth, 110
    unethical *v.,* 35
Illustrator, Adobe, 193
IM. *See* instant messaging
iMac, system unit in, 241
image editors, 194
image search site, Google's, 132
iMovie, 197
inclusion operators (+), 66, 78
incremental backup, 160
Indeed (search engine), 64
index page, 53
individuals, computers for, 12, 13, 15, 26
.info, 59
Infoplease, 64, 65
information, 10. *See also* data; files
    collection of, without consent, 368–369
    computers' role with, 17
    finding, on Web, 63–69
    Internet and, 48, 49
    sharing. *See* sharing information
information kiosks, 314
information overload, 19
information warfare, 388–389
information-processing cycle, 7, 9–11, 26
    communications and, 11
    example of, 11–12
    exercise, 31
    input, 7, 9, 11, 12
    online information for, 12
    output, 7, 10, 12
    processing, 7, 10, 11–12
    storage, 7, 10–11, 12, 293
InfoUSA, 369
infrared, 105–106
Infrared Data Association ports. *See*
        IrDA ports

infringements, copyright, 42, 67, 379
inkjet printers, 291, 304
input (in information-processing cycle),
        7, 9, 11
input devices, 282–288
    bar code readers, 288
    keyboards, 8, 9, 282–285
        ergonomic, 20
        Microsoft Natural Keyboard, 20
        selecting, 273
    microphones, 8, 287
    optical mark readers, 288
    OS and, 150
    pointing devices, 285–287
        joystick, 285, 286
        mice, 8, 9, 273, 285–286
        pointing stick, 285, 286
        stylus, 285, 286
        touch screen, 285, 286
        touchpad, 285, 286
        trackball, 286
    scanners, 287, 288
input/output (I/O) bus, 251
Insert tab, 221–222
insertion point, 283
installing application software, 206–208
instant messaging (IM), 71, 73–74, 78
    netiquette for, 38
    programs
        AOL AIM, 71, 74
        Google Talk, 71
        ICQ, 71
        meebo.com, 71
        Windows Live Messenger, 71, 74
        Yahoo! Messenger, 71
    spimming and, 74, 381
instruction cycle, 246
instruction set, 246
insurance products, 97
integrated application software, 199–200
integrated circuit (IC), 244
integrated circuit cards (ICCs), 303
integrated services digital network. *See*
        ISDN
Intel microprocessors
    comparison of, 265
    evolution of, 249, 250
Intel Museum, 245
intelligence, 329–360. *See also* artificial
        intelligence
intelligent agents, 361, 365
Intelligent Transportation Systems (ITS)
        program, 356
internal drives, 271–272
internal modems, 104
internal peripheral devices, 11
internal speaker, 243
international espionage, 388
international news, 32
Internet. *See also* entries with *cyber;*
        networks; online
    access, 51–53

        cable, 8, 51, 52, 78, 111, 112
        dial-up, 51, 52, 78
        DSL, 8, 51, 52, 78, 111–112
        FiOS, 51, 52, 78
        satellites, 51, 52, 78, 107–108,
            120–122, 124
        through schools, 83
    children's security and, 77
    content, filtering, 77
    control of, 53
    crime. *See* cybercrime
    cyberspace as, 48
    defined, 48
    employment and, 5, 23–24, 26
    ethics and, 22. *See also* ethics
    faxing on. *See* faxes
    fraud on, 88
    gaming. *See* gaming
    growth of, 5, 48, 84
    hard drives, 296–297
    history (online), 48
    information and, 48, 49
    international news and, 32
    interoperability of, 48, 50, 51, 78
    libraries and, 68
    management organizations, 54
        IAB, 54
        ICANN, 54
        IETF, 54
        Internet Solutions, 54
        IRTF, 54
        ISOC, 48, 54
        W3C, 53, 54
    Moore's Law and, 355–356
    netiquette for, 37–38
    as network of networks, 48, 50, 78
    ownership of, 53
    physical structure (online), 51
    piracy on. *See* piracy
    statistics, 84
    telephony. *See* VoIP
    usage
        inequities in, 17
        over-, 25, 26
        percentages of, 48
        responsible, 24–25, 26
    Web *v.,* 53, 78
Internet appliances, 15, 320
Internet Architecture Board (IAB), 54
Internet Corporation for Assigned Names
        and Numbers (ICANN), 54, 60
Internet Crime Complaint Center
        (IC3), 376
Internet Engineering Task Force
        (IETF), 54
Internet Explorer (Microsoft), 55, 57
    anti-phishing feature in, 403
    customizing, 58
    encryption and, 401
    Favorites, 61
    features of, 57
    pop-up blocker and, 403

Internet programs, 197. *See also* browsers; e-mail; instant messaging
Internet Protocol. *See* IP
Internet protocols (TCP/IP), 340
Internet Public Library, 32
Internet Relay Chat (IRC), 71, 74, 78. *See also* instant messaging
  channels on, 74
  mIRC, 71
  Mozilla ChatZilla, 71
  Trillian, 71
Internet Research Task Force (IRTF), 54
Internet service providers (ISPs), 48, 50, 78
  list of, 52, 351
  online services *v.*, 51
  researching, 83
  roles/responsibilities of, 51
  selecting, 351
Internet services, 70–77. *See also* e-mail; instant messaging
  defined, 70
  IRC, 71, 74
  list of, 71
  popular, 71, 78
Internet Society (ISOC), 48, 54
Internet Solutions, 54
Internet storage, 310
Internet2 (I2) project, 48, 84
www.internettutorials.net/search.html, 67
InterNIC, 59
interoperability, 48, 50, 51, 78
interrupt handlers, 150
interrupt request (IRQ), 150
interrupts, 150
I/O (input/output) bus, 251
IP (Internet Protocol), 340
  address, 57, 340
  spoofing, 384
iPhone 3G, 320–321
IRC. *See* Internet Relay Chat
IrDA (Infrared Data Association) ports, 105–106
www.irobot.com, 365
IronKey Secure USB flash drive, 375
IRQ (interrupt request), 150
IRTF. *See* Internet Research Task Force
ISDN (integrated services digital network), 111
ISOC. *See* Internet Society
www.isoc.org/internet/history, 48, 54
ISPs. *See* Internet service providers
ITS (Intelligent Transportation Systems) program, 356

J

jaggies, 193
JiWire, 133
Joint Photographic Experts Group (JPEG), 193

Joost, 335
joysticks, 285, 286
JPEG (Joint Photographic Experts Group), 193

K

KartOO (search engine), 66
Kaspersky Lab's Viruslist site, 385
Kazaa.com, 45, 335
KB (kilobytes), 239
Kbps (kilobits per second), 103, 239
Kennedy Space Center, 392
kernel, 145
key terms/concepts
  chapter 1, 27
  chapter 2, 79
  chapter 3, 127
  chapter 4, 169
  chapter 5, 211
  chapter 6, 259
  chapter 7, 305
  chapter 8, 345
  chapter 9, 397
keyboards, 8, 9, 282–285, 304
  alternative, 283–284
  ergonomic, 20
  Microsoft Natural Keyboard, 20
  PC enhanced, 284
  QWERTY layout, 283
  selecting, 273
keyloggers, 378
keys. *See also* encryption
  encryption, 393
  private, 393, 394
  public, 393
kilobits per second. *See* Kbps
kilobytes (KB), 239
Kingston Technology's Ultimate Memory Guide, 251
kiosks, 286
  information, 314
Kismet robot, 363
know-and-have authentication, 390
Kodak Easyshare printer dock, 318

L

labels, 227
languages. *See also* Web-based languages
  Franklin TGA-490 and, 362
  translation technology for, 362
  VRML, 358
LANs (local area networks), 326, 330–339, 344
  client/server, 15, 331–332
  online information, 338
  P2P, 45, 331, 335, 344
  protocols, 334–339
    Ethernet (10Base-T), 136, 336, 337, 344
    Fast Ethernet (100Base-T), 136, 336, 337, 350

    Gigabit Ethernet, 136, 336, 337
    Token Ring Network, 337
  topologies, 333–334, 344
    bus, 333
    ring, 333, 334
    star, 333–334
  VPN, 331
  WANs *v.*, 344
  wireless, 330
    Wi-Fi, 336–339
LAN-to-LAN connections, with WANs, 341
laptop computers. *See* notebook computers
laser printers, 291, 304
last-mile problem, 109
last-mile technologies, 109–113, 126
  cable modems, 8, 51, 52, 78, 111, 112
  coaxial cable, 104–105, 112
  DSL, 8, 78, 111–112
  ISDN, 111
  leased lines, 112
  MMDS, 112, 126
  selecting, 112
  SONET, 112
  WiMAX, 112, 126
latency, 341
launching application software, 208
layers, network, 334, 336
LCD projectors, 292
LCDs (liquid crystal displays), 289, 304
learning machines, 357. *See also* artificial intelligence
leased lines, 112
Leebow, Ken, 77
legacy technology, 11, 255, 257
lending computers, to science, 338
LexisNexis, 68
libel, 42
libraries, Internet and, 68
licenses
  site, 43, 204, 215
  software, 204–206
Lime Wire, 331, 335, 379
LinkedIn, 74
links. *See* communications channels; hyperlinks
Linksys routers, 140
Linux, 156–157
  PCs *v.* Macs *v.*, 157, 159
  usage, 158
Linux Today, 156
liquid crystal displays. *See* LCDs
The List (www.thelist.com), 52, 351
Listserv, 77
Live ID, 394, 395
Live Search, 63, 64
load, 145
local area networks. *See* LANs
local exchange switch, 108, 109
local loop, 108, 109, 126
location (position) awareness, 125, 375

locked padlock symbol, 98
Loebner Prize Competition, 360
logical operations, 246
logical operators
   AND, 66, 67
   NOT, 66, 67
   OR, 66, 67
login, 147
Logitech Quickcam Pro 9000, 119
lossless compression, 192

M

Mac computers. *See* Apple
Mac OS X, 155, 174
Mac Pro, 241
machine cycle, 246
machine dependent software, 43–44
machine translation (MT) tools, 362
machine-assisted human translation
   (MAHT), 362
Macintosh computers. *See* Apple
macro viruses, 381
macros, 381
www.macfixit, 167
magnetic storage devices, 295, 301. *See*
   also hard disks
Mahalo (search engine), 66
MAHT (machine-assisted human
   translation), 362
Mailings tab, 222
mail-order computers, 274–276
mail-to-fax technology, 120
MailWasher, 73
mainframes, 16
maintenance release, 202
Majordomo, 77
malicious software. *See* malware
malware, 161, 378, 380–382
   adware, 203, 378
   botnets and, 382
   DDoS attacks, 382
   DoS attacks, 382
   keyloggers, 378
   spyware, 203, 378
   Storm, 375
   timebombs, 381
   Trojan horses, 335, 382
   viruses, 175, 378, 380–381
      antivirus software, 161–162, 174
      boot sector, 380–381
      Disk Killer, 380
      downloaded, 61
      e-mail attachments and, 380
      file infectors, 378
      hoaxes, 381
      macro, 381
      Melissa, 384
      variants, 381
      Wazzu, 380
   worms, 381, 384
   zombie computers and, 335, 382

management organizations, for
   Internet, 54
   IAB, 54
   ICANN, 54, 60
   IETF, 54
   Internet Solutions, 54
   IRTF, 54
   ISOC, 48, 54
   W3C, 53, 54
managing
   application software, 147–148, 208–209
   e-mail. *See* e-mail
   files. *See* file management
   memory, OS and, 148–150
markup languages, HTML, 54
mass storage, 293. *See also* storage
massively multiplayer online role-playing
   games (MMORPGs), 198
matching
   chapter 1, 28
   chapter 2, 80
   chapter 3, 128
   chapter 4, 170
   chapter 5, 212
   chapter 6, 260
   chapter 7, 306
   chapter 8, 346
   chapter 9, 398
math coprocessor, 240
mathematical formula, 227
MB (megabytes), 239
Mbps (megabits per second), 103, 239
McAfee
   antispam feature, 73
   Total Protection, 141
   VirusScan Plus, 162
MDS (mobile-dexterous-social) robots, 363
media card readers, 8, 11
media convergence, 113
Media Player, Windows, 71, 196
medicine
   nanomedicine, 354
   tailor-made software for medical offices,
      199
   VR and, 360
meebo.com, 71
megabits per second. *See* Mbps
megabytes (MB), 239
Melissa virus, 384
memory, 10, 251–253. *See also* storage
   devices
   cache, 252–253
   hard disks *v.*, 295
   managing, OS and, 148–150
   nonvolatile, 146
   racetrack, 299
   RAM, 10, 19, 251–252
      sufficient amounts of, 270–271
   ROM, 146
   shaving, 382
   storage devices *v.*, 293–295, 304
   Ultimate Memory Guide, 251

   upgrading, 277
   virtual, 149
   volatile, 145
memory cards
   flash, 11, 302–303, 304
   wireless, 303
menu-driven user interfaces, 151, 153
messaging. *See* e-mail; instant messaging;
   Internet Relay Chat; picture
   messaging; text messaging
Metcalfe, Bob, 355
Metcalfe's Law, 355–356
methane-powered fuel cells, 247
mice, 8, 9, 285–286. *See also* pointing
   devices
   alternatives, 286–287
   selecting, 273
   VisualMouse, 357
   wheel, 285
microbrowsers, 117
microcomputers, 13. *See also* personal
   computers
microphones, 8, 287
microprocessors (processors), 10, 245–251
   AMD, 249
   Intel, 249, 250
      comparison of, 265
      evolution of, 249, 250
   performance, 247
   popular, 249–251
   selecting, 270
Microsoft
   Internet Explorer. *See* Internet
      Explorer
   Money Plus. *See* Money Plus
   Natural Keyboard. *See* Natural
      Keyboard
   Office. *See* Office suite
   search engine. *See* Live Search
   Windows. *See* Windows
Microsoft Works, 200, 216
microwaves, 107
MIDI (Musical Instrument Digital
   Interface), 195
mid-range servers, 16
.mil, 59
minicomputers, 16
minimize, 220
minitower case, 240
mIRC, 71
Misc newsgroups, 76
mission-critical software programs, 21,
   40–41
MMDS (multichannel multipoint
   distribution service), 112, 126
MMORPGs (massively multiplayer online
   role-playing games), 198, 199
mobile phones. *See* cell phones
mobile switching centers (MSCs),
   114–115
   cell phones and, 114–115
   text messaging and, 115

Mobile, Windows, 154–155

mobile-dexterous-social (MDS) robots, 363

modeling, 226

modems (modulators/demodulators), 11, 103–104, 126

  cable, 8, 51, 52, 78, 111, 112

  dial-up, 51, 52, 78

  digital, 111

  DSL, 8, 51, 52, 78, 111–112

  external, 104

  fax, 120

  internal, 104

  networks and, 327

  school networks and, 273

modulation, 103, 126

  protocols, 334

modulators/demodulators. *See* modems

modules, 200

Money Plus (Microsoft), 96

monitoring

  active, 96

  employee, 376

  software for, 376, 402

monitors (displays), 8, 10, 272, 288–291, 304

  CRT, 288–289, 304

  dot pitch of, 272

  LCD, 289, 304

  qualities of, 272

  refresh rate and, 290

  resolutions for, 290

  screen sizes of, 272, 289–290

  tactile, 359

  TVs as, 290

  video cards and, 272

Moore, Gordon, 355

Moore's Law, 355–356

Mosaic, 55

motherboards, 243, 244–253

  chipset on, 251

  components, 244

  memory on. *See* memory

  microprocessors on. *See* microprocessors

  system clock on, 248

Moving Picture Experts Group (MPEG), 196

Mozilla ChatZilla, 71

Mozilla Firefox, 55, 57

  anti-phishing feature in, 403

  Bookmarks, 61

  encryption and, 401

  pop-up blocker and, 403

Mozilla Thunderbird, 71

MP3

  players, 314–315

  sharing, 44, 195

MPEG (Moving Picture Experts Group), 196

MSCs. *See* mobile switching centers

MS-DOS, 157

MSN, 51

MSN Hotmail. *See* Windows Live Hotmail

MSN Messenger. *See* Windows Live Messenger

MSN TV, 320

MT (machine translation) tools, 362

MUDs (multiuser dungeons/dimensions), 198

multichannel multipoint distribution service (MMDS), 112, 126

multicomputer families, 141

multifunction devices, 292–293

multimedia

  defined, 192, 313

  gaming and, 313–314

multimedia and graphics software, 192–197

multimedia authoring systems, 196–197

multimedia devices, 312–323

  audio

    MP3 players, 314–315

    voice recorders, 316

  DVRs, 321–322

  gaming devices, 322

  headsets, 322

  Internet appliances, 15, 320

  portable, 320–321

    iPhone 3G, 320–321

    Samsung Instinct, 321

  TV, 320

  visual

    digital camcorders, 319

    digital cameras, 317–319

    e-books, 316

multiple choice

  chapter 1, 29

  chapter 2, 81

  chapter 3, 129

  chapter 4, 171

  chapter 5, 213

  chapter 6, 261

  chapter 7, 307

  chapter 8, 347

  chapter 9, 399

multiplexing, 109, 126

multiuser dungeons/dimensions (MUDs), 198

.museum, 59

music

  piracy, 31, 32, 44. *See also* piracy

  sharing, P2P networks and, 335

Musical Instrument Digital Interface (MIDI), 195

MySpace, 74, 75

  advertising on, 44

  spam and, 374

myspaceWatch, 77

N

.name, 59

name-brand *v.* generic PCs, 276

nanomedicine, 354

nanorobots, 354

nanotechnology, 353–355

Napster.com, 45, 335

NAS (network access storage), 296

NASA (National Aeronautics and Space Administration), 354, 392

National Aeronautics and Space Administration. *See* NASA

National Cyber Security Alliance, 161

National Do Not Email Registry, 374

National Institute of Standards and Technology, 357

National Nanotechnology Initiative (NNI), 354

National Security Agency (NSA), 395

Natural Keyboard (Microsoft), 20

Navajo Nation, satellites and, 122, 124

navigation pane, 180

NCs. *See* network computers

nesting, 67

.net, 59

NET (No Electronic Theft) Act, 379

Net Nanny, 77

Netgear, 140

Netgrocer, 89

netiquette, 37–38

  www.albion.com/netiquette and, 37

  discussion forums, 37

  e-mail, 37–38

  ethics and, 37–38

  IM, 38

  Internet, 37–38

  text messaging, 38

  Usenet, 77

Netscape Navigator, 55

NetWare, Novell's, 350

network access points, 107, 137, 141

network access storage (NAS), 296

network administrators, 328

Network and Sharing Center, 140

network computers (NCs), 15

network interface cards (NICs), 8, 11, 136, 141, 256, 273, 327, 328

network layers, 334, 336

Network Setup Wizard, 140

networking, social. *See* social networking

networks, 11, 324–351

  advantages of, 329

  application sharing on, 329

  architecture, 334, 336

  categories, 326

  client/server, 15, 331–332

  communications devices and, 327

  defined, 326

  disadvantages of, 329

  file servers and, 328

  fundamentals, 326–329

  home, 134–141

  LANs, 326, 330–339, 344

  modems and, 327

  network of, 48, 50, 78. *See also* Internet

  neural, 360–361

online information about, 329
P2P, 44, 331, 335, 344
power grid and, 334
privacy and, 329
protocols. *See* protocols
school
   modems for, 273
   NICs for, 273
security and, 329
smartphones and, 141
topologies, 333–334, 344
   bus, 333
   ring, 333, 334
   star, 333–334
VPN, 331
WANs, 327, 339–343, 344
wireless, 110, 133, 339
   Evil Twin, 339
   hotspots, 110, 133, 339
   LANs, 330
   piggybacking and, 110, 339
   security and, 110, 133, 339, 387
   Wi-Fi, 336–339
neural networks, 360–361
neurons, 360, 361
new technology file system (NTFS), 296
new/emerging computing technologies, 352–365
news, international, 32
News newsgroups, 76
newsgroups, 75, 76
alt, 77
biz, 77
Comp, 76
Misc, 76
News, 76
Rec, 76
Sci, 76
Soc, 76
standard, 75, 76
Talk, 76
world, 75
Nexi robot, 363
NexTag, 89
NICs. *See* network interface cards
Ning (social networking), 74
NNI (National Nanotechnology Initiative), 354
No Electronic Theft (NET) Act, 379
nodes, 327. *See also* clients
Nokia E90 Communicator, 116
Nokia N82, 125
nonretail online services, 97
nonvolatile memory, 146
Norton (Symantec)
antispam feature, 73
AntiVirus, 162, 203
Internet Security, 141
NOT operator, 66, 67
notebook computers (laptops), 6, 13, 31
convertible, 15
desktop computers *v.,* 268–269

subnotebooks, 15
system unit in, 241
ultraportable, 15
notes pane, 231
NOVA Web site, 402
Novell's NetWare, 350
NSA (National Security Agency), 395
NTFS (new technology file system), 296
numbers
binary, 238, 239
data as, 238–240
decimal, 239
floating point notation and, 240
hexadecimal, 239

O

objects, Access, 228, 230
OCR (optical character recognition), 287
Office Assistant, 361, 365
Office button, 220
Office Clipboard, 223
Office Live, 201
Office suite (Microsoft), 218–235
Access in, 228–230
Excel in, 226–228
online information, 216
Outlook in, 71, 233–234
PowerPoint in, 231–233
shared interface/tools, 220–224
Word in, 225–226
office suites (software suites), 200–202, 210, 216
offline Web page, 64
Ogg Vorbis, 195
OMRs (optical mark readers), 288
on the Web (exercises)
chapter 1, 32
chapter 2, 84
chapter 3, 132
chapter 4, 174
chapter 5, 216
chapter 6, 264
chapter 7, 310
chapter 8, 350
chapter 9, 402
on-board video, 256
1&1, 93
100Base-T (Fast Ethernet), 136, 336, 337, 350
128-bit encryption, 401
1394 ports (FireWire), 255
OnGuard Online, FTC, 377
online. *See also* entries with *cyber;* Internet
banking, 95–96
businesses, starting, 92–94
gaming, 38, 84
going online, 51–53
grocery shopping, 89–91
information sources
   authoritative, 68

citing, 68
libraries and, 68
nonretail services, 97
Online Safety Institute, 77
privacy, 374–375
security. *See* security
services, 51. *See also* AOL; Internet service providers; MSN
sexual predators, 386
shopping, 89–91
stock trading, 96–97
travel reservations, 94–95
OnStar, 122
open source software, 156, 158, 159
OpenOffice, 157
Opera web browser, 56, 403
operating systems (OS), 9
Android mobile, 375
defined, 144
DOS, 157
functions
   handling input/output, 150
   managing applications, 147–148
   managing memory, 148–150
   starting the computer, 145–147
   user interfaces, 151–153, 357
Linux, 156–157, 158, 159
loading, 146
Mac OS X, 155, 174
MS-DOS, 157
multitasking, 148
PC-DOS, 157
single-tasking, 148
UNIX, 155–156
Windows, 153
   Mobile, 154–155
   Server 2008, 154
   timeline, 153
   Vista, 153–154, 174
   XP, 153
Operation Fastlink, 379
optical character recognition (OCR), 287
optical mark readers (OMRs), 288
optical storage devices, 300, 301. *See also* CD technologies; DVD technologies
options/settings for application software, 208
opt-out system, 73
OQO Model 02 computer, 113
OR operator, 66, 67
.org, 59
organizations
backup procedures for, 39
computer ethics for, 39
computers for, 12–13, 15–16, 26
piracy in, 39
OS. *See* operating systems
Outlook (Microsoft), 71, 233–234
Outlook Express. *See* Windows Mail
output (in information-processing cycle), 7, 10, 12

output devices, 288–293
  defined, 288
    CRT, 288–289, 304
    dot pitch of, 272
    LCD, 289, 304
    monitors, 8, 10, 272, 288–291, 304
    qualities of, 272
    refresh rate and, 290
    resolutions for, 290
    screen sizes of, 272, 289–290
    TVs as, 290
    video cards and, 272
  multifunction devices, 292–293
  OS and, 150
  printers, 8, 10, 304
    categories, 272–273
    inkjet, 291, 304
    laser, 291, 304
    photo, 291
    plotters as, 291, 292
    selection of, 273
    thermal-transfer, 291
    toner cartridges, 291
  projectors
    DLP, 292
    LCD, 292
  speakers, 8, 10, 292
    selecting, 273
outsourcing, 31
overusage, of Internet/computers, 25, 26
ownership, of Web/Internet, 53

P

P2P (peer-to-peer) networks. *See* peer-to-peer networks
packaged application software, 199
packet sniffing, 383
packet switching, 340–341, 342, 344
padlock symbol, locked, 98
page description language (PDL), 193
Page Layout tab, 222
pages, 149
paging, 149
Paint (Windows), 193
paint programs, 193
PAN (personal area network), 106
Panda Cam, 119
Panda worm, 384
Panicware, 203
PaPeRo (partner-type personal) robot, 364, 365
Parachute Trainer, VR, 358
parallel ports, 255, 257
parallel processing, 248, 249, 263
parentheses ( ), 66, 67
partitions, 296
partner-type personal (PaPeRo) robot, 35, 364
password guessing, 383
passwords
  authentication and, 390

obtaining, 382–383
  dumpster diving, 383
  packet sniffing, 383
  password guessing, 383
  shoulder surfing, 383
  social engineering, 383
  superuser status and, 383
paths, 59, 178
pattern-recognition software, 361
PayPal, 88, 94, 98
PayPal AuctionFinder, 98
PBS NOVA Web site, 402
PBwiki, 62
PBXs (private branch exchanges), 108
PC card slots, 257
PC enhanced keyboard, 284
PC-DOS, 157
PCI (Peripheral Component Interconnect) bus, 251
PCs. *See* personal computers
PCS (personal communication service), 116
PDAs (personal digital assistants), 15, 117
  convergence and, 117
  Microsoft Windows Mobile and, 154–155
  smartphones and, 117
PDL (page description language), 193
Peapod, 89, 90, 99
peers, 137
peer-to-peer (P2P) networks, 331, 344
  BitTorrent, 331, 335, 379
  controversy in, 335
  Joost, 335
  Kazaa.com, 45, 335
  Lime Wire, 331, 335, 379
  music sharing and, 335
  Napster.com, 45, 335
  privacy and, 335
  security and, 335
  wireless networks as, 137
PEMDAS, 227
perceptual user interfaces, 357
performance
  hard disk, 297–298, 304
  microprocessor, 247
Peripheral Component Interconnect (PCI) bus, 251
peripheral devices, 11
  external, 11
  internal, 11
personal area network. *See* PAN
personal communication service (PCS), 116
personal computers (PCs), 6, 13, 31
  Macs *v.,* 157, 159, 269–270
  Macs *v.* Linux *v.,* 157, 159
  name-brand *v.* generic, 276
  tablet, 13, 15
personal digital assistants. *See* PDAs
personal firewalls, 139, 140, 391, 402

personal information managers (PIMs), 201
personal productivity programs, 190–191. *See also* office suites
Personal Robots Group, 364
petabyte (PB), 239
Pets.com, 91
PGP (Pretty Good Privacy), 395
phishing attacks, 378
  anti-phishing features, Internet Explorer/Firefox and, 403
  spear, 386
phones. *See* cell phones; telephony
photo printers, 291, 318
photo-editing program, 318
Photoshop, Adobe, 194
phrase searching, 67, 78
piconet, 106
picture messaging, 124–125
piggybacking, 110, 339
PIMs (personal information managers), 201
pipelining, 248, 249, 263
piracy, 379
  digital, 14
  illegality of, 43–44
  music, 31, 32, 44
  in organizations, 39
  rates (per country), 379
  reporting, 39
PKI (public key infrastructure), 394
PKZip, 165
placeholder, 231
plagiarism, 41–42
plaintext, 393
platforms, 157, 159, 269–270
platters, 304
plotters, 291, 292
Plug-and-Play (PnP), 146, 254
plug-ins, 56, 70, 71
  Adobe Flash Player, 71
  Adobe Reader, 71
  Adobe Shockwave Player, 71
  Apple QuickTime Player, 71
  RealPlayer, 71
  Windows Media Player, 71
PNG (Portable Network Graphics), 193
PnP (Plug-and-Play), 146, 254
Podcast Directory, 62
podcasts, 62
podslurping, 388
point of presence (POP), 339–340, 344
point-and-shoot digital cameras, 318
pointer, 285
pointing devices, 285–287
  joystick, 285, 286
  mice, 8, 9, 285–286
    selecting, 273
    VisualMouse, 357
  pointing stick, 285, 286
  stylus, 285, 286
  touch screen, 285, 286

touchpad, 285, 286
trackball, 286
pointing sticks, 285, 286
point-of-sale terminals. *See* POS terminals
POP (point of presence), 339–340, 344
pop-up blockers
    Google toolbar and, 403
    Internet Explorer and, 403
    Mozilla Firefox and, 403
Pop-Up Stopper, 203
pop-ups, 203
pornography, child, 45, 77, 395
portability, telephone number, 113
portable multimedia devices, 320–321
Portable Network Graphics (PNG), 193
portals, 64
    shopping, 89, 90
    Yahoo!, 65
ports, 254–257, 263. *See also specific ports*
POS (point-of-sale) terminals, 343
position awareness, 125, 375
positioning performance, 297
POST (power-on self-test), 146
PostScript, 193
power grid, networks and, 334
power supply, 243
power switch, 253–254
power-line networks, home, 137
power-on light, 253
power-on self-test (POST), 146
PowerPoint (Microsoft), 231–233
power-related problems, computers and, 390
.pptx, 233
predators, online, 386
preemptive multitasking, 148
presentation graphics programs, 201
presentations, 233
Pretty Good Privacy (PGP), 395
PriceGrabber.com, 89, 90
www.pricegrabber.com, 350
primary cache, 253
printers, 8, 10, 304
    categories, 272–273
    inkjet, 291, 304
    laser, 291, 304
    photo, 291, 318
    plotters as, 291, 292
    selecting, 272–273
    thermal-transfer, 291
    toner cartridges, 291
Prioritizing Resources and Organization for Intellectual Property (Pro-IP) Act, 379
privacy, 368–386. *See also* security
    anonymity and, 369–370
    data, 39
    defined, 368
    employee monitoring and, 376
    GPS and, 122

information collection, without consent, 368
    location awareness and, 125, 375
    networks and, 329
    P2P networks and, 335
    protecting, 372–376
        at home, 375–376
        online, 374–375
        at work, 376
    rights, 372–373
    social networking sites and, 74–75
    threats, 369–372
        computer crimes *v.,* 377
        cookies, 370–371
        GUIDs, 371
        RFID, 372
        ubiquitous computing, 371–372
privacy seals, 374, 375
private branch exchanges (PBXs), 108
private keys, 393, 394
.pro, 59
processing
    in information-processing cycle, 7, 10, 11–12
    parallel, 248, 249, 263
processing cycle, 246
processors. *See* microprocessors
productivity software. *See* application software
professional workstations, 15
professionals. *See* computer professionals
profile, 147
programs. *See* software programs
Programs and Features utility, 208
Pro-IP (Prioritizing Resources and Organization for Intellectual Property) Act, 379
projectors
    DLP, 292
    LCD, 292
PROM, 252
protecting computer systems, 389–392
protocol stack, 336
protocol suite, 334
protocols (standards), 58, 59, 344
    defined, 334
    FTP, 58, 78
        anonymous, 75, 76
        site access, Windows Explorer and, 75, 76
        WS_FTP Home and, 75
    HTTP, 58
    Internet, 340
    IP, 57, 340
    LAN, 334–339
    modulation, 334
    TCP, 340
    TCP/IP, 340
    WAN, 340–341
    WAP, 117
PS/2 ports, 255, 257
PSTN. *See* public switched telephone

network
public domain software, 43, 205
public key encryption, 393–395
public key infrastructure (PKI), 394
public keys, 393
public location, hotspots and, 133
public safety, security and, 389
public security, encryption and, 394–395
public switched telephone network (PSTN), 108–113, 126
    HelloDirect and, 109
    last-mile problem, 109
    last-mile technologies. *See* last-mile technologies
    multiplexing and, 109, 126
    pathways on, 109
    telephone number portability and, 113
    VoIP and. *See* VoIP
pumping and dumping, 385
pure-play online grocery stores, 90
queries, 228, 230

Q
Query object, 228
Quick Access Toolbar, 220, 221
Quicken, 96
QuickTime, 196
QuickTime Player, 71
quotation marks search operator (" "), 66
quoted size, 289
QWERTY keyboard layout, 283

R
racetrack memory, 299
radio frequency identification (RFID), 372
radio transmissions, 106
    satellite, 120–121
RaFa, 392
RAM. *See* random access memory
random access memory (RAM), 10, 19, 251–252
    sufficient amounts of, 270–271
random access storage devices, 295
random-number generator, NSA's, 395
raster graphics, 193
ray tracing, 194
read-only memory (ROM), 146
real estate listings, 97
real life, virtual life *v.,* 197
RealPlayer, 71
Real-Time Collaborative Criminal Investigation and Analysis tool, 389
Rec newsgroups, 76
recycling
    cell phones, 114, 115–116
    computer systems, 25
    toner cartridges, 291

references, citing, 68
References tab, 222
refresh rate, 290
refurbished computer systems, 276
registers, 246
registration, 205
    of domain names, 59, 84
registration fee, shareware, 43
registry, 146
Reliability and Performance Monitor,
        166–167
remote backups, 33
remote storage (hard disk), 296–297
rental cars, GPS and, 401
replacing cell phones, 131
Report object, 228
https://reporting.bsa.org/usa, 39
reports, 228, 230
    back-end, 94
reset switch, 253
resolutions (monitor), 290
resource, 59
resource extensions, 59
resource names, 59
respect, computer usage and, 36
responsible computer/Internet usage,
        24–25, 26
restore down mode, 220
Review tab, 222
rewritable CD/DVD drives, 33
RFID (radio frequency identification), 372
Ribbon, 221–222
rights, privacy, 372–373
ring topology, 333, 334
rip and tear, 385
risks, security. *See* security
RJ-45 connectors, 105, 136
'Roadrunner' supercomputer, 16
robotics, 364
robots, 364–365. *See also* artificial
        intelligence
    ASIMO, 23, 364, 365
    automation and, 24
    Cog, 363
    computer-guided, 23, 24
    defined, 364
    www.irobot.com, 365
    Kismet, 363
    MDS, 363
    nano-, 354
    Nexi, 363
    PaPeRo, 364, 365
    Personal Robots Group and, 364
    worldwide usage of, 24
rogue programs. *See* malware
ROM (read-only memory), 146, 252
routers, 136, 327, 328
    cable, 141
    DSL, 141
    Linksys, 140
    switches *v.,* 328

rows, 226
RSS feed, 62
Ruckus.com, 45

S

Safari, 70, 403
safe mode, 166
safety. *See* security
safety-critical software programs, 21,
        40–41
Safeway.com, 91
salami shaving, 383
Samsung Instinct, 321
SATA (serial ATA), 257
SATAN (security loophole detection
        program), 389
satellites, 51, 52, 78, 107–108
    DBS, 107
    Echelon and, 122
    GPS and, 107, 121–122
    Navajo Nation and, 122, 124
    satellite radio, 120–121
        SIRIUS, 121
        XM, 121
scams, 97, 385. *See also* fraud
    avoiding, 391
    bogus goods, 385
    pumping and dumping, 385
    rip and tear, 385
scanners, 287, 288
scanning programs, disk, 163–164
Scholar, Google, 68, 69
schools
    acceptable use policy and, 36
    Clemson University's C3B Center, 354
    code of conduct and, 36
    Columbine High School tragedy, 38
    Internet access, 83
    networks
        modems for, 273
        NICs for, 273
schoolwork, Web for, 68–69
Sci newsgroups, 76
science, lending computers to, 338
screen sizes, of monitors, 272, 289–290
screenshots, 217
scroll arrows, 220
scroll bars, 220
SCSI (Small Computer System Interface)
        ports, 255, 257
SDH (synchronous digital hierarchy), 112
SDSL (symmetric digital subscriber line),
        111
Search box, 181
search engines, 63, 78. *See also specific
        search engines*
    AOL, 63, 64
    Ask, 63, 64
    Dogpile, 66
    FindSounds, 66

Google, 63, 64
    green, 64
    Green Maven, 64
    Indeed, 64
    Infoplease, 64, 65
    KartOO, 66
    Live Search, 63, 64
    Mahalo, 66
    online businesses and, 93
    online information about, 67
    specialized, 64
    subject guides *v.,* 63, 78
    top, 63, 64
    Yahoo!, 63, 64
search operators, 64–67
    exclusion (-), 66–67, 78
    inclusion (+), 66, 78
    quotation marks (" "), 66
    wildcards (*), 66, 67
search utility, 163
searches
    Boolean, 66, 67, 78
        AND operator, 66, 67
        NOT operator, 66, 67
        OR operator, 66, 67
        parentheses ( ), 66, 67
    dynamic, 182
    phrase, 67, 78
    techniques for, 64–67
SearchStorage.com, 293
SEC (Securities and Exchange
        Commission), 97
second generation cell phones. *See* 2G cell
        phones
2G cell phones, 116
secondary cache, 253
secondary storage, 295
sectors, 296, 304
    bad, 164, 297
Secure Electronic Transaction (SET), 394
secure mode, 96
secure Web site, 98
Securities and Exchange Commission
        (SEC), 97
security, 387–395
    active monitoring and, 96
    banking and, 96
    biometric authentication and, 242, 390,
        391
    children's. *See* children's security
    corporate espionage and, 387–388
    credit cards and, 97–98
    cyberterrorism and, 388, 389
    electronic voting and, 123
    encryption and, 392–395
    firewalls and, 139, 140, 141, 390–391,
        402
    networks and, 329
    P2P networks and, 335
    protecting computer systems and,
        389–392

public safety and, 389
Real-Time Collaborative Criminal
    Investigation and Analysis tool,
    389
risks, 387–389
stock trading and, 97
STOP and, 389
terrorism and, 388, 389
wireless networks and, 110, 133,
    339, 387
security loophole detection program
    (SATAN), 389
seek time, 297
selecting
    computer systems, 268–274
        hard disks, 271
        internal/external drives, 271–272
        keyboards, 273
        Macs v. PCs, 269–270
        mice, 273
        microprocessors, 270
        modems/NICs, 273
        monitors, 272
        notebooks v. desktop computers,
            268–269
        printers, 272–273
        RAM, 270–271
        sound cards, 273
        speakers, 273
        UPSes, 273
        video cards, 272
    ISPs, 351
    last-mile technologies, 112
selling term papers, 84
September 11th attacks, 388, 394, 395
serial ATA (SATA), 257
serial ports, 255, 257
Server 2008, Windows, 154
servers, 15, 16
    file, 328. See also networks
    mid-range, 16
    Web, 57, 78
SET (Secure Electronic Transaction), 394
SETI@home (http://setiathome.
    berkeley.edu), 338
set-top appliances, 15, 320
setup program, 146
sexual predators (online), 386
shareware, 43, 205, 215
sharing information
    blogs and, 62
    illegally, 44
    networks and, 329. See also home
        networks
    podcasts and, 62
    wikis and, 62
shaving, memory, 382
Shockwave Player, Adobe, 71, 195
shopping (online), 89–91
    portals for, 89, 90
shopping, for computer systems, 267–276

mail-order v. online v. local stores,
    274–276
name-brand v. generic PCs, 276
shopping comparison worksheet, 275
top-of-the-line models v. bargain-bin
    specials, 274
used v. refurbished systems, 276
Shopzilla, 89
short answer
    chapter 1, 30
    chapter 2, 82
    chapter 3, 130
    chapter 4, 172
    chapter 5, 214
    chapter 6, 262
    chapter 7, 308
    chapter 8, 348
    chapter 9, 400
short messaging service. See SMS
shoulder surfing, 383
shutting down computers, 167
sign language, gesture recognition and,
    357
signatures, digital, 393–394
SIIA (Software & Information Industry
    Association), 43
single-lens reflex (SLR) digital cameras,
    318–319
single-tasking operating systems, 148
SIRIUS Satellite Radio, 121
site licenses, 43, 204, 215
64-bit CPU, 247, 248
Skype, 117, 118, 119, 131, 335
SLC. See subscriber loop carrier
sleep mode, 167
slide, 231
slideshow, 233
Sliwa, Curtis, 77
SLR (single-lens reflex) digital cameras,
    318–319
small businesses. See businesses
Small Computer System Interface ports.
    See SCSI (Small Computer System
    Interface) ports
smart appliances, 140, 334
smart cards, 303
smart homes, 334
smart tags, 223–224
SmartMedia, 317
smartphones, 6, 15, 116, 173. See also cell
    phones
    ethics and, 15
    iPhone 3G, 320–321
    networking and, 141
    PDAs and, 117
    Samsung Instinct, 321
    system unit in, 241
SMDS (Switched Multimegabit Data
    Service), 341
SMIL (Synchronized Multimedia
    Integration Language), 196, 197

SMS (short messaging service), 115. See
    also text messaging
Snopes.com, 381
Soc newsgroups, 76
social engineering, 383
social networking, 74–75
    privacy concerns and, 74–75
    sites
        Facebook, 74, 75
        MySpace, 44, 74, 75
        Ning, 74
Social Security numbers, selling,
    369, 396
societal impacts, of computer use, 22
software, 9. See also application
    software
    BSA and, 39
    database. See database programs
    employee monitoring, 376
    firewall. See firewalls
    free, 159, 205, 216
    machine dependent, 43–44
    malicious. See malware
    monitoring, 376, 402
    open source, 156, 158, 159
    OS. See operating systems
    piracy. See piracy
    public domain, 43
    rogue programs. See malware
    shareware, 43, 205, 215
    system, 9, 142–175, 210
    system utilities. See system utilities
Software & Information Industry
    Association (SIIA), 43
software licenses, 204–206
software programs, 9
    content-filtering, Internet and, 77
    database. See database programs
    errors in, 20–21, 26
    lines of code in, 21
    mission-critical, 21, 40–41
    safety-critical, 21, 40–41
software suites. See office suites
Software Update, 165
software validation, 205
solid-state drives (SSDs), 298. See also
    flash drives
solid-state storage devices, 302–303
    ExpressCards, 302
    flash drives, 298, 302, 304
        USB, 11, 33, 298, 300, 304
    flash memory cards, 11, 302–303
    smart cards, 303
SOMA Terror Organization Portal
    (STOP), 389
SONET (synchronous optical network),
    112
songs, illegally copied, 44
SophosLabs, 374
sound card connectors, 257
sound cards, 273

spam, 72–73
CAN-SPAM act and, 73, 374
ChoiceMail and, 72
Cloudmark and, 72
countries and, 374
fighting, 401
filtering out, 72–73, 85
www.ftc.gov/spam and, 73
MailWasher and, 73
McAfee and, 73
MySpace and, 374
opt-out system and, 73
outlawing, 73
prevention, online information, 73
Symantec and, 73
Web beacons and, 73, 373, 402
SpamBully, 73
speakers, 8, 10, 292
internal, 243
selecting, 273
spear phishing, 386
specialized search engines, 64
www.Spectorsoft.com, 376, 402
speculative execution, 248
speech-recognition software, 287, 310, 357
spell checker, 11, 12
spiders, 60
spimming, 74, 381
splatter games, 38
splitters, 141
sponsored sites, 92
spoofing, IP, 384
sports information, 97, 98
spotlight
computer systems, buying/upgrading, 266–279
e-commerce, 86–99
emerging/new computing technologies, 352–365
ethics, 35–45
file management, 176–187
home networks, 134–141
Microsoft Office suite, 218–235
multimedia devices, 312–323
spreadsheet programs, 201
Spybot Search and Destroy, 161
spyware, 203, 378
Spyware Doctor, 203
SSDs (solid-state drives), 298. *See also*
flash drives
stack option, 182
stack, protocol, 336
standalone application software, 199, 210
standard newsgroups, 75, 76
standards. *See* protocols
Staples Contract division, 88
star topology, 333–334
StarOffice suite, 215
Start menu, 180
statistics, Internet, 84
status bar, 220
stealing bandwidth, 109

stock trading (online), 96–97, 99
brokerages and, 97
day trading and, 97
security and, 97
timeliness and, 97
STOP (SOMA Terror Organization
Portal), 389
Stop Cyberbullying Web site, 77
storage (in information-processing cycle),
7, 10–11, 12, 293
auxiliary, 293
mass, 293
storage devices, 10–11, 293–303. *See also*
backups
backups and, 10–11
categories of, 304
design challenges for, 299
hard disks, 10, 11, 295–298
external, 33
Internet, 296–297
magnetic, 295, 301
memory v., 295
NAS, 296
partitions, 296
performance, 297–298, 304
random access, 295
remote storage, 296–297
as secondary storage, 295
selecting, 271
holographic, 303
Internet, 310
magnetic, 295, 301
memory v., 293–295, 304
optical, 300, 301. *See also* CD
technologies; DVD technologies
racetrack memory as, 299
random access, 295
remote, 296–297
solid-state, 302–303
ExpressCards, 302
flash drives, 11, 33, 298, 300, 302, 304
flash memory cards, 11, 302–303
smart cards, 303
wireless memory cards, 303
stored files, browsers and, 56
Storm malware, 375
streaming video sites, 119, 120
strong AI, 363
structural unemployment, 24
structured program design, control
structures, nesting, 67
StuffIt, 174
stylus, 285, 286
subfolders, 177
subject guides, 63, 78. *See also* search
engines
subnotebooks, 15
subscriber loop carrier (SLC), 108, 109
supercomputers, 16, 32
'Roadrunner,' 16
www.top500.org, 16, 32
superscalar architecture, 248

superuser status, passwords and, 383
surround-sound systems, 310
Switched Multimegabit Data Service
(SMDS), 341
switches, 136, 327, 328, 333–334. *See also*
routers
Symantec. *See* Norton
symmetric digital subscriber line (SDSL),
111
symmetric key encryption, 393
Synchronized Multimedia Integration
Language (SMIL), 196, 197
synchronous digital hierarchy (SDH), 112
synchronous optical network (SONET), 112
synthesizers, 292
system clock, 248
system configuration, 146
system requirements, for application
software, 202
system software, 9, 142–175. *See also*
operating systems; system utilities
application software v., 210
defined, 144
System Tools, 173
System Tray, 147
system unit, 8, 10, 236–265
all-in-one computer and, 241
components, 243–244
defined, 240
desktop computer and, 241
iMac and, 241
Mac Pro and, 241
motherboard in, 243, 244–253
notebook and, 241
outside components, 253–257
connectors/ports, 254–257
front panel, 253–254
power switch, 253–254
smartphone and, 241
system utilities (utility programs),
159–167
antivirus software, 161–162, 174
backup software, 159–161
disk defragmentation programs, 164
disk scanning programs, 163–164
file compression utilities, 164–165
file manager, 162–163
loading, 147
system updates, 165
Software Update, 165
Windows Update, 165
troubleshooting and, 165–167

T

T1 lines, 112
T3 lines, 112
tab(s), 221–222
contextual, 222
Home, 221
Insert, 221–222
Mailings, 222

Page Layout, 222
References, 222
Review, 222
View, 222
tabbed browsing, 60
tables (data files), 228, 230
tablet PCs, 13, 15
tactile displays, 359
tags, smart, 223–224
tailor-made application software, 198–199
Talk newsgroups, 76
TB (terabytes), 33, 239, 271
TCP (Transmission Control Protocol), 340
TCP/IP (Internet protocols), 340
teamwork (exercises)
    chapter 1, 31
    chapter 2, 83
    chapter 3, 131
    chapter 4, 173
    chapter 5, 215
    chapter 6, 263
    chapter 7, 309
    chapter 8, 349
    chapter 9, 401
technology
    anonymity and, 369–372
    CD. *See* CD technologies
    DVD. *See* DVD technologies
    emerging/new, 352–365
    globalization and, 24
    growth of, 5
    information sources for, 25
    legacy technology, 11
    structural unemployment and, 24
    translation, 362
    vision, 357
    wearable, 294
    Web-hosted, 201–202
teen usage, of cell phones, 122, 124
telecommunications. *See* communications
telephone connector, 256
telephone modem, 51, 52, 78
telephone number portability, 113
telephone-to-telephone service, VoIP and, 118
telephony. *See also* cell phones; public switched telephone network
    analog technology and, 108
    digital, 108–109, 127
    HelloDirect and, 109
    Internet. *See* VoIP
television (TV). *See also* cable
    AOL TV, 320
    Backseat, 121
    DIRECTTV, 107
    HDTV, 290
    as monitor, 290
    MSN TV, 320
    multimedia devices, 320
templates
    design, 231, 232
    Office, 224

Ten Commandments for Computer Ethics, 37
10Base-T, 336, 337. *See also* Ethernet
terabytes (TB), 33, 239, 271
term papers, for sale, 84
terminals, 16
terminators, 333
terminology managers, 362
terms. *See key terms/concepts*
terrorism
    cyberterrorism and, 388, 389
    public key encryption and, 394–395
    Real-Time Collaborative Criminal Investigation and Analysis tool, 389
    September 11th attacks, 388, 394, 395
    STOP and, 389
text messaging, 124
    e-mail and, 70
    MSCs and, 115
    netiquette for, 38
    SMS as, 115
TFT (Thin Film Transistor), 289
theft, 382. *See also* identity theft
thermal-transfer printers, 291
Thin Film Transistor (TFT), 289
third generation cell phones. *See* 3G cell phones
3G cell phones, 114
Thomas, Eric, 77
1000Base-T (gigabit Ethernet), 136, 336, 337
threads, 75
3-D rendering programs, 194, 195
throughput, 102. *See also* bandwidth
Thunderbird. *See* Mozilla Thunderbird
Tiger Direct, 350
timebombs, 381
time-limited trial versions, 202
Timeline of Computer History site, 7
timeliness, online trading and, 97
title bar, 220
TLD names. *See* top-level domain names
toggle key, 283
Token Ring Network, 337
tokens, 334
toner cartridges, 291
toolbar, Google, 403
top-level domain (TLD) names, 59
    .aero, 59
    .biz, 59
    .com, 59
    .coop, 59
    .edu, 59
    .gov, 59
    .info, 59
    .mil, 59
    .museum, 59
    .name, 59
    .net, 59
    .org, 59
    .pro, 59

top-level folder, 178
top-of-the-line computer systems *v.* bargain-bin specials, 274
topologies (network), 333–334, 344
    bus, 333
    ring, 333, 334
    star, 333–334
www.top500.org, 16, 32
Torvalds, Linus, 156
touch screens, 285, 286
touchpads, 285, 286
tower case, 240
trackballs, 286
tracks, 296, 304
trading. *See* stock trading
transaction acquisition, WANs and, 341, 343
transfer performance, 297
transistor, 244
translation technology, 362
Transmission Control Protocol. *See* TCP
transportation monitoring, 41
transporting data, 33
TransUnion, 369
trap doors, 388
travel reservations (online), 94–95, 99
Travelocity, 94, 95
tree structure, 178
trial versions, time-limited, 202
Trillian, 71
Trojan horses, 335, 382
troubleshooting, 165–167
True.com, 386
truncation, 67
TRUSTe, 374, 375
'try before you buy,' 205. *See also* shareware
Tucows, 205
Turing, Alan, 360
Turing Test, 360
TV. *See* television
TV/sound capture board connectors, 257
twisted pair, 104
typing programs, 198

U

UAH (underground automated highways), 356
ubiquitous computing, 356–360
    AHS and, 356, 365
    biological feedback devices, 357
    chemical detectors and, 359
    digital forensics and, 357, 365
    privacy threats and, 371–372
    tactile displays and, 359
    VR and, 357–359, 365
Ubuntu, 157
uLocate, 375
Ultimate Memory Guide, 251

ultraportables, 15
underground automated highways
    (UAH), 356
unemployment, structural, 24
unethical *v.* illegal actions, 35. *See also*
    cybercrime; ethics
Unicode, 240
Uniform Resource Locators. *See* URLs
uninstalling application software,
    207–208
uninterruptible power supplies (UPSes),
    273
uninterruptible power supply (UPS),
    390
Universal Serial Bus ports. *See*
    USB ports
universities. *See* schools
UNIX, 155–156, 158
updates, 165
    Software Update, 165
    Windows Update, 165
upgrading
    application software, 202, 204
    computer systems, 276–277
    memory, 277
uploading, 61
UPS (uninterruptible power supply),
    390
URLs (Uniform Resource Locators), 42,
    57–58
    components, 58–59, 78
    domain name, 58–59, 78
    path, 59, 78
    protocol, 58, 59, 78
    resource name, 59, 78
U.S. Computer Emergency Readiness
    Team (US-CERT), 388, 392
U.S. Department of Homeland Security
    (DHS), 388
U.S. Department of Transportation
    (USDOT), 356
USB flash drives, 11, 33, 298, 300, 304
    IronKey Secure, 375
USB hub, 256
USB (Universal Serial Bus) ports, 254
US-CERT (U.S. Computer Emergency
    Readiness Team), 388, 392
USDOT (U.S. Department of
    Transportation), 356
used computer systems, 276
Usenet, 75, 76, 77, 78
    Google Groups and, 77
    netiquette on, 77
    newsgroups, 75, 76
        alt, 77
        biz, 77
        standard, 75, 76
        threads and, 75
user interfaces, 151–153
    command-line, 153
    GUIs, 151

menu-driven, 151, 153
    perceptual, 357
utility programs. *See* system utilities

V

validation, software, 205
variants, 381
vector graphics, 193
Verified by Visa, 98
VeriSign logo, 98
Verizon, 51
VGA (Video Graphics Array), 255, 256
video cards, 272
    monitors and, 272
video editors, 196
Video for Windows, 196
Video Graphics Array. *See* VGA
View tab, 222
violence, gaming and, 38
virtual life, real life *v.,* 197
virtual memory, 149
virtual private networks (VPNs), 331
virtual reality (VR), 357–359, 365
    augmented reality and, 359
    data gloves and, 358
    HMD and, 358
    medicine and, 359
    Parachute Trainer, 358
    VRML and, 358
Virtual Reality Modeling Language
    (VRML), 358
viruses, 175, 378, 380–381. *See also*
    malware
    antivirus software, 161–162, 174
    boot sector, 380–381
    Disk Killer, 380
    downloaded, 61
    e-mail attachments and, 380
    file infectors, 378
    hoaxes, 381
    macro, 381
    Melissa, 384
    variants, 381
    Wazzu, 380
Viruslist site, Kaspersky Lab's, 385
vision technology, 357
Vista, Windows, 153–154, 174
VisualMouse, 357
Vmyths.com, 381
Voice over IP. *See* VoIP
voice recognition. *See* speech-recognition
    software
voice recorders, 316
VoIP (Voice over IP), 113, 117–119
    computer-to-phone service and, 118
    configuration, 118
    Joost and, 335
    phone-to-phone service and, 118
    Skype and, 117, 118, 119, 131, 335
    teleconferencing and, 118–119

volatile memory, 145
voting, electronic, 123
VPNs (virtual private networks), 331
VR. *See* virtual reality
VRML (Virtual Reality Modeling
    Language), 358

W

W3C. *See* World Wide Web Consortium
Wallace, Richard, 360
Wallace, Sanford, 374
WANs (wide area networks), 327,
    339–343, 344
    backbones, 339, 340, 344
    Cisco's documentation on, 341
    LANs *v.,* 344
    LAN-to-LAN connections with, 341
    point of presence, 339–340
    protocols, 340–341
        circuit switching, 340–341, 344
        Internet, 340
        online information, 341
        packet switching, 340–341, 342, 344
    transaction acquisition and, 341, 343
WAP (Wireless Application Protocol), 117
warfare, information, 388–389
warm boot, 145
WAV, 195
Wazzu virus, 380
wearable technology, 294
Web, 5, 78. *See also* Internet; *on the Web*
    browsing the, 60–62. *See also* browsers
    connecting to, via browser, 56
    control of, 53
    defined, 53
    information finding on, 63–69
    Internet *v.,* 53, 78
    ownership of, 53
    for schoolwork, 68–69
    spiders on, 60
Web 2.0, 55
Web addresses, 57–60
Web beacons, 73, 373, 402
Web browsers. *See* browsers
Web hosting services, 93
    GoDaddy, 93
    1&1, 93
    Yahoo!, 93
Web pages, 53
    evaluation, rules for, 67–68
    offline, 64
    saving, 61
    typical, 60
Web portals. *See* portals
Web servers, 57, 78. *See also* servers
Web sites, 53. *See also specific Web sites*
    blocking, 77
    revisiting, 83
    secure, 98
    sponsored, 92

Web subject guides, 63, 78. *See also* search engines
Web-based languages, markup languages, HTML, 54
Webcams, 118, 119
  Logitech Quickcam Pro 9000, 119
  online information for, 120
  in public locations, 119
Web-enabled devices, 117. *See also* notebook computers; PDAs; smartphones
  WAP and, 117
Web-hosted technology, 201–202
Weblogs. *See* blogs
Webroot, 203
WebTrust, 374, 375
Weizenbaum, Joseph, 360
WEP (Wired Equivalent Privacy), 133, 338, 387
We:Recycle program, 114
what-if analysis, 226
wheel mouse, 285
Wherify, 375
whistle-blowing, 39
white hats, 384
whiteboards, 119
wide area networks. *See* WANs
Wi-Fi, 336–339
  home networks, 137–138
Wi-Fi Protected Access (WPA), 133, 338, 387
WiFinder (www.wifinder.com), 110
wikis, 62
wiki-wiki, 62
wildcards (*), 66, 67
WiMAX (worldwide interoperability for microwave access), 112, 126
window border, 220
window control buttons, 220
Windows (Microsoft), 153
  Mobile, 154–155
  Server 2008, 154
  timeline, 153
  Vista, 153–154, 174
  XP, 153
Windows Bitmap (BMP), 193
Windows Disk Defragmenter, 164
Windows Explorer
  file management with, 179–184
  FTP site access with, 76, 77

Windows Live Hotmail, 71
Windows Live ID, 394, 395
Windows Live Messenger, 71, 74
Windows Mail, 71
Windows Media Audio (WMA), 195
Windows Media Player, 71, 196
Windows Task Manager, 149
Windows Update, 165
WinZip, 165, 174
wired communications, 102
  home networks, 136–137
    Ethernet, 136–137
    home power-line network, 137
  PSTN and, 108–113, 126
  transmission media
    coaxial cable, 104–105, 112
    fiber-optic cable, 105
    twisted pair, 104
    wireless media *v.,* 104
Wired Equivalent Privacy (WEP), 133, 338, 387
wireless access points, 107, 137, 141
wireless adapter cards, 138, 139
Wireless Application Protocol. *See* WAP
wireless communications, 102
  hotspots, 110, 133, 339
  security and, 110, 133
  transmission media
    Bluetooth, 106–107, 125, 132
    infrared, 105–106
    microwaves, 107
    radio, 106
    satellites, 51, 52, 78, 107–108, 120–122
    wired transmission media *v.,* 104
wireless memory cards, 303
wireless networks, 110, 133, 339
  client/server, 137
  Evil Twin, 339
  home, 137–138
  hotspots and, 110, 133, 339
  LANs, 330
  network access points, 107, 137, 141
  peer-to-peer, 137. *See also* peer-to-peer networks
  piggybacking and, 110, 339
  security and, 110, 133, 339, 387
  Wi-Fi, 336–339
    home, 137–138
WMA (Windows Media Audio), 195

Word (Microsoft), 225–226
word size, 247, 248
word-processing programs, 200, 201
work visas, H1Base, 41
workbooks, 226
Works, Microsoft, 200, 216
worksheets, 226
world newsgroups, 75, 76
World of Warcraft, 198, 199
World Wide Web. *See* Web
World Wide Web Consortium (W3C), 53, 54
worldwide interoperability for microwave access (WiMAX), 112, 126
worms, 381
  Fujack, 384
  Panda, 384
WPA (Wi-Fi Protected Access), 133, 338, 387
WPA2, 387
WS_FTP Home, 75
WWW. *See* Web

X

X.25, 341
xDSL, 111. *See also* DSL
.xlsx, 228
XM Satellite Radio, 121
XP, Windows, 153

Y

Yahoo!
  Mail, 71
    e-mail filter for, 85
  Messenger, 71
  portal, 65
  search engine, 63, 64
  Web hosting service, 93
yottabytes, 239
YouTube, 119, 120

Z

zettabytes, 239
Zip drives, 10
zombie computers, 335, 382